Communications
in Computer and Information Science   1277

Commenced Publication in 2007
Founding and Former Series Editors:
Simone Diniz Junqueira Barbosa, Phoebe Chen, Alfredo Cuzzocrea,
Xiaoyong Du, Orhun Kara, Ting Liu, Krishna M. Sivalingam,
Dominik Ślęzak, Takashi Washio, Xiaokang Yang, and Junsong Yuan

Editorial Board Members

More information about this series at http://www.springer.com/series/7899

Hector Florez · Sanjay Misra (Eds.)

Applied Informatics

Third International Conference, ICAI 2020
Ota, Nigeria, October 29–31, 2020
Proceedings

 Springer

Editors
Hector Florez (ID)
Universidad Distrital Francisco Jose
de Caldas
Bogota, Colombia

Sanjay Misra (ID)
Covenant University
Ota, Nigeria

ISSN 1865-0929   ISSN 1865-0937 (electronic)
Communications in Computer and Information Science
ISBN 978-3-030-61701-1   ISBN 978-3-030-61702-8 (eBook)
https://doi.org/10.1007/978-3-030-61702-8

This Springer imprint is published by the registered company Springer Nature Switzerland AG
The registered company address is: Gewerbestrasse 11, 6330 Cham, Switzerland

Preface

The Third International Conference on Applied Informatics (ICAI 2020) aimed to bring together researchers and practitioners working in different domains in the field of informatics in order to exchange their expertise and to discuss the perspectives of development and collaboration.

ICAI 2020 was held virtually at the Covenant University in Ota, Nigeria, during October 29–31, 2020. It was organized by the Information Technologies Innovation (ITI) research group that belongs to the Universidad Distrital Francisco José de Caldas, Colombia, the Covenant University, Nigeria, and the Federal University of Technology, Minna, Nigeria. In addition, ICAI 2020 was proudly sponsored by Springer and Strategic Business Platforms.

ICAI 2020 received 101 submissions on informatics topics such as artificial intelligence, business process management, cloud computing, data analysis, decision systems, health care information systems, human-computer interaction, learning management systems, simulation and emulation, and software design engineering. Authors of the 101 submissions came from the following countries: Argentina, Brazil, Cameroon, Chile, China, Colombia, Ecuador, France, India, Lithuania, Mexico, Nigeria, Poland, Portugal, South Africa, Spain, and the USA.

All submissions were reviewed through a double-blind peer-review process. Each paper was reviewed by at least three experts. To achieve this, ICAI 2020 was supported by 80 Program Committee (PC) members, who hold PhD degrees. PC members come from the following countries: Argentina, Austria, Brazil, Chile, China, Colombia, Cyprus, Czech Republic, Ecuador, France, Germany, Greece, India, Latvia, Lithuania, Luxembourg, Mexico, The Netherlands, Nigeria, Portugal, Spain, Switzerland, Ukraine, the UAE, the UK, and the USA. Based on the double-blind review process, 35 full papers were accepted to be included in this volume of *Communications in Computer and Information Sciences* (CCIS) proceedings published by Springer. Moreover, seven of the accepted papers are international collaborations.

Finally, we would like to thank Jorge Nakahara, Alfred Hofmann, Leonie Kunz, Ramvijay Subramani, and Alla Serikova from Springer for their helpful advice, guidance, and support in publishing the proceedings.

We trust that the ICAI 2020 conference and proceedings open you to new vistas of discovery and knowledge.

October 2020

Hector Florez
Sanjay Misra

Welcome Message

On behalf of the Local Organizing Committee of ICAI 2020, it was a pleasure to welcome you to the Third International Conference on Applied Informatics (ICAI 2020), held during October 29–31, 2020. We are very proud and grateful to the ICAI Steering Committee for giving us the opportunity to host this year's conference.

ICAI 2020 was planned to take place at the Covenant Univeristy, Ota, Nigeria, which is located in close vicinity to the metropolitan city of Lagos, Nigeria. Ota is an industrial town surrounded by many large-scale industries. Covenant University, which happened to be the venue of the conference, is a gentle departure from the hustle and bustle of the busy metropolitan life in the city of Lagos. It is a serene campus with landscaped surroundings. However, due to the COVID-19 pandemic and considering the safety, security, and health of all the authors and ICAI community, we decided to organize this conference in virtual mode at the Covenant University.

Covenant University is currently among the most prestigious institutions of higher education in Nigeria and offers an excellent setting for the conference. In 2019, Times Higher Education (THE) ranked Covenant University under 400–500 best in Nigeria and West Africa, and 5th on the whole African continent. Founded in 2002, Covenant University is rated the best performing university by the National Universities Commission, Nigeria.

Plenary lectures by leading scientists and several paper sessions provided a real opportunity to discuss new issues and find advanced solutions able to shape recent trends in informatics.

The conference could not have happened without the dedicated work of many volunteers. We want to thank all members of ICAI Organizing Committee for collaborating with us in hosting a successful ICAI 2020 as well as our fellow members of the local organization.

On behalf of the Local Organizing Committee of ICAI 2020, it was our honor to cordially welcome your virtual presence to the Covenant University for this unique event. Your participation and contribution to this conference made it much more productive and successful.

October 2020   Sanjay Misra

Organization

General Chairs

Hector Florez — Universidad Distrital Francisco José de Caldas, Colombia

Sanjay Misra — Covenant University, Nigeria

Honorary Chairs

A. A. A. Atayero — Covenant University, Nigeria

Charles Ayo — Trinity University, Nigeria

Abdullahi Bala — Federal University of Technology Minna, Nigeria

Steering Committee

Jaime Chavarriaga — Universidad de los Andes, Colombia

Cesar Diaz — OCOX AI, Colombia

Hector Florez — Universidad Distrital Francisco José de Caldas, Colombia

Ixent Galpin — Universidad de Bogotá Jorge Tadeo Lozano, Colombia

Olmer García — Universidad de Bogotá Jorge Tadeo Lozano, Colombia

Christian Grévisse — Université du Luxembourg, Luxembourg

Sanjay Misra — Covenant University, Nigeria

Fernando Yepes-Calderon — Children's Hospital Los Angeles, USA

Organizing Committee

Shafi'i Muhammad Abdulhamid — Federal University of Technology Minna, Nigeria

Joseph Adebayo Ojeniyi — Federal University of Technology Minna, Nigeria

Emmanuel Adetiba — Covenant University, Nigeria

Adeyinka Ajao Adewale — Covenant University, Nigeria

Adewole Adewumi — Algonquin College Ottawa, Canada

Adoghe Anthony — Covenant University, Nigeria

Aderonke Atinuke Oni — Covenant University, Nigeria

Amborse Azeta — Covenant University, Nigeria

Joke Badejo — Covenant University, Nigeria

Onyeka Emebo — Covenant University, Nigeria

Azubuike Ezenwoke — Covenant University, Nigeria

Francis Idachaba — Covenant University, Nigeria

Ismaila Idris — Federal University of Technology Minna, Nigeria

Nicholas Iwokwagh — Federal University of Technology Minna, Nigeria

Sanjay Misra	Covenant University, Nigeria
Isaac Odun-Ayo	Covenant University, Nigeria
Modupe Odusami	Covenant University, Nigeria
Morufu Olalere	Federal University of Technology Minna, Nigeria
Jonathan Oluranti	Covenant University, Nigeria
David Omole	Covenant University, Nigeria
Victor Onomza Waziri	Federal University of Technology Minna, Nigeria
Rajesh Prasad	African University of Science and Technology, Nigeria
Isaac Samuel	Covenant University, Nigeria

Workshops Committee

Hector Florez	Universidad Distrital Francisco José de Caldas, Colombia
Ixent Galpin	Universidad de Bogotá Jorge Tadeo Lozano, Colombia
Christian Grévisse	Université du Luxembourg, Luxembourg

International Advisory Committee

Matthew Adigun	University of Zululand, South Africa
Ricardo Colomo-Palacios	Østfold University College, Norway
Luis Fernandez Sanz	Universidad de Alcalá, Spain
Murat Koyuncu	Atilim University, Turkey
Raj Kumar Buyya	The University of Melbourne, Australia
Cristian Mateos	Universidad Nacional del Centro de la Provincia de Buenos Aires, Argentina
Victor Mbarika	Southern University, USA

Program Committee

Fernanda Almeida	Universidade Federal do ABC, Brazil
Francisco Alvarez	Universidad Autónoma de Aguascalientes, Mexico
Hernan Astudillo	Universidad Técnica Federico Santa María, Chile
Cecilia Avila	Fundación Universitaria Konrad Lorenz, Colombia
Jorge Bacca	Fundación Universitaria Konrad Lorenz, Colombia
Carlos Balsa	Instituto Politécnico de Bragança, Portugal
José Barros	Universidade de Vigo, Spain
Xavier Besseron	Université du Luxembourg, Luxembourg
Hüseyin Bicen	Yakin Dogu Üniversitesi, Cyprus
Dominic Bork	Universität Wien, Austria
Raymundo Buenrostro	Universidad de Colima, Mexico
Patricia Cano-Olivos	Universidad Popular Autónoma del Estado de Puebla, Mexico
Ines Casanovas	Universidad Tecnológica Nacional, Argentina
Germán Castañeda	Universidade Estadual de Campinas, Brazil
Elio Castillo	Universidad Nacional de Misiones, Argentina

Jaime Chavarriaga	Universidad de los Andes, Colombia
Erol Chioasca	The University of Manchester, UK
Robertas Damasevicius	Kauno Technologijos Universitetas, Lithuania
Victor Darriba	Universidade de Vigo, Spain
Helio de Oliveira	Universidade Federal de Pernambuco, Brazil
Luis de-la-Fuente-Valentín	Universidad Internacional de La Rioja, Spain
Cesar Diaz	OCOX AI, Colombia
Silvia Fajardo	Universidad de Colima, Mexico
Mauri Ferrandin	Universidade Federal de Santa Catarina, Brazil
Hector Florez	Universidad Distrital Francisco José de Caldas, Colombia
Ixent Galpin	Universidad de Bogotá Jorge Tadeo Lozano, Colombia
Olmer Garcia	Universidad de Bogotá Jorge Tadeo Lozano, Colombia
Javad Ghofrani	Hochschule für Technik und Wirtschaft Dresden, Germany
Raphael Gomes	Instituto Federal de Goiás, Brazil
Daniel Görlich	SRH Hochschule Heidelberg, Germany
Jānis Grabis	Rīgas Tehniskā Universitāte, Latvia
Christian Grévisse	Université du Luxembourg, Luxembourg
Guillermo Guarnizo	Universidad Santo Tomás, Colombia
Jens Gulden	Universiteit Utrecht, The Netherlands
Horacio Hoyos	Rolls-Royce, UK
Gilles Hubert	Institut de Recherche en Informatique de Toulouse, France
Monika Kaczmarek	Universität Duisburg-Essen, Germany
Musonda Kapatamoyo	Southern Illinois University Edwardsville, USA
Rodrigo Kato	Universidade Federal de Minas Gerais, Brazil
Kinshuk	University of North Texas, USA
Diana Lancheros	Universidad de La Salle, Colombia
Robert Laurini	Knowledge Systems Institute, USA
Marcelo Leon	Inicio Universidad Nacional de Loja, Ecuador
Keletso Letsholo	Higher Colleges of Technology, UAE
Tong Li	Beijing University of Technology, China
Isabel Lopes	Instituto Politécnico de Bragança, Portugal
Orlando Lopez	Universidad El Bosque, Colombia
Jose Martinez-Flores	Universidad Popular Autónoma del Estado de Puebla, Mexico
Rytis Maskeliunas	Kauno Technologijos Universitetas, Lithuania
Raul Mazo	Université Paris 1 Panthéon-Sorbonne, France
Hernan Merlino	Universidad Tecnológica Nacional, Argentina
Sergio Minniti	Università degli Studi di Padova, Italy
Sanjay Misra	Covenant University, Nigeria
Ivan Mura	Duke Kunshan University, China
Jonathan Oluratni	Covenant University, Nigeria
Hugo Peixoto	Centro ALGORITMI, Universidade do Minho, Portugal

Diego Peluffo-Ordóñez	Universidad Yachay Tech, Ecuador
Yoann Pitarch	Institut de Recherche en Informatique de Toulouse, France
Florencia Pollo-Cattaneo	Universidad Tecnológica Nacional, Argentina
Filipe Portela	University of Minho, Portugal
Juan Posadas	Universitat Politècnica de València, Spain
Pablo Pytel	Universidad Tecnológica Nacional, Argentina
Luis Rabelo	University of Central Florida, USA
Francisco Ribadas	Universidade de Vigo, Spain
Francklin Rivas	Universidad Técnica Federico Santa María, Chile
Ben Roelens	Open Universiteit, The Netherlands
José Rufino	Instituto Politécnico de Bragança, Portugal
Marcela Ruiz	Zürcher Hochschule für Angewandte Wissenschaften, Switzerland
Simona Safarikova	Univerzita Palackého v Olomouci, Czech Republic
Camille Salinesi	Université Paris 1 Panthéon-Sorbonne, France
Karina Salvatierra	Universidad Nacional de Misiones, Argentina
Christoph Schütz	Johannes Kepler Universität Linz, Austria
Manik Sharma	DAV University, India
Sweta Singh	Savitribai Phule Pune University, India
Inna Skarga-Bandurova	East Ukrainian National University, Ukraine
Modestos Stavrakis	University of the Aegean, Greece
Cristian Triana	Universidad El Bosque, Colombia
German Vega	Centre National de la Recherche Scientifique, France
Manuel Vilares	Universidade de Vigo, Spain
Fernando Yepes-Calderon	Children's Hospital Los Angeles, USA

Contents

Decision Systems

Health Care Information Systems

Human-Computer Interaction

Artificial Intelligence

A Machine Learning Model to Detect Fake Voice

Yohanna Rodríguez-Ortega$^{(\boxtimes)}$ (iD), Dora María Ballesteros (iD), and Diego Renza (iD)

Universidad Militar Nueva Granada, Bogotá, Colombia
{u3900269,dora.ballesteros,diego.renza}@unimilitar.edu.co

Abstract. Nowadays, there are different digital tools that permit the editing of digital content as audio files and they are easily accessed in mobile devices and personal computers. Audio forgery detection has been one of the main topics in the forensics field, as it is necessary to have reliable evidence in court. These audio recordings that are used as digital evidence may be forged and methods that are able to detect if they have been forged are required as new ways of generation of fake content continue growing. One method to generate fake content is imitation, in which a speaker can imitate another, using signal processing techniques. In this work, a passive forgery detection approach is proposed by manually extracting the entropy features of original and forged audios created using an imitation method and then using a machine learning model with logistic regression to classify the audio recordings. The results showed an accuracy of 0.98 where all forged audios were successfully detected.

Keywords: Fake voice · Machine learning · Logistic regression · Imitation

1 Introduction

Digital content like audio recordings, are an important element in the legal and digital forensics field, as they can be used as digital evidence to be analyzed by criminal investigators, since they are stored in computers, mobile phones, pen drives or another kind of storage devices [1]. The rise of new tools that permit the editing of digital content makes the manipulation easier to perform to the content, even if it is related to entertainment or another kind of purpose. Researches use this material in order to know the facts of a crime scene [2]. As a result, it can be the key element used to solve a legal case. Nowadays, some public and private agencies are implementing digital and multimedia sections focused on this category and they give training and certificates in the legal field [3].

There are different kinds of manipulations that can be done to an audio, depending on the kind of source. It is found that there are two main methods: multiple-source manipulation and single-source manipulation [4]. Multiple-manipulation is using more than one source to create the forged audios, and in single-source manipulation the content is altered without using other sources of content. As the audio files found as digital content, they are also a target of forgery. The most common audio forgery methods are deletion/insertion, copy-move and splicing [5].

© Springer Nature Switzerland AG 2020
H. Florez and S. Misra (Eds.): ICAI 2020, CCIS 1277, pp. 3–13, 2020.
https://doi.org/10.1007/978-3-030-61702-8_1

When deletion is applied, some parts of the audio are removed, this kind of forgery can lead to misunderstanding of the facts given in the audio file [4] besides, it is possible to insert audio fragments in the audio file coming from the same audio file [6] as the copy-move method in image manipulation, and this can be used to intentionally mislead. Splicing methods use different audio segments from different sources and then those segments can be assembled in an audio file [7]. This kind of manipulation is known as multiple-source manipulation [4] as mentioned before, these forged audio files can be used as evidence in court. In [8] it was proposed a method based on imitation for obtaining fake voice signals from original voice signals by applying a reordering task of the wavelet coefficients of the original voice signal. An audio generated using this method is also a forged one. Additionally, since GANs (Generative Adversarial Networks) were introduced [9], it is possible to create new content from a training set, which means that is possible to create audio files [10] that do not belong to a person in particular. This is related to speech synthesis which is also known as text-to-speech and its aim is to convert a text input into a speech output [11].

Regarding the detection of forged audios as in the detection of forged images, there are different approaches according to the kind or forgery made to the content. There are two kinds of forgery detection: active and passive approaches [12]. In order to have an active approach it is necessary to have information that is embedded in the digital content like watermarks using hash functions [13] and digital signatures [4]. The information obtained from them is used to assess if the content has been manipulated or not. These techniques are useful when the information of the original content is known. On the other hand, when this previously mentioned information is unknown, it is necessary to have a passive (blind) approach, this kind of approach extracts features from the content and identifying (if the case) the acquisition device, and it is not necessary to have additional information. There are different strategies that are used in order to detect alterations in audio files since some of them leave artifacts when they were edited in some way or manipulated, but forensic detectors are still weak in the detection of forgery when there are medium-high compression levels [14]. The acquisition devices are considered in order to detect manipulation by classifying microphones [15], when this information is obtained, it is possible to see if one audio has been forged, by checking if it has parts of different audios recorded with different microphones. In [16] there is a method which detects copy-move forgery using multi-feature decision having an accuracy of 99.0%. In [5] a blind approach is proposed using a voice activity detection (VAD) method, the purpose is to investigate audio recordings to detect and localize forgery. A method to detect splicing in audio recordings is used in [17] by detecting abnormal differences in the local noise levels in the audio signal.

As new forgery methods are created, not all the tools are able to detect all kinds of forgery and as it is important to have reliable evidence in courtrooms in order to solve a legal case, it is necessary to implement different kinds of computational tools that permit the forgery detection in audio evidence. In this instance, a tool that permits the identification of an audio that has been forged using an imitation process with a machine learning model is proposed. In this document, a false audio recording is an audio obtained by spoofing the voice, and when an original voice recording is transformed using signal processing techniques or machine learning is fake.

This paper is structured as follows: Sect. 2 briefly presents a background related to Machine learning, specifically to logistic regression and metrics of evaluation for classification. Section 3 presents the methodology used in this research. Section 4 shows the results obtained with the procedures and finally conclusions are shown in Sect. 5.

2 Background

This section briefly presents basic machine learning concepts of the topics addressed in the project.

2.1 Logistic Regression

Logistic regression is a machine learning classification technique and its aim is to be in a model that predicts the class of a sample and it is based on probabilities [18]. It is used in binary classification problems and fits the data to the logistic function shown in Eq. (1). This is based on the Sigmoid function (Fig. 1) represented in the model by $\hat{y} = \sigma(\theta^T)$, which gives the probability of a value belonging to a class, as it is a binary classification problem, this function will help to choose between the values "0" or "1" [19].

$$h_\theta(x) = \frac{1}{1 + e^{-\theta^T x}} \tag{1}$$

When $\theta^T x$ gets bigger, the value of the sigmoid function is closer to one. On the other hand, when $\theta^T x$ is small, the sigmoid function is closer to zero. The main purpose is to optimize the parameter θ that are trained. The optimum values of the parameters are found when the cost function shown in (2) is minimized using an optimization algorithm. Where $x^{(i)}$ corresponds to the single training data i; $y^{(i)}$ is the real output of the i data, h is the prediction or output.

$$J(\theta) = -\frac{1}{m} \sum_{i=1}^{m} \left[y^{(i)} log\left(h_\theta\left(x^{(i)}\right)\right) + \left(1 - y^{(i)}\right) log\left(1 - h_\theta\left(x^{(i)}\right)\right) \right] \tag{2}$$

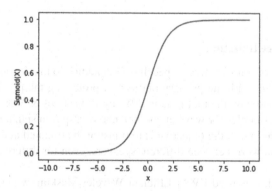

Fig. 1. Sigmoid function

It is important to analyze the performance of a machine learning model and the following metrics are commonly used to analyze them. A confusion matrix (Table 1) that can be binary or multi-class. Also, metrics for precision, recall, F1 score and overall accuracy (Table 2). Where TP is true positive, FP is false positive, TN is true negative, and FN is false negative.

Table 1. Confusion matrix

		Predicted	
		1	**0**
Real	**1**	TP	FN
	0	FP	TN

These metrics are useful when analyzing the performance of the model and it depends in the application that the model will have. When the designer of the model wants to choose the right metrics, it is necessary to analyze the goals that they have and the expected results in the validation and the external test. The ideal results have an error close to zero and it is also necessary to take into account the cost function that is being used when the model is trained [20].

Table 2. Metrics of performances for machine learning

Metric	Equation
Precision	$P = \frac{TP}{TP+FP}$
Recall	$R = \frac{TP}{TP+FN}$
F1 score	$F1 = 2 * \frac{1}{\frac{1}{precision} + \frac{1}{recall}}$
Overall accuracy	$OA = \frac{TP+TN}{TP+FN+FP+TN}$

2.2 Voice to Voice Imitation

Imitation is a way of transforming a speech (secret audio) so that it sounds like another speech (target audio) with the primary purpose of protecting the privacy of the secret audio. It was proposed by the first time in 2012 by Ballesteros & Moreno [8]. It works by re-ordering the samples (or wavelet coefficients) of a speech signal using a mapping process. As seen in Fig. 2, the objective is to transmit the imitated audio instead of the secret audio. It can work between different speakers, even for different languages and genres.

In this method, it is used EWM Efficient Wavelet Masking which is a scheme of speech-in-speech hiding proposed in [21].The adaptation of the speech signals is based

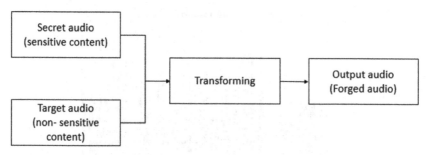

Fig. 2. Flowchart of imitation

on the following hypothesis: any voice (original) signal may seem similar to other voice signal (target) if its wavelet coefficients are sorted. The output is the fake voice recordings. If a person listens to the adapted secret signal, it sounds like a normal audio recording and it is not easy to identify if an audio has been forged using this method by humans. Figure 3 shows an original voice signal, Fig. 4 a target voice signal, and Fig. 5 shows the fake voice signal obtained from the original voice signal.

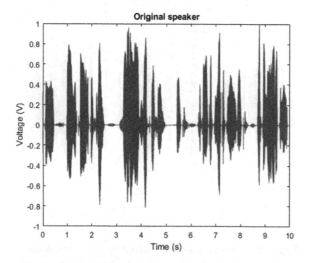

Fig. 3. Graph of the original recording in the time domain

When performing this imitation process, it is crucial to have both voice recordings with the same signal characteristics. As seen in Figs. 3 and 4, they have the same duration of ten seconds, and they were recorded with the same frequency sampling and resolution.

As shown in Figs. 3, 4 and 5, It is possible to see that the target signal and the fake audio signal are very similar, but one is original, and the other has been created by a signal processing algorithm.

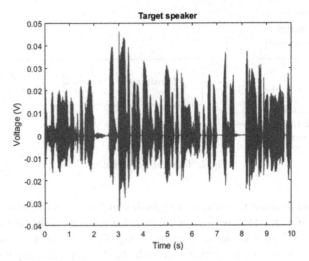

Fig. 4. Graph of the target recording in the time domain

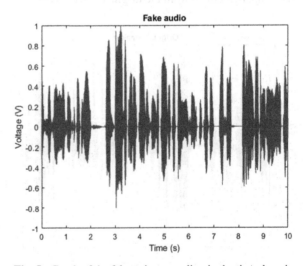

Fig. 5. Graph of the fake voice recording in the time domain

3 Methodology

This section presents the methodology proposed. It has four main steps described in Fig. 6 as follows:

Step 1: Data labeling
Step 2: Feature extraction
Step 3: Post-processing data
Step 4: Machine learning algorithm

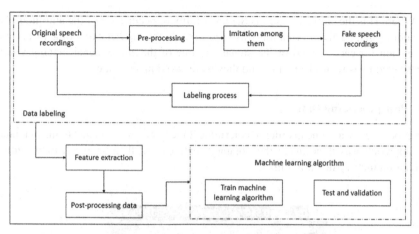

Fig. 6. Flowchart of the general solution

Figure 6 is going to be explained in the following sub-sections:

3.1 Data Labeling

A dataset was created in order to train the machine learning model. First, a set of original audios were recorded with the following characteristics:

- Number of speakers: 43
- Number of original recordings: 1,086
- Languages: Spanish, English, Portuguese, French and Tagalog
- Gender: Female and male
- Sample frequency: 44,100 Hz
- 16 bits
- Duration: 10 s
- Format: .WAV
- Acquisition device: Different devices

Once the audios were recorded, they were normalized. After that, the process of imitation among them was done obtaining a total of 10,000 imitated audio recordings. These audios were generated using the method described in [8]. The labels assigned were "1" for the original audios and "0" for the fake ones.

3.2 Feature Extraction

The entropy of the signal was used to obtain the features of the logistic classifier. Entropy is calculated according to Shannon's equation from [22] as:

$$H = -\sum p_i \log(p_i) \tag{3}$$

Where H is the entropy and p_i is the probability of occurrence of the amplitude i in the audio signal. This information was used to build the dataset extracting 11 entropy values, ten for each second of the signal and one of the entire signal, having a total 11,086 examples with 11 features and they were saved in a.csv file.

3.3 Post-processing Data

The experiment was done in order to determine if the features are related to the outcome, this approach was done using the obtained features and then analyzed them with a correlation matrix shown in Fig. 7.

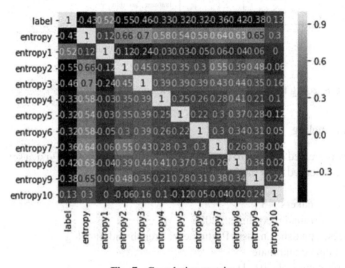

Fig. 7. Correlation matrix

In Fig. 8, the values for two features (two entropies), one for each class (0 and 1) were plotted to observe graphically if it was possible to separate two classes (original and forged audios) with the selected features. In Fig. 8, we can identify by sight that the classification is possible and using all the features (eleven) the process of classification is good.

3.4 Machine Learning Algorithm

In order to classify original and fake audios, a machine learning model was used. Logistic regression, a well-known classification method was chosen in this model. The dataset was divided into a training set, which was 20% of the total amount of examples and a testing set (80%) with random split of the examples. The performance metrics of the model are shown in the following section.

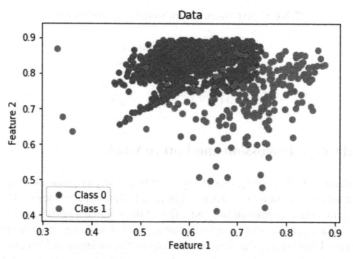

Fig. 8. Graph for two features of the dataset

4   Results

In Table 3, by using the entropy features for the entire signal and for every second of the signal to train the model with logistic regression, it is possible to observe the confusion matrix showing that all the fake audios were correctly classified as fake, but some of the original audios were classified as fake ones (only 36).

Table 3. dataset confusion matrix

		Predicted	
		Fake	**Original**
Real	**Fake**	1989	0
	Original	36	193

Although some of the original audios were classified as fake, the performance of the model using the previously mentioned metrics is very accurate. In Table 4, there are more metrics to measure the performance of the model: precision, recall and F1-score. According to the results, if the system classified a voice recording as original, the confidence about the result is 100%, it means that none of the fake voice recordings was labeled as original voice recording. In other words, if the predicted label is original, the legal authority can trust about this recording and used it as evidence.

Table 4. performance of the model using the dataset

Class	Precision	Recall	F1-Score
0	0.99	1	0.99
1	1	0.87	0.93

5   Conclusions, Discussion and Future Work

The proposed machine learning model was used to classify original and forged audios that were made with an imitation process. The results show an accuracy of 0.98, all fake audios were identified as fake audios and a few of the original audios were classified as fake audios. If a legal authority accepted an audio as evidence, they can trust that it is an original audio. Using entropy as feature, not only for the entire signal but also for every second of the signal, the correlation figures show correlation around 0.5, and then, these features help the classifier to separate original and fake voice recordings.

Our method is limited in the feature extraction, as all features were manually obtained and the model does not learn them automatically. We suggest using features that represent a similar behavior of the distribution, or features that are learned by the model for future work.

References

1. Digital evidence|NIST. https://www.nist.gov/topics/digital-evidence. Accessed 05 Nov 2019
2. A Simplified Guide To Forensic Audio and Video Analysis. http://www.forensicsciencesim plified.org/av/AudioVideo.pdf. Accessed 28 Aug 2019
3. ANSI National Accreditation Board|ANAB. https://www.anab.org/. Accessed 26 Aug 2019
4. Teerakanok, S., Uehara, T.: Digital media tampering detection techniques: an overview. In: Proceedings of IEEE 41st Annual Computer Software and Applications Conference, pp. 170–174. https://doi.org/10.1109/COMPSAC.2017.109, https://doi.org/10.1109/COMPSAC.2017.109
5. Imran, M., Ali, Z., Bakhsh, S.T., Akram, S.: Blind detection of copy-move forgery in digital audio forensics. IEEE Access, 12843–12855. https://doi.org/10.1109/ACCESS.2017.2717842
6. Ali, Z., Imran, M., Alsulaiman, M.: An automatic digital audio authentication/forensics system. IEEE Access, 2994–3007. https://doi.org/10.1109/ACCESS.2017.2672681
7. Chen, J., Xiang, S., Huang, H., Liu, W.: Detecting and locating digital audio forgeries based on singularity analysis with wavelet packet. Multimedia Tools Appl. **75**(4), 2303–2325 (2014). https://doi.org/10.1007/s11042-014-2406-3
8. Ballesteros, D.M., Moreno, J.M.: Highly transparent steganography model of speech signals using Efficient Wavelet Masking. Expert Syst. Appl. **39**(10), 9141–9149. https://doi.org/10.1016/j.eswa.2012.02.066
9. Goodfellow, I.J., et al.: Generative adversarial networks, pp. 1–9. https://arxiv.org/abs/1406.2661
10. Audio Generation with GANs - Neuronio - Medium. https://medium.com/neuronio/audio-generation-with-gans-428bc2de5a89. Accessed 16 Sept 2019

11. Ning, Y., He, S., Wu, Z., Xing, C., Zhang, L.-J.: Review of deep learning based speech synthesis. Appl. Sci. **9**(19), 1–16. https://doi.org/10.3390/app9194050
12. NBA Warif et al.: Copy-move forgery detection: survey, challenges and future directions. J. Netw. Comput. Appl., 259–278 (2016). https://doi.org/10.1016/j.jnca.2016.09.008
13. Gul, E., Ozturk, S.: A novel hash function based fragile watermarking method for image integrity. Multimedia Tools Appl. **78**(13), 17701–17718 (2019). https://doi.org/10.1007/s11 042-018-7084-0
14. Milani, S., Piazza, P.F., Bestagini, P., Tubaro, S.: Audio tampering detection using multimodal features, 4563–4567. https://doi.org/10.1109/ICASSP.2014.6854466
15. Cuccovillo, L., Mann, S., Tagliasacchi, M., Aichroth, P.: Audio tampering detection via microphone classification. In: 2013 IEEE International Workshop on Multimedia Signal Processing. MMSP 2013, pp. 177–182 (2013). https://doi.org/10.1109/MMSP.2013.6659284
16. Xie, Z., Lu, W., Liu, X., Xue, Y., Yeung, Y.: Copy-move detection of digital audio based on multi-feature decision. J. Inf. Secur. Appl., 37–46. https://doi.org/10.1016/j.jisa.2018.10.003
17. Pan, X., Zhang, X., Lyu, S.: Detecting splicing in digital audios using local noise level estimation. In: ICASSP, IEEE International Conference on Acoustics, Speech and Signal Processing - Proceedings, pp. 1841–1844. https://doi.org/10.1109/ICASSP.2012.6288260
18. Isak-Zatega, S., Lipovac, A., Lipovac, V.: Logistic regression based in-service assessment of mobile web browsing service quality acceptability. EURASIP J. Wireless Commun. Netw. **2020**(1), 1–21 (2020). https://doi.org/10.1186/s13638-020-01708-2
19. Javed, A., Ejaz, A., Liaqat, S., Ashraf, A., Ihsan, M.B.: Automatic target classifier for a ground surveillance radar using linear discriminant analysis and logistic regression. In: European Microwave Week 2012: "Space for Microwaves", EuMW 2012, Conference Proceedings, pp. 302–305 (2012)
20. Goodfellow, I.J., Bengio, Y., Courville, A.: *Deep Learning*
21. Ballesteros, D.M., Moreno, J.M.: On the ability of adaptation of speech signals and data hiding. Expert Syst. Appl. **39**(16), 12574–12579 (2012). https://doi.org/10.1016/j.eswa.2012.05.027
22. Shannon, C.E.: A mathematical theory of communication. Bell Syst. Tech. J.. [Online]. Available: http://www.math.harvard.edu/~ctm/home/text/others/shannon/entropy/ entropy.pdf. Accessed 16 Sept 2019

A Q-Learning Hyperheuristic Binarization Framework to Balance Exploration and Exploitation

Diego Tapia[1]($\boxtimes$) , Broderick Crawford[1] , Ricardo Soto[1] ,
Felipe Cisternas-Caneo[1] , José Lemus-Romani[1] , Mauricio Castillo[1] ,
José García[1] , Wenceslao Palma[1] , Fernando Paredes[2] , and
Sanjay Misra[3]

[1] Pontificia Universidad Católica de Valparaíso, Valparaíso, Chile
{broderick.crawford,ricardo.soto,jose.garcia,wenceslao.palma}@pucv.cl,
{diego.tapia.r,felipe.cisternas.c,jose.lemus.r,
mauricio.castillo.d}@mail.pucv.cl
[2] Universidad Diego Portales, Santiago, Chile
fernando.paredes@udp.cl
[3] Covenant University, Ota, Nigeria
sanjay.misra@covenantuniversity.edu.ng

Abstract. Many Metaheuristics solve optimization problems in the continuous domain, so it is necessary to apply binarization schemes to solve binary problems, this selection that is not trivial since it impacts the heart of the search strategy: its ability to explore. This paper proposes a Hyperheuristic Binarization Framework based on a Machine Learning technique of Reinforcement Learning to select the appropriate binarization strategy, which is applied in a Low Level Metaheuristic. The proposed implementation is composed of a High Level Metaheuristic, Ant Colony Optimization, using Q-Learning replacing the pheromone trace component. In the Low Level Metaheuristic, we use a Grey Wolf Optimizer to solve the binary problem with binarization scheme fixed by ants. This framework allowing a better balance between exploration and exploitation, and can be applied selecting others low level components.

Keywords: Hyperheuristics · Binarization framework · Reinforcement learning · Metaheuristics · Combinatorial optimization

1 Introduction

The optimization problems are diverse in the industry, in general they can be considered as a maximization or minimization of an objective function, subject to constrains. In the field of combinatorial optimization, the solutions are coded in variables that take discrete values, this means that the solution to the problem can be an integer, a subset, a permutation or a graph [3], and those have no polynomial solution time, also know as NP-Hard [4]. Given the complexity of solving NP-Hard

© Springer Nature Switzerland AG 2020
H. Florez and S. Misra (Eds.): ICAI 2020, CCIS 1277, pp. 14–28, 2020.
https://doi.org/10.1007/978-3-030-61702-8_2

problems with exact methods, it is that approximate methods are used, sacrificing the guarantee of finding the optimal one, for good solutions [3].

This research proposes a framework, which supported through a Machine Learning (ML) technique, allows to properly decide a binarization scheme in the context of a problem that requires a binary solution. This paper proposes a Hyperheuristic Binarization Framework based on a Machine Learning technique of Reinforcement Learning, particularly Q-Learning, to select the appropriate binarization strategy, which is applied in a Low Level Metaheuristic, in this case Grey Wolf Optimizer, solving a Optimization Combinatorial Problem.

This section exposes the general concepts around Metaheuristics, Hyperheuristics and the area of ML. Later, in Sect. 3 the Hyperheuristic Framework supported by Q-Learning is defined, and then in the Sect. 4 propose an implementation using Ant Colony Optimization and Grey Wolf Optimizer, solving the Set Covering Problem. Finally, in Sect. 6 conclusions are made with respect to the improvement potentials when using an automated decision framework, by virtue of improving the search for solutions.

2 Background

2.1 Metaheuristics and Hyperheuristics

In the approximate methods, there are heuristic algorithms, procedures to find solutions that do not guarantee the optimal [15]. Metaheuristics (MH) can then be defined as a generic or higher level heuristic that is more general in problem solving [19], a master strategy that guides and modifies other heuristics to produce solutions beyond those that are normally generated in a local search [28]. Some existing MH in the literature are Tabu Search (TS) [17], Greedy Randomized Adaptive Search Procedure (GRASP) [16], Ant Colony Optimization (ACO) [12] and Genetic Algorithms (GA) [18].

The concept of Hyperheuristics was introduced by P. Cowling et al. [8], to define a higher level of abstraction than current Metaheuristic approaches, which manages which heuristics should be used at any given time. An objective is that Hyperheuristics will lead to more general systems that are able to handle a wide range of problem domains rather than current metaheuristic technology which tends to be customised to a particular problem or a narrow class of problems [5].

2.2 Machine Learning

ML is a field that lies at the intersection of statistics, artificial intelligence and computer science [27], in order to develop models that can learn through experience. These models can be categorized as [2]:

1. Supervised Learning [21]: models are trained with desired input and output pairs, so you can generate outputs from new inputs. There are two major

problem areas: classification and regression. In the first one, you seek to determine a label within a set of possibilities, while the regression problems seek to predict a continuous number. Some models in the literature: Logistic Regression (LR), Decision Trees (DT), Support Vector Machines (SVM), Neural Networks (NN).

2. Unsupervised Learning [6]: only the input data is known, and it seeks to gain knowledge from it. The problems in this area are those of transformation and clustering. In the former, the aim is for the data to be easily understood, for example, by reducing its dimensionality. On the other hand, in clustering, we seek to generate partitions of different groups, where their elements are similar. Some examples from the literature are: K-Means, DBSCAN.

3. Reinforcement Learning [32]: the purpose of the models is to know what decisions to make in order to maximize a reward signal. There are two fundamental characteristics: trial-error and late reward. The above, through an agent capable of perceiving the environment, and making decisions that affect its state. An example is the Q-Learning technique [35].

3 Proposed Framework

The proposed Framework aims to improve selection with respect to the binarization scheme used by Low-Level Metaheuristic (LL-MH). For this purpose, it is used a High-Level Teamwork Hybrid (HLTH) approach, that is to say, that in which a dynamically acquired knowledge is extracted in parallel during the search in cooperation with a LL-MH [33]. From this cooperation, ML technique can learn, to improved the quality metric(s) selected for LL-MH.

As shown in Fig. 1, there is a Two-Level solver, in the low level there is a MH that works in the domain of continuous solutions. In the upper level, there is a MH that has the task of selecting the best binarization scheme to be applied in the lower level. The selection of the binarization scheme is very relevant to maintain an adequate balance between exploration and exploitation, because there are more exploratory binarization schemes than others. For example, the V-Shape transfer function is more exploratory than S-Shape [24], the Elitist operator is more exploratory [26]. This decision is supported by an Reinforcement Learning (RL) technique, specifically Q-Learning.

The High-Level layer uses an RL technique that helps to select based on the quality metrics obtained by the previous decisions, in order to improve the decision making. These quality metrics should show how our solution improves, e.g. solution fitness, ratio of improvement to previous fitness, number of movements to obtain an improvement, or a metric of interest at the discretion of the researcher.

Recall that, RL is a learning algorithm that selects a suitable action based on experience by interacting with the environment. The learner receives a reward or penalty after performing each selected action [7]. This concept its utilized to proposed a mechanism of learning in the high-level MH.

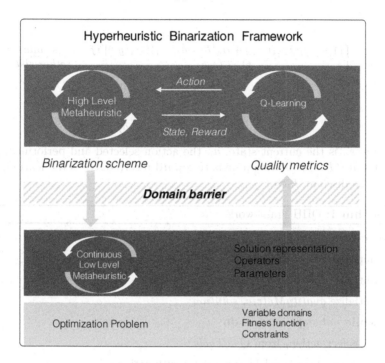

Fig. 1. Hyperheuristic Binarization Framework

3.1 Q-Learning

In Q-Learning, the agent maintains a current policy (the best policy it is figured out so far) and wanders about its environment following that policy. The goal is ultimately to figure out the optimal (smartest possible) policy, that is, the policy which brings in the highest expected rewards over the agent's lifetime. [23]

Dynamic programming usually refers to figuring out policies for agents in Markovian environments where the transition probability P and reward function R are known beforehand, as shown by Eq. 1. From an artificial intelligence perspective, if we have P and R, this is not a very interesting algorithm. Such algorithms are often called model-free algorithms, and RL is distinguished from dynamic programming by its emphasis on model-free algorithms.

Q-Table is a function $Q(s, a)$ over every possible state s and action a that could be performed in that state.

$$Q(s,a) = R(s,a) + \gamma \sum_{s'} P(s'|s,a) max Q(s',a') \tag{1}$$

For consider Q-Learning like ML algorithm, we need to replace the $\sum_{s'} P(s'|s,a)$ and $R(s,a)$, for this, we let them learn from the environment, and we can defined that the agent experience consists in a sequence of different stages or episodes. In the umpteenth episode, the agent:

$$Q_n(s,a) = \begin{cases} (1 - \alpha_n)Q_{n-1}(s,a) + \alpha_n[R(s,a) + \gamma V_{n-1}(y_n)] \; if & \text{s} = \text{s}_n \; and \; a = a_n \\ Q_{n-1}(s,a) & ; otherwise \end{cases}$$

(2)

$$V_{n-1}(y) \equiv max \; Q_{n-1}(y,b) \tag{3}$$

Where, s_n is the current state, a_n the action selected and performed, y_n is the next state, $R(s,a)$ is the immediate reward received, α_n is the learning rate and γ is the discount factor.

Algorithm 1: QHH Framework

---

1 **Procedure** *QHH()*

2   Initialize Set of Actions A;

3   Initialize $Q - Table(A)$ and initial *state*;

4   Initialize *qualityMetric, solution*;

5   **while** *not stop criterion* **do**

6   Select action$_t$ from $Q - Table$

7   Apply Low-Level Metaheuristic with action$_t$

8   Update *qualityMetric, solution*

9   Update $Q - Table$

10   *state* ← state$_{t+1}$

11   **end**

12   Return Best Solution and Best Quality Metric

13 **end**

---

4 Implementation Approach

This section shows an implementation of the framework, using as high level Metaheuristics Ant Colony Optimization and Grey Wolf Optimizer in the low level, solving the Set Covering Problem.

4.1 Set Covering Problem

The Set Covering Problem (SCP) is a classic optimization problem, which can be used to model in different applications and various domains, such as assignment problems, transport networks, among others. This problem is class NP-Hard, so it will be used as an example of implementation in this research [33].

The SCP can be defined as:

$$\text{Minimize} \quad Z = \sum_{j=1}^{n} c_j x_j \tag{4}$$

Subject to

$$\sum_{j=1}^{n} a_{ij} x_j \geq 1 \quad \forall i \in I \tag{5}$$

$$x_j \in \{0, 1\} \quad \forall j \in J \tag{6}$$

Where, $A = a_{ij}$ be a mxn binary matrix with $I = \{1, 2, ..., m\}$ and $J = \{1, 2, ..., n\}$. If $a_{ij} = 1$ then we say that column j cover row i. The cost of selecting column j is c_j. Finally, x_j is the problem decision variable, which indicates whether column j is selected ($x_j = 1$) or not ($x_j = 0$).

4.2 Grey Wolf Optimizer Metaheuristic (Low Level)

Grey Wolf Optimizer (GWO) is inspired in Grey wolves behavior, that are considered as apex predators. The main phases of grey wolf hunting are as follows: i) Tracking, chasing, and approaching the prey, ii) Pursuing, encircling, and harassing the prey until it stops, iii) Attack towards the prey. Grey wolves mostly search according to the position of the α, β and δ. They diverge from each other to search for prey and converge to attack prey [25].

Consider $\overrightarrow{X_1}, \overrightarrow{X_2}, \overrightarrow{X_3}$ Grey wolves (candidates solutions) α, β and δ, respectively. The random parameters $\overrightarrow{A}$, to indicate that grey wolves diverge (exploration) from the prey or converge (exploitation) towards the prey, and $\overrightarrow{C}$, the effect of obstacles to approaching prey in nature.

It is defined, $\overrightarrow{A} = 2\overrightarrow{a}\overrightarrow{r_1} - \overrightarrow{a}$, where components of $\overrightarrow{a}$ are linearly decreased from 2 to 0 over the course of iterations, $\overrightarrow{r_1}$ its a uniform random vector $[0,1]$, and $\overrightarrow{C} = 2\overrightarrow{r_2}$, where $\overrightarrow{r_2}$ uniform random vector $[0,1]$.

$$\overrightarrow{D} = \mid \overrightarrow{C} \cdot \overrightarrow{X_p}(t) - \overrightarrow{X}(t) \mid \tag{7}$$

$$\overrightarrow{X}(t+1) = \overrightarrow{X_p}(t) - \overrightarrow{A} \cdot \overrightarrow{D} \tag{8}$$

where $\overrightarrow{X_p}(t)$ its the position of the grey wolves, later the position of the prey, can be estimate by:

$$\overrightarrow{X}(t+1) = \frac{\overrightarrow{X_\alpha} + \overrightarrow{X_\beta} + \overrightarrow{X_\delta}}{3} \tag{9}$$

Algorithm 2: Grey Wolf Optimizer

---

1 **Procedure** *GWO(binarizationScheme)*

2   Initialize population X (search agents)

3   Initialize parameters a, A, and C

4   Calculate fitness and determine X_α, X_β and X_δ

5   **while** *t less than MaxIterations* **do**

6   **foreach** *x in X* **do**

7   Update the position using Eq. (8)

8   **end**

9   Update a, A and C

10   Apply Binarization (X, binarizationScheme)

11   Calculate fitness of population X

12   Update X_α, X_β and X_δ

13        $t \leftarrow t_{+1}$

14   **end**

15   Return Best Fitness, Best Solution

16 **end**

4.3   Two-Step Binarization

One of the purposes of the Framework is the selection of the appropriate discretization scheme in each iteration of the LL-MH.

It is proposed as a first approach, the two-step binarization as discretization scheme, which works by applying a transfer function, as shown in Table 1, which take the solution from the $\mathbb{R}^n \rightarrow \{Integer Space\}$, and then, finally, apply a binarization operator $\{Integer Space\} \rightarrow \mathbb{Z}^n$ [10], among which are Standard, Complement, Static Probability and Elitist, as shown in Table 2.

Table 1. Transfer Function family

S-shape		V-shape	
Name	Transfer function	Name	Transfer function
S1	$T(d_w^j) = \frac{1}{1+e^{-2d_w^j}}$	V1	$T(d_w^j) = \left| erf\left(\frac{\sqrt{\pi}}{2}d_w^j\right) \right|$
S2	$T(d_w^j) = \frac{1}{1+e^{-d_w^j}}$	V2	$T(d_w^j) = \left| tanh(d_w^j) \right|$
S3	$T(d_w^j) = \frac{1}{1+e^{\frac{-d_w^j}{2}}}$	V3	$T(d_w^j) = \left| \frac{d_w^j}{\sqrt{1+(d_w^j)^2}} \right|$
S4	$T(d_w^j) = \frac{1}{1+e^{\frac{-d_w^j}{3}}}$	V4	$T(d_w^j) = \left| \frac{2}{\pi}arctan\left(\frac{\pi}{2}d_w^j\right) \right|$

Table 2. Binarization function

Binarization Function
$Standard \longmapsto X_{new}^j = \begin{cases} 1 \; if \;\; rand \leq T\left(d_w^j\right) \\ 0 \qquad\quad else \end{cases}$
$Complement \longmapsto X_{new}^j = \begin{cases} Complement\left(X_w^j\right) \; if \;\; rand \leq T\left(d_w^j\right) \\ 0 \qquad\qquad\qquad\quad else \end{cases}$
$StaticProbability \longmapsto X_{new}^j = \begin{cases} 0 \qquad if \;\; T\left(d_w^j\right) \leq \alpha \\ X_w^j \; if \;\; \alpha < T\left(d_w^j\right) \leq \frac{1}{2}(1+\alpha) \\ 1 \qquad if \;\; T\left(d_w^j\right) \geq \frac{1}{2}(1+\alpha) \end{cases}$
$Elitist \longmapsto X_{new}^j = \begin{cases} X_{Best}^j \; if \;\; rand < T\left(d_w^j\right) \\ 0 \qquad\qquad else \end{cases}$

4.4 Ant Colony Optimization (High Level)

The MH Ant Colony Optimization (ACO), inspired by the natural behavior of ants, defines them as a group of agents that through their movements build solutions. These artificial ants communicate with each other by means of a pheromone trail, which increases as the ant prefers certain paths of better quality (fitness). In other words, the pheromone deposited influences the probability of other ants in the colony choosing a certain route [22].

Originally, ACO was applied for the resolution of the Travel Salesman Problem (TSP) [14], a problem that aims to minimize a cost function, regarding the trip made by a salesman in a network, subject to the constraint of visiting each city only once, a Hamiltonian cycle. However, in [22], an adaptation was proposed for subset problems, thus allowing the choice of an element more than once. The SCP has been solved with different MHs succesfully [9,11].

$$Prob_i^{ant}(t) = \begin{cases} \dfrac{\tau_i^\alpha \eta_i^\beta}{\displaystyle\sum_{j \in allowed_{ant}} \tau_j^\alpha \eta_j^\beta} & if \;\; item_i \; in \; allowed_{ant}(t) \\ 0 \quad else. \end{cases} \tag{10}$$

$$\tau_i(t, t+1) = (1-\rho)\tau_i(t) + \sum_{ant} \triangle\tau_i^{ant}(t, t+1) \tag{11}$$

$$\triangle\tau_i^{ant}(t, t+1) = \begin{cases} F(fitness_k) & if \; ant \; incorpore \;\; item_i \\ 0 \;\; else. \end{cases} \tag{12}$$

Where τ is the pheromone trail, which corresponds to the memory of the paths traced by the ants. η is the heuristic information, which allows the ant to have visibility regarding future choices. In addition, α and β correspond to weight parameters for τ and η, respectively, which allow to have a trade-off between exploration and exploitation. ρ is a discount factor for the ant's memory, which is the evaporation of the pheromone. Finally, F is a function of the fitness of each ant, which allows to update the trace of the pheromone, this will depend on the problem, if it is of maximization or minimization.

Algorithm 3: Ant Colony Optimization - Subset Problem

---

1 **Procedure** $ACO()$

2   Initialize total cycles c, total artificial ants A

3   **for** $t = 1$ *to* c **do**

4   **for** $ant = 1$ *to* A **do**

5              $allowed_{ant}$ = set of all items

6   **while** $allowed_{ant}$ *is not empty* **do**

7   Select item $item_i$ with probability Eq. 10

8   Remove $item_i$ from $allowed_{ant}$

9   **end**

10   Calculate $fitness_{ant}$ and Save the best fitness so far

11   **end**

12   Update trails of pheromone on all items with Eq. 11

13   **end**

14   Return Best Solution and Best Fitness

15 **end**

4.5 ACO Hyperheuristic

As indicated in Fig. 1, the framework proposes a high-level Metaheuristic, for this case ACO, aims to select a particular discretization scheme from the set BS as {Transition Function} × {Binarization Operator}. Where, Transition Function is defined by $\{V1, ..., V4, S1, ..., S4\}$ and Binarization Operator by $\{Standard, Complement, StaticProbability, Elitist\}$.

Recall that, the ant's learning is guided by visibility information that is described by η, while τ allows the ant to communicate its previous choices. In order to generate a learning, taking into account the previous decisions, it is proposed to replace the pheromone by a value considering actions previously taken, which have meant a penalty or reward according to the quality metric obtained. This decision is used with a RL approach, using the Q-Learning technique, where the decision in this learning will correspond to which technique of the BS set (*action*) to select in each iteration (*state*) [20].

Algorithm 4: AntHHQ-GWO

1 **Procedure** *AntHHQ-GWO()*

2   Initialize total artificial ants A, *bestQualityMetric*, *bestSolution*

3   Initialize set of binarization schemes BS

4   Initialize Q-Table(BS) and initial *state*

5   **for** $t = 1$ *to iterMax* **do**

6   **for** *ant* $= 1$ *to* A **do**

7   **while** *not stop criterion* **do**

8   Select bs_i with probability Eq. 13

9   Get *qualityMetric* and *Solution* from $GWO(bs_i)$ Algorithm 2.

10   Update *qualityMetric$_{ant}$*

11   **if** *qualityMetric best than bestQualityMetric* **then**

12   Update *qualityMetric* and *bestSolution*

13   **end**

14   Apply *QtableUpdate(qualityMetric, bs$_i$, state)*

15   **end**

16   **end**

17   *state* $\leftarrow$ state$_{t+1}$

18   **end**

19   Return *bestSolution*

20 **end**

In Eq. 13 an ML mechanism is introduced to improve the search and learning capabilities of MH [30], in place of a random choice. For this reason, this knowledge will guide and improve the performance of the search, making the MH intelligent and informed. [34]. This in terms of obtaining a better balance between exploration and exploitation in order to achieve a better convergence to the optimum.

$$Prob_{bs}^{ant}(s) = \frac{Q - Table(s, bs)^{\alpha} \eta_i^{\beta}}{\sum\limits_{j \in BS} Q - Table(s, bs)_j^{\alpha} \eta_j^{\beta}} \tag{13}$$

The importance of having a quality metric information allows you to assign a reward or penalty in Q-Values updates for Q-Table. This update mechanism is shown in the Algorithm 5. Note that, the reward is assigned if the quality metric improves, otherwise it is penalized keeping, for this case, the reward as zero.

Algorithm 5: Q-Table Update

---

1 Procedure *QtableUpdate(qualityMetric,action,state)*

2 $\quad$ Get *Qmax* from Q-Table to *state* -1

3 $\quad$ Set reward $= 0$

4 $\quad$ **if** *qualityMetric best than bestQualityMetric* **then**

5 $\qquad$ | reward $= 1$

6 $\quad$ **end**

7 $\quad$ Obtain *Qnew* by Eq. 2 with *reward, action* and *Qmax*

8 $\quad$ With *Qnew* update all Q-Values for *state*

9 $\quad$ Return Qvalues

10 end

---

5   Experimental Results

The experiments were developed in Python (3.7) language. Experiments were designed to demonstrate a better convergence when supported with a machine learning technique and the performance between Exploration and Exploitation. Instances from the OR library [1] were used for the Set Covering Problem.

Three experiments were designed. The first one is Grey Wolf Optimizer helped with Q-Learning (GWO-Q) for the selection of the Binarization Scheme (BS). The second is GWO supported by a Hyperheuristic Ant Colony Optimization for the selection of the BS (AntHH-GWO). The last experiment is AntHH supported by Q-Learning for the selection of BS in GWO (AntHHQ-GWO).

The purpose is to compare a MH approach supported by a ML technique against a hyperheuristic selection approach: GWO-Q vs AntHH-GWO. On the other side, to observe the changes of the approach by adding a RL technique in a HH Framework: AntHH-GWO vs AntHHQ-GWO (Table 3).

Table 3. Comparative results for experiment and instance

Instance	Optimal	GWO-Q		AntHH-GWO		AntHHQ-GWO	
		Best	Worst	Best	Worst	Best	Worst
SCP.41	429	431	437	433	433	430	433
SCP.51	253	254	270	255	262	255	255
SCP.61	138	141	146	141	143	138	143
SCP.A1	253	258	265	257	258	256	257
SCP.B1	69	69	76	71	71	69	71
SCP.C1	227	231	246	231	231	229	231
SCP.D1	60	61	65	61	61	60	61
SCP.NRE1	29	29	33	29	29	29	29

To complement the above, the Fig. 2 shows the percentage of relative error, Eq. 14, in relation to the optimal of each instance. It is shown that AntHH-Q in front of the two methods, obtains a lower error dispersion, which generates a better convergence, as a result of the balance between Exploration and Exploitation, this improvement can be seen by avoiding premature convergence.

$$Error = \frac{|BestFitness - OptimalFitness|}{OptimalFitness} \qquad (14)$$

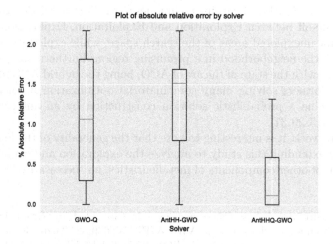

Fig. 2. Absolute relative error by solver.

Figure 3 shows the convergence behaviour of the experimental results obtained for the SCP51 instance for the best performances of each hyperheuristic. It is known that ACO algorithms emphasize Exploration in the initial stages and Exploitation in the final stages, the inclusion of Q-Learning as an intergenerational learning technique, allows more information to be accumulated throughout the iterations, avoiding the premature convergence and increasing its effectiveness.

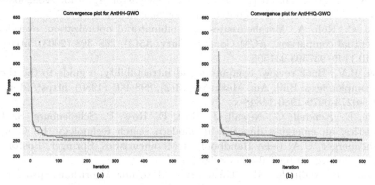

Fig. 3. Best convergence curve comparative AntHH-GWO (a) vs AntHHQ-GWO (b).

6   Conclusions

The proposed Framework allows to automate the decision making about the binarization schemes to be used by some Metaheuristics in the field of continuos. This decision making is made with the learning generated from the strategy that can provide better results in each area of the search space.

With this learning, it is possible to better use the search information, through the quality metrics obtained from the low level, improving with respect to a random selection of the binarization strategy to be used.

Incorporating Machine Learning techniques to the metaheuristics would allow a better trade-off between Exploration and Exploitation. Exploration refers to the search for unexplored areas of the search space, while exploitation refers to the search of the neighborhood in a promising region. Furthermore, our results are consistent with the state of the art of ACO, being the hybrid ACO algorithms the best performers solving many combinatorial optimization problems, these hybrids combine a probabilistic solution construction by an ant colony with local search [13, 29, 31].

As future work, it is interesting to note that the generality of the Framework, would allow extending this study to analyze the exploration and exploitation in the selection of other components of metaheuristics, not necessarily binarization schemes.

Acknowledgements. Felipe Cisternas-Caneo is supported by Grant DI Investigación Interdisciplinaria del Pregrado/VRIEA/PUCV/039.324/2020. Broderick Crawford is supported by Grant CONICYT/FONDECYT/REGULAR/1171243. Ricardo Soto is supported by Grant CONICYT/FONDECYT/REGULAR/1190129. José Lemus-Romani is supported by National Agency for Research and Development (ANID)/Scholarship Program/DOCTORADO NACIONAL/2019 - 21191692. José García is supported by the Grant CONICYT/FONDECYT/INICIACION/11180056.

References

1. Beasley, J.E.: Or-library: distributing test problems by electronic mail. J. Oper. Res. Soc. **41**(11), 1069–1072 (1990). http://www.jstor.org/stable/2582903
2. Bishop, C.M.: Pattern Recoginiton and Machine Learning (2006)
3. Blum, C., Roli, A.: Metaheuristics in combinatorial optimization: overview and conceptual comparison. ACM Comput. Surv. **35**(3), 268–308 (2003). https://doi.org/10.1145/937503.937505
4. Book, R.V.: Book review: computers and intractability: a guide to the theory of NP-completeness. Bull. Am. Math. Soc. **3**(2), 898–905 (1980). https://doi.org/10.1090/s0273-0979-1980-14848-x
5. Burke, E., Kendall, G., Newall, J., Hart, E., Ross, P., Schulenburg, S.: Hyper-heuristics: an emerging direction in modern search technology. In: Glover, F., Kochenberger, G.A. (eds) Handbook of Metaheuristics. Springer, Boston(2006). https://doi.org/10.1007/0-306-48056-5_16
6. Celebi, M.E., Aydin, K. (eds.): Unsupervised Learning Algorithms. Springer, Cham (2016). https://doi.org/10.1007/978-3-319-24211-8

7. Choong, S.S., Wong, L.P., Lim, C.P.: Automatic design of hyper-heuristic based on reinforcement learning. Inf. Sci. (NY). (2018). https://doi.org/10.1016/j.ins.2018.01.005
8. Cowling, P., Kendall, G., Soubeiga, E.: A hyperheuristic approach to scheduling a sales summit. In: Burke, E., Erben, W. (eds.) PATAT 2000. LNCS, vol. 2079, pp. 176–190. Springer, Heidelberg (2001). https://doi.org/10.1007/3-540-44629-X_11
9. Crawford, B., Soto, R., Astorga, G., García, J.: Constructive metaheuristics for the set covering problem. In: Korošec, P., Melab, N., Talbi, E.-G. (eds.) BIOMA 2018. LNCS, vol. 10835, pp. 88–99. Springer, Cham (2018). https://doi.org/10.1007/978-3-319-91641-5_8
10. Crawford, B., Soto, R., Astorga, G., García, J., Castro, C., Paredes, F.: Putting continuous metaheuristics to work in binary search spaces (2017). https://doi.org/10.1155/2017/8404231
11. Crawford, B., Soto, R., Olivares, R., Riquelme, L., Astorga, G., Johnson, F., Cortés, E., Castro, C., Paredes, F.: A self-adaptive biogeography-based algorithm to solve the set covering problem. RAIRO - Oper. Res. **53**(3), 1033–1059 (2019). https://doi.org/10.1051/ro/2019039
12. Dorigo, M., Birattari, M., Stützle, T.: Ant colony optimization artificial ants as a computational intelligence technique. IEEE Comput. Intell. Mag. (2006). https://doi.org/10.1109/CI-M.2006.248054
13. Dorigo, M., Gambardella, L.M.: Ant colony system: A cooperative learning approach to the traveling salesman problem. IEEE Trans. Evol. Comput. (1997). https://doi.org/10.1109/4235.585892
14. Dorigo, M., Maniezzo, V., Colorni, A., Dorigo, M.: Positive Feedback as a Search Strategy. Technical report, 91-016 (1991)
15. Eusuff, M., Lansey, K., Pasha, F.: Shuffled frog-leaping algorithm: A memetic meta-heuristic for discrete optimization. Eng. Optim. (2006). https://doi.org/10.1080/03052150500384759
16. Feo, T.A., Resende, M.G.: A probabilistic heuristic for a computationally difficult set covering problem. Oper. Res. Lett. (1989). https://doi.org/10.1016/0167-6377(89)90002-3
17. Glover, F.: Tabu search-Part II. ORSA J. Comput. (1990). https://doi.org/10.1287/ijoc.2.1.4
18. Holland, J.H.: Genetic algorithms. Sci. Am. (1992). https://doi.org/10.1038/scientificamerican0792-66
19. Hussain, K., Mohd Salleh, M.N., Cheng, S., Shi, Y.: Metaheuristic research: a comprehensive survey. Artif. Intell. Rev. **52**(4), 2191–2233 (2018). https://doi.org/10.1007/s10462-017-9605-z
20. Khamassi, I., Hammami, M., Ghédira, K.: Ant-Q hyper-heuristic approach for solving 2-dimensional Cutting Stock Problem. In: IEEE SSCI 2011 - Symposium Series Computing Intelligent - SIS 2011 2011 IEEE Symposium Swarm Intelligent (2011). https://doi.org/10.1109/SIS.2011.5952530
21. Kotsiantis, S.B.: Supervised machine learning: a review of classification techniques. In: Proceedings of the 2007 Conference on Emerging Artificial Intelligence Applications in Computer Engineering: Real Word AI Systems with Applications in EHealth, HCI, Information Retrieval and Pervasive Technologies, pp. 3–24. IOS Press, NLD (2007). https://doi.org/10.5555/1566770.1566773
22. Leguizamon, G., Michalewicz, Z.: A new version of ant system for subset problems. In: Proceedings of the 1999 Congress on Evolutionary Computation, CEC 1999 (1999). https://doi.org/10.1109/CEC.1999.782655

23. Lones, M.: Sean Luke: essentials of metaheuristics. Genet. Program Evolvable Mach. (2011). https://doi.org/10.1007/s10710-011-9139-0
24. Mafarja, M., Eleyan, D., Abdullah, S., Mirjalili, S.: S-shaped vs. V-shaped transfer functions for ant lion optimization algorithm in feature selection problem. In: ACM International Conference Proceedings Series (2017). https://doi.org/10.1145/3102304.3102325
25. Mirjalili, S., Mirjalili, S.M., Lewis, A.: Grey Wolf Optimizer. Adv. Eng. Softw. (2014). https://doi.org/10.1016/j.advengsoft.2013.12.007
26. Mirjalili, S., Song Dong, J., Lewis, A.: Nature-Inspired Optimizers (2020).https://doi.org/10.1007/978-3-030-12127-3
27. Müller, A.C., Guido, S.: Introduction to Machine Learning with Python: a guide for data scientists (2016). https://doi.org/10.1017/CBO9781107415324.004
28. Muncie, H.L., Sobal, J., DeForge, B.: Research methodologies (1989). https://doi.org/10.5040/9781350004900.0008
29. Solnon, C.: Ants can solve constraint satisfaction problems. IEEE Trans. Evol. Comput. (2002). https://doi.org/10.1109/TEVC.2002.802449
30. Song, H., Triguero, I., Özcan, E.: A review on the self and dual interactions between machine learning and optimisation. Progress Artif. Intell 8(2), 143–165 (2019). https://doi.org/10.1007/s13748-019-00185-z
31. Stützle, T., Hoos, H.H.: MAX-MIN ant system. Futur. Gener. Comput. Syst. (2000). https://doi.org/10.1016/S0167-739X(00)00043-1
32. Sutton, R.S., Barto, A.G.: Reinforcement learning: an introduction 2018. Technical report (2017). https://doi.org/10.1109/TNN.1998.712192
33. Talbi, E.G.: Metaheuristics: From Design to Implementation (2009). https://doi.org/10.1002/9780470496916
34. Talbi, E.G.: Machine learning into metaheuristics: a survey and taxonomy of data-driven metaheuristics, June 2020. https://hal.inria.fr/hal-02745295, working paper or preprint
35. Watkins, C.J., Dayan, P.: Technical note: Q-learning. Mach. Learn. (1992). https://doi.org/10.1023/A:1022676722315

Artificial Neural Network Model for Steel Strip Tandem Cold Mill Power Prediction

Danilo G. de Oliveira[1,3], Eliton M. da Silva[2], Fabiano J. F. Miranda[3],
José F. S. Filho[3], and Rafael S. Parpinelli[1,2(✉)]

[1] Graduate Program in Applied Computing,
Santa Catarina State University – UDESC, Joinville, Brazil
danilo.oliveira@arcelormittal.com.br, rafael.parpinelli@udesc.br
[2] Department of Computer Science, Santa Catarina State University – UDESC,
Joinville, Brazil
elitonmachadod200@gmail.com
[3] ArcelorMittal – Global Research and Development Group,
São Francisco do Sul, Brazil
fabiano.miranda@amcontratos.com.br, jose.francisco@arcelormittal.com.br

Abstract. In the cold rolling of flat steel strips, electric energy consumption is one of the highest expenses. Predicting the power requirements according to the line and product conditions can significantly impact the energy cost and, thus, on the business's profitability. This paper proposes predicting the power requirements of a tandem cold rolling mill of steel strips on a coil-to-coil base applying Artificial Neural Networks (ANN) as a uni-variate regression problem. The tests yielded an MSE of 300.39 kW or 2.4% and are better than the acceptable 5% error margin for this project, indicating that the ANN presented satisfactory results. The application of six full-month worth of data in the trained ANN model showed the excellent correlation of the ANN predictions with the measured data, leading to the conclusion that the system is ready for the deployment for daily use for line engineers. Overall, the results obtained show that the steel industry can highly benefit from Industry 4.0 and Artificial Intelligence technologies.

Keywords: Steel industry · Artificial Intelligence · Industry 4.0 · Regression problem · Automotive industry

1 Introduction

The challenging economic and market conditions faced by the steel industry in the last decade, which resulted from low steel demand and overcapacity, has caused severe changes in how steel producers operate. This challenging market condition concomitant with high raw material prices is driving the steel industry into prioritizing the reduction of operational costs as much as possible to maintain the profitability of the business [1]. In the cold rolling of flat steel strips, electric energy consumption is one of the highest expenses. The tandem cold

H. Florez and S. Misra (Eds.): ICAI 2020, CCIS 1277, pp. 29–42, 2020.
https://doi.org/10.1007/978-3-030-61702-8_3

rolling mill (TCM) studied in this paper, composed of four stands, has a total installed electrical power of 27.0 MW.

Such high-power requirements rest in the fact that steel presents a high resistance to plastic deformation. Thus, it is the material of choice of the automotive industry and is a crucial element in reinforcing the automobile structure to improve the safety of the drivers and other occupants in the event of a car crash. Additionally, to achieve the required mechanical properties to comply with the safety regulations, the strip thickness must be reduced by up to 85% in the cold rolling process, requiring a considerable amount of energy. The mechanical energy required to perform such work is delivered to the mill by electric motors connected to the work rolls by a shaft and gearbox. These motors are responsible for converting electrical energy into mechanical energy.

In the Brazilian electric energy market, high power demanding industries are required to inform the National Electric System Operator the expected power consumption in advance [2]. This procedure allows the entity to predict energy consumption peaks and prevent disruptions caused by insufficient generation. These industries must purchase in advance the right to consume such power at that specific moment and are subject to very high penalties if their actual power requirement exceeds the purchased amount. On the other hand, if the power is not consumed, there are no refunds.

For all these reasons, predicting the power requirements according to line and product conditions can have a significant impact on the energy cost and, thus, on the profitability of the business. In addition to this, there is also a close mathematical relationship between power and energy. This paper proposes predicting the power requirements of a tandem cold rolling mill of steel strips on a coil-to-coil base applying Artificial Neural Networks as detailed hereafter. Since the power requirement is a variable of the continuous domain, the problem at hand is characterized as a uni-variate regression problem [3]. This paper is organized as follows: Sect. 2 brings the background, Sect. 3 describes the proposed approach, Sect. 4 shows the experiments and results obtained, and Sect. 5 shows the conclusion and future research directions.

2   Background

2.1   Data Base and Industry 4.0

As early as 1940, the steel industry has started massive instrumentation of the hot and cold rolling mills. This movement has allowed the gathering of a significant amount of data. This allowed many researchers to work on the modeling of strip rolling, especially between 1940 and 1950 [4]. As a result, rolling mills are considered one of the most successful technological processes of the modern industry [5].

To improve their level of intelligence, Hu et al. and Routh and Pal indicate that several businesses around the world are actively building an overall management and control platform [6,7]. The platform is designed to collect, process, monitor, control, manage and optimize data using technologies such as cloud computing, Internet of Things (IoT), and big data, which can be summarized as what is being called Industry 4.0 [7]. Such movement towards the new intelligent data management is the potential value it can yield [7]. Routh and Pal expect Industry 4.0 to have a total economic potential of USD 3.9 trillion to 11.1 trillion per year in 2025 [7].

Even though the steel industry is heavily instrumented and with massive data-sets at its disposal, this segment has not achieved the same level of data intelligence many other industries have in the path to reach the modern concepts of Industry 4.0 [6]. Most steel enterprises are composed of large scale, complex, and utterly different equipment [5], which makes it very difficult to integrate product data across the production chain, which renders these processes almost an isolated island in the digital world. However, most of these companies are now moving towards more integration between these processes and increasing the business's level of intelligence aiming at the potential value Industry 4.0 concepts can provide [6].

2.2   The Rolling Theory and Modeling

Cold rolling is an efficient economical process for the production of thin sheets and strips for subsequent cold forming operations where the sheet quality is critical in terms of material microstructure, uniformity of mechanical properties, thickness, and surface texture [8]. Figure 1 shows a representation of a four stands tandem cold mill of steel strips. Each stand in this case is composed of one pair of backup rolls and one pair of work rolls, being the last ones responsible for the plastic deformation of the strip. At the exit side of the mill, the steel is coiled for further processing at downstream lines.

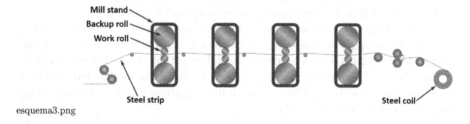

esquema3.png

Fig. 1. Representation of a tandem cold mill with 4 stands. Source: Created by authors.

Many theories for both hot and cold rolling have been put forward in the last century or so beginning with the pioneering works of Sibel and von Karman in 1924 and 1925 [9], where they developed the first equations to predict both rolling force and torque. The latter, in particular, is of great interest for the prediction of mill power requirements since it allows the straight calculation of the power when multiplied by the work roll speed and the efficiency factor of the transformation of electric energy into mechanical energy delivered to the rolls.

Orowan developed the most comprehensive of these theories proposed in the 20Th century in 1943 [9]. He discussed the complicating factor of the deformation's in-homogeneity, the variation of the material yield stress during rolling, and the different friction regimes between rolls and strip observed in the process. Despite the fact it is generally acknowledged as an 'exact' theory of rolling, Orowan's approach is based on inherent assumptions, including plane-strain deformation and no elastic deformation of the work-piece [4].

Nonetheless, the complexity of this method undoubtedly caused later research workers to develop solutions based on simplified assumptions, which allowed analytical expressions to be developed [9]. Unfortunately, this inevitably led to a sacrifice in accuracy, not serious in the case of the estimation of roll force but much more significant in the prediction of roll torque [9], which is a crucial element in predicting the rolling power requirements of the mill.

With the advent of modern electronic computers, better accuracy has been achieved for industrial rolling conditions, in which computing time is critical to provide the mill with the necessary set points for rolling the coming coil. However, yet Alexander has concluded that "none of the existing theories of rolling can ever be expected to predict roll torque with any precision" [9] since the simplifications required to solve the complex, non-linear equations involved in the cold rolling process result in unacceptable incorrect predictions.

Freshwater, in 1996, even after adapting Alexander's solution and using Orowan's inhomogeneous method, concluded that there were significant differences between prediction and experimental results when rolling copper strips with tensions [8], which is often the case when rolling steel strips due to significant higher material hardness.

However, most TCMs rely on an online rolling model for the prediction of several set points, including rolling power. This model is frequently monitoring process measured data and comparing them with its predictions for the last few products. The differences (or model inaccuracies) are fed into a special adaption algorithm designed to adjust various model parameters to compensate these errors by a learning procedure [8]. Unfortunately, this strategy is efficient only when measured process data is readily available so that this adaption algorithm can play its part before each new calculation. So, even though this model is accurate enough for the problem at hand, it is not suitable for predicting energy consumption several days in advance.

The finite-element method, which originated in the structural analysis field, has been rapidly expanded to a wide range of non-structural problems for which exact solutions cannot be found with existing techniques [6]. When applied to a roll of steel strips, this method can simulate the deformation of the metal in the roll gap and predict the roll contact stresses, the total rolling load, and the torque of rolling [5]. The precision reported in many different works is unmatched by any other method, and this approach is frequently used as a benchmark to evaluate the accuracy of different models [7]. On the other hand, the necessary computing resources and the time to achieve a fully converged solution limits this technique's general application to case studies rather than an everyday tool for predicting rolling conditions.

Alternatively to the classical, analytical rolling theory, or the accurate but costly finite-element method, novel approaches, such as soft computing techniques, are becoming common in the steel industry. There has been considerable focus on artificial Neural Networks in the recent past as it is widely applicable as an approximation for problems with highly non-linear, complex data [6].

2.3   Artificial Neural Networks

An Artificial Neural Network (ANN) is generally comprised of a collection of artificial neurons that are interconnected to perform some computation on input data and create output patterns [10]. Even though these artificial neural networks are usually arranged in a complex architecture of several neurons arranged in different layers and with many interconnections, the calculations involved are relatively simple.

ANN is a type of model well established in machine learning and has also become competitive to regression and statistical models regarding usefulness [11]. Nowadays, they are widely used for uni- and multi-variable regression problems because of their excellent self-learning properties, fault tolerance, non-linearity, and advancement in input to output mapping [11]. Different artificial neural network architectures have been proposed since the 1980 s, and one of the most influential is the multi-layer perceptrons (MLP) [12]. This architecture is the most used in many different forecasting applications because of its inherent pattern-recognition capability, relatively simple configuration, and high speed [12].

Typically an MLP is composed of several layers of neurons. The first layer is responsible for receiving the external information and feeding it to the ANN, while the last layer is an output layer where the problem solution is obtained [12]. There are one or more intermediate layers between these two layers, also called hidden layers, which are the core of the artificial neural network. The interconnections between the neurons located in the hidden layers are responsible for storing the input and output variables' relationship. Thus, ANNs are well suited for problems whose solutions require knowledge that is difficult to specify but for which there are enough data or observations available for the training of the network [12].

Training is the iterative process that determines the weights (or the significance) of each input of each neuron in the network. These weights are initially defined in a stochastic fashion and are adjusted according to the error between the expected value (referred to as the target) and the actual output of the network calculation. This scenario is known as supervised learning. As these weights are adjusted, and the error reduces in each iteration, one could say that the ANN is learning and the weights store the knowledge the network is acquiring from the data-set.

The problem with such data-driven modeling approaches, as ANNs, is that the underlying rules governing the behavior of the process are not always evident, and observations are often masked by noise in industrial conditions. Nevertheless, in some situations, this approach provides the only feasible way to solve real-world problems [12].

Another advantage of the ANNs is their generalization capacity. After learning from the data presented to them during the training procedure, neural networks can often correctly infer the unseen part of a population even if the sample data contain noisy information [12]. With the right architecture and configuration, they can also be used to learn and generalize from very complex, non-linear data-sets without any prior knowledge or assumptions about how each input variable influences the outputs.

The next section provides examples of the application of ANN in works related to this project.

2.4   Related Work

The application of soft computing techniques in the steel industry remotes to the early 1990s [6]. The application of such techniques for predicting energy consumption or power requirements has not been found in the literature, but its use in different process variables provided valuable insight during the development of this project.

In their work, Lee and Lee, back in 2002, have applied artificial neural networks for improving the accuracy of roll-force modeling in a hot strip rolling mill [14]. They observed that, in order to maintain the efficiency of the ANN in accurately predicting the roll-force on the long-term, frequent retraining must be performed by an engineer. According to them, the cause for this behavior is frequently changing process conditions, and future work would focus on implementing an automatic training procedure.

One can argue that Lee and Lee left one or more variables out of their neural network training, which would explain such long-term behavior of the ANN [14]. However, it is often the case to have faulty sensors or equipment operating not in its ideal conditions in industrial applications. The authors of this paper, based on their industrial and practical modeling experience, agree with Lee and Lee and are also implementing functionalities in this system that will allow frequent retraining of the ANN to compensate for any changes in process variables or line conditions such as new products being added to the portfolio.

Gudur and Dixit have shown that neural networks can also be used as a large data-set generator [13] . In their paper, an ANN has been trained to emulate with acceptable accuracy the calculations of a finite-element model of tandem cold mill roll force and torque and then generate a large amount of data which was later used in a fuzzy inference model. According to them, this approach provided the required data-set without the prohibitive computational costs of the finite-element model and provided insight into the power of this pattern-recognition algorithm [13].

Hu et al. have reviewed and cited more than 60 papers concerning the application of soft computing techniques in the steel industry [6]. They observed that most of these researches focused on improving rolling force and torque calculations, flatness predictions and actuators, production flow and scheduling optimizations, thickness and temperature control, and other process variables [6]. Hu et al. also noted an increase in recent years in using such techniques to improve the processing of the strip and provide better quality to the customer and reduce production losses [6]. None of these works, however, concern the prediction of power requirements or energy consumption.

Mosavi et al., in their systematic review of the application of machine learning to energy systems, have cited more than 100 documents comprising residential and industrial consumption prediction, the design of distribution and generation energy system of cities and hole countries [15].

Green computing is the use of computers and related technology in the study and practice of environmentally sustainable computing that includes, for example, systems' energy efficiency maximization reducing the impact of carbon emissions on our environment [16]. The steel industry is well-known for its relatively high emissions, and it is being pushed throughout the world to reduce its environmental impact [1]. However, the review made by Mosavi et al. have not found references of its application in steel manufacturing [15].

The researches mentioned above and the research proposed in this paper are applications related to green computing since it provides the means not only to reduce costs but also to preserve the environment by providing a better understanding of the correlation between process parameters and power requirements. But in the specific case of this paper, these concepts are applied to an industry which is not yet benefiting from all the advantages Industry 4.0 and Artificial Intelligence can bring to the business and to the environment.

The following sections detail the methodology used in this work, the experiments conducted throughout the development of this project, and discussions on the results as well.

3 Proposed Method

The objective is to predict the required motor power of a steel strip tandem cold mill. The system is modeled to predict the necessary power of all four stands of the mill. Hence, the problem at hand is a uni-variate regression problem. Figure 2 depicts the flowchart of the proposed method. The process starts with the data collection followed by the pre-processing step that prepares data to build the ANN model. Next, the data split phase separates the data-set into training, validation, test, and application portions. The next step creates the ANN architecture that is used in the train/validation step. The trained model is used in the test and application phases. In the following, each step is described in detail.

The data collection consists of the extraction of the selected data. The selected variables are shown in Table 1. They are the average exit line speed (AvgS), the average target line speed (AvgTgS), the coil weight (Wg), the entry coil thicknesses (EntrTh), the exit coil thicknesses (ExitTh), the total coil reduction (Red), the coil width (Wd), the strip hardness (SH), the coil running time (CRT), and the average total required power (AvgP). From Table 1, the first

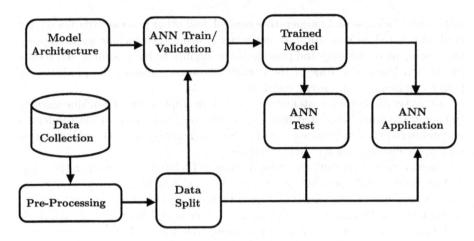

Fig. 2. Flowchart showing the proposed method.

column shows the variable identification, the second column shows variables description, the third column shows the variable domain followed by its range, the fifth column shows the variable unit, and the last column informs which variables are used as input and output of the model. The first nine variables are the independent ones and represent the ANN input data. The last variable is the dependent variable and represents the neural network output data. As it can be noticed in the third column of Table 1, the output variable to predict is from continuous domain characterizing the problem to be solved as a univariate regression problem. The dataset is not available to download due to company restrictions.

The next stage corresponds to the pre-processing of the collected data, followed by removing empty and not-a-number values since problems in the data

Table 1. Description of the input and output variables of the model.

Item	Description	Domain	Range	Unit	Usage
AvgS	Average exit line speed	Real	[85.0 – 910.0]	mpm	Input
AvgTgS	Average target line speed	Real	[230 – 900]	mpm	Input
Wg	Coil weight	Real	[0.6 – 37.5]	t	Input
EntrTh	Entry coil thickness	Real	[1.8 – 4.8]	mm	Input
ExitTh	Exit coil thickness	Real	[0.35 – 2.70]	mm	Input
Red	Total coil reduction	Real	[35.0 – 85.0]	%	Input
Wd	Coil width	Real	[750 – 1878]	mm	Input
SH	Strip hardness	Real	[64.0 – 150.0]	kgf/mm^2	Input
CRT	Coil running time	Real	[0.002 – 4.600]	h	Input
AvgP	**Average total required power**	**Real**	**[2551.9 – 19489.8]**	**kW**	**Output**

collection system cause these, and then scaling. The scaling algorithm plays a fundamental role in this process as the variables involved in this project present completely different ranges and physical units, as Table 1 indicates. The selected scaling algorithm was the MinMaxScaller as it compresses the data within -1 and 1. The most significant advantage of the algorithm is that it keeps the original data distribution [17]. However, this algorithm is susceptible to outliers. Another essential step in the pre-processing of the data consists of the detailed verification of the dataset range.

The database is composed of 14 months worth of production. This data-set is split into two main portions: the first eight months and the last six months. The first eight months are used in the training/validation/test procedures. The last six months are used to simulate the application of the ANN in a monthly prediction. This procedure was defined to mimic the conditions this system will endure over the years when used by line engineers to predict real power requirements. Following this procedure, the line engineers can retrain the ANN in the case of changing line conditions, for example, or new products are added to the production schedule.

The training/validation/test data (represented by eight months of data) are split in 80% for training and 20% for testing the model. Concerning the training data, 20% is separated and used for validation of the model before testing. All data separation is performed at random using Uniform distribution.

The ANN architecture employed in this work comprises seven input nodes representing the input variables, three hidden layers with 30 nodes each, and one output node representing the output variable. The hyperbolic tangent is used as activation function. The model architecture was empirically defined. The *Adam* optimizer was employed to train the model with a learning rate of 0.001. Also, a mini-batch of size 32 was employed.

During the training procedures, the Mean Absolute Error (MAE) and the Mean Squared Error (MSE) are being kept track of both training and validation. The stop criterion has been defined as the mean squared error of the validation procedure.

4   Experiments and Results

This project was developed on Python3 with Tensorflow as the main library. An Intel(R) Core(TM) i9-9900K CPU @3.60 GHz, 62 GB RAM, equipped with an NVIDIA Geforce Titan V 12 GB, was used in experiments.

To verify the robustness of the model, the cross-validation procedure was employed [18] with the number of folds set to 10. The cross-validation consists in splitting the training data (8 months dataset) into ten folds. Each fold is used once to validate the model generated using the remaining folds. In this cross-validation experiment, 1000 epochs were employed. The average and standard deviation of the MSE resulting from the cross-validation are 8.45×10^{-4} and 1.06×10^{-4}, which were considered very low for the problem at hand. The cross-validation processing time was 2 h and 27 min.

Figure 3 depicts the evolution of the MAE and MSE metrics (y-axis) over the epochs (x-axis) using the standard data separation (80%–20% as described in Sect. 3). The behavior of both these metrics and the training shows that the algorithm did not find local attractors since it followed a smooth curve throughout the entire procedure. However, as the orange line of MSE in Fig. 3 shows, the validation, or generalization capability of the network, have not improved in the last 100 of the 827 epochs (limited to 1000), and the training stopped to prevent over-fitting of the ANN. The training processing time took 25 min.

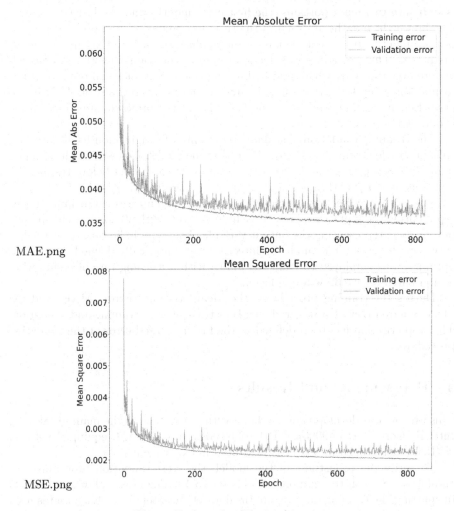

Fig. 3. Train and validation history.

The test results of the trained network are shown in Fig. 4, which compares real coil average required power and the predicted required power of the test data. The tests yielded an MSE of 300.39 kW or 2.4% and are better than the acceptable 5% error margin for this project. The distribution of most of the points around the ideal diagonal indicates that the neural network presented satisfactory results.

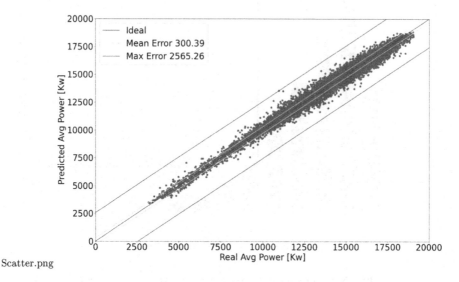

Scatter.png

Fig. 4. Comparison between real coil average required power and predicted average required power.

Figure 5 shows the same data of Fig. 4 but grouping the data by percentage of MSE. This representation clearly shows that 90.1% of the tested coils presented a predicted mean squared error of less than 5.0% in comparison with the real measured power value and more than 50% of the cases, the MSE was lower than 2.0%, which are at least 34% better than the existing online model explained in Sect. 2.2. Considering that the ANN does not retrofit line measurements on a coil-to-coil basis to adjust its inaccuracies (as does the online model used in this comparison), the results obtained are promising.

The last step of the prediction model is applying the trained model in the remaining six months of unseen data. The aim is to ensure the model is ready for daily use by line engineers. A monthly visualization of the prediction also provides relevant insight into how accurate the MLP artificial neural network has performed. Figure 6 shows the results for this scenario, which shows the sum of measured and predicted required power of every coil separated according to the month of production for the six remaining months. Figure 6 indicates a strong correlation between the sum of total monthly predictions and real measured power.

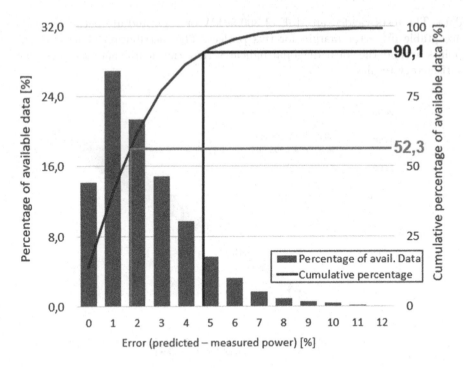

Fig. 5. Coil quantity (y-axis) per absolute error (x-axis).

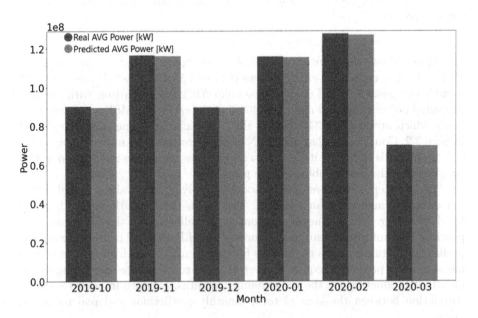

Fig. 6. Comparison between real monthly required power and predicted required power.

5   Concluding Remarks and Future Works

The generation of electric energy for an entire country requires planing and coordination. Therefore, high demanding industries, such as a tandem cold rolling mill facility, have to predict the required power with great accuracy to reduce energy contract costs.

The steel industry have massive databases at its disposal and highly instrumented equipment but there is much to be done to effectively use these advantages to drive the business into Industry 4.0 concepts. However many enterprises are focusing efforts on improving the steel industry intelligence.

The present work brings the concept of applying Industry 4.0 and Artificial Intelligence together to address a practical industrial issue that is the reduction of electric energy costs by predicting the required electric power.

The output variable, the required power, is a continuous variable leading the problem at hand to a uni-variate regression problem. Hence, it was applied a multi-layer perceptron artificial network resulting in a mean squared error of 2.4%. The cross-validation procedure presented a very low standard deviation, which indicates that the selected architecture is robust for the problem at hand and proves once more the MLP's pattern-recognition capability.

The comparison of a full-month worth of data predicted by the network against values measured online also indicate the excellent correlation of the ANN predictions with the measured data leading to the conclusion that this system is ready for the deployment for daily use for line engineers.

However, even though the prediction of the power requirement is essential information for controlling the cold mill production cost, the total energy consumption has a much more significant impact on the business's profitability. Thus, the development of a model for the prediction of total energy consumption is considered a topic for future study. Another future research direction is to approach the problem by using time series prediction. Also, we intend to explore other supervised learning prediction methods and compare them with the results obtained by the proposed approach.

Acknowledgements. The authors are thankful to ArcelorMittal Vega (Sao Francisco do Sul, SC, Brazil) and the FAPESC agency for providing financial support. We gratefully acknowledge the support of NVIDIA Corporation with the donation of the Titan V GPU used for this research.

References

1. Ministerial Meeting on the Global Forum on Steel Excess Capacity(GFSEC) Held. https://www.meti.go.jp/english/press/2019/1026-001.html. Accessed 29 Jul 2020
2. ONS, ONS - Operador Nacional do Sistema Elétrico, ONS - Operador Nacional do Sistema Elétrico. http://ons.org.br:80/paginas/sobre-o-ons/o-que-e-ons. Accessed 02 Jul 2020
3. Mohammadi, S.: Neural network for univariate and multivariate nonlinearity tests. Stat. Anal. Data Min. ASA Data Sci. J. **13**(1), 50–70 (2020)

4. Roberts, W.L.: Cold Rolling of Steel. M. Dekker, New York (1978)
5. Lenard, J.G.: Primer on Flat Rolling. Elsevier Ltd. 2nd edn. (2014)
6. Hu, Z., Wei, Z., Sun, H., Yang, J., Wei, L.: Optimization of metal rolling control using soft computing approaches: a review. Arch. Comput. Methods Eng. (2019)
7. Routh , K., Pal, E.T.: A survey on technological, business and societal aspects of Internet of Things by Q3. In: 2017, 3rd International Conference On Internet of Things: Smart Innovation and Usages (IoT-SIU), pp. 1–4 (2018)
8. Freshwater, I.J.: Simplified theories of flat rolling, part I. The calculation of roll pressure, roll force and roll torque. Int. J. Mech. Sci. **38**, 633–648 (1996)
9. Alexander, J.M.: On the theory of rolling. Proc. R. Soc. Lond. Ser. A, Math. Phys. Sci. **326**(1567), 535–563 (1972)
10. Brownlee, Jason: Clever Algorithms: Nature-Inspired Programming Recipes, 1st edn. LuLu, Abu DhabiAbu Dhabi (2011)
11. Abiodun, O.I., et al.: State-of-the-art in artificial neural network applications: a survey. Heliyon **4**(11), e00938 (2018). https://doi.org/10.1016/j.heliyon.2018.e00938
12. Zhang, C., Patuwo, B.E., Hu, M.Y., The state of the art: Forecasting with artificial neural networks. Int. J. Forecast. **14**, 35–62 (1998)
13. Gudur, P.P., Dixit, U.S.: An application of fuzzy inference for studying the dependency of roll force and roll torque on process variables in col flat rolling. Int. J. Adv. Manuf. Technol. **42**, 41–52 (2009)
14. Lee, D., Lee, Y.: pplication of neural-network for improving accuracy of roll-force model in hot-rolling mill. Control Eng. Pract. **10**(4), 473–478 (2002)
15. Mosavi, A., et al.: State of the art of machine learning models in energy systems, a systematic review. Energies **12**(7), 1301 (2019)
16. Singh, S.: Green computing strategies challenges. In: 2015 International Conference on Green Computing and Internet of Things (ICGCIoT), pp. 758–760 (2015)
17. Kotsiantis, S., Kanellopoulos, D., Pintelas, P.E.: Data preprocessing for supervised learning. Int. J. Comput. Sci. **1**, 111–117 (2006)
18. Perrotta, F., Parry, T., Neves, L.C.: Application of machine learning for fuel consumption modelling of trucks. In: IEEE International Conference on Big Data (Big Data), Dec 2017, pp. 3810–3815 (2017)

Fairly Ranking the Neediest in Worldwide Social Systems. An Artificial Intelligence Approach Born in Cov2 Pandemic Outbreak

Alvin Gregory[1]([⊠]) [iD], Eduardo Yepes Calderon[2] [iD], Fernando Jimenez[1] [iD],
J. Gordon McComb[4] [iD], and Fernando Yepes-Calderon[2,3] [iD]

[1] Universidad de los Andes, Cra. 1 18a 12, Bogotá, Colombia
{ad.gregory,fjimenez}@uniandes.edu.co
[2] GYM Group SA, Carrera 78 A No. 6-58, Cali, Colombia
eduardo@gym-group.org
[3] SBP LLC, 604 Beach CT, Fort Pierce, FL 34950, USA
fernando.yepes@strategicbp.net
[4] Children's Hospital Los Angeles,
1300 N Vermont Avenue No. 1006, Los Angeles, CA 90027, USA
gmccomb@chla.usc.edu

Abstract. Without a clear view about how long the Cov2 will continue affecting the humankind, governments are facing a multi striking menace with no precedents. The first big challenge was to define whether trying to block contamination or curing the sick. The question seemed to have two answers depending on the established medical capacity of each country. However, in less than two months, even the leaders of wealthy countries had to admit that there was only one answer: obligated isolation. Less wealthy countries adopted confinement, but soon, they encounter a more lethal endanger. These societies are modest for a myriad of reasons. They have weak economies with unemployment rates above 10% and labor informality, ranging from half of the workforce. Leaders started sending to confinement people who work for a wage and who cannot accumulate money. Forcibly, governments activated their social emergency protocols, and the disfavored start receiving the aid. Here rises another dimension of the current dilemma. How to assure that benefits reach the right homes? How long should the aid last?

This document describes the complexity of being fair in delivering goods to the neediest in social ecosystems that lack a good reputation. Where the recipients of the benefits, often present themselves as permanently impoverished. A system where these two groups of the social structure – decision-makers and recipients of aid – find a commonplace of mutual convenience that drains the countries' unsupervised public treasuries.

The proposed solution employs machine-learning in the core to fairly classifying society's most vulnerable members. The system incorporates a decision layer where morals and ethics are abstracted and remain unmodifiable, creating a fraud-free platform.

© Springer Nature Switzerland AG 2020
H. Florez and S. Misra (Eds.): ICAI 2020, CCIS 1277, pp. 43–55, 2020.
https://doi.org/10.1007/978-3-030-61702-8_4

Keywords: Artificial intelligence · Social aid systems · Fighting corruption

1   Introduction

Although the Covid-19 has a low lethally index [12], it has a rapid spreadability [6]. The virus uses mucus secretion to travel from an infected individual to a new host, but it can also travel in the form of aerosols and using third agents in the form of fomites [16]. Since humans are the vectors, social contact favors contamination. Less wealthy countries faced contagion, trying to flatten the number of positives for the COVID19 in the timeline. Such as strategy requires confinement [13]; therefore, citizens working for a wage and informal workforce started suffering a shortage in nurture and capacity to buy the essentials, such as water, energy, medicine, and self-care elements.

Social covering systems in the world share the following core concept: the community is a holistic entity, and governments assist the neediest using part of the funds collected within the same society.

Governments around the world declared a state of emergency and released laws to protect the neediest [8]. Identifying people in need might be feasible in developed countries. Not the case of developing countries, where the planning departments filter out individuals who do not comply with the rules to receive the aid using improvised criteria.

The current cov2 pandemic made visible and old issue. In general, one can see that social programs follow a global tendency, and changes in the amount of the Gross Domestic Product (GDP) percentage invested by the governments might depend on who rules the nations [9] Documented precedents of social programs worldwide are provided by the United States government's social security administration at https://www.ssa.gov/policy/docs/progdesc/ssptw/.

These reports were collected from the Social Security Programs throughout the world survey conducted by the International Social Security Association (ISSA) in partnership with the U.S. Social Security Administration (SSA). Biyearly monitoring records since 2002 for Europe [1], Asia [11], and since 2003 for Africa [2] and the Americas [2] are publicly available in the link of the US social security administration provided above.

The 2019 reports of social programs, in particular, gather information about programs in five main categories:

- Old age, disability, survivors
- Sickness and maternity
- Work injury
- Unemployment
- Family allowances

An extensive review of social programs' effectiveness in Latin America and the Caribbean [3] reported difficulties in targeting the right individuals. A similar review regarding the European social programs [10] suggests the dismantlement of the system. The precluding reason includes the lack of inclusion of the youth, inequality, and the fact that poverty never stops growing in the last decade. Independent reviews of US and Canada were not found in the bibliographic study.

According to the reports, the social systems comply with their purpose, and the nations are progressively improving their citizens' quality of life. However, those reports can only determine if a country is covering its citizens' needs in the factors defined by the international organizations that monitor these social variables.

There are other factors associated with inequality, generation of misery, and general deterioration of wellness that governmental reports can not consider in their indexes regarding social aid. It has to do with corruption on both sides of the subsidiary pipeline. Due to the extraordinary social conditions forced by the current pandemic, governments have lessened the controls, and corruption increased [7].

Since the pandemic seems to last longer than initially predicted, the social platforms forcibly continue to provide help in an ecosystem that lacks a good reputation, and thus, several questions arise:

- How can we assure that social aids are delivered to the neediest?
- How to know that people are using the aid to the purpose they have been created?
- How to return confidence to the citizens in the contributory regime regarding the use of funds?

To give respond to these critical questions, we present a strategy based on artificial intelligence, where the machine uses a conceptual layer loaded with moral and ethical features to learn how to rank the individuals according to their social status and dynamic social features eliminating human biasing.

2   Materials and Methods

As we previously stated, the social programs around the world follow an international directive that pretends to cover the neediest citizens with the basics and provides an environment where equality is the goal.

Colombia in South-America is a real challenge. Their social system is stratified. A social labeling mechanism perceived by nationals of other countries as official segregation and adds complexity to the decision tree. The current development uses the structure established in Colombia as a proof-of-concept due to its intrinsic intricacy. The implementation of the current methods in other social systems is straightforward.

In Colombia, people receive a public social aid in function of a wealthiness score that is stratified, and in many cases it leads to corruption.

Data gathering and visualization was accomplished using Evalu@ www.evalualos.com [17].

2.1   Variables

Fairness Regarding Age. Since this model is based on justice criteria, multiple variables were taken into account to prioritize specific individuals due to their current conditions. As it can be seen in Fig. 1, the population between 0 to 15, and 83 to 120 years old, have a negative impact in their wealthiness score, which leads to a prioritization of aid. The formulation used to perform that figure of fairness can be seen in Eq. (1).

$$
Age(x) = \begin{cases} \left(\frac{27}{20}\right) x - 20 & if \ \ 0 \le x \le 20 \\ \left(\frac{3}{25}\right) x + \left(\frac{23}{5}\right) & if \ \ 20 < x \le 45 \\ \left(\frac{-3}{25}\right) x + 15.4 & if \ \ 45 < x \le 70 \\ \left(\frac{-27}{50}\right) x + 44.8 & if \ 70 < x \le 120 \end{cases}
\tag{1}
$$

Fairness Regarding Time. Furthermore, as the population tends to get non-expiring aid, the function presented in Eq. (2) was developed to introduce another notion of correctness: help is given to improve a condition and should not be provided for life. The mathematical expression that quantifies this principle of rightness penalizes the recipient by exponentially reducing the operator's negativity while time t increases ($t = 0$). The resulting figure is presented in Fig. 2.

$$
f(t) = \begin{cases} e^{\frac{t}{50}} - 11 & if \ 0 \le t < 120 \\ 0 & if \ \ t > 120 \end{cases}
\tag{2}
$$

Fairness Regarding Aid. Social programs target individuals but have a strong family-oriented notion. Therefore, an aid given to an individual affects all members of the family in their scores. To represent this behavior, we have introducing weights depending on two possible roles by aid, the direct recipient (personal) or member of a family with benefits (home). The weights given to training the model are in Table 1.

- ColMayor: Given to underprivileged elders, without pension, or to those who live in extreme poverty or indigence [15].
- FamAcc: Given to families with underage children, that requires financial help to have healthy nutrition and permanence in school, among other needs [14].
- Jouth in Action (JEA): Money transferred to the youth in poverty and vulnerability conditions to help them continue with their technical or professional carriers [4].
- Victim: Given to those who have been victimized because of armed conflict in Colombia [5].

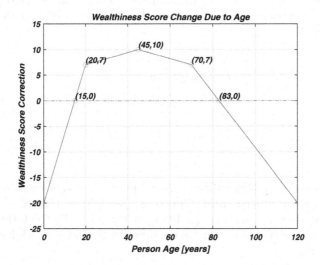

Fig. 1. Wealthiness Score correction regarding individual's age. The rationale here describes a parabolic weight along the age curse of an individual. This ethical concept forces the system to favor the oldest and the youngest as well.

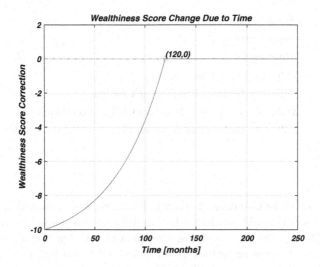

Fig. 2. Wealthiness score correction regarding the individual's time being benefited. The function describes a moral criterion that forces the individuals to use the aid in a limited frame-time.

Table 1. Table of weighs per aid. In social systems around the world, an individual is labeled as either recipient or person living with a recipient of an aid. The operators are Boolean. Here, weights are provided to reflect the social impact of factor that programs pretend to cover.

Aid	Person	Home
ColMayor	10	−2
FamAcc	15	−5
JEA	15	10
Victim	−10	−2

Fairness Regarding Disabilities. Social program authorities often overestimate disabilities in crucial times. Moreover, disability is treated as a Boolean operator that does not distinguish levels of calamity. To treat the disability according to the level of affliction, we use different weights for each listed impairment (Table 2).

Table 2. Table of weights depending upon disabilities. The numbers in this table define the justice taught to the machine regarding the different disabilities and how they affect the day-by-day of a human being.

Index	Disability	Weight
0	None	0
1	Total Blindess	−15
2	Total Deafness	−2
3	Muteness	−3
4	Difficulty of moving	−8
5	Difficulty bathing, dressing, self-feeding	−10
6	Difficulty going outside without help or company	−5
7	Difficulty understanding or learning	−20

Fairness Regarding Current Activity. Furthermore, when making decisions, a fair social system should consider what an individual is doing (Activity in Last Period - ALP), prioritizing those who are unemployed. On the other hand, the weights gave to workers or retired individuals with a pension, neither sum nor subtract to the decision making (Table 3).

Table 3. Table of weights according to Activity in the Last Period (ALP). With the aim of providing an environment of equal access to opportunities, the machine learns about the labor condition and involves this conditioning in the decision-making stage.

Index	Activity in Last Period	Weight
0	Without Activity	−3
1	Working	0
2	Looking for a job	−10
3	Studying	−5
4	Household Chores	−8
5	Rentier	0
6	Retired	−15
7	Invalid	−20

2.2 Dataset

Since there is not an existent correlation between the implemented variables, we made all the possible combinations between the variables previously presented, by applying:

$$nCr = \frac{n!}{r!(n-r)!} \tag{3}$$

Giving a total of 127 combinations, repeated 100 times with randomly created values for *Disability, ALP, Age, Time,* and the current wealthiness score given by the government. Therefore, the Machine Learning model implemented was trained with 12.7 thousand samples.

2.3 IBM Watson

In order to train this Machine Learning model, IBM Watson was used, implementing a regression model. After training, the metrics seen in Table 4 were obtained implementing hold-out (90% train, 10% test).

Table 4. IBM Watson machine learning model metrics.

Metric	Score
Root Mean Square Error	0.005
R^2	1
Mean Absolute Error	0.004
Mean Squared Error	0
Median Absolute Error	0.004

3   Results

To test the model, eleven randomly created individuals were used as testing set. They were all set with the same initial conditions Table 5, only varying in their age and wealthiness score. In order to make it more understandable, all individuals are active workers with no disabilities and no aid. An animated graphical representation was performed, being able to see the dynamic when applying a new factor to a certain individual. A bar graph representing these initial values can be seen in Fig. 3.

In a time-lapse testing, individuals were naturally changing over time their wealthiness score due to an incremental in both their age and time being benefited. As the purpose was to check how an individual score changes because of a given aid or a change in their physical and work-related condition, some changes to certain individuals were performed. The final states and wealthiness scores are presented in Table 6, as well in Fig. 4 in a graphical representation of the results, simulating 20 years of benefits (Table 7).

Table 5. Initial Conditions in the AI ranking process.

PERSON	COLMAYOR Person	COLMAYOR Home	FamAcc Person	FamAcc Home	JEA Person	JEA Home	VICTIM	Disability	ALP	AGE [Years]	TIME [Months]	Wealthy Score
Carmen	0	0	0	0	0	0	0	0	1	21	0	87
Maria	0	0	0	0	0	0	0	0	1	43	0	65
Sofia	0	0	0	0	0	0	0	0	1	33	0	55
Monica	0	0	0	0	0	0	0	0	1	18	0	90
Enrique	0	0	0	0	0	0	0	0	1	55	0	23
Felipe	0	0	0	0	0	0	0	0	1	60	0	15
Sebastian	0	0	0	0	0	0	0	0	1	67	0	30
Andres	0	0	0	0	0	0	0	0	1	73	0	63
Laura	0	0	0	0	0	0	0	0	1	35	0	45
Alvin	0	0	0	0	0	0	0	0	1	45	0	10
Nelfy	0	0	0	0	0	0	0	0	1	65	0	43

Table 6. Ranking after random conditioning and timing.

PERSON	COLMAYOR Person	COLMAYOR Home	FamAcc Person	FamAcc Home	JEA Person	JEA Home	VICTIM	Disability	ALP	AGE [Years]	TIME [Months]	Wealthy Score
Carmen	0	0	0	0	0	0	0	4	1	41	240	95
Maria	0	0	0	0	0	0	0	0	1	63	240	69
Sofia	0	0	0	0	0	0	0	0	1	53	240	71
Monica	0	0	0	0	0	0	1	0	1	38	240	99
Enrique	0	0	0	1	0	0	0	0	1	75	240	52
Felipe	0	0	0	0	0	0	0	0	1	80	240	27
Sebastian	0	0	0	0	0	0	0	6	1	87	240	16
Andres	0	0	0	0	0	0	0	0	1	93	240	52
Laura	0	0	0	0	0	0	0	0	1	55	240	59
Alvin	0	0	1	0	0	0	0	0	1	65	240	31
Nelfy	1	0	0	0	0	0	0	0	6	85	240	37

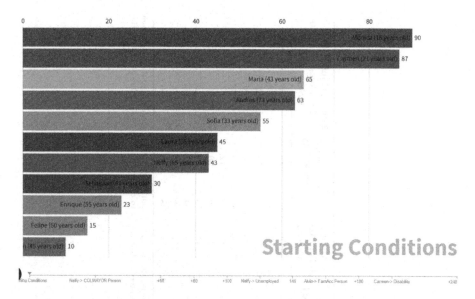

Fig. 3. Starting Conditions of wealthiness score of eleven randomly created individuals.

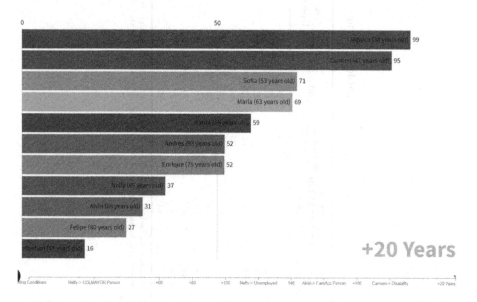

Fig. 4. Reformation of wealthiness score after +20 years of study and condition changing for certain individuals.

Table 7. Results

Person	Initial Score	Monica-> Victim Person	Nelfy-> COLMAYOR Person	Sebastian-> Disability	+60	+80	+100	Nelfy-> Unemployed	140	Alvin-> FamAcc Person	+180	Carmen-> Disability	220; Enrique-> FamAcc-Home	+240
Carmen	87	84	67	94	104	78	82	108	112	87	97	89	92	95
Maria	65	62	70	53	93	59	59	79	84	47	84	67	82	69
Sofia	55	54	74	47	52	52	48	65	57	50	91	55	52	71
Monica	90	84	75	67	62	78	79	96	82	105	100	98	96	99
Enrique	23	22	43	23	12	28	25	28	20	29	45	16	34	52
Felipe	15	13	17	12	13	6	16	37	8	22	29	12	27	27
Sebastian	30	27	38	32	21	26	26	18	46	35	16	30	26	16
Andres	63	58	70	50	68	61	55	69	70	67	56	59	74	52
Laura	45	44	43	40	39	56	55	47	71	61	64	54	63	59
Alvin	10	10	25	30	21	13	8	24	28	34	12	14	14	31
Nelfy	43	41	45	41	43	53	40	44	27	36	38	26	26	37

Change of wealthiness score due to specific factors applied to certain individuals along the time span study (240 months). Recall that there is not a deterministic approach in this classification. The AI implementation uses the moral and ethics layer empowered by the concepts presented in Sect. 2 to create an abstract layer that influences the decisions made by the machine.

4 Discussion

Artificial intelligence has been used for many applications, including but not limited to medical imaging, market segmentation, buying trending and prediction, self-driving cars, and assisted surgery. However, application in politics and public management are in their early stages. Politics, like other activities involving human decision-making, carries with the stigma of the biasing. In other fields, individual reasoning or arguably selfish acting would be perceived as a result of preference or experience with no exceptional consequences in the outcome of the action, even in the presence of convenience. That is not the case with politics were decisions have an impact on public Budget. Here, decisions that result in benefits for the public employee, relatives, or friends will be labeled as corruption, negatively affecting the image of the already deteriorated public sector.

With artificial intelligence, decisions can be made by machines previously trained to behave with ethics; therefore, biasing is inherently unfeasible.

In the development presented in this document, we configure a conceptual layer that provides ethical input built upon correctness features translated to numerical values. In the training sessions, the machine learns from these ethical concepts and modify a score that ends by ranking the citizens according to their needs and economic profile. With the presented strategy, it is possible to include learning notions never envisaged before, such as aid expiration. When the machine learns about expiration, aid recipients are forced to improve their conditions before the automation moves their scores to the non-eligible zone. The mechanisms to determine when a benefit should expire responds to a complex operation that involves the involvement and joining time of all other social programs run by governments.

The social-program-assisting tool created is capable of automatically choosing the neediest without the risk of being unfair or convenient on both sides of the subsidized pipeline, the politician side, and the social program recipients' side. More importantly, for the first time of humanity, the crowd in the contributing side would remain unruffled about the real purpose of social programs and how the social funds are used.

5 Conclusions

In this project we present a modern way to re-rank individuals in a more moral and ethical way than it is done today.

The three rules for automation presented by Asimov in his book I, robot, have gained relevance in the recent boom of artificial intelligence. Whether automation can harm humans is arguably crucial for all possible applications; therefore, the rules for human preservation and obedience might not be mandatory for some implementations. Another scope of the same problem relies on the fact that machines can learn from a set of tendentious principles, in which case, corruption would appear in their decision. Such a scenario is possible only if the human feeds unethical notions in the machines' learning process.

Asimov was predictive but forgot to include the human factor in which case, the instructions for the machines would need to include a fourth directive: Once operative, do not listen to humans.

References

1. Social Security Administration: Social security programs throughout the world: Europe. HEW Publications No. 76–11805(13) (1976)
2. Social Security Administration: Social security programs throughout the world: the Americas. HEW Publication No. 76–11805(13) (1976)
3. Bouillon, C.P., Tejerina, L.R.: Do We Know What Works? A Systematic Review of Impact Evaluations of Social Programs in Latin America and the Caribbean (2011). https://doi.org/10.2139/ssrn.996502
4. de Colombia, G.: Jóvenes en acción (2020). https://prosperidadsocial.gov.co/sgpp/transferencias/jovenes-en-accion/
5. de Colombia, G.: Unidad para la atención y reparación integral a las víctimas (2020) http://unidadvictimas.gov.co/es/ayuda-humanitaria/54344
6. Eslami, H., Jalili, M.: The role of environmental factors to transmission of SARS-CoV-2 (COVID-19). AMB Express **10**(1), 1–8 (2020). https://doi.org/10.1186/s13568-020-01028-0
7. Gallego, J.A., Prem, M., Vargas, J.F.: Corruption in the times of Pandemia. SSRN Electron. J. (0044) (2020). https://doi.org/10.2139/ssrn.3600572
8. Gentilini, U., et al.: Social Protection and Jobs Responses to COVID-19: a real-time review of country measures week's special feature on delivery includes summaries from case studies 11 (2020)
9. Groskind, F.: Ideological influences on public support for assistance to poor families. Soc. Work (United States) **39**(1), 81–89 (1994). https://doi.org/10.1093/sw/39.1.81
10. Hermann, C.: Crisis, structural reform and the dismantling of the European Social Model(s). Econ. Ind. Democr. **38**(1), 51–68 (2017). https://doi.org/10.1177/0143831X14555708
11. International Social Security Association: Social Security Programs Throughout the World: Asia and the Pacific, 2014(13), p. 259 (2012)
12. Kumar, M., Taki, K., Gahlot, R., Sharma, A., Dhangar, K.: A chronicle of SARS-CoV-2: part-I - epidemiology, diagnosis, prognosis, transmission and treatment. Sci. Total Environ. **734**(336), 139278 (2020). https://doi.org/10.1016/j.scitotenv.2020.139278
13. López, L., Rodó, X.: The end of social confinement and COVID-19 re-emergence risk. Nat. Hum. Behav. **4**(July) (2020). https://doi.org/10.1038/s41562-020-0908-8
14. Plataforma de Seguridad Alimentaria y Nutricional (PSAN): Familias en acción (2020). https://plataformacelac.org/programa/481
15. de Solidaridad Pensional, F.: ¿qué es el programa colombia mayor? (2020). https://www.fondodesolidaridadpensional.gov.co/portal/normatividad/finish/50/19.html

16. Yao, M., Zhang, L., Ma, J., Zhou, L.: On airborne transmission and control of SARS-Cov-2. Sci. Total Environ. **731**, 139178 (2020). https://doi.org/10.1016/j.scitotenv.2020.139178d
17. Yepes-Calderon, F., Yepes Zuluaga, J.F., Yepes Calderon, G.E.: Evalu@: an agnostic web-based tool for consistent and constant evaluation used as a data gatherer for artificial intelligence implementations. In: Florez, H., Leon, M., Diaz-Nafria, J.M., Belli, S. (eds.) ICAI 2019. CCIS, vol. 1051, pp. 73–84. Springer, Cham (2019). https://doi.org/10.1007/978-3-030-32475-9_6

Intelligent Digital Tutor to Assemble Puzzles Based on Artificial Intelligence Techniques

Sara M. Cachique[1][ID], Edgar S. Correa[2][ID], and C. H. Rodriguez-Garavito[1(✉)][ID]

[1] Faculty of Engineering, Universidad de la Salle, Bogota, Colombia
{scachique18,cerodriguez}@unisalle.edu.co
[2] Faculty of Engineering, Pontificia Universidad Javeriana, Bogota, Colombia
e_correa@javeriana.edu.co

Abstract. The potential of applying image processing tools and artificial intelligence in learning processes is identified. This article presents the development of a digital tutor that helps solve a puzzle. Point cloud technology is used to identify each person's interaction dynamically in space. The proposed methodology is developed in several stages. The first stage consists of the acquisition and pre-processing system for adquaring the user environment. The second stage consists of recognizing the piece in the puzzle, at this stage it is necessary to develop a database of the particular puzzle. In the identification process, the PCA algorithm is implemented as a complementary strategy to the use of the neural network. The last stage implements a general search algorithm as the core of the decision system. This methodology is presented as an iterative process and evolves over time according to the interaction with the user. The results are presented through confusion matrix which exhibits a performance of 92.7% assertiveness. Finally, the potential of using this methodological structure in different cognitive processes with puzzles with different levels of difficulty is raised.

Keywords: 3D Image-Processing · Intelligent-tutor · Search-algorithms · ANN · PCA

1 Introduction

Currently, the development of technologies in the world has increased, requiring people who are competent in areas such as science, technology, engineering and mathematics, known as STEM outcomes (Science, Technology, Engineering and Mathematics). According to the Office of the Chief Economist of the United States, STEM occupations have increased over the past 10 years by almost 24.4% while other occupations have increased by 4% [21]. In this context, the automation of the human learning process is presented as a tool for developing STEM skills.

© Springer Nature Switzerland AG 2020
H. Florez and S. Misra (Eds.): ICAI 2020, CCIS 1277, pp. 56–71, 2020.
https://doi.org/10.1007/978-3-030-61702-8_5

Research in human learning area is widely discussed in the literature, in Bloom [1] authors have shown that a person with a personalized tutor significantly improves the performance of learning process, results show improvement above 90% in contrast to conventional learning processes in groups. Personalized tutoring with robotic systems has begun to receive attention of scientists, but it is still relatively little explored [2]. Despite investments of tens of billions of dollars, the problem of development education at global scale remains unsolved [3]. An interesting approach in which Robots focuses on learning and interacting with children is proposed by a study that covers the effects of two different social roles of a robot "peer vs. tutor" on children's tasks [4]. Other social skills, such as teamwork, are investigated using cutting-edge technologies such as virtual reality [5].

Image processing has positioned itself as a powerful field in the process of interaction with the environment, applied research shows this [6–8]. In this research, image processing is an important component since it allows interaction with the decision-making system based on artificial intelligence techniques.

The potential of point cloud technology is identified because it presents the possibility of interacting in three-dimensional space. This field of research has been developing through cumulative effort provided by a free software community [11]. Other studies evaluate the effects of using the Kinect camera as a depth and color sensor, effects related to precision and resolution in the mapping of three-dimensional spaces [12]. While other works present the detection of human activity [13]. These works demonstrate the potential of using this technology as a base tool to detect the interaction of a person in space, in this research, related to the pieces of a puzzle.

Assisted learning has been the subject of research in various fields of knowledge. The computer-assisted dental patient simulator, DentSim is a significant advance that has enabled dental students to acquire cognitive-motor skills in a multimedia environment [14]. It is a high-tech unit developed from the classic dental simulator. Not only can this system standardize and improve the students' dexterity, but also does the training module make preparations easier to be visualized and provide immediate feedback, real-time user-generated evaluation by using advanced imaging and simulation technologies via the built-in 3D scanning system [15]. The feedback that the researchers propose has two interesting characteristics. The first is based on real-time focus and the second is based on image processing, the latter consists of generating the 3D image from the spatial information provided by the instrument head. In this context, the research presented in this document could be useful since it would allow sensory fusion with the system already implemented. In this sense, the main contribution of this research is how image processing as a tool to capture reality is integrated with artificial intelligence tools to interact with the user and lead to a digital-intelligent tutor. Another similar investigation reports the use of a digital tutor to accelerate knowledge acquisition and improve their preparation for the civilian workforce, this tutor to develop veterans' technical expertise and employability [16].

At a technological level, this tutor is based on a computer-assisted learning system and the only interaction with the user is through the keyboard and mouse of a computer. This approach has been presented in several investigations in different fields of application [17,18]. It would be of great research value if this type of computer-assisted system integrates interaction with the user as developed in the methodological proposal of this research. The main contribution of the methodological proposal presented in this document is based on the possibility of monitoring all the interactions of students through image processing. It is presented as a useful tool in the search to develop structures to capture the social skills of students that allow the instructional management of warmth, commitment and determination. It would be a complement to computer-assisted systems that visualize education as children interacting with online learning systems where based on past performance and algorithms offer what each student needs to know [19]. The biggest recent advance in smart tutors is presented by IBM and Pearson [20]. They have partnered to develop intelligent dialogue-based tutoring systems. This development is based on advances in machine learning and natural language processing to create a Watson dialog-based tutor (WDBT). In this sense, the main contribution of this research is presented as a methodological development that would allow the integration of image processing as useful information to the systems currently developed. Although the field of artificial intelligence is growing rapidly and specifically the area of computer vision and it is of investigative value to present how these advances are integrated into different fields of action. In this case, the learning systems that could be as varied as people and areas of knowledge exist.

In this article a puzzle is presented as a case study, the methodological structure of the research proposal is developed. This is structured in three stages, the first stage covers the acquisition and pre-processing system based on the acquisition of a point cloud. The second stage consists of generating a part identification system based on artificial intelligence techniques to finally generate a decision-making system by executing a general search algorithm. This process is presented iteratively using a graphical interface. The structure of this document is developed as follows: in section two the methods are put forth, in section three the experimental configuration of the methodological proposal is presented, in section five the experimental results are shown and finally in section six the discussion of the results and conclusions.

2   Methods

Our intelligent tutor is aimed at children from 3 years of age onwards, as it is a very important stage for asserting skills related to learning and cognitive development. To start the tutor, it is required to have access to a computer with the programme settings, follow the tutor's instructions, and finally it is recommended that an adult be responsible for the child.

This kind of system could be useful by stakeholders as: teachers, peers, schools and educational institutions and those who wish to incorporate the intelligent tutors in their learning programs.

This tutor is developed in several phases, integrating image processing techniques, machine learning and Search algorithms (see Fig. 1).

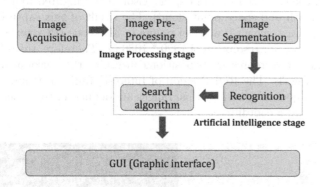

Fig. 1. General outline of the methodology

2.1 Acquisition System and Image Processing

Puzzle Selection. The pieces of the puzzle contain geometric figures of pictorial type and strong primary colors, in order to call children attention when solving this puzzle, as well a minimum amount of 12 pieces, for a level of complexity appropriate for children, the dimensions of the puzzle are 40 × 30 cm. The size of each piece is 10 × 10 cm for easy manipulation (see Fig. 2).

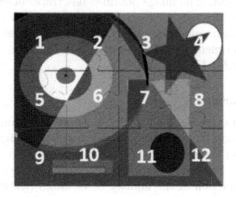

Fig. 2. Puzzle with labels

Image Acquisition and Pre-processing. The Kinect 2 v2 camera was chosen for its outstanding features, including image resolution, a field of view, computer connection, and compatibility with the operating system. Before capturing the environment, the color sensor and depth sensor are configured to get an RGBD (RGB color depth and space point cloud). The result of this capture is a point cloud called PCraw, which is a set of points in 3D space (PCraw: [x, y, z]), the point cloud has a color resolution of 1920 * 1080 px. Therefore, the reference system of a PCraw point represent its position concerning the sensor at which it was acquired (see Fig. 3). The ROI (Region of Interest) function is implemented to constrain the object in space, for this, ranges are defined in the space associated with the x, y, and z coordinates.

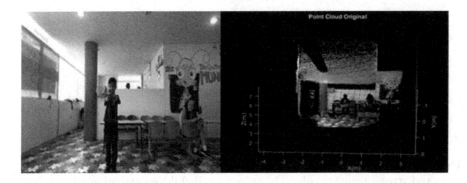

Fig. 3. Color Image and PCraw

Image Segmentation. The image obtained has traces of skin, so a color segmentation is made, taking as a reference the study [9] to HSV of skin images with different tones and their respective histograms to identify the range of values for skin, from this experiment we obtain that the threshold is at $0 < H < 0.18$, $0.5 < S < 0.9$ and $0.2 < V < 0.95$.

2.2 Machine Learning

Principal Components Analysis - PCA. Descriptors contain the raw information for each image, by itself, they have great dimensionality, so makes difficult, the training of the classifier, because it consumes great amount of computational resources, learning time, and/or execution of the program; therefore, a dimensionality reduction of the number of variables (features) of the images must be done.

To carry out dimensionality reduction of the images, PCA was applied, the following steps were taken into account: 1) Average (center the data). 2) Variance, Covariance (How the data set looks). 3) Eigenvectors and eigenvalues of the covariance matrix. 4) Project the data in the dimension where the greatest dispersion of information is observed.

ANN. For the recognition of the puzzle piece in the digital tutor, an artificial neural network is developed, which are networks that simulate the biology of the human brain and its neurons, these are connected to each other, through small programs that are responsible for processing the data and identify the patterns that are indicated with labels.

The neural network takes the descriptors received from the PCA process as inputs, which contains the main information from the puzzle image database and returns the labels that correspond to the selected pieces.

2.3   Search Algorithm

This tool (tutor) generates the next piece for assembling the puzzle based on an uninformed search algorithm, which has no additional information on the problem, generating successors to next states and distinguishing one state that is a solution and another that is not [10], (see Fig. 4).

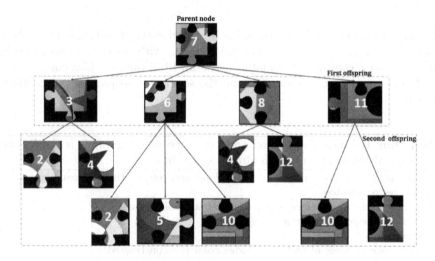

Fig. 4. Uninformed search algortihm scheme

3   Experimental Setup

3.1   Image Acquisition and Pre-processing

In this phase, the point cloud, available further than 0,5 m from camera sensor, corresponding to a piece of puzzle, must be placed in a larger space to obtain a good definition in color and depth. Then it is filtered in space using the pcfit-plane function which is a variant of the RANSAC algorithm (Random Sample Consensus), where the maximum distances of the point cloud are adjusted, and returns a geometric model that describes the plane, additionally returns the indices that are in and out of the plane. These position ranges are entered into a function of the program, which is based on the ROI (region of interest) processing technique, which takes a portion of the image where is the piece held by the user. The information about the location of the puzzle piece in the scene is obtained, the indices of this process return the image in 2D, and then proceeds to crop and eliminate the noise in the (imcropped) image, (see Fig. 5).

Fig. 5. Image with ROI

Image acquisition and pre-processing is related in the algorithm below. Where a spatial filtering is done with the ROI function with restrictive conditions in the X, Y and Z coordinates, to later obtain an RGB image, which contains the puzzle piece and part of the hand, and the segmentation process can continue by color.

Algorithm 1. Image Acquisition and pre-processing, the input is the PCraw and Original Image and return a filtered image in space

---

$pcfitplanef \leftarrow$ extract planes of point cloud and returns the surfaces, the model, and other parameters
$pc - roi = select(pc - raw, index) \leftarrow$ select sub point cloud
$matrixofImage \leftarrow$ create matrix m*n
for i=1:n **do**
    $ind - pix \leftarrow$ values of each color index color is reconstructed
    $Image2D \leftarrow$ create image 2D
    $imcropped \leftarrow$ crop image of piece
end for

3.2 Image Segmentation

In this phase, the ranges of the skin are selected at different color spaces such as: YCrCb, Lab and HSV, where the best segmentation to the skin was made in HSV color space, the ranges gave the following ranges of each channel were: $0 < H < 0.07$, $0.1 < S < 0.52$, $0.3 < V < 0.85$. (see Fig. 6(a)), the result of this final segmentation is shown in (see Fig. 6(b)).

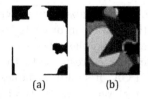

(a)   (b)

Fig. 6. Mask and Segmented image of puzzle piece

3.3 Principal Components Analysis PCA

The database[1] contains the images of each piece, the size of them is 50 * 50 * 3, the information is organized in a data structure as follows: 1) Data of the images 12000 * 7500. 2) Data of the labels that correspond to each image (Part Number), for a supervised learning 1 * 12000. The selected PCA number is (30) since it allows learning the neural network in less time.

3.4 ANN

In this tutor, an artificial neural network called newff was used, which is a feed-forward backpropagation network. This function requires the input arguments such as: Image information referring to the descriptors resulting from PCA; topology of the net; functions to activate layers and at the expected labels associated to each input descriptor. The neural network needs to learn patterns corresponding to each piece of the puzzle.

Algorithm 2. Neural Network the input of ANN is the descriptor of Image and return the label of pieces **L**

$Database \leftarrow$ Database for test
$Database \leftarrow$ Database for train
$net \leftarrow$ newff with the arguments such as: Size Image, number of neurons, activation functions, layers
$Train \leftarrow$ train with network training with the target value and the value obtained
$sim \leftarrow$ simularion with model NN and test image (sample)
Create descriptor of Image new for test
Label **L**
Do the PCA of Descriptor Image
$Label \leftarrow$ Predict piece with NN trained, return the number of piece selected.

---

[1] The entire puzzle database is available at: https://www.dropbox.com/sh/ yirqf4xv7lrs13j/AACMKJb0QaklhsItmjXKD88oa?dl=0.

Input and Output Data. The database was divided into test information (30%) and training information (70%), in order to use one part for neural network training (entered in newff) and the other to check the network learning. The inputs of the neural network correspond to the value resulting from the dimensional reduction with PCA, it's (30) variables, and the outputs of the network correspond to the target vector, it's (12) labels.

Neural Network Architecture. The architecture of a neural network depends on four main parameters: (1) the number of layers in the system; (2) the number of neurons per layer; (3) the degree of connectivity and (4) the type of neural connections. A problem with this level of complexity can be solved with three (3) layers such as the input layer, output layer and hidden layer.

3.5   Uninformed Search Algorithm

There are several Uninformed search strategies, the used is in this tutor is the Breadth-first Search, this type can be implemented for actions that have the same cost and for problems that do not have highly complex searches, such as maze problems, maze problems, missionaries and cannibals problem and others.

This search takes as an strategy, that the first parent node, (root node, in this document, will be called father), is expanded (FIFO ordering principle), a successor list is created by its physical connection with its father in the sense of the assembly order, and subsequently its successor nodes (descendants).

The algorithm works as follows: 1) Start with the initial node that corresponds to the first selected piece of the puzzle. 2) A graph is created, which represents the assembled puzzle. 3). The list of successors corresponds to the links in the graph. 4) The successors (possible solutions) are rearranged randomly, to generate solutions to the next state in the assembly, without the successors repeating.

4   Experimental Results

The initial result of this investigation is a database associated with the case study, this has different perspectives related to rotation and translation, the effects of light variations are introduced and contains images with Gaussian noise and salt and pepper in ranges of 0.01 to 0.1. A total of 12000 images with twelve different pieces. RGB images are 50 * 50 in size for each channel. The first stage is to train the neural network, for this, the input layer of the network is configured. The number of neurons in the input layer of the network must be the size of the descriptor. Initially, the descriptor is the image organized by rows, this configuration has a size of 7500. The PCA algorithm is used to reduce this number of neurons with the aim to improve system performance at the processing time level. The result is a descriptor of 30 elements, therefore a reduction of

Algorithm 3. Seach algorithm the input of the algorithm is the label selected L

```
Create Node; temp var
Create Vector Open VO
Create Vector Close VC
N=length (Puzzle)
while Infinity loop to repeat do
   if void-vector(VO) then
      Return false
   end if
   Node←FirtElement(VO), extract the first label
   VC←add(VC,Node)
   if length(VC)==N then
      Return true
   end if
   function show.next.piece(Node)
   function offspring=sucessor(Node)
   for i=1:length(offspring) do
      if offspring(i)∉ VC then
         VO=add(VO,offspring(i))
      end if
   end for
end while
```

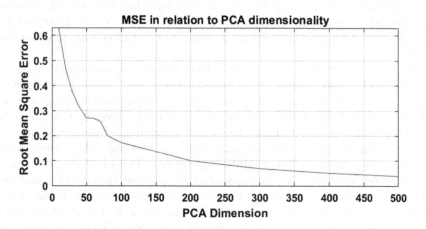

Fig. 7. Root mean square error in relation to PCA dimensionality.

250%. A graph (see Fig. 7) relates the effects of varying the dimension of the descriptor using the PCA algorithm is presented. The results show that with a lower degree of dimensionality, arround 30 PCA, the error does not increase proportionally as PCA components are added.

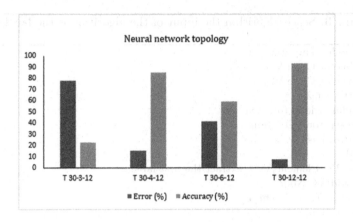

Fig. 8. Performance of four neural network topologies

A neural network with three layers has been defined as a universal classifier. The number of neurons in the input layer is the dimension defined in the PCA algorithm and the number of neurons in the output layer is the number of pieces of the puzzle, in this case, twelve. This approach limits the possible tests to the number of neurons in the intermediate layer, results of using 3 - 4 - 6 - 12 neurons respectively (see Fig. 8) allow it to define that the network topology that generated greater precision in the predictions is the 30-12-12 network (30 input neurons, 12 neurons in the intermediate layer and 12 neurons in the output layer).

The confusion matrix (see Fig. 9) is developed to assess the performance of the model. The configuration of the neural network confusion matrix is defined as 12 × 12, since the puzzle has 12 pieces. From this analysis, a learning accuracy of 92.7% and an error of 7.3% are obtained. The results presented in the confusion matrix allow it to determine the correct functioning of the neural network fed by the image reduced dimensionally with the PCA algorithm. After identifying the image in space it is possible to generate a decision engine. For this, a general search algorithm has been presented. In this case, the level of complexity is low and an "uninformed search algorithm" is defined. Results are presented using a graphical interface (see Fig. 10) On the left side, the graphical interface contains the user interaction functionality. On the right side, the identified pieces are presented and pieces are suggested for the armed. Search algorithm dynamically evolves with user interactions. To evaluate the performance of the integrated system, an evaluation of duration times of each stage of the process is developed. The system startup takes approximately 5 min, this process includes the execution of MatLab software and the compilation of the GUI graphical interface, communication verification (SDK) is also executed, with the Kinect sensor-camera (Fig. 10).

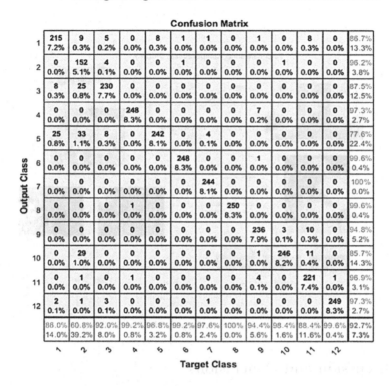

Fig. 9. Confusion matrix

A reference parameter analyzed is the assembling of puzzles in a natural way, for this, a young person takes an average of 2 min in the assembly process, a child takes ten times more depending on age. With the proposed system, five moments are identified, the first moment takes 45 s and consists of "Capturing" the image, the second moment takes less than 20 s and consists of segmenting the captured image, the third stage takes less than 10 s and consists of identifying the puzzle piece by trained neural network, finally, the last stage takes less than 5 s and it consists of generating the suggestion of assembly by means of the search algorithm. The total system takes an average of 25 min to assemble the puzzle because it requires user interaction. A total of 25 tests were performed with different people in a range of 3 to 11 years. It should be noted that the experimentation tests were carried out on a computer with a Windows 10 operating system, 8 GB RAM and an Intel (R) Core (TM) i5 processor.

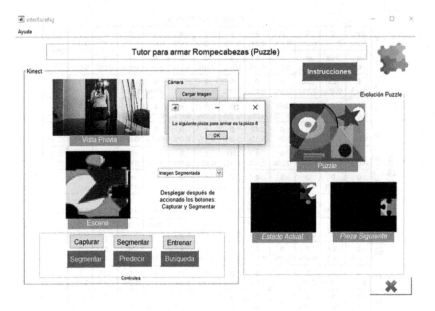

Fig. 10. Graphical interface in MatLab software

5   Discussion and Conclusions

Throughout the development of this work, were addressed two main challenges, the first one was the creation of image database by the using of augmented data as a mixture of real images at different illumination levels and images under artificial noise [22, 23]. Therefore, the decision making algorithm based on uninformed search was also a challenge, it was because the requirement of being flexible to fit the size of a general puzzle, for this problem, a 12-piece search problem.

Therefore, the decision making algorithm based on uninformed search was also a challenge, it because the requirement of being flexible to fit the size of a general puzzle, in this case, a 12-piece search problem.

The use of some artificial intelligence techniques such as neural networks requires an initial knowledge base, in this case it was necessary to develop a data set because the case study is a particular puzzle, however, the possibility of developing an approach to transfer learning is presented as an interesting future job. To evaluate the effects of the initial knowledge level, the developed database is shared.

Since a neural network is configured as the central tool that identifies the piece in space, it is necessary to convert the image as a descriptor. Using an image as a descriptor is impractical. PCA algorithm is used as a powerful tool that allows projecting the image as a lightweight descriptor, impacting in the reduction of the training time of the neural network. The descriptor dimension is defined in 30 components because this value ensures a breaking point where the variations of a greater number of components is not meaningful (see Fig. 7). This stage ensures acceptable convergence times for intermediate performance hardware.

According to the network topology used, different levels of error and accuracy are generated. The network that generates more precision and a lower error rate is desirable. It is observed that the performance of the network is not directly proportional to the number of neurons in the inner layer, so it is necessary to carry out experimental tests to validate the selection of the topology. Implementing a confusion matrix is a useful tool for evaluating the performance of work methodologies that is based on a large number of tests that integrate random components, in this case light variations or noise of different types.

Identifying the piece in space is a complex task since it is the piece that moves in space, however the proposed image processing methodology manages to properly capture the piece's information, and with artificial intelligence tools it is possible to identify the piece at software level, to allow decision making.

In the case study presented in this research, the results suggest that the system reachs of the main objective "to put the puzzle together" as well as the natural assembly process. However, it has the potential to solve more complex problems where the conventional process is limited, given this case, the presented system takes a competitive advantage in the assembly process. Another interesting aspect in which the proposed system becomes relevant focuses on populations of people with limitations related to cognitive abilities. To validate this hypothesis, it is necessary to carry out the technological transfer of the proposed system to this type of population and with experts in the areas of cognitive learning to validate it. The presented research is developed in MATLAB, this suggests that the presented development has the potential to be improved in terms of execution time if it is developed in c++.

References

1. Bloom, B.S.: The 2 sigma problem: the search for methods of group instruction as effective as one-to-one tutoring. Educ. Res. **13**(6), 4–16 (1984). https://doi.org/10.3102/0013189X013006004
2. Gao, Y., Barendregt, W., Obaid, M., Castellano, G.: When robot personalisation does not help: insights from a robot-supported learning study. In: RO-MAN 2018–27th IEEE International Symposium on Robot and Human Interactive Communication, pp. 705–712 (2018). https://doi.org/10.1109/ROMAN.2018.8525832
3. Essa, A., Laster, S.: Bloom's 2 sigma problem and data-driven approaches for improving student success. In: The First Year of College: Research, Theory, and Practice on Improving the Student Experience and Increasing Retention, pp. 212–246. Cambridge University Press (2017). https://doi.org/10.1017/9781316811764.009

4. Zaga, C., Zaga, C., Lohse, M., Truong, K.P., Evers, V.: The effect of a robot's social character on children's task engagement: peer versus tutor. In: Lecture Notes in Computer Science (Including Subseries Lecture Notes in Artificial Intelligence and Lecture Notes in Bioinformatics), 9388 LNCS, pp. 704–713 (2015). https://doi.org/10.1007/978-3-319-25554-5_70

5. Kolomaznik, M., Sullivan, M., Vyvyan, K.: Can virtual reality engage students with teamwork. Int. J. Innov. Sci. Math. Educ. **25**(4), 32–44 (2017)

6. Nourbakhsh, I.R., Sycara, K., Koes, M., Yong, M., Lewis, M., Burion, S.: Human-robot teaming for search and Rescue. In: IEEE Pervasive Computing, vol. 4, no. 1, pp. 72–77 (2005). https://doi.org/10.1109/MPRV.2005.13

7. Murphy, R.R.: Human-robot interaction in rescue robotics. IEEE Trans. Syst. Man Cybern. Part C: Appl. Rev. **34**(2), 138–153 (2004). https://doi.org/10.1109/TSMCC.2004.826267

8. Levitt, T.S., Lawton, D.T.: Qualitative navigation for mobile robots. Artif. Intell. **44**(3), 305–360 (1990). https://doi.org/10.1016/0004-3702(90)90027-W

9. Shaik, K.B., Ganesan, P., Kalist, V., Sathish, B.S., Jenitha, J.M.M.: Comparative study of skin color detection and segmentation in HSV and YCbCr color space. Procedia Comput. Sci. **57**, 41–48 (2015). https://doi.org/10.1016/j.procs.2015.07.362

10. Norvig, P., Russell, S.: Artificial Intelligence: A Modern Approach, 4th edn., pp. 76–84. Pearson, Hoboken (2003)

11. Rusu, R.B., Cousins, S.: 3D is here: point Cloud Library (PCL). In: Proceedings - IEEE International Conference on Robotics and Automation (2011). https://doi.org/10.1109/ICRA.2011.5980567

12. Khoshelham, K., Elberink, S.O.: Accuracy and resolution of kinect depth data for indoor mapping applications. Sensors **12**(2), 1437–1454 (2012)

13. Sung, J., Ponce, C., Selman, B., Saxena, A.: Unstructured human activity detection from RGBD images. In: Proceedings - IEEE International Conference on Robotics and Automation, pp. 842–849 (2012). https://doi.org/10.1109/ICRA.2012.6224591

14. Welk, A., et al.: Computer-assisted learning and simulation lab with 40 DentSim units. Int. J. Comput. Dentistry, **11**(1), 17–40. (2008). ISSN: 14634201 2-s2.0-49049085467

15. Zheng, J., Cao, X., Lin, Y., Zhang, J., Feng, X.: An introduction of DentSim in pre-clinical dental training and practice. Shanghai kou qiang yi xue - Shanghai J. Stomatol. **23**(6), 749–754 (2014)

16. Fletcher, J.D.: The value of digital tutoring and accelerated expertise for military veterans. Educ. Technol. Res. Dev. **65**(3), 679–698 (2017). https://doi.org/10.1007/s11423-016-9504-z

17. Woods, K.: The development and design of an interactive digital training resource for personal tutors. Front. Educ. **5**, 100 (2020) https://doi.org/10.3389/feduc.2020.00100

18. Suebnukarn, S., Haddawy, P.: A collaborative intelligent tutoring system for medical problem-based learning. International Conference on Intelligent User Interfaces, Proceedings IUI, pp. 14–21 (2004) https://doi.org/10.1145/964445.964447

19. Noble, D.D.: The classroom arsenal: military research, information technology and public education. The Classroom Arsenal: Military Research, Information Technology and Public Education, pp. 1–224 (2017) https://doi.org/10.4324/9780203730317

20. Ventura, M., et al.: Preliminary evaluations of a dialogue-based digital tutor. In: Penstein Rosé, C., et al. (eds.) AIED 2018. LNCS (LNAI), vol. 10948, pp. 480–483. Springer, Cham (2018). https://doi.org/10.1007/978-3-319-93846-2_90

21. Noonan, R.: STEM Jobs: 2017 Update. ESA Issue Brief# 02–17. US Department of Commerce (2017)
22. Ding, X., Hu, R.: Learning To see faces in the dark. In: 2020 IEEE International Conference on Multimedia and Expo (ICME), London, United Kingdom, pp. 1–6 (2020) https://doi.org/10.1109/ICME46284.2020.9102816
23. Zhang, Y., et al.: A poisson-gaussian denoising dataset with real fluorescence microscopy images. In: 2019 IEEE/CVF Conference on Computer Vision and Pattern Recognition (CVPR), Long Beach, CA, USA, pp. 11702–11710 (2019) https://doi.org/10.1109/CVPR.2019.01198

Machine Learning Methodologies Against Money Laundering in Non-Banking Correspondents

Jorge Guevara$^{(\boxtimes)}$, Olmer Garcia-Bedoya©, and Oscar Granados©

Universidad de Bogota Jorge Tadeo Lozano Carrera, 4 22-61 Bogota, Colombia
{jorgei.guevarap,olmer.garciab,oscarm.granadose}@utadeo.edu.co

Abstract. The activities of money laundering are a result of corruption, illegal activities, and organized crime that affect social dynamics and involved, directly and indirectly, several communities through different mechanisms to launder illegal money. In this article, we propose a machine learning approach to the analysis of suspicious activities in non-banking correspondents, a type of financial agent that develops some financial transactions for specific banking customers. This article uses several algorithms to identify anomalies in a transaction set of a non-banking correspondent during 2019 for an intermediary city in Colombia. Our results show that some methodologies are more appropriate than others for this case and facilitate to identify the anomalies and suspicious transactions in this kind of financial intermediary.

Keywords: Money laundering · Financial services · Machine learning · Non-banking correspondents

1 Introduction

Money laundering activities have used different mechanisms to launder their illegal money. This money tries to access the legal economy in almost all countries through goods trading, commodities exploitation, real estate transactions, financial transactions, or illegal activities as smuggling. In Colombia, as a global level, the exact amount of money laundering is impossible to estimate because the economic activities are susceptible to money launderers, that who use a dynamical structure. The literature has investigated this old problem with different methodologies. For Colombian case as a criminal and socio-economic approach [26], as a legal approach [27,28], as a political approach, as an economic approach [16], or as a result of drug production [3] to list a few. Other scholars proposed a multidisciplinary approach between artificial intelligence and network science [10] because money laundering is a result of corruption, financial crime, or drug trafficking, and other activities that needs a group of methodologies to fight a growing problem.

© Springer Nature Switzerland AG 2020
H. Florez and S. Misra (Eds.): ICAI 2020, CCIS 1277, pp. 72–88, 2020.
https://doi.org/10.1007/978-3-030-61702-8_6

For other countries, several scholars have implemented diverse machine learning methodologies. First, with a basic statistical model to identify the correlation between risk assessment and suspicious transactions [6]. Second, with the analysis of user's transactions to characterize them based on the behavior of all transactions in a specific dataset [1] or some patterns in suspicious financial transactions or money flow with transaction mining algorithms and frequent pattern mining algorithms [8,9]. Third, with the analysis of bank statements to find patterns that could resemble techniques used to the money laundering process [25]. Fourth, the classification of machine learning algorithms from anti-money laundering typologies, link analysis, behavioral modeling, risk scoring, anomaly detection, and geographic capability to identify the different features and mechanisms of money laundering [5]. Fifth, a combination of structural coupling theory with some data methodologies and algorithms to identify the information redundancy that could affect the money laundering control process [7]. Sixth, the Support Vector Machine (SVM) a machine learning method that trains a data set to identify the outliers [21].

On the other hand, 1.7 billion adults worldwide do not have a basic transaction account according to the World Bank's Universal Financial Access Initiative, the non-bank correspondents (NBC) are the first link for financial inclusion and to reduce poverty. Habitually, they could more close than the traditional financial service providers and could improve the trust in financial service providers trough everyday activities of the adult population. Thus, the non-bank correspondents as a strategy to create a new option for financial inclusion and to integrate customers to the formal financial system are non-financial establishments belong to everyday sectors whose principal activity involves cash. This mechanism facilitates the financial operations of customers in different developing countries, but the non-bank correspondents cannot identify suspicious transactions or implement an anti-money laundering scheme. Additionally, the non-banking correspondents have increased their operations in different regions like China, India, Bangladesh, Pakistan, Indonesia, Turkey, Congo, South Africa, Brazil, Colombia, Ecuador, Mexico, among others with some particular conditions as economic informality that facilitate to criminal organizations the money laundering through traditional or new schemes that they use in financial institutions. In consequence, this kind of correspondent is vulnerable to criminal organizations and illegal activities.

This situation has attracted the attention of scholars from a wide range of disciplines. However, the non-banking correspondent is a new phenomenon to study in the anti-money laundering techniques, and data science methodologies motivate us to create an effective approach. We propose an implementation of algorithmic analysis and visualization that facilitates identifying suspicious activities in non-banking correspondents. Our contribution is detecting unusual transactions in a non-banking correspondent using data analysis and machine learning techniques in a real dataset as well as, empirical rules and others have already known about money laundering. In this article, we apply some tools from machine learning and visualization techniques to identify suspicious transactions in non-bank correspondents, a growing service in Colombia and other developing countries. We used unsupervised machine learning algorithms because test data does not have exit labels.

This article is divided as follows. In Sect. 2, we present some basic terminology employed in the text. Section 3 describes several features of the dataset structure and analysis. The following Sect. 4 presented the results of implemented methodologies and we close the paper with Sects. 5 and 6 that consist of concluding comments and provide directions for future work.

2   Preliminaries

For the reader convenience, in this section, we include some basic notions employed in this work and related to anti-money laundering and several characteristics of non-banking correspondents. First, we explain the SARLAFT normative and the irregular transactions that the financial sector must report to UIAF (Financial Information and Analysis Unit). Secondly, we present how the non-banking correspondents work.

2.1   Risk Management System for Money Laundering and Terrorism Financing (SARLAFT)

Two stages describe the risk management system for money laundering and terrorism financing:

- Risk Prevention. The objective is to prevent the inclusion of the resources from activities related to money laundering or financing of terrorism into the financial system(ML/FT). Thus, all clients should give some information to financial institutions with this purpose.
- Risk Control. Institutions like banks should report irregular transaction related to ML/FT, for that there must have a system that monitors and reduce the risk over these activities.

According to the Colombian Criminal Code of the 64 related crimes with money laundering, the financial transfer is one of the schemes in which financial institutions become vulnerable since they are the ideal agent for this purpose compromising their assets and their reputation.

2.2   Detection and Prevention Methods to Money Laundering and Terrorist Financing

Empirically, unusual transactions have been detected that could be related to ML/FT, although some are current transactions or transactions without due process. In this case, the unusual or suspicious transactions contemplated in the Colombian Criminal Code that could be made at NBC are:

– Withdrawal close to the limits defined in Resolution 285 of 2007 of the Financial Information and Analysis Unit - UIAF. Those amounts are not reported but should be analyzed in some way, for example, one or two transactions close to the limits.
– Withdrawals with the same debit card or with several debit cards at different moments on the same day.
– Reiterative transactions (ex: withdrawals, transfers, deposits) over financial products during a specific period.
– Withdrawals with different cards at the same time (users have a limit of transactions).
– Several debit transactions to the same account during a specific period.
– Balance inquiries repeatedly.

2.3   Non-Banking Correspondents

The non-bank correspondents (NBC) as a strategy to promote the financial inclusion and to integrate customers to the formal financial system are non-financial establishments belong to everyday sectors whose principal activity involves cash as gas stations, drugstores, retail stores, among others. This mechanism facilitates the financial operations of customers, develops new customer interactions in services and products, and creates new benefits through business commissions to the owners of those non-financial establishments.

2.4   Operations in a Non-Banking Correspondent

In the standard scheme, non-banking correspondents carry out several operations like cash in, cash out, and bill payments. In this case, the operations are:

◇ *Saving Deposit.* Deposit to a savings account.
◇ *Current Deposit.* Deposit to a current account.
◇ *Balance Inquiry.* The balance inquiry process associated with current accounts, saving accounts or financial products as credit cards.
◇ *Collection.* The collection process involves pursuing payments of debts or services that have been owed by individuals or companies. This process can be with automatic validation, i.e., the process uses a bar-code or QR code to validate the operation. In the other case, the process is semi-automatic because it needs a specific number as a payment reference that the cashier capture manually. Finally, the collection process involves payments of financial services as consumer credit, mortgages, and credit cards.
◇ *Withdrawal.* A retreat of money that has been deposited in an account previously. This account could be current, savings or special account.
◇ *Transfer.* A transfer is the movement of money from one account to another or others.

3   Materials

Here we explain some relevant information about the datasets, describing the raw data and some data mining processes required to obtain our samples.

3.1 Data Collection

A non-bank correspondent active since 2015 provided the data set used in this article. During 2019, at the end of every day, the non-bank correspondent collected the transaction receipts by date. Additionally, the digital data was downloaded monthly and stored by date. The owner of the non-bank correspondent provided all this evidence to integrate the datasets and initiate the analysis.

The dataset for this research was collected from a non-banking correspondent in Colombia during 2019. From the POS machine (provided by the financial institution) connected to the information system of the financial institution, the non-banking correspondent receives and sends information for each transaction. Each transaction issues a receipt, which is delivered to the transaction holder and the second one as back up for the transaction information that managed by the non-bank correspondent. The data stored in the receipt such as date, time, transaction type, and transaction number is information about each transaction, and this data linked to any of the financial institution's products like debit cards, credit cards, personal accounts, business accounts, or debt numbers.

To analyze and visualize the data and subsequently apply analytical and machine learning techniques, it was important to have the receipts data in a dataset. The financial institution has an information system so that each non-bank correspondent can obtain the operations information except the product number that affects the transaction, i.e. if the transaction is a deposit to a current or savings account, a deposit to a business account or other financial instrument does not record the product number. On the other hand, in the debit card withdrawals, the product number was omitted. However, those data found on the receipt.

To have the complete data in digital and to use adequately the database, it was necessary to integrate some data of receipts to the digital file. For this, we made several tests with the Google Vision API [11] through the OCR service (Optical Character Recognition) and programming code to capture the missing data employing a receipt image. Although the tool could detect the text, it did not have the accuracy to take the complete data due to some physical features of receipts as the thermally printed process. With those findings, we resorted to transcribing the receipt data into the database manually. To confirm the veracity of the process, we compared 100 random samples between transactions in the database and receipts with a result of 100% coincidence.

3.2 Data Analysis

The database has numeric and categorical columns, as well as a column with the transaction date and time. With this structure, the idea is to find unusual transactions that may be related to money laundering in any of the 64 crimes established in the Colombian criminal code.

Although the transaction amounts in a non-bank correspondent have limits and are low compared to transactions at banking institution branches, we observed some particular patterns such as similar transactions, transactions carried out on specific days and times, or with a certain periodicity. The 80% of transactions are withdrawals and savings account deposits (Table 1), additionally, 72% of transactions are closed values, considering that those values usually do not belong to debt or service payments. We try to approach these transactions with behaviors that could become unusual.

Table 1. Relative frequency by transaction type

Type	Code	Frequency
Withdrawal	WITHDRAWAL	0.4286
Savings account deposit	DEPOSIT_SAVINGS	0.3734
Collection	COLLECTION	0.1111
Current account deposit	CURRENT_DEPOSIT	0.0643
Credit card collection	CREDIT_CARD_PASS	0.0096
Transfer	TRANSFER	0.0066
Other collections	PURSE	0.0064

Transactions have value limits, which change depending on the transaction type. Thus, the maximum value for withdrawal is ten Colombian million peso, for transfer is six Colombian million peso, and for other transactions is three Colombian million peso. In consequence, we observed that not consider this difference generates variables' disproportion problem. To resolve this, we divided the raw database considering the three transaction limits. The first dataset for withdrawals (WITHDRAWAL), second for transfers (TRANSFER), and third for other transactions (VARIOUS). From the value, we identified the asymmetric behavior of distributions for the withdrawal database (Fig. 1a) and various database (Fig. 1b), and also how some closed values widely exceed the mean.

Concerning categorical variables, we identify the characteristics count for each variable and especially as savings account product as the most relevant (Fig. 2a), as well as the deposit in this product is the transaction type most relevant (Fig. 2b) for the Various dataset. Meanwhile, the density distribution and various values outside the average ranges are characteristic of the categorical variable of the withdrawal dataset. Namely, the box-plot helped us to indicate whether a distribution skewed and whether there are potential unusual observations (outliers) in the withdrawal dataset (Fig. 2c). Additionally, we eliminated some variables because they did not provide relevant information, and we added other variables extracted from the relevant variables that could strengthen the database. For the withdrawal case, we used the time, and we divided into other variables such as a month, day of the month, day of the week, hour, and time bands, all to obtain other information from the dataset as the frequency by day to list a few (Fig. 2c). Summarize, the dataset consists of 64,000 records,

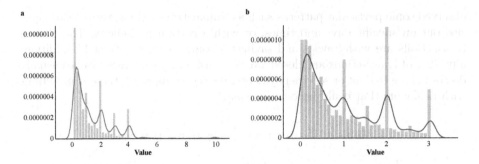

Fig. 1. Value histogram. a. WITHDRAWAL dataset. b. VARIOUS dataset.

and after preprocessing and cleaning, the dataset has 52,512 records and nine variables. We divided this raw dataset into three datasets as we explained above.

4   Unusual Transactions Detection with Machine Learning

This section presents visualization techniques, machine learning algorithms, and the modeling and testing layer of the CRISP-DM [31] methodology. We used unsupervised machine learning algorithms to detect unusual transactions taking account that the data does not have target labels.

Suspicious or unusual movements found in the data analysis are statistical. However, to improve the objective, we used machine learning algorithms to carry out the tests and take advantage of the computational resources, efficiency, and self-learning of those algorithms to detect, visualize, and predict these transactions. The algorithms used for testing are Isolation Forest based on decision trees [15] and One-Class SVM based on support vector machines (SVM) [17]. Of each one, we present a methodological structure, the importance and function of different parameters, and the way to validate them. Although K-Prototype based on clustering is not an algorithm to detect anomalies [13], but helps us to identify some behaviors through segmentation.

According to dataset characteristics, we used the grid search method through the GridSearchCV library of Sklearn in Phyton [19] to determine the optimal values of the hyper-parameters and validate algorithms in the Isolate Forest and One-Class SVM models. This method provides a tool to generate its scoring objects for each algorithm as a result of a score from the analyzed data, which classifies the unusual values as -1 and the normal ones as 1. Besides, with the estimator's function (*score_samples*), we can access the score used to compare the results of the two anomaly detection algorithms. Finally, as a complementary analysis with K-Prototype, we used the elbow method to determine the number of clusters in each dataset [4].

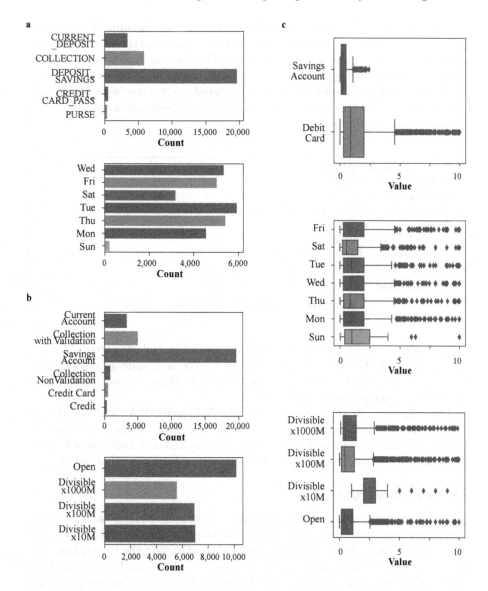

Fig. 2. Categorical variables. a. Transaction type in VARIOUS dataset. b. Product type in VARIOUS dataset. c. Boxplot (Box and whisker plot) in WITHDRAWAL dataset.

4.1 Isolation Forest

It is an unsupervised learning algorithm based on decision trees to detect anomaly in a dataset. Statistically, an anomaly is an observation or event that deviates significantly from other events to raise suspicions that a different mean generated it [15]. Habitually, algorithms define the profile of that is average data and then isolate that is not, but Isolation Forest uses the opposite approach to detect anomalies, i.e., it isolates unusual data immediately. In consequence, anomaly detection is a process of two-stage. The first one builds isolation trees using sub-samples of the training set, i.e., trees are defined by recursive partitioning the training set until instances are isolated or trees reached a limit height l, around to the average tree height defined by the sub-sampling size [15]. Thus, the algorithm structure is:

Input: X - input data, T - number of trees, ψ- subsampling size
Output: a set of T iTrees
1 **Initialize Forest:**
2   set height limit $l =$ ceiling(log2 ψ);
3   **for** $i = 1$ to t **do**
4         $X' \leftarrow$ sample(X, ψ)
5   Forest $\leftarrow$ Forest $\cup$ iTree(X', 0, l)
6   **end**
7 **return Forest**

Algorithm 1. iForest (X, T, ψ)

The second stage passes the test instances through isolation trees to obtain an anomaly score for each instance [15]. This score is a result of the expected path length for each test instance. Thus, this algorithm is more specific and requires less computational resources.

The evaluation of this algorithm for the WITHDRAWAL dataset (Fig. 3) presents the dispersion diagram, where indicates the anomalous transactions. We find that the transaction's value is not the only factor defining data features since there are anomalous and normal points throughout the value range.

4.2 One-Class SVM

The support vector machine (SVM) is a linear classifier based on the margin maximization principle and define the methodology of this algorithm [2,30]. The SVM accomplishes the classification task by constructing the hyperplane that optimally separates the data into two categories, which can be used for both classification and regression tasks and should receive a labeled training data set, defined as follows: $x_1, ...x_n \in \mathcal{X}$, where $n \in \mathbb{N}$ is the number of observations and $\mathcal{X}$ is some set [23]. In this case, the model trained with data of only one class, i.e., the positive information [18]. In other words, this algorithm tries to classify one class of objects and distinguish it from the other possible objects. However, it has to train to reject this object and to define it as an outlier [24]. Also, it infers the standard class properties and from these properties predicts which data is different [17].

To test the detection effect of the classifier based on the One-Class SVM algorithm, we use this methodology with the training and testing data for the WITH-DRAWAL dataset respectively, and the detection result shows in Fig. 4. Newly,

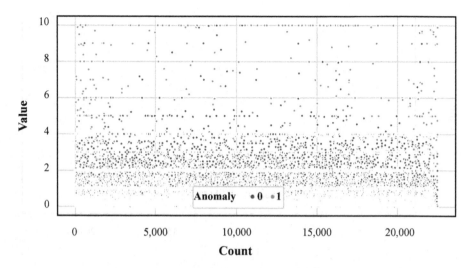

Fig. 3. iForest dispersion diagram for WITHDRAWAL dataset.

the transaction's value is not the only factor defining data features because there are anomalous and normal points throughout the range as well as in the previous algorithm.

4.3   Complementary Analysis

We compared the top ten transactions marked as anomalous by the two algorithms mentioned above (Table 2), and we find how values that we call closed have the highest frequencies in both cases. Also, we observed that values do not represent only the maximum or minimum values in each dataset because of algorithms included other additional variables to the transaction value. As a result, the One-class SVM algorithm shows a homogeneous classification of anomalous and normal values (Fig. 4) than the Isolation Forest algorithm (Fig. 3).

Additionally, as a technique for statistical analysis, we used K-prototype algorithm. This algorithm cluster objects with mixed, numeric, and categorical attributes in a way similar to k-means. Clustering consists of a set of objects that it with the greatest number of similar characteristics grouped, but in this case, objects clustered against k-prototypes instead of k-means, i.e., k-means, based on Euclidean distance, used for the numerical data and k-modes used for categorical variables [12]. However, when applied to numeric data the k-prototypes algorithm is similar to k-means (Table 3).

The purpose of this process was to demonstrate how numeric and categorical attributes interact with each other in the process of clustering and obtain other issues that complement the anomalies analysis. Figure 5 shows clustering in seven groups of the WITHDRAWAL dataset, defining by the elbow technique [4]. These seven clusters show some aspects that could help us to complement the

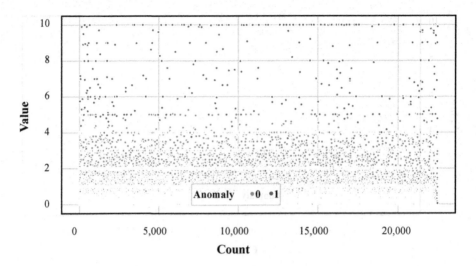

Fig. 4. One-Class SVM dispersion diagram for WITHDRAWAL dataset.

Table 2. Relative frequency of closed values for WITHDRAWAL dataset

iForest		One-Classs SVM	
Value	Frequency	Value	Frequency
4,000,000	0.103234	4,000,000	0.091852
100,000	0.048737	9,999,999	0.036543
200,000	0.042534	1,000,000	0.028148
9,999,999	0.032787	3,000,000	0.021235
300,000	0.025698	100,000	0.020247
1,000,000	0.024369	200,000	0.019753
50,000	0.023039	2,000,000	0.015802
5,000,000	0.021267	50,000	0.014815
400,000	0.019938	5,000,000	0.013827
2,000,000	0.019495	150,000	0.013827

above results. We analyze some elements in cluster 0 to list a few. Several clients withdraw the maximum value of (9,999,999) as a strategy to evade the tax law control of the Financial Information and Analysis Unit (UIAF), which is from 10 million. This situation presented every month, weekday, and day that the non-banking correspondent operates and is a particular feature that needs monitoring. Additionally, withdrawals with specific values or closed values (75% values in cluster 0 are equal to four Colombian million peso) could be a signal of suspicious operations if they integrated with their frequency and temporality, like

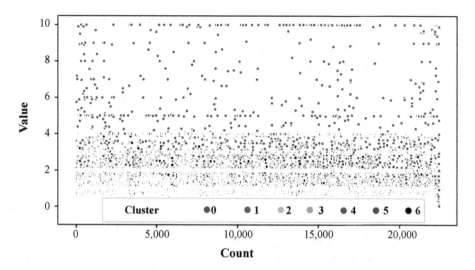

Fig. 5. Clustering for WITHDRAWAL database.

the case of the maximum values in other clusters. Namely, the cluster analysis is a powerful tool to complement the anomalies' analysis as long as characteristics from clusters can be identified and integrated because of each cluster covers a homogeneous space in the entire sample space.

Finally, we confirm a baseline approach with the statistical analysis. In Fig. 1a, we identified a long tail from five Colombian million pesos to ten million values on the x-axis, which indicates that those values skewed towards 10 million. Also, the first graph in Fig. 2c confirms that withdrawals with debit cards have unusual values starting at 5 Colombian million pesos. Therefore, if we compare the results of One-Class SVM in Fig. 4, we observed that the values on the y-axis after 5 million are unusual, which is confirming that seen above. Another example (1a) shows how some closed values like 1, 2, 3, and 4 million deviate from normal values. We could compare those values with Table two where the most common unusual values are 1, 2, 3, and 4 million.

5 Discussion

Anomaly detection algorithms can detect anomalous transactions directly and consistently with results of previous exploratory analyzes, while the clustering algorithm identified different behaviors in datasets. Although the detection of anomalies in bank transactions is not something new, if it is limited in the case of non-bank correspondents since beyond being a financial service in non-financial establishments, they have the particularity of developing in socio-economic, cultural, and particular geographical environments. These environments require the definition of policies and the design of technological tools that reduced the growing problem of money laundering. Likewise, algorithms allowed identifying

Table 3. Cluster statistical description for withdrawal database

Measure	Value	Month	Day_month	Weekday	Time
Cluster 0. Count 2,226					
min	2,500,000	1	1	0	8
25%	3,500,000	5	10	1	14
50%	4,000,000	7	15	2	15
75%	4,000,000	9	21	3	16
max	9,999,999	12	31	6	19
Cluster 1. Count 3,768					
min	1,600,000	1	1	2	7
25%	250,000	3	4	4	10
50%	600.000	5	8	4	11
75%	1,500,000	6	12	5	14
max	4,390,000	10	19	6	18
Cluster 2. Count 3,203					
min	3,000	1	11	0	8
25%	250,000	2	20	1	14
50%	630,000	3	25	2	15
75%	1,500,000	5	28	3	16
max	4,000,000	7	31	5	18
Cluster 3. Count 4,016					
min	3,500	1	1	0	8
25%	260,000	4	8	0	9
50%	734,000	7	13	1	10
75%	1,900,000	9	19	2	10
max	4,190,000	12	30	3	12
Cluster 4. Count 2,634					
min	2,000	1	12	2	8
25%	230,000	5	21	3	9
50%	600,000	7	25	4	10
75%	1,500,000	10	28	5	11
max	4,190,000	12	31	5	16
Cluster 5. Count 3,496					
min	1,300	6	4	0	11
25%	210,000	8	16	1	14
50%	598,000	10	20	2	15
75%	1,527,500	11	25	4	16
max	3,590,000	12	31	5	18
Cluster 6. Count 3,166					
min	3,000	1	1	0	11
25%	240,000	3	4	1	15
50%	650,000	5	8	1	16
75%	1,535,000	7	12	2	16
max	3,860,000	10	18	4	18

in greater detail the operations of several users, especially in the use of some financial products. In this case, we identified some user operations exceeded the maximum amounts defined by the Colombian Tax Code, as well as an unusual situation: the use of an account every 35 h during the period, something that is not usual in personal accounts (Fig. 6). The anomaly detection algorithms allowed us to improve results by adjusting hyper-parameters and available validations. However, for anomaly detection, we need to combine algorithm processes that robustness the tool and obtain detecting results more specific and for each cluster.

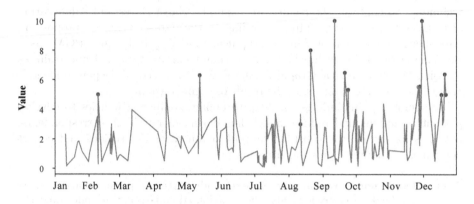

Fig. 6. Anomalies example of a specific user.

On the other hand, when identifying movements of a non-bank correspondent, a new problem arises that adds to money laundering and that is the robbery vulnerability [14,22]. They have this risk because of an increase in operations levels that makes them targets of common and organized crime. Some statistical metrics defined that non-banking correspondents could have operations on average between five to ten times greater than a store, a gas station, or a drugstore in a traditional operation day. Also, non-banking correspondents could have operations as a banking branch. In consequence, non-banking correspondents must have professional advice from financial institutions in cash management, money laundering, and other risks because of the criminal organizations that dedicate to money laundering and other illegal activities evolve permanently. Namely, those situations could affect the benefits and reduce the number of non-banking correspondents.

6 Conclusion

The main focus of this article is how machine learning and visualization algorithms serve to identify anomalies in a set of transactions of a non-banking correspondent. This work sheds light on this problem by introducing some algorithms that can create a new perspective about financial transactions in a kind of financial agent that grows in different countries, especially, in developing countries as Bangladesh, Brazil, China, Colombia, Ecuador, India, Mexico, Pakistan, among others, as well as how is the money laundering activities in specific socioeconomic environments.

We identified some research topics to explore. First, the analysis of agents in big cities or some hot-spots in countries with a special growth of these kinds of financial intermediaries. Another approach for future research would be algorithms to identify anomalies using supervised and unsupervised machine learning techniques to confront the results, for example, Naive Bayes and Adaboosting algorithms to list a few. Third, according to the dataset type, we propose an implementation of a probabilistic graphical modeling technique (PGM) as a Bayesian network for unsupervised data that facilitate to model uncertainties by using Directed Acyclic Graphics [20,29]. Fourth, we could deepen to identify anomalies in each cluster using the result of segmentation.

In summary, our findings can help to define monitoring policies to develop preventive actions and reduce money laundering in non-bank correspondents, but it is important the constant support of financial institutions and expert personnel to counter a growing situation.

Acknowledgements. We have the support of administrative personnel and cashiers of some non-banking correspondents who contributed empirically to understand the business particularities.

References

1. Rao, A.A., Kanchana, V.: Dynamic approach for detection of suspicious transactions in money laundering. Int. J. Eng. Technol. **7**(3.10), 10–13 (2018). https://doi.org/10.14419/ijet.v7i3.10.15619
2. Adankon, M.M., Cheriet, M.: Support vector machine. In: Li, S.Z., Jain, A. (eds.) Encyclopedia of Biometrics, pp. 1303–1308. Springer, Boston (2009). https://doi.org/10.1007/978-0-387-73003-5_299
3. Bayona-Rodríguez, H.: Money laundering in rural areas with illicit crops: empirical evidence for Colombia. Crime Law Soc. Change **72**(4), 387–417 (2019). https://doi.org/10.1007/s10611-019-09822-z
4. Bholowalia, P., Kumar, A.: EBK-means: a clustering technique based on elbow method and k-means in WSN. Int. J. Comput. Appl. 105(9) (2014). https://doi.org/10.5120/18405-9674
5. Chen, Z., Van Khoa, L.D., Teoh, E.N., Nazir, A., Karuppiah, E.K., Lam, K.S.: Machine learning techniques for anti-money laundering (AML) solutions in suspicious transaction detection: a review. Knowl. Inf. Syst. **57**(2), 245–285 (2018). https://doi.org/10.1007/s10115-017-1144-z
6. Cindori, S., et al.: Money laundering: correlation between risk assessment and suspicious transactions. Financ. Theor. Pract. **37**(2), 181–206 (2013). https://doi.org/10.3326/fintp.37.2.3

7. Demetis, D.S.: Fighting money laundering with technology: a case study of bank x in the UK. Decis. Support Syst. **105**, 96–107 (2018). https://doi.org/10.1016/j.dss.2017.11.005
8. Drezewski, R., Dziuban, G., Hernik, L., Paczek, M.: Comparison of data mining techniques for money laundering detection system. In: Proceedings - 2015 International Conference on Science in Information Technology: Big Data Spectrum for Future Information Economy, ICSITech 2015, pp. 5–10 (2016). https://doi.org/10.1109/ICSITech.2015.7407767
9. Drezewski, R., Sepielak, J., Filipkowski, W.: System supporting money laundering detection. Digital Invest. **9**(1), 8–21 (2012). https://doi.org/10.1016/j.diin.2012.04.003
10. García-Bedoya, O., Granados, O., Cardozo, J.: Ai against money laundering networks: the Colombian case. J. Money Laundering Control (2020). https://doi.org/10.1108/JMLC-04-2020-0033
11. GoogleCloud: Vision AI. https://cloud.google.com/vision
12. Huang, Z.: Extensions to the k-means algorithm for clustering large data sets with categorical values. Data Min. Knowl. Discovery **2**(3), 283–304 (1998). https://doi.org/10.1023/A:1009769707641
13. Ji, J., Bai, T., Zhou, C., Ma, C., Wang, Z.: An improved k-prototypes clustering algorithm for mixed numeric and categorical data. Neurocomputing **120**, 590–596 (2013). https://doi.org/10.1016/j.neucom.2013.04.011
14. Kumar, A., Parsons, A., Urdapilleta, E., Nair, A.: Expanding Bank Outreach through Retail Partnerships: Correspondent Banking in Brazil. The World Bank, Washington (2006)
15. Liu, F.T., Ting, K.M., Zhou, Z.H.: Isolation forest. In: 2008 Eighth IEEE International Conference on Data Mining, pp. 413–422. IEEE (2008). https://doi.org/10.1109/ICDM.2008.17
16. Loayza, N., Villa, E., Misas, M.: Illicit activity and money laundering from an economic growth perspective: A model and an application to Colombia. J. Econ. Behav. Organ. **159**, 442–487 (2019). https://doi.org/10.1016/j.jebo.2017.10.002
17. Manevitz, L.M., Yousef, M.: One-class SVMs for document classification. J. Mach. Learn. Res. **2**, 139–154 (2001)
18. Muller, K., Mika, S., Ratsch, G., Tsuda, K., Scholkopf, B.: An introduction to kernel-based learning algorithms. IEEE Trans. Neural Networks **12**(2), 181–201 (2001). https://doi.org/10.1109/72.914517
19. Pedregosa, F., et al.: Scikit-learn: Machine learning in python. J. Mach. Learn. Res. **12**, 2825–2830 (2011)
20. Pham, D.T., Ruz, G.A.: Unsupervised training of Bayesian networks for data clustering. Proc. Roy. Soc. Math. Phys. Eng. Sci. **465**(2109), 2927–2948 (2009). https://doi.org/10.1098/rspa.2009.0065
21. Prakash, A., Apoorva, S., Amulya, K.H., Kavya, T.P., Prashanth Kumar, K.N.: Proposal of expert system to predict financial frauds using data mining. In: 2019 3rd International Conference on Computing Methodologies and Communication (ICCMC), pp. 1080–1083, March 2019. https://doi.org/10.1109/ICCMC.2019.8819709
22. Sánchez-González, C., Prada-Araque, D., Erazo-Inca, F.: El aporte de los corresponsales no bancarios a la inclusión financiera. Desarrollo Gerencial **12**(1), 1–23 (2020). 10.17081/dege.12.1.3599
23. Schölkopf, B., Platt, J.C., Shawe-Taylor, J., Smola, A.J., Williamson, R.C.: Estimating the support of a high-dimensional distribution. Neural Comput. **13**, 1443–1471 (2001). https://doi.org/10.1162/089976601750264965

24. Shin, H.J., Eom, D.H., Kim, S.S.: One-class support vector machines–an application in machine fault detection and classification. Comput. Ind. Eng. **48**(2), 395–408 (2005). https://doi.org/10.1016/j.cie.2005.01.009

25. Singh, K., Best, P.: Anti-money laundering: using data visualization to identify suspicious activity. Int. J. Acc. Inf. Syst. **34**, 100418 (2019). https://doi.org/10.1016/j.accinf.2019.06.001

26. Thoumi, F.E.: Political Economy and Illegal Drugs in Colombia. Lynne Rienner Publishers, Boulder (1995)

27. Thoumi, F.E., Anzola, M.: Asset and money laundering in Bolivia, Colombia and Peru: a legal transplant in vulnerable environments? Crime Law Soc. Change **53**(5), 437–455 (2010). https://doi.org/10.1007/s10611-010-9235-8

28. Thoumi, F.E., Anzola, M.: Can AML policies succeed in Colombia? Crime, Law and Soc. Change **57**(1), 1–14 (2012). https://doi.org/10.1007/s10611-011-9331-4

29. Thulasiraman, K., Swamy, M.: 5.7 acyclic directed graphs. In: Graphs: Theory and Algorithms, p. 118. Wiley, New York (1992)

30. Vishwanathan, S., Murty, M.N.: SSVM: a simple SVM algorithm. In: Proceedings of the 2002 International Joint Conference on Neural Networks, IJCNN 2002 (Cat. No. 02CH37290), vol. 3, pp. 2393–2398. IEEE (2002)

31. Wirth, R., Hipp, J.: CRISP-DM: towards a standard process model for data mining. In: Proceedings of the 4th International Conference on the Practical Applications of Knowledge Discovery and Data Mining, pp. 29–39. Springer, London (2000)

Predicting Polypharmacy Side Effects Based on an Enhanced Domain Knowledge Graph

Ruiyi Wang, Tong Li[✉], Zhen Yang, and Haiyang Yu

Beijing University of Technology, Beijing, China
wangruiyi@emails.bjut.edu.cn
{litong,yangzhen,yuhaiyang}@bjut.edu.cn

Abstract. The use of multiple drugs, termed Polypharmacy, is a common prescription for treatment. However, Polypharmacy is likely to cause unknown side effects, which can seriously affect patients' health. Given the complexity of the Drug-Drug Interactions (DDIs), recent approaches mainly leverage knowledge graphs to predict DDIs, formulated as a multi-relational link prediction problem. The accuracy of such approaches relies on the comprehensibility of the established knowledge graphs. In this paper, we explore the factors of DDIs in-depth and propose an effective DDIs prediction method based on reasonable domain knowledge. Specifically, we established a comprehensive knowledge graph, which takes the interrelationships among drugs, genes, and enzymes into account, on top of a baseline knowledge graph. We then train and apply a Convolutional Neural Network (CNN) to predict the type and probability of DDIs among drug pairs. We verify the impact of different factors on performance. Under the same data conditions as the baseline, the results of which show that the accuracy of our proposal is 12% higher than the baseline approach.

Keywords: Drug-Drug Interactions · Knowledge graph · Link prediction · Convolutional Neural Network

1 Introduction

DDIs and their associated Adverse Drug Reactions (ADRs) are serious public health hazards. Every year, a large amount of human and material resources are invested in the treatment of diseases caused by ADRs. Thus it can be seen that drug side effects not only seriously harm health but also cause huge economic losses.

Polypharmacy therapy is currently a promising disease-fighting strategy that involves the simultaneous use of multiple drugs in combination therapy, also known as drug combination. A significant consequence of polypharmacy therapy for patients is that the risk of side effects is much higher than taking only one drug. There is, however, a huge amount of drugs, so it is impossible to test all

© Springer Nature Switzerland AG 2020
H. Florez and S. Misra (Eds.): ICAI 2020, CCIS 1277, pp. 89–103, 2020.
https://doi.org/10.1007/978-3-030-61702-8_7

possible interaction drug pairs in actual drug trials, and rare side effects are difficult to observe in drug trials. Therefore, side effects from drug combinations are difficult to identify trials manually [2,22].

For the above reasons, it is particularly important to predict DDIs through available data and relevant methods. The critical interaction tasks in drug development mainly include the Drug-Target Interactions prediction task and the Drug-Drug Interactions (DDIs) prediction task [25]. Besides, the causes of ADRs are related to a variety of factors, such as drug chemical formula, molecular drug structure, drug pathway, and other factors. However, different factors have different effects on DDIs. Among the existing methods, some DDIs prediction methods utilize plain text information, which the same as us. Next, we focus on the methods, which use plain text.

In the DDIs prediction methods, which utilize plain text information, few multi-relation prediction methods can achieve high accuracy and flexibly add feature information. We introduce three typical DDIs methods. Most of the text-only DDIs prediction methods mainly use the method of Graph Convolutional Neural Network (GCN) [26,30], or the method based on the similarity of ADR characteristics [1,3,23,28], and the traditional machine learning method [4,7,15,29]. Most predictions only predict whether a reaction occurs between the drug pairs, rather than the reaction types of drug pairs.

In this paper, we propose a novel polypharmacy side effect prediction method based on an enhanced domain knowledge graph. Specifically, the contributions of our proposal consist of the following parts:

- We deeply explore the factors that influence DDIs, based on the results of identifying the genes and enzymes as two main factors.
- Based on our investigation of drug interactions, we propose a complete method to characterize the relationship between drug pairs and establish a comprehensive knowledge graph that includes drug, gene, and enzyme.
- We use CNN to build a classification method for predicting DDIs and conduct experiments to evaluate its performance. The results turn out that our method is better than the baseline.

The remainder of this paper is organized as follows. Section 2 briefly introduces three typical DDIs prediction methods and existing problems. Section 3 mainly introduces our data processing method and DDIs prediction method. Section 4 introduces our experimental dataset, specific experimental setup, baseline method, and experimental results. Section 5 discusses possible problems with our current approach. Section 6 summarizes the work of this paper and discusses the future research direction.

2   Related Work

This section mainly introduces the three kinds of existing DDIs prediction methods: GCN related method, the characteristic similarity of DDIs reaction related method, and the traditional machine learning method related method. In addition, we introduce the ConvE model, which uses 2D convolutions to link prediction in knowledge graphs [9], and explain why we base our proposal on this model.

Graph Convolutional Neural Network-Based Approaches. Decagon [30] is the first method to implement the prediction of DDIs. It integrates the multiple GCN method [8,10,11,13,19], and integrate these GCN methods for DDIs prediction. Although Decagon first implements the prediction of DDIs, its prediction effect is not good. Based on Decagon, Tri-Graph [26] method improves prediction accuracy to a certain extent. Although it reduces the calculation time and space by splitting a graph into three subgraphs, it is not reasonable to compare different spaces' embedding. At the same time, GCN methods are not as flexible and convenient as our method, and it needs to follow some additional rules to make the graph difficult to expand.

DDIs of Characteristic Similarity-Based Approaches. In the prediction method of ADRs in the early years, most of them adopt the method based on similarity [1,3,23,28], the main realization of ADRs prediction is to prediction drug unknown side effects. The ADRs prediction method [3] add gene-related data and implement edge prediction by forming a feature matrix through drug-gene and DDIs. The DDI method based on similarity [1,5,28] adding a variety of characteristics of drugs, to incorporate multiple databases, just superposition of information interaction between the drug and other characteristics. Those methods prefer to semantic features of data. However, drug entities have various expressions, and each drug has multiple names. Too much emphasis on semantic expression may be limited.

Traditional Machine Learning Methods-Based Approaches. Those methods use different machine learning classifiers. For example, Liu et al. [15] use logistic regression, naive Bayes, K-means, random forest, and SVM to establish a prediction method integrating pharmaceutical chemical and biological information. Bresso et al. [4] use decision trees and logistic regression to identify and describe the common side effects of several drugs. Zhang et al. [29] improved and optimized the SVM method, implemented ADRs prediction, and solved the problem of multi-label tasks and data imbalance. Compare to ours, the accuracy that such methods calculate complex graphs and DDI prediction is lower. Due to the relatively simple method, when facing large complex graphs, the data contains multiple reaction types, prone to overfitting. It is difficult to accurately predict the different types of drug interactions that occur between drug pairs.

ConvE Model. ConvE model [9] is the first method that combines the CNN model and knowledge graph linking prediction task, and it is suitable for a large knowledge graph. ConvE model is a multi-layer CNN model for link prediction, mainly use for highly connected complex knowledge graphs. This model has a high parameter efficiency. Its performance is the same as DistMult [27] and R-GCN [19] under the condition of parameter reduction of 8 times and 17 times. We consider DDIs prediction as a multi-link prediction task. The comprehensive knowledge graph we construct is characterized by many kinds of entities, complex entity relationships, and high entity connectivity. Therefore, we choose the ConvE model as the basis of our work, which is suitable not only for the multi-relational link prediction task but also for the comprehensive knowledge graph we construct.

In this paper, we use the ConvE model as the basis of our work. We construct our method based on the ConvE model, which combines the advantages of the ConvE model and is more suitable for DDIs.

3   Method

We propose our method, which is a predictive method of DDIs based on CNN. The method is divided into two parts: data processing (3.1) and the prediction method (3.2). Figure 1 shows two parts.

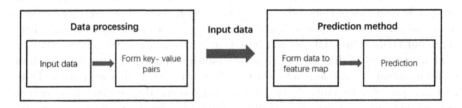

Fig. 1. Our method steps

The prediction method is mainly divided into six steps. The first two steps are to reconstruct and connect head and tail entities embedding (Steps 1 and 2). The resulting matrix then uses as the convolution layer's input (Step 3). Input the resulting Hessian eigenmaps tensor vectorize from Step 3, and project into a K-dimensional space (Step 4 and 5). The score calculates with all relational objects (Step 6). The steps are shown in Fig. 2.

3.1   Data Preprocessing

We establish a comprehensive knowledge graph (shown in Fig. 3) that takes the interrelationships among drugs, genes, and enzymes. In this comprehensive knowledge graph, we divided four types of reactions: drug-drug, drug-gene, gene-gene, and drug-enzyme. Among them, drug-drug has a variety of different reaction types; different kinds of interactions occur between two drugs.

The steps of the ConvE model for preprocessing the ternary data are as follows. A triple is a data structure composed of head entities, relations, and tail

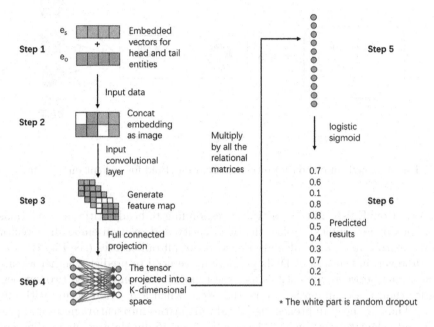

Fig. 2. The specific steps of the prediction method employed in this paper

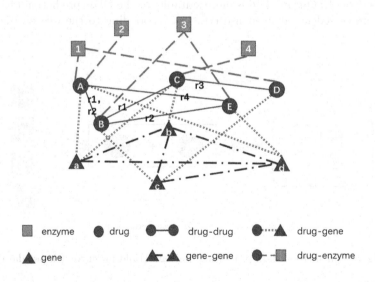

Fig. 3. Knowledge graph of DDIs with three entities

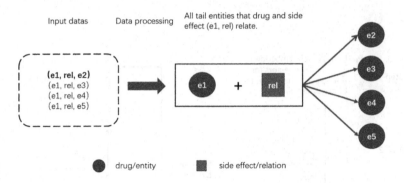

Fig. 4. ConvE model data processing diagram (Bold for current input data)

entities. ConvE lists all tail entities corresponding to head entities and relations (i.e., positive examples). Splice the head entity and relation embedding vector to the feature map, and calculate the scores of all tail entities (see Fig. 4).

However, in the task of DDIs prediction, we need to predict whether a reaction occurs between two entities and the type of reaction between two entities, rather than the combination of another drug when a reaction occurs with one drug. Thus, we need to process head and tail entities into feature maps and predict and calculate scores with relations. Besides, in our dataset, many different types of DDIs often occur between the two entities. Therefore, based on the characteristics of the above dataset related to the DDIs task, we build our method based on ConvE. Our method is more suitable for the DDIs prediction task. The data is processed for all response types corresponding to the two entities (see Fig. 5).

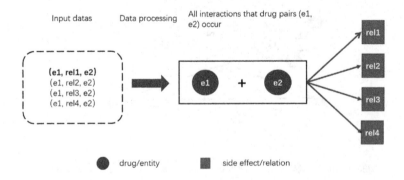

Fig. 5. Our method data processing diagram (Bold for current input data)

3.2   Prediction Method

In this work, based on the improvement of data processing, our input has also changed. Our overall implementation steps are as follows: the interaction relationship between head and tail entities takes as input. The convolutional layer and the full connection layer are used for methods to obtain two-dimensional convolution embedding, and the score is calculated. Figure 2 shows the concrete implementation steps of the method.

The scoring function is defined as:

$$\psi_r(e_s, e_o) = f(vec(f([\overline{e_s}; \overline{e_o}] * \omega))W)r_r \tag{1}$$

Triples (s,r,o) in which the head entity is s, the tail entity is o, the relation entity is r. The score of a triple (s,r,o) is defined as $\psi(s, r, o) = \psi_r(e_s, e_o) \in \mathbb{R}$. The vectors e_s and e_o is denote the subject and object embedding. $e_s, e_o, r_r \in \mathbb{R}^k$. $\overline{e_s}$ and $\overline{e_o}$ is 2D reshaping of e_s and e_o, $[\overline{e_s}; \overline{e_o}]$ connect the embedding vectors of $\overline{e_s}$ and $\overline{e_o}$ into "image" form (step 1 and step 2), where $\overline{e_s}, \overline{e_o} \in \mathbb{R}^{k_w * k_h}$, $k = k_w * k_h$. CNN model is especially suitable for image processing. When applying the CNN model in our method, our data need to be processed to form an "image". Using "image" form data as input, our method can process high-dimensional data well and accurately acquire data characteristics.

After concatenating the head entity and tail entity, we input it into a 2D convolutional layer with filters ω. This step aims to reduce the dimensionality of the "image" we have formed and increase the non-linear expression ability of the method. The output is a feature map tensor $\tau \in \mathbb{R}^{cmn}$ (step 3), where c is the number of 2D feature maps with dimensions m and n. $vec(\tau)$ is reshaping τ, make full connect projection (step 4), and then multiply the W matrix (step 5). We project the tensor τ into the K-dimensional space by multiplying the W matrix, then matching the relation embedding r_r via an inner product. Step 4 and Step 5 are preparing to calculate the prediction scores. Finally, inputting entity matrix of e_s and e_o into sigmoid and compute scores (step 6). To improve the computational efficiency, we get all relationships scores, and we prevent overfitting by random dropout.

Most of the existing DDIs prediction methods are predicted by constructing graph structures containing drugs and gene entities, which data are sparse graph structures. This structure is not only consuming large amounts of memory space but also must satisfy the graph structure rules. Thus, it is difficult to add other entities of characteristics. For example, if we want to add drug-gene data in the Decagon, this gene does not exist in the node of the existing gene-gene graph, so this data cannot be combined. However, we adopt the triplet data, only store the data relationships in memory space, initializing embedded vectors of the entities and relationships. Use our method, the data of various entity types can be added flexibly without considering graph structure problems and avoid unnecessary waste of memory space.

4   Evaluation

This section describes the dataset we use, the specific experimental steps, and the analysis of our results. We carry out experiments on a comprehensive knowledge graph. It is divide into two experiments. First, we divide the comprehensive knowledge graph into three graphs: containing information about drug interaction, drug and protein interaction, drug, gene, and enzyme interaction. Then we take three subgraphs as input, experiment separately, and evaluate the method's performance under different subgraphs. Different subgraphs are embedded in the same way. Under the same conditions as the baseline, the result concludes that our method experimental performance is 12% higher than baseline, and AUROC achieved 96% accuracy. Protein information increases the results by 7%. The drug-enzyme data increased the experimental results by 1% when they are used to predict DDIs. Second, we evaluated our method's predictive accuracy for different side effects on the dataset containing drugs and proteins. The result is that our method has a good effect on the side effect of abuse type. Our method has achieved good results in the task of DDIs prediction.

4.1   Dataset

The dataset use in this paper is mainly divide into two parts. The first part uses partial data from the Decagon, which combines five types of data: SIDER database [14], OFFSIDES database [22], TWOSIDES database [22], Protein Interaction Network [6,16,18,20], and STITCH Database [21]. The second part uses enzyme data from Drugbank.

Decagon Dataset. Decagon's drug network combines the following three sources. The SIDER database is the database of drug side effects, obtain in drug experiments. The OFFSIDES database is a summary of ADRs obtained outside the drug experiment, in the report of drug side effect. The TWOSIDES database is for DDIs. Decagon's protein function network combines four sources of protein interaction data on the human genome, a total of 19085 genes, and 719402 physical interactions. By STITCH, the interaction between drug and gene in the database information connects to the rest of the databases. Finally, the knowledge graph contains two entities: drugs and protein, three types of relation: drug-drug, drug-gene, and gene-gene.

Drugbank Dataset. Based on Decagon Dataset, this paper obtains necessary information on drugs through the SIDER database, connects existing drug entities with Drugbank database [24]. We select drugs containing enzyme and add the data related to the enzyme. We refer to some papers and finally conclude that, except gene, the enzyme is the factor that has a greater impact on the drug side effect. Mohamed et al. conclude that DDIs have little to do with the disease that drug treats [17]. However, DDIs are related to gene and enzyme, and these two factors are the main factors that influence drug interactions. Therefore, we add data related to the enzyme to the dataset.

Finally, we select the dataset containing 30 reaction types. A total of 38,616 drug-drug reaction types and 389 drugs is select, and through the drugs, it includes 30 drug-drug reaction types, 12096 drug-genes, and 71,281 gene-gene 1753 drug-enzyme, 19,083 genes, and 163 enzymes are select. All data information are shown in Table 1. We end up with a knowledge graph of drugs, gene, enzyme, shown in Fig. 1.

Table 1. Dataset list

Dataset	Number of entities	Number of edges
Drug-drug	389	38616
Drug-gene	19472	12096
Gene-gene	19083	71281
Drug-enzyme	552	1753

4.2 Experiment

Dataset Setup. We treat the DDIs prediction problem as a multi-relational link prediction problem and divide all the data into the training set, test set, and validation set. The training set contains 80% data, and the validation set and test set each contain 10% data. Avoid information leakage, after data preprocessed, each entity combination only appears once in the dataset. Each piece of data contains all the reaction types under the entity combination. For example, drug A and drug B may have multiple side effects, and in the data of drug A and drug B, all the reactions of drug A and drug B are list.

Since most knowledge graphs are direct graphs, take a triple data (head entity, relationship, tail entity) as an example: (Obama, is, the President of the United States). The default is a directed graph in the calculation process, because (the President of the United States, is, Obama) this data is not tenable. Our graph is undirected. For example, drug A and drug B interact, and there is no positional differentiation between head and tail entities. To solve this problem, we split each data into two data (drug A, reaction, drug B) (drug B, reaction, drug A). We process all the data into the form of key-value pairs to calculate. We encode all the entities and relations and randomly initialize them into two embedded matrices. We do the same embedding randomly initialize for all different types of nodes.

Baseline. Decagon is chosen as the baseline because both the Decagon's method task and our method task predict DDIs and regard DDIs as the multi-relation link prediction problem. Our method and Decagon both can predict the type of DDIs. There are four types of interaction in the dataset: drug-drug, drug-gene,

gene-gene, drug-enzyme. Baseline contains three types: drug-drug, drug-gene, gene-gene. To compare with baseline, we use three types of knowledge graph and the same dataset. We reuse part of the original code of ConvE and modify it to achieve the task of DDIs prediction. Hidden drop is 0.3, the learning rate is 0.002, embedding dim is 200 by default.

Evaluation Indicator. There are three evaluation indexes, Area Under the Receiver-Operating Characteristic (AUROC), Area Under the Precision-Recall Curve (AUPRC), and Average Precision at 50 (AP@50), which are the same as the baseline used for the experiment. AUROC is the area under the curve. The abscissa is the probability of judging the positive sample as positive. The ordinate is the probability of judging the negative sample as positive. AUROC curve is one of the most common indexes to evaluate classifier classification performance in medical and machine learning papers. Meanwhile, in some methods, AUROC is the most used as the evaluation standard [12,30]. In DDIs predictions, our task is to find the likelihood of a reaction between two drugs. Therefore, the higher the AUROC value, the better.

AUPRC is an area under the recall rate curve. In practical application, most of the time, the positive and negative samples are not average. In this situation, AUROC can keep the score constant, and it is not a good measure of the classifier's quality under such conditions. The x-coordinate of AUPRC is the recall rate. The y-coordinate is the accuracy, and the value is the area under the curve, the higher the AUPRC value, the better. When the distribution of positive and negative samples is not average, especially in the dataset where the number of negative samples is far larger than that of positive samples, AUPRC can more effectively measure the method's quality. In our experiments, the negative samples are 11 times as much as the positive samples. Our method's characteristics could return in computing entities combine reaction with all types of ratings, so there are many more negative samples than positive samples. Especially in practice, the number of negative samples is much larger than the number of positive samples. So our method has an advantage. AP@50 is the hit rate of the positive sample in the top 50 predictions.

Table 2. The experimental results

	AUROC	AUPRC	AP@50
Baseline (drug,gene)	0.86	0.30	0.11
Our method (drug,gene)	0.96	0.71	0.90
Our method (drug,gene,enzyme)	**0.97**	**0.71**	**0.91**
Our method (drug)	0.89	0.70	0.87

Result. The results of our method and baseline under the same subgraph and the results of our method under different subgraphs are shown in Table 2. We verify the improvement of drug-gene, gene-gene, and drug-enzyme in predicting DDIs, respectively. Using our method to predict DDIs and add gene data makes AUROC a more significant promotion. Adding enzyme data to the prediction accuracy has some improvement, but not as good as the promotion effect in gene data. When three entities add to the dataset, we can get the best prediction result. On the whole, the effect of our method under the same dataset is better than the baseline.

Table 3. AUROC ranked top 10 side effects

Side effect	AUROC
Abuse	0.984
Acne rosacea	0.978
Fascitis plantar	0.976
Cholecystitis chronic	0.975
Joint effusion	0.974
Eye infection	0.974
Otitis media	0.971
Chest wall pain	0.971
Acute sinusitis	0.971
Hesitancy	0.971

Table 3 shows the top 10 DDIs prediction results by AUROC among the 30 drugs. Among all the AUROC values of DDIs, the accuracy of abuse is the highest 0.984, and the accuracy of Scotoma is the lowest 0.948.

4.3 Analysis

In this part, we analyze from the following three aspects: construction of comprehensive knowledge graph, experimental design, analysis of experimental results. We analyze the influence of the three parts of the existing design on the experimental results and the existing problems.

Comprehensive Knowledge Graph Construction. In constructing our comprehensive knowledge graph, knowledge fusion, and word sense disambiguation are the biggest problems we encounter. There are many existing databases related to drugs. However, different databases focus on different points, such as some databases focus on the records of gene relationships, and some databases focus on the records of drug pathways. Drugbank focuses on recording relevant information about individual drugs themselves, including the main components of drugs, indications of drugs, enzymes, and more other information expect drug pairs interactions. Therefore, we chose to connect with the drug and gene interaction data from Decagon. However, drugs have multiple names. We may lose a part of the enzyme data when matching the two databases by drug names, resulting in a relatively small amount of enzyme data.

Experimental Design. In this section, we analyze the factors that may affect the experimental results in two types of experiments we conducted. In the first experiment, our experiments compared the effects of different entity data on the DDIs prediction. We conclude that adding gene-related data to predict DDIs has a significant effect. In contrast, adding enzymes have little effect on improving accuracy. However, part of the reason may be that there are more gene-related data than enzyme data. Different amounts of data may be the reason that the gene-gene data caused the facilitation. Two factors contribute to the data imbalance problem. First, the reason for less enzyme-related data is the drug name matching process loses that part of the drug enzyme's data. Second, the amount of enzymes data in Drugbank is smaller than the amount of existing gene data. In the second experiment, we compared the predictive accuracy of our method for different side effect type. The experimental results obtained in the dataset include genes and drugs. Thus, the differences in the accuracy of predicting different side effects may be as follows: the amount of data related to different side effects is different, and the sensitivity of our method to different molecular types of drugs is different.

Experimental Results. According to the hypothesis of ConvE, our method is more suited to capture the specificity between the relationship of drug pairs. In our dataset, each kind of relations involving at least thousands of data means a relationship associated with a variety of drugs. Different drug nodes have differences, but the drug pairs with large differences may have the same side effects. Our method can capture the constraint condition. Besides, our method is more suitable for the situation where there are more negative samples than positive samples. Therefore, it has a significant improvement in our results.

5 Discussion

In this section, we discuss factors that may affect the effectiveness of our experiments. Firstly, due to the limited experimental conditions, when we input a large amount of data, the experimental time is too long to obtain the corresponding experimental results. Therefore, we can only select a part of the data for the experiment under limited conditions. We finally select about 120,000 experimental data. Thus, the accuracy of experimental results is limited, representing some drugs and some DDIs types contained in the dataset. Secondly, since the protein entity's numbers are larger than the drug entity's numbers, the prediction results of protein data greatly influence the overall prediction results.

Finally, we maintain the super parameters the same with baseline and do not conduct specific parameter adjustment experiments. The experimental results may also be affected after the parameter adjustment experiment.

In the following work, under the existing experimental conditions, we can seek a method with lower time complexity to solve the long experimental time problem while ensuring the number of data. At the same time, we can also extract more drug entities and DDIs data from reports and literature through natural language processing to expand the number of drug entities. Finally, we can supplement the reference experiment in future work to seek the optimal solution as much as possible.

6   Conclusion and Future Work

This paper studies the prediction of DDIs. We regard the problem of multi-drug DDIs prediction as a multi-relation link prediction problem. We propose our method to implement the prediction of DDIs types and DDIs probability of drug pairs. Studying the factors affecting side effects in-depth and chose to add enzymes that significantly impact DDIs. We use triple type data to construct a comprehensive knowledge graph containing drugs, genes, and enzymes. Triple data solves the problem that the traditional graph structure does not easily add information, and we improve prediction accuracy. Our method can predict the interaction of three entities in the dataset: drug, gene, and enzyme, and significantly superior to the baseline. We also evaluated the impact of other types of entities on the prediction of DDIs, among which gene has a greater impact.

In the future, we can make efforts in the following three aspects: Firstly, constructing a richer comprehensive knowledge graph, such as considering drug molecular structure issues and adding data types other than plain text. Secondly, we can solve the problem of data fusion as much as possible, add more valid data to the dataset, and reduce unnecessary data loss. Thus, we can make an effort to construct a more balanced, comprehensive knowledge graph. Finally, we can explore more suitable methods for predicting DDIs, further optimize our method, and improve the accuracy of DDIs.

Acknowledgements. This work is partially supported National Natural Science of Foundation of China (No.61902010), Beijing Excellent Talent Funding-Youth Project (No.201800002-0124G039), and Engineering Research Center of Intelligent Perception and Autonomous Control, Ministry of Education.

References

1. Abdelaziz, I., Fokoue, A., Hassanzadeh, O., Zhang, P., Sadoghi, M.: Large-scale structural and textual similarity-based mining of knowledge graph to predict drug-drug interactions. J. Web Semantics **44**, 104–117 (2017)
2. Bansal, M., et al.: A community computational challenge to predict the activity of pairs of compounds. Nat. Biotechnol. **32**(12), 1213–1222 (2014)

3. Bean, D.M., et al.: Knowledge graph prediction of unknown adverse drug reactions and validation in electronic health records. Sci. Rep. **7**(1), 1–11 (2017)
4. Bresso, E., et al.: Integrative relational machine-learning for understanding drug side-effect profiles. BMC Bioinform. **14**(1), 207 (2013)
5. Burkhardt, H.A., Subramanian, D., Mower, J., Cohen, T.: Predicting adverse drug-drug interactions with neural embedding of semantic predications, bioRxiv p. 752022 (2019)
6. Chatr-Aryamontri, A., et al.: The biogrid interaction database: 2015 update. Nucleic Acids Res. **43**(D1), D470–D478 (2015)
7. Cheng, F., Zhao, Z.: Machine learning-based prediction of drug-drug interactions by integrating drug phenotypic, therapeutic, chemical, and genomic properties. J. Am. Med. Inform. Assoc. **21**(e2), e278–e286 (2014)
8. Defferrard, M., Bresson, X., Vandergheynst, P.: Convolutional neural networks on graphs with fast localized spectral filtering. In: Advances in Neural Information Processing Systems, pp. 3844–3852 (2016)
9. Dettmers, T., Minervini, P., Stenetorp, P., Riedel, S.: Convolutional 2D knowledge graph embeddings. In: Thirty-Second AAAI Conference on Artificial Intelligence (2018)
10. Gilmer, J., Schoenholz, S.S., Riley, P.F., Vinyals, O., Dahl, G.E.: Neural message passing for quantum chemistry. arXiv preprint arXiv:1704.01212 (2017)
11. Hamilton, W., Ying, Z., Leskovec, J.: Inductive representation learning on large graphs. In: Advances in Neural Information Processing Systems, pp. 1024–1034 (2017)
12. Hu, B., Wang, H., Wang, L., Yuan, W.: Adverse drug reaction predictions using stacking deep heterogeneous information network embedding approach. Molecules **23**(12), 3193 (2018)
13. Kipf, T.N., Welling, M.: Semi-supervised classification with graph convolutional networks. arXiv preprint arXiv:1609.02907 (2016)
14. Kuhn, M., Letunic, I., Jensen, L.J., Bork, P.: The sider database of drugs and side effects. Nucleic Acids Res. **44**(D1), D1075–D1079 (2016)
15. Liu, M., et al.: Large-scale prediction of adverse drug reactions using chemical, biological, and phenotypic properties of drugs. J. Am. Med. Inform. Assoc. **19**(e1), e28–e35 (2012)
16. Menche, J., et al.: Uncovering disease-disease relationships through the incomplete interactome. Science **347**(6224) e156–e199 (2015)
17. Mohamed, S.K., Nounu, A., Nováček, V.: Biological applications of knowledge graph embedding models. Briefings in Bioinformatics (2020)
18. Rolland, T., et al.: A proteome-scale map of the human interactome network. Cell **159**(5), 1212–1226 (2014)
19. Schlichtkrull, M., Kipf, T.N., Bloem, P., van den Berg, R., Titov, I., Welling, M.: Modeling relational data with graph convolutional networks. In: Gangemi, A., et al. (eds.) ESWC 2018. LNCS, vol. 10843, pp. 593–607. Springer, Cham (2018). https://doi.org/10.1007/978-3-319-93417-4_38
20. Szklarczyk, D., et al.: The string database in 2017: quality-controlled protein-protein association networks, made broadly accessible. Nucleic Acids Res., p. gkw937 (2016)
21. Szklarczyk, D., Santos, A., von Mering, C., Jensen, L.J., Bork, P., Kuhn, M.: Stitch 5: augmenting protein-chemical interaction networks with tissue and affinity data. Nucleic Acids Res. **44**(D1), D380–D384 (2016)

22. Tatonetti, N.P., Patrick, P.Y., Daneshjou, R., Altman, R.B.: Data-driven prediction of drug effects and interactions. Sci. Trans. Med. **4**(125), 125ra31–125ra31 (2012)
23. Timilsina, M., Tandan, M., d'Aquin, M., Yang, H.: Discovering links between side effects and drugs using a diffusion based method. Sci. Rep. **9**(1), 1–10 (2019)
24. Wishart, D.S., et al.: Drugbank 5.0: a major update to the drugbank database for 2018. Nucleic Acids Res. **46**(D1), D1074–D1082 (2018)
25. Xin, C., Xien, L., Ji, W.: Research progress on drug representation learning. J. Tsinghua Univ. (Science and Technology) **60**(2), 171–180 (2020)
26. Xu, H., Sang, S., Lu, H.: Tri-graph information propagation for polypharmacy side effect prediction. arXiv preprint arXiv:2001.10516 (2020)
27. Yang, B., Yih, W.t., He, X., Gao, J., Deng, L.: Embedding entities and relations for learning and inference in knowledge bases. arXiv preprint arXiv:1412.6575 (2014)
28. Zhang, W., Chen, Y., Liu, F., Luo, F., Tian, G., Li, X.: Predicting potential drug-drug interactions by integrating chemical, biological, phenotypic and network data. BMC Bioinform. **18**(1), 18 (2017)
29. Zhang, W., Liu, F., Luo, L., Zhang, J.: Predicting drug side effects by multi-label learning and ensemble learning. BMC Bioinform. **16**(1), 365 (2015)
30. Zitnik, M., Agrawal, M., Leskovec, J.: Modeling polypharmacy side effects with graph convolutional networks. Bioinformatics **34**(13), i457–i466 (2018)

Prostate Cancer Diagnosis Automation Using Supervised Artificial Intelligence. A Systematic Literature Review

Camilo Espinosa[1], Manuel Garcia[1], Fernando Yepes-Calderon[2,4], J. Gordon McComb[3], and Hector Florez[1(✉)] ⓘ

[1] Universidad Distrital Francisco Jose de Caldas, Bogota, Colombia
elmonachoa@gmail.com, manuel-alejo2000@hotmail.com,
haflorezf@udistrital.edu.co
[2] SBP LLC - RnD Department, 604, Fort Pierce, FL 34950, USA
fernando.yepes@strategicbp.net
[3] Children's Hospital Los Angeles, 1300 N Vermont Ave 1006,
Los Angeles, CA 90027, USA
gmccomb@chla.usc.edu
[4] GYM Group SA - Departamento I+R, Cra 78A No. 6-58, Cali, Colombia
fernando@gym-group.org

Abstract. Prostate cancer (PCa) is the most frequent genre-specific malignancy and the fourth overall behind lung, breast, and colon cancers. PCa is diagnosed non-invasively with serum prostate-specific antigen assay, digital rectal examination, and trans-rectal ultrasound and invasively with multiple rectal biopsies from which a Gleason score is assigned. The biopsy tissue is subject to sampling error and cellular interpretation that in turn can lead to disagreement as to whether treatment is needed, and if so, the method and the extent of therapy. Magnetic resonance (MR) imaging is proving to be progressively useful in evaluating PCa. New sequences are continually being introduced that are proving to be even more accurate in determining the extent and degree of tumor malignancy than other imaging modalities. The MR images, however, are evaluated by radiologists whose interpretation is subjective. This study reviews the currently available artificial intelligence and machine learning techniques that may eliminate the need for multiple rectal biopsies and provide a more uniform classification of these malignancies. Also, the evaluation of treatment outcome can be better assessed with more precise tumor size and classification. This paper investigates and analyzes projects related to prostate cancer's automatic diagnosis using artificial intelligence.

Keywords: Prostate cancer · MR images · Prostate automatic segmentation · Supervised classification · Machine learning · Artificial intelligence

© Springer Nature Switzerland AG 2020
H. Florez and S. Misra (Eds.): ICAI 2020, CCIS 1277, pp. 104–115, 2020.
https://doi.org/10.1007/978-3-030-61702-8_8

1   Introduction

Like breast cancer for women, prostate cancer is one the most common for men, accounting for 1'276.106 new cases in 2018 and killing 358.989 men the same year [18]. Diagnosis usually starts with an elevated serum prostate (PSA) and a digital rectal examination (DRE). If the findings are of concern, the next test is transrectal ultrasound (TRUS). The process continues with the invasive transrectal biopsies performed in multiple regions of the organ to increase sampling. The extracted tissue is analyzed histologically, yielding a Gleason score (G-Score). The biopsy tissue is subject to sampling error and cellular interpretation, leading to disagreements about whether treatment is needed and the scope and method to treat. Contrary to computer tomography (CT), magnetic resonance (MR) proves to be progressively useful in evaluating prostate cancer. New sequences are continuously being introduced and have proved to be more precise in determining the extent and degree of malignancy. Additionally, MR does not use the harmful ionizing radiation present in CT and other imaging methods such as positron emission tomography (PET), digital tomosynthesis (DTS), and single positron emission computed tomography (SPECT). Currently, radiologists evaluate and derive verdicts from MR images, a process that is subject to interpretation once again.

The development of artificial intelligence (AI) has the potential to accurately and non-invasively determine the volume of the tumors, the degree of malignancy, and the response to therapy [21].

This study is a review of current AI and machine learning strategies that are proposed to evaluate MR images of prostate cancer automatically and accurately.

The document's structure is composed as follows: Sect. 2 shows method employed to develop a systematic literature review (SLR) where criteria, data extraction, quality verification, and search process have been devised. In Sect. 3, we present the investigation's results with each study's descriptions and compare accuracy and complexity.

2   Method

This study developed a Systematic Literature Review (SLR) based on the guidelines proposed by Kitchenham [11].

2.1   Research Questions

- RQ1. Which software for prostate cancer diagnosis uses artificial intelligence?
- RQ2. Which artificial intelligence techniques are implemented to classify MR images?
- RQ3. Which measurement methods exist for diagnostic in prostate cancer?

2.2 Search Process

Search Strategy. The search strategy implemented in this SLR was the Population, Intervention, and outcome strategy suggested by Kitchenham [11], which allows us to generate a suitable search chain.

- **Population.** The population in this document is defined by the software for prostate cancer diagnosis, where the keywords are `prostate cancer` AND `software`.
- **Intervention.** The implementation requires study of automatic segmentation and classification. Then, the keywords are: `automatic classification` OR `machine learning` OR `artificial intelligence`.
- **Outcome** The expected result is prostate cancer diagnosis with his measure. Then, the keywords are `diagnosis` AND `measure`.

Selected Journals and Conferences. The selected sources were found in the following digital databases: Scopus, IEEE Xplore, Springer Link, and Science Direct. The time-range in which the sources were searched was from 2015 to 2019, as shown in Table 1.

The search sentences are:

- **Scopus:**
  ```
  TITLE-ABS-KEY (("prostate cancer") AND (("artificial
  intelligence") OR ("machine learning") OR ("automatic
  segmentation"))) AND ("diagnosis")
  ```
- **IEEE:**
  ```
  (("prostate cancer") AND (("artificial intelligence") OR
  ("machine learning") OR ("automatic segmentation"))) AND
  ("diagnosis")
  ```
- **Springer Link:**
  ```
  ALL(("prostate cancer") AND (("artificial intelligence") OR
  ("machine learning") OR ("automatic segmentation"))) AND
  ("diagnosis")
  ```
- **Science Direct:**
  ```
  (("prostate cancer") AND (("artificial intelligence") OR
  ("machine learning") OR ("automatic segmentation"))) AND
  ("diagnosis")
  ```

2.3 Inclusion and Exclusion Criteria

The criteria are defined by directly related information in the case of the inclusion criteria (IC) and complementary information in the case of the exclusion criteria (EC).

Table 1. Pre-selected articles

Database	Found	Duplicates	Pre-selected
Scopus	12	2	6
IEEE Xplore	10	1	7
SpringerLink	7	0	2
ScienceDirect	5	1	3

The IC are the following:

- **IC1** Studies which refers to classifiers or automatic machines for prostate cancer diagnosis.
- **IC2** Studies in which prostate MR images are manipulated with automatic segmentation techniques.
- **IC3** Studies which refers to an automatic measurement for prostate cancer diagnosis.

The EC are the following:

- **EC1** Studies which do not focus on prostate cancer.
- **EC2** Studies in which general MR images are manipulated with automatic segmentation techniques.
- **EC3** Studies which do not use a measurement for prostate cancer diagnosis.

2.4 Data Extraction

The following data was extracted from the pre-selected articles shown in Table 2:

- Type of the article (journal or conference) with its reference.
- Author's data with their affiliations.
- Date of the document.
- Database where the article is located.
- DOI (Digital Object Identifier).
- Abstract of the article with its topic area.
- Keywords of the article.

Table 2. Selected articles

Database	Pre-selected	Selected
Scopus	6	3
IEEE Xplore	7	3
SpringerLink	2	1
ScienceDirect	3	1

2.5   Quality Verification

The studies exposed in Table 2 had to pass through the following verification criteria (VC) for an optimal study with the collected information:

- **VC1** Does the article contain information that can answer the research questions?
- **VC2** Does the article include a good explanation about its content?
- **VC3** Does the study deal about the research?
- **VC4** Was the article published in journals or conferences?
- **VC5** Does the article have a good accuracy in its results?

Finally, the selected journals and conferences articles are show in Table 3.

Table 3. Selected journals and conferences

Name	SJR H index
Proceedings of the National Academy of Science	699
Journal of biomedical optics	123
Computerized Medical Imaging and Graphics	63
BioSMART	2
European Radiology	134
IEEE Transactions on Medical Imaging	195
2015 IEEE International Conference on Image Processing (ICIP)	97
Journal of Magnetic Resonance Imaging	142

3   Results

Prostate-cancer diagnosis based on artificial intelligence (AI) is a logical path of development. The AI's goal is to find cancerous areas on prostate images – often MRI – improving the accuracy of diagnosis. Several authors have pursued automation employing all sorts of image modalities and AI classifiers.

Fehr *et al.*, [7] proposed an automatic Gleason score (G-score) estimation using MR T2 weighted image (T2W) and apparent diffusion coefficient (ADC) maps for the transitional zone (TZ) and peripheral zone (PZ). The images require pre-processing and registration. In Fehr's outline, a support vector machine (SVM) uses texture features extracted from mp-MRI intensity and the gray level co-occurrence matrix (GLCM), consisting of energy, entropy, correlation, homogeneity, and contrast to yield a G-score appraisal. Also, the system has an accuracy of 87%, the sensitivity of 87%, and specificity of 84%.

Nguyen *et al.*, [14] implemented a random forest (RF) algorithm to classify light interference microscopy (SLIM) images from prostate biopsy to produce a G-score number. The RF was trained with a tissue microarray (TMA) composed by H&E biopsies and a feature vector histogram for determining which pixel in the SLIM is a lumen, gland, or stroma with an accuracy of 0.82 measurements by the receiver operating characteristic (ROC) curve with its area under the curve (AUC).

Giannini et al., [8] introduced a method to explore the prostate's PZ exclusively. The strategy uses T2W images with CAD (Computer-Aided Detection) to indicate candidate cancer zones. Additionally, Giannini's method requires image registration in order to standardize them. Prostate segmentation was defined by identifying a rectangular region by each slice of the mp-MRI, then the rectangle was segmented by the Hough transformation. Feature extraction develops the intensity of the ADC maps and T2W images, while pharmacokinetics act as an SVM classifier to discriminate between normal and tumor voxels. Later a false-positive (segmented tissues that are not cancerous) reduction are made to exclude them; the system has an accuracy of 91%.

Peyret et al., [15] proposed an algorithm of Multispectral Linear Binary Pattern (MLBP), this handles Multispectral images, where the image features are obtained, and the texture is analyzed to get intensity. The images are next divided into blocks, with each block having feature vectors. Each block makes a codebook that is classified with SVM. This method reports an accuracy of 93.7%.

Wang et al. [22] developed an AI mechanism that mimics the Prostate Imaging Reporting and Data System (PI-RADS v2). This procedure uses T1-weighted imaging (T1WI), T2WI, diffusion-weighted imaging (DWI), as well as dynamic contrast-enhanced (DCE) imaging. Wang analyzes the images with a radial basis function (RBF) and determines verdicts with an SVM classifier.

A study called Focalnet is described in Cao et al., [2] in which the diagnosis and lesion detection is made using a pre-registered mp-MRI for prostate cancer with a convolutional neural network (CNN) using Gleason the to characterizes the aggressiveness of the tumor. Focalnet also uses a mutual finding loss (MFL), which allows identifying the optimal features in a T2W and ADC images for the CNN training phase. The T2W image is used for assessing intensity variation. Thus, Focalnet has an accuracy of 80.5% and a sensitivity of 79.2%.

In another study, Reda et al., [17] implemented a CAD system for DW-MRI to find the benign and malignant tissue in the prostate. They employed a non-negative matrix factorization (NMF) to segment the prostate with DW-MRI. Also, the ADC values are calculated for feature extraction, as refined by a Gauss-Markov Random Field (GGMRF). The cumulative distribution function (CDF) universalized the benign and the malignant features extracted to train a stacked nonnegativity constraint autoencoder (SNCAE). The CAD system has an accuracy of 100% in a dataset consisting of 53 cases.

Ginsburg et al. proposes another CAD system [9], which arguments mp-MR images with a Gleason score to obtain a diagnosis. The features were extracted using the intensities of the MRI measure of concordance using an intra-class correlation coefficient (ICC) and the ROC curve determining the AUC. Two logistic regression (LR) were used to classify the feature sets, the first to classify

a PZ and the second to detect cancerous regions in the TZ. The CAD had an
accuracy of 73% to 86% utilizing the AUC.

Table 4. Features of the studies

Authors	Type of machine learning	Type of diagnosis score	Type of imaging
Fehr *et al.*	SVM	G-score	T2W
Nguyen *et al.*	RF	G-score	SLIM
Giannini *et al.*	SVM	NA	T2W
Peyret *et al.*	SVM	NA	Multispectral
Wang *et al.*	SVM	PI-RADS v2	mp-MRI
Cao *et al.*	CNN	NA	T2W
Reda *et al.*	SNCAE	NA	DWI
Ginsburg *et al.*	LR	G-Score	mp-MRI

Some authors [7,8,22] use image registration for standardization, given that
the multiparametric MRI has to be aligned correctly for this use. Some others
instead manipulate the images directly, employing the SLIM imaging technique
on prostate biopsy tissue [14]. Moreover, transforming the images from multispectral to grayscale allows a better feature extraction of the image without any
standardization for the pixels [15]. The technique based on segment classification by MRI to extract features from each pixel in the image is common to all
presented procedures. Machine learning (frequently SVM) will train and later
diagnose new images using these features. Then, the system depicts the regions
where tumor cells are found [8,15]. Other approaches implement a Gleason Score
to measure malignancy of the prostate cancer [7,14]. The PI-RADS can also be
employed as a grading measure [22].

Table 4 notes the frequent use of the SVM as a machine learning option to
develop the topics of interest.

The standard workflow for machine learning implementation is PCa is shown
in Fig. 1. [8,23] begins with the training process. First, the classifier needs the
training data that, in this case, are mp-MRI focused on the prostate; the images
then are preprocessed, asserting standardization. The next step consists of using
feature extraction on the preprocessed images to decide each pixel's most suitable
classification method.

When the SVM classifier is trained and a new image is obtained, it has to
do the feature extraction and put it into the classifier ending with an estimated
segmentation that separates the organ from the surrounding tissue.

Another way to do this process is with a CNN like the case of Cao *et al* [2],
which works modifying the data obtained, as seen in Fig. 2, taking the original
MR image and its corresponding segmented image in the first instance. The

next step is a convolution that consists of a mathematical operator between a determined filter matrix (in this case is a 3×3 matrix) and the image, getting a new matrix for the feature extraction. Then a max-pooling consisting of a sample window with a specific value (in this case 2×2) runs through the entire image where the value of the higher pixel in the selecting window is recovered and put it into a new matrix of reduced dimensions. The convolution and max-pooling can be repeated many times as need, with the last step being the output layer to give the prostate's estimated segmentation.

4   Discussion

Cancer is the second cause of death globally, only surpassed by cardiovascular diseases. The World Health Organization (WHO) reported 9.6 million casualties worldwide among all cancer types being prostate, the fourth most insidious disease type, accounting for 1.275.106 cases [1]. Prostate cancer (PCa) is the most deadly genre-specific affliction of this type, considering that lung (2.09 million cases), breast (2.09 million cases), and colorectal (1.80 million cases) ranking

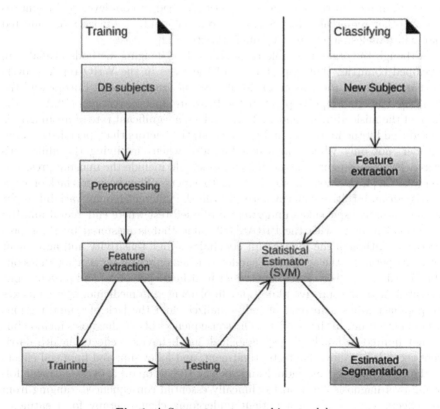

Fig. 1. A Support vector machine model

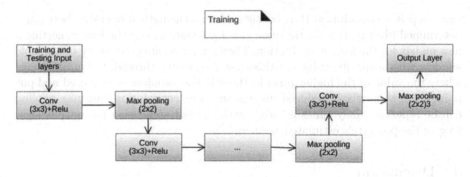

Fig. 2. A convolutional neural network model

in the top three deadly cancers, affect both males and females. Recall that all reported numbers are global for 2018.

Another significant factor in prostate cancer is its independence of socio-economic inputs. A retrospective study showed that men older than 65 established in developed countries have 3.75 times more probability of suffering the disease than men in the same age-range established in non-developed countries [16]. Another remarkable fact is that Afro-descendants are twice more affected than white males, according to global statistics [22].

Although the organ is visible through in-place imaging methods available in developed countries that apport most of the cases in the WHO reports, over-diagnosis has been the reason for 20–40% of the listed cases in Europe and the US [3,5]. The cited reports point at the Prostate Specific Antigen (PSA) as the cause of the misleading diagnosis. Nevertheless, a significant rate of misdiagnosis is produced by the myriad of highly interpretative factors that specialists should consider, not only while diagnosing but also when classifying the affliction's degree. Exacerbating misdiagnosing causes should include the unusual presentations of PCa [4] that complicate the tasks to experts. The observer's lack of accuracy is not an intuitive concept derived from the inherent human variability; for the specifics, five specialists underwent a blinded test where endorectal mpMRI was provided along with the PIRASDv2 guide that is mastered by these professionals. Although the manuscript concludes a high sensitivity and agreement between operators, the agreement's index reached only 58% for scoring all lesions [10]. Overdiagnosis is a severe concern for healthcare personnel and patients, but it is intrinsic of the curative philosophy implemented in medicine, where indexes are population-based instead of individualized, and the lack of quantifications favors fluctuations in the verdicts. The consequences of overdiagnosis include but are not limited to labeling's psychological and behavioral effects; health detriment secondary to invasive tests, treatment, and follow-up; and financial effects on the overdiagnosed individual and society [19]. Moreover, overtreatment following overdiagnosis can lead to clinically essential consequences, ranging from side effects, e.g., sepsis in a patient undergoing chemotherapy for treatment, higher rates of myocardial infarction, and suicide have been reported in men with prostate cancer in the year after diagnosis [6,20].

Artificial intelligence (AI) applied to medical imaging has presented a robust alternative to generating clinical verdicts. Machines yield reproducible results, and the capacity to infer rules when we feed them successful experiences as supervisory elements in the learning process makes them capable of overcoming the performance of any automation envisaged before. Authors with expertise in multidisciplinary domains have acknowledged the impact and potential of AI [12,13].

In medical imaging, the AI is mostly used to classify, and thus exert separation of structures in the images, often called segmentation. However, it is ubiquitous to see applications where the automation consists of delivering a verdict. The two approaches mentioned here can appear in the same application, an AI-based segmentation followed by a verdict that uses a supervisory factor, the retrospective diagnosis.

In the case of PCa, the authors have devoted their time to locate lesions using the classifying methods shown in Table 4. The listed classifying methods intend to mimic the PIRADS directives to deliver a grade that could be a Gleason score or any other metric. One can generalize a pipeline where the methods cited in this review can fit to partial or in full extense.

Automatic cancer detection and grading through the image are desired to avoid risky and uncomfortable examination. As mentioned before in this document, artificial intelligence seems to be the right tool to accomplish this complex task. The performed LSR allowed us to know the techniques and current state of art-technology applied to the problem of segmenting the prostate. The authors have used two approaches. The first approximation consists of using a classifier – very often an SVM – fed with features extracted from the image. Then, The classifier is trained to create a separating hyper-plane represented in a statistical estimator. The found hyper-plane exerts separation between the prostate and surrounding tissue. The second approach uses neuronal networks. Here the images are fed to the system, and different features are automatically extracted in a multi-layer implementation. In the two most used approaches, masks manually extracted layer by layer from the training images are used as supervisory elements. Reported accuracy ranges from 88–95%; however, and despite the abundance of implementations intended to segment the prostate automatically, none has reported such instrument being used in the clinics.

To reach a level of implementation, developers should go farther than detecting the prostate's boundaries. An algorithm that detects changes either in the form of the masks or in the organ tissue directly should be in place to yield the numbers needed in further detection and grading pipeline stages. The resulting quantification should be used as features in a new machine learning implementation where the histology results should accomplish the supervision of the learning.

5 Conclusions

Multiple methods are used to determine prostate cancer's presence and its classification as to the degree of malignancy. Unfortunately, various qualitative features are subject to interpretation that in turn can lead to disagreement as to whether treatment is needed, and if so, the scope and method to treat. The use of artificial intelligence with machine learning can provide a more uniform and objective measurement of these tumors using MR imaging characteristics alone, obviating the need for other testing modalities, especially multiple biopsies. Also, the evaluation of treatment outcome can be better assessed with more precise tumor classification. The presented review shows that artificial intelligence is a potent instrument to yield compelling verdicts on prostate cancer diagnosis. Moreover, these machine-produced verdicts are reproducible and render the uncomfortable testing unnecessary.

References

1. Bray, F., Ferlay, J., Soerjomataram, I., Siegel, R.L., Torre, L.A., Jemal, A.: Global cancer statistics 2018: GLOBOCAN estimates of incidence and mortality worldwide for 36 cancers in 185 countries. CA Cancer J. Clin. **68**(6), 394–424 (2018)
2. Cao, R., et al.: Joint prostate cancer detection and gleason score prediction in mp-MRI via focalnet. IEEE Trans. Med. Imaging **38**(11), 2496–2506 (2019)
3. Draisma, G., et al.: Lead time and overdiagnosis in prostate-specific antigen screening: importance of methods and context. J. Natl. Cancer Inst. **101**(6), 374–383 (2009). https://doi.org/10.1093/jnci/djp001
4. Elabbady, A., Kotb, A.F.: Unusual presentations of prostate cancer: a review and case reports. Arab J. Urol. **11**(1), 48–53 (2013). https://doi.org/10.1016/j.aju.2012.10.002
5. Etzioni, R.: Overdiagnosis due to prostate-specific antigen screening: lessons from U.S. prostate cancer incidence trends. CancerSpectrum Knowl. Environ. **94**(13), 981–990 (2002). https://doi.org/10.1093/jnci/94.13.981
6. Fang, F., et al.: Immediate risk of suicide and cardiovascular death after a prostate cancer diagnosis: cohort study in the United States. J. Natl Cancer Inst. **102**(5), 307–314 (2010). https://doi.org/10.1093/jnci/djp537
7. Fehr, D.: Automatic classification of prostate cancer gleason scores from multiparametric magnetic resonance images. Proc. Natl. Acad. Sci. **112**(46), E6265–E6273 (2015)
8. Giannini, V.: A fully automatic computer aided diagnosis system for peripheral zone prostate cancer detection using multi-parametric magnetic resonance imaging. Comput. Med. Imaging Graph. **46**, 219–226 (2015)
9. Ginsburg, S.B.: Radiomic features for prostate cancer detection on MRI differ between the transition and peripheral zones: preliminary findings from a multi-institutional study. J. Magn. Reson. Imaging **46**(1), 184–193 (2017)
10. Greer, M.D., et al.: Accuracy and agreement of PIRADSv2 for prostate cancer mpmri: a multireader study. J. Magn. Reson. Imaging **45**(2), 579–585 (2017)
11. Kitchenham, B.: Procedures for undertaking systematic reviews: Joint technical report. http://www.inf.ufsc.br/aldo.vw/kitchenham.pdf (2004)

12. Lecun, Y., Bengio, Y., Hinton, G.: Deep learning. Nature **521**(7553), 436–444 (2015). https://doi.org/10.1038/nature14539

13. Miller, D.D., Brown, E.W.: Artificial intelligence in medical practice: the question to the answer? Am. J. Med. **131**(2), 129–133 (2018). https://doi.org/10.1016/j.amjmed.2017.10.035

14. Nguyen, T.H., et al.: Automatic gleason grading of prostate cancer using quantitative phase imaging and machine learning. J. Biomed. Opt. **22**(3), 036015 (2017)

15. Peyret, R., Khelifi, F., Bouridane, A., Al-Maadeed, S.: Automatic diagnosis of prostate cancer using multispectral based linear binary pattern bagged codebooks. In: 2017 2nd International Conference on Bio-engineering for Smart Technologies (BioSMART), pp. 1–4. IEEE (2017)

16. Quinn, M., Babb, P.: Patterns and trends in prostate cancer incidence, survival, prevalence and mortality. Part I: international comparisons. BJU Int. **90**(2), 162–173 (2002). https://doi.org/10.1046/j.1464-410X.2002.2822.x

17. Reda, I., et al.: Computer-aided diagnostic tool for early detection of prostate cancer. In: 2016 IEEE International Conference on Image Processing (ICIP), pp. 2668–2672. IEEE (2016)

18. Siegel, R.L., Miller, K.D.: (2018) cancer statistics. CA Cancer J. Clin. **68**(1), 7–30 (2018)

19. Singh, H., et al.: Overdiagnosis: causes and consequences in primary health care. Can. Fam. Physician **64**(9), 654–659 (2018)

20. Villers, A., Grosclaude, P.: Épidémiologie du cancer de la prostate. Article de revue. Medecine Nucleaire **32**(1), 2–4 (2008). https://doi.org/10.1016/j.mednuc.2007.11.003

21. Vegega, C., Pytel, P., Pollo-Cattaneo, M.F.: Evaluation of the bias in the management of patient's appointments in a pediatric office. ParadigmPlus **1**(1), 1–21 (2020)

22. Wang, J., Wu, C.J., Bao, M.L., Zhang, J., Wang, X.N., Zhang, Y.D.: Machine learning-based analysis of MR radiomics can help to improve the diagnostic performance of PI-RADS v2 in clinically relevant prostate cancer. Eur. Radiol. **27**(10), 4082–4090 (2017). https://doi.org/10.1007/s00330-017-4800-5

23. Yepes-Calderon, F., Nelson, M.D., McComb, J.G.: Automatically measuring brain ventricular volume within PACS using artificial intelligence. PLOS ONE **13**(3), 1–14 (2018). https://doi.org/10.1371/journal.pone.0193152

The Bio-I Capsule. Preventing Contagion of Aerial Pathogens with Real-Time Reporting in Evalu@

Fernando Yepes-Calderon[2,4]([✉]), Andres Felipe Giraldo Quiceno[1],
Jose Fabian Carmona Orozco[1], and J. Gordon McComb[3]

[1] Quality Live Concept LLC,
2741 Pleasant Cypress Circle, Kissimmee, FL 34741, USA
feli@qlconcept.com
[2] SBP LLC - RnD Department,
604 Fort Pierce, FL 34950, USA
fernando.yepes@strategicbp.net
[3] Children's Hospital Los Angeles,
1300 N Vermont Avenue 1006, Los Angeles, CA 90027, USA
gmccomb@chla.usc.edu
[4] GYM Group SA - Departamento I+R,
Cra 78A No. 6-58, Cali, Colombia
fernando@gym-group.org

Abstract. During the current pandemic produced by Cov2, physicians and biologists have received attention. They have done a great job. However, these professionals help the already sick people who are, by now, less than 1% of the population. This tendency is an old conceptual mistake of medicine: we put more effort into curing than preventing. This sort of tradition-biasing directive explains why we are spending tons of resources curing people, while most of the global population remains unprotected.

We need to set up our efforts to protect healthy people. They add to 99% of the current population. They are also the workforce that we need to re-activate the economies. We cannot hide forever, neither send our people to face an invisible enemy.

As a response to the question: how can we prevent contagion efficiently? We have created the bio-I capsule to bring back the crowd's confidence so they can develop their lives and re-activate the economy.

We are facing a retrovirus. The last pathogen of this kind was HIV announced in 1986. HIV is still there because creating a vaccine to fight is not straightforward. While attacking the retrovirus, we also compromise fundamental cell functions. For our sake, we shall assume that Cov2 will remain there longer than expected.

Recall also that pathogens are potent when they are inside the hosts' bodies. Nevertheless, if we keep them outside, they will get denaturalized easily. An effective strategy to avoid contamination will also kill the current menace and any other pathogen coming in the future.

© Springer Nature Switzerland AG 2020
H. Florez and S. Misra (Eds.): ICAI 2020, CCIS 1277, pp. 116–128, 2020.
https://doi.org/10.1007/978-3-030-61702-8_9

The Bio-I capsule is an effective barrier against nanoscopic pathogens, and this manuscript presents details of its specifications and constructions along with the scientific reasons for its creation.

Keywords: Coronavirus 2 outbreak · Airborne pathogens · Droplets contagion · Fomites contagion · Artificial intelligence · Evalu@ data centralizer

1   Introduction

A retrovirus outbreak occurred in Wuhan (China) in December 2019 and spread to the country in two days [7]. The outbreak was declared a Public Health Emergency of International Concern on 30 January 2020. On 11 February 2020, the health world organization (WHO) announced a name for the new coronavirus (Cov2) disease: COVID-19 [10]. On the 27th June 2020, the WHO reported 10'080.115 million infected humans and 501.262 deaths worldwide.

The Cov2 is a member of the coronavirus family as a group of pleomorphic bodies with diameters between 80 and 160 nm (10^{-9} m scale) [6]. Scientific reports state that Cov2 is more contagious than Cov1; this is due to a 10 to 20 times more powerful linking between the S-protein and the ACE-2 enzyme [7]. The S-protein is present in the virus's spikes, and the ACE-2 enzyme is the receptor present in respiratory cells [8]. The pathogen arrives at the back of the throat and moves to the lungs producing alveolar inflammation [9]. Once inside the hosting cell, the retrovirus uses the cell machinery that expresses proteins to create new versions of the virus and accelerate the invasion.

According to WHO, The Cov2 spreads efficiently from human to human in a ratio of 1:3. Scientists have estimated that droplets produce by cough and sneezing are responsible for the dissemination [3]. However, retrospective research performed around the recent H1N1 outbreak (2009) suggested that aerosols and fomites can also be a medium for contamination [1]. Before the Cov2 outbreak, researchers found airborne adenovirus pathogens in a test performed at the Durham international airport. The viral aerosols were positive in 17% of the explored places [1].

There is compelling evidence of aerosols present and being contagious in confined places with recirculating air. Airplanes represent a controlled environment where most of the research has been developed [11,13]. There is also evidence that a person sitting down two chairs away from a confirmed positive H1N1 in an airplane, resulted positive after 9.5 h in the cabin [13] withdrawing the one-chair-free strategy suggested by WHO. In [1], the authors corroborated that traveling subjects were screened with a questionnaire and temperature readings in the vector, and these controls were ineffective.

H1N1, adenovirus, and H5N1 have diameters in the 80 to 120 nm range, the same diameters found of the Cov2; therefore, transmission mechanisms are common to all these pathogens and experience gained during precedent outbreaks is useful while affronting the current pandemic. During the H5N1 outbreak, the

Canadian pandemic plan and the US department of health proposed using N95 filters instead of masks. The argument was that aerosols could be contagious.

Aerosols settling is not linear. The following statements refer to the particles' diameter and settling time after releasing them from a 3 m distance above the floor presented by [11]:

- 100 um takes 10 s.
- 20 um takes 4 min.
- 20 um takes 4 min.
- Particles smaller than 3 um never settle.

Since Cov2 particles are 1000 times smaller than 3 um, they can be airborne. The Cov2 can travel from human-to-human longer distances than 2 m in aerosols and fomites and not only directly through droplets. Considering the Cov2 pathogen's size, the particle capacity to infect in aerosol or fomite form, and the fact that scientists have reported contagion occurrences through the eyes, masks end by being ineffective.

Currently, there are no mechanisms to control Cov2 spreading produced by positive asymptomatic patients. If contagion keeps growing, finding nanoscopic pathogens will naturally rise in places frequented by humans. Aerosols and fomites are spreading mechanisms that we can not control. However, in the understood that nanoscopy pathogens could be anywhere, blocking their access is the most effective strategy to avoid contagion.

This document presents a strategy to prevent contagion by airborne particles. The approach consists in blocking the access to the human respiratory system while providing a comfortable option to remain in close contact.

2   Materials and Methods

The presented solution is a hardware-firmware-software device intended for personal protection. It consists of a capsule covering the head that blocks droplets, airborne particles, and isolates vulnerable entry points to indirect contagion by fomites. The capsule covers the whole head, including eyes, and presents a motorized system to keep a filtered oxygen supply.

The system is built with light materials and designed to adjust and support the maximum head circumference anatomically. Ergonomics has been included in the design to allow a human using it for more than 16 h.

2.1   The Visor

The anterior capsule element is a thermoformed visor built in a bio-compatible material that is also translucent. Polyethylene terephthalate (PET) with a 3 mm thickness has been successfully used for the purpose, but other materials, including anti-scratch ones, have also been tested. The visor is designed to keep the human visual field intact; therefore, lateral eye scanning is as natural as when no device is used. A variant of the visor includes a double layer construction that retards condensation on humid environments. The visor permits to see face gesticulation, so human interaction is not perturbed by wearing the device. The visor does not distort light, so reading and other activities that require visual attention are not perturbed or precluded by using the invention.

2.2 Engines and Oxygen Supply

The oxygen pushed inside the capsule is filtered using replaceable N95 filters. A lightweight engine located in the anterior-lower part of the capsule propels a fan that pushes air through the filter to the device's interior. The propelling system creates a positive pressure environment inside the capsule, and thus, particles can not travel inside the capsule. Instead, particles are repelled. A variant of the innovation uses two engines. One engine is located in the visor's anterior-lower part and one more on top of the visor. When both devices are turned on, the flux of air is increased, so it is possible to use it in low-pressure places where oxygen is scarce. The two engines are called the injector and the extractor. The injector pushed air into the capsule while the extractor takes out the used air. Within these blocks, spare spaces is created to add a pathogen killing strategy based on light.

A lithium-ion battery located on top of the capsule provides energy to the engine or engines in the extended versions using anti-corrosive wiring.

2.3 The Fabric

The visor is closed with around the back of the head and the neck with 100% polyester fabric. The fabric is thermally attached to the visor, avoiding spaces or bubbles. A version of the fabric is designed to protect health-care individuals mainly – but useful for any user – comes with a zipper or self-adhesive material (velcro) so the user can escape from the device without touching the exposed parts.

2.4 Sensor, Telecommunications and Internet of Things

The capsule counts with an internet of things (IoT) device based on an ESP32 chip that provides Bluetooth and wifi capabilities. The communications system can send and receive data using IoT dedicated networks such as the one globally provided by sigfox [14]. Sensors, initially temperature, humidity, heart rate, and accelerometer, and proximity are integrated within the capsule. The IoT reports the variables provided by the sensors to the data centralizer Evalu@ [12], available at www.evalualos.com. The IoT can also report other metabolic variables or even global positioning system coordinates. The capsule can share the data read from the sensors with handheld devices such as mobile phones and tablets using the Evalu@ app available on Apple and Android stores.

2.5 Artificial Intelligence Services

Individual and population-based services using artificial intelligence are accessible through Evalu@. The artificial intelligence services include but are not limited to GPS shielding, GPS tracking, early diagnosis of infections by the metabolic response in temperature and heart rate, unstable displacement among several others that might result from crossing the variables read, and feeding them as features a Machine Learning implementation.

3 Results

In Fig. 1, the visor [102] presents on the top, the air extractor [103], the batteries holder 101, and the electronics and sensors cage [104]. The receptacle [104], allocates the ESP32 or any other programmable device and various sensors such as temperature, humidity, proximity, and accelerometer.

In Fig. 2, a version of the capsule with one engine – injector – while extraction is passively performed by right and left valves ([201] and [202], respectively). Also, Fig. 2, the neck whole 203 is visible just behind the air injector unit [204]. Note in [204], the presence hatches [205] that direct the air towards the visor – not shown here – so condensation is detached.

In the one-engine version, electronics and communications remain active in receptacle [104].

Figure 3 shows the visor [102] attached to the polyester fabric [301]. The boundary [302] is thermally sealed. The fabric adjusts gently to the neck [303] of the user. Since [102] is transparent, more details of the extractor [204] are visible. Note the flux-adjusting holes [306] that balance the flux air inside the capsule. The elements labeled [304] are adjusting screws. The chassis [305] is the boundary element that defines the in and outside the capsule.

Figure 4 shows the air injector from the bottom to the top. The device [401] is the retaining screw. The [104] keeps the filter [402] in place and also allows for filter replacement. The chassis [305] is the boundary [403] between fabric and the visor. In Fig. 4 below [403] defines the inside the capsule while above [403]; defines the outside of the capsule.

Element [404] is the engine, and part [204] is the air distributor.

In Fig. 5, the communications system is depicted. The ESP32 or any other programmable device resides in the container [104]. The programmable device provides the capsule with wifi [503] and Bluetooth [502] capabilities in both directions. Additionally, the programmable device can communicate with proprietary data networks such as SigFox [507] using the universal asynchronous protocol (UART) [504]. These proprietary networks permit communication in places where conventional networks are not available.

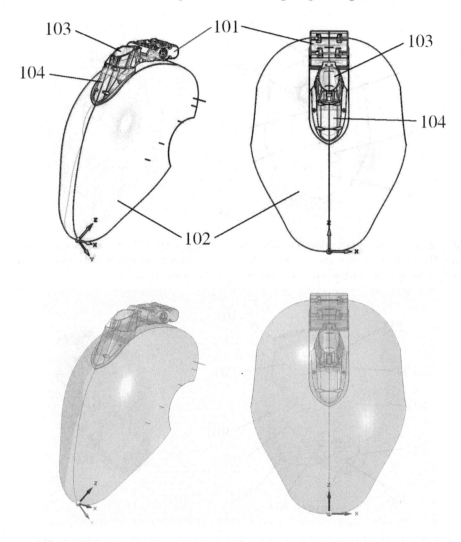

Fig. 1. Visor and superior attached elements. Two views of the visor showing the batteries container, the electronics allocation and the extractor for the two-engines version of the capsule. On-top the drawings of the design, on the bottom, 3D models in stl format

Regardless of the communication system used, all data sharing paths will use a cloud computing structure to move information – see data links [506], [508] and [509] in Fig. 5. Data links [502] and [503] will always be bi-directional to exert control actions on the capsule or in the mobile app. By now, the SigFox works uni-directionally.

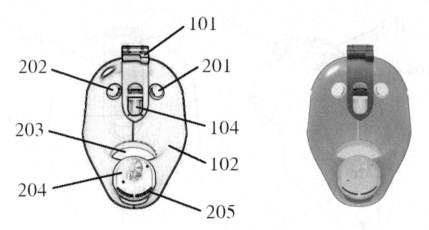

Fig. 2. Top view of the visor. The one-engine version of the visor with escape valves, and the elements inside the capsule. The elements inside the capsule are present for both version – one-engine and two-engines – of the innovation

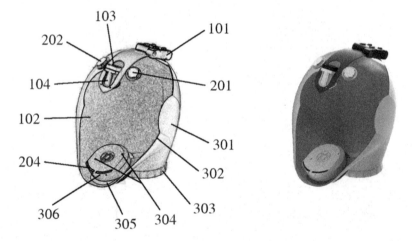

Fig. 3. The Bio-I capsule showing the visor, the fabric, and the air-injector details

The cloud (public or proprietary) is used to feed the Evalu@ server using link [510]. Evalu@ is a data centralizer intended for artificial intelligence implementations available at www.evalualos.com.

The created devices combine hardware-firmware-software to provide the user with comfort, reliability, and effective protection against aerial pathogens like Cov2. The reader can observe the final product in Fig. 6 and its packaging in Fig. 7.

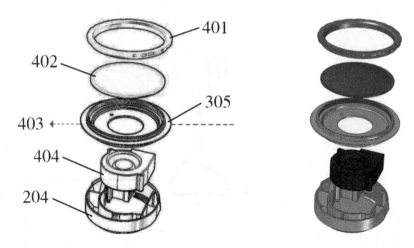

Fig. 4. Construction details of the air injector

4   Discussion

Since the cov2 pandemic outbreak's announcement, humanity intended to approach the problem from a curative perspective. Today, society, in general, know
more about the invasion mechanisms of the retrovirus inside the body than
how the pathogen reaches the throat—the WHO has delivered the information
about transmission by chunks. Initially, the transmission mechanisms were solely
droplets; therefore, masks where recommended. With the mask, human droplets
– average diameter of 8.35 μm – might be critically trapped. However, that is an
average; in fact, human droplets can have diameters of 620 nm, and several of
the masks produced and used during the Cov2 pandemic are, by far, ineffective
protecting the aerial ways due to scale.

Later, when the economy started being a severe issue, and concerns about
finding the pathogen in crowded places arose, the WHO announced the possibility of finding the Cov2 particle in the form of aerosols. Consequently, contagion
risk is exceptionally high in places with recirculating air, such as airplanes, shop-
ping centers, and offices with central cooling systems. In the presence of airborne
nanometric pathogens, the initially suggested masks are rendered useless, and
this is something that most of the population still ignores. The next announcement should be the transmission by fomites, a mechanism mentioned in the
scientific literature next to the droplets and aerosols, but with few or none diffusion in the media. The fomites would put humanity in a scary situation where
pets' accessories, presents, and other inert objects might serve the pathogens to
travel from one host to another.

The most protected individuals in nowadays society are the physicians and
health care providers. They are using uncomfortable protection equipment, some
designed for environments different from hospitals and health care tasks. The
most publicized personal-protection-equipment for health-care providers adhere

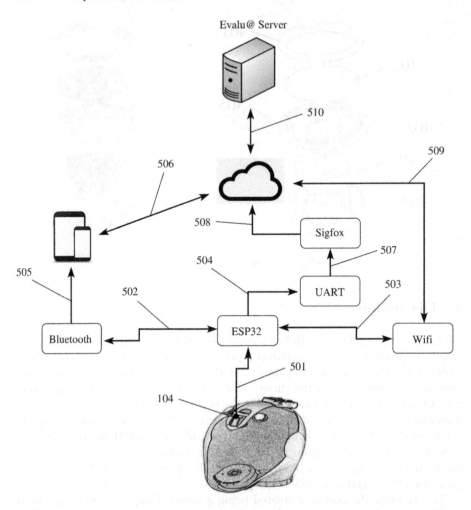

Fig. 5. Connectivity capabilities and artificial intelligence service. The capsule will be of personal use in the current pandemic condition and will protect humans in further airborne menaces. When connected to a data centralizer, artificial intelligence start playing a key role in anticipating the location of asymptomatic prospects and virus contagion paths to creating digital barriers.

to a wide range of specifications and levels of protection [5]. The NIOSH mask complies with the N95 specification but does not cover the eyes. Recall that scientists have presented compelling evidence for the pathogens infecting trough the eyes [2]. Isolating visors and N95 masks are a comfortable combination but still lets the airborne particles reach the airways. The contact masks of series 3M 6000, NS 7600, 3M 6900 lack the positive-pressure specification; therefore gives space for a contagion probability. Besides, these kinds of masks have been

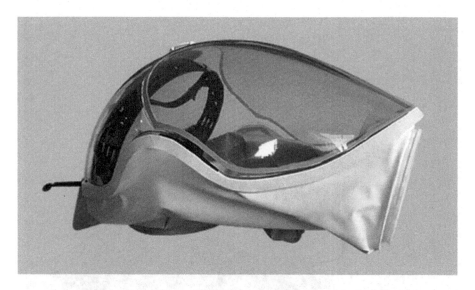

Fig. 6. Standard Bio-I capsule. Final presentation of the Bio-I device.

reported to lacerate the skin in extended periods of work creating entry points for pathogens [4].

Regardless of the protective device of preference, citizens and physicians should know and understand the risks to make informed decisions about the life-threatening particles that currently menace us. As for usability, if the contagion keeps going up, using full-face barrier devices for prolonged periods will not be a matter of preference, will be mandatory.

Regarding the price, the 3M 6800 respirator using negative pressure and without the added connectivity services, is currently offered at 336 USD in Amazon. The most expensive Bio-I version is offered at a 109 USD promotional price in the Kickstarter's campaign but will be sold at 299 once the campaign ends.

Since the Bio-I is a solution to a worldwide life-threatening menace, we do not envisage the device being sold without a strategy involving political and governmental input. In that sense, the cost of the capsule and associated services would need to be covered by the universal health and social programs of the countries.

As for Bio-I, development perspectives are countless and, when connected to the data centralizer Evalu@, a myriad of services become available, including those based on artificial intelligence concerning real-time monitoring the health of the individuals, identification, and location of asymptomatic prospects and creation of digital fences.

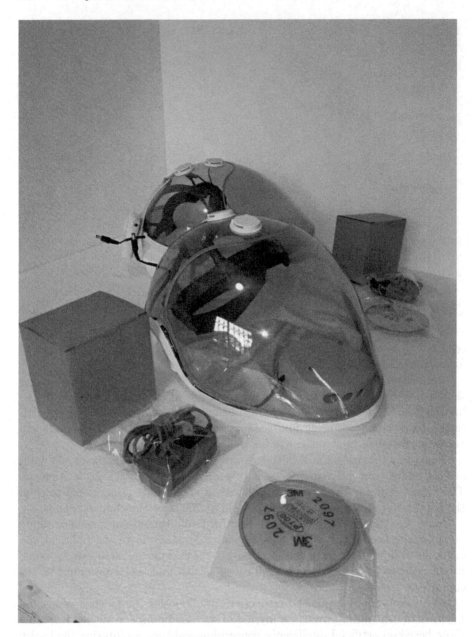

Fig. 7. Bio-I capsule and accessories in the packing. A N95 filter, the lithium-ion battery and a charger are packed with the capsule

5   Conclusions

The Cov2 is one of the myriads of under-micrometric-scaled pathogens that can harm humans. Several of them were reported by scientists even decades ago. Our tendency to cure instead of preventing have us cornered by an announced menace. The same tendency has pushed humankind to use more resources to cure the sick than trying to stop contagion effectively. The same tendency to desperately act with legacy mindsets has us waiting for a vaccine. We have not considered that a robust strategy to stop transmission would leave the current retrovirus or any further aerial pathogen outside human metabolism, where these particles are weak and denaturalize with ease. Such a strategy, driven with care, would put us in the track to finish this and any other similar menace sooner than any other known or proposed approach.

References

1. Bailey, E.S., Choi, J.Y., Zemke, J., Yondon, M., Gray, G.C.: Molecular surveillance of respiratory viruses with bioaerosol sampling in an airport. Trop. Dis. Travel Med. Vaccines **4**(1), 11 (2018). https://doi.org/10.1186/s40794-018-0071-7
2. Coroneo, M.T.: The eye as the discrete but defensible portal of coronavirus infection. Ocular Surf. (2020). https://doi.org/10.1016/j.jtos.2020.05.011
3. Correia, G., Rodrigues, L., Gameiro da Silva, M., Gonçalves, T.: Airborne route and bad use of ventilation systems as non-negligible factors in SARS-CoV-2 transmission. Med. Hypotheses **141**(April), 109781 (2020). https://doi.org/10.1016/j.mehy.2020.109781
4. Gefen, A., Ousey, K.: Update to device-related pressure ulcers: SECURE prevention. COVID-19, face masks and skin damage. J. Wound Care **29**(5), 245–259 (2020)
5. Holland, M.: COVID-19 Personal Protective Equipment (PPE) for the emergency physician. Vis. J. Emerg. Med. **19**(January), 1–6 (2020). https://doi.org/10.1016/j.visj.2020.100740
6. Hospital, H., Bradburne, A.F., Tyrrell, D.A.J.: The propagation of "coronaviruses" in tissue-culture. Archiv für die gesamte Virusforschung **28**, 133–150 (1969). https://doi.org/10.1007/BF01249379
7. Kumar, M., Taki, K., Gahlot, R., Sharma, A., Dhangar, K.: A chronicle of SARS-CoV-2: part-I - epidemiology, diagnosis, prognosis, transmission and treatment. Sci. Total Environ. **734**(336), 139278 (2020). https://doi.org/10.1016/j.scitotenv.2020.139278
8. Li, R., et al.: Substantial undocumented infection facilitates the rapid dissemination of novel coronavirus (SARS-CoV-2). Science **368**(6490), 489–493 (2020). https://doi.org/10.1126/science.abb3221
9. Liu, N., et al.: Prevalence and predictors of PTSS during COVID-19 outbreak in China hardest-hit areas: gender differences matter. Psychiatry Res. **287**(March), 112921 (2020). https://doi.org/10.1016/j.psychres.2020.112921
10. Shereen, M.A., Khan, S., Kazmi, A., Bashir, N., Siddique, R.: COVID-19 infection: origin, transmission, and characteristics of human coronaviruses. J. Adv. Res. **24**, 91–98 (2020). https://doi.org/10.1016/j.jare.2020.03.005

11. Tellier, R.: Review of aerosol transmission of influenza A virus. Emerg. Infect. Dis. **12**(11), 1657–1662 (2006). https://doi.org/10.3201/eid1211.060426
12. Yepes-Calderon, F., Yepes Zuluaga, J.F., Yepes Calderon, G.E.: Evalu@: an agnostic web-based tool for consistent and constant evaluation used as a data gatherer for artificial intelligence implementations. In: Florez, H., Leon, M., Diaz-Nafria, J.M., Belli, S. (eds.) ICAI 2019. CCIS, vol. 1051, pp. 73–84. Springer, Cham (2019). https://doi.org/10.1007/978-3-030-32475-9_6
13. Young, N., et al.: International flight-related transmission of pandemic influenza A(H1N1)pdm09: an historical cohort study of the first identified cases in the United Kingdom. Influenza Other Respir. Viruses **8**(1), 66–73 (2014). https://doi.org/10.1111/irv.12181
14. Zuniga, J.C., Ponsard, B.: Sigfox System Description. IETF 97, p. 9 (2016). https://www.ietf.org/proceedings/97/slides/slides-97-lpwan-25-sigfox-system-description-00.pdf

Business Process Management

A Grammatical Model
for the Specification of Administrative Workflow
Using Scenario as Modelling Unit

Milliam Maxime Zekeng Ndadji[1,2]([⊠]) [iD], Maurice Tchoupé Tchendji[1,2] [iD],
Clémentin Tayou Djamegni[1] [iD], and Didier Parigot[3]

[1] Department of Mathematics and Computer Science,
University of Dschang, PO Box 67, Dschang, Cameroon
{ndadji.maxime,maurice.tchoupe}@univ-dschang.org, dtayou@yahoo.com
[2] FUCHSIA Research Associated Team, Rennes, France
[3] Inria, Sophia Antipolis, France
didier.parigot@inria.fr
https://project.inria.fr/fuchsia/

Abstract. Process modelling is a crucial phase of Business Process Management
(BPM). Despite the many efforts made in producing process modelling tools,
existing tools (languages) are not commonly accepted. They are mainly criticised
for their inability to specify both the tasks making up the processes and their
scheduling (their lifecycle models), the data they manipulate (their information
models) and their organizational models. Process modelling in these languages
often results in a single task graph; such a graph can quickly become difficult to
read and maintain. Moreover, these languages are often too general (they have a
very high expressiveness); this makes their application to specific types of processes complex: especially for administrative processes. In this paper, we present
a new language for administrative processes modelling that allows designers to
specify the lifecycle, information and organizational models of such processes
using a mathematical tool based on a variant of attributed grammars. The approach imposed by the new language requires the designer to subdivide his process
into scenarios, then to model each scenario individually using a simple task graph
(an annotated tree) from which a grammatical model is further derived. At each
moment then, the designer manipulates only a scenario of the studied process:
this approach is more intuitive and modular; it allows to produce task graphs that
are more refined and therefore, more readable and easier to maintain.

Keywords: Administrative process modelling · Workflow language ·
Grammars · Artifact · Accreditation

1 Introduction

Workflow technology aim at automating business processes[1]. To do so, it provides
a clear framework composed of two major entities: (1) a *workflow language* for the

---

[1] A *business process* is a set of tasks that follow a specific pattern and are executed to achieve a
specific goal [1]. When such processes are managed electronically, they are called *workflows*.

© Springer Nature Switzerland AG 2020
H. Florez and S. Misra (Eds.): ICAI 2020, CCIS 1277, pp. 131–145, 2020.
https://doi.org/10.1007/978-3-030-61702-8_10

description of such processes in a (generally graphical) format that can be interpreted by (2) a software system called *Workflow Management System* (WfMS). The role of WfMS is to facilitate collaboration and coordination of various actors involved in the distributed execution of processes' tasks: in this way, workflow reduces the automation of business processes to their modelling in *workflow languages*; process modelling (specification) is therefore a crucial phase of workflow management[2].

Several tools have been developed to address process modelling. Among the most well-known are the BPMN standard (*Business Process Model and Notation*[3]) [13] based on statecharts, and the YAWL language (*Yet Another Workflow Language*) [1] which uses a formalism derived from that of Petri nets. Despite the significant research progress around these tools (often qualified as "*traditional tools*"), they are not commonly accepted. Indeed, they are often criticized for not being based on solid mathematical foundations [8], for having a much too great expressiveness compared to the needs of professionals in the field [22] and/or for not being intuitive [8].

Another important criticism often levelled at traditional workflow languages is the fact that they treat data (process *information model*) and users (part of process *organizational model*) as second-class citizens by highlighting tasks and their routing (process *lifecycle model*). To precisely remedy this, researchers have developed over the last two decades and under the initiative of IBM, the artifact-centric [15] approach to the design and execution of business processes. This one, revisited in several works [2–4,7,9–11], proposes a new approach to workflow management by focusing on both automated processes and data manipulated using the concept of "*business artifact*" or "*artifact*" in short. An artifact is considered as a document that conveys all the information concerning a particular case of execution of a given business process, from its inception in the system to its termination. A major shortcoming of artifact-centric models is that, after designing a given business process, it's difficult to manage it out of the context for which it was designed: specification and execution context (the WfMS on which it must be executed) are strongly coupled. In fact, in artifact-centric approaches the process specification is done with artifact modelling and artifacts are usually tailored to dedicated collaborative systems; process designers are then obliged to take into account certain details related to the workflow execution technique during the modelling phase: it is therefore difficult to consider these approaches exclusively as business process modelling tools since they are context dependant.

Another mentioned shortcoming of existing process modelling approaches is that they concentrate the modelling of a given process into a single task graph. Not only does this not allow designers to explicitly express the entire control flow of certain types of processes, but the resulting specifications are generally not easy to read, to maintain and to evolve. These concerns were first raised by Wil M. P. van der Aalst et al. [19,21]. They provide a solution to this by introducing the concept of *proclet*; they thus propose to deal with several levels of granularity assigned to lightweight workflow

---

[2] The *Workflow Management Coalition* (it is the organization responsible for developing standards in workflow) defines *workflow management* as the modelling and computer management of all the tasks and different actors involved in executing a business process [1].

[3] BPMN was initiated by the *Business Process Management Initiative* (BPMI) which merged with *Object Management Group* (OMG) in 2005.

processes (proclets) in charge of orchestrating their execution. The modelling of each level of granularity is therefore done using a smaller task graph. We find this vision very interesting. However, the notion of granularity manipulated in [19] is not very intuitive and seems, as for artifact-centric models, intimately linked to the execution model of proclets. In the case of an administrative process[4] $\mathcal{P}_{op}$, we think it would be more affordable to partition its task graph according to a characteristic that is natural to it. Knowing that such a process is naturally composed of a set of execution scenarios and can be represented by a finite set $\{S_{op}^1, \ldots, S_{op}^k\}$ of *representative scenarios*[5] (see Sect. 3.2) known in advance, we propose to use the "scenario" as the modelling unit .

All the above-mentioned shortcomings of traditional workflow languages confirm that there is still a need of scientific innovation in the field of business process modelling. This paper presents a new *Language for the Specification of Administrative Workflow Processes* (LSAWfP) based on the concept of attributed grammars (a specification of business processes by the means of attributed grammars is also presented in [5]). LSAWfP is built in a more traditional way and then, unlike the artifact-centric approaches, it allows process modelling independently of a workflow execution technique. Opposed to traditional workflow languages, LSAWfP provides coherent tools to model both processes' lifecycle model, information model and organizational model. Additionally, LSAWfP uses the "scenario" as the modelling unit: a given process modelling consists to the modelling of each of its representative scenario. Designers can thus focus on the modelling and the maintenance of process' parts rather than handling the whole process at a time: this seems to be more intuitive, modular and easier, and can also be further well composed with the level of granularity splitting approach proposed by [19].

LSAWfP is especially tailored for administrative processes modelling: its expressiveness is then built to fit the needs of such processes. Its modelling approach can be described as follow: from the observation that one can analyse the textual description of a given administrative process to exhibit all its possible representative execution scenarios leading to its business goals, LSAWfP proposes to model each of these scenarios by an annotated tree called a *representative artifact* in which, each node corresponds to a task of the process, and each hierarchical decomposition (a node and its sons) represents a scheduling of these tasks. From these representative artifacts, are derived an attributed grammar $\mathbb{G}$ called the *Grammatical Model of Workflow* (GMWf). The symbols of a given GMWf represent the process tasks and each of its productions represents a scheduling of a subset of these tasks; intuitively, a production given by its left and right hand sides, specifies how the task on the left hand side precedes (must be executed before) those on the right hand side. Thus, the GMWf of a process contains both its *information model* (modelled by its attributes) and its *lifecycle model* (thanks to the set of its productions). Once the GMWf is obtained, LSAWfP proposes to add organizational information (*organizational model*) modelled by two lists: L_{P_k} which contains actors involved in the process and $L_{\mathcal{A}_k}$ which contains their *accreditations*. These lists

---

[4] According to the classification framework of [12], administrative processes are those for which all cases are known; tasks are predictable and their sequencing rules are simple and clear.

[5] We refer to a representative scenario as any execution scenario that, in combination with other representative scenarios, can generate a (potentially infinite) set of other scenarios.

aim at modelling actors, their roles and the different perceptions they have on a given process. Thus, with LSAWfP, the model (subsequently called *a Grammatical Model of Administrative Workflow Process* - GMAWfP -) of a given administrative process $\mathcal{P}_{op}$ is an executable grammatical specification given by a triplet $\mathbb{W}_f = \left(\mathbb{G}, \mathcal{L}_{P_k}, \mathcal{L}_{\mathcal{A}_k}\right)$.

The rest of this manuscript is organised as follows: after describing a running example (the peer-review process) in Sect. 2, we present more formally and with illustrations, the proposed language in Sect. 3. A discussion on its expressiveness and on some ongoing works is conducted in Sect. 4. Finally, Sect. 5 is devoted to the conclusion.

2   A Running Example: The Peer-Review Process

As running example, we will use the peer-review process. A brief description of it inspired by those made in [19], can be the following one:

- The process starts when the editor in chief (*EC*) receives a paper for validation;
- Then, the *EC* performs a pre-validation after which he can accept or reject the submission for various reasons (subject of minor interest, submission not within the journal scope, non-compliant format, etc.); let us call this **task "A"**;
- If he rejects the submission, he writes a report (**task "B"**) then notifies the corresponding author (**task "D"**) and the process ends;
- Otherwise, he chooses an associated editor (*AE*) and sends him the paper for the continuation of its validation;
- The *AE* prepares the manuscript (**task "C"**) and contacts simultaneously two experts for the evaluation of the paper (**tasks "E1"** and **"E2"**); if a contacted expert refuses to participate, the *AE* contacts another one (iteration on **task "E1"** or **"E2"**). Otherwise, the expert (referee) can start the evaluation;
- Each referee reads, seriously evaluates the paper (**tasks "G1"** and **"G2"**) and sends back a report (**tasks "H1"** and **"H2"**) and a message (**tasks "I1"** and **"I2"**) to the *AE*;
- After receiving reports from all referees, the *AE* takes a decision and informs the *EC* (**task "F"**) who sends the final decision to the corresponding author (**task "D"**).

From the description above, one can identify all the tasks to be executed, their sequencing, actors involved and the tasks assigned to them. For this case, four actors are involved: an editor in chief (*EC*) which is responsible for initiating the process, an associated editor (*AE*) and two referees (*R*1 and *R*2).

Figure 1 shows the orchestration diagrams corresponding to the graphical description of this peer-review process using the widely used process-centric notations BPMN (*Business Process Model and Notation*) and WF-Net (*Workflow Net*). As usual, tasks are ordered using *sequential flow*, {*And, Or*}-*Splits* and {*And, Or*}-*Joins*. Each diagram resumes the *main scenarios* of the studied process.

3   A Language for the Specification of Administrative Workflow Processes (LSAWfP)

In this section, we present the new language LSAWfP that allows to specify administrative workflow processes independently of a workflow execution technique.

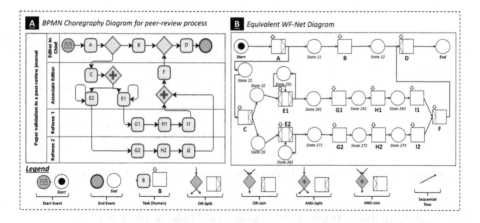

Fig. 1. Orchestration diagrams of the peer-review process.

3.1 Artifacts as Control Flow Graphs

Let's consider an administrative process $\mathcal{P}_{op}$ to be modelled. By definition (of administrative process), its set $\mathbb{T}_n = \{X_1, \ldots, X_n\}$ of tasks is known in advance. In traditional workflow languages like BPMN or WF-Net, the control flow between its tasks is represented using a directed graph that can contain cycles (see Fig. 1). Such a graph allows the modelling of the potentially infinite set[6] of $\mathcal{P}_{op}$'s execution scenarios. Let's note however that each $\mathcal{P}_{op}$'s execution scenario can also be modelled using an annotated tree t_i called *artifact*. Indeed, starting from the fact that a given scenario S_{op}^i consists of a subset $\mathbb{T}_m \subseteq \mathbb{T}_n$ of $m \leq n$ tasks to be executed in a specific order (in parallel or in sequence), one can represent S_{op}^i as a tree t_i in which each node (labeled X_i) potentially corresponds to a task $X_i \in \mathbb{T}_m$ of S_{op}^i and each hierarchical decomposition (a node and its sons) corresponds to a scheduling: the task associated with the parent node must be executed before those associated with the son nodes; the latter must be executed according to an order - parallel or sequential - that can be specified by particular annotations "⨾" (is sequential to) and "∥" (is parallel to) which will be applied to each hierarchical decomposition. The annotation "⨾" (resp. "∥") reflects the fact that the tasks associated with the son nodes of the decomposition must (resp. can) be executed in sequence (resp. in parallel). To model iteration, nodes can be recursive in an artifact: i.e a node labelled X_i may appear in subtrees rooted by a node having the same label X_i.

Considering the running example (the peer-review process), two of its execution scenarios can be modelled using the two artifacts art_1 and art_2 in Fig. 2. In particular, we can see that art_1 shows how the task "Receipt and pre-validation of a submitted paper" assigned to the *EC*, and associated with the symbol A (see Sect. 2), must be executed before tasks associated with the symbols B and D that are to be executed in sequence.

---

[6] This is the case when there is one or more iterative routing (materialized by cycles in the task graph) on tasks.

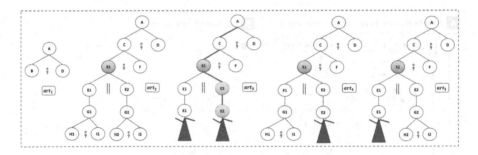

Fig. 2. Representative artifacts of a paper validation process in a peer-review journal.

3.2 Representative Artifacts and Grammatical Model of Workflow

Representative Artifacts. As mentioned earlier (see Sect. 3.1), the set of execution scenarios for a given administrative process can be infinite. This is the case of our running example process in which we can iterate on tasks $E1$ and $E2$ without limit and thus generate an infinite set of execution scenarios. In these cases, the designer cannot list this set of scenarios in order to model each of them. It is then necessary to substitute this one by a finite set $\{S_{op}^1, \ldots, S_{op}^k\}$ of scenarios said to be *representative*. Each representative scenario can then be modelled by a so called *representative artifact*.

For a given process, the set of its representative artifacts is obtained by adding to the finite set of artifacts modelling its nominal scenarios (those leading to its different business goals without iteration), those representing the modelling of its alternative scenarios (these are scenarios in which at least one iteration have been made). Operationally, when designing an alternative scenario artifact, the designer must prune it at each first iteration encountered: i.e the designer must prune each branch of an alternative scenario artifact as soon as he encounters a node labelled for the second time by a same label along a path starting from the root. In fact, one could assume that to design the representative artifacts of a given business process, the designer begins by identifying the initial tasks of it (i.e., the tasks that can start one of its execution scenarios); each of these tasks will thus constitute the root of several representative artifacts. To construct the set $arts_{X_{0_i}}$ of representative artifacts rooted in a given initial task X_{0_i}, the designer will:

(1) Construct an artifact *art* having X_{0_i} as the single node (root);

(2) Then, he will determine the set $follow = \left\{ \left(X_{1_{i_1}}, \ldots, X_{m1_{i_1}} \right), \ldots, \left(X_{1_{i_n}}, \ldots, X_{mn_{i_n}} \right) \right\}$ of task combinations (each combination is either sequential or parallel[7]) that can be immediately executed after the execution of X_{0_i}. For each combination $\left(X_{1_{i_j}}, \ldots, X_{mj_{i_j}} \right)$, the designer will create a new artifact art_j by expanding the node X_{0_i} of *art* such that in art_j, the tasks $X_{1_{i_j}}, \ldots, X_{mj_{i_j}}$ are the child nodes of X_{0_i}.

---

[7] If a given combination $\left(X_{1_{i_j}}, \ldots, X_{mj_{i_j}} \right)$ is sequential (resp. parallel), its tasks are to be (resp. can be) executed sequentially (resp. in parallel).

(3) It will then only remain to recursively develop (using the principle of (2)) each leaf node of the new artifacts until representative artifacts (those that describe an execution scenario in its entirety) are obtained.

This construction principle emphasizes the fact that one does not loose information by pruning an artifact when encountering a given node X for the second time in the same branch. In such a case, it is not necessary to develop X a second time since the designer has enumerated (in several artifacts) all the possibilities (scenarios) of continuing the execution of the process after the execution of the task associated with X. As we will see in Sect. 3.2, these possibilities will be coded in a grammar and thus, the execution scenarios characterized by several iterations on X, will indeed be specified in the language. When constructing a representative artifact, the pruning of a branch is therefore systematic when a node is encountered for the second time; no matter how many nodes generate an iteration in the same branch.

Figure 2 presents the five representative artifacts of our running example process. The artifacts art_1 and art_2 model the two nominal scenarios: art_1 models the scenario in which the EC directly rejects the paper while art_2 models the case where the paper is evaluated by referees ($R1$ and $R2$) without the AE having to contact more than two experts (no iteration on tasks $E1$ and $E2$). The artifacts art_3, art_4 and art_5 represent the infinite set of alternative scenarios in this example. In art_3 in particular, we can see that the designer has pruned at node $E2$ which appeared for the second time in the same branch.

Grammatical Model of Workflow. From the finite set of representative artifacts of a given process, it is possible to extract an abstract grammar[8] that represents the underlying process's lifecycle model: it is this grammar that we designate by the expression *Grammatical Model of Workflow (GMWf)*.

Let's consider the set $\{t_1, \ldots, t_k\}$ of representative artifacts modelling the k representative execution scenarios of a given process $\mathcal{P}_{op}$ of n tasks ($\mathbb{T}_n = \{X_1, \ldots, X_n\}$). Each t_i is a derivation tree for an abstract grammar (a GMWf) $\mathbb{G} = (S, \mathcal{P}, \mathcal{A})$ whose set of symbols is $S = \mathbb{T}_n$ (all process tasks) and each production $p \in \mathcal{P}$ reflects a hierarchical decomposition contained in at least one of the representative artifacts. Each production is therefore exclusively of one of the following two forms: $p : X_0 \rightarrow X_1 \, ° \ldots °\, X_n$ or $p : X_0 \rightarrow X_1 \parallel \ldots \parallel X_n$. The first form $p : X_0 \rightarrow X_1 \, ° \ldots °\, X_n$ (resp. the second form $p : X_0 \rightarrow X_1 \parallel \ldots \parallel X_n$) means that task X_0 must be executed before tasks $\{X_1, \ldots, X_n\}$ and these must be (resp. that can be) executed in sequence (resp. in parallel). A GMWf can therefore be formally defined as follows:

Definition 1. *A Grammatical Model of Workflow (GMWf) is defined by* $\mathbb{G} = (S, \mathcal{P}, \mathcal{A})$ *where :*

– *S is a finite set of **grammatical symbols** or **sorts** corresponding to various **tasks** to be executed in the studied business process;*

---

[8] It is enough to consider the set of representative artifacts as a regular tree language: there is therefore an (abstract) grammar to generate them.

- $\mathcal{A} \subseteq S$ is a finite set of particular symbols called **axioms**, representing tasks that can start an execution scenario (roots of representative artifacts), and
- $\mathcal{P} \subseteq S \times S^*$ is a finite set of **productions** decorated by the annotations "$\mathring{,}$" (is sequential to) and "$\|$" (is parallel to): they are **precedence rules**. A production $P = (X_{P(0)}, X_{P(1)}, \cdots, X_{P(|P|)})$ is either of the form $P : X_0 \to X_1 \mathring{,} \ldots \mathring{,} X_{|P|}$, or of the form $P : X_0 \to X_1 \| \ldots \| X_{|P|}$ and $|P|$ designates the length of P right-hand side. A production with the symbol X as left-hand side is called a X-production.

Let's illustrate the notion of GMWf by considering the one generated from an analysis of the representative artifacts obtained in the case of the peer-review process (see Fig. 2): the derived GMWf is $\mathbb{G} = (S, \mathcal{P}, \mathcal{A})$ in which the set S of grammatical symbols is $S = \{A, B, C, D, S1, E1, E2, F, G1, G2, H1, H2, I1, I2\}$ (see Sect. 2); the only initial task (axiom) is A (then $\mathcal{A} = \{A\}$) and the set $\mathcal{P}$ of productions is:

$$
\begin{array}{llll}
P_1 : A \to B \mathring{,} D & P_2 : A \to C \mathring{,} D & P_3 : C \to S1 \mathring{,} F & P_4 : S1 \to E1 \| E2 \\
P_5 : E1 \to G1 & P_6 : E2 \to G2 & P_7 : E1 \to E1 & P_8 : E2 \to E2 \\
P_9 : G1 \to H1 \mathring{,} I1 & P_{10} : G2 \to H2 \mathring{,} I2 & P_{11} : B \to \varepsilon & P_{12} : D \to \varepsilon \\
P_{13} : F \to \varepsilon & P_{14} : H1 \to \varepsilon & P_{15} : I1 \to \varepsilon & P_{16} : H2 \to \varepsilon \\
P_{17} : I2 \to \varepsilon
\end{array}
$$

There may be special cases where it is not possible to schedule the tasks of a scenario using the two (only) forms of production selected for GMWf. For example, this is the case for the peer-review process wherein task C precedes tasks $E1$, $E2$ and F, tasks $E1$ and $E2$ can be executed in parallel and precede F (see Sect. 2). In such cases, the introduction of a few new symbols known as *(re)structuring symbols* (not associated with tasks) can make it possible to produce a correct scheduling. For the peer-review process example, the introduction of a new symbol $S1$ allows us to obtain the following productions: $P_3 : C \to S1 \mathring{,} F$ and $P_4 : S1 \to E1 \| E2$ which properly model the required scheduling and avoid the usage of the malformed production $p : C \to E1 \| E2 \mathring{,} F$ (see in Fig. 2, art_2, the node $S1$—in gray—). To deal with such cases, the previously given GMWf definition (Definition 1) is slightly adapted by integrating the (re)structuring symbols; the resulting definition is as follows:

Definition 2. *A **Grammatical Model of Workflow** (GMWf) is defined by $\mathbb{G} = (S, \mathcal{P}, \mathcal{A})$ wherein $\mathcal{P}$ and $\mathcal{A}$ refer to the same purpose as in definition 1, $S = \mathcal{T} \cup \mathcal{T}_{Struc}$ is a finite set of **grammatical symbols** or **sorts** in which, those of $\mathcal{T}$ correspond to **tasks** of the studied business process, while those of $\mathcal{T}_{Struc}$ are (re)structuring symbols.*

3.3   Modelling the Information Model of Processes with GMWf

As formalized in Definition 2, a GMWf perfectly models the tasks and control flow of administrative processes (lifecycle model). In this section we discuss the specification of processes-related data (*the information model*) in LSAWfP.

It is not easy to model the structure of business processes data using a general type as they differ from one process to another. For the current work, tackling the automated processes data structure has no proven interest because it does not bring any added value to the proposed model: a representation of these data using a set of variables associated with tasks is largely sufficient. However, it should be noted that in existing data-driven modelling approaches like the Guarded Attribute Grammar (GAG) model [5], these variables typically have two parts to allow designers to model each task's (1) preconditions or input data required for its actual execution, and (2) post-conditions or output data produced during its execution. In addition, dependency relationships between data are often modelled.

In this work, the potential manipulated data by a given process task is represented using an *attribute* embedded in the nodes associated with it. To materialise this adjustment, we update for the last time the definition of GMWf. We thus associate with each symbol, an attribute named *status* allowing to store all the data of the associated task; its precise type is left to the discretion of the process designer. The new definition of GMWf is thus the following one:

Definition 3. *A **Grammatical Model of Workflow** (GMWf) is defined by* $\mathbb{G} = (\mathcal{S}, \mathcal{P}, \mathcal{A})$ *wherein* $\mathcal{S}$, $\mathcal{P}$ *and* $\mathcal{A}$ *refer to the same purpose as in definition 2. Each grammatical symbol* $X \in \mathcal{S}$ *is associated with an attribute named **status**, that can be updated when tasks are executed;* $X.status$ *provides access (read and write) to its content.*

3.4   An Organizational Model for LSAWfP

Because business processes are generally carried out collectively, it is important to model actors an to set up mechanisms to ensure better coordination between them and to eventually guarantee the confidentiality of certain actions and data: this is the purpose of *accreditation*. The accreditation of a given actor provides information on its rights (permissions) relatively to each sort (task) of the studied process's GMWf. We propose here, a simple but non-exhaustive nomenclature of rights. It is inspired by the one used in UNIX-like operating systems. Three types of accreditation are therefore defined: accreditation in reading *(r)*, writing *(w)* and execution *(x)*.

1. *The accreditation in reading (r)*: an actor accredited in reading on sort X must be informed of the execution of the associated task; he must also have free access to its execution state (data generated during its execution). We call an actor's *view*, the set of sorts on which he is accredited in reading.

2. *The accreditation in writing (w)*: an actor accredited in writing on sort X can execute the associated task. To be simple, any actor accredited in writing on a sort must necessarily be accredited in reading on it.

3. *The accreditation in execution (x)*: an actor accredited in execution on sort X is allowed to ask the actor who is accredited in writing in it, to execute it (realization of the associated task). More formally, an accreditation is defined as follows:

Definition 4. *An **accreditation** $\mathcal{A}_{A_i}$ defined on the set $\mathcal{S}$ of grammatical symbols for an actor A_i, is a triplet $\mathcal{A}_{A_i} = \left(\mathcal{A}_{A_i(r)}, \mathcal{A}_{A_i(w)}, \mathcal{A}_{A_i(x)} \right)$ such that, $\mathcal{A}_{A_i(r)} \subseteq \mathcal{S}$ also called **view** of actor A_i, is the set of symbols on which A_i is accredited in reading, $\mathcal{A}_{A_i(w)} \subseteq \mathcal{A}_{A_i(r)}$ is the set of symbols on which A_i is accredited in writing and $\mathcal{A}_{A_i(x)} \subseteq \mathcal{S}$ is the set of symbols on which A_i is accredited in execution.*

The accreditations of various actors must be produced by the workflow designer just after modelling the scenarios in the form of representative artifacts. From the task assignment for the peer-review process in the running example (see Sect. 2), it follows that the accreditation in writing of the EC is $\mathcal{A}_{EC(w)} = \{A,B,D\}$, that of the AE is $\mathcal{A}_{AE(w)} = \{C,S1,E1,E2,F\}$ and that of the first (resp. the second) referee is $\mathcal{A}_{R_1(w)} = \{G1,H1,I1\}$ (resp. $\mathcal{A}_{R_2(w)} = \{G2,H2,I2\}$). Since the EC can only execute the task D if the task C is already executed (see Fig. 2), in order for the EC to be able to ask the AE to execute this task, he must be accredited in execution on it; so we have $\mathcal{A}_{EC(x)} = \{C\}$. Moreover, in order to be able to access all the information on the peer-review evaluation of a paper (task C) and to summarize the right decision to send to the author, the EC must be able to consult the reports (tasks $I1$ and $I2$) and the messages (tasks $H1$ and $H2$) of the different referees, as well as the final decision taken by the AE (task F). These tasks, added to $\mathcal{A}_{EC(w)}$[9] constitute the set $\mathcal{A}_{EC(r)} = \mathcal{V}_{EC} = \{A,B,C,D,H1,H2,I1,I2,F\}$ of tasks on which it is accredited in reading. By doing so for each of other actors, we deduce the accreditations represented in Table 1.

Table 1. Accreditations of the different actors taking part in the peer-review process.

Actor	Accreditation
EC	$\mathcal{A}_{EC} = (\{A,B,C,D,H1,H2,I1,I2,F\},\{A,B,D\},\{C\})$
AE	$\mathcal{A}_{AE} = (\{A,C,S1,E1,E2,F,H1,H2,I1,I2\},\{C,S1,E1,E2,F\},\{G1,G2\})$
R1	$\mathcal{A}_{R1} = (\{C,G1,H1,I1\},\{G1,H1,I1\},\emptyset)$
R2	$\mathcal{A}_{R2} = (\{C,G2,H2,I2\},\{G2,H2,I2\},\emptyset)$

Since the (re)structuring symbols are not associated with tasks and were only introduced to adjust the control flow, their execution neither requires nor produces data. Therefore, the accreditation in writing and execution on them may be best left to the designer's appreciation; he will then make the assignment by referring to the execution model he will use later. To this end, he could use the same principle for the assignment of these accreditations in the case of concrete process' tasks. However, one could by default consider that all actors are accredited in reading on (re)structuring symbols; this would make these symbols visible to all of them and would guarantee that the adjustment of the control flow will be effective for all of them even if they have partial perceptions of the process.

3.5   Summary: Definition of LSAWfP

To summarise, we state that in LSAWfP, an administrative process $\mathcal{P}_{op}$ is specified using a triplet $\mathbb{W}_f = (\mathbb{G}, L_{P_k}, L_{\mathcal{A}_k})$ called *a Grammatical Model of Administrative Workflow Process* (GMAWfP) and composed of: a GMWf, a list of actors and a list of their accreditations. The GMWf is used to describe all the tasks of the studied process and their scheduling, while the list of accreditations provides information on the role played by each actor involved in the process execution. A GMAWfP can then be formally defined as follows:

---

[9] Recall that we consider that one can only execute what he sees.

Definition 5. *A **Grammatical Model of Administrative Workflow Process** (GMAWfP)* $\mathbb{W}_f$ *for a given business process, is a triplet* $\mathbb{W}_f = \left(\mathbb{G}, \mathcal{L}_{P_k}, \mathcal{L}_{\mathcal{A}_k}\right)$ *wherein* $\mathbb{G}$ *is the studied process (global) GMWf,* $\mathcal{L}_{P_k}$ *is the set of k actors taking part in its execution and* $\mathcal{L}_{\mathcal{A}_k}$ *represents the set of these actors accreditations.*

4 Ongoing and Perspective Work on LSAWfP

In this section, we present some of the work being currently done on LSAWfP while assessing what has already been done and presented in this paper.

4.1 On the Expressiveness of LSAWfP

Let's consider a specification $\mathbb{W}_f = \left(\mathbb{G}, \mathcal{L}_{P_k}, \mathcal{L}_{\mathcal{A}_k}\right)$ of a given business process $\mathcal{P}_{op}$. As described above, its organizational model that expresses and classifies/assigns the resources that must execute its tasks is given by the couple $\left(\mathcal{L}_{P_k}, \mathcal{L}_{\mathcal{A}_k}\right)$ of $\mathbb{W}_f$. Its informational model that describes the data structure being manipulated is given by the type of the attribute *status* associated with each task. Its lifecycle model that provides information on tasks and their sequencing (coordination) is given by the GMWf $\mathbb{G}$ of $\mathbb{W}_f$. Thus, we can conclude that LSAWfP has the major expected characteristics of a workflow language according to [1].

The GMWf effectively allows the designers to specify all the basic control flows (sequential, parallel, alternative and iterative) which can be found in traditional workflow languages. Figure 3 gives for each type of basic control flow its BPMN notation and the corresponding notations (artifact and associated productions) in LSAWfP as described below:

- the sequential flow between two tasks A and B can be expressed either by a production p of the form $p : A \rightarrow B$, or by a production q of the form $q : S \rightarrow A \, \S \, B$ in which S is a (re)structuring symbol (see Fig. 3(a));
- the parallel flow between two tasks A and B is expressed using a production p of the form $p : S \rightarrow A \parallel B$ (see Fig. 3(b));
- the alternative flow (choice) between two tasks $A1$ and $A2$ is expressed using two productions $p1$ and $p2$ such that $p1 : S \rightarrow A1$ and $p2 : S \rightarrow A2$; S is a (re)structuring symbol expressing the fact that after "execution" of S, one must execute either task $A1$ or task $A2$ (see Fig. 3(c)).
- iterative routing (repetition) is expressed using recursive symbols. Thus the productions $p1 : A \rightarrow B$, $p2 : B \rightarrow C$ and $p3 : B \rightarrow A$ express a potentially (transitive) iterative flow on the task A (see Fig. 3(d)); $P_7 : E1 \rightarrow E1$ in the running example also expresses a direct iterative flow on $E1$ (see Fig. 2).

One avenue we are currently exploring is that of measuring the expressiveness of LSAWfP in relation to workflow patterns [20]. This will allow us to characterize precisely the class of processes that this language can model.

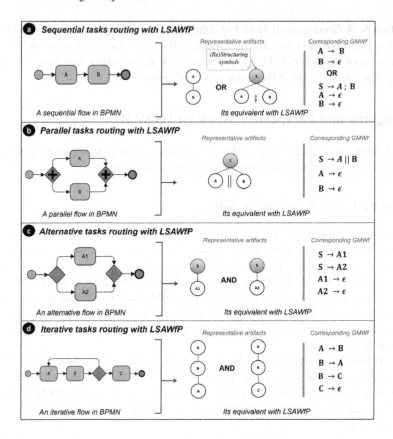

Fig. 3. Illustrating basic control flows with LSAWfP.

4.2 Towards an Artifact-Centric Model of Processes Design and Distributed Execution Based on Cooperative Edition of a Mobile Artifact

We are also working to produce an artifact-centric model of business process management. In this model inspired by the work of Badouel et al. on cooperative editing [6,14,16–18], the process tasks are executed by the various actors with the help of software that they pilot. These software agents are autonomous, reactive and communicate in peer to peer mode by exchanging an artifact (considered as "mobile") edited cooperatively. This mobile artifact is an annotated tree that represents the execution status of the process at each moment. For this purpose, it contains information on the tasks already executed, on the data produced during these executions and on the tasks ready to be executed.

When the mobile artifact is received at a given execution site, the local agent executes an update protocol whose purpose is to reveal the tasks ready to be executed locally by the local actor. The execution of the tasks by the local actor is done using a specialized editor and can be assimilated to the edition of a structured document since its actions cause the received mobile artifact (the tree) to be updated, by expanding

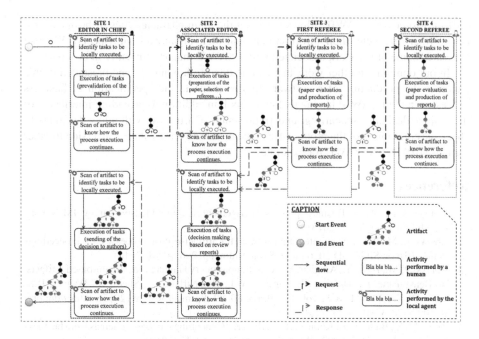

Fig. 4. An overview of the artifact-centric execution of the peer-review process.

some of its leaf nodes into sub-trees and by assigning values to the "status" attributes of some other nodes. When all the tasks ready to be locally executed have been executed, the artifact is sent to other agents for further execution of the process if necessary.

To run the peer-review process described in Sect. 2 with the artifact-centric model being built, four agents controlled by four actors (the *EC*, the *AE*, the *R*1 and the *R* agents) will be deployed. Figure 4 sketches an overview of exchanges that can take place between those four agents. The scenario presented there corresponds to the nominal one in which the paper is pre-validated by the *EC* and therefore, is analysed by a peer review committee. The artifact-centric execution is triggered on the *EC*'s site by introducing (in this site) an artifact reduced to its root node. During its transit through the system, this artifact grows. Note that there may be situations where multiple copies of the artifact are updated in parallel; this is notably the case when they are present on site 3 (first referee) and 4 (second referee).

5   Conclusion

In this paper, we have proposed a new workflow language called LSAWfP which allows, through a simple grammar-based formalism, to specify administrative business processes. Like any traditional workflow language, LSAWfP allows to specify basic flows (sequential, parallel, alternative and iterative) that are generally found in workflow models; particularly, it focuses on the modelling of each of the process scenario using an artifact. Moreover, LSAWfP allows to model the main characteristics of business processes (their lifecycle, their informational and their organizational aspects). We also presented some of the work associated with LSAWfP that are currently in progress.

In our opinion, an other work that can be done following the one presented in this paper, is the production of a software tool to assist in the specification of business processes in the LSAWfP language. Such a tool, in addition to providing interfaces for the graphic design of scenario graphs (representative artifacts), will allow designers to check the correctness of the produced specifications and ensure their conversion to other formats (BPMN and YAWL for example).

References

1. Van der Aalst, W.M.: Business process management: a comprehensive survey. ISRN Software Engineering 2013 (2013)
2. Abi Assaf, M.: Towards an integration system for artifact-centric processes. In: Proceedings of the 2016 on SIGMOD 2016 Ph.D. Symposium, pp. 2–6. ACM (2016)
3. Abi Assaf, M., Badr, Y., Amghar, Y.: A continuous query language for stream-based artifacts. In: Benslimane, D., Damiani, E., Grosky, W.I., Hameurlain, A., Sheth, A., Wagner, R.R. (eds.) DEXA 2017. LNCS, vol. 10439, pp. 80–89. Springer, Cham (2017). https://doi.org/10.1007/978-3-319-64471-4_8
4. Assaf, M.A., Badr, Y., El Khoury, H., Barbar, K.: Generating database schemas from business artifact models. Int. J. Inf. Technol. Comput. Sci. 2, 10–17 (2018)
5. Badouel, E., Hélouët, L., Kouamou, G.E., Morvan, C., Fondze Jr., N.R.: Active workspaces: distributed collaborative systems based on guarded attribute grammars. ACM SIGAPP Appl. Comput. Rev. 15(3), 6–34 (2015)
6. Badouel, E., Tchendji, M.T.: Merging hierarchically-structured documents in workflow systems. Electron. Notes Theor. Comput. Sci. 203(5), 3–24 (2008). https://doi.org/10.1016/j.entcs.2008.05.017
7. Boaz, D., Limonad, L., Gupta, M.: BizArtifact: artifact-centric business process management, June 2013 (2013). https://sourceforge.net/projects/bizartifact/. Accessed 12 Dec 2019
8. Börger, E.: Approaches to modeling business processes: a critical analysis of BPMN, workflow patterns and YAWL. Softw. Syst. Model. 11(3), 305–318 (2012). https://doi.org/10.1007/s10270-011-0214-z
9. Deutsch, A., Hull, R., Vianu, V.: Automatic verification of database-centric systems. ACM SIGMOD Rec. 43(3), 5–17 (2014)
10. Hull, R., Narendra, N.C., Nigam, A.: Facilitating workflow interoperation using artifact-centric hubs. In: Baresi, L., Chi, C.-H., Suzuki, J. (eds.) ICSOC/ServiceWave -2009. LNCS, vol. 5900, pp. 1–18. Springer, Heidelberg (2009). https://doi.org/10.1007/978-3-642-10383-4_1
11. Lohmann, N., Wolf, K.: Artifact-centric choreographies. In: Maglio, P.P., Weske, M., Yang, J., Fantinato, M. (eds.) ICSOC 2010. LNCS, vol. 6470, pp. 32–46. Springer, Heidelberg (2010). https://doi.org/10.1007/978-3-642-17358-5_3
12. McCready, S.: There is more than one kind of workflow software. Computerworld 2, 86–90 (1992)
13. BP Model: Notation (BPMN) version 2.0. OMG Specification, Object Management Group, pp. 22–31 (2011)
14. Zekeng Ndadji, M.M., Tchoupé Tchendji, M.: A software architecture for centralized management of structured documents in a cooperative editing workflow. In: M. F. Kebe, C., Gueye, A., Ndiaye, A. (eds.) InterSol/CNRIA -2017. LNICSSITE, vol. 204, pp. 279–291. Springer, Cham (2018). https://doi.org/10.1007/978-3-319-72965-7_26

15. Nigam, A., Caswell, N.S.: Business artifacts: an approach to operational specification. IBM Syst. J. **42**(3), 428–445 (2003)
16. Tchoupe Tchendji, M.: Une Approche Grammaticale pour la Fusion des Réplicats Partiels d'un Document Structuré: Application à l'Édition Coopérative Asynchrone. Ph.D. thesis, Université de Rennes I (France), Université de Yaoundé I (Cameroun) (2009)
17. Tchoupé Tchendji, M., Djeumen, R.D., Atemkeng, M.T.: A stable and consistent document model suitable for asynchronous cooperative edition. J. Comput. Commun. **5**(08), 69 (2017)
18. Tchoupé Tchendji, M., Zekeng Ndadji, M.M.: Tree automata for extracting consensus from partial replicas of a structured document. J. Softw. Eng. Appl. **10**(05), 432 (2017)
19. Van Der Aalst, W.M., Barthelmess, P., Ellis, C.A., Wainer, J.: Proclets: a framework for lightweight interacting workflow processes. Int. J. Coop. Inf. Syst. **10**(04), 443–481 (2001)
20. Van Der Aalst, W.M., ter Hofstede, A.H.: Workflow patterns put into context. Softw. Syst. Model. **11**(3), 319–323 (2012). https://doi.org/10.1007/s10270-012-0233-4
21. Van Der Aalst, W.M., Mans, R., Russell, N.C.: Workflow support using proclets: divide, interact, and conquer. IEEE Data Eng. Bull. **32**(3), 16–22 (2009)
22. Muehlen, M., Recker, J.: How much language is enough? Theoretical and practical use of the business process modeling notation. Seminal Contributions to Information Systems Engineering, pp. 429–443. Springer, Heidelberg (2013). https://doi.org/10.1007/978-3-642-36926-1_35

Cloud Computing

A Linux Scheduler to Limit the Slowdown Generated by Volunteer Computing Systems

Jaime Chavarriaga[✉], Antonio de-la-Vega, Eduardo Rosales,
and Harold Castro

Computing and Systems Engineering Department,
Universidad de los Andes, Bogotá, Colombia
{ja.chavarriaga908,aj.de10,ee.rosales24,hcastro}@uniandes.edu.co

Abstract. Volunteer computing systems leverage idle resources on voluntarily enabled desktops to execute CPU-intensive jobs. When these systems execute simultaneously to tasks performed by the end-user (i.e., the person who runs applications on the shared desktop), a slowdown can be generated and the end-user may perceive it. Since slowdown is a key factor to either encourage or discourage end-users to donate their computing resources, volunteer computing systems often aim at reducing it by limiting CPU consumption. This introduces a trade-off in using the available processing resources. On the one hand, if the processor is fully idle then resources are underutilized. On the other hand, significant slowdown still can be generated in presence of other CPU-intensive end-user tasks. In contrast to fixing CPU consumption, we tackle this problem by modifying the *Linux Scheduler* to implement scheduling policies that determine whether a volunteer computing system can execute a job by dynamically considering the potential slowdown that it may introduce. By implementing our policies, we found the utilization of idle resources is improved and the slowdown the end-user experiences is effectively limited. Our evaluation results show that our approach overcomes state-of-the-art CPU limiting techniques such as the *CPUlimit* and *cgroups*.

1 Introduction

Volunteer Computing is a form of distributed system where public participants, known as volunteers, share their idle computing resources in order to contribute to computationally expensive projects [5]. Existing *volunteer computing systems* such as BOINC[1] and HTCondor[2] consist of thousands of desktops providing a huge amount of memory and processing for scientific projects [3]. According to its website, BOINC alone accounts more than 800,000 volunteer computers and

---

[1] https://boinc.berkeley.edu/.

[2] https://research.cs.wisc.edu/htcondor/.

© Springer Nature Switzerland AG 2020
H. Florez and S. Misra (Eds.): ICAI 2020, CCIS 1277, pp. 149–164, 2020.
https://doi.org/10.1007/978-3-030-61702-8_11

supplies more than 21.69 PetaFLOPS to initiatives such as SETI@Home[3] and Rosetta@Home[4].

When volunteer computing systems execute simultaneously to tasks performed by the *end-user* (i.e., the person who runs applications on the shared desktop), a slowdown can be generated and the end-user may perceive it. Since slowdown is a key factor to either encourage or discourage end-users to donate their computing resources, volunteer computing systems often aim at reducing it by fixing CPU consumption to a limit. For instance, BOINC and HTCondor can be configured to limit CPU consumption to a specific percentage.

Nonetheless, fixing a CPU consumption limit introduces a trade-off in using the available processing resources. On the one hand, when a desktop is fully idle, then resources are underutilized. On the other hand, significant slowdown can still be generated to the end-user when the number of executing processes exceeds the number of CPU cores.

In a previous work [17], we found that, each time a volunteer computing job is executed, end-user tasks increased their execution time in a percentage that varied depending on the total number of CPU cores currently busy. There, we outlined a scheduling policy that monitors CPU core consumption to determine whether a volunteer computing job can be executed while generating a tolerated slowdown to end-user tasks.

This paper presents a twofold solution to limit the slowdown produced by volunteer computing jobs: (1) an automated test to determine a *processor-specific profile* that indicates, when multiple jobs and end-user tasks are being executed, the slowdown produced to the latter; and (2) a modification to the *Linux Scheduler* that uses that profile to determine if a new job should execute considering the number of active cores in the desktop and a predefined limit for slowdown.

Our evaluation shows that this approach outperforms modern CPU limiting techniques such as *CPULimit* and cgroups, along with existing options for low priority processes such as *nice* and the SCHED_IDLE scheduler class. In contrast to such techniques, our scheduler generated a slowdown lower than a predefined 15% limit while executing from 1 up to 8 CPU-intensive volunteer jobs.

The rest of this paper is organized as follows. Section 2 introduces the design of the Linux scheduler and of the CPULimit and cgroups tools as background work. Section 3 presents our analysis of the slowdown generated by introducing new processes in a modern CPU. Section 4 describes our modification on the Linux scheduler. Section 5 compares our approach to other existing tools and techniques. Section 6 presents related work. Finally, Sect. 7 concludes the paper and presents future work.

2   Background

We modified the Linux scheduler to determine whether a volunteer computing job should run by considering the slowdown that its execution could generate

---

[3] http://setiathome.ssl.berkeley.edu/.
[4] https://boinc.bakerlab.org/.

to an end-user. This section describes the design of the Linux scheduler and of other subsystems and tools that limit CPU consumption.

2.1 Linux Scheduler

In an operating system, the *scheduler* is a kernel subsystem that assign computation tasks, represented as processes and threads, to hardware resources that complete the work [1]. Each process and thread is assigned to a CPU (a processor, CPU core or processor thread) according to a predefined algorithm known as a *scheduling policy*. In modern systems, different tasks may be executed using different policies. For instance, it is possible that some tasks run on a real-time policy while others run on a prioritized preemptive one.

Linux Scheduling Classes. Starting with Linux 2.6.23, scheduling policies are implemented using modules known as *scheduling classes* [1]. A typical Linux distribution has four scheduling classes that implement six scheduling policies: (1) the *fair_sched_class*, a.k.a., the Completely Fair Scheduler (CFS) class, implements the SCHED_NORMAL and SCHED_BATCH policies for typical user-defined tasks[5], (2) the *rt_sched_class* implements the realtime SCHED_FIFO and SCHED_RR policies, (3) the *dl_sched_class* implements the Earliest Deadline First (EDF) SCHED_DEADLINE policy, and (4) the *idle_sched_class* defines a SCHED_IDLE for lowest-priority tasks. There is an additional *stop_sched_class* that supports the per-CPU stop tasks and does not manage end-user tasks.

Internally, each scheduling class is implemented using a *sched_class* structure with hooks (i.e., function pointers) to functions that implement the policies. At start-up, Linux builds a linked list with the scheduling classes. The priority of the classes is determined by their position in the list. The kernel first asks the *dl_sched_class* if a task must run to meet a deadline. Then it asks the *rt_sched_class* if a realtime task must be executed. Later, it asks the *fair_sched_class* for a normal task to run and, finally, it asks the *idle_sched_class* for running lowest-priority processes. Intuitively, tasks managed by a scheduling class only run when the classes with higher priority do not execute tasks in all the CPUs of the machine.

The Linux kernel provides means to change the scheduling policy for a task. The *sched_setscheduler* kernel function can be used to set both the scheduling policy and the associated parameters. At command line, programs such as *chrt* can be used to modify the policy and its parameters.

2.2 CPU Limiting Techniques

There are some techniques and tools to limit, or at least reduce, the amount of CPU that a task can use. A user can (1) assign a *nice value* to reduce its priority, (2) change the scheduling policy to SCHED_IDLE, (3) include the task

---

[5] Some documentation and user-space tools refer to SCHED_NORMAL as SCHED_OTHER.

into a cgroup, or (4) use tools such as *cpulimit* to limit the percentage of CPU that the task can use.

Setting a Nice Value for a Task. Users can provide a *nice value*, between −20 and 19 (default 0), as a hint for the initial or the next priority value for a normal task [1]. In Linux, the priority for a normal process is used to determine the CPU time assigned to its execution. This priority cannot be set manually. Instead, it is updated dynamically, rewarding I/O-bound tasks and punishing CPU-bound tasks by adding or subtracting from the task's priority. Basically, providing a higher nice value (e.g., 19) suggests to the *fair_sched_class* to reduce the priority of the process and reduce the time assigned to it. The user cannot use *nice values* to enforce a limit to the CPU used by the task.

Using the SCHED_IDLE Class. Users can change the scheduling class of a process to SCHED_IDLE. Processes in this class will only be executed if no real-time or normal task is available to run in one of the CPUs in the machine. SCHED_IDLE processes can be considered as the ones with the lowest priority. However, just like with the nice value, users cannot use the SCHED_IDLE class to enforce limits to the amount of CPU that the tasks can use.

Assigning the Task to a *cgroup*. Modern Linux kernels allow users to create a *cgroup*, a collection of processes that obey limits to resources such as CPU, memory and I/O, that these processes can use [15]. In a cgroup, the CPU usage can be limited (1) by using a *relative share* or (2) by using hard limits with the *Ceiling enforcement parameters.*

The relative share of CPU time available to a cgroup can be specified using cpu.shares. Two cgroups with the same cpu.shares will receive the same CPU time. Tasks in a cgroup with the double of the cpu.shares will receive twice as much CPU time. However, when the tasks in a cgroup are idle, the unused CPU cycles are assigned to the other groups. Thus, the resulting usage of CPU may be greater than the percentage defined by the shares.

Hard limits can be defined using cpu.cfs_quota_us and cpu.cfs_period_us. They specify the total amount of time for which all the tasks in a group can run during each period of time (in microseconds). For instance, if a task should access a single CPU till 0.2 s out of every second, it is possible to include it into a cgroup with cpu.cfs_quota_us set to 200,000 and cpu.cfs_period_us to 1,000,000. Note that using hard limits under-utilizes the CPUs when the desktop is idle.

Using Tools Such as CPULimit[6]. These tools monitor the percentage of CPU used by a process and, if it starts to consume more than a limit, it sends a SIGSTOP signal to pause its execution. When the process have consumed less than the limit and it is paused, they send a SIGCONT signal to resume the process. At the end, the monitored process does not consume more than the specified limit. In contrast to other solutions, cpulimit uses percentage values to define the limits to the CPU time, instead of shares and time quotas. It works by limiting a single process and cannot be used to limit a group of processes.

---

[6] https://github.com/opsengine/cpulimit.

2.3   Slowdown to End-User Tasks

Volunteer computing systems use the aforementioned techniques aiming to inter-
fere as little as possible with end-user tasks. In this paper, we use the *slowdown*
of a process, i.e., the ratio between its actual execution time and its optimal execution time (on an ideal system) [12], to analyze this interference. The slowdown
metric can be interpreted as the overhead incurred on a process by the existence
of other processes in the same machine.

We can mention, at least, two reasons for a process slowdown: (1) *CPU and
resource contention* that increase the time that a process must wait and (2)
dynamic overclocking technologies that may reduce the overall frequency scale
and therefore increase the time required to perform end-user tasks on a processor.

CPU Contention. All the processes running in a computer share resources
such as the CPU and the memory. Intuitively, a slowdown may be caused when
the system tries to execute concurrently more processes than the available CPU
cores. In this case, these processes must share CPU cores and, therefore, require
more time to perform the same tasks.

Dynamic Overclocking. Modern processors incorporate a dynamic frequency
scaling subsystem that changes the clock-speed of each CPU based on its load,
temperature and power consumption. Also known as *throttling*, this technique
aims at conserving power and reducing the amount of heat generated by the
chip. They may reduce the speed of the processors and, therefore, produce a
slowdown to end-user tasks.

For instance, *Intel Turbo Boost* is the frequency scaling subsystem of modern
Intel Core i5 and i7 processors [7]. There, the operating frequency of the processor
changes dynamically. The upper limit of the frequency is determined by the
model of the processor and the number of active CPU cores at any given instant.
In this paper, a CPU core is considered *active* (busy, occupied) if it is operating
normally and it is considered *inactive* (idle) if it has some circuits turned off due
to inactivity [7]. For instance, Table 1 shows the frequency steps and limits for
the Core i7-4770 @3.40 GHz processor. The base operating frequency is 3.4 GHz.
The processor allows up to five 100 MHz frequency steps (up to 3.9 Ghz) when
just one or two CPU cores are active, four steps when three CPU cores are active
(up to 3.8 GHz) and three frequency steps (up to 3.7 GHz) when two or more
CPU cores are active.

Different models of processors may differ in features such as the number of
cores, algorithms for frequency scaling and for power saving.

Table 1. Intel Turbo Boost, frequency table for Core i7-4770@3.40 GHz [8]

Core i7-4770@3.40 GHz				
Active Cores	4C	3C	2C	1C
Max Bin Upside	3	4	5	5
Max Frequency	3.7GHz	3.9 GHz	3.9 GHz	3.9 GHz

3   Analyzing the Slowdown to End-User Tasks

As part of our solution, we defined an automated analysis to determine, for a specific processor model, the slowdown introduced by a new volunteer computing job to concurrent executing end-user tasks. This section describes how it works.

3.1   Automated Analysis

We are interested in finding an automated way to determine when a new volunteer computing job interferes with the performance of end-user tasks. Considering that each model of a processor may have a different number of CPU cores, different algorithms for frequency scaling and different processing modes, we defined an automated technique that collects information on a real machine. This technique produces a *processor profile* that we can later use to instruct the Linux scheduler which criteria must be met to run volunteer computing jobs.

Our automated analysis is based on the experiments we used to measure the slowdown produced by volunteer computing jobs on Intel Turbo Boost processors [17]. We defined two sets of tasks: *foreground processes* that represents end-user tasks running on a desktop, and *background processes* that represents volunteer computing jobs introduced by a volunteer computing system. We measured how much the execution time of the foreground processes were affected by introducing a new background process.

We defined a base line by determining the time spent by a foreground process to calculate a set of Fibonacci numbers in the absence of background process. Then, we measured the time spent by the same process when a background process is started at the same time. We measured the time combining from 1 up to 8 foreground processes with 1 up to 8 background processes. The slowdown was calculated as the ratio of increment on the time spent by the foreground processes running along the background processes over the time spent by the foreground processes alone.

Table 2 shows the results of our tests using tasks that calculate, each one, the 80th Fibonacci number 200 million times on an Intel Core i7-4770. In the top row, it shows the time spent by the foreground processes without any background process. For instance, a single foreground process took 47.2302 s and three processes 48.5095 s. The next rows show the time spent by the foreground processes when they run concurrently to other background processes. When three foreground tasks ran with three background processes, they took 56.0948 s. We estimate that the slowdown generated was 16% by using the ratio of the difference over the time spent without background processes, i.e., $slowdown = (56.0948 - 48.5095)/48.5095 = 16\%$.

The resulting data of the automated process is used to define a heuristic to determine when a process can be executed without generating a slowdown greater than a given value. For instance, consider that we are interested on running volunteer computing systems without producing a slowdown greater than 13%. The Table 3 shows a 1 in the combination of foreground and background processes where the slowdown is less than that limit. A 0 is shown otherwise.

Table 2. Average processing time using normal processes. our baseline.

(a) Running foreground processes without background tasks:(time in seconds)							
	FG 1	FG 2	FG 3	FG 4	FG 5	FG 6	FG 7	FG 8
BG 0	47.2302	47.2827	48.5095	52.4097	57.5743	59.9892	60.1932	62.2737

(b) Running foreground processes with 1 to 8 background tasks:							
	FG 1	FG 2	FG 3	FG 4	FG 5	FG 6	FG 7	FG 8
BG 1	47.2738	48.8317	52.6690	53.9087	57.9467	59.9785	62.8760	60.9190
BG 2	48.5122	51.9415	54.0763	59.0677	59.2200	61.5075	62.1845	60.9080
BG 3	48.9185	54.3118	56.0948	61.3075	62.1273	61.4953	63.1912	63.7873
BG 4	53.6465	56.3275	55.4507	59.9658	60.9147	61.9265	61.5837	65.1315
BG 5	55.0017	53.5483	56.4258	61.1692	60.5322	60.8180	61.4748	63.0038
BG 6	54.2303	57.6698	54.9595	63.5222	61.2905	62.7773	62.6492	63.7760
BG 7	54.7598	58.3053	58.0022	60.8363	64.0060	61.8783	63.0517	66.7110
BG 8	58.6400	57.9192	57.6157	60.9000	65.4618	61.1715	63.1287	65.0787

(c) Slowdown caused by 1 to 8 background tasks:							
	FG 1	FG 2	FG 3	FG 4	FG 5	FG 6	FG 7	FG 8
BG 1	0%	4%	9%	7%	2%	3%	5%	2%
BG 2	3%	10%	12%	13%	4%	5%	4%	3%
BG 3	4%	15%	16%	18%	8%	4%	5%	5%
BG 4	14%	19%	14%	15%	6%	3%	4%	5%
BG 5	16%	13%	16%	17%	5%	4%	4%	2%
BG 6	15%	22%	13%	22%	7%	7%	5%	2%
BG 7	16%	23%	20%	17%	11%	5%	5%	7%
BG 8	24%	22%	19%	17%	14%	5%	5%	5%

Table 3. Combinations where the slowdown on foreground processes caused by normal processes is less than 13%

	FG 1	FG 2	FG 3	FG 4	FG 5	FG 6	FG 7	FG 8
BG 1	1	1	1	1	1	1	1	1
BG 2	1	1	1	0	1	1	1	1
BG 3	1	0	0	0	1	1	1	1
BG 4	0	0	0	0	1	1	1	1
BG 5	0	0	0	0	1	1	1	1
BG 6	0	0	0	0	1	1	1	1
BG 7	0	0	0	0	1	1	1	1
BG 8	0	0	0	0	0	1	1	1

Note, for instance, that running at the same time two foreground processes with two background processes generates a slowdown below 13%. In contrast, running three foreground and three background processes generates more slowdown than the limit.

3.2 Discussion

The slowdown generated by introducing a new process vary depending on the number of foreground and background processes. Although the background processes ran with the maximum *nice* value, i.e., a 19 value, they compete for CPU time and then affect the processing power assigned to the foreground processes.

Considerations on the Model of Processor. All our tests were performed using a computer with an Intel Core i7-4770, the processor mentioned above (§ Sect. 2.3). This processor has four cores and supports the Hyper-Threading and the Turbo Boost features. Linux detects this processor as a machine with eight CPUs (i.e., 4 physical CPU cores, each one with 2 threads). When the computer runs few tasks, as Linux is Hyper-Threading aware, the scheduler tries to assign the tasks each one to a different physical CPU. Our data suggests that the slowdown vary depending on the number of CPU cores that are active.

When the number of foreground processes does not exceed the number of physical CPUs, i.e., between 1 to 4 foreground processes in our data, it is possible to introduce one or two background processes without producing a slowdown greater or equal to 13%. In contrast, introducing three or more background processes caused a slowdown greater than that limit. In such cases, on the one hand, the number of foreground and background processes goes further the number of physical CPUs and they start to share these cores. On the other hand, the activation of additional cores produces a reduction of the CPU clock speed. Both affect the computing power for each process can use and produces the slowdown.

On the contrary, when the number of foreground processes exceeded the number of physical CPUs, i.e., more than 4 processes in our data, all the cores were active and the CPU frequency remained at the lowest value. There, introducing new background processes did not generate a slowdown greater than 13%.

Considerations for Other Processors. The slowdown data vary from one model of processor to the other. We have collected data on different processors and the slowdown vary depending on the number of CPUs detected by Linux and on features such as Hyper-Threading and TurboBoost that have been activated. To define a heuristic for a processor, such as the shown in Table 3, it is necessary to collect the corresponding slowdown data using our test suite for that purpose.

4 The Proposed Linux Scheduler

We used the slowdown analysis presented above to create a new Linux scheduler class that only runs tasks when they do not produce a slowdown on end-user tasks that exceed a predefined limit. In our scheduler, the tasks introduced by the volunteer computing system are only executed when our previous analysis show that it will not generate a slowdown greater than 13%.

4.1 Linux Scheduler Class

We defined a new *Unacloud* scheduler class. The Linux source code was modified to include *unacloud_sched_class*, a new *sched_class* node, between the existing *fair_sched_class* and the *idle_sched_class*. This scheduling class runs when there is an idle CPU but no normal program to execute. Each time our scheduler is called, it checks all the CPUs in the desktop and determines how many CPU cores are executing normal tasks and how many are running tasks in our scheduling policy. Then, if the combination of the number of foreground and background processes do not cause a slowdown greater than the limit, our scheduler sets a new task to run. The tasks in our policy only run if the foreground/background tasks combination generates a slowdown below the limit.

4.2   Evaluation

We evaluated our scheduler using the same analysis we performed to measure the slowdown using normal processes. We simulate foreground and background processes using CPU-intensive tasks, in concrete, using a program that calculates the 80th Fibonacci number 200 million times. Foreground processes are normal processes running with the default nice value, while the background processes run as tasks managed by our scheduler.

Table 4 shows a summary of our evaluation. It presents the average time and slowdown after running the test five times. Note, in the lower table, that the slowdown remains in less than 15% all the time. In contrast to the tasks running as normal processes (§ Table 2), the foreground process took between 0% to 5% in the 45.3% of the combinations. Foreground processes had a slowdown of less than 10% in the 87.5% of the combinations.

5   Evaluation Against Existing Solutions

The goal of our scheduler is to support volunteer computing platforms willing to produce the least possible slowdown to the user tasks. This section presents a comparison of our approach to other existing solutions, namely by (i) using the SCHED_IDLE, (ii) using *cgroups* and (iii) using the *cpulimit* tools.

5.1   Comparing to SCHED_IDLE

Table 5 shows the slowdown produced when the foreground processes run with the SCHED_NORMAL scheduler with the default *nice* value, and the background processes run with the SCHED_IDLE scheduler aimed to lowest-priority tasks.

Note that, although we used low-priority tasks, the foreground processes were affected. The slowdown of these processes was greater than 15% in the 37.5% of the combinations. Only the 21.8% of the combinations had a slowdown of less than 5%. The 42.2% had a slowdown of less than 10%. In contrast, in our scheduler the 45.3% of the combinations had a slowdown of less than 5% and the 87,5% had one of less than 10%.

Table 4. Average processing time using our Linux Scheduling class

(a) Running foreground processes without background tasks: (time in seconds)

	FG 1	FG 2	FG 3	FG 4	FG 5	FG 6	FG 7	FG 8
BG 0	47.2222	47.3702	48.5104	49.8910	57.9766	58.8800	60.6362	65.5346

(b) Running foreground processes with 1 to 8 background tasks:

	FG 1	FG 2	FG 3	FG 4	FG 5	FG 6	FG 7	FG 8
BG 1	47.3082	47.5674	48.7818	52.0798	57.3706	58.7496	64.7536	62.9110
BG 2	49.8138	48.6638	51.0784	52.8884	57.4864	60.2134	60.7400	66.8582
BG 3	49.9168	48.8830	52.3488	56.0840	57.8100	59.6658	63.3586	67.0838
BG 4	50.4164	49.4090	52.1454	54.7120	58.7878	59.5874	62.2136	65.2870
BG 5	51.2666	50.4660	52.0468	56.9768	58.4302	59.7084	62.2246	61.4986
BG 6	50.4546	49.7742	51.6072	55.2576	59.9628	61.9928	61.1844	62.2284
BG 7	50.5014	49.8362	51.9050	56.1324	60.5994	62.2582	61.6470	64.0830
BG 8	50.1192	49.7682	51.9232	56.7538	61.9174	62.6970	63.2898	66.2396

(c) Slowdown caused by 1 to 8 background tasks:

	FG 1	FG 2	FG 3	FG 4	FG 5	FG 6	FG 7	FG 8
BG 1	0%	1%	1%	5%	3%	1%	7%	7%
BG 2	5%	3%	5%	6%	3%	2%	1%	14%
BG 3	6%	3%	8%	12%	2%	1%	5%	3%
BG 4	7%	4%	7%	10%	2%	2%	3%	5%
BG 5	9%	7%	7%	14%	3%	2%	4%	5%
BG 6	7%	5%	6%	11%	5%	5%	2%	6%
BG 7	7%	5%	7%	13%	5%	6%	2%	9%
BG 8	6%	5%	7%	14%	7%	6%	4%	13%

Table 5. Average slowdown using SCHED_IDLE

	FG 1	FG 2	FG 3	FG 4	FG 5	FG 6	FG 7	FG 8
BG 1	0%	3%	6%	8%	8%	4%	3%	8%
BG 2	3%	5%	11%	10%	8%	11%	4%	7%
BG 3	5%	11%	16%	17%	15%	9%	5%	14%
BG 4	9%	16%	29%	22%	21%	6%	2%	5%
BG 5	11%	25%	28%	23%	15%	12%	3%	8%
BG 6	12%	17%	34%	23%	21%	13%	3%	13%
BG 7	8%	38%	32%	24%	17%	7%	6%	14%
BG 8	22%	33%	40%	24%	17%	11%	3%	9%

5.2 Comparing to Cgroups

Table 6 shows our evaluation using cgroups with diverse configurations. For each scenario, we defined two process groups: one for the foreground processes and another one for the background processes. These groups were configured by defining cpu.shares where the foreground group can use the 100% of all the cores while the background only were allowed to use a value among 10%, 20%, 30%, 40% and 50%.

Note that, even when the cpu.shares gives background processes the 10% of the CPUs assigned to the foreground processes, the latter produced a slowdown greater than 15% in the 35.9% of the combinations. The number of combinations with a slowdown greater than 15% increased as the assigned proportion of CPU grew. When the proportion gives a 50% of the CPUs to the background processes, the 65.6% of all the combinations had a slowdown greater than 15%.

Table 6. Average slowdown using cgroups

cpu.shares equivalent to 10%

FG	1FG	2FG	3FG	4FG	5FG	6FG	7FG	8
BG 1	0%	6%	6%	6%	4%	4%	4%	10%
BG 2	3%	4%	14%	10%	8%	9%	6%	13%
BG 3	8%	11%	15%	17%	16%	8%	3%	9%
BG 4	16%	15%	14%	21%	14%	8%	8%	9%
BG 5	13%	18%	14%	24%	19%	9%	3%	15%
BG 6	15%	23%	14%	24%	13%	8%	12%	18%
BG 7	24%	27%	17%	23%	14%	8%	8%	18%
BG 8	30%	31%	17%	23%	13%	12%	4%	14%

cpu.shares equivalent to 20%

FG	1FG	2FG	3FG	4FG	5FG	6FG	7FG	8
BG 1	0%	6%	11%	9%	6%	9%	4%	15%
BG 2	3%	6%	7%	12%	10%	12%	11%	15%
BG 3	6%	12%	12%	25%	16%	12%	7%	18%
BG 4	15%	12%	20%	32%	19%	14%	12%	13%
BG 5	13%	20%	15%	29%	16%	10%	23%	19%
BG 6	14%	21%	17%	32%	17%	9%	12%	20%
BG 7	24%	28%	20%	33%	15%	11%	12%	26%
BG 8	33%	31%	24%	34%	17%	9%	10%	24%

cpu.shares equivalent to 30%

FG	1FG	2FG	3FG	4FG	5FG	6FG	7FG	8
BG 1	0%	5%	7%	7%	13%	6%	15%	16%
BG 2	3%	8%	14%	11%	8%	15%	17%	28%
BG 3	10%	10%	16%	12%	11%	10%	13%	20%
BG 4	17%	8%	10%	24%	12%	15%	15%	27%
BG 5	13%	15%	11%	29%	14%	9%	14%	27%
BG 6	14%	16%	9%	24%	12%	14%	17%	31%
BG 7	27%	21%	21%	26%	14%	16%	14%	30%
BG 8	33%	27%	27%	26%	17%	10%	17%	30%

cpu.shares equivalent to 40%

FG	1FG	2FG	3FG	4FG	5FG	6FG	7FG	8
BG 1	0%	5%	7%	17%	4%	7%	6%	18%
BG 2	3%	6%	8%	10%	11%	7%	19%	33%
BG 3	9%	9%	10%	15%	16%	16%	21%	41%
BG 4	17%	12%	10%	25%	18%	17%	19%	26%
BG 5	13%	19%	10%	32%	17%	19%	19%	34%
BG 6	14%	21%	13%	24%	16%	16%	19%	36%
BG 7	27%	29%	28%	30%	17%	19%	19%	42%
BG 8	33%	29%	30%	33%	20%	18%	21%	46%

cpu.shares equivalent to 50%

FG	1FG	2FG	3FG	4FG	5FG	6FG	7FG	8
BG 1	0%	8%	4%	11%	4%	7%	8%	16%
BG 2	2%	5%	9%	13%	9%	8%	21%	30%
BG 3	7%	3%	13%	14%	13%	24%	36%	43%
BG 4	17%	10%	18%	22%	18%	21%	30%	38%
BG 5	13%	10%	19%	24%	18%	20%	28%	44%
BG 6	14%	19%	28%	23%	20%	22%	29%	45%
BG 7	23%	22%	31%	23%	15%	21%	34%	51%
BG 8	34%	25%	37%	26%	21%	24%	33%	58%

5.3 Comparing to Cpulimit

Table 7 shows our evaluation using cpulimit with different values. For each scenario, foreground processes ran as normal processes with the default *nice* value, while the background processes ran monitored by cpulimit to not exceed the 10%, 20%, 30%, 40% or 50% of a CPU.

Note that cpulimit defines limits based on the use of a single CPU. In our testing machine, the configured value is a percentage of one of the eight detected CPUs in the Intel Core i7-4770. In contrast, when we defined cgroups with a proportion of `cpu.shares`, any value represents a percentage of all the eight CPUs. For instance, while using cgroups a limit of 10% corresponds to the 10% of all the CPUs (the 80% of a single CPU), using cpulimit the 10% corresponds to the 1,2% of all the CPUs (the 10% of a core).

When we ran the background process with 10% of a CPU, the effect on the foreground processes is negligible. Additionally, when these processes ran up to the 20% of a CPU, the slowdown only exceeded the 15% in three combinations. The number of combinations where the slowdown exceeds the 15% increases as

Table 7. Average slowdown using cpulimit

cpulimit equivalent to 10%									cpulimit equivalent to 20%								
FG	1FG	2FG	3FG	4FG	5FG	6FG	7FG	8	FG	1FG	2FG	3FG	4FG	5FG	6FG	7FG	8
BG 1	0%	0%	1%	2%	1%	1%	3%	4%	BG 1	0%	1%	3%	9%	5%	2%	4%	8%
BG 2	1%	5%	3%	6%	1%	2%	6%	7%	BG 2	1%	2%	2%	7%	3%	2%	4%	6%
BG 3	0%	2%	3%	3%	3%	1%	8%	5%	BG 3	1%	2%	2%	9%	3%	2%	2%	7%
BG 4	1%	2%	2%	4%	3%	2%	5%	5%	BG 4	1%	4%	3%	6%	3%	4%	7%	10%
BG 5	1%	2%	3%	5%	2%	2%	2%	7%	BG 5	2%	3%	5%	6%	3%	2%	2%	12%
BG 6	2%	3%	3%	5%	2%	2%	5%	7%	BG 6	3%	4%	5%	7%	4%	2%	6%	15%
BG 7	2%	3%	3%	6%	3%	4%	9%	9%	BG 7	2%	5%	7%	7%	2%	2%	9%	18%
BG 8	2%	3%	3%	6%	2%	4%	11%	10%	BG 8	3%	6%	7%	8%	2%	5%	13%	20%

cpulimit equivalent to 30%									cpulimit equivalent to 40%								
FG	1FG	2FG	3FG	4FG	5FG	6FG	7FG	8	FG	1FG	2FG	3FG	4FG	5FG	6FG	7FG	8
BG 1	0%	1%	5%	5%	1%	4%	5%	8%	BG 1	0%	5%	4%	6%	3%	5%	5%	6%
BG 2	2%	3%	3%	7%	2%	4%	5%	8%	BG 2	0%	3%	4%	6%	9%	3%	5%	7%
BG 3	1%	3%	5%	6%	3%	4%	4%	8%	BG 3	3%	4%	7%	6%	3%	3%	3%	12%
BG 4	1%	4%	6%	8%	2%	2%	5%	9%	BG 4	3%	5%	8%	7%	2%	4%	10%	19%
BG 5	2%	5%	6%	9%	4%	6%	10%	13%	BG 5	4%	7%	9%	9%	5%	10%	19%	28%
BG 6	3%	7%	9%	10%	4%	4%	16%	19%	BG 6	4%	8%	11%	13%	8%	15%	31%	37%
BG 7	4%	8%	10%	11%	7%	7%	25%	28%	BG 7	7%	11%	14%	17%	14%	24%	42%	49%
BG 8	5%	9%	12%	13%	8%	17%	34%	38%	BG 8	8%	14%	17%	25%	22%	37%	54%	61%

cpulimit equivalent to 50%								
FG	1FG	2FG	3FG	4FG	5FG	6FG	7FG	8
BG 1	0%	3%	7%	7%	8%	1%	2%	2%
BG 2	7%	4%	6%	7%	7%	1%	7%	8%
BG 3	2%	5%	11%	10%	7%	3%	10%	21%
BG 4	3%	7%	9%	10%	6%	6%	22%	33%
BG 5	4%	10%	12%	17%	7%	19%	35%	47%
BG 6	6%	13%	15%	23%	11%	30%	47%	60%
BG 7	11%	15%	21%	27%	18%	46%	63%	78%
BG 8	12%	21%	26%	35%	30%	61%	80%	99%

the CPU assigned to the tasks grows. When the limit is defined to the 40% or the 50% of a CPU, the combinations with a slowdown greater than 15% are the 26.6% and the 40.6% of the total.

5.4 Summary

Our evaluation shows that the proposed Linux scheduler minimizes the performance drop that the foreground processes suffer when they are executed alongside CPU-intensive background processes.

SCHED_IDLE: In contrast to running the background processes with a high *nice* value or the SCHED_IDLE policy, our scheduler did not produce a slowdown greater than 15% SCHED_IDLE produced a slowdown greater than 15% in 37.5% of the combinations.

cgroups: Comparing our scheduler to cgroups, while our scheduler does not produced a slowdown greater than 15%, cgroups produced a slowdown greater or equal to 15% in the 35.9% of the combinations when we used a *cpu.shares* proportion that gives to the background processes the 10% of the CPUs. The slowdown increased as the *cpu.shares* proportion grew. When the background processes were limited to 50% of the CPUs, the slowdown values greater than 15% grew to 65.6% of the combinations.

CPULimit: Comparing our approach with cpulimit, that tool produces less slowdown when the proportion of CPU is very low. When cpulimit is set to 10% of a CPU, none of the foreground processes produced a slowdown greater than 15%. When the background processes ran with a cpulimit of 40% or 50%, the combinations with a slowdown greater than 15% grew to 26.6% and 40.6% of the total. In contrast, our scheduler did not produced a slowdown greater than 15%.

6 Related Work

Both slowdown and the ways to limit it have been widely studied in parallel programming [12]. There, the need for coordinating multiple tasks in different computers introduces delays that affect the execution time of the tasks. Many proposals aim to design and deploy the distributed systems in a way that these delays are as minimum as possible. In contrast, our research is focused on limiting the slowdown produced to end-user tasks that do not participate in the distributed processing.

Slowdown in Volunteer Computing. Many authors have proposed techniques to reduce the slowdown of the jobs running in the volunteer computing system. For instance, some works propose strategies to allocate interdependent jobs into near located desktops [2] or by using multi-objective optimization techniques [18]. However, these works are not focused on the slowdown produced to other applications.

Vyas and Subhlok [19] analyzed the slowdown produced by running volunteer computing on clusters. They evaluated three Linux kernel versions, the 2.4, 2.6 and a specially configured 2.6-tuned kernel, to determine which produced the least slowdown when these jobs run as low-priority processes. As conclusions, they defined guidelines to configure the kernel for these clusters. In addition, they argued for the support of *zero priority processes* in the OS schedulers which could "virtually eliminate the impact of volunteer computing on host applications [19]."

Slowdown and Fairness in Linux Systems. The Linux Scheduler have been subject of a lot of research. Initial works were focused on improving the performance of the initial O(N) scheduler [11,16]. Additional work were focused on improving the fairness and preventing the starvation of GUI applications running along CPU-bound tasks [10,20]. Further research was focused on supporting advanced scheduling policies [6,13], enhancing virtualization [9] and improving the efficiency in multiprocessors [4] and big-little architectures with heterogeneous processors [21]. Recently, some research have been focused on reducing idle cores in systems with a large number of processors [14]. However, none of these works aimed at implementing zero priority processes such as the suggested by the above authors.

7 Conclusions

Existing solutions to limit the CPU usage and reduce the priority of processes in Linux do not prevent Volunteer Computing platforms to produce a slowdown on the user's tasks. We developed a novel technique to limit the slowdown that the introduced tasks may cause: We created a new linux scheduling class that runs these tasks only if it considers that they will not produce a significant slowdown. The scheduler checks how many CPU cores are already executing tasks and use a processor-specific heuristic to determine if the new one may produce a performance drop. Our evaluation shows that this scheduler is able to produce a slowdown in user's tasks lesser than 15%, even when we introduced eight CPU-intensive background tasks.

We compared our approach with traditional techniques such as using the nice value, the SCHED_IDLE, the cgroups and CPUlimit tools. In contrast with these solutions, our scheduler was able to run combinations from 1 to 8 foreground processes and 1 to 8 background processes without producing any slowdown on foreground greater than the predefined limit.

Our evaluation considered CPU-intensive foreground user tasks. However, users typically run interactive applications that are different, i.e., I/O-bound tasks. We consider that our scheduler may prevent the slowdown to these processes too. An evaluation of the benefits of using our scheduler with interactive applications remains in the future work.

Our scheduler runs applications (such as virtual machines) when they will not affect other high-priority tasks. Existing cloud providers such as Google and Amazon offer low-priority virtual machines (VMs) to reduce the cost of batch workloads. We consider that our scheduler can be used in these scenarios. Further research is required to integrate our solution to existing cloud platforms.

References

1. Aas, J.: Understanding the Linux 2.6.8.1 CPU Scheduler. Technical report, SGI (2005)
2. Anderson, D.: Local scheduling for volunteer computing. In: Parallel and Distributed Processing Symposium, IPDPS 2007, pp. 1–8. IEEE (2007)
3. Anderson, D.P., Christensen, C., Allen, B.: Designing a runtime system for volunteer computing. In: SC 2006 Conference, p. 33 (2006)
4. Bryant, R., Hawkes, J.: Linux scalability for large NUMA systems. In: Linux Symposium, vol. 76 (2003)
5. Durrani, M.N., Shamsi, J.A.: Volunteer computing: requirements, challenges, and solutions. J. Netw. Comput. Appl. **39**, 369–380 (2014)
6. Faggioli, D., Checconi, F., Trimarchi, M., Scordino, C.: An EDF scheduling class for the Linux kernel. In: the Real-Time Linux Workshop (2009)
7. Intel Turbo Boost Technology in Intel Core Microarchitecture (Nehalem) Based Processors (2008). https://goo.gl/kvA1YZ
8. Intel Core i7–4770 Processor Specifications (2013). https://goo.gl/jjH5yT
9. Jiang, W., et al.: CFS optimizations to KVM threads on multi-core environment. In: Parallel and distributed systems, ICPADS 2009, pp. 348–354 (2009)
10. Jones, M.T.: Inside the Linux 2.6 completely fair scheduler. IBM Developer Works Technical Report 2009 (2009)
11. Kravetz, M., Franke, H., Nagar, S., Ravindran, R.: Enhancing Linux scheduler scalability. In: Proceedings of the Ottawa Linux Symposium (2001)
12. La'adan, O., Barak, A.: Inter process communication optimization in a scalable computing cluster (chap. 4). In: Annual Review of Scalable Computing, pp. 121–180. World Scientific Publishing (1999)
13. Lelli, J., Lipari, G., Faggioli, D., Cucinotta, T.: An efficient and scalable implementation of global EDF in Linux. In: Workshop on Operating Systems Platforms for Embedded Real-Time Applications, OSPERT 2011, pp. 6–15 (2011)
14. Lozi, J.P., Lepers, B., Funston, J., Gaud, F., Quéma, V., Fedorova, A.: The Linux scheduler: a decade of wasted cores. In: 11th European Conference on Computer Systems, p. 1. ACM (2016)
15. Menage, P.: CGroups, Linux Kernel Documentation (2006). https://www.kernel.org/doc/Documentation/cgroup-v1/cgroups.txt
16. Molloy, S.P., Honeyman, P.: Scalable Linux scheduling. In: USENIX Technical Conference, Boston (2001)
17. Rosales, E., Sotelo, G., de la Vega, A., Diaz, C.O., Gómez, C.E., Castro, H.E.: Harvesting idle CPU resources for desktop grid Computing while limiting the slowdown generated to end-users. Cluster Comput. **18**(4), 1331–1350 (2015). https://doi.org/10.1007/s10586-015-0482-4
18. Rubab, S., Hassan, M.F., Mahmood, A.K., Shah, N.M.: Bin packing multiconstraints job scheduling heuristic for heterogeneous volunteer grid resources. In: Fourth International Conference on Computer Science & Computational Mathematics, ICCSCM 2015 (2015)
19. Vyas, D., Subhlok, J.: Volunteer computing on clusters. In: Frachtenberg, E., Schwiegelshohn, U. (eds.) JSSPP 2006. LNCS, vol. 4376, pp. 161–175. Springer, Heidelberg (2007). https://doi.org/10.1007/978-3-540-71035-6_8

20. Wong, C.S., Tan, I., Kumari, R.D., Wey, F.: Towards achieving fairness in the Linux scheduler. ACM SIGOPS Oper. Syst. Rev. **42**(5), 34–43 (2008)
21. Yu, K., Han, D., Youn, C., Hwang, S., Lee, J.: Power-aware task scheduling for big. Little mobile processor. In: 2013 International SoC Design Conference (ISOCC), pp. 208–212. IEEE (2013)

Reliability Analysis in Desktop Cloud Systems

Carlos E. Gómez[1,2]($\boxtimes$), Jaime Chavarriaga[1], and Harold E. Castro[1]

[1] Computing and Systems Engineering Department, Universidad de Los Andes,
Bogota, Colombia
{ja.chavarriaga908,hcastro}@uniandes.edu.co
[2] Universidad del Quindío, Armenia, Colombia
carloseg@uniquindio.edu.co

Abstract. Although users of desktop clouds perceive these platforms
as typical cloud infrastructure (IaaS) services, these platforms must face
reliability threats not found in traditional clusters and data centers.
Desktop Clouds are opportunistic platforms that offer cloud computing services using computers that people use for their daily activities.
For instance, platforms such as CernVM and UnaCloud, harvest idle
resources on computer labs to run clusters of virtual machines and support scientific applications. These platforms must deal with interruptions
and interference caused by the users on the desktops and the applications they run. In this paper we describe diverse strategies we propose
to increase the reliability in desktop cloud platforms. First, we present a
reliability analysis based on extended threat propagation chains. Then,
we describe mitigation strategies for the identified threats. Finally, we
discuss some evaluations we performed.

Keywords: Reliability · Fault tolerance · Threat propagation chains ·
Global snapshot · Checkpointing

1 Introduction

Desktop clouds (DC) are opportunistic platforms that offer Cloud Computing
services on common desktop computers [1]. While users perform daily activities, significant computing resources are idle. DC exploit these idle resources to
execute virtual machines (VMs), totally configured, without disturbing users.

Some examples of DC are *UnaCloud* [14] and *CernVM*[1] [15], which use computers located on university or business campuses to offer some infrastructure
services (IaaS), which can be computational support in academic and scientific
projects, in this case, without using dedicated hardware. In this model, desktop
users' applications run concurrently with VMs managed by DCs [9].

DCs are more susceptible to service failures than traditional cloud platforms
since its infrastructure is not based on dedicated data centers neither dedicated

---

[1] https://cernvm.cern.ch/.

© Springer Nature Switzerland AG 2020
H. Florez and S. Misra (Eds.): ICAI 2020, CCIS 1277, pp. 165–180, 2020.
https://doi.org/10.1007/978-3-030-61702-8_12

hardware. However, the presence of computer users at the same time that VMs are running is the most critical aspect in the operation of a DC. It is possible that the tasks executed by a DC are affected by interference and interruptions caused by the applications that the users on the computers run. Typically DCs, do not offer warranties on the execution of the tasks sent to the platform. It is the responsibility of the user of the DC to verify the correct execution of their VMs. Therefore, the DC have in the reliability one of the aspects in which there is work to be done.

This article is an extended version of a work presented by us in [10]. Here, we present a more general reliability analysis based on extended threat propagation chains and considering different implementations of DCs. We describe the faults that DCs can be experienced and propose mitigation strategies to increase the reliability in these systems.

The paper is organized as follows. In Sect. 2 we give a background, describing DC systems and the threats propagation chains used in this paper. Sect. 3 presents our fault analysis for DCs covering not only the faults, errors and failures, but also the consequences of failures, the actor causing the faults and a comprehensive mitigation strategy to face them. In Sect. 4 we present our approach for providing a scalable provisioning of VMs, and Sect. 5 summarizes our global snapshot solution to deal with VM execution failures in a DC. The conclusion and future work are in the final section.

2   Background

Desktop cloud (DC) systems take advantage of idle capacity of computers in a campus to provide infrastructure (IaaS) services. These systems combine ideas from virtualization and volunteer computing to offer computing resources to academic and scientific projects. For DC users, the system offers infrastructure just like any other cloud platform. Desktop Clouds run VMs on desktops in a university computer labs or a business campus [3]. In this section we briefly introduce the fundamentals of DCs and the threat propagation chains that we use to analyze the reliability of these systems.

2.1   Desktop Cloud Systems

DC systems have received multiple names in the literature. There are many papers describing these solutions using names such as volunteer cloud [7,11,13], non-dedicated cloud [1], nebulas [6] peer-to-peer cloud [2], ad hoc cloud [12] and opportunistic cloud [14]. These platforms, or their users, may use dedicated or volunteer nodes to provide infrastructure (IaaS) services according to the needs or policies defined in the system. Some of those projects have noted the difficulties of providing a reliable service on unreliable computing resources.

UnaCloud [14] is our implementation of a DC. this platform was designed and developed exclusively to support opportunistic cloud services, where the users using the desktops do not perceive that additional processing is executed in their machines. This platform, in use since 2011, is used currently to run diverse scientific applications on virtual clusters running on the computer labs in the Universidad de los Andes, Colombia.

2.2 Operation of Desktop Cloud Systems

We have identified two phases in the operation of DCs in order to better understand the different anomalies a DC may experiment: (1) conditioning phase and, (2) operation phase. These phases are described below.

Conditioning. The conditioning phase groups five activities: (1) Preparation of virtual images (VIs). It refers to the creation and configuration of VIs. It includes the operating system and applications with all their dependencies. (2) Creating a cluster. The DC user creates a cluster as a set of VIs. (3) Request to deploy a cluster. The user of the DC requests a specific number of MVs to be executed for each VI in the cluster. (4) Scheduling. The system allocates the VMs to the PMs of the computer room. (5) Provisioning. It consists of sending the files from the VIs to the selected PMs, creating the VMs and configuring them according to the requirements of the DC users.

Operation. The operation phase groups two activities: (1) VM management. The DC performs the following operations on the VMs: to start, to reconfigure, to turn-off. (2) Monitoring. The DC obtains usage statistics of both PMs and VMs. The DC controls the execution of VMs.

2.3 Threats Against Dependability

In this section we present the basic concepts of dependability in computer systems along with the threats propagation chain.

According to Avizienis [5], "dependability of a system is the ability to avoid failures that are more frequent and severe than is acceptable". The same author in [4] establishes, the threats against the reliability of a computer system are: faults, errors and failures.

Fault. It refers to a type of software-level interruption. In computing, also known as *trap* or *exception*. It is a strange condition, anomaly or defect in a computer system that leads to an error. An error does not necessarily occur as an immediate consequence because the environment can activate a fault or not.

Error. Manifestation of a fault (anomaly or interruption) in a system. Part of the state of the system that as a consequence of a fault, is responsible for leading to a failure.

Failure. Event in the system that occurs when the service delivered is not correctM; that is, when the service does not comply with specifications because it is not well specified, or because it produces unexpected results.

These threats can be seen as a chain in which an anomaly or interruption can cause an error, and in turn, an error can lead to a failure in the service, as can be seen in Fig. 1. Upon completion of the succession of these events, a computer system can deliver incorrect services or stop providing the service.

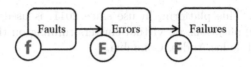

Fig. 1. Threats propagation chain

To illustrate the concept of the propagation of threats against dependability, consider the case of a user who turns off a computer where a VM that is part of the DC is running. In this case, the interruption in the execution of the computer causes a connection error to the software agent in the PM. This error leads to a service failure in which the DC agent in the PM is not accessible. It is important to note that several faults (anomalies or interruptions) can cause the same error, and in the same way, several errors can lead to the same failure.

3   Desktop Cloud Fault Analysis

3.1   Extended Threats Propagation Chain

In this section we present a DC fault analysis, in order to understand the faults that can occur in a DC. Two years ago, we presented a characterization of the faults that could occur in DC platforms, analyzing *UnaCloud* our case study.

With about 10 years running *UnaCloud*, as a real implementation of a DC, we have accumulated a valuable experience that allows us to identify the problems in its operation, both in the conditioning phase and in the operation phase. However, this time we want to make a more general analysis to understand the reliability of DC in an abstract context, which can be applied to any DC.

A DC can experience service faults at any time. The cause of a fault can not always be determined since, considering the threats propagation chain shown in Fig. 1, different faults (anomalies or interruptions) can lead to the same error and several errors can cause same service failure. This can be caused, among others, because: (1) the desktop computer was turned off, or (2) the PM was restarted.

To perform our fault analysis, we initially used the threats propagation chain (§ Fig. 1). Consider the example in Fig. 2, in which a failure in the system is analyzed due to the impossibility of copying the VI in the selected computer to execute a VM based on that VI. In this example, the failure occurs because one of the files that make up the VI can not be copied, which in turn is due to insufficient disk space on the destination computer.

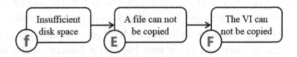

Fig. 2. Example of the threats propagation chain

Although it can clearly be understood that there is a fault (insufficient disk space) that can cause an error (a file can not be copied) and this error can provoke a specific failure for the service (the VI can not be copied), this threats propagation chain is quite limited in the identification of the problem and its corresponding solution.

In the operation of a DC, this fault occurs when, in the scheduling, the DC server selects a specific computer to host the VI, but the selected computer does not have enough space on the disk, causing that the VI can not be copied. In this case, the result of not being able to copy VI in the PM is that the DC user will not be able to use a VM based on the VI.

In [10], we proposed extending the threats propagation chain to include the author or user causing the fault and their mitigation strategies, as well as the consequences of service failures. By taking into account these new elements, we will be able to better distinguish the threats in our DC and, in this way, facilitate the automation of corrective measures.

Figure 3 shows the same example of the extended threats propagation chain, which includes the actor or user causing the fault (anomaly or interruption), a mitigation strategy proposed to face the faults, and the consequence of the failure.

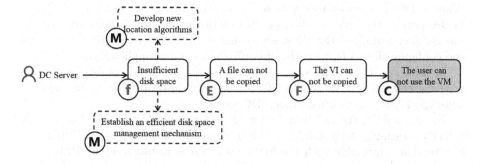

Fig. 3. Example of extended threats propagation chain

In this case, we have two suggestions to mitigate these faults: (1) modify the location algorithms, so that they consider the available capacity of the hard disk of each eligible computer before assigning the VMs to the corresponding PMs and, (2) establish an efficient disk space management mechanism.

Therefore, we will perform the analysis of the faults using the extended threats propagation chain (§ Fig. 4), through which not only the actor or the user that causes the fault can be determined, but also the consequences of the failures. In addition, it allows us to include some strategies to face the faults that affect the normal functioning of the DC.

This analysis includes the most relevant failures that we have identified, two in the conditioning phase and two in the operation phase:

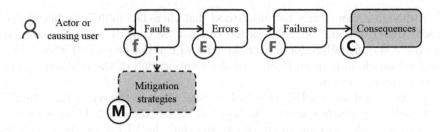

Fig. 4. Extended threats propagation chain

(1) the hypervisor can not configure the VM; (2) the VI can not be copied; (3) the VMs that run on the same PM are not accessible; and (4) the DC server can not communicate with the client.

It is important to highlight that the fault analysis must be carried out periodically, since new threats may arise according to the evolution of the platform, the applications that are being executed and the behavior of the users.

3.2   The Hypervisor Can Not Configure the VM

When a DC user wants to create a cluster, the VIs must exist on the server. In this part of the process, the intervention of the DC user is definitive for the successful execution of the VMs, given that it is the DC user who must create and configure their VIs, with the operating system and applications.

In addition, these VIs must comply with the essential conditions for the proper execution of VMs in the DC. These conditions are difficult to meet for non-expert users, as is usual among DC users.

For example, if the DC user (*actor or user causing U_1*) installed an unsupported operating system (*fault f_1*), or he did not install the hypervisor extensions in a version compatible with the hypervisor that is installed in the PMs (*fault f_4*), the VI that uploads to the server will not be compatible with the DC (*error E_1*).

Table 1. Faults in the preparation of a VI

Notation	Fault
f_1	The operating system is not supported
f_2	The network adapter is not configured in bridge mode
f_3	The IP address is not static
f_4	The Hypervisor extensions have not been installed or the version does not correspond
f_5	The superuser account is not correct
f_6	The superuser password supplied does not match

On the other hand, if the superuser account in the VI is not properly configured (*fault f_5*) or the password of the superuser supplied for the VI does not correspond with the configured password (*fault f_6*), the hypervisor can not log in to the MV (*error E_2*). In either case, if the VI is not compatible with the DC or the hypervisor can not log in to the VM, the hypervisor can not configure the VM (*failure F_1*). Therefore, the DC user can not use the VM (*consequence C_1*).

In Table 1 we list the faults ($f_1 - f_6$) that the DC user can cause in the preparation of an VI.

As already mentioned, the these faults arise from the conditions required to run VMs in a DC, and although these conditions are specific to the *UnaCloud* context, in reality, any implementation of a DC could establish yours, therefore, it is important to consider them.

To face these faults, we propose that the DC be easy to use for researchers, thus they can create VIs easily.

The mitigation strategy we propose is to offer a catalog of preconfigured VIs created by expert users (*mitigation strategy M_1*).

Figure 5 shows the extended chain of threat propagation that lead to failure F_1.

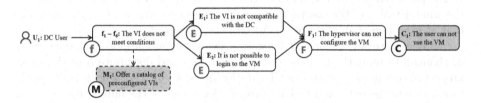

Fig. 5. F_1 — The hypervisor can not configure the VM

Note that we are using the notation in Table 2 to identify the elements that are part of the extended threats propagation chain that leads to the failure F_1. This notation will be used in the rest of the paper.

Table 2. Notation to identify the elements of the extended chain of threat propagation to dependability

Element	Notation
Actor or user causing	U_i
Fault	f_i
Error	E_i
Failure	F_i
Consequence	C_i
Mitigation strategy	M_i

3.3   The VI Can Not Be Copied

In the conditioning phase the DC user prepares the VIs and uploads them to the server. With the VIs available in the DC, this user can create a cluster and request its deployment. The DC server schedules the location of the VMs and performs the provisioning, which consists of the transmission of the VIs to the assigned PMs, the creation of the VMs and their configuration.

The *failure* F_2 occurs when a VI can not be copied to the assigned PM by the DC Server. As a result, VMs based on that VI can not be created (*consequence* C_2).

We identified two faults that prevent VIs from being copied correctly. First, it can happen that at least one of the files that is part of a VI can not be copied (*error* E_3) because the destination computer does not have enough space on the disk (*fault* f_7). To mitigate this fault, we suggest establishing an efficient disk space management mechanism (mitigation strategy M_2).

Second, the same *error* E_3 can occur due to network congestion (*fault* f_8) during the transmission of the VIs. The intensive use of the network due to the transmission of the bulky VIs by the DC server (actor or user causing U_2), added to the potential use by the users of the PMs (*actor or user causing* U_3) or by the administrator of the computer room (*actor or user causing* U_4), it can cause that at least one of the files of the VI can not be copied.

To deal with an episode of network congestion, we propose to establish a mechanism to limit the transfer of replicated data and distribute over time the process of copying files with the VIs (*mitigation strategy* M_3). Figure 6 allows us to appreciate the extended threats propagation chain of the failure F_2.

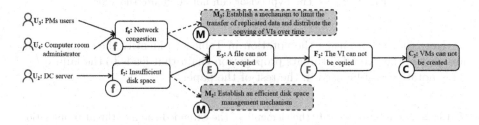

Fig. 6. F_2 — The VI can not be copied

It is important to note that the faults f_7 and f_8 show that the scalability in the provisioning is a serious difficulty in a DC. Therefore, implementing these identified mitigation strategies can help address not only these faults at the individual level, but also contribute significantly to improving the scalability of a DC.

3.4   The VMs that Run on the Same PM Are Not Accessible; the DC Server Can Not Communicate with the Client

In the operation phase of a DC, it may happen that, at a given moment, the VMs that are running in the same PM are not accessible (*failure* F_3) or that the DC client in a PM is not accessible (*failure* F_4).

These two failures F_3 and F_4, are very related. According to our analysis, the *failure* F_3 can happen because the hypervisor does not respond (*error* E_4).

The faults f_9 to f_{11}, can be the cause of the E_4 error. f_9: the PM has been turned off; f_{10}: the PM has been restarted; f_{11}: the hypervisor is blocked.

The three faults can be caused by a deliberate or accidental action by PM users (*actor or originator user* U_3) or by the computer room administrator (*actor or causing user* U_4); the interruption in the execution of the VMs that run on the same PM by hypervisor blocked (*fault* f_{11}) it is a situation that can happen to the hypervisor (*actor or causing user* U_5) in the middle of its execution. The consequences of the failure F_3 depend on the particular application that is currently running on the VM (*consequence* C_3).

To mitigate the effect of the fault because a desktop computer was turned off (f_9), we propose that, if the PM is going to be put into service in a relatively short time, save the state of the execution of the system that runs in the DC and resume execution in the same PM from the last stored state (*mitigation strategy* M_4). However, if resuming the execution of the host will be more delayed, we can use the same mitigation strategy, but recovering its execution on another computer (*mitigation strategy* M_5), strategy that could also be applied if the fault it is because the PM has been reset (fault f_{10}). If the hypervisor is blocked (fault f_{11}), our proposal is to restart the hypervisor (*mitigation strategy* M_6).

The F_4 failure can occur when the DC client does not respond (*error* E_5), due to the faults f_9 and f_{10} already mentioned or because the DC client (*actor or originator user* U_6) is blocked (*fault* f_{12}). In this case, the mitigation strategies identified for the faults f_9 and f_{10} are the same as for the (*failure* F_3), that is, the mitigation strategies (M_4 and M_5), along with the strategy (M_7, which consists of restarting the DC client.

The failure (F_4) has different consequences, depending on the state of the deployment, due to lack of communication between the DC server and client. For example, it is not possible to create new VMs (*consequence* C_1), it is not possible to request new deployments (*consequence* C_4), it is not possible to request files for new VIs (*consequence* C_5) or VMs on the same PM do not report status to the DC server (*consequence* C_6).

Figure 7 shows the extended threats propagation chain for the failures (F_3) and (F_4).

Thanks to the extended threats propagation chain, it was possible, on the one hand, to identify in greater detail the most relevant faults in the conditioning and operation phase for a DC, and on the other hand, to propose strategies to face them.

This analysis allows us to direct efforts in two directions: (1) Develop an efficient solution that allows the DC to make scalable provisioning of VMs. (2)

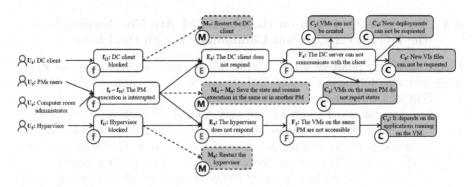

Fig. 7. The VMs that run on the same PM are not accessible; the DC server can not communicate with the client

Develop a solution that allows the DC to save the execution state of a system running on VMs, and resume the execution from a saved state, using the same or other PMs, if necessary.

In the following two sections we describe the implementation of the mitigation strategies that we developed to face the identified faults.

4   Scalable Provisioning of Virtual Machines

One of the results of the DC fault analysis allowed us to identify the weaknesses in the conditioning phase. We found two critical aspects that affect this phase: (1) The preparation of the VIs is carried out by the DC users. If a VI does not meet one or more of the established conditions, the hypervisor will not be able to correctly configure the VMs based on that VI and the VMs will not be provisioned. (2) The provisioning of multiple VMs is a fragile process with limitations in scalability. The files of the VIs are voluminous and must be transmitted through the network and stored on desktop computers. On the one hand, it is necessary to implement an efficient disk space management mechanism. On the other hand, the transmission of VIs congests the network and is very delayed.

4.1   Mitigation Strategies for Scalable Provisioning

We have implemented three mitigation strategies that in order to provide scalable provisioning of VMs in a DC.

Offer a Catalog of Preconfigured VIs. All IaaS providers allow their users to create and execute instances (VMs) with the operating system and some basic applications previously installed and configured. In particular, the analyzed DC has based its service model in which the DC user can run their usual environment to make it easier to use. As a consequence, the DC user must create and configure the VIs, and send them to the server in order to use these VIs in the deployment of their clusters and, in this way, to execute their applications.

Although it is true that for the user it may be easier to run their applications in a very similar or identical environment to the one he usually uses, it is also true that complying with the required conditions imposed by the DC for the successful provisioning of VMs is a difficult task for its users.

Having a catalog of VIs to create VMs from them would allow DC users to access DC services more quickly using a VI correctly prepared by expert users.

Establish an Efficient Disk Space Management Mechanism. The hypervisors offer several writing modes on virtual hard drives. The writing mode selected for each disk determines its behavior after the write operations of a VM and determines the operation of the *snapshots*.

It is very common for a DC to use virtual disks in normal write mode, in which VMs can read and write as computers do on real disks. This write mode on the disks used in the VMs works very well when there is only one VM running on each PM. However, when it is necessary to run more than one VM on the same computer, it is possible that the VMs have a significant part of the content of their virtual disk in common. Unfortunately, each VM of a DC has its disk in a separate file, which typically occupies several GB.

A disk in multiattach writing mode can be connected to multiple VMs and these can be run at the same time. When connecting each VM to a multiattach disk, a differential disk is created to save the modifications of that VM with respect to the original disk, keeping isolated the individual content of each VM. multiattach mode is used to share files that are rarely modified. In this way, the modified blocks are stored in differential disks that remain relatively small and the content is saved only once. Only fixed-size virtual disks can be configured as multiattach writing disks in the current version of *Oracle VirtualBox*[2].

Therefore, we suggest to employ multiattach writing mode disks as a mechanism for an efficient disk space management in DCs.

Establish a Mechanism to Limit the Transfer of Replicated Data and Distribute the Copying of VIs over Time. As a complement to the two previous strategies, the mechanism to limit the transfer of replicated data consists of preloading the preconfigured VIs created by expert users using discs in multiattach writing mode. These VIs or templates are copied to the disks of desktop computers at times of low utilization or when maintenance is performed, according to the planning made by the administrator of the computer rooms. The objective is that the templates are copied in the computers of the rooms without this process affecting the network or the work of the users of the PMs.

---

[2] https://www.virtualbox.org.

4.2 Preliminary Evaluation

To evaluate the mitigation strategies in the scalable provisioning of VMs, we analyzed the use of disk space and the VM provisioning time.

Use of Disk Space. We seek to answer the following research question: What is the benefit of using multiattach disks instead of using normal disks in the disk space occupied by one or several VMs in the same PM?

Figure 8 shows the behavior of the use of disk space to host from 1 to 8 VMs with the same operating system and some applications. A VI occupying 3.01 GB was used to carry out this test. It can be noted that as the number of VMs in the same PM increases, disk space increases at a rate of 3.01 GB per VM if disks are used in normal write mode, while the growth is 250 MB if the disks used have the multiattach write disk configured. However, the multiattach disk requires a special configuration that makes the first VM larger.

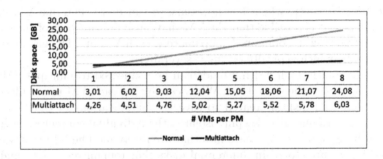

Fig. 8. Disk space of VMs: normal vs multiattach write modes

It is evident, according to the Fig. 8, that the use of multiattach disks is much more efficient than the use of normal disks, with respect to the use of disk space, given the possibility of having VMs that have in common a significant part of its content.

VM Provisioning Time. The creation of VMs can be analyzed by comparing the time used to create a VM using normal disks and multiattach, as we propose in the mitigation strategy. In this case, the research question we wanted to answer is the following: What is the benefit of using multiattach disks instead of using normal disks in the VM provisionng time of one or more VMs on the same PM?

In order to answer this question, we first analyze the time of creating a VM on a PM using normal and multiattach disks. The creation time of a VM includes the transmission of the VI to the PM. For the analysis of the creation time of VMs, when using normal disks, we create a second VM and compare the time it takes to create them. It is not necessary to create more VMs, since the creation of an additional VM behaves as if it were the second VM. For the second VM, the creation is done through the cloning of the VM.

Figure 9 shows the provisioning times of VMs for this test.

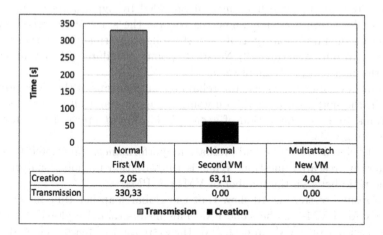

Fig. 9. VM provisioning time

It can be noted that the provisioning time of the first VM using normal disks includes 330.33 s of transmission and 2.05 s of creation, for a total time of 332.38 s. Provisioning a second VM with normal disks is done by cloning the VM, which lasts 63.11 s, and there is no transmission of the VI, since a first VM already exists. The cloning time is directly proportional to the size of the disk.

Finally, the provisioning time of a VM, when using multiattach disks, is approximately 4 s. In this case, it is indifferent whether it is the first MV or a later one. When the disk is preloaded, it does not require the transmission of the VI files.

Provisioning times using the suggested mitigation strategies show that it is possible to offer scalable provisioning of VMs in DC systems.

5   Global Snapshot of a Distributed System Running on Virtual Machines

When the DC is in operation and the VMs are running, the DC user may lose the work done so far if the execution of the VMs is interrupted. As a mitigation strategy we propose to save the state of the whole system and resume execution in the same PMs or in others, if it becomes necessary.

In [8] we proposed a global snapshot protocol for its application in the context of DCs over TCP/IP networks. In this work, we obtain consistent global snapshots for general distributed systems running on the VMs of a DC preserving communications in progress when resuming execution. Our protocol maintains the semantics of the system without modifying applications on VMs or the hypervisors.

We extended the snapshot function provided by hypervisors for individual VMs to offer a solution that allows us to save the state of the whole system considering the limitations of a DC and the following principles for the solution: (1) No extra infrastructure, (2) No single points of failure, (3) Low impact on DC performance, and (4) Lightweight.

In our development, we use the reliability mechanisms of the TCP protocol, colors in the nodes to mark the outgoing datagrams and filtering of incoming datagrams, and the adaptation of a *one-phase commit* protocol to control the participating PMs.

We develop a prototype and evaluate its performance. We wanted to answer the following research question: What is the variation in global snapshot time and the ratio between the number of VMs per PMs?

The results of the Fig. 10 show that the global snapshot time increases significantly for 4 VMs on the same PM. This means that if a global snapshot is obtained with 1 or 2 VMs in each PM, the system offers reasonable and highly consistent global snapshot times.

However, when obtaining global snapshots with 4 VMs in the same PM, there is a significant increase in global snapshot time, which allows us to conclude that if we want to offer this alternative as a mitigation strategy, it is convenient to avoid systems that have more than 2 VMs on the same PM.

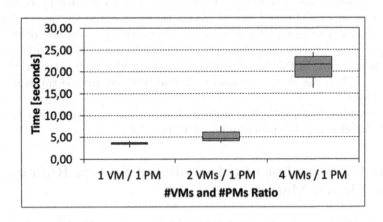

Fig. 10. Global snapshot time by #VMs and #PMs ratio

6   Conclusion and Future Work

This article presents a reliability analysis for desktop cloud systems. It includes a desktop cloud fault analysis based on extended threat propagation chains, which allows us to understand in a broad way the failures in the operation of a DC and its causes. The extended chain includes information of the actor causing the faults, the consequences of failures, and some mitigation strategies that can help face the faults. We found in our analysis that main factors that may affect provisioning of VMs in a DC are the use of disk space and the transmission of virtual images over the network. In addition, regarding the execution of the VMs, we identified that applications and actions performed by users in the desktops may cause the loss of the work done. To improve the reliability of DCs we propose: (1) we propose to use preloaded VIs in the disks of PMs, using disks in multiattach writing mode, and (2) provide means to obtain global snapshots of distributed systems running on virtual machines to resume failed executions. For the future, we have considered the use of monitoring information to improve decisions regarding VMs allocation and scheduling. We are also considering new analyzes and experiments to validate the findings presented in this paper.

References

1. Alwabel, A., Walters, R.J., Wills, G.B.: A view at desktop clouds. In: International Workshop on Emerging Software as a Service and Analytics (ESaaSA 2014), Barcelona, Spain, pp. 55–61. ScitePress (2014)
2. Amoretti, M., Grazioli, A., Zanichelli, F.: An autonomic approach for p2p/cloud collaborative environments. Peer-to-Peer Networking Appl. **9**(6), 1226–1241 (2016)
3. Anderson, D.P.: Volunteer computing: the ultimate cloud. ACM Crossroads **16**(3), 7–10 (2010)
4. Avizienis, A., Laprie, J.C., Randell, B., Landwehr, C.: Basic concepts and taxonomy of dependable and secure computing. IEEE Trans. Dependable Secure Comput. **1**(1), 11–33 (2004)
5. Avižienis, A.: A visit to the jungle of terminology. In: 2017 47th Annual IEEE/IFIP International Conference on Dependable Systems and Networks Workshop (DSN-W), pp. 149–152. IEEE, Denver (2017)
6. Chandra, A., Weissman, J.B.: Nebulas: Using distributed voluntary resources to build clouds. In: Workshop on Hot Topics in Cloud Computing (HotCloud 2009), San Diego, CA, USA, pp. 1–5. USENIX (2009)
7. Cunsolo, V.D., Distefano, S., Puliafito, A., Scarpa, M.: Volunteer computing and desktop cloud: the cloud@ home paradigm. In: Eighth IEEE International Symposium on Network Computing and Applications (NCA 2009), pp. 134–139. IEEE, Cambridge (2009)
8. Gómez, C.E., Castro, H.E., Varela, C.A.: Global snapshot of a distributed system running on virtual machines. In: 2017 29th International Symposium on Computer Architecture and High Performance Computing (SBAC-PAD), pp. 169–176. IEEE, Sao Paulo (2017)
9. Gómez, C.E., Chavarriaga, J., Bonilla, D.C., Castro, H.E.: Global snapshot file tracker. In: Florez, H., Diaz, C., Chavarriaga, J. (eds.) ICAI 2018. CCIS, vol. 942, pp. 90–104. Springer, Cham (2018). https://doi.org/10.1007/978-3-030-01535-0_7
10. Gómez, Carlos E., Chavarriaga, Jaime, Castro, Harold E.: Fault characterization and mitigation strategies in desktop cloud systems. In: Meneses, Esteban, Castro, Harold, Barrios Hernández, Carlos Jaime, Ramos-Pollan, Raul (eds.) CARLA 2018. CCIS, vol. 979, pp. 322–335. Springer, Cham (2019). https://doi.org/10.1007/978-3-030-16205-4_24

11. Marosi, A., Kovács, J., Kacsuk, P.: Towards a volunteer cloud system. Future Gener. Comput. Syst. **29**(6), 1442–1451 (2013)
12. McGilvary, G.A.: Ad hoc cloud computing. Ph.D. thesis, The University of Edinburgh (2014)
13. Mengistu, Tessema M., Alahmadi, Abdulrahman M., Alsenani, Yousef., Albuali, Abdullah, Che, Dunren: cuCloud: volunteer computing as a service (VCaaS) System. In: Luo, Min, Zhang, Liang-Jie (eds.) CLOUD 2018. LNCS, vol. 10967, pp. 251–264. Springer, Cham (2018). https://doi.org/10.1007/978-3-319-94295-7_17
14. Rosales, E., Castro, H., Villamizar, M.: UnaCloud: opportunistic cloud computing infrastructure as a service. In: Second International Conferences on Cloud Computing, GRIDs, and Virtualization (CLOUD COMPUTING 2011), Rome, Italy, pp. 187–194. ThinkMind (2011)
15. Segal, B., et al.: LHC cloud computing with CernVM. In: 13th International Workshop on Advanced Computing and Analysis Techniques in Physics Research (ACAT 2010), Jaipur, India, p. 004. PoS (2010)

Data Analysis

A Case-Based Approach to Assess Employees' Satisfaction with Work Guidelines in Times of the Pandemic

Ana Fernandes[1] , Margarida Figueiredo[2] , Almeida Dias[3] , Jorge Ribeiro[4] ,
José Neves[3,5] , and Henrique Vicente[5,6(✉)]

[1] Departamento de Química, Escola de Ciências e Tecnologia, Universidade de Évora, Évora,
Portugal
anavilafernandes@gmail.com

[2] Departamento de Química, Escola de Ciências e Tecnologia, Centro de Investigação em
Educação e Psicologia, Universidade de Évora, Évora, Portugal
mtf@uevora.pt

[3] Instituto Politécnico de Saúde do Norte, CESPU, Famalicão, Portugal
a.almeida.dias@gmail.com

[4] Instituto Politécnico de Viana do Castelo, Rua da Escola Industrial e Comercial de
Nun'Álvares, 4900-347 Viana Do Castelo, Portugal
jribeiro@estg.ipvc.pt

[5] Centro Algoritmi, Universidade do Minho, Braga, Portugal
jneves@di.uminho.pt

[6] Departamento de Química, Escola de Ciências e Tecnologia, REQUIMTE/LAQV,
Universidade de Évora, Évora, Portugal
hvicente@uevora.pt

Abstract. The actual pandemic crisis posed new challenges for organizations that had to adapt new working procedures to prevent infection. In this context, monitoring employee satisfaction is paramount, but a very difficult task. To respond to this challenge, a workable problem-solving methodology was developed and tested. It examines the dynamics between *Logic Programming* and the *Laws of Thermodynamics* for *Knowledge Representation and Reasoning*. Such formalisms are consistent with a computer-based approach based on *Case-Based Reasoning*, the ultimate goal of which is to assess employee satisfaction in water analysis laboratories. The model was trained and tested with real data, collected through questionnaires, exhibiting an overall accuracy of 85.9%.

Keywords: COVID–19 · Human resources management · Organizational performance · Water laboratories · Case-Based reasoning

1 Introduction

The health sector is central to the well-being of society, and people become gradually more important to the proper functioning of such area. Indeed, the COVID–19 pandemics are a major challenge for health, for organizations and for society. On the other hand,

© Springer Nature Switzerland AG 2020
H. Florez and S. Misra (Eds.): ICAI 2020, CCIS 1277, pp. 183–196, 2020.
https://doi.org/10.1007/978-3-030-61702-8_13

work activities are potential sources of exposure to the virus due to the closeness of employees and customers when acting according to their obligations [1]. Maintaining the health of professionals who continue to work is therefore essential to control the spread of the disease. Last but not least, and according to the guidelines announced by the World Health Organization, all organizations had to introduce new operating procedures such as social distance in order to avoid the spread of the virus [2]. In order to maintain the productivity and satisfaction of customers and employees, all new processes and working measures must be understood and accepted by each one [3]. The entire team should be satisfied, as employee satisfaction is highly linked to productivity, personal fulfillment, and customer satisfaction. However, assessing employee satisfaction is a difficult task that comprises a variety of issues that depend on both the employee and the organization [4–6]. The present work aims to assess the satisfaction of the employees of water analysis laboratories with the new working methods in connection with the pandemic crisis.

The article is composed by five sections. Afterwards to a brief introduction to the problem, the basics used in the study are discussed, specifically the notion of *Entropy*, the procedures of *Logic Programming (LP)* for *Knowledge Representation and Reasoning (KRR)* [7–9] and a computer-based approach to *Case-Based Reasoning (CBR)* [10, 11]. Sections 3 presents the methodology and data processing, whereas in Sect. 4 the results are presented and discussed taking into account the notion of *Entropy* [12]. Finally, in Sect. 5, the main conclusions pointed out and future work are delineated.

2 Literature Review

2.1 Thermodynamics and Knowledge Representation and Reasoning

The methodology used in this article is grounded on thermodynamics, and aims to present the practices of *KRR* as an energy conversion process [9, 12, 13]. In order to illustrate the basics of the method, the first two laws of thermodynamics were taken into account, attending that one is faced to a dynamic system, i.e., that moves continuously from state to state. The *First Law* or the *Energy Saving Law* establishes that the total energy of an isolated system is constant, although it can take different forms. The *Second Law* is concerned with *Entropy*, i.e., the state of order of a system, establishing that in an isolated system the entropy never decreases. These qualities meet one's viewpoint of *KRR* practices. In fact, such does are inspired by the processes of energy degradation in an isolated system, which can be described as, viz.

- *exergy*, also denominated as energy ready for use or work ready for use, and corresponds to the energy fraction that may be used in an arbitrary way by a system, providing a measurement of its entropy, being figured by the dark zones (Fig. 2, Sect. 3.2);
- *vagueness*, i.e., that corresponds to the energy values that were or were not used, being represented by the dark regions with circles (Fig. 2, Sect. 3.2); and
- *anergy*, that can be set as an available energetic potential, i.e., the energy that was not consumed at moment, being denoted in Fig. 2 by the dark surfaces with asterisks [12, 13].

Several advances to *KRR* are based on the *LP* architype, namely in *Model* and *Proof Theory*. The problem-solving method used in this work is based on *Proof Theory* and is applied to logic programs that use an extension of the *LP* language [7] in the form of a finite summative of clauses, viz.

{

    $\neg p \leftarrow not\ p, not\ exception_p$

    $p \leftarrow p_1, \cdots, p_n, not\ q_1, \cdots, not\ q_m$

    $?\ (p_1, \cdots, p_n, not\ q_1, \cdots, not\ q_m)\ (n, m \geq 0)$

    $exception_{p_1}, \quad \cdots \quad, exception_{p_j}\ (0 \leq j \leq k),\ being\ k\ an\ integer\ number$

}

Program 1. A generic example of a *Logic Program*.

The former clause stands for the closure of the predicate, ",", symbolizes the "*logical and*", whereas "*?*" is a domain atom indicating "*falsity*". Finally, p_i, q_j, and p are positive atoms or atoms preceded by the classical negation sign $\neg$ [7]. Indeed, $\neg$ is used for strong negation, whereas *not* represents *negation-by-failure*, i.e., a failure in proving a declaration that was not expressed explicitly. Following this this line of thought, each program contains a number of abducibles expressed as exceptions to the extensions of the predicates included in the program, viz.

$$exception_{p_1}, \cdots, exception_{p_j}\ (0 \leq j \leq k),\ being\ k\ an\ integer\ number$$

designating data/information/knowledge that cannot be discarded. Clauses of the type, viz.

$$?(p_1, \cdots, p_n, notq_1, \cdots, notq_m)(n, m \geq 0)$$

stand for invariants, i.e., terms or expressions that determine the context and guide the understanding of the universe of discourse [8, 13].

2.2 Case-Based Reasoning

In the broadest sense, *CBR* can be labelled as the practice of solving new problems centered on solutions to parallel ones by reusing and adapting their solutions [10, 11]. In fact, the basic postulate that serves as the basis for *CBR* is *analog problems can be solved with analog solutions*. Various descriptions of the *CBR* can be found in the literature that converge to a model that includes the steps knowledge representation, retrieving, reusing, repairing, and maintaining. Neves et al. [14–16] presents an extended *CBR* cycle that includes a case optimization process, taking two new metrics into account, i.e., the *Quality-of-Information* (*QoI*) and the *Degree-of-Confidence* (*DoC*) on the solution so far obtained. The similarity measure is calculated using *QoI* and *DoC*, which allows the search space for similar cases to be narrowed.

3 Case Study

3.1 Methods

The study was performed in a water laboratory in southern Portugal. The participants' ages varied between 18 to 60 years (mean age 38 ± 20 years old), with 61% female and 39% male. A questionnaire to assess employee satisfaction with the new pandemic crisis procedures was created and used for a cohort of 64 personnel. The questionnaire was formed by into two segments, the initial one containing common questions (such as age, gender, educational qualifications, seniority and department within the organization), while the second covered points for assessing employees' satisfaction with the current restrictions.

3.2 Data Processing

Aiming to gather evidences related with the satisfaction of the employees concerning the new procedures related with the pandemic crisis, the participants were requested to mark the alternative(s) that best reflect their feelings concerning each item. In the case of the participant mark more than one alternative, he/she is also requested to specify the tendency of his/her answer, i.e., i.e., growing tendency (*Very Dissatisfied → Very Satisfied*) or the opposite (*Very Satisfied → Very Dissatisfied*) as displayed in Fig. 1. Taking into account the cohort dimension, the answer alternatives were given in a four items Likert scale, *viz.*

(4) *Very Satisfied*, (3) *Satisfied*, (2) *Dissatisfied*, (1) *Very Dissatisfied*

The answer alternatives are in accordance a four items Likert type scale with the *decreasing tendency*, to be in terms with the *First Law of Thermodynamics*, i.e. *from (4) Very Satisfied, (3) Satisfied, (2) Dissatisfied*, to *(1) Very Dissatisfied*, and from *(1) Very Dissatisfied), (2) Dissatisfied, (3) Satisfied*, to *(4) Very Satisfied* with the *increasing tendency*, to be in terms with the *Second Law of Thermodynamics*.

The items to be considered were structured in three distinct groups, i.e., *Training Related with COVID–19 Items – Four Items* (TRI – 4), *Resources Related Items – Four Items* (RRI – 4), and *Cleaning and Disinfection Related Items – Four Items* (CDRI – 4). The former one contains the items, viz.

I1 – The syllabus of COVID–19 in individual training procedures;
I2 – The usefulness of COVID–19 training in the context of the organization to which I belong;
I3 – The usefulness of COVID–19 training in a personal context; and
I4 – The applicability of COVID–19 training in daily assignments.

TRAINING (RELATED WITH COVID–19) ITEMS	Very Satisfied	Satisfied	Dissatisfied	Very Dissatisfied	Decreasing Trend	Increasing Trend
S1. The syllabus of COVID–19 training actions.	☐	☒	☐	☐	☐	☐
S2. The usefulness of COVID–19 training in the context of the organization.	☒	☒	☐	☐	☐	☒
S3. The usefulness of COVID–19 training in a personal context.	☐	☐	☐	☐	☐	☐
S4. The applicability of COVID–19 training in daily tasks.	☒	☒	☐	☐	☐	☒

Fig. 1. A fragment of employee #1's answers to COVID–19 training items included in the second part of the questionnaire.

The second group was built according to the particulars, viz.

I5 – Implementation of distance measures of at least 2 meters (signal lines on the ground) between employees;
I6 – The suitability of personal protection equipment during chemical tests;
I7 – The suitability of personal protection equipment during microbiological tests; and
I8 – The suitability of personal protection equipment during sample collection.

Finally, the third one comprises the specifics, viz.

I9 – Disinfectant gel availability at the entrance to the rooms;
I10 – Disinfection of contact surfaces with the employees between each use;
I11 – Disinfection of hands with alcohol at 70° or alcohol-based solution, between each service/employee; and
I12 – Cleaning of common spaces (e.g. bar; WC; service rooms data holders).

In order to transpose the qualitative information into a quantitative one all calculation details for *Training Related Items – Four Items* (*TRI – 4*) are presented, in order to illustrate the process. The answers of the employee #1 to the *TRI – 4* group are present in Table 1. Taking into account that the answers to *I2* and *I4* were *Satisfied (3)* → *Very Satisfied (4)*, it reveals an increase tendency on the employee's satisfaction, corresponding to a decrease in entropy. For *I1* the answer was *medium (3)*; a fact that is self-explanatory, while for *I3* no alternative were marked, configuring an ambiguous situation, i.e., vague, where the energy expended is unknown, but ranging between 0 and 1.

Table 1. Answers of the employee #1 to *TRI – 4*.

Items	Scale							
	entropy increasing tendency →			*entropy decreasing tendency* →				
	(4)	(3)	(2)	(1)	(2)	(3)	(4)	*Vagueness*
I1		×						
I2						×	×	
I3								×
I4						×	×	

With regard to the different types of energy, *exergy* corresponds to the well-defined answers, i.e. the cases where only one alternative was marked. Indeterminacy (i.e., *vagueness*) occurs when no alternatives or more than one alternative have been marked and *anergy* corresponds to the energy not yet used. Figure 2 and Fig. 3 show the conversion of the information contained in Table 1 into the diverse types of energy described above (*exergy*, *vagueness* and *anergy*). Taking into consideration that the marks on the axis match to each one of the possible scale alternatives, the employees' opinion is encouraging in the cases where occur a decrease of entropy (I2 and I4), as presented in Table 2.

4   Results and Discussion

The data presented in Table 2 can be organized in terms of the extent of the predicate *training related items* (*tri – 4*) in the form, *viz.*

$$tri - 4 : \textbf{\textit{EX}}ergy, \textbf{\textit{VA}}gueness, \textbf{\textit{AN}}ergy, Employee\,Satisfaction\,Assessment,$$
$$Quality-of-Information \rightarrow \{True, False\}$$

The scope and formal description of the predicate *tri – 4* are present in Table 3 and in Program 2.

The calculation of *Employee Satisfaction Assessment* (*ESA*) and the *Quality-of-Information truth values* (*QoI truth values*) for the different terms or clauses that make the *tri – 4* predicate's extent are now given in the form, *viz.*

- *ESA* is found as $\sqrt{1 - ES^2}$ (Fig. 4), which leads to, viz.

$$ESA_{BCS} = \sqrt{1 - (0.42)^2} = 0.9; \text{ and}$$

$$ESA_{WCS} = \sqrt{1 - (0.89 + 0)^2} = 0.46$$

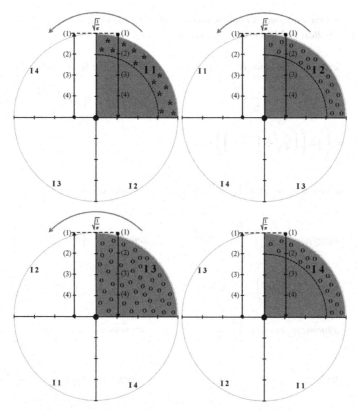

Fig. 2. Estimation of energy types for the diverse items respecting to the answers of employee #1 to the *TRI – 4*. The dark zones stand for *exergy*, dark areas with circles denote *vagueness* and dark regions with asterisks characterize *anergy*.

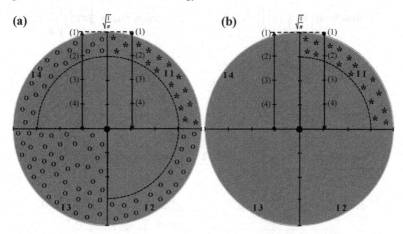

Fig. 3. The global evaluation of the contribution of employee #1 to the team's satisfaction in answering *TRI – 4* in the *Best* (a) and in the *Worst* (b) *Case Scenarios*.

Table 2. Assess the employee's contribution to evaluating the team's satisfaction in responding to *TRI − 4* for the *Best* and *Worst Case Scenarios*.

Items	Best Case Scenario (BCS)	Worst Case Scenario (WCS)
I1	$exergy_{I_1} = \frac{1}{4}\pi r^2 \Big]_0^{\frac{3}{4}\sqrt{\frac{1}{\pi}}} =$ $= \left(\frac{1}{4}\pi \left(\left(\frac{3}{4}\sqrt{\frac{1}{\pi}}\right)^2 - 0\right)\right) = 0.14$	$exergy_{I_1} = \frac{1}{4}\pi r^2 \Big]_0^{\frac{3}{4}\sqrt{\frac{1}{\pi}}} = 0.14$
	$vagueness_{I_1} = \frac{1}{4}\pi r^2 \Big]_{\frac{3}{4}\sqrt{\frac{1}{\pi}}}^{\frac{3}{4}\sqrt{\frac{1}{\pi}}} = 0$	$vagueness_{I_1} = \frac{1}{4}\pi r^2 \Big]_{\frac{3}{4}\sqrt{\frac{1}{\pi}}}^{\frac{3}{4}\sqrt{\frac{1}{\pi}}} = 0$
	$anergy_{I_1} = \frac{1}{4}\pi r^2 \Big]_{\frac{3}{4}\sqrt{\frac{1}{\pi}}}^{\sqrt{\frac{1}{\pi}}} = 0.11$	$anergy_{I_1} = \frac{1}{4}\pi r^2 \Big]_{\frac{3}{4}\sqrt{\frac{1}{\pi}}}^{\sqrt{\frac{1}{\pi}}} = 0.11$
I2	$exergy_{I_2} = \frac{1}{4}\pi r^2 \Big]_0^{\frac{3}{4}\sqrt{\frac{1}{\pi}}} = 0.14$	$exergy_{I_2} = \frac{1}{4}\pi r^2 \Big]_0^{\sqrt{\frac{1}{\pi}}} = 0.25$
	$vagueness_{I_2} = \frac{1}{4}\pi r^2 \Big]_{\frac{3}{4}\sqrt{\frac{1}{\pi}}}^{\sqrt{\frac{1}{\pi}}} = 0.11$	$vagueness_{I_2} = -\frac{1}{4}\pi r^2 \Big]_{\frac{4}{4}\sqrt{\frac{1}{\pi}}}^{\frac{4}{4}\sqrt{\frac{1}{\pi}}} = 0$
	$anergy_{I_2} = \frac{1}{4}\pi r^2 \Big]_{\sqrt{\frac{1}{\pi}}}^{\sqrt{\frac{1}{\pi}}} = 0$	$anergy_{I_2} = -\frac{1}{4}\pi r^2 \Big]_{\sqrt{\frac{1}{\pi}}}^{\sqrt{\frac{1}{\pi}}} = 0$
I3	$exergy_{I_3} = \frac{1}{4}\pi r^2 \Big]_0^0 = 0$	$exergy_{I_3} = \frac{1}{4}\pi r^2 \Big]_0^{\sqrt{\frac{1}{\pi}}} = 0.25$
	$vagueness_{I_3} = \frac{1}{4}\pi r^2 \Big]_0^{\sqrt{\frac{1}{\pi}}} = 0.25$	$vagueness_{I_3} = \frac{1}{4}\pi r^2 \Big]_{\sqrt{\frac{1}{\pi}}}^{\sqrt{\frac{1}{\pi}}} = 0$
	$anergy_{I_3} = \frac{1}{4}\pi r^2 \Big]_{\sqrt{\frac{1}{\pi}}}^{\sqrt{\frac{1}{\pi}}} = 0$	$anergy_{I_3} = \frac{1}{4}\pi r^2 \Big]_{\sqrt{\frac{1}{\pi}}}^{\sqrt{\frac{1}{\pi}}} = 0$
I4	$exergy_{I_4} = \frac{1}{4}\pi r^2 \Big]_0^{\frac{3}{4}\sqrt{\frac{1}{\pi}}} = 0.14$	$exergy_{I_4} = \frac{1}{4}\pi r^2 \Big]_0^{\sqrt{\frac{1}{\pi}}} = 0.25$
	$vagueness_{I_4} = \frac{1}{4}\pi r^2 \Big]_{\frac{3}{4}\sqrt{\frac{1}{\pi}}}^{\sqrt{\frac{1}{\pi}}} = 0.11$	$vagueness_{I_4} = \frac{1}{4}\pi r^2 \Big]_{\sqrt{\frac{1}{\pi}}}^{\sqrt{\frac{1}{\pi}}} = 0$
	$anergy_{I_4} = \frac{1}{4}\pi r^2 \Big]_{\sqrt{\frac{1}{\pi}}}^{\sqrt{\frac{1}{\pi}}} = 0$	$anergy_{I_4} = \frac{1}{4}\pi r^2 \Big]_{\sqrt{\frac{1}{\pi}}}^{\sqrt{\frac{1}{\pi}}} = 0$

Table 3. The extent of the predicate *tri – 4*, obtained using the answers of the employee #1 to *TRI – 4*.

Group	Ex BCS	VA BCS	AN BCS	ESA BCS	Qol BCS	EX WCS	VA WCS	AN WCS	ESA WCS	Qol WCS
TRI – 4	0.42	0.47	0.11	0.91	0.58	0.89	0	0.11	0.46	0.11

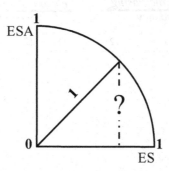

Fig. 4. *ESA* evaluation.

ES represents the exergy's consumed. Thus, for the *Best Case Scenario ES*, stands for *exergy*, while for the *Worst Case Scenario ES* denotes (*exergy + vagueness*).

- The *Qol truth values* are evaluated as *(1 − ES/Interval length)* [13], leading to, viz.

$$Qol \; truth \; values_{BCS} = 1 - 0.42 = 0.58$$

$$Qol \; truth \; values_{WCS} = 1 - (0.89 + 0) = 0.11$$

where, by definition, *interval length* was set to 1 (one).

{

¬ *tri – 4 (EX, VA, AN, ESA, Qol truth values)*

← *not tri – 4 (EX, VA, AN, ESA, Qol truth values)*,

not exception$_{tri-4}$ (EX, VA, AN, ESA, Qol truth values)

tri – 4 (0.42, 0.47, 0.11, 0.91, 0.58).

}

Program 2. The extent of the *tri – 4* predicate for the *Best Case Scenario*.

In addition to Table 1, Table 4 and Table 5 show employee #1's answers to the *RRI − 4* and *CDRI − 4* groups.

Table 4. Answers from employee #1 to *RRI − 4* and *CDRI − 4*.

Group	Items	Scale							
		entropy increasing tendency →			entropy decreasing tendency →				
		(4)	(3)	(2)	(1)	(2)	(3)	(4)	Vagueness
RRI − 4	I5	×							
	I6						×	×	
	I7					×			
	I7								×
CDRI − 4	I9					×	×		
	I10		×						
	I11								
	I12								×

Table 5. The *tri − 4*, *rri − 4* and *cdri − 4* predicates' scopes computed in conformity with the answers of the employee # 1 to *TRI − 4*, *RRI − 4* and *CDRI − 4*.

Groups	Ex BCS	VA BCS	AN BCS	ESA BCS	Qol BCS	EX WCS	VA WCS	AN WCS	ESA WCS	Qol WCS
TRI − 4	0.42	0.47	0.11	0.91	0.58	0.89	0	0.11	0.46	0.11
RRI − 4	0.45	0.26	0.19	0.89	0.55	0.81	0	0.19	0.59	0.19
CDRI − 4	0.40	0.30	0.30	0.92	0.60	0.70	0	0.30	0.71	0.30

4.1 A Symbolic, Logic Method to Evaluate Employee's Satisfaction

Computational Logic can be understood in the broadest sense as a problem-solving methodology, in which the problems and the respective solutions are expressed in logic terms so that a computer can execute them using deductive/inductive interpretations methods. This section presents the logic program that takes into account employee opinions regarding their satisfaction with the new procedures related to the coronavirus crisis. This framework brings into being the basis for an assessment of the level of the *Employee's Satisfaction Assessment (ESA)* and a measure of its *Sustainability (Qol truth values)*, an assembly of *truth values* belonging to the interval *0...1*.

{

/* The subsequent sentence specifies that the extent of predicate tri – 4 is based on the explicitly itemized clauses and the ones that cannot be dropped */

¬ tri – 4 (EX, VA, AN, ESA, QoI truth values)

← not tri – 4 (EX, VA, AN, ESA, QoI truth values),

not exception$_{tri-4}$ (EX, VA, AN, ESA, QoI truth values)

/* The following sentence stands for an axiom of tri – 4*/

tri – 4 (0.42, 0.47, 0.11, 0.91, 0.58).

/* The subsequent sentence specifies that the extent of predicate rri – 4 is based on the explicitly itemized clauses and the ones that cannot be dropped */

¬ rri – 4 (EX, VA, AN, ESA, QoI truth values)

← not rri – 4 (EX, VA, AN, ESA, QoI truth values),

not exception$_{rri-4}$ (EX, VA, AN, ESA, QoI truth values)

/* The following sentence stands for an axiom of rri – 4*/

rri – 4 (0.45, 0.26, 0.19, 0.89, 0.55).

/* The subsequent sentence specifies that the extent of predicate cdri – 4 is based on the explicitly itemized clauses and the ones that cannot be dropped */

¬ cdri – 4 (EX, VA, AN, ESA, QoI truth values)

← not cdri – 4 (EX, VA, AN, ESA, QoI truth values),

not exception$_{cdri-4}$ (EX, VA, AN, ESA, QoI truth values)

/* The following sentence stands for an axiom of cdri – 4*/

cdri – 4 (0.40, 0.30, 0.30, 0.92, 0.60).

}

Program 3. The make-up of the LP for assessing the contribution of employee #1's in the evaluation of the team's satisfaction for the *Best Case Scenario*.

4.2 A Case-Based Approach to Process Employee's Satisfaction

In this study a cohort of 64 employees was involved. The *Database/Knowledge Base/Case Base* is now obtained by validating the theorem, viz.

$$\forall(EX_1, VA_1, AN_1, ESA_1, QoI\ truth\ values_1, \cdots,$$
$$\cdots, EX_3, VA_3, AN_3, ESA_3, QoI\ truth\ values_3),$$
$$\big(tri{-}4(EX_1, VA_1, AN_1, ESA_1, QoI\ truth\ values_1),$$
$$rri{-}4(EX_2, VA_2, AN_2, ESA_2, QoI\ truth\ values_2),$$
$$cdri{-}4(EX_3, VA_3, AN_3, ESA_3, QoI\ truth\ values_3))$$

in all possible ways, i.e., generating every possible sequencing of the terms/clauses of the extents of predicates *tri – 4*, *rri – 4* and *cdri – 4*, viz.

$$\{\{tri{-}4(EX_1, VA_1, AN_1, ESA_1, QoI\ truth\ values_1),$$
$$rri{-}4(EX_2, VA_2, AN_2, ESA_2, QoI\ truth\ values_2),$$
$$cdri{-}4(EX_3, VA_3, AN_3, ESA_3, QoI\ truth\ values_3)\}, \cdots\} \approx$$
$$\approx \{\{tri{-}4(0.42, 0.47, 0.11, 0.91, 0.58), rri{-}4(0.45, 0.26, 0.19, 0.89, 0.55),$$
$$cdri{-}4(0.40, 0.30, 0.30, 0.92, 0.60)\}, \cdots\}$$

Regardless of encouraging results, the current *CBR* systems don't be versatile enough to be used in all domains. Often, users are forced to adopt the similarity methods imposed by the system, despite they do not completely adjusted to their needs [11, 14]. To meet this challenge, the alternative *CBR* cycle suggested by Neves et al. [14–16] was adjusted taking into account the global *Employee Satisfaction Assessment* (*ESA*) and the employees *QoI truth values*. For the *Best Case Scenario*, they can be calculated in the form, viz.

$$\{\{(ESA_{tri-4} + ESA_{rri-4} + ESA_{cdri-4})/3\}, \cdots\}_{BCS} \approx$$
$$\approx \{\{(0.91 + 0.89 + 0.92)/3 = 0.90\}, \cdots\}_{BCS}$$

and, *viz.*

$$\{\{(QoItruthvalues_{tri-4} + QoItruthvalues_{rri-4} +$$
$$+ QoItruthvalues_{cdri-4})/3, \cdots\}_{BCS} \approx$$
$$\approx \{\{(0.58 + 0.55 + 0.60)/3 = 0.58\}, \cdots\}_{BCS}$$

Thus, when handled with a new occurrence, the system is search and retrieve the cases that match in certain degree the new case specifications, and act accordingly [14–16].

5 Conclusions and Future Work

Employees' satisfaction is an old topic, but simultaneously a very current one, since it is closely related to productivity. The actual pandemic crisis brought new challenges to organizations, which had to adjust themselves to new requirements to avoid contagion. From this perspective the *ESA* is of utmost importance. Despite to be a challenging task, it is very hard to achieve since imply to manipulate distinct variables with numerous and multifaceted interconnections among them. In this study, the development of an *ESA–CBR* model is presented, with which the satisfaction of employees with the new work guidelines due to the actual pandemic crisis is assessed. It takes the advantages of the synergies between Logic Programming and the Laws of Thermodynamics for Knowledge Representation and Reasoning, together with a computational approach that uses Case-Based Reasoning. The model was tested with real data collected through questionnaires exhibiting an overall accuracy of 85.9%. On the other hand, the weights of the case attributes can be defined so that the bandwidth of the search space can be selected for comparable cases at runtime. Regarding subsequent work, it will take new factors into account, namely issues relating to occupational medicine or the organizational climate. In addition, the study is to be extended to a larger sample in order to examine the role of additional variables like age, gender or the academic and social training of employees on their emotions and feelings.

Acknowledgments. This work has been supported by FCT – Fundação para a Ciência e Tecnologia within the R&D Units Project Scope: UIDB/00319/2020

References

1. Portuguese Goverment: Establishes exceptional and temporary measures regarding the epidemiological situation of the new Coronavirus, COVID–19. Decree-Law No. 10-A/2020 of 13 March (2020)
2. World Health Organization: Laboratory Biosafety Guidance Related to Coronavirus Disease (COVID–19) & #x200E;– Interim Guidance. WHO Edition, Geneve (2020)
3. World Health Organization: Cleaning and Disinfection of Environmental Surfaces in the Context of COVID–19 & #x200E;– Interim Guidance. WHO Edition, Geneve (2020)
4. Alfes, K., Shantz, A.D., Truss, C., Soane, E.C.: The link between perceived human resource management practices, engagement and employee behaviour: a moderated mediation model. Int. J. Hum. Resour. Manag. **24**, 330–351 (2013)
5. Berman, E.M., Bowman, J.S., West, J.P., Van Wart, M.R.: Human Resource Management in Public Service: Paradoxes, Processes, and Problems. SAGE Publications Inc., Thousand Oaks (2020)
6. Petrescu, A.I., Simmons, R.: Human resource management practices and employees' job satisfaction. Int. J. Manpower **29**, 651–667 (2008)
7. Neves, J.: A logic interpreter to handle time and negation in logic databases. In: Muller, R., Pottmyer, J. (eds.) Proceedings of the 1984 Annual Conference of the ACM on the 5th Generation Challenge, pp. 50–54. ACM, New York (1984)
8. Fernandes, B., Vicente, H., Ribeiro J., Capita, A., Analide, C., Neves, J.: Fully informed vulnerable road users – simpler, maybe better. In: Proceedings of the 21st International Conference on Information Integration and Web-based Applications & Services (iiWAS2019), pp. 600–604. Association for Computing Machinery, New York (2020)
9. Figueiredo, M., et al.: An assessment of students' satisfaction in higher education. In: Vittorini, P., Di Mascio, T., Tarantino, L., Temperini, M., Gennari, R., De la Prieta, F. (eds.) MIS4TEL 2020. AISC, vol. 1241, pp. 147–161. Springer, Cham (2020). https://doi.org/10.1007/978-3-030-52538-5_16

10. Aamodt, A., Plaza, E.: Case-based reasoning: foundational issues, methodological variations, and system approaches. AI Commun. **7**, 39–59 (1994)
11. Richter, M.M., Weber, R.O.: Case-Based Reasoning: A Textbook. Springer, Berlin (2013)
12. Wenterodt, T., Herwig, H.: The entropic potential concept: a new way to look at energy transfer operations. Entropy **16**, 2071–2084 (2014)
13. Neves, J., et al.: Entropy and organizational performance. In: Pérez García, H., Sánchez González, L., Castejón Limas, M., Quintián Pardo, H., Corchado Rodríguez, E. (eds.) Hybrid Artificial Intelligent Systems. Lecture Notes in Computer Science, vol. 11734, pp. 206–217. Springer, Cham (2019)
14. Vilhena, J., Vicente, H., Martins, M.R., Grañeda, J., Caldeira, F., Gusmão, R., Neves, J., Neves, J.: A case-based reasoning view of thrombophilia risk. J. Biomed. Inform. **62**, 265–275 (2016)
15. Neves, J., et al.: Waiting time screening in healthcare. In: Jung, J.J., Kim, P., Choi, K.N. (eds.) BDTA 2017. LNICSSITE, vol. 248, pp. 124–131. Springer, Cham (2018). https://doi.org/10.1007/978-3-319-98752-1_14
16. Ferraz, F., Vicente, H., Costa, A., Neves, J.: Analysis of dyscalculia evidences through artificial intelligence systems. J. Softw. Networking **2016**, 53–78 (2016)

A Data-Driven Approach for Automatic Classification of Extreme Precipitation Events: Preliminary Results

J. González-Vergara[1,2]([✉]), D. Escobar-González[3], D. Chaglla-Aguagallo[1,2], and D. H. Peluffo-Ordóñez[1,2,4]

[1] Yachay Tech University, San Miguel de Urcuquí Canton, Ecuador
juan.gonzalez@yachatech.edu.ec
[2] SDAS Research Group, Ibarra, Ecuador
[3] Empresa Pública Metropolitana de Agua Potable y Saneamiento
(EPMAPS–Agua de Quito), Quito 17-03-0330, Ecuador
[4] Corporación Universitaria Autónoma de Nariño, Pasto, Colombia
http://www.sdas-group.com

Abstract. Even though there exists no universal definition, in the South America Andean Region, extreme precipitation events can be referred to the period of time in which standard thresholds of precipitation are abruptly exceeded. Therefore, their timely forecasting is of great interest for decision makers from many fields, such as: urban planning entities, water researchers and in general, climate related institutions. In this paper, a data-driven study is performed to classify and anticipate extreme precipitation events through hydroclimate features. Since the analysis of precipitation-events-related time series involves complex patterns, input data requires undergoing both pre-processing steps and feature selection methods, in order to achieve a high performance at the data classification stage itself. In this sense, in this study, both individual Principal Component Analysis (PCA) and Regresional Relief (RR) as well as a cascade approach mixing both are considered. Subsequently, the classification is performed by a Support-Vector-Machine-based classifier (SVM). Results reflect the suitability of an approach involving feature selection and classification for precipitation events detection purposes. A remarkable result is the fact that a reduced dataset obtained by applying RR mixed with PCA discriminates better than RR alone but does not significantly hence the SVM rate at two- and three-class problems as done by PCA itself.

Keywords: SVM · Forecasting · Extreme precipitation · Relief · PCA · Feature selection · Data driven

D.H. Peluffo-Ordóñez—This work is supported by SDAS Research Group, EPMAPS and Yachay Tech University.

H. Florez and S. Misra (Eds.): ICAI 2020, CCIS 1277, pp. 197–209, 2020.
https://doi.org/10.1007/978-3-030-61702-8_14

1   Introduction

Climate modelling is often used by decision makers to minimize the risk related to extreme weather, saving important amounts of money and ultimately, human lives. Models are based on physical processes and well-studied differential equations. Numerical Weather Prediction (NWP) models based on such realm are the core of many systems, being itself a huge discipline [1]. NWP allows researchers predict weather with long periods of time in advance, leaving then a short-to-medium range forecast and even generates an extensive range of global, atmospheric and marine forecasts [2]. Although being of great scope, several factors might stop researchers and decision makers to further develop NWP models. Remarkable challenges encompass optimal computational time, affordable power generation and lack of top-notch hardware like parallel computation centers or better processors [3] -plus the monetary constraints to acquire them.

In the other hand, Data Science models have gained popularity in many fields of investigation [4]. Specifically, the so-named *Data-Driven* approaches have gained attention in the understanding of earth systems, e.g. hydrology, atmospheric processes and climate problems [5]. Several works have already taken advantage of this methodology, from classic Neural Networks [6], Machine Learning [7,8] to modern Deep Learning algorithms [9]. The goal of this article is to choose the features that have the greatest impact in extreme precipitation events, thereby reducing the dimension of a training dataset suitable for an AI/ML algorithm. Thus, this work presents a Data-Driven approach to tackle classification of extreme precipitation events. Results from this classification could be used to anticipate an extreme precipitation event within an hour in advance.

The rest of the article is organized as follows. Section 2 outlines the preprocessing, feature selection and explains the SVM classification. Section 3 compares the results of the feature selection and shows results of the SVM. Finally, Sect. 4 states the conclusion and future works.

2   Materials and Methods

This article follows the CRISP-DM methodology to develop the data mining process thereof. Broadly speaking, the steps followed in this article are summarized in Fig. 1. Particularly, the data management, pre-processing and training tasks are performed using open source libraries from Python [10,11] and R [12].

Business Understanding	Data Understanding	Data Preparation	Modeling	Evaluation	Deployment
Due to the amount of data that the multivariate time series generates, it is needed to capture and understand the most relevant information while being capable of creating optimum models that anticipate extreme precipitation events.	Initial data is a set of multivariate time series collected from various sources. The collected data is known to contain sparse information and a wide range of values. Furthermore, duplicates, missing values, and size homogeneity are also a found.	This article employs several methods used to produce a high quality dataset. Techniques for managing information, mitigating erroneous values and solving issues named in the Data Understanding section are accomplished. Besides, data is processed by feature selection algorithms with the goal of selecting the most relevant information	A supervised machine learning method that takes as inputs data acquired from feature selection algorithms is applied. In effect, a kernel SVM algorithm is executed several times to conduct two- and three-class classification problems and measure the performance yielded by each dataset	In this phase, the different approaches of feature selection are evaluated by analyzing a Box Plot diagram of accuracy for each classification through each training dataset. As expected, variables that influence the most at precipitation events are established.	The article seeks to show preliminary results of an exploratory analysis of the dataset. This project underlies the baseline for future projects which might develop regression algorithms in neural networks, deep learning, or in general AI-related.

Fig. 1. CRISP-DM methodology for data mining process.

2.1 Database

Data used in this article are obtained from *"Estación Científica Agua y Páramos"* (ECAP) [13], *"Empresa Pública Metropolitana de Agua Potable y Saneamiento de Quito"* (EPMAPS) [14] and *"Fideicomiso Mercantil Fondo Ambiental para la Protección de las Cuencas y Agua"* (FONAG) [15]. The purpose of ECAP is to coordinate the development of research projects and generate knowledge about water and the Andean Paramo. Data from ECAP is recorded with a frequency of 5 min in 30 pluviometric stations and 12 climatological stations. In addition to pluviometry, several hydroclimate features are registered, namely: *Temperature, Relative Humidity, Solar Irradiance, Pressure, Wind speed* and *Wind Direction*. Specifically, this article uses data from stations C02-Rumihurco and C04-Rumipamba, ranging from late 2017 to mid 2020 with 270,645 samples and 94,232 samples, respectively. An overall description of the obtained data is presented in Fig. 2, where the tables includes count (samples), mean, std, min, max, as well as the 25th, 50th (same as the median) and 75th percentile.

	Value (°)	Value (%)	Value (hPa)	Value (W/m2)	Value (°C)	Value (m/s)	Value (mm)
count	270645.000000	270645.000000	270645.000000	270645.000000	270645.000000	270645.000000	270645.000000
mean	120.111297	80.997873	665.326875	160.749472	9.015922	2.063146	0.010707
std	86.599145	14.831381	1.112139	264.722837	2.243214	2.631695	0.091532
min	0.000000	13.000000	661.300000	0.000000	2.900000	0.000000	0.000000
25%	52.000000	70.000000	664.500000	0.000000	7.300000	0.800000	0.000000
50%	84.000000	82.000000	665.400000	2.000000	8.600000	1.500000	0.000000
75%	172.000000	95.000000	666.100000	219.000000	10.700000	2.800000	0.000000
max	360.000000	100.000000	668.800000	1331.000000	24.200000	232.800000	6.800000

(a) Station C02-Rumihurco Statistical Description.

	Value (°)	Value (%)	Value (hPa)	Value (W/m2)	Value (°C)	Value (m/s)	Value (mm)
count	94232.000000	94232.000000	94232.000000	94232.000000	94232.000000	94232.000000	94232.000000
mean	228.235005	81.160858	684.760118	154.528754	10.093179	1.178067	0.017746
std	96.448052	16.721472	1.240791	274.321987	3.077449	0.871993	0.135356
min	0.000000	0.000000	680.700000	0.000000	0.000000	0.000000	0.000000
25%	128.000000	68.000000	683.900000	2.000000	7.700000	0.600000	0.000000
50%	295.000000	86.000000	684.800000	2.000000	9.200000	1.100000	0.000000
75%	316.000000	95.500000	685.700000	181.000000	12.700000	1.600000	0.000000
max	360.000000	100.000000	688.200000	1417.000000	28.400000	111.100000	5.800000

(b) Station C04-Rumihurco Statistical Description.

Fig. 2. Statistical description of data obtained from stations C02-Rumihurco and C04-Rumipamba. Each table shows the central tendency, dispersion and shape of a dataset's distribution

Throughout this article, the following matrix notation is to be considered:

- Station Matrix $\mathbf{X}^s \in \mathbb{R}^{N \times D}$ and its Precipitation vector $\mathbf{p}^s \in \mathbb{R}^N$ where $s \in \{1, 2\}$ indicates the station, N is the sample size, and D is the number of feature.
- Extreme Event Matrix $\mathbf{X_e} \in \mathbb{R}^{m \times D}$ and its Extreme Precipitation vector $\mathbf{p_e} \in \mathbb{R}^n$ where $e = 1, \ldots 13$ are the events, m is the extreme precipitation event sample size and D is number of features.
- Training Matrix with all features $\mathbf{T} \in \mathbb{R}^{n \times D}$, Reduced Training Matrix with Feature Selection made by PCA $\widehat{\mathbf{T}}^1 \in \mathbb{R}^{n \times d}$, Reduced Training Matrix with Feature Selection made by RR $\widehat{\mathbf{T}}^2 \in \mathbb{R}^{n \times d}$ and the Reduced Training Matrix with Feature Selection made by Cascading approach $\widehat{\mathbf{T}}^3 \in \mathbb{R}^{n \times d}$, such that n is the training sample size and d is the number of selected features, with $d < D$ and $n < N$.

2.2 Data Cleaning

To produce both high quality data and valid results, well-established pre-processing techniques are highly desirable. The here-used pre-processing stage is as follows: First, each $\mathbf{X}^s$ is built from feature vectors containing different sample sizes with empty and repeated values. In order to have size homogeneity, duplicate samples were deleted and an inner joint was employed instead. Secondly, a linear interpolation process -obtained from the slope equation- is applied to handle missing values:

$$\frac{y - y_0}{x - x_0} = \frac{y_1 - y_0}{x_1 - x_0},$$
$$y = \frac{y_0(x_1 - x) + y_1(x - x_0)}{x_1 - x_0}, \tag{1}$$

where y is the missing data in position x and $(x_0, y_0), (x_1, y_1)$ are the consequent points. Additionally, PCA and RR are corresponded with centered data obtained as:

$$\mathbf{W_i} = (\bar{\mathbf{Y}}_i - \mathbf{Y_i}), \tag{2}$$

such that $\bar{\mathbf{Y}}_i$ is the column mean of feature $\mathbf{Y_i}$ and $\mathbf{W_i}$ is the centered feature vector. Finally, for the SVM training, data dispersion was handled by standardization:

$$z = \frac{x - \mu}{\sigma}, \tag{3}$$

where z is the scaled data point, μ is the mean of the training samples and σ is a biased estimator for the standard deviation.

2.3 Data Relevance and Feature Selection

Due to information volume and computational resources surrounding hydroclimatic data, this matter can be treated as a Big Data problem. Although interpretation of hydroclimatic features may be intuitive for experienced weather researchers, they become complex variables to decode because of their sampling frequency and their pseudo-randomly nature. For example, Pressure throughout the day has sinusoidal-like behavior; features Solar Irradiance, Wind Speed and Temperature commonly display its highest peaks around noon and lowest at night and early morning, see Fig. 3a. On the other hand, when extreme precipitation events happen, as shown in Fig. 3b, some descriptive characteristics display a similar but fuzzy pattern before a precipitation event. Following are some of such descriptive characteristics:

- Sudden drop in Temperature and Solar Irradiance.
- Significant increase in Relative Humidity and Wind Speed.
- Hard drop of Pressure prior to a storm and sudden increase in the beginning of the storm.

Particularly, the main idea of the feature relevance analysis is to apply PCA, RR and the combination of the both of them to several Extreme Event Matrices $\mathbf{X_e}$. The goal is to distinguish information only relevant to extreme precipitation events. Then, the SVM compares what feature selection method yields better accuracy, *idem quod* what feature selection method creates the better training $\widehat{\mathbf{T}}^i$. Algorithm1 is based on the following premise to identify extreme precipitation events: If the absolute value of the difference between current value of precipitation $[i]$ and the next value of precipitation $[i + 1]$ is greater than one and the accumulated precipitation from that moment to one hour later is greater than 15 mm, then the value of precipitation $[i]$ is the start of the extreme precipitation event. In particular, not all extracted events from Algorithm 1 are used, this article is interested only in events that occurred around afternoon and there was minimum to no precipitation before the events had started.

Algorithm 1: Extreme precipitation extraction

Input   : Station Matrix $\mathbf{X^s} \in \mathbb{R}^{N \times D}$; Precipitation vector $\mathbf{p^s} \in \mathbb{R}^N$
Output: Extreme Event Matrix $\mathbf{X_e} \in \mathbb{R}^{m \times D}$; Extreme Precipitation vector $\mathbf{p_e} \in \mathbb{R}^n$.

1 event=0
2 for $i \leftarrow 0$ to N do
3   if *(abs(Precipitation vector[i] - Precipitation vector[i+1]) > 1)* *(sum(Precipitation vector[i] : Precipitation vector[i+12]) > 15)* then
4   for $j \leftarrow 0$ to D do
5   data= Station Matrix[i-12 : i+12][j]
6   Extreme Event Matrix[event].append(data)
7   Extreme Precipitation vector.append(Precipitation vector[i-12 : i+12])
8   end for
9   event+=1
10   end if
11 end for

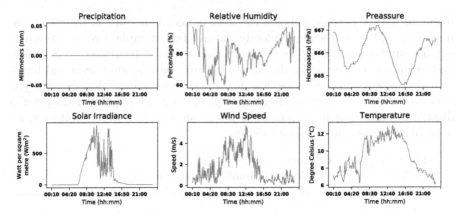

(a) Features from C02-Rumihurco Station in a day without precipitation.

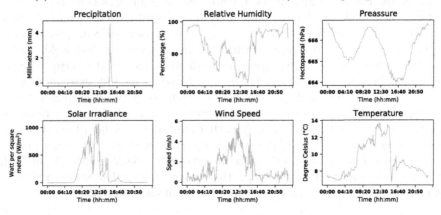

(b) Features from C02-Rumihurco Station in a day of an extreme precipitation event.

Fig. 3. Features from C02-Rumihurco Station. Each plot has 289 data points, equivalently to one day of sampling.

The feature relevance analysis starts by assigning each feature a variable *counter* $= 0$ when the feature selection method begins. For every $\mathbf{X_e}$, if a feature is selected, then *counter*$+ = 1$. The purpose is to build the Training Matrix $\widehat{\mathbf{T^i}}$ with the features that are selected the more times for each method. The core ideas behind the feature selection are summarized here:

- **Principal Component Analysis**
  Feature selection made by PCA is based on [16], where the relevance is granted by the contribution of each feature with respect to the variance explained. This criteria chooses features that have the most relevance to the inner product between the absolute value of each feature's eigenvector with the variance. The relevance of the *ith* feature is expressed as:

$$\xi_i = \langle |\lambda_i|, v_i \rangle,$$

$$\Xi_i = \frac{\xi_i}{\sum_{j=1}^{d} \xi_j}, \tag{4}$$

where ξ_i is the relevance of the i-th feature, $|\lambda_i|$ is the vector containing the absolute values of the principal components for the i-th feature, v is the PC variance vector and Ξ_i is the relevance of such feature with respect to the accumulated relevance. Therefore, PCA-based feature selection is set by choosing the three features with greater Ξ the most times. Besides, note that Cumulative Variance Explained showed that in all events three PCs were enough to account most information.

– **Regressional Relief-F**

As a part of the Relief family of algorithms, feature selection made by RR is based on the Relief-F extension of the original Relief algorithm [17]. Hence, the selection delivered by RR depends on random selection of instances, distance between nearest instances and the probability that two instances are different:

$$W[A] = \frac{\mathbf{P}_{\text{diffC|diffA}}\mathbf{P}_{\text{diffA}}}{\mathbf{P}_{diffC}} - \frac{(1 - \mathbf{P}_{diffC|diffA})\mathbf{P}_{diffA}}{1 - \mathbf{P}_{diffC}}, \tag{5}$$

where the quality estimation $W[A]$ of attribute (feature) A is obtained using Bayes' rules such that $\mathbf{P}_{diffA}$ is the probability of a different value of attribute A given the nearest instance, $\mathbf{P}_{diffC}$ is the probability of a different prediction given the nearest instance, $\mathbf{P}_{diffC|diffA}$ is the probability of a different prediction given the different value of A and its and nearest instances. This article executed RR to obtain three features with the greater quality estimation $W[A]$.

Accordingly, features having the greatest counter from each technique form the training matrices that are input to the SVM. Likewise, a cascading approach derived from adding the counter given by PCA to the counter given by RR is analysed. In that sense, once both techniques have selected their best ranked features, the combination of PCA & Relief yields a different training dataset. It should be noted that each data matrix is provided with a precipitation vector holding continuous values. For classification purposes, these vectors are later transformed to a two-class or three-class label vector. Also, the above explained methods are used to compare two perspectives of performing feature selection. The approach with which RR addresses the feature selection, i.e. entropy, in contrast to the approach taken by PCA, e.g. dispersion of information.

2.4   Training

The SVM was originally proposed by Cortes and Vapnik [18] in the 90's and have became a popular algorithm for Supervised Learning [19]. There are several variations of SVM and its applications are found in many disciplines [20]. The SVM algorithm can be used on early stages of many Data-driven applications as a baseline point for later comparison with more modern methods. This is due to its effectiveness to work in high dimensional spaces, relatively memory efficient and stability. The algorithm constructs a hyper-plane represented in a high dimensional space containing the input data points. The classification is achieved by maximizing the distance between the hyper-plane and the data points. This means that given the user specified support vectors, a *Margin* that separates the hyperplane is built, as seen in Fig. 4.

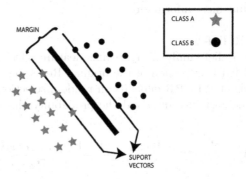

Fig. 4. A hyper-plane separating two classes. The Support Vectors contains a subset of three training samples of each class

Briefly put, solving a SVM is a quadratic programming problem. Let us say that a Training Matrix $\mathbf{T} \in \mathbb{R}^{n \times D}$ and its training label vector $\mathbf{y} \in \mathbb{R}^n$ are to be separated by a hyper-plane $f(\mathbf{t}) = \mathbf{w}^\top \mathbf{t} + b$, then the SVM turns to be an optimization over $\mathbf{w}$ as follows:

$$\underset{w}{\text{maximize}} \quad \frac{1}{2} \| w \|^2,$$
$$\text{subject to} \quad y_i w^\top t + b = 1..$$
(6)

Many real-world datasets, as is the case, are not linearly separable and requires a *Soft-Margin*. That is, introduce a slack variables that controls the distance of the point on the wrong side of the hyper-planes [21]. Furthermore, the *Kernel Trick* allows for mapping the original feature space of the dataset into a higher-dimensional. It makes a non separable problem to be separable in a higher-dimensional space [22]. This work uses a Radial Basis Function (RBF) kernel defined as:

$$K(\mathbf{y_i}, \mathbf{y_j}) = \mathbf{exp}(-\gamma \| \mathbf{y_i} - \mathbf{y_j} \|^2),$$
(7)

where $\| \mathbf{y}_i - \mathbf{y}_j \|^2$ is the distance of two feature vectors and γ is a user-defined parameter that scales the distance.

To evaluate the selected features resulting from Sect. 2.3, two- and three-class problems are considered and classified with SVM with a RFB kernel setting *gamma* = 100 and regularization parameter $C = 1$. Equally important, the SVM is used to forecast an extreme precipitation event within an hour before its beginning. For that purpose, the Training Precipitation vector is transformed to a label vector.

In the case of the two-class problem, training data is balanced, having equally amount of points for each class. Labeling is carried out as follows: The *Label* = 0 is given to all extreme precipitation event data and means that an extreme event is near or happening; *Label* = 1 is assigned to random sample data and means no danger of extreme event is close or happening. Whereas, for the three-class problem, the *Label* = −1 is given to data previous to an extreme precipitation event and means that an extreme event is near; *Label* = 0 is assigned to data acquired since the moment when the extreme precipitation event started and means an extreme event is happening; *Label* = 1 is analog to the two-class problem. The training dataset for the two-class problem consists of $n = 624$, $e = 13$ and $m = 24$, which is equivalent to 13 extreme precipitation events, each of sample size 24, corresponding to 312 samples for each label. The training dataset for the three-class problem consists of $n = 481$, $e = 13$ and $m = 24$, which is equivalent to 13 extreme precipitation events, each of size 24, corresponding to 169 samples of *Label* = −1, 143 of *Label* = 0, and 169 of *Label* = 1.

To evaluate the classification performance of the considered algorithm, the conventional accuracy is used, stated as the ratio of correct predictions over $n_{samples}$:

$$accuracy(y_i, \hat{y}_i) = \frac{1}{n_{samples}} \sum_{i=0}^{n_{samples}-1} 1(y_i = \hat{y}_i), \tag{8}$$

where $\hat{y}_i$ is the predicted value of the i-th sample and y_i is the corresponding true value. To validate the stability of each training set, the SVM undergoes 100 repetitions in which the accuracy is measured. For the sake of visual comparisons, a box plot is used.

3   Results

Experimental results proceed from examining each $\mathbf{X_e}$ through PCA and RR plus visual explanation of the figures. Reading Fig. 5a it is clear that PCA and RR strongly disagree on Relative Humidity and Wind Direction; it is not clear which features are the most relevant, in PCA the feature Pressure ties Solar Irradiance and Pressure ties Temperature in RR. Interpretation resulting from Fig. 5a might be related to Wind Direction due to its cardinal essence, therefore it is immediately discarded from the datasets. On the other hand, relevance analysis done without Wind Direction shows subtle homogeneity, see Fig. 5b where in both cases Temperature is the most relevant feature but both methods strongly disagree in Solar Irradiance and Wind Speed. Provided that Wind Direction is removed, it seems as if PCA and RR better judge the features. Relevance as stated by PCA ranks in top three Temperature, Relative Humidity and Solar Irradiance. Meanwhile, RR ranks in the top three Temperature, Pressure and Wind Speed. Likewise, when adding results from both methods a new feature selection can be derived. Table 1 displays the results of applying both methods in a cascading approach.

Table 1. Cascading approach: combination of RR & PCA feature selection

RR			PCA			Cascade	
Feature	Counter		Feature	Counter		Feature	Counter
Relative Humidity	6		Relative Humidity	12		Relative Humidity	18
Pressure	10	+	Pressure	6	=	Pressure	16
Solar Irradiance	2		Solar Irradiance	8		Solar Irradiance	10
Temperature	12		Temperature	13		Temperature	25
Wind Speed	9		Wind Speed	0		Wind Speed	9

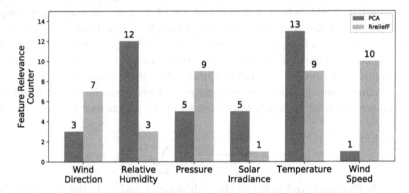

(a) Feature relevance made by PCA and RR in extreme precipitation events of C02-Rumihurco and C04-Rumipamba with all features

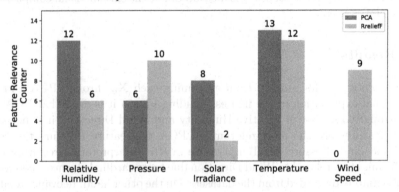

(b) Feature relevance made by PCA and RR in extreme precipitation events of C02-Rumihurco and C04-Rumipamba without Wind Direction

Fig. 5. Feature relevance according to PCA and RR. The Y axis show how many times each feature was selected as relevant.

Table 2. Mean accuracy of each training dataset after a 100 repetitions.

Two-Class SVM		Three-Class SVM	
Dataset	**Mean Accuracy**	**Dataset**	**Mean Accuracy**
Complete	84.481	Complete	79.983
PCA	85.891	PCA	79.066
RR	76.320	RR	72.298
Cascade (PCA & RR)	81.474	Cascade (PCA & RR)	78.149

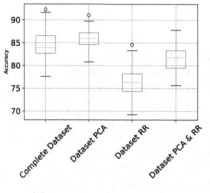

(a) Two-class SVM Boxplot

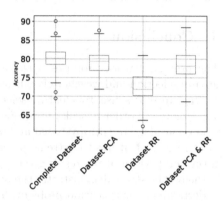

(b) Three-class SVM Boxplot

Fig. 6. Boxplot diagram of accuracy performances for the training datasets after executing 100 repetitions in each SVM

The resulting selected features can be seen as if one method, RR, highlights the influence of the entropy among variables and the other, PCA, remarks the influence of the dispersion among variables. Hence, combining both approaches might select most relevant features according to entropy and dispersion.

Finally, Fig. 6 depicts two boxplot diagrams of the accuracy achieved by the training datasets after executing 100 repetitions in each SVM. In both cases, features selected by PCA proved to be the most relevant to extreme precipitation events. In the case of the two-class SVM the training dataset resulting from PCA performs better than all of the others. Figure 6 exhibits cases in both SVM where accuracy can reach values above or close to 90% using the correct data but it should be noted that values could go down as low as 70% or 65% when the wrong data is used. In general, mean accuracy from Complete dataset and the PCA dataset are almost the same, as can be observed in Table 2.

The comparison of accuracy in both SVM shows that classification executed when using a dataset obtained from PCA and the Complete Dataset perform very similar. This reflects that when working with hydroclimate datasets, if the proper features are selected then results can be good as if using all features.

Consequently, the two-class SVM showed that its classification task could be enhanced using features selected by means of standard PCA analysis. Three-class SVM evidenced the same pattern of similarity between the PCA dataset and the complete dataset, although the latter performed almost insignificantly better. This opens the window to apply more sophisticated techniques as Kernel PCA. The experiments revealed that the combination of both approaches, PCA and RR, does not imply that the result might successfully improve the quality of the feature selection nor the classification task. Despite that the combination of RR with PCA outputs better accuracy than RR alone, it did not outperformed the complete training set nor the set given by PCA alone.

4   Conclusion

The presented work proposes a Data-Driven approach towards hydroclimatic feature selection and weather classification that could be used for one hour forecasting. In that sense, two feature selection methods and a combination of both are explored in order to seek improvement in the results of a SVM classifier. The paper considers an entropy-based and dispersion-based analysis of data to select most relevant features to extreme precipitation events. The core of the analysis is the comparison of the result given by PCA, RR and the combination of both of them. The study demonstrates the quality of each feature selection method by undertaking a classification problem through a two-class SVM and a three-class SVM.

Furthermore, based on experimental results, it can be stated that hydroclimate features in the South America Andean Region are better selected by the data dispersion-based approach.

Future works can be devoted to compare more sophisticated feature selection algorithms in hydroclimate dataset or include results from this article to develop regression algorithms in neural networks, deep learning or other related AI technique.

Acknowledgments. This work is supported by SDAS Research Group (www.sdas-group.com).

References

1. McGuffie, K., Henderson-Sellers, A.: Forty years of numerical climate modelling. Int. J. Climatol. J. R. Meteorol. Soc. **21**(9), 1067–1109 (2001)
2. Lynch, P.: The origins of computer weather prediction and climate modeling. J. Comput. Phys. **227**(7), 3431–3444 (2008)
3. Bauer, P., Thorpe, A., Brunet, G.: The quiet revolution of numerical weather prediction. Nature **525**(7567), 47–55 (2015)
4. Jordan, M.I., Mitchell, T.M.: Machine learning: trends, perspectives, and prospects. Science **349**(6245), 255–260 (2015)
5. Ganguly, A.R., et al.: Data-driven solutions. Climate 2020: Degrees of Devastation, pp. 82–85 (2018)

6. Maqsood, I., Khan, M.R., Abraham, A.: An ensemble of neural networks for weather forecasting. Neural Comput. Appl. **13**(2), 112–122 (2004). https://doi.org/10.1007/s00521-004-0413-4

7. Radhika, Y., Shashi, M.: Atmospheric temperature prediction using support vector machines. Int. J. Comput. Theor. Eng. **1**(1), 55 (2009)

8. Xingjian, S.H.I., Chen, Z., Wang, H., Yeung, D.Y., Wong, W.K., Woo, W.C.: Convolutional LSTM network: a machine learning approach for precipitation nowcasting. In: Advances in Neural Information Processing Systems, pp. 802–810 (2015)

9. Mehrkanoon, S.: Deep shared representation learning for weather elements forecasting. Knowl.-Based Syst. **179**, 120–128 (2019)

10. McKinney, W.: Data structures for statistical computing in python. In: van der Walt, S., Millman, J. (eds.) Proceedings of the 9th Python in Science Conference, pp. 56–61 (2010)

11. Pedregosa, F., et al.: Scikit-learn: Machine learning in Python. J. Mach. Learn. Res. **12**, 2825–2830 (2011)

12. Team, R.C.: R: a language and environment for statistical computing. R Foundation for Statistical Computing, Vienna, Austria (2014)

13. EPMAPS-FONAG. Estación Científica Agua y Páramo. http://www.fonag.org.ec/web/estacion-cientifica-agua-y-paramos/

14. EPMAPS. Empresa Pública Metropolitana de Agua Potable Y Saneamiento. https://www.aguaquito.gob.ec/

15. Echavarria, M.: Financing watershed conservation: the Fonag water fund in Quito, Ecuador. In: Selling Forest Environmental Services, pp. 105–115. Routledge (2012)

16. Peluffo Ordoñez, D.H., Lee, J.A., Verleysen, M., Rodriguez, J.L., Castellanos-Dominguez, G.: Unsupervised relevance analysis for feature extraction and selection. a distance-based approach for feature relevance. In: 3rd International Conference on Pattern Recognition Applications and Methods (ICPRAM 2014) (2015)

17. Robnik-Šikonja, M., Kononenko, I.: Theoretical and empirical analysis of Relieff and RRelieff. Mach. Learn. **53**(1–2), 23–69 (2003). https://doi.org/10.1023/A:1025667309714

18. Cortes, C., Vapnik, V.: Support-vector networks. Mach. Learn. **20**(3), 273–297 (1995). https://doi.org/10.1007/BF00994018

19. Kotsiantis, S.B., Zaharakis, I.D., Pintelas, P.E.: Machine learning: a review of classification and combining techniques. Artif. Intell. Rev. **26**(3), 159–190 (2006). https://doi.org/10.1007/s10462-007-9052-3

20. Hsu, C.W., Chang, C.C., Lin, C.J., et al.: A practical guide to support vector classification (2003)

21. Chen, D.R., Wu, Q., Ying, Y., Zhou, D.X.: Support vector machine soft margin classifiers: error analysis. J. Mach. Learn. Res. **5**, 1143–1175 (2004)

22. Hofmann, M.: Support vector machines-kernels and the kernel trick. Notes 26(3), (2006)

A Data-Driven Method for Measuring the Negative Impact of Sentiment Towards China in the Context of COVID-19

Laura M. Muñoz[1], Maria Fernanda Ramirez[2], and Jorge E. Camargo[3(✉)]

[1] Facultad de Ingeniería, Universidad Distrital Francisco José De Caldas,
Bogotá, Colombia
lmmunoza@correo.udistrital.edu.co
[2] Facultad de Ciencias Económicas, Universidad Nacional de Colombia,
Bogotá, Colombia
mframirezs@unal.edu.co
[3] Departamento de Ingeniería de Sistemas e Industrial,
Universidad Nacional de Colombia, Bogotá, Colombia
jecamargom@unal.edu.co

Abstract. Social media is a valuable source of information that allows to study people opinions of many events that happen every day. Nowadays social networks are one of the most important communication methods that people use. Feelings towards nations can be measured today thanks to the advances in machine learning and big data. In this paper we present a method to identify if there are negative sentiments towards China as a result of the COVID-19 virus. The method is based on sentiment analysis and extracts information from the Twitter social network. This analysis was done with the VADER library, a rule-based tool that provides classification algorithms. A dataset of 30,000 tweets was built for three time windows: December 2019 (before the pandemic), March 2020 (month in which the pandemic was confirmed by the World Health Organization), and May 2020 (when some countries started the de-escalation phase). Results show that sentiments became negative towards China and social network data allows to confirm this situation.

Keywords: Sentiment towards China · Text mining · VADER · Machine learning · COVID-19

1 Introduction

Nowadays, social networks are a medium that allows users to express their point of view and emotions through text, images, or videos. In particular, the social network Twitter is a popular medium that allows to access to all kinds of information such as breaking news [6,10,17–19], information on international interest, trending topics, and other domains [5,9,12,14,24]. This social network allows to access to comments and opinions of users, in which they express their feelings

© Springer Nature Switzerland AG 2020
H. Florez and S. Misra (Eds.): ICAI 2020, CCIS 1277, pp. 210–221, 2020.
https://doi.org/10.1007/978-3-030-61702-8_15

through short text messages, which may be the result of reactions to different news and publications from different sources such as mass media or accounts of private users [11].

The emergence of COVID-19 has been the most important news of 2020, an epidemic originated in the city of Wuhan in China. Over the months it expanded globally, until it became the main pandemic of the 21st century, due to its level of expansion and contagion and the effects at economic and social level [13]. The origin of this virus generated speculation worldwide against China and the handling that was given to the virus at the beginning. This put China as the center of attention during the first months of 2020, although since 2018 this country had been presenting trade differences with the United States, which generated a global impact due to the global importance of these two economies.

Sentiment analysis is a challenging tasks in machine learning applied to text. Particularly, text classification by sentiment polarity refers to the positivity or negativity of the sentiment represented by the text. There are prominent difficulties in classifying text by polarity when text is too short, as it is the case in Twitter in which text does not exceed 140 characters [22].

In this paper, we aim to establish the change that the image and feelings towards China have had in the global situation context due to COVID-19 emergence and its expansion, compared to the moment before the pandemic started. We propose a method based on machine learning techniques, specifically sentiment analysis [20]. The method uses also Natural Language Processing (NLP) over a set of tweets published before and during the pandemic. Tweets were crawled from Twitter taking into account if they had mentions to the word "China" as part of its text content or involved hashtags.

With this analysis it is possible to establish whether the sentiments and the image of China have changed at different points in time between December 2019 and May 2020. By setting different time windows marked by relevant events. It was possible to identify changes in sentiments through the social network.

As part of the results, we found that the general sentiment towards China went from a mainly neutral state, for December 2019, to be negative in the months of March and May 2020. The tweets with the highest number of likes are those related to political and social issues, unlike what was expected within the context of the pandemic.

This paper is organized as follows: In Sect. 2 we present references of interest for this analysis; in Sect. 3 we present materials and methods; Sect. 4 describes results and findings; and finally, the main conclusions and future work are presented in Sect. 5.

2   Related Work

In recent studies, social media data has been used to study sentiments from some nations towards other. In [1] authors propose a method for detecting sentiment between nations using Twitter data. The objective was to identify the feelings between nations through social networks, and on the use of contextual polarity.

Initially they had four labels to classify tweets: positive, negative, objective and irrelevant. First, they identify the country of origin of the tweets or the user, then they filter the tweets that do not refer to a country and irrelevant topics such as restaurants, food, concerts, among others. Next They used different classification methodologies (logistic regression classifiers, relevance classifier, and contextual sentiment analysis) using characteristics selected by them. Finally, they identify the sentiment towards the country using three labels: positive, negative, and objective. Lastly, they evaluated the precision of their classifiers and show the correlation between public opinion polls and international alliance relation.

In [7] it is proposed a system for tracking relationships between nations using news. In this work the authors propose a model for detection of feelings. The contribution of this model is that it integrates information such as predicates, nouns, and proper names and identify the situation in context. They hypothesize that the relevance of verbal predicates is that information that has to do with relationships is almost always encoded with verbal predicates. Finally, they compare their RMN (Relation Modeling Network) model with the LARN (Linguistically aware relationship network) model, by doing tests on undergraduate students, where they show that the majority of students chose the RMN model.

In [23] authors evaluated online public sentiments towards China using a Twitter discourse during the 2019 Chinese national day. They filter the database in English, Traditional Chinese, and Simplified Chinese and have certain hashtags, to feed the base. The techniques used by them for the analysis were the dictionary method and SVM (support vector machine). Something very interesting about this project is that they made a spatial analysis of both positive and negative comments for each country referring to China. In this study authors show that India had positive comments, and on the other hand, the United States and China stood out in the largest number of both positive and negative comments. They also showed the frequency of words used in this database; some of the most common words were 70th, Military, national, police, and republic. Results showed that the most negative tweets were in the English language.

3   Method and Materials

This section describes the 5 stages of the proposed method. Figure 1 depicts the overall method: (1) Crawling of tweets for 3-time windows; (2) Data preprocessing; (3) Sentiment analysis methodology; (4) Score computation; and (5) Visualization and analysis of the obtained results.

3.1   Tweets Crawling

Tweets were collected for 3-time windows, each window of 3 consecutive days for 3 months or different moments. The first window represents the time before the pandemic and it is between 12/01/2019 and 12/03/2019. The second one was established in the month of March, in this month the World Health Organization (WHO) officially assessed that COVID-19 was a pandemic [15]; the window

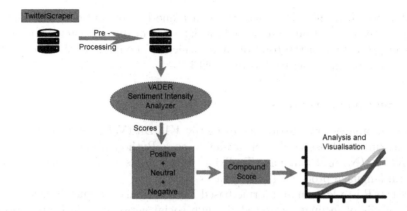

Fig. 1. Overview of the proposed method. We crawl tweets using the API Twitter filtering by the English language. Then, pre-processing was made over this set of tweets. After that, we applied the Sentiment analysis tool named VADER, which allow to score sentiment. Finally, we normalize a sum of scores obtaining a compound score, which is used for visualization and analysis.

begins on 03/29/2020 and runs until 03/31/2020. The third window was in the month of May, moment in which some countries ended the quarantine or started the de-escalation phase [16]; the window was established between 05/29/2020 and 05/31/2020.

The tool used for the collection of tweets was the Python *twitterscraper*[1] library, which allows to filter tweets for different time windows, as well as for words and hashtags. Tweets were filtered for each time window and had to contain the word "China", either in the content of the tweet or as a hashtag, taking into account the word in uppercase, lowercase, or capitalized. Since the objective of the analysis was to compare sentiment towards China before and during the pandemic, no other additional words were included, since it was intended to keep the time windows homogeneous and comparable.

3.2 Data Pre-processing

For each window, 10,000 tweets were downloaded, so we collected a total of 30,000 tweets for our study. Once tweets were downloaded, the Python *langdetect*[2] library was used to select those tweets that are in English language. Duplicated tweets were eliminated. In this process, an average of 3,144 tweets were excluded per time window. Finally, for the analysis stage, after pre-processing, 6,797 tweets were kept for the December time window, 6,953 for March and 6,357 for May.

Since our interest was to know the general sentiment about China, no variables or filters were included by countries, and only English-language tweets were used. These tweets could come from people at anyplace in the world.

---

[1] https://pypi.org/project/twitter-scraper/.
[2] https://pypi.org/project/langdetect/.

It is worth noting that Twitter has a request limit and does not allow to scrap all the tweets that were posted during a day or durign a time window, but a small percentage of the total of them, which is about 1% of the tweets. This is a restriction that Twitter has in its API.

3.3 Sentiment Analysis

Sentiment analysis was performed using the *VADER* (Valence Aware Dictionary and sentiment Reasoner)[3] tool, available as a Python library, and as one of the *NLTK* (Natural Language ToolKit)[4] library tools, which is widely used for natural language processing (NLP) tasks.

VADER is a lexicon and a rule-based Python libary specifically designed for the analysis of feelings expressed through social networks, which appropriates a series of rules or heuristics as tools to improve the analysis [8]. Regarding the lexicon, VADER includes a detailed list of emoticons, acronyms, and words commonly used in social networks. Each word has a score calculated using the Wisdom of the Crowd (WotC) methodology [21], where different trained individuals assigned a score between −4 and 4 to each word, and the mean is obtained to get the score of each word.

Regarding the heuristics or rules used to measure the intensity of the feelings contained in a text, five rules were contemplated:

1. *Exclamation point*: the number of exclamation points (!!) denotes intensity.
2. *Capitalization*: using uppercase, ALL-CAPS, to emphasize or increase the intensity of a feeling.
3. *Intensifiers*: using words that modify the intensity of the text. For example: extremely, marginally, incredibly.
4. *The conjunction "but"*: the dominant feeling of the text is the one that follows once the conjunction "but" is used.
5. *Negation*: cases in which negation changes the polarity of the text. For example: "the food there was not so good".

The VADER library has several advantages over other libraries and sentiment analysis tools. According to [8], the main advantages of this library are:

- It has shown outstanding results when analyzing information from social networks, since both, the lexicon and the grammar rules, are fine-tuned for the interpretation of the language used in microblog-like context.
- It has a capacity for classifying tweets as good, and even better, than other eleven classification methods and lexicons with which it was compared, among these are Inquiry Word Count (LIWC), General Inquirer (GI), Affective Norms for English Words (ANEW), Sen-tiWordNet (SWN), among others, and algorithms like Naive Bayes, Support Vector Machine and Maximun Entropy.

---

[3] https://pypi.org/project/vaderSentiment/.
[4] https://www.nltk.org/.

– It does not require training information or previous classification, since it is a rule-base type classification that has a "human-curated gold standard sentiment lexicon". Therefore, in the analysis carried out, information of classification errors is not obtained, given that for the use of this library it is not necessary to divide the data set into a training group and a test group.

3.4   Score Computation

Once each element of the tweet has its respective score, the library's "polarity score" function is used. This function takes the whole text as an argument and returns a dictionary-like object with four continuous measures, three of them denoting the probability that the tweet is positive, neutral or negative, and the fourth corresponds to a "compound score".

The *compound score* corresponds to an indicator that is calculated from the summation of the scores obtained for each feature according to the lexicon and it is normalized [2] between −1 and +1, where −1 corresponds to a feeling extremely negative and +1 extremely positive. This measure aims to synthesize the sentiment of the tweet into a single continuous indicator, which syncretizes the analysis in an aggregated measure.

Equation 1 describes the normalization function,

$$NormalizedScore = \frac{x}{\sqrt{x^2 + \alpha}},$$ (1)

where x is the individual score, and α is a constant set to 15 that represents the maximum expected value [2].

For example, with a text like "Not bad at all", we got a positive score = 0.487, neutral = 0.513, negative = 0.0, and a compound score = 0.431, where the summation of the first three scores is equal to 1 [3]. This can be interpreted as a tweet has a probability of belonging to each class, but the highest indicates that the tweet belongs to it.

3.5   Analysis and Visualization

Once the positive, neutral, negative and compound scores have been calculated, we proceed to the last stage of the methodology, which consists in comparing the sentiments of tweets that contain the word or hashtag "China". We analyzed the 3-time windows employing the visualization of the score trends of scores. For this task we used the *Matplotlib* and *Seaborn* libraries, which are Python libraries that are common tools for visualization tasks.

4   Results and Discussion

Figure 2 shows a bar graph with the mean of the scores. For the window of December (date before the pandemic), the mean of the compound score was positive with an score of 0.006, this implies that *neutral – positive* comments prevail. During March and May, when WHO declared the pandemic state, the compound score became *negative* with an average score of −0.122 and −0.089, respectively. This first results show a variation in the sentiment implicit in the tweets that refer to China, where March had the most *negative* compound score.

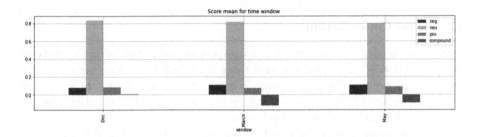

Fig. 2. Bar graph with the mean of the scores comparing the three time windows.

Despite the focus on the compound score, it is important to note that December reflects a small balance between negative and positive score, but in March and May the negative score increases with respect to the positive score, especially for March, and it is reflected in the compound score. It is worth mentioning that for this type of analysis the neutral field usually has the highest score due to the number of tweets where the weight of the words, both positive and negative, are very similar, such as sarcastic comments that imply great challenges for natural language libraries.

Now, we aim to identify which is the most common type of interaction with tweets and how this is related to the feelings towards China. The most common types of interaction were *likes*, above *retweets* and *replies*. Figure 3 shows a scatter plot discriminated by time window, where the relationship between the number of likes and the compound score was compared. It can be seen that the highest number of likes occurred in March with 15,918 likes for a tweet with negative compound score. Also, in the same month, there was a high reaction to a positive comment. However, the reaction to the negative comment has twice as many comments.

Table 1 shows the highest number of likes that each time window had, in March the interactions shot up, but for May they decreased considerably.

The tweet with the highest number of likes among the 3 windows can be seen in the Fig. 4.

Table 1. Highest number of *likes* for each time window

Window time	Number of *likes*
Dec	5,434
March	15,918
May	3,495

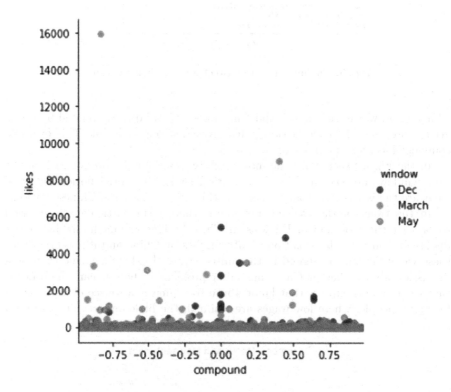

Fig. 3. Scatter plot of the number of *likes* for each window.

```
"You're the incompetent Idiot.
You've been sitting in Congress for decades and
didn't have enough common sense to write legislation to stop China
from making and manufacturing our products, especially our medicines.
The idiocy starts with you.....boo!"
```

Fig. 4. Text of the tweet whit highest number of likes for the three windows.

There is a notion that the text of the tweet has a negative sentiment related where the user complains about the importation of products and medicines from

```
What cruelty?
Is the first step act cruel?
Is record low black unemployment cruel?
Is preventing China's rape of US jobs cruel?
Is stopping illegal immigration cruel?
Is Making America Great Again Cruel?
```

December

```
Seriously, fuck those guys. I'm so damn sick of their BS.
They are rooting for people to die,
the economy to collapse and people to suffer.
Absolutely un American for a group of people who called him
racist for the China travel ban in January.
```

March

```
No one has shown more hatred than Donald Trump.
Hatred towards Obama.
Hatred with your unconstitutional Muslim ban.
Hatred with your wall that Mexico still hasn't paid for.
Hatred with your immigration policy.
Hatred with your attack on the media.
Hatred with your China bashing.
```

May

Fig. 5. The most negative tweet for each window time.

China. Also, words like "idiot" and "incompetent" are directly related to a negative score, and the exclamation point gives a stronger weight. This example comment has a compound score of −0.8356.

In the Fig. 5 tweets with the most negative compound score for each of the time windows are shown. This visualization let is got a brief notion about of what are the issues that lead to negative thinking towards the Chinese nation.

In the tweet of the December window, there is in particular "Is it cruel to prevent the violation of US jobs in China?" This comment highlights the dissatisfaction with the violation of labor rights by China and if it is cruel that these violations are prevented in the united states. In this magazine there is a discussion about whether China has labor problems, where it can be observed that the opinions express that labor abuse by China is a source of indignation for many people, where low wages are claimed, the little opportunity to find a

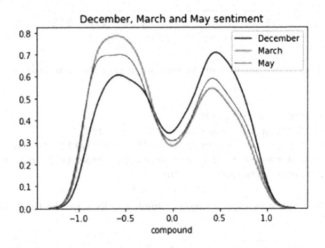

Fig. 6. Distplot graph comparing the compound score for the three time windows.

decent job in China, wage discrimination for women among others [4]. For the March window, the economic field is again related in the negative comment and for the May window there is talk of hatred promoted towards China, where the word "hatred" is used several times, which makes its negative score even higher.

Finally, Fig. 6 shows the density function graph of the compound score for each month. It can be seen that the window of December has the highest density on the positive axis of the compound on a range close to 0.5. However, for March and May there is a higher density on the negative axis of the compound in a range close to -0.5 to -0.8. Nevertheless, the density of the negative compound for May decreases slightly respect to March, this is reflected in the positive axis the compound, where the density of May is slightly higher.

In this figure, records with a compound score strictly equal to zero were removed, that is to say, comments with neutral sentiment, in order to have a better visualization of the data. However, the decrease in the curve is explained by the scores close to zero.

4.1 Discussion of the Method

The results obtained from a computational perspective show that VADER is an improved, more complete, and efficient method since it does the measurement feelings about a specific topic automatically, through word selection. it is a highlight that this method is improved and more complete because it also classifies acronyms, exclamation marks, and emojis, that for this type of analysis done on social networks is important to have on mind when determining a feeling. This inclusion in particular makes this method stand out from the other methods used for sentiment analysis that do not take this new information into account (emojis, acronyms, and exclamations). To verify its effectiveness, a search was made for the comment with the highest number of likes, which was in March and as previously shown, the compound score was -0.8356 and when reading the comment, it can be seen that it is a comment with sentiment negative. Based on this, this work can be used in case studies related such as the popularity of a politician, a country, a product, or any specific topic on platforms such as social networks that handle large volumes of information to analyze feelings of automated way.

5 Conclusions and Future Work

This paper presented a method to establish if there are negative feelings towards China. The information was downloaded from Twitter social network and a sentiment analysis was performed using a sentiment analysis strategy to tweets in 3 different time windows. A dataset of 30,000 tweets was built for three time windows: December 2019 (before the pandemic), March 2020 (month in which the pandemic was confirmed by the World Health Organization), and May 2020 (when some countries started the de-escalation phase). For this purpose we used the VADER library, which provided us sentiment analysis functionalities to analyze our Twitter dataset. Particularly, this library provide classification algorithms that allow for each word, emoji and exclamation signs to get a final score.

Results showed that for the December window most of the comments had a neutral - positive compound score, but March and May had a predominant negative compound score. By December 2019 there is a neutral - positive sentiment, but in March and May 2020, the sentiment towards China was neutral - negative. This result allow us to conclude that the sentiments towards China decreased due to the COVID-19.

Our work could be used in other contexts to automatically measuring the feelings that a country causes to other nations as a result of different types of actions.

In a future work we want to find the reasons why this sentiment towards China became negative, by identifying the different causes for the negative sentiment, in order to clarify if the feelings are mainly due to the pandemic, or if they are also related to other issues such as politics or economics. We also want to apply other machine learning techniques such as latent topics analysis for identifying what are the most important topics that emerge from text data. As future work we want to establish if there are significant differences between the scores of each window time by means of statistical hypothesis testing.

References

1. Chambers, N., et al.: Identifying political sentiment between nation states with social media, pp. 65–75 (2015). https://doi.org/10.18653/v1/D15-1007
2. Chatterjee, S., Krystyanczuc, M.: Python social media analytics. Analyze and visualize data from Twitter. YouTube, GitHub, and more, pp. 112–114. Packt Publishing Ltd., Birmingham, Mumbai (2017)
3. C.J., H.: Vader-sentiment-analysis. (2014). https://github.com/cjhutto/vader Sentiment
4. Crothall, G., Franceschini, I., Friedman, E., Gallagher, M.: Does china have a jobs problem? (2018). https://www.chinafile.com/conversation/does-china-have-jobs-problem
5. Culnan, M.J., McHugh, P.J., Zubillaga, J.I.: How large u.s. companies can use twitter and other social media to gain business value. MIS Quarterly Executive **9** (2010)
6. Golbeck, J., Grimes, J.M., Rogers, A.: Twitter use by the u.s. congress. J. Am. Soc. Inf. Sci. Technol. **61**(8), 1612–1621 (2010). https://doi.org/10.1002/asi.21344
7. Han, X., Choi, E., Tan, C.: No permanent friends or enemies: tracking relationships between nations from news (2019)
8. Hutto, C., Gilbert, E.: Vader: A parsimonious rule-based model for sentiment analysis of social media text (2015)
9. Ioanid, A., Scarlat, C.: Factors influencing social networks use for business: Twitter and Youtube analysis. Procedia Eng. **181**, 977–983 (2017). https://doi.org/10.1016/j.proeng.2017.02.496. 10th International Conference Interdisciplinarity in Engineering, INTER-ENG 2016, 6–7 October 2016, Tirgu Mures, Romania

10. Kim, S.K., Park, M.J., Rho, J.J.: Effect of the government's use of social media on the reliability of the government: focus on twitter. Public Manage. Rev. **17**(3), 328–355 (2015). https://doi.org/10.1080/14719037.2013.822530

11. Lee, K., Palsetia, D., Narayanan, R., Patwary, M.M.A., Agrawal, A., Choudary, A.: Twitter trending topic classification. In: 2011 IEEE 11th International Conference on Data Mining Workshops, pp. 251–258. Washington, DC, USA (2011)

12. Linda, S.L.A.I.: Social commerce - e-commerce in social media context. World Acad. Sci. Eng. Technol. **72**, 39–44 (2010)

13. Malik, Y., et al.: Emerging coronavirus disease (covid - 19), a pandemic public health emergency with animal linkages: current status update. The Indian J. Animal Sci. **90**(8), 3 (2020). In Processing

14. Mata, F.J., Quesada, A.: Web 2.0, social networks and e-commerce as marketing tools. J. Theor. Appl. Electron. Commerce Res. **9**, 56–69 (2014)

15. Organization, W.H.: Coronavirus disease 2019 (covid-19) situation report - 51 (2020). https://www.who.int/docs/default-source/coronaviruse/situation-reports/20200311-sitrep-51-covid-19.pdf?sfvrsn=1ba62e57_10

16. Organization, W.H.: Coronavirus disease 2019 (covid - 19) situation report - 99 (2020). https://www.who.int/docs/default-source/coronaviruse/situation-reports/20200428-sitrep-99-covid-19.pdf?sfvrsn=119fc381_2

17. de Rosario, A.H., Sáez-Martín, A., del Carmen Caba-Pérez, M.: Using social media to enhance citizen engagement with local government: Twitter or facebook? New Media Soc. **20**(1), 29–49 (2018). https://doi.org/10.1177/1461444816645652

18. Small, T.A.: e-government in the age of social media: an analysis of the canadian government's use of twitter. Policy Internet **4**(3–4), 91–111 (2012). https://doi.org/10.1002/poi3.12

19. Sobaci, M.Z., Karkin, N.: The use of twitter by mayors in turkey: Tweets for better public services? Govern. Inf. Quarterly **30**(4), 417–425 (2013). https://doi.org/10.1016/j.giq.2013.05.014

20. Sobrino, J.: Análisis de sentimientos en twitter (tesis de maestría), p. 98. Universitat Oberta de Catalunya, Barcelona (2018)

21. Surowiecki, J.: The wisdom of crowds: why the many are smarter than the few and how collective wisdom shapes business, economies, societies, and nations. pp. xxi, 296 pages. New York, USA (2005)

22. Vargas-Calderón, V., Sánchez, N., Calderón-Benavides, L., Camargo, J.: Sentiment polarity classification of tweets using an extended dictionary. Inteligencia Artif. **21**(62) (2018). https://doi.org/10.4114/intartif.vol21iss62pp1-12

23. Xu, Y., He, Q., Ni, S.: Evaluating online public sentiments towards china: a case study of english and chinese twitter discourse during the 2019 chinese national day (2020)

24. Zhao, W.X., Li, S., He, Y., Chang, E.Y., Wen, J., Li, X.: Connecting social media to e-commerce: cold-start product recommendation using microblogging information. IEEE Trans. Knowl. Data Eng. **28**(5), 1147–1159 (2016). https://doi.org/10.1109/TKDE.2015.2508816

A Virtual Wallet Product Recommender System Based on Collaborative Filtering

David Rodolfo Prieto-Torres[(✉)] and Ixent Galpin

Facultad de Ciencias Naturales e Ingeniería Universidad Jorge Tadeo Lozano,
Bogotá, Colombia
{davidr.prietot,ixent}@utadeo.edu.co

Abstract. Nowadays, there are several options when it comes to making use of products that facilitate financial services to people through virtual wallets. A recommender system quickly provides customers with what they are looking for and helps discover new products that they like. In this paper, a recommender system is proposed that can be customized according to the variables implemented by Movii, a company in the Colombian FinTech sector, taking as input transaction records that indicate the frequency of use of each product, which can be understood as ratings of these products. To determine the model that will implement the recommender system that will be deployed, different models are evaluated, such as techniques based on collaborative filtering. In our evaluation, we found that the model that recommends the most popular products is the one that offers the best performance in recommending a product to users. Thus, it is possible to generate some estimated recommendations on the services available by the company, involving users who consume the available services.

Keywords: Recommender system · Fintech · Collaborative filtering · Prediction

1 Introduction

FinTech is an acronym for *Financial Technology*, referring to an interdisciplinary topic that combines finance, technology management and innovation management. This concept is used to describe any innovative idea that improves financial services processes, by proposing technological solutions according to different business situations. On the other hand, the proposed ideas could also lead to new business models or even new businesses which involve customers with financial products and services [9].

Movii[1] is the first FinTech in Colombia to offer a virtual wallet by means of a digital platform. It is based on an application in which users can have immediate access to various *products* through a cell phone with an Android or iOS operating system. Those products include an account or electronic wallet, a

---

[1] https://www.movii.com.co.

H. Florez and S. Misra (Eds.): ICAI 2020, CCIS 1277, pp. 222–234, 2020.
https://doi.org/10.1007/978-3-030-61702-8_16

debit card without procedures or processes to pay on the Internet and shops, the possibility of making free transfers between accounts, paying bills, among others. The marketing area at Movii faces the difficulty of defining which products to effectively recommend to the clients or users of the application. Therefore, it seeks to create a solution that meets the needs of the actors involved in the use of the products. To do this, we identify the most worthwhile products to recommend so that a user will continue using the app.

In this work, the predictive data process carried out by companies in the FinTech sector for their decision-making is observed and analyzed, intervening with the creation of a predictive analytical model, implementing technological resources to improve their productivity in product sales, keeping track of their progress. Various algorithms for recommender systems are evaluated and the best performing algorithm is selected. The result is a study carried out on the products sold by a company that belongs to the FinTech sector, related to the products offered to customers.

Currently, the vast majority of measurement models have focused on individual organizations, with companies measuring performance at strategic, tactical, and operational levels with metrics that address different types of customer services. These collaboration models are based on a clear definition of what is expected for the processes of the organizations. Companies use standardized metrics, evaluating and using benchmarking services to benchmark against other entities and perform gap analysis [14].

Companies are made up of different areas, which seek to do their best to offer quality digital products to their customers, thus being the interest and importance in obtaining a support tool in their decision-making, exploring different methods for the exploitation of data.

The purpose of developing this predictive analytics model is not only contemplated by making sales predictions, but also to analyze customers to find out about their greatest interactions with some of the products offered. Once the analysis has been carried out, a better experience can be provided with the other items offered by the company, managing to integrate the stakeholders.

This paper is structured as follows: Sect. 2 describes related work. Section 3 describes the understanding of business and data, and Sect. 4 the preparation of data. Section 5 describes the process for data modeling and evaluation and selection of the best performing recommendation algorithm, and Sect. 6 describes the deployment of the recommender system. Section 7 concludes the paper.

2   Related Work

Table 1 presents recommender systems that have been developed in the financial domain. As can be seen from the table, most of the recommender systems currently developed focus on recommending investments to different trading funds in financial companies, e.g., [5,13]. However, as done in our work, recommender systems are used for recommending products to customers, as is the case with [1,3,8]. However, none of these systems seem to base recommendations on the number of user transactions of other products.

Table 1. Recommender systems used in the Financial Domain

Paper	Application	Input data	Techniques
[13]	Predictions in the stock market	Public stock data from Yahoo or Google	UBCF
[5]	Suggestions investment assets to a large panel of investors	Financial investment information by a major European bank	BPR-MF
[8]	Predictive systems in the process of delivery of personalized customer services for the recommendation of the products of a banking entity	Multiple sets of instances were generated randomly based on INE (2017) for different groups of clients, who were assigned various products	CF combined with content-based filtering
[16]	Fuzzy scoring expending model, the importance score of each product for each customer can be generated as input of the collaborative filter method	User demographic data and product purchase data from financial sector	CF, content-based filtering and hybrid approach
[2]	Rating system using machine learning that will check the potential of the startups to become successful so that the potential investor can determine if the startup is worth investing in and to prototype and implement the system like this	The dataset was obtained using the data.world service. From the service, the .csv document was received with the statistics of Kickstarter platform, which is the crowdfunding platform for startups in different areas	Supervised and unsupervised machine learning algorithms
[3]	A prediction of recommendations of particular items for a particular consumer is based on the updated singular value decomposition while receiving the ratings and updating the singular value decomposition	Rating on item are received from consumers as a sequential stream of data	SVD
[15]	Coupling relationship between users and financial products and transaction behavior between users and users	MovieLens and BCSs datasets	CB algorithm based on user reference clustering
[10]	Multiobjective binary integer programming model to allocate sponsored recommendations considering a dual objective of maximizing ad revenue and user utility	The data is from an online grocery retailer in the United States, operating in 12 states and Washington D.C., with unique stock-keeping units (SKUs), unique users and orders	UBCF
[17]	Interpolation-based recommender system that exploits the collaborative filtering and the Indexing HDMR method	The data set is imported to MS SQL Server Management Studio to manipulate. There are unique customers, unique products and purchases in the data set	CB and content-based filtering
[1]	Evaluation of multi-label classification techniques and recommender systems for cross-selling purposes in the financial services sector	The dataset represents its Belgian customer base on December 1, 2016, containing unique customers and unique products	UBCF

As is evident from Table 1, it can be seen that a broad range of techniques have been used for recommender systems in the financial domain. These include User-Based Collaborative Filtering (UBCF), Bayesian Personalized Ranking (BPR-MF), Collaborative Filtering (CF), and Singular Value Decomposition (SVD). For this reason, it is important to carry out an empirical evaluation to determine the recommender model to deploy for our FinTech product recommender system.

3   Preliminaries

The methodology contemplated for the development of the recommender system is focused on the architecture based on the life cycles of projects for mining and data analytics. According to [4], CRISP-DM (Cross Industry Standard Process for Data Mining) proposes a methodology for data mining projects, providing guidance for their execution, starting with an analysis of the business problem and then transforming it into a technical data mining problem.

3.1   Business Understanding

Movii is a company in the SEDPE[2] category, defined as an entity supervised by the Financial Superintendence, which can obtain savings from the public only to offer the services of payments, money orders, transfers, collection and savings [12]. In this way, it allows citizens to have an electronic means of payment to carry out their transactions. Likewise, they can obtain funds from natural or legal persons through electronic deposits, and in turn provide transactional financial services. It currently has more than 700,000 active users and 34 products available for users of the mobile app, and is made up of different areas such as commercial, marketing, product, IT, among others.

3.2   Data Understanding

Requirements gathering sessions carried out with the technology area at Movii established that there is an Online Transaction Processing (OLTP) data source which is responsible for carrying out the transactional processing of the mobile application. There are two namespaces in the database that contain the information in the following two categories:

- Transactional and descriptive tables for pay-as-you-go product top-ups, money orders, sale of virtual pins, among others.
- Transactional and descriptive tables of the product purchases with debit card that the application offers for its users.

---

[2] SEDPE is an abbreviation in Spanish meaning *Specialized Companies in Electronic Deposits and Payments*.

The data, comprising the transactional history of the movements generated by the mobile application, is structured using the relational entity model with the relevant integrity constraints as appropriate. It is worth mentioning that it is an append-only model, i.e., there is no data deletion carried out.

An ETL (Extraction, Transformation and Loading) process allows entities to move data from different sources, with appropiate mappings, cleaning and other transformations. The data is loaded to a target database and/or data warehouse for posterior analysis, or to another Operational Data Store (ODS) to support an additional operational business process. Amazon Web Services (AWS) is a well-known clould service provider that enables such processes to take place. In our system, we implement an architecture as the one shown in Fig. 1, using Python as the main coding language. As can be seen in the architecture diagram, we run services such as EC2 for ETL script execution, S3 to support a data lake for loading information, Redshift [6] as a target data store, EMR with R previously installed for processing of large loads, and Amazon QuickSight [11] as a company reporting tool.

The execution frequency of upload is approximately every five minutes from the origin (OLTP database) to destination (Amazon Redshift database) via scheduled tasks. The understanding of the stored and transformed information is required for the creation of the recommender system based on the models provided by the company.

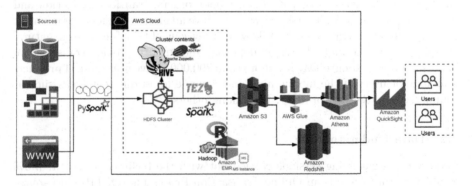

Fig. 1. Operational Data Store architecture diagram

4   Data Preparation

Amazon Redshift (RS) is a fully managed petabyte-scale AWS cloud data storage service. The information of the business models required to develop the recommender system are housed in said columnar database. Monthly, approximately 400,000 transactions are generated between the products used by the users of the application, classified by the company's operational area by means of identifiers previously mapped the information with their respective transactional filters.

Table 2. Classification of products by number of transactions.

Product_id	Transaction_count	Product_id	Transaction_count
1101	213404	2801	7161
1201	50273	2802	4856
1301	739609	3003	4832
1303	19768	3004	178553
1501	4081	3101	632
1701	388364	3102	3385
1801	10991	3103	4
2102	6028	3104	194
2106	212122	3201	16563
2201	1184	4102	6028
2202	642576	4201	77210
2203	196964	6101	107352
2205	31732	6802	1801381
2206	193041	6804	238952
2208	1177	7101	165520
2301	110966	7102	77657
2702	82604		

The data that we use to build the recommender models is extracted according to the requirements specified by the company. Additionally, a clean data extraction is performed from the RS database for training and testing the algorithms to be evaluated:

- For the *training* dataset: We extract data via an SQL query grouping the users and product codes, generating a count per transaction, applying the following filters: Exclusion of unnecessary (operational) products and users who have less than four products used in the transactions history; inclusion of users with active status and successful transactions.
- For the *test* dataset: We extract data via an SQL query in the same manner as for the training set, however we include all users regardless of the number of products used.

Table 2 presents an example of the results dataset with the number of transactions for each financial product.

5   Modelling and Evaluation

5.1   Modelling

recommenderlab [7] is an R package that provides a framework for testing and developing recommendation algorithms. recommenderlab supports rating data sets such as 1 to 5 stars as well as binary (0–1) scales. It comes with the following, inbuilt recommendation algorithms: User-based collaborative filtering (UBCF), Element-based collaborative filtering (IBCF), SVD with mean column imputation (SVD), popular items (POPULAR), items chosen at random for comparison (RANDOM), among others. However, we note that it is an extensible framework and enables users to create their own custom algorithms for evaluation.

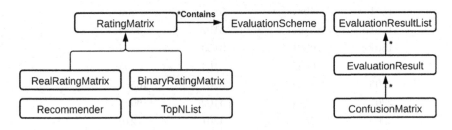

Fig. 2. UML class diagram for the recommenderlab [7] package.

recommenderlab is implemented using formal classes in the object-oriented programming S4 class system for R. Figure 2 shows the main classes and their relationships; the package provides a common interface for rating data `rating-Matrix` implementing many methods typically available for array-like objects. For example, `dim()`, `dimnames()`, `colCounts()`, `rowCounts()`, `colMeans()`, `rowMeans()`, `colSums()` and `rowSums()`. Also, `sample()` can be used to sample users (rows) and `image()` produces an image graph depicting a rating matrix [7].

Initially the data is taken by the columns `user_id` (user ID or mobile number), `product_id` (product identifier) and `transaction` (number of transactions per user and product), from the generated training information in a CSV file.

Once loaded in an R dataframe variable, a conversion to a matrix is performed by means of a function called `acast`, organizing users in rows, products in columns and number of transactions as values. For the modeling of the recommender system, the number of ratings is taken as a qualification. The assumption we make here is that the more transactions a user carries out involving a particular product, the higher the subjective user preferences towards that product. Thus, we use the transaction count as a proxy for the rating in the recommender system that we deploy in Sect. 6.

The normalization of the input data is required in order to standardize the values, correcting for the scale effect that comes from the different level of ranges of the users in their ratings. This is necessary in order to make users comparable, as a user who has been a customer for a longer amount of time is likely to have a higher range of transaction counts compared to a relatively new user. There are two methods to normalize supported by recommenderlab: subtracting the mean, and subtracting the mean and dividing by the standard deviation. For standardization (see Fig. 3) the `normalize()` function is called. This function applied to the raw rating matrix in row-wise (i.e., per user) using the `range` method. We

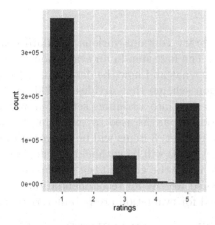

Fig. 3. Distribution of standardized ratings.

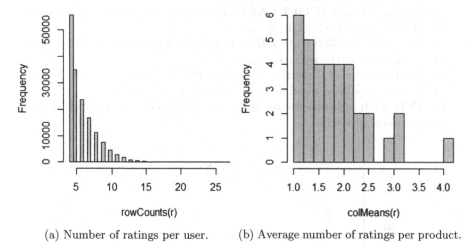

(a) Number of ratings per user.   (b) Average number of ratings per product.

Fig. 4. Histograms showing rating distributions.

specify a ranges from 1 to 5 with the parameter `on.constant = quiet`. In this way, we avoid a skew in the data caused by the presence of older vs. newer users, given that as mentioned before, older users are likely to have a higher number of transactions.

`realRatingMatrix` is a sparse matrix recommenderlab data structure. The resulting normalized matrix has `item` × `product` dimensions of 160682×35 with 939654 ratings in total.

The histograms in the Fig. 4 show that there are unusually many users with ratings (number of normalized transactions) of around 1. The average number of ratings per product, shown in Fig. 4b, resembles a geometric distribution along with the previous histogram with a mean above 2.

5.2   Evaluation

The recommenderlab library contains various standard evaluation methods for recommender systems. The first step in an evaluation is to create an evaluation scheme that determines what and how the data is used for training and testing. We create an evaluation scheme that divides 70,000 users from the extracted training data set, segmented into a training set (90%) and a test set (10%). The cross validation method (cross) is used by executing the algorithm evaluation at k = 10 folds. For the test set, 3 items will be delivered to the recommendation algorithm and the other items will be withheld to calculate the error. We set the definition of a positive using the goodRating = 4 threshold, thus classifying the scores that are considered worthy for recommendation.

The algorithms used for evaluation are parameterized in the following form:

- For the **Random Elements (RANDOM)** algorithm no value is parameterized, therefore param = NULL is applied.
- The **Popular Items (POPULAR)** method does not parameterize any values, therefore param = NULL is applied.
- For **User-based collaborative filtering (UBCF)**, the nearest 15 neighbors are obtained using the parameter nn = 15.
- For **Item-based collaborative filtering (IBCF)**, we specify that the nearest 15 items should be obtained using the parameter k = 15.
- For **SVD with column-mean imputation (SVD)** we specify an approximation range of k = 15.

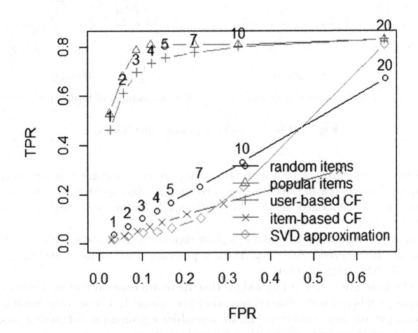

Fig. 5. Comparison of ROC curves for several recommender methods

The evaluation method used is `topNList`, combining the values within a vector to evaluate the recommendation lists top-1, top-2, top-3, top-4, top-5, top-7, top-10 and top-20. The `plot()` function of R is used to generate the graphs of Receiver Operating Characteristic (ROC) and precision-recall (see Figs. 5 y 6), using the `annotate` to score points depending on the selected curves with the length of the list.

It is observed that for the previously selected data set and the given evaluation scheme, the POPULAR and UBCF methods outperform all other evaluated methods. In the Fig. 5 it can be seen that they are above the other methods, since for each length of the top-N list method, they provide a better combination of true positive rate (TPR) and false positive rate (FPR). A similar trend is evident in Fig. 6, where the POPULAR method shows the highest precision and recall values.

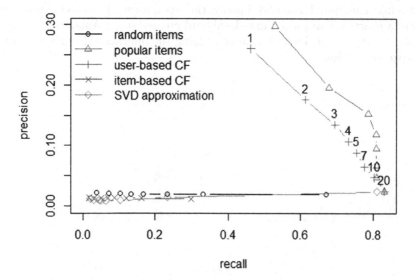

Fig. 6. Comparison of precision-recall curves for several recommender methods.

6 Deployment

The creation of the recommender is carried out by means of the `Recommender()` constructor function, using the POPULAR recommendation method for which we reported the best results in Sect. 5. We take the training data set as a reference, calling the recommender with the variable `recom`. The test data set is loaded into the algorithm by reading the CSV file where all the users to which the recommender will be applied are, executing the process of converting the matrix data, normalization and conversion to a matrix `realRatingMatrix` seen in the modeling phase described in Sect. 5.1.

`Predict` is a function of recommenderlab that returns predictions of lists or objects for top-N methods or qualifications. This function returns an object of class `topNList` that contains a top-N list for each active user. The following values are configured for the recommender system:

- `object`: The variable `recom`, the recommender object, is returned.
- `newdata`: Loading the data of the active users, which uses the previously loaded variable with the test dataset.
- `n` is the maximum number of recommended items in each list. `n=5` is specified, extracting 5 recommended elements.

Once `predict` is executed, the `bestN` function is implemented, returning the best product to recommend for each of the lists. Finally, a dashboard is created, shown in Fig. 7 in a tool available to the end user. After the final execution of the algorithm, the variable is converted to a list type and the data is exported to a data lake configured using S3. Finally, the recommended products classified in different charts are displayed in a dashboard created using Amazon QuickSight, for analysis by people interested in consuming the information in the marketing department at Movii.

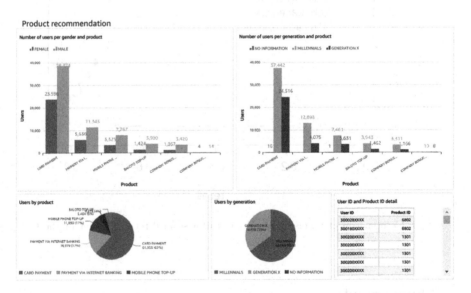

Fig. 7. Dashboard with the products to recommend generated by the recommender system.

7 Conclusion

In this paper, we have proposed a recommender system for a FinTech company based on collaborative filtering. We follow the phases proposed by the CRISP-DM methodology for data analytics projects. We understood the business of a

FinTech company, involving the stakeholders and generating a knowledge base for the development of the recommender system. We studied and understood the information from the data sources, getting to know the extraction, transformation and loading process implemented in the data currently in the company. We analyzed the important data for the creation of the recommender system, classifying the training and test data sets. We modelled the input data, applying standardization and normalization in the training information. We evaluated different evaluation methods for the recommender system, and identified the best methods as being Popular and UBCF. We displayed the information generated using a dashboard, using the data generated by the recommender system. Future work could usefully investigate the incorporation of other important data types into FinTech companies, as well as the ratings of the company's mobile app.

References

1. Bogaert, M., Lootens, J., Van den Poel, D., Ballings, M.: Evaluating multi-label classifiers and recommender systems in the financial service sector. Eur. J. Oper. Res. **279**(2), 620–634 (2019)
2. Bogdanova, M.: Fintech underwriting using machine learning (2019)
3. Brand, M.E.: On-line recommender system, US Patent 7,475,027 (Jan 6 2009)
4. Cobos, C., Zuñiga, J., Guarin, J., León, E., Mendoza, M.: CMIN-herramienta case basada en CRISP-DM para el soporte de proyectos de minería de datos. Ingenieria e investigación **30**(3), 45–56 (2010)
5. Gigli, A., Lillo, F., Regoli, D.: Recommender systems for banking and financial services. In: RecSys Posters (2017)
6. Gupta, A., et al.: Amazon redshift and the case for simpler data warehouses. In: Proceedings of the 2015 ACM SIGMOD International Conference on Management of data, pp. 1917–1923 (2015)
7. Hahsler, M.: recommenderlab: A framework for developing and testing recommendation algorithms. Technical report (2015)
8. Hernández-Nieves, E., Hernández, G., Gil-González, A.B., Rodríguez-González, S., Corchado, J.M.: Fog computing architecture for personalized recommendation of banking products. Expert Syst. Appl. **140**, 112900 (2020)
9. Leong, K., Sung, A.: FinTech (Financial Technology): what is it and how to use technologies to create business value in fintech way? Int. J. Innov. Manage. Technol. **9**(2), 74–78 (2018)
10. Malthouse, E.C., Vakeel, K.A., Hessary, Y.K., Burke, R., Fuduric, M.: A multi-stakeholder recommender systems algorithm for allocating sponsored recommendations. In: RMSE@ RecSys (2019)
11. Nadipalli, R.: Effective Business Intelligence with QuickSight. Packt Publishing Ltd, Birmingham (2017)
12. Pérez, C., Pacheco, B.H., et al.: Beneficios potenciales de un incremento en el uso de los medios de pago electrónicos en colombia (2016)
13. Sayyed, F., Argiddi, R., Apte, S.: Collaborative filtering recommender system for financial market. Int. J. Eng. Adv. Technol. (IJEAT) ISSN pp. 2249–8958 (2013)
14. Stefanovic, N.: Proactive supply chain performance management with predictive analytics. Sci. World J. **2014**, (2014)

15. Xue, J., Zhu, E., Liu, Q., Wang, C., Yin, J.: A joint approach to data clustering and robo-advisor. In: Sun, X., Pan, Z., Bertino, E. (eds.) ICCCS 2018. LNCS, vol. 11063, pp. 97–109. Springer, Cham (2018). https://doi.org/10.1007/978-3-030-00006-6_9
16. Yang, C.L., Hsu, S.C., Hua, K.L., Cheng, W.H.: Fuzzy personalized scoring model for recommendation system. In: ICASSP 2019–2019 IEEE International Conference on Acoustics, Speech and Signal Processing (ICASSP), pp. 1577–1581. IEEE (2019)
17. Yücel Kasap, Ö.: A polynomial modeling based algorithm in Top-N recommendation. Ph.D. thesis, Bahçeşehir University Graduate School of Natural and Applied Sciences (2018)

Evaluating Models for a Higher Education Course Recommender System Using State Exam Results

Jenny Mayerly Díaz-Díaz[✉] and Ixent Galpin[✉]

Facultad de Ciencias Naturales e Ingeniería, Universidad Jorge Tadeo Lozano,
Bogotá, Colombia
{jennym.diazd,ixent}@utadeo.edu.co

Abstract. When young people approach the end of their schooling, they are faced with a plethora of often daunting decisions, including whether to go to University or other further education institution, and what further education course is most suitable for them. In this paper, we propose using result data obtained from the Colombian *Saber 11/T&T/Pro* state exams as input for a higher education course recommender system. We compare five different recommender models by analyzing precision, recall, ROC curves and prediction error. Our findings are that user-based collaborative filtering, and the model that recommends the most popular courses, are the ones that perform best. We note that while the context of this work is in Colombia, most other countries have similar or equivalent state exams. It can therefore be expected that our research findings can be more generally applied to other contexts. As further work, we hope to deploy this recommender system as a mobile telephone application for young people to use to help them choose higher education courses.

Keywords: Recommender system · Collaborative filtering · Higher education courses

1 Introduction

When young people approach the end of their schooling, they are faced with a plethora of often daunting decisions, including whether to go to University or a further education institution, and what further education course is most suitable for them. This paper addresses the problems regarding the question of what to study at University. For many completing high school and making the leap to the adult world, it is perhaps one of the most difficult decisions that they face. For most, it is not clear what their professional field of action will be, or where they should study. In this paper, we propose a Recommender System (RS) to

This work is supported by Minciencias from the Call for Research Proposals 804-2018, Project Grant 115680463846.

advise students finishing secondary school on further education courses suitable for them.

Recommender Systems [12] are typically useful in settings where there is a broad range of items to choose from. For example, in a movie recommendation setting such as [4], based on preferences elicited from users, a typical RS approach is to recommend movies to a user based on preferences of users with similar tastes, as is the case with User-based Collaborative Filtering (UBCF) [5]. The problem of selecting a higher education course is unlike that of selecting a movie to watch. While a person may watch a movie relatively frequently, most people only choose a further education course once in their lives, due to the time and financial costs entailed by this decision. Furthermore, the consequences of choosing an incorrect movie are typically, at worst, a couple of hours of wasted time. In contrast, making the wrong decision when leaving school can have significant ramifications for the rest of that person's life.

Recommending the best higher education course to study using a technique such as UBCF may be especially challenging due to, as mentioned previously, the relatively small number of higher education courses a person typically takes in their lives. This means that there is likely to be very few ratings per user. In effect, everyone in the rating dataset may turn out to be a cold-start user [9]. To circumvent this potential issue, in this paper we propose using the scores obtained for the various state exams as a proxy for ratings in a Recommender System. In Colombia, there are two sets of state exams: *Saber 11* is typically taken during eleventh grade, when nearing the end of school. *Saber Pro* and *Saber T&T* are taken when the higher education course, for professional or technical courses respectively. These can be taken as an indication of how successful the student was in that course, given that the content of the exams is related to the higher education course taken.

The *Saber 11* exam is broken down into different thematic modules such as, for example, language comprehension or mathematical reasoning. Our proposal involves using the score for each thematic module to predict how well a student will do in the *Saber Pro* or *Saber T&T* exams, using classical recommender system techniques. Based on the predicted *Saber Pro* or *Saber T&T* scores, we can then recommend the most suitable higher education courses to the student. In this paper, we evaluate the performance of various RS technique approaches using recommenderlab [3], a framework in R that enables the comparison of different recommendation methods, to determine the most suitable approach for such a recommender system.

This paper is structured as follows: Sect. 2 presents a background on the Colombian state exams, and various recommender system algorithms which we evaluate. In Sect. 3, we describe related work. Section 4 detailed the data sources used, how they were integrated, and the application of normalization techniques. We subsequently, in Sect. 5, illustrate how the deployment of the algorithm would be, by illustrating the example recommendation output with different techniques. Section 6 describes the experimental evaluation carried to determine the performance of the aforementioned recommender system techniques. Finally, Sect. 7 concludes.

2   Background

2.1   Colombian State Exams

For a large number of young people it is clear that they want to continue studying, but they do not know what subject to study, or what higher education institution is the most suitable for them. In Colombia, the *ICFES*[1] state entity offers educational evaluation services at all levels, and in particular, supports the National Ministry of Education in conducting state exams, such as the *Saber 11* exam, which aims to evaluate eleventh grade students to enable them to access higher education. Furthermore, it acts as an important barometer to monitor the quality of education offered by secondary education establishments. It can also be taken by those who have already obtained school-leaving baccalaureate diploma, or have passed a baccalaureate validation exam. On the other hand, the state *Saber Pro* exam is aimed at students who have passed 75% of the credits of their respective professional university education programs.

Saber 11 Exam: The *Saber 11* exam is designed to assess the degree of development of skills of students who are finishing eleventh grade at School. The results are used by different actors in the educational system and beyond, *viz.*:

- it provides students with elements for their self-evaluation and the development of their life project.
- it allows higher education institutions to select suitable candidates for their education programs and to monitor their academic progress.
- it offers educational establishments references for their self-evaluation processes and orientation of their pedagogical practices.
- allows educational authorities to build quality indicators.

Annually, approximately 600,000 students take the *Saber 11*.

Exam Saber Pro and T&T: The *Saber Pro and T&T* exam has a compulsory first section for all those who take the exam, which is made up of 5 modules that assess generic skills (critical reading, quantitative reasoning, citizenship skills, written communication and English). In addition, there are modules associated with specific themes and contents that students have the possibility to take according to their area of study.

Approximately 400,000 students take the *Saber Pro and T&T* exams every year.

---

[1] ICFES is an abbreviation in Spanish for *Colombian Institute for the Evaluation of Education*. See https://www.icfes.gov.co/.

2.2   Recommender System Algorithms

This section briefly summarizes several algorithms used by Recommender Systems and which are supported by recommenderlab, which are used for the evaluation in Sect. 6.

- *User-based Collaborative filtering (UBCF)*: This algorithm produces recommendations that are made based on the terms of similarity between users. In other words, this algorithm recommends items that are of the same affinity as other users. The objects to be recommended are chosen from those that have received the highest score from other users with similar tastes or interests, thus reflecting a similar pattern of preferences [2].
- *Item-based Collaborative filtering (IBCF)*: This algorithm recommends items based on items that are deemed to be similar to those preferred by that user [6].
- *Singular value decomposition (SVD):* This algorithm is based on matrix factorization. Broadly speaking, it reduces the number of features in the user element ratings matrix by reducing its dimensions [7].
- *Random:* This algorithm selects items at random to the user.
- *Popular:* This algorithm recommends items based on their overall popularity, based on those which have the highest scores.
- *Rerecommend:* This algorithm recommends items which have been previously highly rated. It has two variants: recommendHPR recommends items according to the highest predicted ratings for a user. recommendMF recommends the most frequent item in a user item rating matrix.
- *Hybrid Recommender:* The approach combines the recommendation algorithms mentioned previously, according to the weights specified.

3   Related Work

The choice of a technical or professional career is an important act in the life of a person, for which a study was developed to make a recommendation of a possible professional or technical study option, with the support of an efficient tool and the objective of evaluating the knowledge of a grade eleven student, which is the *Saber 11* exam, by simplifying these classification elements, a more effective and subjective prediction is made for the user.

As a first measure, the different recommendation systems allow us to help make a better recommendation for the user and regret that in the field of education it is not well used [10,13]. For the majority of the objective users they lack the necessary knowledge to carry out decision making and that this in turn guides them to select the best option.

The recommendation systems with the academic profiles in the student stage and in the higher education of the base users, offers an alternative to users who want to continue with the next educational stage, that is, their higher education.

There are different techniques or forms for the implementation of a recommendation system, based on the similarity metrics and the information available to form the catalog, which will serve as the main source for the recommender when making the classification [11].

Most of the recommendation models are based on calculating different statistics that provide the number of possibilities of recommendation to the user on a given item, although some differ from the techniques and information on the academic characteristics of the students [1].

There are several documentations on the analysis carried out on education, where some focus on high school students applying various classification algorithms, which assesses the importance of education based on different metrics, providing great collaboration with teachers [8].

4   Data Preparation

4.1   Data Sources

In order to build the recommender models evaluated in this paper we used three datasets:

- The results of the *Saber 11* exam spanning the periods 2012-1 to 2015-1 comprising 1,751,870 records, corresponding to candidates registered with a high school educational establishment (i.e., we did not include records from candidates who took the exam independently).
- The results from *Saber Pro* and T&T between the years 2016 to 2018, comprising 657,443 records.
- A reference dataset to enable us to map minor identity card numbers to adult identity card numbers. This was necessary because in Colombia these identity documents use different numbering schemes. This dataset is created from the registration questionnaire used during the registration for the *Saber Pro* and Saber T&T exams.

The distribution of the results for the *Saber 11* exam is shown in Fig. 1a, and the combined results for the *Saber Pro* and *T&T* exams is shown in Fig. 1b. Note that the result ranges between the exams differ. The scores for the *Saber 11* exam are in the range of 0 to 100, whereas for the *Saber Pro* and *T&T* exams they are in the range of 0 to 300.

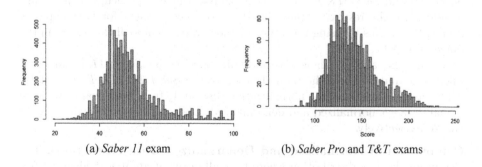

(a) *Saber 11* exam   (b) *Saber Pro* and *T&T* exams

Fig. 1. Histograms showing results for Colombian state exams.

4.2   Integration of Data Sources

In order to create a user × item ratings matrix, we combined these sources into a single dataframe as follows:

- Join between *Saber Pro/Saber T&T* variable that indicates the identity document that the student used when taking *Saber 11* and the identity document variable registered in *Saber 11*.
- Join between variables of identity documents reported at the time of registering for *Saber Pro/Saber T&T* and *Saber 11*.
- Phonetic Join between *Saber* Pro students who did not find their *Saber 11* registration with the previous steps and students registered in *Saber 11*. This phonetic join takes into account names, surnames, gender and date of birth.

This dataset generated contains a sample of 2,142 users with their respective results from both exams. These results are found as variables in columns. An excerpt of the dataframe resulting from the integration of the data sources is shown in Table 1.

Table 1. Excerpt of the Final dataset showing dataframe resulting from integration of data sources.

User	Social sciences	English	Reading	Maths	Science	Architecture	Business
1	64	95	71	86	100	205	
2	61	85	64	65	62		
3	67	90	62	61	65		
4	51	85	59	67	66		
5	60	60	59	55	55		225

4.3   Data Normalization

As can be seen from the histograms in Fig. 1, the results for the *Saber 11* and *Saber Pro* and *Saber T&T* exams have different ranges. As such, it is necessary to normalize the results so that they have the same ranges for both types of exams. We do this by using the scalar method, which scales all the results in the range of 0 to 1.

Figures 2a and 2b show the normalization of the *Saber 11* exam data. Figures 2c and 2d show the normalization of the *Saber Pro/T&T* exam data. After having carried out the normalization separately from both exams, we have a final data set normalized and denormalized, as shown in the following Fig. 2f and 2e respectively.

Comparison of Normalized and Denormalized Data Histograms. The histogram shows a distribution where they all occur at an almost identical frequency and the most frequent positive ratings with a steady decline toward the rating. Since this distribution may be the result of users with a biased rating, we look at the rating distribution after normalization below (Fig. 3).

As shown in Fig. 4 the distribution of the scores is closer to a normal distribution after unifying the two data sets.

5   An Example Run

After the algorithms have been evaluated together, each one will be implemented to evaluate their respective predictions.

User-Based Collaborative Filtering (UBCF). To predict the evaluation that a user will make of an item that has not yet been seen, users with similar profiles are searched and the evaluations of these other users on the item are used as an estimate of the user's evaluation. The prediction was made based on the following top-N recommendation (N = 3) for the first 11 selected users. Note that the figure is omitted for space reasons.

Item-Based Collaborative Filtering (IBCF). To predict the estimation or evaluation that a user will make of an item that he/she has not yet seen, other similar items that have had or received ratings and that the user has also rated are searched. Estimates are used the user has made similar items as a prediction of their assessment or score on the item. This recommendation system could be confused with the content-based one, the difference is that each item is not defined by its attributes but by the score it has received. The prediction was made based on the following top-N recommendation (N = 3) for the first 11 selected users, as evidenced by the results in Fig. 5a.

RE-RECOMMEND. In Fig. 5b the prediction will be displayed, according to the following top-N recommendations (N = 3) for the first 11 selected users.

SVD. In Fig. 5c the prediction is displayed, according to the following top-N recommendations (N = 3) for the first 11 selected users

Popular Recommender. In this case, the model has a list of top-N recommendations (N = 3) for the first 11 selected users, where it shows popularity of professional and technical careers. Note that the result is not shown here for space reasons.

Hybrid Recommender. Create and combine recommendations using various recommendation algorithms and given the weight of weights, such as:

Case 1, in Fig. 5d:

```
method = "UBCF" Peso = 0.6
method = "POPULAR" Peso = 0.3
method = "IBCF" Peso = 0.1
```

Case 2, not shown for space reasons:

```
method = "UBCF" Peso = 0.3
method = "POPULAR" Peso = 0.5
method = "IBCF" Peso = 0.2
```

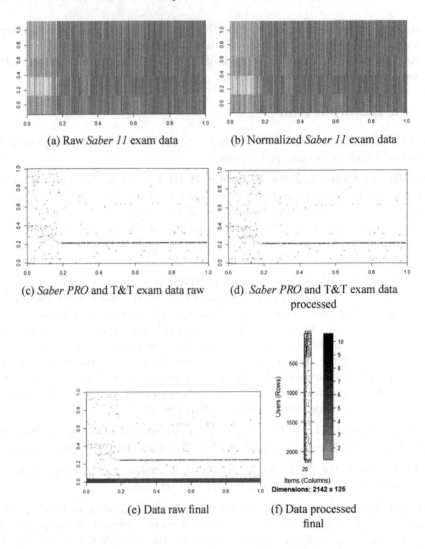

(a) Raw *Saber 11* exam data

(b) Normalized *Saber 11* exam data

(c) *Saber PRO* and T&T exam data raw

(d) *Saber PRO* and T&T exam data processed

(e) Data raw final

(f) Data processed final

Fig. 2. Normalization of the exam data

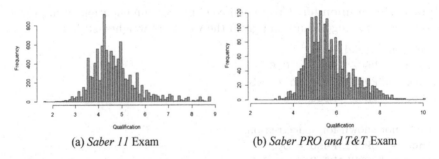

(a) *Saber 11* Exam

(b) *Saber PRO and T&T* Exam

Fig. 3. Histograms showing distributions of exam scores after normalization.

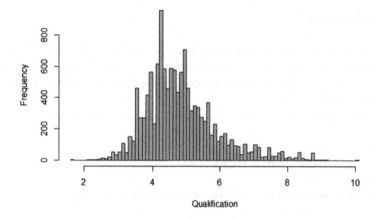

Fig. 4. Histogram showing distribution resulting from normalization of the integrated data set.

(a) IBCF algorithm  (b) Rerecommend algorithm

(c) SVD algorithm 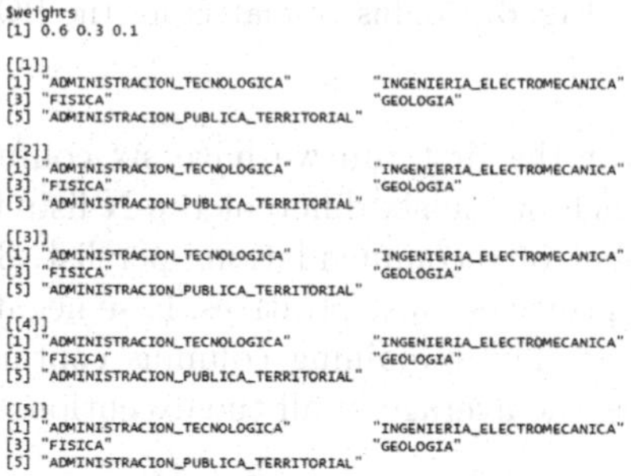 (d) Hybrid algorithm Case 1

Fig. 5. Prediction result for different algorithms

6   Evaluation

For our evaluation, a cross-validation scheme was created (K = 10). We specified the given = 3 parameter, meaning that for test users, all but three randomly selected items are withheld for evaluation. The parameterization of the evaluation scheme was as follows:

```
scheme <- evaluationScheme(dtev, method="cross", k=10 given=3,goodRating=5)
scheme
Evaluation scheme with 3 items given
Method: 'cross-validation' with 10 run(s).
Good ratings: >=5.000000
Data set: 2142 x 125 rating matrix of class 'realRatingMatrix' with 12850 ratings.
```

We use the evaluation scheme created to evaluate the popular recommendation method. We evaluated the recommendation lists of top-1, top-3, top-5, top-10, top-15 and top-20:

```
resultsPopular <- evaluate(scheme, method="POPULAR", type =
"topNList", n=c(1,3,5,10,15,20))
```

The result is the classification report for the four runs, as shown on Fig. 6.

	TP	FP	FN	TN	precision	recall	TPR	FPR
1	0.3194444	0.6805556	0.7129630	120.2870	0.31944444	0.4148418	0.4148418	0.005618585
3	0.3333333	2.6666667	0.6990741	118.3009	0.11111111	0.4330900	0.4330900	0.022037987
5	0.3379630	4.6620370	0.6944444	116.3056	0.06759259	0.4403893	0.4403893	0.038534230
10	0.3472222	9.6527778	0.6851852	111.3148	0.03472222	0.4501217	0.4501217	0.079793326
15	0.3657407	14.6342593	0.6666667	106.3333	0.02438272	0.4647202	0.4647202	0.120974613
20	0.3750000	19.6250000	0.6574074	101.3426	0.01875000	0.4708029	0.4708029	0.162233390

Fig. 6. Confusion matrix for the POPULAR recommendation algorithm

For the first run we have six confusion matrices represented by rows, one for each of the six different top-N lists that we used for the evaluation. n is the number of recommendations per list. TP, FP, FN, and TN are the inputs for true positives, false positives, false negatives, and true negatives in the confusion matrix. The remaining columns contain the performance calculated. Figure 7 shows the average of all the executions of the evaluation results.

	TP	FP	FN	TN	precision	recall	TPR	FPR
1	0.2259259	0.7740741	0.8180556	120.1819	0.22592593	0.3010066	0.3010066	0.006392765
3	0.2449074	2.7550926	0.7990741	118.2009	0.08163580	0.3249361	0.3249361	0.022771260
5	0.2643519	4.7356481	0.7796296	116.2204	0.05287037	0.3500705	0.3500705	0.039145927
10	0.2819444	9.7180556	0.7620370	111.2380	0.02819444	0.3656503	0.3656503	0.080339572
15	0.2962963	14.7037037	0.7476852	106.2523	0.01975309	0.3776552	0.3776552	0.121560225
20	0.3027778	19.6972222	0.7412037	101.2588	0.01513889	0.3844237	0.3844237	0.162846984

Fig. 7. Average number of executions

The results of the evaluation plotted on the ROC curve shown in Fig. 9a is the curve of the true positive rate (TPR) against the false positive rate (FPR), which indicates that in iterations 3, 5 and 10 it represents a moderately perfect diagnostic value.

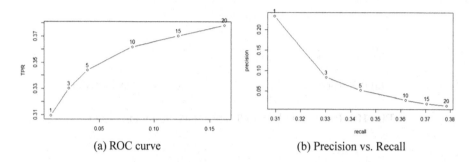

(a) ROC curve   (b) Precision vs. Recall

Fig. 8. Results of the POPULAR recommendation algorithm

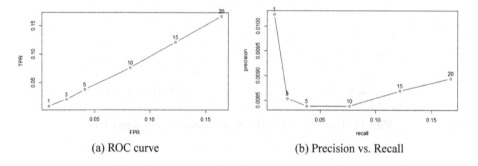

(a) ROC curve   (b) Precision vs. Recall

Fig. 9. Results for the RANDOM recommendation algorithm

For Fig. 8b where we write down the curve with the size of the list N = 1 it is higher with respect to recall of the other iterations.

Algorithm Evaluation. We will evaluate the results of the RANDOM, UBCF, IBCF and SVD algorithms

- Random Algorithm
  In Fig. 9a it shows a random classification, since list N is located along the diagonal line or as the non-discrimination line is known.
  In Fig. 9b, it is evident that the precision is much more effective when the iteration N = 1, however its recall is better with respect to the other iterations.

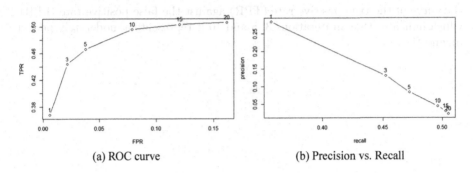

(a) ROC curve

(b) Precision vs. Recall

Fig. 10. Results for the UBCF recommendation algorithm

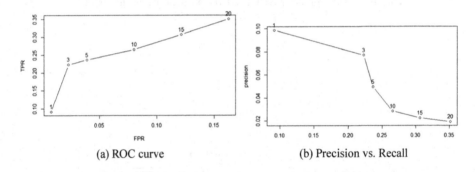

(a) ROC curve

(b) Precision vs. Recall

Fig. 11. Results for the IBCF recommendation algorithm

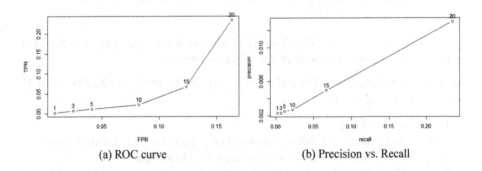

(a) ROC curve

(b) Precision vs. Recall

Fig. 12. Results for the SVD recommendation algorithm

- UBCF Algorithm
  The results of the evaluation on the ROC curve shown in Fig. 10a is the curve of (TPR) with respect to (FPR). The curve indicates that in iterations 3, 5 and 10 it represents a fairly good diagnostic value and even almost the same as the Popular algorithm.
  In Fig. 10b, it can be seen that in the N = 1 iteration it has a greater precision with respect to the other iterations, however the iterations 10, 15 and 20 are predominant in recall.
- IBCF Algorithm
  For this algorithm, the evaluation on the ROC curve shown in Fig. 11a. The curve indicates that in iterations 5, 10 and 15 they remain slightly constant, therefore their result is quite good.
  In Fig. 11b, a drastic change is evident in the N = 5 iteration, since its precision is lower with respect to the recall of the other iterations.
- SVD Algorithm
  The SVD algorithm, as regards its result of the ROC curve, does not have a favorable diagnostic, since even the N = 20 iteration is good, as can be seen in Fig. 12a.
  In Fig. 12b, iterations 1, 3, 5 and 10 are the result of the best recall, however in terms of precision it was not, but it was for iterations 15 and 20.

6.1 Comparison of Recommendations

Comparison of various recommendation algorithms is one of the main functions of Recommenderlab [3]. That is why we jointly evaluate these algorithms using the CROSS method. We then use the evaluation scheme to compare the five recommendation models:

```
algorithms <- list(
"random items" = list(name="RANDOM", param=NULL),
"popular items" = list(name="POPULAR", param=NULL),
"user-based CF" = list(name="UBCF", param=list(nn=50)),
"item-based CF" = list(name="IBCF", param=list(k=50)),
"SVD approximation" = list(name="SVD", param=list(k = 50)))
resultsalgorcross <- evaluate(scheme, algorithms, type = "topNList", n=c(1, 3, 5, 10, 15,
20))
```

Figures 13a and 13b shows the prediction time and the model time for each algorithm included in the execution list, using four-fold cross validation.

Figure 14a is the ROC curve of the 5 algorithms. Together we observe that the Popular, IBCF, UBCF algorithms have a better diagnosis regarding the recommendations of a professional or technical career, with respect to the Random algorithm and SVD not they were so efficient in diagnosing.

Regarding Fig. 14b, it is observed that the UBCF, POPULAR and IBCF algorithms have a better recall with respect to the other remaining algorithms, additionally the RANDOM algorithm has a lower precision and a constant in its recall and the SVD algorithm has a lower precision and recall with respect to the other algorithms evaluated.

```
RANDOM run fold/sample [model time/prediction time]
        1   [0sec/0.08sec]
        2   [0.01sec/0.1sec]
        3   [0sec/0.12sec]
        4   [0sec/0.1sec]
        5   [0sec/0.06sec]
        6   [0sec/0.09sec]
        7   [0sec/0.09sec]
        8   [0sec/0.09sec]
        9   [0.01sec/0.08sec]
       10   [0.02sec/0.09sec]
POPULAR run fold/sample [model time/prediction time]
        1   [0sec/0.56sec]                                  IBCF run fold/sample [model time/prediction time]
        2   [0sec/0.62sec]                                          1   [0.1sec/0.07sec]
        3   [0sec/0.67sec]                                          2   [0.1sec/0.09sec]
        4   [0.02sec/0.62sec]                                       3   [0.11sec/0.08sec]
        5   [0.01sec/0.8sec]                                        4   [0.11sec/0.09sec]
        6   [0.02sec/0.5sec]                                        5   [0.11sec/0.06sec]
        7   [0sec/0.55sec]                                          6   [0.14sec/0.08sec]
        8   [0.02sec/0.54sec]                                       7   [0.11sec/0.08sec]
        9   [0sec/0.56sec]                                          8   [0.12sec/0.08sec]
       10   [0sec/0.57sec]                                          9   [0.09sec/0.09sec]
UBCF run fold/sample [model time/prediction time]                  10   [0.11sec/0.08sec]
        1   [0sec/0.6sec]                                   SVD run fold/sample [model time/prediction time]
        2   [0sec/0.54sec]                                          1   [0.07sec/0.2sec]
        3   [0sec/0.67sec]                                          2   [0.06sec/0.15sec]
        4   [0.02sec/0.67sec]                                       3   [0.08sec/0.19sec]
        5   [0sec/0.54sec]                                          4   [0.07sec/0.19sec]
        6   [0sec/0.6sec]                                           5   [0.05sec/0.17sec]
        7   [0sec/0.61sec]                                          6   [0.06sec/0.16sec]
        8   [0sec/0.74sec]                                          7   [0.08sec/0.2sec]
        9   [0sec/0.56sec]                                          8   [0.09sec/0.21sec]
       10   [0.01sec/0.5sec]                                        9   [0.07sec/0.18sec]
                                                                   10   [0.08sec/0.26sec]
```

(a) RANDOM, POPULAR and UBCF   (b) IBCF and SVD

Fig. 13. Evaluation of the five algorithms

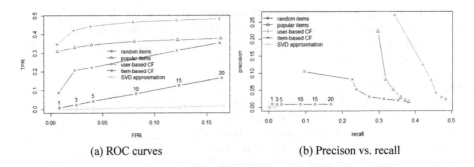

(a) ROC curves   (b) Precison vs. recall

Fig. 14. Comparison of performance for the five RS models

6.2   Comparison of Predicted Ratings

We evaluate not the top recommendations, but how well the algorithm ratings can predict. Plotting the results shows a bar graph with the mean root error and the mean absolute error as shown in Fig. 15, the one with the largest error is the Random algorithm and the one with the least error is the Popular algorithm

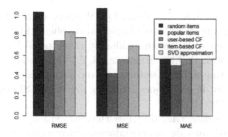

Fig. 15. Comparison of RMSE, MSE and MAE for recommendation methods

7   Conclusions

In this paper, we have shown that it is possible to cast the Colombian state exam results as a user × item recommendation matrix to construct a Recommender System for recommending higher education courses to young people. We evaluate five different recommender system models. The worst performing model is the SVD approximation, which has worse results than the random baseline. The best results are obtained using the user-based collaborative filtering and popular models. We note that while the context of this work is in Colombia, most other countries have similar or equivalent state exams. It can therefore be expected that our research findings can be more generally applied to other contexts. As further work, we hope to deploy this recommender system as a mobile application for young people to use to help them choose higher education courses.

References

1. Caprar, G.V., et al.: Longitudinal analysis of the role of perceived self-efficacy for self-regulated learning in academic continuance and achievement. J. Educ. Psychol. **100**(3), 525 (2008)
2. Goldberg, D., Nichols, D., Oki, B.M., Terry, D.: Using collaborative filtering to weave an information tapestry. Commun. ACM **35**(12), 61–70 (1992)
3. Hahsler, M.: recommenderlab: a framework for developing and testing recommendation algorithms. Tech. rep. (2015)
4. Harper, F.M., Konstan, J.A.: The movielens datasets: history and context. ACM Trans. Interact. Intell. Syst. (TIIS) **5**(4), 1–19 (2015)
5. Herlocker, J.L., Konstan, J.A., Terveen, L.G., Riedl, J.T.: Evaluating collaborative filtering recommender systems. ACM Trans. Inf. Syst. (TOIS) **22**(1), 5–53 (2004)
6. Kitts, B., Freed, D., Vrieze, M.: Cross-sell: a fast promotion-tunable customer-item recommendation method based on conditionally independent probabilities. In: Proceedings of the Sixth ACM SIGKDD, pp. 437–446 (2000)
7. Koren, Y., Bell, R., Volinsky, C.: Matrix factorization techniques for recommender systems. Computer **42**(8), 30–37 (2009)
8. Lakkaraju, H., et al.: A machine learning framework to identify students at risk of adverse academic outcomes. In: Proceedings of the 21th ACM SIGKDD International Conference on Knowledge Discovery and Data Mining, pp. 1909–1918 (2015)

9. Liu, N.N., Meng, X., Liu, C., Yang, Q.: Wisdom of the better few: cold start recommendation via representative based rating elicitation. In: Proceedings of the Fifth ACM Conference on Recommender Systems, pp. 37–44 (2011)

10. López, M.B., Montes, A.J.H., Ramírez, R.V., Hernández, G.A., Cabada, R.Z., Estrada, M.L.B.: Emoremsys: sistema de recomendación de recursos educativos basado en detección de emociones. Revista Ibérica de Sistemas e Tecnologias de Informação **17**, 80–95 (2016)

11. Olguín, G.M., de Jesús, Y.L., de Celis Herrero, M.P.: Métricas de similaridad y evaluación para sistemas de recomendación de filtrado colaborativo. Revista de Investigación en Tecnologías de la Información **7**(14), 224–240 (2019)

12. Ricci, F., Rokach, L., Shapira, B.: Introduction to recommender systems handbook. In: Ricci, F., Rokach, L., Shapira, B., Kantor, P.B. (eds.) Recommender Systems Handbook, pp. 1–35. Springer, Boston (2011). https://doi.org/10.1007/978-0-387-85820-3_1

13. Torres, E.: Evaluación del uso de algoritmos colaborativos para orientar académicamente al alumnado en bachillerato. Departamento de Informática-Universidad de Jaén **143** (2007)

Future Scenarios of Water Security: A Case of Bogotá River Basin, Colombia

Andres Chavarro[1], Monica Castaneda[2], Sebastian Zapata[2(✉)],
and Isaac Dyner[2]

[1] Institucion Universitaria Politecnico Gran Colombiano, Bogotá, Colombia
achavarr@poligran.edu.co
[2] Universidad Jorge Tadeo Lozano, Bogotá, Colombia
{mcastanr,szapatar,idyner}@unal.edu.co

Abstract. Bogotá is the largest city in Colombia, it is the capital district and 20% of the Colombian population live there. Public reports have suggested that the vulnerability of water supply system in this city is high, mainly because of inadequate water resource management, climate variability, and population growth. This paper proposes a computational model to assess the long-term effects of delays in water plants and droughts on the water security of the Bogotá river basin, Colombia. The computational model is based on systemic approach, in particular, water planning on the supply side is studied in detail. The main conclusion that can be drawn is that under a Business as Usual (BAU) scenario, the study area will experiment a risk of water security. To avoid a risky situation for water security, the construction time of water plants should be lower than 9 years. The contribution of this work is to raise the awareness of policy makers about the risk of shortage.

Keywords: System dynamics · Water supply · Delays in water plants · Water demand

1 Introduction

Bogotá is a city in the center of Colombia, it is an engine of the Colombian economy, as it generated almost 25% of Colombia's Gross Domestic Product by 2018 [38].

Bogotá's water resources come from the river basin on the eastern Andean mountain range region [39]. During the last two decades, public reports suggested that the vulnerability of the Bogotá River Basin is high [40,41]. i.e., the capacity of the water supply system to cover water demand is not enough [40]. The causes of risk water shortages in the Bogotá river basin are [41]: first, inadequate management of the territory; second, lack of systematic approach of water resources management; third, problems of scarcity due to variability and climate change. Next, these causes are deepened. Some authors agree that the inadequate management of territory in Bogotá increases risk of water shortages [1]. Given

© Springer Nature Switzerland AG 2020
H. Florez and S. Misra (Eds.): ICAI 2020, CCIS 1277, pp. 251–265, 2020.
https://doi.org/10.1007/978-3-030-61702-8_18

that Bogotá has high population density, this leads to inadequate management of the territory expressed as urban growth without long-term planning [2]. This entails disorderly growth of the city [3,4], pressure for urban expansion [36], solutions for housing in areas of flood risk and destruction of ecosystems [5]. In consequence, the urban edge is expanding threating paramos – a rare and unique ecosystem that produces natural water that flows to Colombian rivers [6].

Additionally, territorial plans in paramos have not been implemented, the delimitation of these areas is not clear, and fines for breaching environmental legislation do not repair the environmental damage to paramos [36].

According to some specialists the risk of water shortages in Bogotá is much more related to management than to a real crisis of scarcity. In this regard, the authors have highlighted the following problems: (i) the institutional design of water, i.e., the supply system is not based on a holistic approach, there are flaws of planning, confusion between institutions and poor water allocation; (ii) there is a lack of economic or administrative instruments to manage the river basin;(iii) the infrastructure to guarantee the availability of water in Bogotá and the region is not enough [7].

Regarding the climate change effects over water resources, these effects are: the increase of temperature and consequently water consumption, the shifts in hydrological cycles i.e., precipitation patterns, and the frequency of floods. In other words, the level of uncertainty produced by climate change on water resources involves a risk to water supply. In particular, there is empirical evidence of these climate change effects on the Bogotá region [35]. This, combined with the population growth and consequently greater use of land exacerbate the environmental flows such as water. In fact, Buytaert and De Bievre [8] estimated that this situation could increase water demand in Bogotá even up to 50% by 2050. Which is risky, because of the lack of adaptation strategies for Bogotá in response to previous environmental changes, as well as the possible delays in the construction of water plants.

In this context, it is useful to build a computational model to assess the long-term effects of delays in water plants and droughts on the water security of the region, which may help to raise the awareness of policy makers about the risk of shortages. This research may be considered a relevant contribution to the study area, given the importance of the region to the country, and the lack of literature applied to this study area (Bogotá river basin).

In order to achieve this, the document is organized as follows: The second section indicates the use of systems dynamics in the field of water resources management in the international and local context. In the third section, the study area is characterized. In the fourth part of the document, a description of the model is made through the presentation of the dynamic hypothesis and the presentation of the flows and levels model. The results of the different scenarios and public policy measures that respond to the proposed challenge are shown in the fifth section. Finally, the discussion of the results and conclusions of the investigation are made in the last section.

2   Literature Review

This section offers a review of the main studies developed to understand the complexity behind management of water resources from a System Dynamics (SD) approach. Although, there are no studies that use System Dynamics (SD) for water supply in Colombia, the panorama on a planetary scale is different.

Water security is the capacity of a country or region to face water-related disasters, and safeguard access to water for the sustainable development at social, economic, and ecological level [9]. To ensure water security in a region is challenging due to its complexity. As water security involves many political, technological and biophysical processes; which are characterized by many interactions and nonlinear interrelationships [9,10]. In addition, these complexity features are reinforced by the uncertainty of future water availability and water demand, which are driven by changing processes – economic, geo-political, demographic, and climatic [11].

An important concept related to water security is the water environment carrying capacity. It is defined as "the largest population and economic scale that the water environment can support in a specific region during a period of time without an adverse impact on the local water environment" [12,13]. In these papers, water security may be understood as a process, which comprises two stages [14–17]. First, determining the water environment carrying capacity to cover current and future water demand without hindering the environmental flow. Second, the water resource management. Next a literature review regarding these issues is presented.

2.1   Determining the Water Environment Carrying Capacity

Some important studies have addressed the topic of water environment carrying capacity, Zhou et al. [18], Hanjra and Qureshi [19] and Wang et al. [20] analyse the role of the drivers that impact global food supply and demand, particularly, the impact of increasing water scarcity on global food security. It emerged from the analysis that, the demand for food and water will be increased due to the population and income growth. The subsequent increase in water scarcity will impact food security and socioeconomic conditions. In fact, feeding the 2050 population will leave a water gap of about 3300 km^3 even after applying water management measures to improve water availability.

In contrast, other researchers have used China as case study [21,22]. Such is the case for Yang et al. [23], who propose a method to assess the water environment carrying capacity. To achieving this, they developed a System Dynamics (SD) model applied to China. This model considered the population size, economic growth and their coupling effects on water resources. Results show that water resources constraints may lead to economic stagnation.

Li et al. [24] presented a SD model to establish the WRCC in Beijing city. They concluded that under the status quo scenario, the WRCC will declined over time. In this sense, water saving policies and pollution control investment are key policies to ensure the sustainable utilization of water.

Yang et al. [25] combined a SD model and an analytic hierarchy process (AHP) to evaluate WRCC for Xian, proposing five scenarios to improve the WRCC. They concluded that the current socio-economic development of this city is unsustainable. The key to changing the trend is to improve irrigation efficiency and increase investment in irrigation infrastructure. A similar proposal was developed by Wang et al. [13], who also combined an AHP and SD model applied to Bosten lake basin, China. Their results showed that the growth rate of water demand and reutilization rate in the industrial sector, increase the WRCC.

2.2 Water Resource Management

According to Chen and Wei [9], water resource management consists of designing the rational used of water, based on scientific principles. SD models have been used around the world to support water resource management. Such is the case of Mirchi et al. [26], who described the importance of SD to water resource management, demonstrating how SD tools may help to conceptualize water resource problems through a holistic approach. Also, Tidwell et al. [27] used a SD model to support water resource management for a three-county region in north-central New Mexico. They found that treating the model as an instructive tool instead of a predictive tool, allows planners to better visualize the problem as well potential solutions.

Similarly, in the US, Stave [28] proposed a strategic-level SD model focused on water management which was applied to Las Vegas, Nevada. The purpose of this paper was to build awareness between public, about the value of water conservation.

Qi and Chang [29] proposed an SD model to forecast water demand, they considered the relationship between water demand and macroeconomic environment. The case study was Manatee County, Florida. They concluded that socioeconomic factors such as economic development, income, real estate status, and health care level were having an important influence on domestic water demand.

Niazi et al. [30] studied a strategy to minimize evaporative water losses and groundwater depletion, and also to provide water to expanded agricultural activities. They found that this may be achieved through aquifer storage and recovery, as well as water storage in an ephemeral river. This proposal may be successful if converge next factors: central technical planning, aquifer storage and recovery strategies and farmer engagement and education. They used an SD model applied to Sirik region of Iran.

Moncada et al. [33] studied assessed water stress vulnerability in small Andean basins in this paper is concluded that climate variability, increases vulnerability and water shortages. And the absence of strategies cause vulnerability.

Finally, Hossein and Zarghami [31] assessed different water supply scenarios for the Shiraz City, using a SD model. Findings suggested that the city must focus on city resources in the next decade to eliminate water shortages. Also, a Monte Carlo analysis in the SD model suggested that the shortage is more sensitive to the irrigation efficiency than the treated wastewater rate and the dam capacity.

This research may be considered a relevant contribution to the study area, given the importance of the region to the country, and the lack of literature applied to this study area (Bogotá river basin). The contribution of this work is to raise the awareness of policy makers about the risk of shortages associated to construction delays of water plants.

3   Case Study: Bogotá River Basin

This research focuses on the region, which water demand is supplied by the Bogotá river Basin. Its territory extends about 9,645 km^2, this area includes 53 municipalities of the basin and the city of Bogotá [39]. This region mainly consumes surface water provided by four paramos. These paramos are: Chingaza, Guacheneque, Guerrero and Sumapaz. These paramos are located in the corners of the region, and the Chingaza paramo supplies about 70% of the water demand in the region [32] (see Fig. 1).

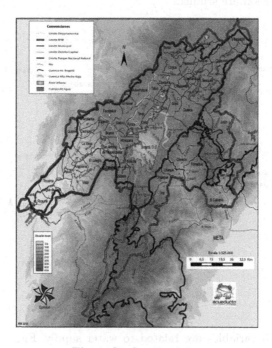

Fig. 1. Study area map.

4 Model Description

The water supply system in the study area is influenced by the relationship between water consumption and water supply capacity. This relationship is depicted in Fig. 2. As may be observed in Fig. 2, system margin is calculated as a ratio that involves water consumption and water supply; if this ratio increases, it inuences the management of the system from the demand side, which has an effect on water consumption from industrial, agricultural and domestic sector (negative feedback loop B1). When the system margin increases, it inuences the management of the system from the supply side, leading to build water plants (production capacity), which in the long-term inuences system margin (negative feedback loop B2). Water consumption reduces water availability, this depends on natural water outflows and water inflows (see negative feedback loop B3), the latter is also influenced by the land use policy (see negative feedback loop B4).

Feedback loop B4 is related to policies to increase the water available through a better land use, such as the protection of lands with high water resources Fig. 2

Figure 2 shows the main components of the built-in SD model. With this model, the long-term effects of delays in water plants and droughts on the water security of the region are studied.

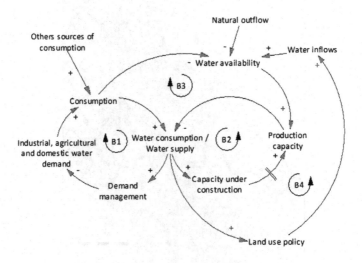

Fig. 2. Dynamic hypothesis.

In Fig. 3, two variables are related to water supply. First, water reservoir which refers to the availability of water resource. Second, supply capacity which refers to the production capacity, i.e., the water plants and water pipelines.

Water reservoir and supply capacity, along with the water consumption are used to calculate the system margin (SM). A detailed equation is shown below (See Eq. 1). Under normal conditions, the system margin varies between 0 and 1.

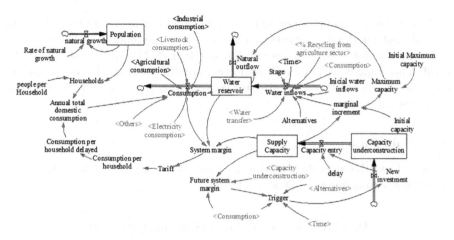

Fig. 3. Stocks and flows diagram.

The system margin may vary due to: the expansion of water sources, new reservoirs, basin transfers, as well as the expansion of production capacity, i.e., more or better water plants. Likewise, there may be negative variations in supply due to long droughts, reduction of water production in paramos or surface effluents.

$$SM(t) = \frac{[min(SC(t), WR(t)) - C(t)]}{C(t)} \tag{1}$$

Supply capacity (SC) is depicted by a integral equation (See Eq. 2), it indicates that the rate of change for the supply capacity for one unit of time is equivalent to the capacity entry (CE). Which is the water plant projects, 9 years after their construction end.

$$SC(t) = \int CE(t)\,dt + SC(t_0) \tag{2}$$

According to Eq. 3, the water plant projects are accumulated in the capacity under construction variable (CUC). Which depends on new investment (NI), and the water plants that are built, i.e. the capacity entr (CE).

$$CUC(t) = \int [NI(t) - CE(t)]dt + CUC(t_0) \tag{3}$$

Regarding the water reservoir (WR), its equation may be observed in Eq. 4. The rate of change for the water reservoir for one unit of time is equal to water inflows (WI), minus consumption (C) and minus natural outflow (NO).

$$WR(t) = \int [WI(t) - C(t) - NO(t)]\,dt + WR(t_0) \tag{4}$$

The water consumption per each sector is modeled using the historical growth rate. Except for the domestic consumption, where the number of households is forecasted, and the water consumption per household depends on the water tariff. The number of household projection is built using the historical growth rate, the effect of water tariff on water consumption per household is simulated using historical data.

4.1 Main Data

Table 1 shows the main data used to feed the computational model. These data is important to define the initial conditions.

Table 1. Main data used in the computational model.

Variable	Data [units]	Font size and style
Water consumption	$778.291\,m^3$	[38]
Water power capacity	$860\,Mm^3/yr$	[3,4]
System margin	10.3%	Own calculation
Population	8.000.000	[38]
Annual population growth rate	1.5%	[38]

5 Findings

5.1 Scenarios

Three scenarios are briefly described in this section. The system margin, the water consumption and water supply capacity are studied for a simulation period between 2018 to 2050. The first scenario illustrates the Business as Usual (BAU) scenario, it is based on current water supply plan, where the construction time for water plants is about 9 years [3]. The second scenario shows the impact of delay in construction of water plants, a construction time of 12 years is assumed. Under the third scenario, the construction time for water plants is about 9 years, i.e., delays are not considered. Also, the third scenario presents the effect of drought during 2026 on the water security. In Colombia, droughts caused by the weather phenomenon El Niño are usual, here it is assumed a drought in the worst moment for the system, to measure the robustness of the water supply system. Table 2 summarizes the simulation scenarios.

Table 2. Description of the scenarios.

Variable	Scenario 1	Scenario 2	Scenario 3
Time water plants construction 9 years	x		x
Time water plants construction 12 years		x	
Droughts			x

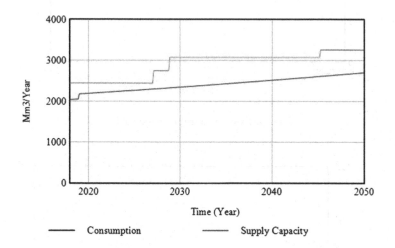

Fig. 4. Water consumption versus water supply capacity, scenario 1.

5.2   Simulation Results

Under Fig. 4, water supply satisfies water consumption during the simulation period, however, the risk of water scarcity by 2026 is high, as during this year the gap between water supply and consumption becomes smaller. Water supply capacity shows a particular behavior, the steps represent the entrance of water plants by 2027, 2028 and 2045.

By 2026 system margin is about 6% and it increases when water plants are built by 2027 and 2028. After this, system margin falls until the entrance of a new water plant by 2045. System margin has the trend of being reduced in time, this is because of the continuous growth of water consumption, water consumption also grows by steps but remains after this constant (see Fig. 5).

For scenario 2, Fig. 6 shows a risk of water scarcity by 2029. Although, the risk of water scarcity occurs 3 years later in comparison to the first scenario, this time the risk is greatest. The gap between water supply and consumption becomes smaller than for scenario 1. In fact, the system margin is reduced to 4% by 2029, according to Fig. 7. This behavior is explained by the longer delay in water plant construction.

Under scenario 2, the entrance of water plants occurs by 2030, 2032 and 2049, as can be observed in Fig. 7. The behavior of system margin in scenario 2

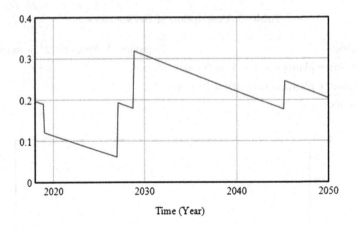

Fig. 5. System margin, scenario 1.

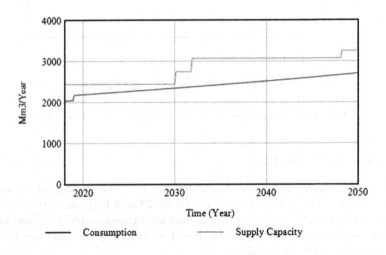

Fig. 6. Water consumption versus water supply capacity, scenario 2.

is very similar to scenario 1, notwithstanding, scenario 2 is out of phase regarding scenario 1.

Under the third scenario a drought was assumed by 2026, as can be observed in Fig. 8, the gap between water supply and consumption becomes smaller. After this, the water supply system reacts with the entrance of water plants by 2027, 2028 and 2045. This is the riskiest scenario for water security, given that the system margin falls to −1%, as can be observed in Fig. 9.

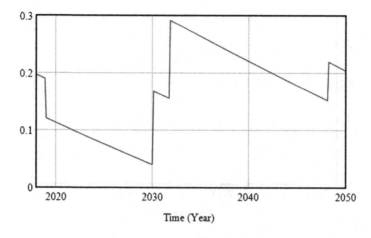

Fig. 7. System margin, scenario 2.

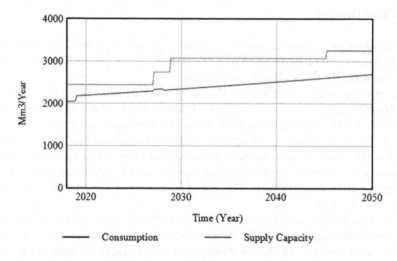

Fig. 8. Water consumption versus water supply capacity, scenario 3.

Scenario 3 and scenario 1 are different between 2026 and 2027, i.e., during the drought. After drought finishes, the system margin presents increases and water plants are built. The entrance of water plants occurs by 2027, 2029 and 2045.

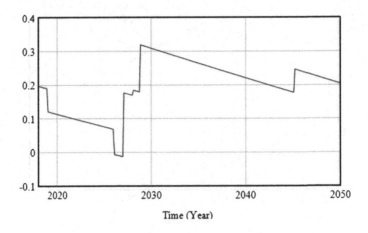

Fig. 9. System margin, scenario 3.

6   Conclusions

This article was successful reaching its aim, as it proposed a computational model to assess the long-term effects of delays in water plants and droughts on the water security of the Bogotá river basin.

In summary, this paper argued that a systemic approach to the water security, should include the water supply and demand side. Although, this paper is only focused on analyzing two aspects of the water supply side due to space constraints. These aspects are the effect of delays in construction of water plants, as well as the effect of a strong drought on the water security. This research may be considered a relevant contribution to the study area, given the importance of the region to the country, and the lack of literature applied to this study area (Bogotá river basin).

The main conclusion that can be drawn is that under a BAU scenario, the study area will experiment a risk of water security. As the water demand keeps growing and the delays in the construction of water plants are important, about 9 years.

If the construction of water plants lasts 12 years instead of 9 years, the consequences to water security will be the worse than under the BAU scenario.

More importantly, if a drought caused by the Niño phenomenon occurs when the gap between water supply and water consumption becomes narrow, this could be catastrophic to water security in the study area. To prevent this situation, the construction time of water plants should be lower than 9 years.

Future research should consider the potential effects of water demand and supply management on water security. Particularly, the effects of water saving, efficiency progress, water tariffs, water recycling and reuse. Likewise, to assess the sustainability of different water policies.

References

1. Pares-Ramos, I.K., Alvarez-Berrios, N., Aide, T.M.: Contrasting patterns of urban expansion in Colombia, Ecuador, Peru, and Bolivia between 1992 and 2009. AMBIO **42**, 29–40 (2013)
2. Ricardo, L.: El papel del agua en una ciudad como Bogota. Revista Ciudades Estados y Politica **1**, 51–60 (2013)
3. Aldana, A.C., Osorio, S.C.: El urbanismo y la planeación moderna. Glocalidades en la formación de la modernidad urbana de Medellín. Historia y sociedad **26**, 17–51 (2013)
4. Aldana, A.C., Osorio, S.C.: Landscape and urban planning informal urban development in Latin American urban peripheries. Spatial assessment in Bogotá, Lima and Santiago de Chile. Landsc. Urban Plan. **165**, 267–279 (2017)
5. Andrade, G.I., Castro, L.G.: Degradación, pérdida y transformación de la biodiversidad continental en Colombia Invitación a una interpretación socioecológica. Ambiente y Desarrollo **165**, 54–74 (2012)
6. Cardenas-Agudelo, M.: La gestión de ecosistemas estratégicos proveedores de agua. Gestión y desarrollo **1**, 109–121 (2013)
7. Molina-prieto, C.A., Victoria-morales, M.I.: Diversidad social y reasentamiento de población, un reto más en la recuperación del río Bogotá. Revista Nodo **7**, 23–42 (2012)
8. Buytaert, W., Bievre, B.De: Water for cities: the impact of climate change and demographic growth in the tropical Andes. Water Resour. **48**, 1–13 (2012). https://doi.org/10.1029/2011WR011755
9. Chen, Zhihe, Wei, Shuai: Application of system dynamics to water security research. Water Resour. Manag. **28**(2), 287–300 (2013). https://doi.org/10.1007/s11269-013-0496-8
10. Zeitoun, M., et al.: Reductionist and integrative research approaches to complex water security policy challenges. Glob. Environ. Chang. **39**, 143–154 (2016). https://doi.org/10.1016/j.gloenvcha.2016.04.010
11. Proskuryakova, L.N., Saritas, O., Sivaev, S.: Global water trends and future scenarios for sustainable development: the case of Russia. J. Clean. Prod. **170**, 867–879 (2018). https://doi.org/10.1016/j.jclepro.2017.09.120
12. Lu, Y., Xu, H., Wang, Y., Yang, Y.: Evaluation of water environmental carrying capacity of city in Huaihe River Basin based on the AHP method: a case in Huai'an City. Water Resour. Ind. **18**, 71–77 (2017). https://doi.org/10.1016/j.jclepro.2017.09.120
13. Wang, Y., Zhou, X., Engel, B.: Water environment carrying capacity in Bosten Lake basin. J. Clean. Prod. **199**, 574–583 (2018). https://doi.org/10.1016/j.jclepro.2018.07.202
14. Grizzetti, B., Lanzanova, D., Liquete, C., Reynaud, A., Cardoso, A.C.: Assessing water ecosystem services for water resource management. Environ. Sci. Policy **61**, 194–203 (2016). https://doi.org/10.1016/j.envsci.2016.04.008
15. Henriques, C., Garnett, K., Weatherhead, E.K., Lickorish, F.A., Forrow, D., Delgado, J.: The future water environment–using scenarios to explore the significant water management challenges in England and Wales to 2050. Sci. Total Environ. **512**, 381–396 (2015). https://doi.org/10.1016/j.jclepro.2018.07.202
16. Liu, R.Z., Borthwick, A.G.: Measurement and assessment of carrying capacity of the environment in Ningbo, China. J. Environ. Manag. **92**, 2047–2053 (2011). https://doi.org/10.1016/j.jenvman.2011.03.033

17. Wei, S., Yang, H., Song, J., Abbaspour, K.C., Xu, Z.: System dynamics simulation model for assessing socio-economic impacts of different levels of environmental flow allocation in the Weihe River Basin, China. Eur. J. Oper. Res. **221**, 248–262 (2012). https://doi.org/10.1016/j.ejor.2012.03.014

18. Zhou, X.Y., et al.: Space-time approach to water environment carrying capacity calculation. J. Clean. Prod. **149**, 302–312 (2017). https://doi.org/10.1016/j.jclepro.2017.02.110

19. Hanjra, M.A., Qureshi, M.E.: Global water crisis and future food security in an era of climate change. Food Policy **35**, 365–377 (2010). https://doi.org/10.1016/j.foodpol.2010.05.006

20. Wang, T., Xu, S.: Dynamic successive assessment method of water environment carrying capacity and its application. Ecol. Indic. **52**, 134–146 (2015). https://doi.org/10.1016/j.ecolind.2014.12.002

21. Wang, Y.J., Qin, D.H.: Influence of climate change and human activity on water resources in arid region of Northwest China: an overview. Adv. Clim. Chang. Res. **8**, 268–278 (2017). https://doi.org/10.1016/j.accre.2017.08.004

22. Zhang, S., et al.: Technology research progress, problems and prospects of mine water treatment technology and resource utilization in China water treatment technology and resource utilization. Crit. Rev. Environ. Sci. Technol. **50**, 331–383 (2020). https://doi.org/10.1080/10643389.2019.1629798

23. Yang, J., Lei, K., Khu, S., Meng, W.: Assessment of water resources carrying capacity for sustainable development based on a system dynamics model: a case study of Tieling City, China. Water Resour. Manag. **29**, 885–899 (2020). https://doi.org/10.1016/j.jenvman.2018.09.085

24. Li, Z., Li, C., Wang, X., Peng, C., Cai, Y., Huang, W.: A hybrid system dynamics and optimization approach for supporting sustainable water resources planning in Zhengzhou City, China. J. Hydrol. **556**, 50–60 (2018). https://doi.org/10.1016/j.jhydrol.2017.11.007

25. Yang, Z., Song, J., Cheng, D., Xia, J., Li, Q., Ahamad, M.I.: Comprehensive evaluation and scenario simulation for the water resources carrying capacity in Xi'an city, China. J. Environ. Manag. **230**, 221–233 (2019). https://doi.org/10.1016/j.jenvman.2018.09.085

26. Mirchi, A., Madani Jr., K., Watkins, D., Ahmad, S.: Synthesis of system dynamics tools for holistic conceptualization of water resources problems. Water Resour. Manag. **26**(9), 2421–2442 (2012). https://doi.org/10.1007/s11269-012-0024-2

27. Tidwell, V.C., Passell, H.D., Conrad, S.H., Thomas, R.P.: System dynamics modeling for community-based water planning: application to the Middle Rio Grande. Aquat. Sci. **66**(4), 357–372 (2004). https://doi.org/10.1007/s00027-004-0722-9

28. Stave, K.A.: A system dynamics model to facilitate public understanding of water management options in Las Vegas, Nevada. J. Environ. Manag. **67**(4), 303–313 (2003). https://doi.org/10.1016/S0301-4797(02)00205-0

29. Qi, C., Chang, N.B.: System dynamics modeling for municipal water demand estimation in an urban region under uncertain economic impacts. J. Environ. Manag. **92**(6), 1628–1641 (2011). https://doi.org/10.1016/j.jenvman.2011.01.020

30. Niazi, A., Prasher, S.O., Adamowski, J., Gleeson, T.: A system dynamics model to conserve arid region water resources through aquifer storage and recovery in conjunction with a dam. Water **6**(8), 2300–2321 (2014). https://doi.org/10.3390/w6082300

31. Hossein, M., Zarghami, M.: Should water supply for megacities depend on outside resources? A Monte-Carlo system dynamics simulation for Shiraz, Iran. Sustain. Cities Soc. **44**, 163–170 (2019). https://doi.org/10.3390/w6082300

32. Gil, E., Tobon, C.: Hydrological modelling with TOPMODEL of Chingaza páramo, Colombia. Rev. Fac. Nac. Agron. **69**, 7919–7933 (2016). https://doi.org/10.15446/rfna.v69n2.59137

33. Moncada, A., Escobar, M., Betancourth, A., Vélez-Upegui, J., Zambrano, J., Alzate, L.: Modelling water stress vulnerability in small Andean basins: case study of Campoalegre River basin, Colombia. Int. J. Water Resour. Dev. 1–18 (2016). https://doi.org/10.1080/07900627.2019.1699780

34. Author, F., Author, S.: Title of a proceedings paper. In: Editor, F., Editor, S. (eds.) CONFERENCE 2016, LNCS, vol. 9999, pp. 1–13. Springer, Heidelberg (2016). https://doi.org/10.10007/1234567890

35. Cities and Climate Change. PSCRS. Springer, Cham (2020). https://doi.org/10.1007/978-3-030-40727-8_5

36. INSTITUTO DE INVESTIGACIÓN DE RECURSOS BIOLÓGICOS ALEXANDER VON HUMBOLDT: urbano-rural de la localidad de Suba, 2nd edn. Instituo Von Humboldt, Bogota (2016)

37. Author, A.-B.: Contribution title. In: 9th International Proceedings on Proceedings, pp. 1–2. Publisher, Location (2010)

38. DANE Departamento Administrativo Nacional de Estadisticas. https://www.dane.gov.co/. Accessed 4 May 2020

39. Acueducto de Bogota. https://www.acueducto.com.co/. Accessed 4 Jan 2020

40. IDEAM. http://institucional.ideam.gov.co/jsp/812. Accessed 1 Feb 2020

41. Huitaca CAR. https://www.car.gov.co/uploads/files/5b9a94fe1389d.pdf. Accessed 1 Mar 2019

42. Acueducto de Bogota. https://www.acueducto.com.co/. Accessed 1 Mar 2020

Inverse Data Visualization Framework (IDVF): Towards a Prior-Knowledge-Driven Data Visualization

M. Vélez-Falconí[1,2(✉)], J. González-Vergara[1,2], and D. H. Peluffo-Ordóñez[1,2,3]

[1] Yachay Tech University, San Miguel de Urcuquí, Ecuador
martin.velez@yachaytech.edu.ec
[2] SDAS Research Group, Pasto, Colombia
[3] Corporación Universitaria Autónoma de Nariño, Pasto, Colombia
https://www.sdas-group.com/

Abstract. Broadly, the area of dimensionality reduction (DR) is aimed at providing ways to harness high dimensional (HD) information through the generation of lower dimensional (LD) representations, by following a certain data-structure-preservation criterion. In literature there have been reported dozens of DR techniques, which are commonly used as a pre-processing stage withing exploratory data analyses for either machine learning or information visualization (IV) purposes. Nonetheless, the selection of a proper method is a nontrivial and -very often- toilsome task. In this sense, a readily and natural way to incorporate an expert's criterion into the analysis process, while making this task more tractable is the use of interactive IV approaches. Regarding the incorporation of experts' prior knowledge there still exists a range of open issues. In this work, we introduce a here-named Inverse Data Visualization Framework (IDVF), which is an initial approach to make the input prior knowledge directly interpretable. Our framework is based on 2D-scatter-plots visuals and spectral kernel-driven DR techniques. To capture either the user's knowledge or requirements, users are requested to provide changes or movements of data points in such a manner that resulting points are located where best convenient according to the user's criterion. Next, following a Kernel Principal Component Analysis approach and a mixture of kernel matrices, our framework accordingly estimates an approximate LD space. Then, the rationale behind the proposed IDVF is to adjust as accurate as possible the resulting LD space to the representation fulfilling users' knowledge and requirements. Results are greatly promising and open the possibility to novel DR-based visualizations approaches.

Keywords: Dimensionality reduction · Interaction model · Kernel functions · Data visualization

D. H. Peluffo-Ordóñez—This work is supported by Yachay Tech University and SDAS research group (www.sdas-group.com).

© Springer Nature Switzerland AG 2020
H. Florez and S. Misra (Eds.): ICAI 2020, CCIS 1277, pp. 266–280, 2020.
https://doi.org/10.1007/978-3-030-61702-8_19

1   Introduction

High-dimensional (HD) data requires an arduous and extensive analysis that exceeds the human senses and may even deceive the human perception. The wide and ubiquitous field of Computer Science refers to the HD data analysis as an Information Visualization (IV) problem. The area of IV aims to generate natural visual representations to simplify the data interpretation by the user. Particularly, the visualization approaches powered by low-dimensional (LD) spaces (mainly at 2D or 3D) represent a very appealing and outstanding alternative. In this connection, the Dimensionality Reduction (DR) techniques have taken place as a crucial stage for such approach, here named as DR-based IV. According to [1], the most remarkable DR techniques reported by literature are the original versions and variants of Principal Component Analysis (PCA), Classical Multidimensional Scaling (CMDS), locally linear embedding (LLE), Laplacian eigenmaps (LE), Stochastic Neighbor Embedding (SNE). Besides strengths and weaknesses of each DR method, there are some approaches to select a DR algorithm [2,3]. As a result, there is growing necessity for an interactive approaches enabling (even non-expert) users assess each method and select the one(s) that best fit(s) the data set.

The state of the art reports some approaches to add interactivity through a so-called Interaction Models (IM) [4] such as: geometric [5], equalizer-like [6], color-based [7], geodesic [8] models, and among others, as extensively reviewed in [9]. The intuition behind these models is to find a kernel matrix, create a linear combination between kernel matrices, and adjust the weights in order to obtain the desired representation [10]. Since methods as LLE, LE, and ISOMAP [11] are susceptible to be represented as kernel matrices, it is possible to explore the DR of the data from a linear combination of kernel matrices using a Kernel DR method, namely Kernel PCA (KPCA) [12]. The task of selecting an appropriate kernel (or multiples kernels) and their criteria within a KPCA framework is challenging-even for experts. More detailed interactive tools - as those based on IM and kernel matrices [9] - propose diverse interfaces for dynamic selection of kernel combination approaches. In order to pick to the best kernel, the users should explore multiple options - e.g. try several kernels and their combinations. As natural, the option that a kernel that perfectly suits the user's needs does not exist is also possible. However, these mechanisms are not efficient enough when user has no a proper interpretation of the data structure.

As an alternative to tackling these issues, in this paper, we present a novel interactive DR based on choosing/setting a suitable kernel for KPCA from the lower dimensional space defined by a user. Specifically, we introduce a here-named Inverse Data Visualization Framework (IDVF). Broadly, IDVF works as follows: It uses spectral DR techniques based on kernels. Its visualization consist of 2D-scatter-plots. Then, to capture either the user's knowledge or requirements, users are requested to provide changes or movements of data points in such a manner that resulting points are located where best convenient according to the user's criterion. Subsequently, we estimates an approximate LD space from a mixture of kernel matrices inputting to a KPCA approach. Therefore, the main goal of IDVF is to adjust as accurate as possible the resulting LD space to the representation fulfilling users' knowledge and requirements. Results are greatly promising and open the possibility to novel DR-based visualizations approaches.

The rest of this paper is organized as follows: Sect. 2 briefly explains the theoretical background on kernels and DR. Sections 4 and 5 present the experimental setup and results, respectively. Finally, Sect. 6 gathers the concluding remarks and future works.

2   Theoretical Background

This section is structured as follows: Sect. 2.1 briefly explains the KPCA approach used in this work. Finally, Sect. 2.2 mentions a possible mixture of such matrices.

2.1   Kernel PCA

PCA has been extended in different non-linear generalization. One of the most remarkable ones is KPCA, which is based on mapping onto higher-dimensional space and the kernel trick to estimate the principal components from a non-linear representation. The principles of KPCA are widely described in [13–16].

The kernel trick maps the input samples onto a so-named high-dimensional feature space $\mathcal{F}$. The kernel function $\kappa(\boldsymbol{x}_1, \boldsymbol{x}_2)$ satisfies that $\kappa(\boldsymbol{x}_1, \boldsymbol{x}_2) = \langle \phi(\boldsymbol{x}_1), \phi(\boldsymbol{x}_2) \rangle$.

Where $\phi(\cdot)$ maps $\mathbb{R}^{n \times D}$ onto $\mathcal{F}$ and $\langle \cdot, \cdot \rangle$ stands for inner product. The benefit of the kernel trick is the fact that the inner product on the feature space can be replaced by a kernel function and reduce a problem from $\mathcal{F}$ to $\mathbb{R}^n$. KPCA optimization problem can be understood as an eigenvalue problem formulated over a Gram or kernel matrix $\boldsymbol{K}$ holding pairwise kernel function values. A fully matrix development of KPCA is introduced in [16].

2.2   Mixtures of Kernel Matrices

A kernel matrix or Gram matrix is a square, symmetric positive definite matrix, such that its entries can be represented by a kernel function [17]. In this sense, as discussed in [18], the linear combination of kernel matrices is a also a kernel Matrix [18]. By taking advantage of this property, multiple kernel analysis for dimensionality reduction [2], and interaction models for visualization [4] have been proposed.

Let us define the matrix $\widetilde{\boldsymbol{K}}$ as a linear combination of kernels matrices, as follows:

$$\widetilde{\boldsymbol{K}}\left(\boldsymbol{X}_{n \times D}\right) = \sum_{i=1}^{m} \alpha_i \boldsymbol{K}^{(i)}\left(\boldsymbol{X}_{n \times D}\right) \quad \text{if } \alpha_i \geq 0 \text{ and if } \alpha_i \in \mathbb{R}. \tag{1}$$

where $\boldsymbol{K}^{(m)}\left(\boldsymbol{X}_{n \times D}\right)$ is a multidimensional matrix which carries the m different kernel matrices.

3   Proposed Inverse Data Visualization Framework (IVDF)

3.1   Outline

The interactive IV methods are commonly used to obtain the best DR set from a linear combination of kernel matrices, which becomes a mixture Kernel Matrix ($\widetilde{K}$) to input a kernel-based DR method - such as KPCA. The linear combination coefficients are manipulated by an interface [6]. Previous works [5–7,19] have reported different interaction models based on linear mixtures, wherein the users may select the methods within an intuitive approach. Yet, the use of these interfaces to determine structure of the data represents an ardours task. Proposed Inverse Data Visualization Framework (IDVF) tunes the coefficients of the kernel matrices in order to achieve the best approximation of DR structure provided by the user. In such vein, the user avoids manual adjustment of the weights. Given a scatter plot of a DR structure of a High Dimensional Data set, the main idea of IDVF is to find the advantageously Mixture Kernel Matrix $\widetilde{K}$. The expected result is to get a similar low dimensional data set to the structure by applying KPCA ($\widetilde{K}$).

3.2   Method Flowchart

Figure 1 depicts the IDVF workflow.

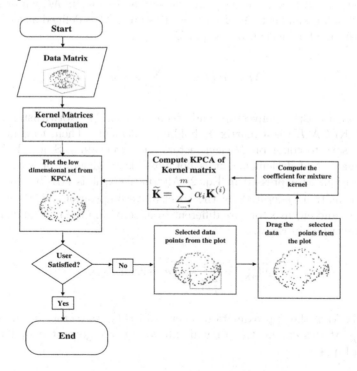

Fig. 1. Proposed IVDF flowchart. It seeks for the best coefficients, which used as weighting factors for a mixture of kernel matrices best represent a desired, low-dimensional space when applying KPCA.

The IDVF works as follows: Considering a high-dimensional (3D for quick test), input data matrix, we calculate a set of kernel matrices. Then, we can estimate a low-dimensional representation and plot an initial lower-dimensional (2D) representation. Over such representation, the user can pick up a data point and decide its final location. Next, our algorithm seeks for the weighting factors or coefficients, which best approximate the desired low-dimensional representation by following a KPCA-based DR applied over a linear combination of kernel matrices regarding obtained coefficients. This process iterates until the user manually stops.

3.3   Estimating the Coefficients for the Mixture of Kernels

In broad terms, the rationale of IDVF is to estimate the coefficients or weighting factors for a mixture of kernel matrices, which is aimed to map $X_{n \times D}$ onto $Y_{n \times d}$ such that $d < D$, and $Y_{n \times d}$ approximates the desired space (pointed out graphically by the user) $\widehat{Y}_{n \times d}$. Once the user define the low dimensional $\widehat{Y}$ through a graphic interface, we need to estimate coefficients of the mixture matrix $\widetilde{K}$ to subsequently apply KPCA($\widetilde{K}$) for producing a matrix Y that best approximates to $\widehat{Y}$. However, building the matrix $\widetilde{K}$ is not a trivial task, and there is no a linear or straightforward relationship between $\widetilde{K}$ and $\widehat{Y}$. Our solution consist in generating a square and symmetric matrix $\widehat{M}$, whose spectral decomposition is similar to $\widehat{Y}$. To achieve this goal, M is defined as the spectral decomposition of Y, as can be seen in Eq. 2:

$$M = VDV^{-1} = \sum_{i=0}^{D} \lambda_i v_i v_i^{\top}. \tag{2}$$

where $\lambda_i v_i$ are the eigenvectors and eigenvalues of M. Notwithstanding, the result of KPCA(K) is a matrix Y holding d elements. Then, to compute M, it is necessary to count on D eigenvectors and eivenvalues. Since, Y is a low-dimensional set of d elements, it is not possible to generate a exact spectral decomposition, as expressed in Eq. 2. Alternatively, it is possible to generate an approximation generated by the spectral decomposition $\widehat{M}^*$, such that d eigenvalues and eigenvectors are different from zero, and the remaining ones are null, as described in Eq. 3:

$$\widehat{M}^*_{n \times n} = \sum_{j=1}^{d} \lambda_j v_j v_j^{\top} \text{ with } d \leq D. \tag{3}$$

Matrix $\widehat{M}$ is the approximation generated by d eigenvectors v_j and d eigenvalues λ_j. At this extent, the original values of Y are generated by KPCA, as shown in Eq. 4:

$$\text{KPCA}(K(X_{n \times D})) = Y_{n \times d} = \{y_1, ..., y_d\}, \tag{4}$$

where the d terms from Y are constructed by the d eigenvalues and eigenvectors, according to shortcut expression used in [20].

$$y_j = \sqrt{\lambda_j} v_j. \tag{5}$$

Therefore from Eqs. 3 and 5, an approximation of M can be expressed as:

$$\widehat{M}^* = \sum_{j=0}^{d} \sqrt{\lambda_j} \sqrt{\lambda_j} v_j v_j^\top = \sum_{j=0}^{d} y_j y_j^\top \text{ with } v_j \lambda_j \in Y. \tag{6}$$

Since $\widehat{Y}$ is constructed by the user modification of y_j, $\widehat{y_j}$ can be expressed as presented in Eq. 7:

$$\widehat{y}_j = \sqrt{\hat{\lambda}_j} \widehat{v}_j, \tag{7}$$

where $\widehat{v}_j$ is any vector that multiply by a constant $\hat{\lambda}_j$ return the vector $\widehat{y}_j$. $\widehat{M}$ is constructed by applying Eq. 6 on Eq. 7, so:

$$\widehat{M} = \sum_{j=0}^{d} \sqrt{\hat{\lambda}_j} \sqrt{\hat{\lambda}_j} \widehat{v}_j \widehat{v}_j^\top = \sum_{j=0}^{d} \widehat{y}_j \widehat{y}_j^\top \text{ with } \widehat{y}_j \in \widehat{Y}. \tag{8}$$

Then, $\widehat{M}$ is expected to approximate $\widetilde{K}$, and can be defined as:

$$\text{vec}\left(\widetilde{K}(X)\right) = \sum_{i=1}^{m} \alpha_i K^{(i)}(X) = \left(K^{(0)} \ \ldots \ K^{(m)}\right) \left(\alpha_0 \ldots \alpha_m\right)^\top. \tag{9}$$

From previous equation, we can appreciate that there exists a linear relationship between $\widehat{M}$ and $\widetilde{K}$ as expressed in Eq. 10:

$$\left(K^{(0)} \ \ldots \ K^{(m)}\right) \left(\alpha_0 \ldots \alpha_m\right)^\top = \text{vec}(\widehat{M}). \tag{10}$$

Since $\widehat{M}$ and $K^{(i)}$ are beforehand calculated, the unique unknown variable is α. A simplest approach to estimated α is as follows:

$$\left(\alpha_0 \ldots \alpha_m\right)^\top = \left(\text{vec}(K^{(0)}) \ \ldots \ \text{vec}(K^{(m)})\right)^\dagger \text{vec}(\widehat{M}), \tag{11}$$

where $(\cdot)^\dagger$ stands for pseudo-inverse matrix. As shown in Eq. 1, knowing α, we can readily calculate $\widetilde{K}$ as:

$$\widetilde{K} = \left(K^{(0)} \ \ldots \ K^{(m)}\right) \left(\alpha_0 \ldots \alpha_m\right)^\top. \tag{12}$$

Thus, $\text{KPCA}(\widetilde{K})$ generate a d dimensional set $\widehat{Y}$ being similar to Y.

4 Experimental Setup

4.1 Databases

For experiments, we consider three toy datasets. These database are commonly used for DR experiments in different papers as [7], which are three-dimensional and holds some topology and geometry interesting for DR purposes, namely:

1. S 3D: A surface in form of the uppercase letter S.
2. Spherical Shell: A spherical surface.
3. Swiss Roll: A Swiss-roll-like manifold.

All previous datasets are generated by random points, setting $N = 200$ and $D = 3$. Figure 2 shows views of the datasets' scatter plots.

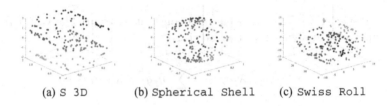

    (a) S 3D   (b) Spherical Shell   (c) Swiss Roll

Fig. 2. Databases used for the experiment

4.2 Kernels for DR

This paper takes advantage of the equivalent matrices as performing a DR process, when using neighborhood structure preservation through KPCA, as explained in [12].

Classical Multidimensional Scaling
The kernel version approximation of CMDS is based in a distance matrix D, and it is double centered. For this article D is based on the euclidean distance [16].

$$K_{\text{CMDS}} = \frac{1}{2}(I - 1_N 1_N^T)D(I - 1_N 1_N^T). \tag{13}$$

Isometric Mapping
The Kernel Isomap calculate the kernel matrix, the two first steps of the Isomap algorithm are performed. It constructs the neighborhood graph and compute the geodesic distances which is defined as D^2. Then, the Mercer Kernel matrix is applied as [11,21,22], where K_{Isomap} is positive definite if $c \geq c^*$:

$$K_{\text{Isomap}} = K\left(D^2\right) + 2cK\left(D\right) + \frac{1}{2}c^2 H. \tag{14}$$

Laplacian Eigenmaps

The kernel LE constructs an Laplacian matrix L, from the neighborhood relations graph W and its corresponding degree D, as follows: $L = D - W$. Then, the KLE is defined as the pesudoinverse of the Laplacian matrix as [12,23,24]:

$$K_{\text{LE}} = L^{\dagger}. \tag{15}$$

Locally Linear Embedding

The Kernel LLE builds a weight matrix W and defines a matrix M, so that $M = (I_n - W^{\top})(I - W)$ and compute the maximum eigenvalue c of M. Then, its kernel matrix can be written as [25–27]:

$$K_{\text{LLE}} = (cI_n - M). \tag{16}$$

Table 1 gathers other well-known kernel functions [28] used in this work.

Table 1. Kernel Functions and its definitions

Kernel function	Definition
Linear	$x^{\top} y$
Polynomial	$(\gamma x^{\top} y + c)^D$
Sigmoid	$\tanh(\gamma x^{\top} y + c)$
Radial basis function	$\exp(-\gamma \parallel x - y \parallel^2)$
Laplacian	$\exp(-\gamma \parallel x - y \parallel_1)$

4.3 Parameter Settings and Method

The experiment was executed with 100 different kernel matrices $\{K^{(1)}, \ldots K^{(100)}\}$. Some of the kernel matrices were obtained by varying the Gram Matrices hyper-parameters. Next, the definition of the considered set of kernels: $K^{(100)}$ is generated by:

- $K^{(1)} = K_{\text{CMDS}}$.
- $\{K^{(2)} \ldots K^{(10)}\} = K_{\text{LE}}$ with neighborhood from 2 to 10.
- $\{K^{(11)} \ldots K^{(19)}\} = K_{\text{LLE}}$ with neighborhood from 2 to 10.
- $\{K^{(20)} \ldots K^{(28)}\} = K_{\text{Isomap}}$ with neighborhood from 2 to 10.
- $K^{(29)} = K_{\text{linear}}$.
- $K^{(30)} = K_{\text{polinomial}}$ setting the degree as 3.
- $K^{(31)} = K_{\text{sigmoid}}$ $\sigma = 1$.
- $K^{(32)} = K_{\text{laplacian}}$ $\sigma = 1$.
- $\{K^{(31)} \ldots K^{(100)}\} = K_{\text{RBF}}$ with γ chosen from $\{0.0001 \ldots 1.2\}$.

4.4   Quality Measure

Lee and Verleysen [29], introduced a formal evaluation measurement of dimensionality reduction in form of a ranking-based metric. Let as denote $L < D$ and $|\cdot|$ the set cardinality, the authors represent δ_{ij} as the distance between two elements (ξ_i, ξ_j) of high dimensional dataset $\Xi = \{\xi_i \ldots \xi_n\} \subset \mathbb{R}^D$. Analogously, d_{ij} is the distance between two elements (x_i, x_j) of the low dimensions dataset $X = \{x_i \ldots x_j\} \subset \mathbb{R}^L$. Then, the rank of ξ_j with respect to ξ_i in $\mathbb{R}^D$ is given by $\rho_{ij} = |\{k|\delta_{ik} < \delta_{ij} \text{ or } (\delta_{ik} = \delta_{ij} and 1 \le k < j \le n\})|$, while the Rank of x_j with respect to x_i in $\mathbb{R}^L$ is given by $r_{ij} = |\{k|d_{ik} < d_{ij} or (d_{ik} = dij$ and $1 \le k < j \le n\})|$. Thus, reflexive ranks are set to zero $(\rho_{i,i} = r_{i,i} = 0)$ and non-reflexive ranks belong to $\{1, \ldots, n - 1\}$. The definition of a co-ranking matrix allows to compare different rank based criteria. It is defined as $Q_{kl} = |\{(i,j) : \rho_{ij} = k \wedge r_{ij} = l\}|$,

The core of the *Quality Criterion* of [29] - just as highlighted by [30] - is the matrix $Q_{NX}(K) = \frac{1}{KN} \sum_{k=1}^{K} \sum_{l=1}^{L} Q_{kl}$. Hence, the plot presented here is the result from $R_{NX}(K) = \frac{(N-1)Q(K)-K}{N-1-K}$, where $Q_{NX} = 1$ represents the ideal K-ary neighborhood agreement. A full description of the algorithm is given in [31,32].

5   Results and Discussion

The experiments performed in this article seek two aims: The first one is to compare the DR result made by user manipulation with the DR outcomes produced by KPCA using the mixture kernel $\widetilde{K}$. The second one is to contrast the quality curve of the original space of the data with the DR produced by CMDS, KPCA inputted with the CMDS kernel, and the mixture kernel. Consequently, Sect. 5 starts by showing a demo of the interactive visualization. Following, the section is divided into three Subsects. (5.1, 5.2, and 5.3), one for every database mentioned in Subsect. 4.1. Each subsection starts with two plots illustrating the two dimensional representations of the database using CMDS and K_{CMDS} (Figs. 4, 5, and 6). Next, Figs. 7, 8, and 9 group presents the manipulated representation of the dataset at their left-column, the middle-column the two dimensional representation of a Mixture Kernel computed accordingly to the plot in the left-column, and the right-column the quality curve described in Sect. 4.4; the rows are the different trials made by the user. The average agreement rate R_{NX} of the quality curve is used to compare the similarity among the manipulate data and the mixture kernel [9]. Additionally, given that K_{CMDS} generates first dimensional reductions, the results shows the quality curve of K_{CMDS} and CMDS. To check efficiency of this Kernel is compared to the lineal method CMDS.

Demo

Figure 3 shows a view of an interface for proposed IDVF. The left-scatter-plot can be manipulated by the user to set the desired low-dimensional space, while the right-one depicts the obtained representation given by the mixture of kernels.

Figure 3 shows a view of the developed interface. Find a demo at https://sdas-group.com/gallery/.

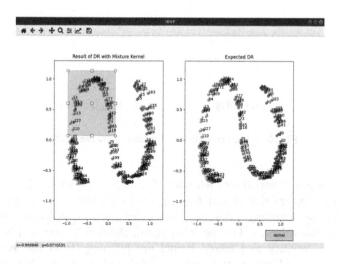

Fig. 3. View of the IDVF interface. Both the scatter plot of the desired and the obtained low-dimensional representations are displayed.

5.1   Results for S 3D

Figure 4 shows the scatter plot of the resultant embedding from both the conventional CMDS and its kernel version applied on KPCA.

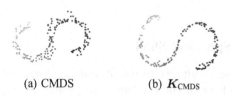

(a) CMDS   (b) $\boldsymbol{K}_{\text{CMDS}}$

Fig. 4. Dimentionality reduction of S 3D

Figure 7 shows a comparative of quality curves. Regarding its area under the curve of R_{NX}, such curves can be organized from the highest to the lowest as follows: CMDS, $\boldsymbol{K}_{\text{CMDS}}$, mixture of kernels, and user-given embedding. At its upper-row and middle-row, we can observe that the user-provided and mixture-of-kernels embeddings exhibit similar quality curves.

5.2   Results for Swiss Roll

Figure 5 shows the scatter plots for Swiss Roll dataset.

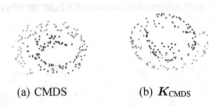

(a) CMDS   (b) K_{CMDS}

Fig. 5. Dimentionality reduction of Swiss Roll

Results on Fig. 8 varied on each trial. The upper-row shows that the quality curves of the Mixture Kernel and K_{CMDS} are barely the same, however the one given by the user handling has a low performance and slight differences between the two mentioned before. On the other hand, the middle-row and bottom-row show that the quality and mixed kernel are far away from the K_{CMDS} and CMDS outcomes. However, the user-provided and mixture-of-kernels embeddings exhibit similar curves.

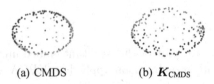

(a) CMDS   (b) K_{CMDS}

Fig. 6. Dimentionality reduction of Spherical Shell

5.3   Results for Spherical Shell

Figure 9 shows some results in terms of scatter plots and quality curves: At its upper-row, the effect of the mixture using some kernels is depicted, which exhibits better performance than CMDS and K_{CMDS}, even when keeping a direct relationship with the user-provided embedding. At the middle-row, the results are far away from the quality reached by CMDS and K_{CMDS}, however user-provided and mixture-of-kernels embeddings remain similar. Finally, for the curves of bottom-row, we can appreciate that they are close to each other, but still the best performance is given by CMDS and K_{CMDS}.

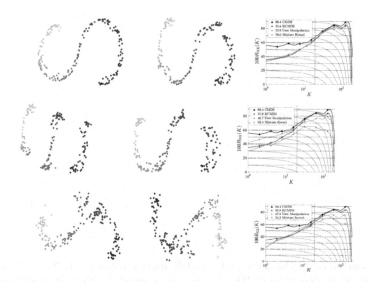

Fig. 7. Selected results for several trials of DR approximations of KPCA using mixture kernel, and quality curve for CMDS, K_{CMDS}, user-provided embedding and the mixture of kernels outcomes over the S3D dataset.

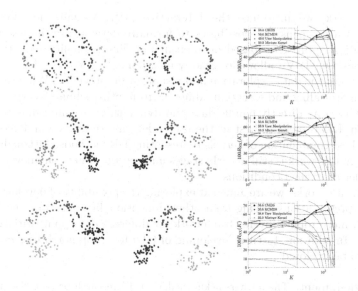

Fig. 8. Selected results for several trials of DR approximations of KPCA using mixture kernel, and quality curve for CMDS, K_{CMDS}, user-provided embedding and the mixture of kernels outcomes over the Swiss Roll dataset.

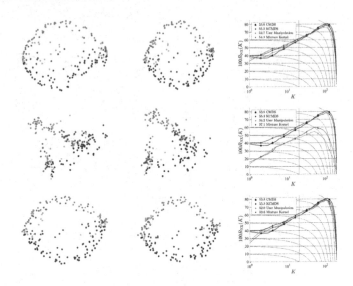

Fig. 9. Selected results for several trials of DR approximations of KPCA using mixture kernel, and quality curve for CMDS, K_{CMDS}, user-provided embedding and the mixture of kernels outcomes over the `Spherical Shell` dataset.

6   Conclusion

In this work, we introduce the Interactive Data Visualization Framework (IDVF), which opens the possibility to formally develop new interactive data visualization approaches based on mixtures of dimensionality reduction (DR) techniques. Our IDVF allows for readily incorporating the users' knowledge and expertise into the data exploration and visualization processes. What makes this approach appealing and essentially different from other similar works is the fact that the user can directly handle data and dynamically accomplish a new representation. IDVF seeks to best fit the user's data interpretation and accordingly find the best combination of kernels representing DR methods. Although already promising, this work is still in early stages and reports results on known datasets and under controlled conditions.

For future works, we are aimed at exploring the possibility of developing novel kernel representations arising from other dimensionality reduction methods, as well as a more robust inverse framework for different data point variations and datasets. In addition, further developing of GUI for a top-notch user experience is also to be explored.

Acknowledgment. The authors acknowledge to the research project "Desarrollo de una metodología de visualización interactiva y eficaz de información en Big Data" supported by Agreement No. 180 November 1st, 2016 by VIPRI from Universidad de Nariño.

Authors thank the valuable support given by the SDAS Research Group (www.sdas-group.com).

References

1. Peluffo Ordoñez, D.H., Lee, J.A., Verleysen, M.: Recent methods for dimensionality reduction: a brief comparative analysis. In: 2014 European Symposium on Artificial Neural Networks, Computational Intelligence and Machine Learning (ESANN 2014) (2014)
2. Peluffo-Ordóñez, D.H., Castro-Ospina, A.E., Alvarado-Pérez, J.C., Revelo-Fuelagán, E.J.: Multiple kernel learning for spectral dimensionality reduction. CIARP 2015. LNCS, vol. 9423, pp. 626–634. Springer, Cham (2015). https://doi.org/10.1007/978-3-319-25751-8_75
3. Liu, S., Maljovec, D., Wang, B., Bremer, P.T., Pascucci, V.: Visualizing high-dimensional data: advances in the past decade. IEEE Trans. Vis. Comput. Graph. **23**(3), 1249–1268 (2016)
4. Ortega-Bustamante, M.C., et al.: Introducing the concept of interaction model for interactive dimensionality reduction and data visualization. In: Gervasi, O., et al. (eds.) Computational Science and its Applications - ICCSA 2020. ICCSA 2020. Lecture Notes in Computer Science, vol. 12250. Springer, Cham (2020). https://doi.org/10.1007/978-3-030-58802-1_14
5. Salazar-Castro, J., Rosas-Narváez, Y., Pantoja, A., Alvarado-Pérez, J.C., Peluffo-Ordóñez, D.H.: Interactive interface for efficient data visualization via a geometric approach. In: 2015 20th Symposium on Signal Processing, Images and Computer Vision (STSIVA), pp. 1–6. IEEE (2015)
6. Rosero-Montalvo, P., et al.: Interactive data visualization using dimensionality reduction and similarity-based representations. In: Beltrán-Castañón, C., Nyström, I., Famili, F. (eds.) CIARP 2016. LNCS, vol. 10125, pp. 334–342. Springer, Cham (2017). https://doi.org/10.1007/978-3-319-52277-7_41
7. Peña-ünigarro, D.F., et al.: Interactive visualization methodology of high-dimensional data with a color-based model for dimensionality reduction. In: XXI Symposium on Signal Processing, vol. 2016, pp. 1–7 (2016)
8. Salazar-Castro, J.A., et al.: Dimensionality reduction for interactive data visualization via a Geo-Desic approach. In: 2016 IEEE Latin American Conference on Computational Intelligence (LA-CCI), pp. 1–6. IEEE (2016)
9. Umaquinga-Criollo, A.C., Peluffo-Ordóñez, D.H., Rosero-Montalvo, P.D., Godoy-Trujillo, P.E., Benítez-Pereira, H.: Interactive visualization interfaces for big data analysis using combination of dimensionality reduction methods: a brief review. In: Basantes-Andrade, A., Naranjo-Toro, M., Zambrano Vizuete, M., Botto-Tobar, M. (eds.) TSIE 2019. AISC, vol. 1110, pp. 193–203. Springer, Cham (2020). https://doi.org/10.1007/978-3-030-37221-7_17
10. Weinberger, K.Q., Sha, F., Saul, L.K.: Learning a kernel matrix for nonlinear dimensionality reduction. In: Proceedings of the Twenty-First International Conference on Machine Learning, p. 106. ACM (2004)
11. Choi, H., Choi, S.: Kernel ISOMAP. Electron. Lett. **40**(1), 1612–1613 (2004)
12. Ham, J., Lee, D.D., Mika, S., Schölkopf, B.: A kernel view of the dimensionality reduction of manifolds. In: Proceedings of the Twenty-First International Conference on Machine Learning, vol. 47. ACM (2004)
13. Mika, S., Schölkopf, B., Smola, A.J., Müller, K.R., Scholz, M., Rätsch, G.: Kernel PCA and de-noising in feature spaces. In: Advances in Neural Information Processing Systems, pp. 536–542 (1999)
14. Washizawa, Y.: Subset basis approximation of kernel principal component analysis. Principal Component Analysis, vol. 67 (2012)

15. Bengio, Y., Vincent, P., Paiement, J.F., Delalleau, O., Ouimet, M., LeRoux, N.: Learning eigenfunctions of similarity: linking spectral clustering and kernel PCA. Technical report, Technical report 1232, Departement d'Informatique et Recherche Oprationnelle (2003)

16. Peluffo-Ordóñez, D.H., Lee, J.A., Verleysen, M.: Generalized kernel framework for unsupervised spectral methods of dimensionality reduction. In: 2014 IEEE Symposium on Computational Intelligence and Data Mining (CIDM), pp. 171–177. IEEE (2014)

17. Lanckriet, G.R., Cristianini, N., Bartlett, P., Ghaoui, L.E., Jordan, M.I.: Learning the kernel matrix with semidefinite programming. J. Mach. Learn. Res. 5(Jan), 27–72 (2004)

18. Bishop, C.M.: Pattern Recognition and Machine Learning. Information Science and Statistics. Springer, New York (2006). https://doi.org/10.1007/978-1-4615-7566-5. Softcover published in 2016

19. Salazar-Castro, J.A., et al.: A novel color-based data visualization approach using a circular interaction model and dimensionality reduction. In: Huang, T., Lv, J., Sun, C., Tuzikov, A.V. (eds.) ISNN 2018. LNCS, vol. 10878, pp. 557–567. Springer, Cham (2018). https://doi.org/10.1007/978-3-319-92537-0_64

20. Pedregosa, F., et al.: Scikit-learn: machine learning in Python. J. Mach. Learn. Res. 12, 2825–2830 (2011)

21. Tenenbaum, J.B., De Silva, V., Langford, J.C.: A global geometric framework for nonlinear dimensionality reduction. Science 290(5500), 2319–2323 (2000)

22. Choi, H., Choi, S.: Robust kernel ISOMAP. Pattern Recogn. 40(3), 853–862 (2007)

23. Belkin, M., Niyogi, P.: Laplacian eigenmaps and spectral techniques for embedding and clustering. In: Advances in Neural Information Processing Systems, pp. 585–591 (2002)

24. Belkin, M., Niyogi, P.: Laplacian eigenmaps for dimensionality reduction and data representation. Neural Comput. 15(6), 1373–1396 (2003)

25. Roweis, S.T., Saul, L.K.: Nonlinear dimensionality reduction by locally linear embedding. Science 290(5500), 2323–2326 (2000)

26. Donoho, D.L., Grimes, C.: Hessian eigenmaps: locally linear embedding techniques for high-dimensional data. Proc. Natl. Acad. Sci. 100(10), 5591–5596 (2003)

27. DeCoste, D.: Visualizing mercer kernel feature spaces via kernelized locally-linear embeddings (2001)

28. Belanche Muñoz, L.A.: Developments in kernel design. In: ESANN 2013 proceedings: European Symposium on Artificial Neural Networks, Computational Intelligence and Machine Learning, Bruges, Belgium, 24–26 April 2013, pp. 369–378 (2013)

29. Lee, J.A., Verleysen, M.: Quality assessment of dimensionality reduction: rank-based criteria. Neurocomputing 72(7–9), 1431–1443 (2009)

30. Mokbel, B., Lueks, W., Gisbrecht, A., Hammer, B.: Visualizing the quality of dimensionality reduction. Neurocomputing 112, 109–123 (2013)

31. Lee, J.A., Verleysen, M.: Scale-independent quality criteria for dimensionality reduction. Pattern Recogn. Lett. 31(14), 2248–2257 (2010)

32. Lee, J.A., Renard, E., Bernard, G., Dupont, P., Verleysen, M.: Type 1 and 2 mixtures of Kullback-Leibler divergences as cost functions in dimensionality reduction based on similarity preservation. Neurocomputing 112, 92–108 (2013)

The Application of DBSCAN Algorithm to Improve Variogram Estimation and Interpretation in Irregularly-Sampled Fields

O. O. Mosobalaje[1]([⊠]) [iD], O. D. Orodu[1], and D. Ogbe[2]

[1] Department of Petroleum Engineering, Covenant University, Ota, Nigeria
olatunde.mosobalaje@covenantuniversity.edu.ng
[2] African University of Science and Technology, Abuja, Nigeria

Abstract. The empirical variogram is a measure of spatial data correlation in geostatistical modeling and simulations. Typically, the empirical variogram is estimated for some defined lag intervals by applying method of moments on an underlying variogram cloud. Depending on the distribution of pair-wise lag values, the variogram cloud of an irregularly-sampled field may exhibit clusteredness. Issues of noisy, uninterpretable and inconsistent empirical variogram plots are commonly encountered in cases of irregularly-sampled fields with clustered variogram clouds. An insightful diagnosis of these problems and a practical solution are the subject of this paper. This research establishes the fact that these problems are caused by the neglect of variogram cloud cluster configurations when defining lag intervals. It is here shown that such neglect hinders the optimal use of spatial correlation information present in variogram clouds. Specifically, four sub-optimal effects are articulated in this paper as the consequence of the neglect.

Consequently, this research presents an efficient cluster-analysis – driven technique for variogram estimation in cases of irregularly-sampled fields with clustered variogram clouds. The cluster analysis required for this technique is implemented using an unsupervised machine learning algorithm known as Density-based Spatial Clustering of Applications with Noise (DBSCAN). This technique has been applied to a real field to obtain a stable, interpretable and geologically consistent variogram plot. It has also been applied to a synthetic field and was found to give the lowest estimation error among other techniques. This technique would find usefulness in geo-modeling of natural resource deposits wherein irregular sampling is prevalent.

Keywords: Cluster analysis · DBSCAN · Variogram cloud · Lag tolerance · Variogram estimation · Irregular sampling

Nomenclature

C_{ID}	Cluster Identifier
$\vec{h}$	Lag vector, m
Δh	Lag distance tolerance, m
i	Loop counter

© Springer Nature Switzerland AG 2020
H. Florez and S. Misra (Eds.): ICAI 2020, CCIS 1277, pp. 281–295, 2020.
https://doi.org/10.1007/978-3-030-61702-8_20

N	Number of clusters
$Z(u_i)$	Value of a random variable attribute at location $\boldsymbol{u_i}$
$Z\left(u_i + \vec{h}\right)$	Value of a random variable attribute at location $u_i + \vec{h}$
$\gamma\left(\vec{h}\right)$	Variogram, squared unit of attribute

1 Introduction

The concept of variogram as a measure of data spatial correlation in a random field is at the core of geostatistical modeling and simulation. The ultimate geostatistical goal of optimal prediction of attributes values at unsampled locations in a random field often requires a variogram model. There are various (but equivalent) conceptual definitions of variogram. Each definition makes reference to data pairs representing values of the same attribute sampled some distance apart from each other. One member of such a pair, $Z(u_i)$, is arbitrarily designated as 'head' and the other, $Z\left(u_i + \vec{h}\right)$, as 'tail'; u_i and $u_i + \vec{h}$ are coordinates of the sampled points. The separation distance vector between the head and the tail for any such pair is known as lag vector $\vec{h}$ for that pair. The theoretical variogram $\gamma\left(\vec{h}\right)$ is thus defined (for a given lag vector) as half the expected value of squared difference between the head data and the tail data [1].

The theoretical variogram cannot be obtained since the infinte number of data realizations required is prohibitive. Therefore, an estimator of the theoretical variogram becomes necessary. The empirical variogram (sample/experimental variogram) which serves as such estimator is the variogram value obtained from limited sample data using method of moments. In practice, a licit function (smooth curve) is fitted to the plot of estimated empirical variogram versus lag values to yield what is known as variogram model. Obtaining the variogram model requires proper interpretation of the estimated empirical variogram. Variogram interpretation entails making inferences on key parameters of the variogram model as well as on the anisotropy of the random field. The estimation of the experimental variogram and its interpretation is the subject of this paper.

Fundamentally, the variogram for a given geospatial data pair (i.e. point-pair) is known as pair variogram and is defined as half the squared difference between the pair values. For a given random field, a plot of all possible pair variograms against their respective lag distances is known as variogram cloud. Bringing the method of moment into context, the empirical variogram for a given lag $\vec{h}$ is therefore one-half the average of pair variograms of all pairs separated by $\vec{h}$. However, practical field constraints during sampling campaigns introduces some randomness into the actual sample locations such that only very few pairs are separated exactly by h distance units [2]. This is true even for regularly-spaced sampling plan. In order to ensure sufficient numbers of pairs are available for the estimation, the averaging is done over intervals of lag values (both distance and direction); not on exact lag values. The empirical variogram plot is thus estimated from a variogram cloud by plotting averages of pair variogram values within some defined lag intervals against averages of lag values in those intervals.

While this lag-interval averaging approach solves the foregoing challenge in the case of regularly-sampled fields; it is insufficient for irregularly-sampled fields with clustered variogram clouds. Issues of noisy, uninterpretable and inconsistent empirical variogram plots are commonly encountered in cases of irregularly-sampled fields with clustered variogram clouds. This research establishes the fact that these problems are caused by the neglect of variogram cloud cluster configurations when defining lag intervals. Consequently, the research presents an efficient lag-clusters averaging approach in estimating empirical variogram of irregularly-sampled fields with clustered variogram clouds. This approach is based on an unsupervised machine learning concept known as cluster analysis. The cluster analysis required for this approach is implemented by deploying an algorithm known as Density-based Spatial Clustering of Applications with Noise (DBSCAN). The significance of this approach could be seen in the prevalence of irregular sampling in petroleum exploration since wells (sampling points) are preferentially positioned in clusters in order to maximize production. The next section of this paper presents an insightful diagnosis of the problem by highlighting the sub-optimal issues caused by the disregard of variogram cloud cluster configuration. Thereafter, the proposed approach is presented and is shown to be effective in handling the highlighted sub-optimal issues. Furthermore, the proposed approach is applied to a real field case. Ultimately, using a synthetic field case, an error analysis comparing the proposed approach with existing approaches is conducted.

2   Sub-optimal Issues with Clustered Variogram Clouds

A variogram cloud is deemed clustered if some lag intervals are dense with plotted points (point-pairs); some intervals only have sparse point-pairs while some intervals have none. Indeed, clustered variogram clouds may occur in regularly and irregularly sampled fields. However, such occurrence in regularly sampled fields could be handled using the conventional lag interval approach. The challenges encountered when such clustered variogram clouds occur in irregularly sampled fields is the subject of this paper. It suffices to note here that not all irregularly-sampled fields give clustered variogram clouds. Rather, the occurrence of clusters is due to the non-uniform distribution of lag distance values in such variogram clouds. The non-uniformity of such distribution may be attributable to field constraints, preferential in-fill drilling or the geometry of the resource deposit [3]. This distribution is best elucidated by adding a marginal histogram to the lag distance axis of the variogram cloud as presented in Fig. 1. In the figure, it is discernible that at any point on the axis, the density of point-pairs in the variogram cloud correlates with the height of the histogram bars. For example, high frequency lag intervals (e.g. 0–500; 1500–2000; 3000–3500 etc.) constitute the high density regions (clusters) of the variogram cloud.

While these clusters are the custodians of the spatial correlation to be measured as empirical variogram; their configurations are neglected in the existing techniques of setting lag intervals. In order to show this neglect, a brief description of these techniques is presented here. The most common technique is the lag-tolerance technique used in GSLIB – an open-source geostatistical software [4]. In this technique, a set of discrete lag values h are chosen; and tolerance values Δh are set along with each lag value. While lag values are chosen with considerations for sample spacing, tolerance values are typically set as half of lag spacing [5]. The range $h \pm \Delta h$ makes up a lag interval. All point-pairs

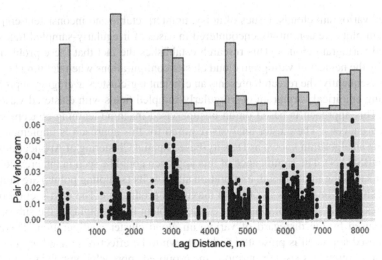

Fig. 1. A typical clustered variogram cloud (bottom) and its lag distance histogram (top).

having lag values in that range are allocated to that particular lag interval. In lag-bin technique, the entire range of lag values is simply divided into small intervals of lags called lag bins; similar to bins used in constructing histograms in descriptive statistics. This technique is implemented in gstat – an open-source R package for geostatistical modeling and simulations [6]. In this paper, these two foregoing techniques are termed traditional techniques. Clearly, in these traditional techniques, cluster configurations are not considered in choosing lag interval parameters such as lag/tolerance values and bin boundaries. This neglect causes a mismatch between chosen parameters and the cluster configurations. The mismatch does not promote an optimal use of spatial correlation information present in the variogram cloud point-pairs. Four (4) sub-optimal issues resulting from this mismatch as identified and articulated in this research are here presented.

First, a certain lag interval may straddle (combine) variogram cloud point-pairs from two adjacent clusters in the cloud. We refer to this as the straddle effect. Each cluster is unique and holds vital spatial correlation information about the range of lag values it covers which may not necessarily coincide with the set lag interval. Hence, straddling point-pairs from two clusters results in 'mixing' two different pieces of information; this does not work well for the estimation as the uniqueness of each piece is lost thereby. Secondly, a lag interval may split a single cluster in the variogram cloud into separate adjacent lag intervals. We refer to this as the split effect. Such splitting has the effect of reducing the amount of variogram cloud point-pairs contributing to the estimation at the resulting lag intervals; thereby rendering the estimated experimental variogram unrepresentative. Thirdly, the two aforementioned sub-optimal issues may actually occur together; i.e. a portion of a cluster may be split from the cluster and straddled with a portion split from an adjacent cluster. We refer to this as the split-straddle effect. In this case; the clusters loosing those split portions produces estimates that are less representative while the combined split portions lose uniqueness. Finally, a lag interval may span a sparse region of the variogram cloud with only few point-pairs; not sufficient to yield a representative empirical variogram estimate at that lag interval. We refer to this as the sparsity effect. Point-pairs at such sparse regions should actually be treated as noise as they are primarily responsible for large fluctuations (instability) in empirical variogram plots. Concisely, straddle effect causes loss of uniqueness; split effect and sparsity effect cause unrepresentativeness; and split-straddle effect diminishes both uniqueness and representativeness. Some of these sub-optimal issues defined here manifest in the field case adopted for this work; and are highlighted in Sect. 4 of this paper. These sub-optimal issues turn out to have negative impacts on the criteria for acceptable empirical variogram plots. These criteria are: stability (estimates not excessively noisy); interpretable structure; and consistency with geologic information [5].

The third lag interval setting technique is the flexible lag technique proposed by Yupeng and Miguel [7]. In this technique, lag values are strategically positioned at the denser regions of the variogram cloud and appropriate tolerance values are set. This technique utilizes a neural network algorithm known as self-organizing maps (SOM) to optimally partition the variogram cloud into "better-informed" regions with centers (neurons) at the denser regions. While the flexible lag technique as conceptualized by Yupeng and Miguel [7] is an excellent solution to the sub-optimal issues; the SOM algorithm upon which it is based has limitations when applied to variogram cloud plots. First, the SOM algorithm does not remove noise (sparse point-pairs) in the variogram cloud. As evident in results presented in Sect. 5, the inability to exclude noise slightly reduced the effectiveness of this technique. In fact, some lag intervals generated using the SOM algorithm consisted entirely of noise point-pairs (the sparsity effect); such intervals introduced fluctuations to the variogram plots. Furthermore, at convergence, the neurons are not necessarily located at the core of the dense regions of the cloud. Some neurons even appear at coordinate locations where there are no point-pairs; they are merely surrounded by point-pairs. Cases of this are reported in Sect. 5. This may result in the straddle, split or split-straddle effects. Lastly, the SOM algorithm requires that the number of clusters be specified ab initio by the human user. The output of the process is sensitive to this specification. Making this specification would entail a visual inspection of the variogram cloud in order to count the number of apparent clusters present therein; this may be cumbersome! Further still, there is no guarantee that the clusters detected by the SOM algorithm would be the same as those visually detected; SOM algorithm may erroneously devote some neurons (clusters) to noise point-pairs. Comprehensive discussions of the SOM algorithm are available in an NPTEL document [8]. Kapageridis [3] proposed variable lag technique. While the variable lag technique is based on k-means clustering algorithm; its operation is essentially equivalent to the SOM-based flexible lag technique and shares similar limitations. Actually, Kapageridis [3] hinted that k-means was chosen for its simplicity and suggested that a more efficient algorithm be considered. All these limiting issues are done away with in the DBSCAN-aided technique here proposed.

3   DBSCAN-Aided Technique for Variogram Estimation

In addressing the sub-optimal issues highlighted in Sect. 2; this work presents a cluster-analysis – driven technique for estimating empirical variogram in irregularly-sampled fields exhibiting clustered variogram cloud. At the core of this technique is the cluster analysis algorithm known as Density-based Spatial Clustering of Applications with Noise (DBSCAN). Al-Fuqaha presented comprehensive discussions on DBSCAN and other clustering algorithms [9]. The choice of the DBSCAN algorithm for this application is predicated on some of its strengths that are certainly appropriate in handling the sub-optimal issues earlier discussed. Foremost is the unique ability of DBSCAN to detect noise data. Such data are not assigned to any cluster; in effect, they are excluded. This functionality helps to deal with the sparsity effect. Furthermore, the working of DBSCAN is based on the density of the objects (point-pairs). This makes it possible for the algorithm to identify natural clusters uniquely without permitting the straddle/split effects and without the user needing to specify the number of clusters. It defines clusters uniqueness based on density of the objects; i.e. the areal extent of a cluster is only terminated as objects become sparse. This way, it would not be possible to straddle two clusters separated by a sparse region neither would it be possible to split a cluster naturally held together by common density. The algorithm is known to perform poorly with high dimensional space and with nested clusters (i.e. cluster within cluster) [10]. Fortunately, these situations do not feature in variogram clouds; a variogram cloud is a two-dimensional space.

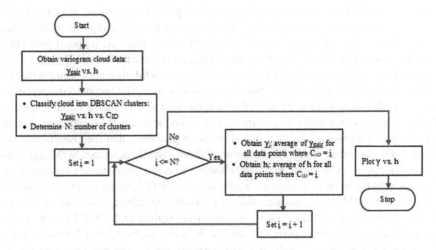

Fig. 2. A flowchart of the DBSCAN-aided empirical variogram estimation technique.

The DBSCAN algorithm measures density at point p in the domain as the numbers of objects within a circle of radius *Eps* centered at p. Such circle is taken to be dense if it contains a number of objects equal to or greater than a user-specified threshold value *MinPts*. An implementation of DBSCAN would require two user input parameters: *Eps* and *MinPts*. The number of clusters identified by the DBSCAN algorithm is significantly sensitive to the values of these parameters; hence their values should be set carefully. Fortunately, Al-Fuqaha [9] includes a scheme to rightly specify these parameters. In implementing DBSCAN in R statistical environment, packages *dbscan* [11] or *fpc* [12] may be used. Package "dbscan" contains function kNNdist that may aid the specification of *Eps* and *MinPts*. Upon successfully classifying the variogram cloud point-pairs into clusters; the empirical variogram can be estimated as the average of all point-pairs in each cluster. This workflow is depicted in the Fig. 2. In this work, the implementation of this workflow is scripted in version 3.6.3 of R [13].

4   Real Field-Case Application

The DBSCAN-based technique is here applied to the porosity attribute of a section of the Nigerian heavy oil and natural bitumen deposits located north of Agbabu, southwest Nigeria. Agbabu field is located in the Dahomey basin which contains deposits of heavy oil and natural bitumen. Adegoke et al. [14] measured weight percent bitumen and water saturations of 583 core samples retrieved from forty (40) wells drilled on the 17 km^2 Agbabu study area. Mosobalaje et al. [15] deployed basic principle of volumetric proportions to compute and generate reservoir porosity database from the existing Adegoke et al. [14] raw database. On the basis of some considerations in Mosobalaje et al., [15], some data points have been excluded from this porosity database. The resulting database containing 408 core porosity data is the subject of the application. The geologic map of the outcrop sections of the deposits showing the Agbabu field is available in Reference [16]. Also, a figure showing the locations of the wells within the Agbabu field is available in Reference 15.

A variogram map reported in Mosobalaje et al., [17] reveals that the major direction of porosity spatial continuity in the Agbabu field is approximately 90° (east-west direction). This is consistent with geologic information in Obaje [18] that sediments in the Dahomey basin (encompassing Agbabu field) are deposited in an east-west direction. The result of an attempt to estimate (using lag-bin technique) and plot the empirical variogram for the 90° direction, with a tolerance of 22.5° is shown in Fig. 3. The plot exhibits various problematic issues. Large fluctuations and absence of interpretable variogram structure are evident in the plot. Furthermore, the variogram plot reaches a sill value of 0.0045 (i.e. the variance of the data) at a lag distance value of about 2000 m. By implication, the range value for the 90° azimuth would then be 2000 m. However, this value is not consistent with prior geologic information that suggests the 90° azimuth as the major direction of continuity. The range for the 45° azimuth has been estimated to be longer [17]. Being the direction of major continuity, the 90° directional variogram should have the maximum range. In investigating these issues, it is observed that they are attributable to the neglected clustering trend of point-pairs in the variogram cloud. Figure 4 shows the variogram clouds obtained using the lag-bin and lag-tolerance techniques. In this figure, point-pairs grouped into same interval/bin have been plotted with same plotting symbol.

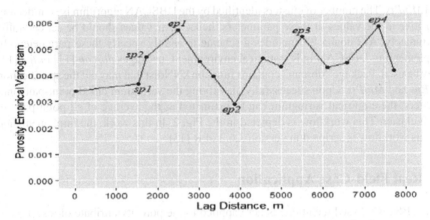

Fig. 3. 90° Directional variogram plot for the Agbabu field porosity data.

It is observed that the grouping in each of these techniques fails to honor the natural clusters present in the cloud. This situation leads to some of the sub-optimal issues. Specifically, the sparsity, split and split-straddle effects all featured in this case, as annotated in Fig. 4. For instance, the fluctuations noticed in Fig. 3 are largely caused by the four (4) extreme points (labelled ep1, ep2, ep3, ep4). These four points are consequences of Bins 5, 8, 11 and 14 in the variogram cloud plot (Fig. 4, top). Each of these bins has very few point-pairs (sparsity effect); hence, the estimated variogram could not be representative. The binning made each of these categories stand alone; whereas, they should have been merged with adjacent clusters or be disregarded in the variogram estimation. Also, Bins 3 and 4 in Fig. 4 (top) belongs to same cluster; and should have been binned together to produce a single variogram estimate more representative than any of Points sp1 and sp2 (in Fig. 3).

In resolving these issues, the DBSCAN algorithm was applied to classify the variogram cloud into clusters; and to delete the sparse point-pairs. Figure 5 is the result of the application of DBSCAN algorithm to the variogram cloud. Six (6) natural clusters are identified. On the basis of the identified clusters; the empirical variogram values are estimated (as cluster averages) and plotted as presented in Fig. 6. It is observed that all the problematic issues are resolved in the DBSCAN-aided variogram plot. Foremost, the plot now exhibits an interpretable variogram structure, with a clear sill, nugget and range. Expectedly, the sill value is about 0.0045 which is the variance of the data. Furthermore, of the four directional variograms obtained (0°, 45°, 90° and 135°); the 90° direction has the longest range of about 3000 m. This is consistent with the result obtained using variogram map, and with geologic information in Obaje [18]. Also, the variogram plot shows minimal fluctuations and becomes rather stable.

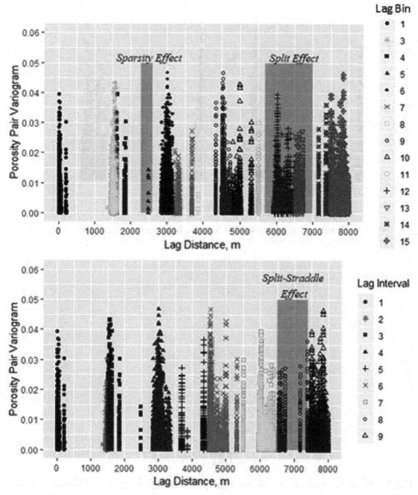

Fig. 4. 90° directional variogram cloud for Agbabu field porosity data: lag-bin technique (top); lag-tolerance technique (bottom).

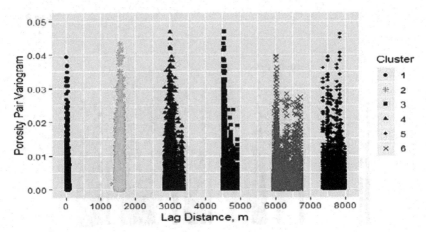

Fig. 5. 90° directional variogram cloud for Agbabu field porosity data: DBSCAN-clustered.

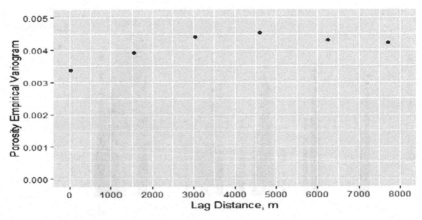

Fig. 6. 90° directional variogram plot for Agbabu field porosity data: DBSCAN-aided.

5   Synthetic Field-Case Application: Comparative Error Analysis

A 3D random field is here synthesized with a specified variogram model as the input, using unconditional Gaussian simulation. The value of the input variogram model at any lag value becomes the true variogram value at that lag. The deviation (error) of estimated empirical variogram from this true variogram is obtained, for each technique featured in this paper. The four techniques considered are: lag-bin, lag-tolerance, SOM-aided (flexible lag) and DBSCAN-aided (lag cluster). Essentially, the 3D field is set up to mimic Agbabu field; having same dimensions and being sampled at same locations. In simulating the field, it was discretized into a $40 \times 13 \times 100$ grid. Gridblock dimensions in x-, y-, and z-axis are 400 m, 400 m and 1 m, respectively. The parameters of the synthetic random field are listed in Table 1.

Table 1. Parameters of the 3D synthetic random field

Parameter	Value
Data mean	0.2415
Nugget	0.001
Partial sill	0.0034
Major range	3000 m
Variogram model type	Spherical
Major direction of spatial continuity	$90°$
Minor direction of spatial continuity	$0°$
Dip angle for the major direction of continuity	$0°$
Anisotropy type	Geometric
Anisotropy ratios	0.5 (for first minor range) 0.1 (for second minor range)

One hundred realizations of the random field were simulated, sampled and subjected to this analysis. Realization 61 is chosen for this presentation because its exhaustive data reproduces the input variogram model fairly well. Figure 7 is the $90°$ directional variogram clouds; with the point-pairs classified according to their respective lag bins/intervals or clusters. On the basis of these classified variogram clouds; the empirical variogram plot obtained using the techniques are presented in Fig. 8. The true (input model) variogram values are also plotted for comparison purposes.

Four metrics are used in comparing the performance of these techniques. These are: stability (minimal fluctuations); interpretability of spatial correlation structure; variogram model reproduction; and mean absolute percentage deviation from variogram model. Deutsch had listed stability and interpretability as part of the criteria for acceptable variogram plots [5]. Variogram model reproduction has been identified as a key factor in the behavior of geostatistical prediction models [19]. It is observed in Fig. 8 that the variogram plot for DBSCAN-aided technique is the most stable and presents the most interpretable spatial correlation structure. Furthermore, the DBSACN-aided estimates match the input variogram model the closest; this is also evident in its lowest mean absolute percentage deviation.

The absolute deviations of the estimates from the true values are presented in Fig. 9. The DBSCAN-aided technique exhibited the least errors. Notably, the DBSCAN-aided technique had the lowest errors at lags values below the range (3000 m). Considering the importance of short-scaled spatial structure, it is desirable to have minimal errors at short lags distances. The absolute errors averaged over 100 realizations are presented in Fig. 10. The average error plots show similar trends.

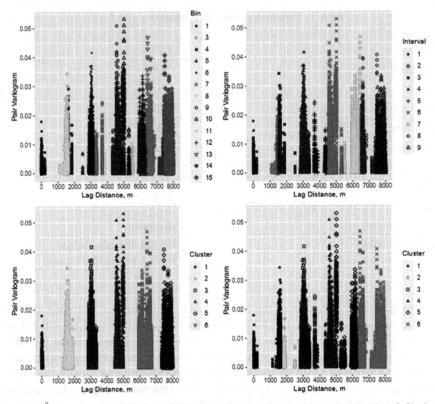

Fig. 7. 90° directional variogram cloud for Realization 61: lag-bin technique (top left); lag-tolerance technique (top right); DBSCAN-aided technique (bottom left); and SOM-aided technique (bottom right)

Meanwhile, in all these performance metrics and error plots, the SOM-aided technique closely follows the DBSCAN-aided technique. This underscores the fact that the two cluster-analysis – driven techniques possess clear advantages over the traditional techniques. The inability of the SOM algorithm to exclude noise (sparsity effect) and to prevent splitting or straddling effects is responsible for the slight reduction in its performance, as discussed in Sect. 2. Notably, the highest error in the SOM-aided technique occurred at a lag value of about 2000 m, for both Realization 61 error plot and average error plot. The variogram estimate at this lag corresponds to the second cluster in the SOM-classified variogram cloud (Fig. 7, bottom right). First, this second SOM-cluster split the natural cluster present between 1000 m and 2000 m lag distances; and then straddled a portion of it with the sparse points present at around 2500 m. This is a case of sub-optimality due to split-straddle effect. More so, this second SOM-cluster contains only few point-pairs; leading to sparsity effect. These two effects reduced the accuracy of estimation at this lag, for the SOM-aided technique.

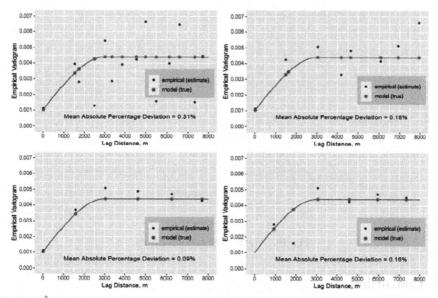

Fig. 8. 90° directional variogram plots for Realization 61: lag-bin (top left); lag-tolerance (top right); DBSCAN-aided (bottom left); and SOM-aided (bottom right).

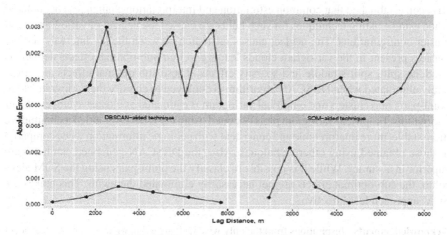

Fig. 9. Absolute error plots for Realization 61.

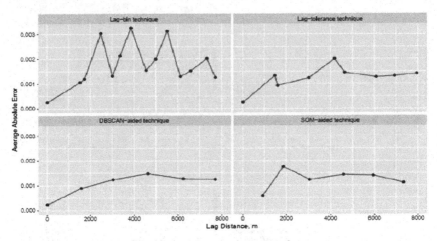

Fig. 10. Average absolute error plots.

6 Conclusion

Essentially, this work proposes a DBSCAN-aided technique for estimating variogram in irregularly-sampled fields with clustered variogram clouds. This technique incorporates variogram cloud cluster configurations into the estimation of empirical variogram. It has been established that common estimation and interpretation challenges encountered when using existing techniques for such fields are caused the neglect of variogram cloud cluster configurations. The neglect causes mismatch between the lag intervals and the clusters present in the variogram clouds leading to four sub-optimal effects defined as straddle, split, split-straddle and sparsity effects. These sub-optimal effects are effectively eliminated when DBSCAN algorithm is deployed to classify the variogram cloud point-pairs into clusters and empirical variogram is estimated as cluster-averages of pair variograms. Empirical variogram plots obtained using the DBSCAN-aided technique are more stable, more interpretable and consistent with geologic information when compared to those obtained using other techniques. Also, the DBSCAN-generated estimates are superior in accuracy. While it is possible to classify the point-pairs using the SOM algorithm; the sub-optimal effects are not necessarily eliminated therewith. This makes the SOM approach less effective.

Acknowledgements. Inspirations from the only wise God are acknowledged. Dr. A. A. Adepelumi facilitated access to previous report of the Geological Consultancy Unit of Obafemi Awolowo University. Publication support from Covenant University Centre for Research, Innovation and Discovery (CUCRID) is also appreciated.

References

1. Li, M., Zhao, Y.: Geophysical Exploration Technology: Applications in Lithological and Stratigraphic Reservoirs. Elsevier, Amsterdam (2014)

2. Zuur, A., Ieno, E.N., Smith, G.M.: Analyzing Ecological Data. Springer, New York (2007)
3. Kapageridis, I.K.: Variable lag variography using k-means clustering. Comput. Geosci. **85**, 49–63 (2015). https://doi.org/10.1016/j.cageo.2015.04.004
4. Deutsch, C.V., Journel, A.: GSLIB: Geostatistical Software Library and User's Guide. Oxford University Press, New York (1998)
5. Deutsch, J.L.: Experimental variogram tolerance parameters (2015). http://www.geostatistic slessons.com/lessons/variogramparameters
6. Pebesma, E.J.: Multivariable geostatistics in S: the gstat package. Comput. Geosci. **30**, 683–691 (2004). https://doi.org/10.1016/j.cageo.2004.03.012
7. Yupeng, L., Miguel, C.: A flexible lag definition for experimental variogram calculation. Int. J. Min. Sci. Technol. **21**, 207–211 (2011)
8. National program on technology enhanced learning (NPTEL). Unsupervised learning (2013). http://14.139.172.204/nptel/CSE/Web/102106023/ch9_Competitive%20Learning_3.pdf
9. Al-Fuqaha, A.: Clustering analysis (2014). https://cs.wmich.edu/alfuqaha/summer14/cs6530/lectures/ClusteringAnalysis.pdf
10. Saraswathi, S., Sheela, M.I.: A comparative study of various clustering algorithms in data mining. Int. J. Comput. Sci. Mob. Comput. **3**, 422–428 (2014)
11. Hahsler, M., Piekenbrock, M.: DBSCAN: density based clustering of applications with noise (DBSCAN) and related algorithms. R package version 1.1-1 (2017). https://CRAN.R-project.org/package=dbscan
12. Hennig, C.: fpc: flexible procedures for clustering. R package version 2.1-11.1 (2018). https://CRAN.R-project.org/package=fpc
13. R Core Team R: a language and environment for statistical computing. R Foundation for Statistical Computing, Vienna (2020). https://www.R-project.org/
14. Adegoke, O.S., et al.: Geotechnical investigations of the Ondo State bituminous sands – Volume I: geology and reserves estimate. Geological Consultancy Unit, Department of Geology, University of Ife, Nigeria (1980)
15. Mosobalaje, O.O., Orodu, O.D., Ogbe, D.: Descriptive statistics and probability distributions of volumetric parameters of a Nigerian heavy oil and bitumen deposit. J. Pet. Explor. Prod. Technol. **9**(1), 645–661 (2018). https://doi.org/10.1007/s13202-018-0498-4
16. Falebita, D.E., Oyebanjo, O.M., Ajayi, T.R.: A geostatistical review of the bitumen reserves of the upper Cretaceous Afowo formation, Agbabu area, Ondo State, Eastern Dahomey basin, Nigeria. Pet. Coal **56**, 572–581 (2014)
17. Mosobalaje, O.O., Orodu, O.D., Ogbe, D.: Estimating and modeling of spatial variability of volumetric attributes of a Nigerian heavy oil and bitumen deposit. In: 2019 SPE Nigerian Annual International Conference and Exhibition (2019)
18. Obaje, N.G.: Geology and Mineral Resources of Nigeria. Lecture Notes in Earth Sciences, vol. 120. Springer, Berlin (2009). http://dx.doi.org/10.1007/978-3-540-92685-6_9
19. Deutsch, C.V.: Geostatistical Reservoir Modeling. Oxford University Press, New York (2002)

Decision Systems

A Multi-objective Evolutionary Algorithms Approach to Optimize a Task Scheduling Problem

Nicolás Cobos, Ixtli Barbosa, Germán A. Montoya,
and Carlos Lozano-Garzon[✉]

Systems and Computer Engineering Department,
Universidad de los Andes, Bogotá, Colombia
{n.cobos,iy.barbosa,ga.montoya44,calozanog}@uniandes.edu.co

Abstract. Nowadays, the size of the problems to be solved in the business world has increased largely; since companies have more resources and more demand for products and services from customers. As a result, different meta-heuristics have been developed in the computing world with the aim of finding an optimal solution in a shorter runtime. Involving a real-life case, this paper will present the approach of a multi-objective task scheduling model, solved with evolutionary algorithms; specifically, NSGA-II and SPEA2. In addition, a mathematical model was proposed and its solution was calculated in order to obtain results that allow us to compare the accuracy of the results obtained by the proposed algorithms. The running time and total cost of the task scheduling were the metrics for the evaluation of the results. Between the evolutionary algorithms, NSGA-II obtained the best results in both metrics.

Keywords: Multi-Objective Evolutionary Algorithms ·
Multi-objective optimization · NSGA-II · SPEA2 · Task scheduling

1 Introduction

The problem of resource allocation is referred to as: "the problem that seeks to find the optimal allocation of a fixed amount of resources to a certain number of activities in such a way that it minimizes the cost generated by the allocation" [1]. This problem is often implemented with a *minimax* in the objective function; this kind of function has been studied a lot for its simplicity and versatility since it can be adapted to be used to represent a large number of problems. An example of its extension and generalization is the relationship with the high-tech industries; in these companies, this problem has been connected with the production planning to maximize their efficiency [1].

The most basic formulation of the resource allocation problem according to Handbook of Combinatorial Optimization [1] is presented in the set of Eqs. 1.

© Springer Nature Switzerland AG 2020
H. Florez and S. Misra (Eds.): ICAI 2020, CCIS 1277, pp. 299–312, 2020.
https://doi.org/10.1007/978-3-030-61702-8_21

$$minimize(maximize_{1 \leq j \leq n}(f_j(x_j))$$

subject to:

$$\sum_{j=1}^{n} x_j = N, \tag{1}$$

$$x_j \geq 0, \forall j$$

Regarding the use of evolutionary algorithms to solve the resource allocation problem, it can be said that it is a topic from the 2010s. One of the most relevant paper was written by Xia and Shen [2], in this paper the authors addressed the allocation of resources in a cloud computing system in order to maximize the utility that a company receives from each user it serves and to satisfy the required level of service (latency, availability, etc.). To solve this, they used three types of algorithms: a genetic algorithm (GA), an ant colony algorithm with a genetic algorithm (ACO-GA), and a quantum genetic algorithm (QGA). Furthermore, a mapping process was used between the resource allocation matrix and the chromosomes of each algorithm, searching for pairs of resources based on the availability matrices of ACO-GA, and coding the differences in values between the resources used and the minimum resource required by QGA. With extensive simulation, the authors proved that evolutionary algorithms, in this case the quantum one, have a better performance than other alternative solutions such as dynamic programming or other meta-heuristics.

There is a similar work to that carried out in this project, the authors combine an evolutionary algorithm with a greedy algorithm to make a task allocation for multi-agent systems [3]. Authors argue that the evolutionary algorithm (in this case D-NSGA III) is specifically used to optimize different targets simultaneously, thus ensuring diversity of responses and search capacity; and the combination of the evolutionary algorithm with the greedy serves to improve the ability to search for local optimums.

This paper is based on a real problem where there is a number of tasks that need to be fulfilled by agents on a business day. So, in order to do that, the scheduling must assign the work orders to the agents so they can complete the activities. Constraints that were taken into account involve the available hours that a worker has on a certain day, the abilities that the worker has, and the ones that a certain work order requires. At the same time, two objective functions are set to be optimized: minimize the total cost of scheduling and minimize the maximum amount of orders that a single agent completes in a day.

The first step to solve this problem was to propose a mathematical model. Then, that mathematical model was translated into an optimization model in Java and Python; the next step was to implement the different solving methods. The linear solving method was implemented in Python with the help of Pyomo [4], which is a collection of Python software packages to formulate optimization models. Meanwhile, the evolutionary algorithms were implemented in Java using JMetal [5], which is an object-oriented Java-based framework for multi-objective optimization with meta-heuristics.

The main goal of this work was to establish which of the solving methods is optimal. For this, it was proposed that the metrics to compare were the results of the objective functions (total cost of scheduling, the maximum amount of work orders completed by an agent in a day), and the time it takes the algorithm to get to the final solution.

The remainder of this paper is organized as follows. In Sect. 2, the general problem will be stated. In the third one, the mathematical optimization model approach will be explained. In Sect. 4, there will be an explanation of the implementation of the mathematical model in Python and Java. And finally, we will discuss the results and future work of the project.

2   General Problem Statement

The problem used in this paper exemplifies the actual condition of some Colombian company that needs a making decision app that supports the day by day agent task scheduling. Each task is required by one company client, and it is necessary to specify at least three parameters: a specific limited time to attend the task, the required skills to do the activity, and the location where the activity is going to take place. In relation to the first parameter, if the time limit is surpassed and the activity has not been attended this will represent a monetary cost for the company because they will break the Service Level Agreement (SLA) previously covenanted with the client.

The agents that solve the activities are company employees, and we need to have some characteristics defined: they have a skill set, a defined working time, an hourly wage defined by the company, and a starting location in the city. It is important to remark that some agents need to go to the central office before they start with the tasks, but some others can just go directly from their house to the location of the activity.

The company defined five optimization attributes:

- Cost: this attribute is related to the agent's salary; the company wants to use the agents with the highest hourly wage in the activities that really need them to be solved. This saves the company operation costs because they will be spending less money on payroll.
- Distances traveled by the agents: this attribute, does not need a deeper explanation; the company expects that an agent does not have to go across the whole cite to take care of a task if there is another one available and closer.
- Fairness of activities assigned to the agents: the third attribute, is related to giving an equal amount of work to all the agents. Sometimes, occurs that some agents have to work all day without rest meanwhile some others just have one task scheduled. In order to promote equality, the company wants the difference in allocation between agents to be as small as possible.
- Matching abilities between the task and the agent: This attribute, maximize the number of matching skills between the task and the agent assigned. This can be confusing because it will make no sense to assign someone how does

not have the skills to an activity; but in some cases, this is happening. In an ideal world, the company will hire as many people as needed; but in the real-world, the resources are limited so they have to do what they can; for this reason, it is common to see employees unqualified in certain activities. Although this is planed, it is wanted to happen with the minimum possible frequency.

- Number of orders solved before the limit time: The last attribute, maximize the number of orders solved before the limit time of each task, according to the SLA. The company wants to fulfill their responsibilities as much as possible.

3   Mathematical Optimization Model Approach

The first step was to determine the sets in the problem. For this, the files that the company had given us were reviewed; from them, it was deduced that the problem could be represented taking into account only this four attributes: orders, employees, hours, and skills. To be more realistic with the number of tasks that can be done in one day, we decide to add an estimate of the transportation time between it.

The sets, and parameters required by our mathematical model are described in the Table 1.

Table 1. Notations of the proposed model.

Sets	Description
E	Set of employees
O	Set of orders
H	Set of working time hours available
S	Set of skills
Parameters	Description
B_{es}	Binary parameter that represents if an employee $e \in E$ has the skill $s \in S$
C_{os}	Binary parameter that represents if an order $o \in O$ require the skill $s \in S$
D_{eh}	Binary parameter that represents if an employee $e \in E$ has availability at time $h \in H$
F_e	Integer parameter that represents the hourly wage of the employee $e \in E$

For this multi-objective proposal, we defined the decision variable as the relation between the employees, orders and hours. This relation is represented through the binary variable X_{eoh} which takes the value of 1 if the employee $e \in E$ goes to the activity $o \in O$ at the hour $h \in H$ (see Eq. 2).

$$X_{eoh} = \begin{cases} 1 \text{ employee } e \in E \text{ goes to the activity } o \in O \text{ at the hour } h \in H \\ 0 \text{ otherwise} \end{cases} \quad (2)$$

3.1 The Objective Function

Considering the main needs for the decision making app, we select only the cost and fairness attributes as part of the main function.

For the cost, we minimize the sum of all the employees' hourly wage multiplied by the sum of all the hours and all the tasks in X_{eoh} as you can see in Eq. 3.

$$min \sum_{e \in E} F_e \sum_{h \in H} \sum_{o \in O} X_{eoh} \tag{3}$$

For fairness, we decided to minimize the variable P, this variable represents the number of agent tasks for the agent with the most assigned activities (see Eq. 4).

$$min \quad P$$
$$where: P = max(\sum_{h \in H} \sum_{o \in O} X_{eoh}) \qquad \forall e \in E \tag{4}$$

3.2 Model Constraints

In order to fulfill the initial optimization requirements, the attributes that were not used for the objective function were modeled as constraints.

The first constraint is related to the fact that an order can only be assigned to one employee at a specific time (see Eq. 5).

$$\sum_{h \in H} \sum_{e \in E} X_{eoh} = 1 \qquad \forall o \in O \tag{5}$$

The next constraint is close related with the previous one, it is desirable that all the orders are attends at the working day, as you can see in Eq. 6.

$$\sum_{o \in O} X_{eoh} \leq 1 \qquad \forall e \in E \quad \forall h \in H \tag{6}$$

Our third constraint ensures that an agent e can only be assigned to an order o at a specific hour h if he has the available time to fill it (see Eq. 7).

$$D_{eh} \geq X_{eoh} \qquad \forall e \in E \quad \forall h \in H \quad \forall o \in O \tag{7}$$

And the final constraint seeks that an employee e must have at least the same skills that the order o requires, as you can see in Eq. 8.

$$B_{es}X_{eoh} \geq C_{os}X_{eoh} \qquad \forall e \in E \quad \forall h \in H \quad \forall o \in O \quad \forall s \in S \tag{8}$$

4   Implementation

As previously mentioned, based on the data files provided by the company, we established some assumptions as: a regular day involved 10 working hours, and there were 2 skills that the task needed and/or the workers might have. Also, from the files, we got that a task lasts approximately 15 min.

After having worked with different optimization frameworks, the ones that provided what we required were Pyomo and JMetal. Pyomo is a Python-based, open-source optimization modeling language with a diverse set of optimization capabilities [6], and JMetal is an optimization framework based on Java [7].

4.1   Meta-heuristics Implementation

Taking into account that the company wants to find a set of optimal solutions, we select the use of Multi-Objective Evolutionary Algorithms (MOEA) because they allow us to find the Pareto front in a single run [8]. Specifically, algorithms Non-dominated Sorting Genetic Algorithm (NSGA-II) and Strength Pareto Evolutionary Algorithm (SPEA-II) were implemented.

NSGA-II and SPEA2. In this section, we show the original pseudocodes for NSGA-II [9] and SPEA2 [10]. These pseudocodes were the basis to solve our resource allocation problem, which are presented in the Algorithms 1 and 2.

Algorithm 1. NSGA-II Pseudocode.

1: *Initialize P*
2: $P' = Non \cdot dominated \cdot sort(P)$
3: *StopRunning = false*
4: **while** StopRunning is false **do**
5:     *Generate F fronts from P'*
6:     *Apply Crossover and Mutation to F*
7:     $D = selection(F)$
8:     $N = combine(F, D)$
9:     $P' = Non \cdot dominated \cdot sort(N)$
10: **end while**
11: *return P'*

The pseudocode for the Non-dominated Sorting Genetic Algorithm (NSGA-II) (Algorithm 1) is described in more detail in the following items:

- A population P is initialized, which corresponds to a set of possible solutions of our problem (line 1).
- The previous solutions are ordered (in a non-dominated manner) and classified in different fronts F (lines 2 and 5).
- Crossover and Mutation are applied to the best fronts F (line 6).

Algorithm 2. SPEA2 Pseudocode.

 1: *Set G = numberOfGenerations*
 2: *Initialize P*
 3: *S = ∅*
 4: **for** 1 to G **do**
 5:     *Apply Fitness to P and S*
 6:     *Define S with feasible solutions*
 7:     *Add non dominated solutions from P and S to S*
 8:     *Apply Truncation to S if its capacity is exceeded*
 9:     *Apply Tournament Selection to S*
10:     *Apply Crossover and Mutation to S*
11: **end for**
12: *return S*

- Once the fronts F are selected, a new population D is created (line 7).
- F and D populations are combined to create a new population N (line 8).
- The previous feasible solutions of N are ordered in a non-dominated manner (line 9).
- A crowd-sorting process is performed to the best front's solutions (line 9).
- A new population is created (line 9).
- If a stop-condition was achieved, we show the final population obtained. Otherwise, we use the previous population to recalculate again the algorithm (lines 4 and 11).

Likewise, the pseudocode for the Strength Pareto Evolutionary Algorithm (SPEA-II) (Algorithm 2) is detailed in the following items:

- A number of generations is established. Notice that a high value of this number allows us to find better solutions (line 1).
- A population P is initialized, which corresponds to a set of possible solutions of our problem (line 2).
- An empty set S is created. This set will be composed of non-dominated solutions (line 3).
- Fitness of P and S is calculated, and the population S is established according to the objective functions and constraints of our problem (lines 5 and 6).
- Non-dominated solutions from P and S are added to S (line 7).
- If the size of S exceeds a determined value, the Truncation operator is applied for deleting repeated solutions (line 8).
- The Tournament Selection process is applied to S in order to select just one individual from a comparison of two random individuals according to their fitness (line 9).
- Crossover and Mutation are applied to S to obtain more variations of the solutions (line 10).
- If the limit of iterations has not been exceeded, we proceed to do another "for" iteration. Otherwise, we show the final population obtained (lines 4 and 12).

It is important to remark that, given the framework limitations the decision variable, for the NSGA-II, were handled as integers, with an inferior limit of 0 and a superior limit of 1; and, for the SPEA2 was established to be binary.

Encoding Chromosome Definition. An evolutionary algorithm can generate many solutions, at which each solution is called *Individual*, and a collection of individuals is called *Population*. Each individual is established using a template called *Chromosome*. In essence, a chromosome encodes information related to decision variables or parameters, and, also, its structure defines the way the fitness function is calculated. A chromosome can be either numerical, binary, symbols, or characters depending on the problem [11].

In order to implement individuals based on our chromosome in JMetal, we need to make a minor adjustment to our decision variable. As we observed in Eq. 2, our decision variable X_{eoh}, depends on three sets; which is why it should be modeled as a three-dimensional array (see Fig. 1). Unfortunately, the selected framework only allows the implementation of chromosomes as a one-dimensional arrays. Therefore, we proposed a "translation" in order to comply with the framework requirements (see Fig. 2).

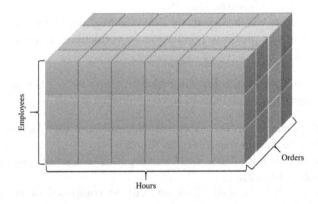

Fig. 1. Original chromosome proposed based on the mathematical model

Taking into account the previous consideration, the chromosome developed by us will be briefly explained. A solution obtained by our evolutionary algorithm is equivalent to the values of each decision variable previously mentioned in the mathematical model formulation. Since the decision variables of this problem are binary, a solution (individual) will be an array of binary elements. Due to there are a high amount of decision variables involved in a relatively big scenario, if the individuals are generated randomly, the computer would take an excessive amount of time to find a feasible solution. To solve this problem, some modifications were applied to the function that creates individuals. The most important aspect of these modifications consists of verifying that each work order was solved in the day only once.

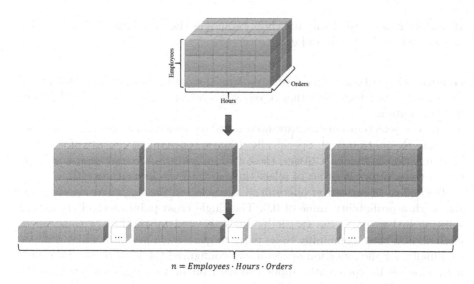

Fig. 2. Final chromosome proposed

The previous modification is explained as follows. First, imagine a scenario with 5 work orders, 4 work hours and 3 agents to fulfill that order. The number of decision variables in this case would be 60 because there is one variable for each combination of the three elements. Each order would be associated to 12 decision variables, involving the combination of each of the hours and workers. To ensure the condition previously mentioned, the process of creating an individual started with a cycle. For each of the work orders the following procedure was executed: choose a random number between 0 and the number of decision variables associated with each order minus one (in this case: $12 - 1 = 11$). Then, you assign that order in that specific index (in terms of the problem, this means to place a 1 in the index and leave the rest of the variables with 0). This ensures that each one of the work orders will be fulfilled just once. After this procedure, maybe the individual created implicates that the employee attends two different work orders in the same work hour, which must be avoided. To solve this problem, each time an order is assigned to the worker, there is a previous checking process to guarantee that there is no other order assigned in that hour.

Generation of Initial Population. It is important to highlight that we modified the original creation process implemented in JMetal. In the framework, the chromosome creation is completely random; when we testing our proposal with this implementation, a high execution time was presented to find a feasible solution. Therefore, based on [3], we decided to modify this process in order to create our chromosomes as a feasible solutions, allowing the algorithm to find solutions faster. This technique improved dramatically the execution time of the algorithm. Finally, we define 100 chromosomes as the initial population size; this size was selected by trial and error.

Genetic Operators. The next step was the selection and configuration of the genetic operators (selection, crossover, and mutation) to be used in our implementation.

For the selection operator we used a binary tournament operator in order to create the mating pool. Specifically, Binary Tournament consists of selecting randomly two individuals. After, these two individuals are evaluated according to its fitness values in order to select the one with the best fitness [12].

Related to the crossover operator, it was selected the single cross point operator with a probability value of 0.9. The single cross point method consists of splitting in two parts the two individuals selected by the binary tournament method, and then, combining these parts to generate a new individual [11].

Finally, for the mutation operator was configured the bit flip mutation function, which is independently applied to each bit in a solution and changes the value of the bit [13]; the probability assigned to this operator was 1 divided by the total number of variables ($p = \frac{1}{|E| \cdot |H| \cdot |O|}$).

Completion Criteria. Based on the experimentation carried out, it was defined that the completion criteria is the number of generations; 250 generations were specifically defined since any increase in this value did not generate improvements to the solution found. In other words, 250 generations were enough to obtain the best results of our specific problem.

4.2 Mathematical Model Implementation

On the other hand, with the Pyomo framework, the implementation followed the three-dimension matrix proposed in the mathematical model so there was no issue with the index use.

The real issue with Pyomo occurred when we tried to implement the fairness optimization attribute because we were not allowed to do the min-max optimization. Our solution propose was to make an adaptation to the model inspired by the ϵ-constrain technique. Basically, this technique allows us to optimize an objective function as a constraint in cases where is difficult to implement all objective functions. In other words, an objective function is included as a constraint in the model, but at the expense of not being included as an objective function anymore. More details of this technique are described in [14]. In this sense, we defined a new constraint that set a maximum limit to the number of orders that could be assigned to an employee. In order to see the model behavior with different maximum limits, we configured the model to run several times changing the limit between the values that the other methods suggested.

The other parts of the model were implemented just as shown in the mathematical model.

5   Experimental Results

With the aim of verifying the correct performance of the model and the proposed algorithms, we defined two main scenarios according to the typical situations of order scheduling on the enterprise. The first one is made up by 150 orders, 30 employees and 10 working hours; whiles for the second scenario have been configured 75 orders, 15 employees and also 10 working hours. Also was defined the following assumptions:

- Each employee has a different hourly wage.
- 2 possible activities and employee skills.
- Not all employees possess all the skills and not all orders require all skills.

5.1   Experimental Results for the First Proposed Scenario

The proposed algorithms finds a feasible solution to the task scheduling problem set up; the Pareto Front obtained is shown in Fig. 3 and the values are presented in Table 2. As expected, the mathematical model presented the best Pareto front since mathematical optimization methods guarantee to find optimal solutions, while meta-heuristic optimization methods cannot guarantee that; for this reason, NSGA-II and SPEA2 Pareto Fronts are not equal to Pyomo's Pareto Front. However, NSGA-II Pareto Front is closer to Pyomo's Pareto Front than SPEA2 Pareto Front, whereby NSGA-II obtained better feasible solutions than SPEA2.

Comparing the execution times of the algorithms deployed, it was found that NSGA-II executed in around 11 s, SPEA2 did it in 24.1 s and the linear optimization algorithm that Pyomo executes in 330 s to obtain the solutions. Finally, in terms of execution time, NSGA-II was the fastest approach.

Table 2. First scenario results

P value	NSGA-II cost	SPEA2 cost	Pyomo cost (ϵ-constraint)
6	$ 13.590.000,00	–	$ 12.000.000,00
7	$ 12.960.000,00	$ 13.365.000,00	$ 10.675.000,00
8	$ 12.525.000,00	$ 13.290.000,00	$ 13.675.000,00
9	–	$ 13.210.000,00	$ 13.675.000,00

5.2   Experimental Results for the Second Proposed Scenario

For the second scenario, the Pareto fronts of the three methods are presented in Fig. 4 and the values are shown in Table 3. As similar to the first scenario, the mathematical model presented the best Pareto front, and also, NSGA-II Pareto Front is closer to Pyomo's Pareto Front than SPEA2 Pareto Front, whereby NSGA-II obtained again better feasible solutions than SPEA2.

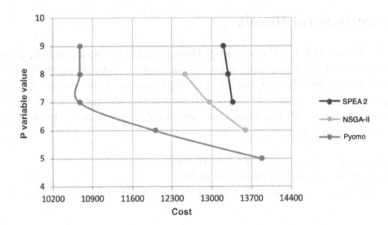

Fig. 3. Fist scenario Pareto fronts.

The execution times of our algorithms are the following, for the NSGA-II was around 3 s, SPEA2 did it in 7 s and the Pyomo optimization runs took 2500 s.

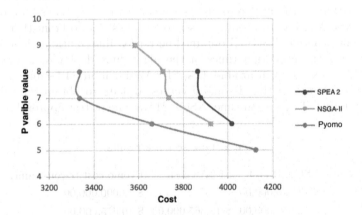

Fig. 4. Second scenario Pareto fronts.

Table 3. Second scenario results

P value	NSGA-II cost	SPEA2 cost	Pyomo cost (ϵ-constraint)
6	\$ 3.925.000,00	\$ 4.020.000,00	\$ 3.660.000,00
7	\$ 3.735.000,00	\$ 3.880.000,00	\$ 3.340.000,00
8	\$ 3.710.000,00	\$ 3.865.000,00	\$ 3.340.000,00
9	\$ 3.585.000,00	–	\$ 3.340.000,00

6   Conclusions and Future Works

In this work, we presented a mathematical optimization model and meta-heuristic approaches for a particular task scheduling problem. Specifically, evolutionary algorithms such as NSGA-II and SPEA2 were implemented and adapted to our problem in order to obtain feasible solutions. In this sense, several components such as chromosome, crossover, and mutation methods were presented. The NSGA-II and SPEA2 results were compared against the optimal results offered by the mathematical optimization model.

As expected, the best Pareto front was obtained by the mathematical optimization model (Pyomo implementation), and the second and third places were for NSGA-II and SPEA2, respectively. In terms of execution time, NSGA-II was the fastest in the evaluated scenarios, while SPEA2 and the mathematical optimization model obtained the second and last place, respectively. That is, mathematical optimization model always obtained the worst execution times. In this sense, if a company requires optimal solutions without execution time requirements, we recommend to use a mathematical optimization approach. However, if a company needs to obtain solutions as soon as possible, a mathematical optimization approach is not suitable, whereby it is recommended to use a meta-heuristic. Therefore, for our particular problem, we suggest to use the NSGA-II evolutionary algorithm.

According to future works, we propose to complement this work by adding the following capabilities:

- Offer path solutions for each employee in order to accomplish the orders taking into account time requirements and other limitations.
- Obtain resource allocation solutions for many working days, instead of one day.
- Test our scenarios by implementing more meta-heuristics such as Particle Swarm Optimization and Ant Colony.
- For large amounts of data, offer solutions by implementing parallelized methods.

References

1. Katoh, N., Shioura, A., Ibaraki, T.: Resource allocation problems. In: Pardalos, P., Du, D.Z., Graham, R. (eds.) Handbook of Combinatorial Optimization. Springer, New York (2013). https://doi.org/10.1007/978-1-4613-0303-9_14
2. Xia, W., Shen, L.: Joint resource allocation using evolutionary algorithms in heterogeneous mobile cloud computing networks. China Commun. **15**(8), 189–204 (2018)
3. Zhou, J., Zhao, X., Zhang, X., Zhao, D., Li, H.: Task allocation for multi-agent systems based on distributed many-objective evolutionary algorithm and greedy algorithm. IEEE Access **8**, 19306–19318 (2020)
4. Center for Computing Research at Sandia National Laboratories: Pyomo. http://www.pyomo.org/

5. Khaos Investigación. JMetal. https://jmetal.github.io/jMetal/
6. Hart, W.E., et al.: Pyomo-Optimization Modeling in Python, 2nd edn. Springer, Heidelberg (2017). https://doi.org/10.1007/978-3-319-58821-6
7. Durillo, J., Nebro, A.: JMetal: a Java framework for multi-objective optimization. Adv. Eng. Softw. **42**(10), 760–771 (2011)
8. Deb, K.: Multi-Objective Optimization using Evolutionary Algorithms. Wiley-Interscience Series in Systems and Optimization. Wiley, West Sussex (2001)
9. Deb, K., Pratap, A., Agarwal, S., Meyarivan, T.: A fast and elitist multiobjective genetic algorithm: NSGA-II. IEEE Trans. Evol. Comput. **6**(2), 182–197 (2002)
10. Zitzler, E., Laumanns, M., Thiele, L.: SPEA2: improving the strength pareto evolutionary algorithm. Institut für Technische Informatik und Kommunikationsnetze (TIK) **103**, 5–6 (2001)
11. Tan, K.C., Khor, E.F., Lee, T.H.: Multiobjective Evolutionary Algorithms and Applications. Advanced Information and Knowledge Processing Series. Springer, Heidelberg (2004). https://doi.org/10.1007/1-84628-132-6
12. Rahman, R., Ramli, R., Jamari, Z., Ku-Mahamud, K.: Evolutionary Algorithm with Roulette-Tournament Selection for Solving Aquaculture Diet Formulation. Hindawi Publishing Corporation, London (2016)
13. Chicano, F., Sutton, A., Whitley, L., Alba, E.: Fitness probability distribution of bit-flip mutation. Evol. Comput. **23**(2), 217–248 (2014)
14. Mavrotas, G.: Effective implementation of the e-constraint method in multi-objective mathematical programming problems. Appl. Math. Comput. **213**, 455–465 (2009)

Diabetes Classification Techniques: A Brief State-of-the-Art Literature Review

Jeffrey O. Agushaka and Absalom E. Ezugwu[(⊠)]

School of Mathematics, Statistics, and Computer Science, University of KwaZulu-Natal, King Edward Road, Pietermaritzburg 3201, KwaZulu-Natal, South Africa
218088307@stu.ukzn.ac.za, Ezugwua@ukzn.ac.za

Abstract. Clinical data on diabetes patients are readily available in many countries and research directories. These data are not necessarily in the same format or do not contain error-free or clear information about diabetes. These incomprehensive and non-homogenous data are a great source of conflict for the practitioner and the research communities. Applying Computational Intelligence on these datasets makes it easier for patterns and relationships to be identified, and useful information or conclusions can be derived. Diabetes diagnosis falls under the data classification problem and so much literature exists in this subject area. This study aims to survey as much literature as can be found on the application of computational intelligence for diabetes classification from 2010–2020. Articles indexed in Scopus, IEEE, Web of Science, Google Scholar, and other scholarly databases were searched for up-to-date articles and the Preferred Reporting Items for Systematic Reviews and Meta-Analyses (PRISMA) was used for article selection. We selected articles after inclusion and exclusion criteria were applied. We discuss the commonly used diabetes classification algorithms and datasets. Finally, a taxonomy based on whether the algorithms are standalone or hybrid and whether they are a variant of major algorithms or a comparative study is presented.

Keywords: Diabetes · Classification · Algorithms · Blood sugar · Computational intelligence

1 Introduction

In situations where the quantity of insulin produced by the pancreas is not enough or cells in the body are no longer reactive to insulin, which means the blood glucose is not absorbed by the cells, these result in a condition known as diabetes mellitus [1]. Diabetes is a chronic disease and a global health threat; it is neither a respecter of economic status nor racial or national boundaries. It can lead to health challenges like renal (kidney) failure, heart disease, stroke, and blindness, etc. Currently, diabetes is among the top 10 causes of death in humans [2]. The International Diabetes Foundation (IDF) estimates that the prevalence of diabetes, type 1 and type 2 (diagnosed and undiagnosed), will reach 700 million people (10.9% of the global population) within the age range of 20–79 years by the year 2045 if adequate prevention measures are not taken. This is a significant rise from 151 million (4.6%) in 2000 and 463 million (9.3%) in 2019. Despite this, many

© Springer Nature Switzerland AG 2020
H. Florez and S. Misra (Eds.): ICAI 2020, CCIS 1277, pp. 313–329, 2020.
https://doi.org/10.1007/978-3-030-61702-8_22

countries still lack a national diabetes plan, and a greater part of the population has little or no essential health coverage needed for halting the rise of diabetes. Also, Africa is projected to have a 143% increase in diabetes prevalence from 19 million in 2019 to 47 million in 2045; this is significantly high and implores for intervention [2].

The criteria for early diagnosis of diabetes are still in its early stages and constantly changing as more about diabetes is known. Many diagnostic criteria exist in studies for estimating diabetes. The American Diabetes Association (ADA) diagnostic criteria in 2019 proposed a criteria of Fasting Plasma Glucose (FPG) concentration $\geq$95 mg/dL or 5.3 mmol/L or HbA1c $\geq$ 6.5% or 1 h Oral Glucose Tolerance Test (OGTT) $\geq$180 mg/dL or 10 mmol/L or 2 h OGTT $\geq$155 mg/dL or 8.6 mmol/L or 3 h OGTT $\geq$140 mg/dL or 7.8 mmol/L [3]. Other clinical and demographic signs are also used in the diagnosis of diabetes, for example, sex, age, cardiovascular disease, body mass index (BMI), diabetes pedigree/genetic, sedentary lifestyle, etc.

There is an unwavering rise in the amount of data kept on diabetes and a corresponding rise in the number of countries that have records on the disease (from 131–138 out of 221 countries) [2]. These data are not necessarily homogenous; neither are they comprehensive. Various diagnostic tests are employed for the diagnosis of diabetes, and conclusions may be based on the World Health Organization (WHO) or the American Diabetes Association (ADA) criteria. Though closely related, the differences cannot be ignored. Also, the sampling population used, the responses achieved, the age groups invited, etc., are potential sources of conflict for the practitioner. Computational intelligence can help make the data useful by deriving relationships and patterns from these extensive data.

Diabetes diagnosis falls under the data classification problem; certain features are identified during the diagnosis phase, and based on these features, a conclusion is made (whether diabetic or not). Data classification is a technique that is employed in computational intelligence, particularly machine learning to predict or allocate a class label to a set of features in a dataset.

Many attempts at using computational intelligence for classification or diagnosis of diabetes exist in literature with varying levels of success. However, the focus of most of the reviews is on some selected algorithms and seldom on all (more selective than a comprehensive survey). This is understandable because of the high turnover of research daily on the subject matter. To the best of our knowledge, no survey has included traditional, deep learning and metaheuristics approach to diabetes classification.

Therefore, this study aims to survey as much literature as can be found on the application of computational intelligence techniques for diabetes classification. This will include traditional, deep learning and metaheuristics methods. We paid attention to new research that had not been reported in previous surveys and shed more light on state of the art. More specifically, we report on the following: i) a comprehensive survey that includes metaheuristic approaches to diabetes classification alongside the traditional and deep learning approaches, and ii) classification of the approaches into single, hybrid or comparative studies.

The rest of the paper is organized as follows: Sect. 2 presents the related work, Sect. 3 discusses the methodology, and major algorithms used for diabetes classification are presented in Sect. 4. Finally, Sect. 5 presents the conclusion and future research direction.

2   Related Work

The success of the application of computational intelligence in the classification of diabetes has led to a tremendous number of publications in journals and conference proceedings [5–11]. Therefore, in this study, we explore some of the significant contributions that have been made so far by different researchers in this domain.

Sun and Zhang [4] reported on articles related to decision tree (DT), support vector machine (SVM), artificial neural network (ANN), clustering, and association rules. They went further to compare deep learning (deep Convolutional Neural Networks (CNN), deep belief network (DBN), and deep recurrent neural networks (RNN)) with conventional machine learning methods. This is more selective than a detailed survey of the application of machine learning in diabetes classification. The study presented in [12] surveyed articles on the application of ML and DL techniques on diabetes predictions published between 2013–2019, proposed an ensemble of rarely used classifiers, and obtained an accuracy of 68%–74%. Similarly, Contreras and Vehi [13] reviewed the latest articles (2010–2018). They proposed a functional taxonomy for applications of artificial intelligence in diabetes management within this period and found that Artificial Intelligence (AI) is further strengthened by the availability of genetic data. The categorization of feature selection algorithms based on search strategy, evaluation criteria, and data mining tasks was presented in [14]. Presenting a similar approach of a taxonomy of the algorithms, [15] categorized the algorithms into single or hybrid, mentioning their pros and cons. Their findings show that the hybridization of techniques yields promising results. Gujral's findings showed that as compared to hybrid approaches that yield better results, single approaches to diabetes detection yield less superior results for early diabetes deduction [16]. Kavakiotis et al. [17] presented a systematic review paying attention to diabetes prediction and diagnosis, complications, family pedigree or genetic background and environment, and health care and management. Their finding showed that diabetes prediction and diagnosis is the most researched area.

The authors in [18] tried to explain using existing literature, why the clinical application of successes recorded by computational intelligence in classification and diagnosis of diabetes, is still elusive. Their findings showed that the underlying statistical structure of the dataset is unknown, the risk score used is unsophisticated, and there is a need to find an algorithm that will best suit clinically. The impact of classification algorithms in diabetes data analysis was reported in [19]; they surveyed articles on the application of Naïve Bayes, Decision trees, KNN and SVM and found that within their context of the survey, the C4.5 algorithm gave a better performance than the other algorithms studied. However, their survey was not extensive because they left out the neural networks and others. A survey that focused not only on classification algorithms but also advances in glucose and lifestyle monitoring sensors, clinical decision support systems (CDSSs) for both self-disease management and healthcare professionals is presented in [20]. They concluded by stating that more data from sensor-based systems should be integrated with the electronic health record as this will further increase the performance of the computational techniques used.

The diversity, strength, and flexibility of nature-inspired computing (NIC) to solve problems, particularly in the medical field, have spurred many pieces of research. The availability and promising results of these researches have led to surveys in the application of NIC in diabetes classification. Application of Genetic Algorithms (GA), Ant Colony Optimization (ACO), Particle Swarm Optimization (PSO), and Artificial Bee Colonies (ABC) in disease diagnosis is the focus of [21]. Their findings showed that GA is more widely used in medical diagnosis, and they observed that the accuracy recorded by these algorithms in early diagnosis of diabetes amongst others is 70%–99.2%, and the hybrid of these nature inspire algorithms yielded more promising results than when used individually. Another survey [22] reported GAs as the best performing algorithm, and the study revealed the lack of researches that show a clear relationship between grouping problem features and best-suited algorithm, suggesting this as future work.

A comparative analysis of selected papers that were published in the period from 2008 to 2017 is given in [23]. They found that the most used type of ANN in literature is a multilayer feedforward neural network with the Levenberg-Marquardt learning algorithm. In their survey, [24] reported that the focus of AI researches in area type 2 diabetes mellitus care was on screening and diagnosis of the disease. Specifically, machine learning methods accounted for 71% of the applied techniques and support vector machine (21%), and Naive Bayesian (19%) were the commonly used algorithms. Another survey that included the top 100 cited articles on statistical methods and machine learning algorithms up to the end of 2017 was presented in [25]. They reported that the future is in hybridization, where more powerful results can be obtained by hybridizing new prediction and classification methods such as Extreme Learning Machines. The effort of study in [26] is the current (2019) review of literature on diabetes prediction; they used a combination of search words "diabetes, prediction and machine learning" on databases like Science Direct, PubMed, Springer link, IEEE Explore and Taylor and Francis.

Table 1 gives a summary of related literature. In building the body of our related work, we looked at surveys from 2010–2020. Credit to the researchers for the work they have done is reported; however, we observed that most of them were not extensive enough (this is understandable because the number of classification algorithms used is numerous). The ability to hybridize these algorithms made the rate of the rollout of articles pertaining to their use in the classification of diabetes high.

Table 1. Summary of related work

Reference	Algorithms covered	Year of review	Remark
Sun & Zhang [4]	DT, SVM, ANN, AR and DL	2019	This is more selective than a detailed survey of application of machine learning in diabetes classification

(continued)

Table 1. (*continued*)

Reference	Algorithms covered	Year of review	Remark
Larabi-Marie-Sainte et al. [12]	All the ML and DL techniques published in the last six years	2019	Ensembled rarely used classifiers and obtained an accuracy of 68%–74%
Contreras & Vehi [13]	141 related articles	2018	They proposed a functional taxonomy
Jain & Singh [14]	Review on feature selection approaches	2018	The categorization of feature selection was based on search strategy, evaluation criteria and data mining tasks
Kalantari et al. [15]	71 articles on application of CI in medical	2018	Their findings show that hybridization of techniques yields promising results
Kavakiotis et al. [16]	103 articles related to prediction and diagnosis in DM	2017	They found that diabetes prediction and diagnosis is the most researched area
Gujral [17]	20 Literatures were surveyed for early diabetes detection	2017	Findings show that hybrid approaches yield better results
Kaur & Sharma [21]	GA, ACO, PSO and ABC	2017	GA is more widely used in medical diagnosis
Alić et al. [23]	Selected papers from 2008 to 2017	2017	The aim is to show which best classifier method is the most appropriate for the diseases.
Current work	*All computational intelligence (including metaheuristics) application in DM*	*Up to date (2020)*	*Survey articles offer researchers pool of the state-of-art on related subject area and can serve as a guide for their research (avoid reinventing the wheel)*

3 Methodology

We searched for and retrieved articles indexed in Scopus, IEEE, Web of Science, Google Scholar, and other databases (24th January 2020). Preferred Reporting Items for Systematic Reviews and Meta-Analyses (PRISMA 2009) flow diagram was used for article selection [27]. The keywords used were "Computational Intelligence and Diabetes," "Machine learning and diabetes," and "Data mining and diabetes." The result for each of these searches was enormous; therefore, we excluded articles earlier than in 2010. Then we physically examined the remaining articles, excluding all articles that dealt with other aspects of diabetes and not classification or prediction. We also excluded articles used in other related survey research, and the remaining articles were included in our research. Finally, articles were selected after inclusion, and exclusion criteria were applied. Figure 1 gives the summary of publications per year, the data until 2016 is taken from [17], and we obtained the rest from Google scholar search. The goal is to bring to bear up-to-date state-of-art in diabetes classification using computational intelligence. A detailed survey is presented subsequently.

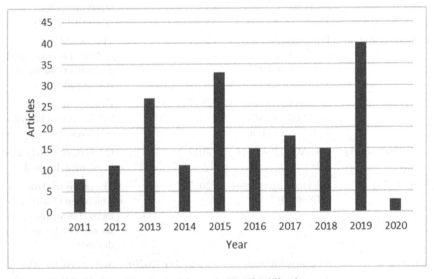

Fig. 1. Articles and year of publication

4 Major Diabetes Classification Algorithms

In this section, we discuss algorithms used in the classification of diabetes to date, and we propose a taxonomy based on whether they are standalone or hybrid and whether they are a variant of a major algorithm or a comparative study.

A comparative study of the implementation of these classification algorithms by researchers gives a new insight into the behavior of the algorithms in different datasets.

Wei et al. [28] investigated how each and a combination of the preprocessing methods improved the accuracy of DNN, DT, SVM, LR classifiers on the Pima Indian dataset, and results showed the best technique had 77.86% accuracy using 10-fold cross-validation. The bases for these comparisons are unclear. Similarly, [29] did an exploratory analysis on the Pima Indian dataset, used KNN, LR, DT, RF, Gradient Boosting, SVM and NN as classifiers and the accuracy (79.7%) of RF was the best.

Mohammadian et al. [30] carried out a comparative study of the implementation of the following classifiers: KNN, DT, NB, RF, AdaBoost, QDA, MLP-NN, SVM and Gaussian process on the UCI diabetic retinopathy dataset. They also integrated multiple image processing algorithms in literature and used them for feature extraction. The accuracy of the classifiers was affected by the different tuneable parameters, and the results showed that the Gaussian process outperformed others in detecting cases with diabetic retinopathy. Using the same dataset, [31] applied LR, SVM and RF with the aim of finding the most accurate for DM prediction and their results showed that RF surpassed all others in prediction accuracy because it paid more importance to the features of the dataset. In the same vein, [32] preprocessed the Pima Indian dataset, selected significant features using backward elimination and then Logistic Regression, Decision Trees, Random Forest, Support Vector Machine (SVM), and Adaptive Boosting, were used for prediction. SVM with linear kernel performed superior to others. Using Naive Bayes, SVM, Random Forest, Simple CART on the Pima Indian dataset, [33] did a comparative study, and their results showed SVM outperformed others with an accuracy of 0.79 (79%).

A performance study of machine learning tree classifiers such as Random Forest, C4.5, Random Tree, REPTree, and Logistic Model Tree (LMT) is given in [34]. Their results showed that the Logistic Model Tree (LMT) classifier achieved the highest accuracy of 79.31%. A study is presented in [35] on the Canadian Primary Care Sentinel Surveillance Network (CPCSSN) dataset. Two (2) algorithms were used in combination with risk factors and random under sampling, oversampling, and k-medoids sampling techniques to generate balanced training sets. The goal is to improve the predictive accuracy of the classifiers. Their results showed that Naïve Bayes with K-medoids under-sampling technique performed better than with random under-sampling, over-sampling, and no sampling.

Exploring the capabilities of GMM (Gaussian mixture model), ELM (Extreme Learning Machine), SVM, Logistic regression and ANN to predict early onset of diabetes, [36] found that the highest accuracy was recorded by ANN (0.89). In [37], the authors aimed to analyse and compare Random Forest (RF), SVM, k-NN, CART and LDA algorithms. They preprocessed the dataset with 10-fold cross validation and 3 iterations and results showed that RF algorithm with (0.99) predicted the data more correctly and accurately. The purpose of [38] was to evaluate the performance of six computational intelligence techniques (ANN, SVM, logistic regression, kNN, classification tree, and Naïve Bayes) for the classification of diabetic and non-diabetic samples (Pima Indian). In this study, logistic regression classifier recorded the highest classification accuracy (78%) and highest F 1 measure (0.84).

Using the Pima Indian dataset, [39] applied different techniques like Gradient Boosting, Logistic Regression and Naïve Bayes for the diagnosis of diabetes disease. They used KNN for reduction of bias and gradient boosting had a prediction highest accuracy of 86%. An attempt was made in [40] to improve the accuracy of AdaBoost, LogicBoost, RobustBoost, Naïve Bayes and Bagging as applied on the Pima Indian dataset. Bagging gave the highest accuracy of 81.77%. [41] aimed at finding the best classifier amongst Support vector machine, Naïve Bayes and Decision tree, on PCA reduced Pima Indian dataset. Naïve Bayes had the highest accuracy of 77.36%. Similarly, [42] checked for the best amongst classification algorithms like Support vector machine, Naïve Bayesian and C4.5 and reported C4.5 algorithms as the best algorithm suited for predicting diabetes disease.

Five (5) algorithms, namely SVM-linear, RBF, k-NN, ANN, and MDR were used in [43] on the Pima Indian. From their experiments, it shows that SVM-linear model had the best accuracy of 0.89. [44] applied many classification algorithms on Pima Indian diabetes dataset in other to check the performance of those algorithms. C4.5 recorded a classification rate of 91%. A risk prediction model for type 2 diabetes was built in [45], and their result shows that the neural network model recorded the highest accuracy (82.4%), specificity (90.2%), and AUC (0.7949).

A study on use of non-invasive parameters and machine learning algorithms (LR, k-NN, and SVM with five-fold cross-validation) to predict future risk of Type 2 diabetes on health data from Kuwait is given in [46], the k-NN recorded highest with AUC values of 0.83, 0.82, and 0.79 respectively for 3-, 5-, and 7-year prediction periods. The authors in [47] used decision tree, random forest and neural network on the dataset from hospital physical examination in Luzhou, China to predict diabetes mellitus. The dataset is highly unbalanced as the authors used principal component analysis (PCA), minimum redundancy maximum relevance (MRMR) to reduce the dimensionality and five-fold cross-validation. Results showed that random forest reached the highest accuracy of 0.8084. A comparison of the performance of classification algorithms in identifying patients who are at risk of developing T2D is given in [48] and they gave a list of predictor variables important for prediction for T2D progression.

Another approach by researchers is to propose novel models (in most cases a hybrid of existing models). Knowing the optimal number of neurons in the pattern layer of RBFNN remains an unsolved problem. [49] tried to solve this problem by proposing a model that combines cluster validity index with k-means algorithm which is then applied over the Pima Indian diabetes dataset and other synthetic datasets in class by class fashion. In a similar vein, [50] used Bat-based clustering algorithm as inputs for the RBFNN. This approach reduced the complexity of [49] by producing fewer patterns and increased the accuracy of the RDFNN by avoiding unbalanced clustering. Five datasets chosen from UCI repository having different attribute types were used in [51] for diabetes classification using a proposed hybrid nature-inspired classification algorithm. Attribute (dimensional) reduction was achieved by combining rough set with the chaos Firefly-Levy Flight algorithm and the resultant dataset was fed as input to the type-2 fuzzy logic system. They found the minimum number of attributes from high dimensional dataset that can efficiently increase the performance of the classification algorithm.

The authors in [52] identified some drawbacks of existing classifiers (need for good dataset, only one dataset, well skewed etc) and proposed one (a mixture of fuzzy logic, neural network and case base reasoning) that solved it. [53] developed a reinforcement learning-based evolutionary fuzzy rule-based system for diabetes diagnosis. Their results produced a more compact, interpretable and accurate rule base that is a promising alternative for diagnosis of diabetes. Using the Pima Indian dataset, [54] did a study on Gaussian process (GP)-based classification technique using three kernels namely: linear, polynomial and radial basis kernels. The application of K-Means and genetic algorithms for dimension reduction by integrating SVM for diabetes diagnosis is given in [55]. K-Means was used for removing the noise from Pima Indian dataset, genetic algorithms for optimal set of features and Support Vector Machine (SVM) as classifier, the proposed model recorded an average accuracy of 98.79%.

A hybrid combination of feature selection technique and the multilayer perceptron is given in [56, 57] evaluated the Pima Indian dataset repository using random forest along with feature selection method (forward selection and backward elimination based on entropy evaluation) and achieved a classification accuracy of 84.1%. A hybrid approach for modelling type 2 diabetes mellitus progression is proposed in [58]. HMM is combined with Newton's Divided Difference Method (NDDM) to develop the model to investigate the future diabetes incidents. [59] employed PCA and PSO algorithms for feature reduction prior to the classification of the Pima Indian diabetes dataset and localized diabetes dataset from Bombay Medical Hall, India using logistic regression, K-Nearest Neighbor, ID3 DT, C4.5 DT, and Naïve Bayes algorithms, less computation time and increased accuracy was achieved. The effectiveness of gradient boosted classifier on a preprocessed (Spearman method) Pima Indian dataset was shown in [60]. The efficacy of extreme learning machine (ELM) is proven with respect to fast learning capability and quick diabetes prediction when compared to other classifiers in the work of [61].

The objective of the study in [62] was to validate the performance of the Framingham Diabetes Risk Scoring Model (FDRSM) using a Hidden Markov Model (HMM). There was an increase in the area under receiver operating characteristic curve (AROC) of 86.9% from 78.6% and 85% reported in previous studies on the same dataset. A study using the real-life diabetes mellitus data acquired from four main hospitals located in the north-western region of Nigeria is given by [63]. A mean accuracy of 98.75% was achieved. In the opinion of [64], recomputing all the training data to construct the classification model whenever a dataset changes, is a problem. They proposed a model that is a combination of noise removal (principal component analysis (PCA)), classification method (support vector machine (SVM)) and clustering techniques (expectation maximization (EM)). Incremental situation was achieved using incremental noise removal method (IPCA) and incremental classification (ISVM) method and results were promising.

Ensemble Learning Approach is also gaining the attention of researchers. [65] used the MLP, SVM, and DT as ensemble at first level classifiers; with LR as the second level classifier. In [66], an ensemble of boosting algorithm with perceptron algorithm in other to improve performance of perceptron algorithm was proposed. Their results showed an improvement of 3% in terms of accuracy. Similarly, [67] proposed an ensemble of three classifiers (support vector machine, artificial neural network, and Naïve Bayes) by adjusting weight based on each classifier's capability and history of making correct predictions. An effective diabetes mellitus classification algorithm on imbalanced data with missing values was proposed in [68]. Their result showed the proposed algorithm achieved 87.10% classification accuracy. The study carried out in [69] presented a new learning technique based on the hybridization of SVMs and evolutionary algorithms and results are promising. The algorithm proposed in [70] essentially selects features from the Pima Indian diabetes dataset with more impact using the Goldberg's genetic algorithm in the preprocessing stage and then uses the multi objective evolutionary fuzzy classifier for classification. The classifier accuracy is improved to 83.0435%. The adaptation to K*-Means for noise removal, genetic algorithm (GA) for optimal feature selection and for SVM classifier on Pima Indian dataset is given in [71] with results showing an increase in accuracy of 1.351%.

5 Summary of Major Algorithms Reviewed

In this section, a collation of the major algorithms which were not previously reported in other published reviews in the literature are presented. The collation of all the articles presented in the current study is based on the way the researchers proved or reported their algorithms and results. Most authors implemented different groups of the existing classification models (without any effort to improve on them) on Pima Indian (commonly used) or any other dataset. Sometimes preprocessing was done and sometimes not, and the results obtained are compared amongst the group implemented. The model with the highest accuracy or other criteria is reported as the best. Others compared their result with that obtained by different authors; however, the basis of this comparison most often is not stated. Table 2 gives a summary of the studies that made a comparison of the regular algorithms that they implemented.

Table 2. Summary of standard algorithms used for diabetes classification

Dataset	Major algorithm	Others	Preprocessing	Result	Year	Ref
Pima Indian	DNN, DT, SVM and LR		Impute, scale and normalization	77.86%	2018	[28]
	LR, SVM and RF		–	RF surpassed all in prediction accuracy	2018	[31]
	KNN, LR, DT, RF, Gradient Boosting, SVM and NN		Replacing with median values and multiple imputations (MICE)	RF outperformed others with accuracy of 79.7%	2018	[29]

(continued)

Table 2. (*continued*)

Dataset	Major algorithm	Others	Preprocessing	Result	Year	Ref
	LR, DT, RF, SVM and Adaptive Boosting		Backward elimination was used to get significant attributes	SVM with linear kernel performs superior than others	2018	[32]
	ANN, SVM, LR, KNN, Classification Tree, And NB		–	Logistic regression classifier outperformed all other (78%)	2018	[38]
	Gradient boosting, logistic regression and Naïve Bayes		KNN imputation for predicting values and to reduce bias	Gradient boosting has prediction accuracy of 86%,	2019	[39]
	AdaBoost, LogicBoost, RobustBoost, NB and Bagging		–	Bagging performed the highest accuracy of 81.77%	2019	[40]
	Gradient Boosting, Random Forest, Neural Networks		Replaced missing values, Spearman method	Gradient boosting models outperforms	2019	[60]
Dataset from Bombay medical hall	LR, KNN, ID3 DT, C4.5 DT, and NB.		PCA and PSO algorithms for feature reduction	The proposed approach showed superiority over the traditional classification	2020	[59]

In the same fashion, some authors tried to improve on the existing classification algorithms. This improvement mostly comes in the form of combining two or more models into one powerful model. Some authors used one of the existing algorithms for preprocessing or dimensionality reduction of the dataset before applying another for classification. Other authors improved one algorithm, say the KNN algorithm, and used this improvement as intelligent guesses for others, say the number of input layers for ANN. These and many more are the hybridization approach. Table 3 gives a summary of the hybrids. On the other hand, Table 4 gives a summary of the efforts that are standalone. Here, the authors proposed new or improve existing ones in such a way that they were not a combination of other efforts, but were self-containing.

Table 3. Summary of hybrid algorithms used for diabetes classification

Dataset	Major algorithm	Others	Preprocessing	Result	Year	Ref
Pima Indian	Ensemble of SVM, ANN and NB		Wrapper Method	The proposed approach beats each single classifier in the ensemble	2014	[67]
	Random Forest (RF)	Naïve Bayes (NB)	NB and ADASYN to reduce class imbalance	The DMP_MI achieved accuracy of 87.10%	2019	[68]
	SVMs	Evolutionary algorithms.	–	The proposed technique offers a good enough accuracy	2006	[69]
	SVM	K*-Means, GA	K*-Means for noise removal, GA for optimal feature selection	Increase in accuracy by 1.351%	2017	[71]

Table 4. Summary of standalone algorithms used for diabetes classification

Dataset	Major algorithm	Others	Preprocessing	Result	Year	Ref
Pima Indian	Multi Objective Evolutionary Fuzzy Classifier		Goldberg's Genetic algorithm	The classifier rate is improved to 83.0435%	2017	[70]
	ISVM		IPCA	A better accuracy (0.9795)	2016	[64]
PIMA database and others	Extreme Learning Machine (ELM)		–	The efficiency of ELM is proven	2019	[61]

6   Conclusion and Future Direction

The success of the application of computational intelligence in diabetes classification has led to a high turnover in publications on the subject matter. This explosion has made it difficult to know the trajectory of research in the field and hence the need for a regular up-to-date survey of articles. Great effort has been dedicated to this end; however, new endeavors are reached by researchers, and the need to include them in the state-of-the-art survey is the path we took in this research. We also identified that after preprocessing the dataset for missing values, most algorithms proceeded with the classification, not accounting for the fact that the values were computed and were actual data. Pre-processing can lead to loss of information, which then affects the accuracy of the algorithm and incorrect conclusion. Also, most of these proposed classification algorithms were tested on a single dataset or in situations where multiple datasets were used; however, the statistical properties of the datasets were not properly studied. The statistical properties of these datasets are very important as they play a significant role in the accuracy of the results obtained. Clustering algorithms have shown great promise in feature selection or dimensionality reduction. However, the selection of the number of clusters is not automated (intelligent guesses). Nature-inspired computations like GA and PSO have shown great promise for both feature selection and disease prediction. There is a great number of these metaheuristics algorithms whose strength can be tested in diabetes prediction and dimensionality reduction.

References

1. Diabetes mellitus. (n.d.) Concise Dictionary of Modern Medicine. McGraw-Hill (2002). https://medical-dictionary.thefreedictionary.com/diabetes+mellitus. Accessed 9th Mar 2020
2. International Diabetes Foundation. IDF Diabetes Atlas, 9th edn. Brussels, Belgium (2019). https://www.diabetesatlas.org
3. American Diabetes Association. Classification and diagnosis of diabetes: Standards of medical care in diabetes – 2018. Diabet. Care **41**(Suppl 1), S13–27 (2018). https://doi.org/10.2337/dc18-s002
4. Sun, Y.L., Zhang, D.L.: Machine learning techniques for screening and diagnosis of diabetes: a survey. Tehnički vjesnik **26**(3), 872–880 (2019)
5. Kelarev, A.V., Stranieri, A., Yearwood, J.L.: Empirical study of decision trees and ensemble classifiers for monitoring of diabetes patients in pervasive healthcare. In: Proceedings of the International Conference on Network Based Information Systems (2012). https://doi.org/10.1109/NBiS.2012.20
6. Kaur, G., Chhabra, A.: Improved J48 classification algorithm for the prediction of diabetes. Int. J. Comput. Appl. **98**(22), 13–17 (2014). https://doi.org/10.5120/17314-7433
7. Baitharu, T.R., Pani, S.K., Dhal, S.K.: Comparison of kernel selection for support vector machines using diabetes dataset. J. Comput. Sci. Appl. **3**(6), 181–184 (2015)
8. Rau, H.H., Hsu, C.Y., Lin, Y.A., et al.: Development of a web-based liver cancer prediction model for type II diabetes patients by using an artificial neural network. Comput. Methods Progr. Biomed. **125**, 58 (2016). https://doi.org/10.1016/j.cmpb.2015.11.009
9. Mamoshina, P., Vieira, A., Putin, E., et al.: Applications of deep learning in biomedicine. Mol. Pharm. **13**(5), 1445–1454 (2016). https://doi.org/10.1021/acs.molpharmaceut.5b00982
10. Ravi, D., Wong, C., Deligianni, F., et al.: Deep learning for health informatics. IEEE J. Biomed. Health Inf. **21**(1), 4–21 (2017). https://doi.org/10.1109/JBHI.2016.2636665
11. Cheruku, R., Edla, D.R., Kuppili, V.: SMRuleMiner: spider monkey based rule miner using novel fitness function for diabetes classification. Comput. Biol. Med. **81**, 79–92 (2017). https://doi.org/10.1016/j.compbiomed.2016.12.009
12. Larabi-Marie-Sainte, S., Aburahmah, L., Almohaini, R., Saba, T.: Current techniques for diabetes prediction: review and case study. Appl. Sci. **9**(21), 4604 (2019)
13. Contreras, I., Vehi, J.: Artificial intelligence for diabetes management and decision support: literature review. J. Med. Internet Res. **20**(5), e10775 (2018)

14. Jain, D., Singh, V.: Feature selection and classification systems for chronic disease prediction: A review. Egypt. Inf. J. **19**(3), 179–189 (2018)
15. Kalantari, A., Kamsin, A., Shamshirband, S., Gani, A., Alinejad-Rokny, H., Chronopoulos, A.T.: Computational intelligence approaches for classification of medical data: state-of-the-art, future challenges and research directions. Neurocomputing **276**, 2–22 (2018)
16. Gujral, S.: Early diabetes detection using machine learning: a review. Int. J. Innov. Res. Sci. Technol. **3**(10), 57–62 (2017)
17. Kavakiotis, I., Tsave, O., Salifoglou, A., Maglaveras, N., Vlahavas, I., Chouvarda, I.: Machine learning and data mining methods in diabetes research. Comput. Struct. Biotechnol. J. **15**, 104–116 (2017)
18. Shankaracharya, D.O., Samanta, S., Vidyarthi, A.S.: Computational intelligence in early diabetes diagnosis: a review. Rev. Diabet. Stud. RDS **7**(4), 252 (2010)
19. Saravananathan, K., Velmurugan, T.: Impact of classification algorithms in diabetes data: a survey. In: 3rd International Conference on Small Medium Business, pp. 271–275 (2016)
20. Zarkogianni, K., et al.: A review of emerging technologies for the management of diabetes mellitus. IEEE Trans. Biomed. Eng. **62**(12), 2735–2749 (2015)
21. Kaur, P., Sharma, M.: A survey on using nature inspired computing for fatal disease diagnosis. Int. J. Inf. Syst. Model. Des. (IJISMD) **8**(2), 70–91 (2017)
22. Ramos-Figueroa, O., Quiroz-Castellanos, M., Mezura-Montes, E., Schütze, O.: Metaheuristics to solve grouping problems: a review and a case study. Swarm Evol. Comput. **53**, 100643 (2020)
23. Alić, B., Gurbeta, L., Badnjević, A.: Machine learning techniques for classification of diabetes and cardiovascular diseases. In: 2017 6th Mediterranean Conference on Embedded Computing (MECO), pp. 1–4. IEEE, June 2017
24. Abhari, S., Niakan Kalhori, S.R., Ebrahimi, M., Hasannejadasl, H., Garavand, A.: Artificial intelligence applications in type 2 diabetes mellitus care: focus on machine learning methods. Healthc. Inf. Res. **25**(4), 248–261 (2019)
25. Pekel, E., Özcan, T.: Diagnosis of diabetes mellitus using statistical methods and machine learning algorithms. Sigma J. Eng. Nat. Sci./Mühendislik ve Fen Bilimleri Dergisi **36**(4) (2018)
26. Dzakiyullah, N.R., Burhanuddin, M.A., Ikram, R.R.R., Ghani, K.A., Setyonugroho, W.: Int. J. Innov. Technol. Explor. Eng. **8**(12), 2199–2205 (2019). https://doi.org/10.35940/ijitee.l2973.1081219
27. Liberati, A., Altman, D.G., Tetzlaff, J., Mulrow, C., Gøtzsche, P.C., et al.: The PRISMA statement for reporting systematic reviews and meta-analyses of studies that evaluate health care interventions: explanation and elaboration. PLoS Med. **6**(7), e1000100 (2009). https://doi.org/10.1371/journal.pmed.1000100
28. Wei, S., Zhao, X., Miao, C.: A comprehensive exploration to the machine learning techniques for diabetes identification. In: 2018 IEEE 4th World Forum on Internet of Things (WF-IoT), pp. 291–295. IEEE, February 2018
29. Barhate, R., Kulkarni, P.: Analysis of classifiers for prediction of type ii diabetes mellitus. In: 2018 Fourth International Conference on Computing Communication Control and Automation (ICCUBEA), pp. 1–6. IEEE, August 2018
30. Mohammadian, S., Karsaz, A., Roshan, Y.M.: A comparative analysis of classification algorithms in diabetic retinopathy screening. In: 2017 7th International Conference on Computer and Knowledge Engineering (ICCKE), pp. 84–89. IEEE, October 2017
31. Dutta, D., Paul, D., Ghosh, P.: Analysing feature importances for diabetes prediction using machine learning. In: 2018 IEEE 9th Annual Information Technology, Electronics and Mobile Communication Conference (IEMCON), pp. 924–928. IEEE, November 2018

32. Kohli, P.S., Arora, S.: Application of machine learning in disease prediction. In: 2018 4th International Conference on Computing Communication and Automation (ICCCA), pp. 1–4. IEEE, December 2018

33. Mir, A., Dhage, S.N.: Diabetes disease prediction using machine learning on big data of healthcare. In: 2018 Fourth International Conference on Computing Communication Control and Automation (ICCUBEA), pp. 1–6. IEEE, August 2018

34. Vigneswari, D., Kumar, N.K., Raj, V.G., Gugan, A., Vikash, S.R.: Machine learning tree classifiers in predicting diabetes mellitus. In: 2019 5th International Conference on Advanced Computing & Communication Systems (ICACCS), pp. 84–87. IEEE, March 2019

35. Perveen, S., Shahbaz, M., Keshavjee, K., Guergachi, A.: Metabolic syndrome and development of diabetes mellitus: predictive modeling based on machine learning techniques. IEEE Access 7, 1365–1375 (2018)

36. Komi, M., Li, J., Zhai, Y., Zhang, X.: Application of data mining methods in diabetes prediction. In: 2017 2nd International Conference on Image, Vision and Computing (ICIVC), pp. 1006–1010. IEEE, June 2017

37. Kumar, P.S., Pranavi, S.: Performance analysis of machine learning algorithms on diabetes dataset using big data analytics. In: 2017 International Conference on Infocom Technologies and Unmanned Systems (Trends and Future Directions) (ICTUS), pp. 508–513. IEEE, December 2017

38. Dwivedi, Ashok Kumar: Analysis of computational intelligence techniques for diabetes mellitus prediction. Neural Comput. Appl. 30(12), 3837–3845 (2017). https://doi.org/10.1007/s00521-017-2969-9

39. Birjais, Roshan., Mourya, Ashish Kumar., Chauhan, Ritu, Kaur, Harleen: Prediction and diagnosis of future diabetes risk: a machine learning approach. SN Appl. Sci. 1(9), 1–8 (2019). https://doi.org/10.1007/s42452-019-1117-9

40. Rawat, V., Suryakant, S.: A classification system for diabetic patients with machine learning techniques. Int. J. Math. Eng. Manage. Sci. 4, 729–744 (2019). https://doi.org/10.33889/ijmems.2019.4.3-057

41. Thammi Reddy, A., Nagendra, M.: Minimal rule-based classifiers using PCA on pima-Indians-diabetes-dataset. Int. J. Innov. Technol. Explor. Eng. 8(12), 4414–4420 (2019). https://doi.org/10.35940/ijitee.l2476.1081219

42. Pandeeswary, P., Janaki, M.: Performance analysis of big data classification techniques on diabetes prediction. Int. J. Innov. Technol. Explor. Eng. 8(10), 533–537 (2019). https://doi.org/10.35940/ijitee.j8840.0881019

43. Kaur, H., Kumari, V.: Predictive modelling and analytics for diabetes using a machine learning approach. Appl. Comput. Inf. (2019). https://doi.org/10.1016/j.aci.2018.12.004

44. Rajesh, K., Sangeetha, V.: Application of data mining methods and techniques for diabetes diagnosis. Int. J. Eng. Innov. Technol. (IJEIT) 2(3), 224–229 (2012)

45. Xie, Z., Nikolayeva, O., Luo, J., Li, D.: Peer reviewed: building risk prediction models for type 2 diabetes using machine learning techniques. Prev. Chronic Dis. 16 (2019)

46. Farran, B., AlWotayan, R., Alkandari, H., Al-Abdulrazzaq, D., Channanath, A., Thangavel, A.T.: Use of non-invasive parameters and machine-learning algorithms for predicting future risk of type 2 diabetes: a retrospective cohort study of health data from Kuwait. Front. Endocrinol. 10, 624 (2019)

47. Zou, Q., Qu, K., Luo, Y., Yin, D., Ju, Y., Tang, H.: Predicting diabetes mellitus with machine learning techniques. Front. Genet. 9, 515 (2018)

48. Talaei-Khoei, A., Wilson, J.M.: Identifying people at risk of developing type 2 diabetes: a comparison of predictive analytics techniques and predictor variables. Int. J. Med. Inf. 119, 22–38 (2018)

49. Cheruku, R., Edla, D.R., Kuppili, V.: Diabetes classification using radial basis function network by combining cluster validity index and BAT optimization with novel fitness function. Int. J. Comput. Intell. Syst. **10**(1), 247 (2017). https://doi.org/10.2991/ijcis.2017.10.1.17

50. Edla, D., Cheruku, R.: Diabetes-finder: a bat optimized classification system for type-2 diabetes. Procedia Comput. Sci. **115**, 235–242 (2017). https://doi.org/10.1016/j.procs.2017. 09.130

51. Muwal, S., Narender, K.: A hybrid nature-inspired classification technique for medical diagnosis. Int. J. Comput. Appl. **153**(4), 32–38 (2016). https://doi.org/10.5120/ijca20169 12003

52. Thirugnanam, M., Kumar, P., Srivatsan, S., Nerlesh, C.R.: Improving the prediction rate of diabetes diagnosis using fuzzy, neural network, case based (FNC) approach. Procedia Eng. **38**, 1709–1718 (2012). https://doi.org/10.1016/j.proeng.2012.06.208

53. Mansourypoor, F., Asadi, S.: Development of a reinforcement learning-based evolutionary fuzzy rule-based system for diabetes diagnosis. Comput. Biol. Med. **91**, 337–352 (2017)

54. Maniruzzaman, M., et al.: Comparative approaches for classification of diabetes mellitus data: machine learning paradigm. Comput. Methods Prog. Biomed. **152**, 23–34 (2017)

55. Santhanam, T., Padmavathi, M.S.: Application of K-means and genetic algorithms for dimension reduction by integrating SVM for diabetes diagnosis. Procedia Comput. Sci. **47**, 76–83 (2015)

56. Hegde, S., Hedge, R.: Symmetry based feature selection with multi layer perceptron for the prediction of chronic disease. Int. J. Recent Technol. Eng. **8**(2), 3316–3322 (2019). https:// doi.org/10.35940/ijrte.b2658.078219

57. Raghavendra, S., Santosh Kumar, J.: Performance evaluation of random forest with feature selection methods in prediction of diabetes. Int. J. Electr. Comput. Eng. **2088–8708**, 10 (2020)

58. Perveen, S., Shahbaz, M., Ansari, M.S., Keshavjee, K., Guergachi, A.: A hybrid approach for modeling type 2 diabetes mellitus progression. Front. Genet. **10**, 1076 (2020). https://doi.org/ 10.3389/fgene.2019.01076

59. Choubey, Dilip Kumar., Kumar, Prabhat., Tripathi, Sudhakar, Kumar, Santosh: Performance evaluation of classification methods with PCA and PSO for diabetes. Netw. Model. Anal. Health Inform. Bioinform. **9**(1), 1–30 (2019). https://doi.org/10.1007/s13721-019-0210-8

60. Beschi Raja, J., Anitha, R., Sujatha, R., Roopa, V., Sam Peter, S.: Diabetics prediction using gradient boosted classifier. Int. J. Eng. Adv. Technol. **9**(1), 3181–3183 (2019). https://doi.org/ 10.35940/ijeat.a9898.109119

61. Suvarnamukhi, B., Seshashayee, M.: Big data processing system for diabetes prediction using machine learning technique. Int. J. Innov. Technol. Explor. Eng. **8**(12), 4478–4483 (2019). https://doi.org/10.35940/ijitee.l3515.1081219

62. Perveen, S., Shahbaz, M., Keshavjee, K., Guergachi, A.: prognostic modeling and prevention of diabetes using machine learning technique. Sci. Rep. **9**(1), 1–9 (2019). https://doi.org/10. 1038/s41598-019-49563-6

63. Sohail, N., Jiadong, R., Muhammad, M., Tahir, S., Arshad, J., Verghese, A.: An accurate clinical implication assessment for diabetes mellitus prevalence based on a study from Nigeria. Processes **7**, 289 (2019). https://doi.org/10.3390/pr7050289

64. Nilashi, M., Ibrahim, O., Mardani, A., Ahani, A., Jusoh, A.: A soft computing approach for diabetes disease classification. Health Inf. J. **24** (2016). https://doi.org/10.1177/146045821 6675500

65. Fitriyani, N.L., Syafrudin, M., Alfian, G., Rhee, J.: Development of disease prediction model based on ensemble learning approach for diabetes and hypertension. IEEE Access **7**, 144777–144789 (2019). https://doi.org/10.1109/access.2019.2945129

66. Mirshahvalad, R., Zanjani, N.: Diabetes prediction using ensemble perceptron algorithm, pp. 190–194 (2017). https://doi.org/10.1109/cicn.2017.8319383

67. Li, L.: Diagnosis of diabetes using a weight-adjusted voting approach, pp. 320–324 (2014). https://doi.org/10.1109/bibe.2014.27
68. Wang, Q., Cao, W., Guo, J., Ren, J., Cheng, Y., and Davis, D.N.: DMP_MI: an effective diabetes mellitus classification algorithm on imbalanced data with missing values. IEEE Access, p. 1 (2019). https://doi.org/10.1109/access.2019.2929866
69. Stoean, R., Stoean, C., Preuss, M., El-Darzi, E., Dumitrescu, D.: Evolutionary support vector machines for diabetes mellitus diagnosis, pp. 182–187 (2006). https://doi.org/10.1109/is.2006.348414
70. Ravindranath, V., Ra, S., Ramasubbareddy, S., Remya, S., Nalluri, S.: Genetic algorithm based feature selection and MOE Fuzzy classification algorithm on Pima Indians Diabetes dataset, pp. 1–5 (2017). https://doi.org/10.1109/iccni.2017.8123815
71. Bhatia, K., Syal, R.: Predictive analysis using hybrid clustering in diabetes diagnosis, pp. 447–452 (2017). https://doi.org/10.1109/rdcape.2017.8358313

Learning from Students' Perception
on Professors Through Opinion Mining

Vladimir Vargas-Calderón[1]([✉]) [iD], Juan S. Flórez[1] [iD], Leonel F. Ardila[1] [iD],
Nicolas Parra-A.[1] [iD], Jorge E. Camargo[2] [iD], and Nelson Vargas[2]

[1] Laboratorios de Investigación en Inteligencia Artificial y Computación de Alto
Desempeño, Human Brain Technologies, Bogotá, Colombia
{vvargasc,jsflorezj,lfardilap,nparraa}@unal.edu.co
[2] System Engineering Department, Fundación Universitaria Konrad Lorenz, Carrera
9 Bis No. 62 - 43, Bogotá, Colombia
{jorgee.camargom,nelsona.vargass}@konradlorenz.edu.co
http://hubrain.co

Abstract. Students' perception of classes measured through their opinions on teaching surveys allows to identify deficiencies and problems, both in the environment and in the learning methodologies. The purpose of this paper is to study, through sentiment analysis using natural language processing (NLP) and machine learning (ML) techniques, those opinions in order to identify topics that are relevant for students, as well as predicting the associated sentiment via polarity analysis. As a result, it is implemented, trained and tested two algorithms to predict the associated sentiment as well as the relevant topics of such opinions. The combination of both approaches then becomes useful to identify specific properties of the students' opinions associated with each sentiment label (positive, negative or neutral opinions) and topic. Furthermore, we explore the possibility that students' perception surveys are carried out without closed questions, relying on the information that students can provide through open questions where they express their opinions about their classes.

Keywords: Students' satisfaction · Natural language processing ·
Polarity analysis

1 Introduction

Having a clear picture of students' perception on their classes, professors, and university facilities enables educational institutions to propose strategies to improve in many areas. It has been suggested by many studies that positive students' perception on the learning environment is correlated with higher academic achievement [3,5,14,16,35]. Therefore, not only can universities improve the quality of their professors, their class content as well as learning facilities, but they also can improve –as a consequence– their students' academic achievement, leading to an overall improvement of the education quality.

© Springer Nature Switzerland AG 2020
H. Florez and S. Misra (Eds.): ICAI 2020, CCIS 1277, pp. 330–344, 2020.
https://doi.org/10.1007/978-3-030-61702-8_23

The call for action is clear. However, in order to propose and implement effective improvement strategies, one needs to measure the students' perception. Typical ways of doing this is through evaluations carried out at the final stage of each academical period where students grade their professors in several aspects. These evaluations normally consist of an online questionnaire with closed questions, and some open questions where students give their opinions about the class and their professors. Closed questions questionnaire can be tedious for students, leading to low response rates [1,20,21,33,34,38,44]. Closed questions are helpful for the fast interpretation of results with statistical tools. These questions are designed to measure professors' performance on specific topics such as how engaging the class is, punctuality, among others. On the other hand, open questions provide students with a free space to express their opinions. Of course, gathering and interpreting data from open questions responses is a much more challenging task than making statistics from closed questions. Nonetheless, the amount of useful information found in students' opinions is a valuable source that is rarely exploited.

The latest advances in machine learning and natural language processing (NLP) techniques can be used to build tools that facilitate the analysis of large amounts of opinions generated by students. Particularly, sentiment analysis is suited to identify and quantify how positively or negatively students feel about their professors. These machine learning applications have only been recently explored [15]. For instance, Naïve Bayes has been used to classify students' opinions in social media [30]. Also, Latent Dirichlet Allocation (LDA) [7] has been used to model topics along with sentiment analysis to explore opinions from students [27]. Some studies using tools from machine learning have been conducted in the field of students' perception analysis. The majority of them have addressed the issue of performing sentiment analysis of the students' comments [19,36], and others have tried to identify topics in suggestions and opinions left by students [18], thus, we develop a joint approach were state of the art tools from NLP are used to perform both sentiment analysis and identify topics of interest in the students' comments.

Nonetheless, we must stress that researchers have for long worked on similar problems of assessing customer satisfaction from written opinions including public election forecasting [13,37,40], sales [26] and trading prediction [45], marketing price prediction [4], among others. The common pipeline for performing opinion mining consists of the following general steps [23,39]: i) retrieval of opinions from public databases, ii) cleaning of the opinions (including discarding some opinions due to quality issues, stemming, tokenisation, among others), iii) prediction of a quantity of interest such as polarity, sentiment strength, among others.

In this paper, we combine state-of-the-art methods in an NLP-based pipeline for classifying the sentiment of students' opinions. We then use these results to predict the ratings given to the professors by the students by means of supervised learning algorithms. Furthermore, we perform LDA to discover latent topics that are central in students' opinions. With the power of question answering systems [28], we envision students' perceptions surveys having only open questions that are fast to answer, reaching high levels of response rates, and also extracting the most relevant information, which comes from the students' opinions. These opinions are then mined with methods like the one we propose to analyse how students truly feel about their professors and classes.

The structure of this paper is as follows. In section methods and materials a brief description of the data and its prepossessing is presented. Next, in the results the analysis of model performance as well as the statistical analysis of the obtained results is scrutinised. Recommendations for future perspectives in the research of the subject as well as an outlined of the conclusions are listed in the final part of the manuscript.

2   Methods and Materials

2.1   Data

The data used for our study was taken from an anonymised data set from the Konrad Lorenz University in Bogotá, Colombia, which contained around 5,700 professor performance evaluations as perceived by their students. Evaluations from the 2018–2020 period were contained in the data set, accounting for 937 courses (773 undergraduate and 164 graduate courses). The information from the evaluations was separated in two tables. The data included in the first table was:

- Subject code: an code that uniquely identifies each subject by year.
- Comment: a comment from a student to the professor of the corresponding subject.

The data in the second table was:

- Subject code: a code that uniquely identifies each subject by year.
- Number of students: the number of students in the corresponding subject.
- Professor's pedagogical and disciplinary aspects: a score from 1 to 5. This is an average over all students' evaluations.
- Professor's evaluation: a score from 1 to 5 referring to the evaluations carried out by the professor. This is an average over all students' evaluations.
- Professor's interpersonal relations: a score from 1 to 5. This is an average over all students' evaluations.
- Education level: a binary label taking the values "undergraduate" and "posgraduate" for the corresponding subject.

2.2   Polarity Prediction and Topic Modelling

The methodology for modelling topics in our corpus and for predicting polarity is shown in Fig. 1. Not every comment made by students was taken into account. We filtered out those comments with less than 5 words or 10 characters, as they do not contain a lot of information. We ended up with around 4,900 comments that we used for training, validating and testing the methodology hereafter presented. These comments made by undergraduate and graduate students from the years 2018, 2019 and 2020 were annotated by humans with one of three polarity classes: positive, neutral and negative. An example of a positive comment is: "Thanks for the rigorousness in your subject and for your pedagogy to transmit to us your acquired knowledge". An example of a negative comment is: "I suggest the professor to be a bit more organised with respect to time and e-mail reading".

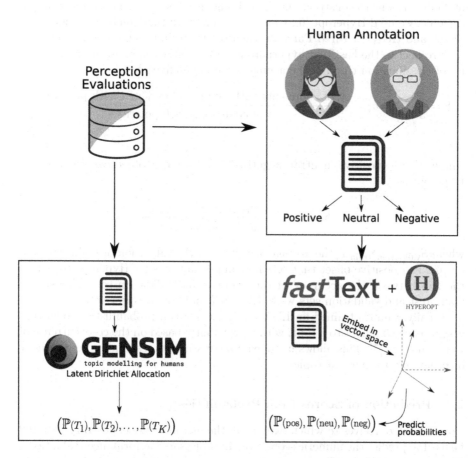

Fig. 1. Flow diagram for polarity prediction and topic modelling. First, the raw comments from students are annotated by humans. Then, FastText vectors are obtained for each of them, with a corresponding probability of belonging to one of three polarity classes: positive, negative or neutral. This model's hyperparameters are optimised with Hyperopt. Also, an LDA model from Gensim [31] is trained to classify texts into latent topics.

Each comment from a student passes through a pre-processing stage where stopwords are removed, all characters are lower-cased, punctuation symbols are removed, and words are stemmed. Then, FastText is used to build a polarity classification model. FastText is a natural language processing method to embed text in low-dimensional vector spaces based on the co-occurrence of words within a context [8,22]. The embedding procedure allows FastText to extract latent semantic features encoded into the embedding vector space's dimensions, similar to its predecessor Word2Vec [24]. The polarity classification model is intended to distinguish which regions of the low-dimensional space correspond to one of the three polarities. Because of the low quantity of comments, we selected a total of 20 dimensions to construct the embedding vector space. To tune its hyperparameters we used Hyperopt [6], which is a framework that combines randomised search and tree-structured Parzen estimators to optimise an objective function with respect to the FastText hyperparameters. In our case, we measure the quality of classification through the average accuracy defined by

$$S = \frac{1}{3} \sum_{i \in P} a_i, \quad a_i = \frac{\# \text{ of comments with polarity } i \text{ predicted with polarity } i}{\# \text{ of comments with polarity } i},$$

(1)

where $P = \{\text{positive, neutral, negative}\}$. We set the objective function for Hyperopt as

$$- S_{\text{validation}} + \frac{|S_{\text{training}} - S_{\text{validation}}|}{1 - S_{\text{training}} + \epsilon},$$

(2)

where $S_{\text{validation/train}}$ is the average accuracy for the validation or train sets, and $\epsilon = 0.2$ is a positive offset that sets how important it is for Hyperopt to reduce the gap between the accuracy of the training and validation sets. The size of train, test and validation sets were 64%, 20% and 16%, respectively.

Finally, we also trained an LDA model, which is a probabilistic model that assigns each comment to a topic with a probability based on the co-occurrence of words in texts [7]. This allows us to examine if students respond more positively or negatively to different topics.

2.3   Prediction of Scores from Probabilities

Now, we ask ourselves to which extent can the methodology exposed in Sect. 2.2 be used to predict the numeric score given in professors' performance evaluations. We create a prediction framework where we try to predict numerical scores only from information deduced from the students' comments. This procedure has the potential to give us insights on what is the participation rate of students in open-ended questions along with its relation to the quantitative score given to the course. The prediction is done with XGBoost [10], which is a widely successful gradient boosting algorithm for regression and classification. We are not interested in precisely predicting the score. Instead, we want to distinguish if students have very high, high or a moderate quality perception of their professor. Therefore, we split the evaluation scores in three groups: very high scores (from

4.5 to 5.0), high scores (from 4.0 to 4.5) and moderate scores (less than 4.0). The classification model takes as an input a FastText vector corresponding to the comments of a class, as well as other features such as the LDA probabilities that those comments belong to one of the K latent topics. Therefore, we use XGBoost to predict, for each class, the average score that students give to their professor based solely on the comments.

For each course we have the average score given by students to that course and the comments registered by students to an open-ended question done at the end of the semester. There may be some students that score the class numerically but do not give any written feedback and vice-versa. This motivates the use of state of the art NLP tools to find out to what extent the average numerical score of a course can be recovered from the comments of the students who took the course. Since there are more courses with high scores than courses with moderate scores we perform a data balancing in order to have the same amount of courses with average grades above and below 4.4, and that balanced data is used to optimise the hyperparameters of the classifier, which in this case is the gradient boosting classifier (XGBoost). After the best hyperparameters were found, the classifier was trained using the complete unbalanced original data.

3   Results

With the pre-processed data, we trained the FastText model and used Hyperopt to find the best hyperparameters. To measure the precision of this model (see Eq. (1)), we use the confusion matrix, which is an error matrix that contains in the diagonal the number of correct predictions for each category, whereas the number of wrong predictions for each category are in the elements outside of the diagonal. Confusion matrices for the train and test sets are shown in Fig. 2. We observed a high number of correct predictions for the categories positive and negative, both in the train and test sets, but a low number of correct predictions in the neutral category, especially in the test set. This can be due to the small number of neutral comments in the data, or in the difficulty of defining a neutral comment in the annotation process. On the contrary, this effect does not happen for positive and negative comments because the amount of these comments is much higher than the neutral comments. The value of accuracy in the train and test sets is 0.821 and 0.749, respectively, which is stable through the last steps of optimisation, giving evidence that no over-fitting occurs. These results improve over similar pipelines such as the one presented in Ref. [9], where high-quality Spanish tweets were annotated by Spanish Society for Natural Language Processing (SEPLN in Spanish). Studies using that dataset (which is similar in data imbalance to ours) also found difficulty in correctly predicting the neutral class [11,17], probably because of data imbalance, as it was identified in a previous study [2], or because words related to neutral comments might contain sentiment, as indicated in Ref. [12].

Since the FastText model produces the probabilities that a comment is classified as positive, negative or neutral, we can look at the capability of the prediction when the assigned probability is low or high. We analyse this situation in

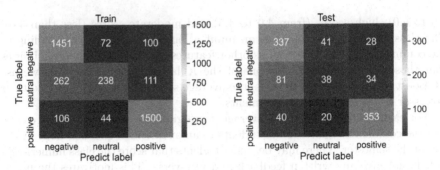

Fig. 2. Confusion matrices for train and test sets for the FastText model that predicts comment polarity.

Fig. 3. For a given threshold of probability that the model classifies a comment in a category, the "percentage above threshold" is the percentage of comments whose probability is greater than the threshold, while the "percentage correct" is the fraction of comments correctly assigned to a class. We observe, as expected, that the higher the threshold the lower the percentage of comments that have a probability assignation above that threshold. Also, as the assigned probability threshold increases, more comments are correctly classified. These observations are helpful if one wants to make automation decisions about classifying polarity. For instance, an automation rule could be: predict a polarity for a text, if the polarity exceeds a given threshold, take the prediction as the truth, else give the text to a human so that the human classifies it.

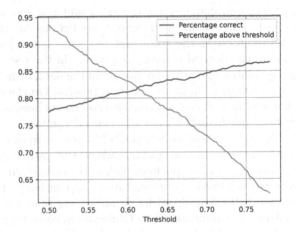

Fig. 3. Percentage of correct comments classified with probability greater than a threshold, and percentage of comments with assigned probability greater than a threshold.

For real applications of the model, it is necessary to know the principal topics in the comments with the aim of decision-making within the institutions. We did this with LDA. This model requires a specific number of topics. We found that a number of topics $K = 5$ was experimentally good because it allowed us to have good interpretability. Since LDA assigns each comment the probability of belonging to one of the K topics, those comments with high topic probabilities are representative of those latent topics. Reading the representative comments and looking at the most used words in each latent topic, we were able to assign a topic label to each latent topic. The topics are shown in Table 1.

Table 1. Topics found with LDA. For each topic we present a relevant negative comment.

#	Topic	Topic Interpretation	Representative comment
0	Excellent methodology, practice, dynamic class, school-like, more feedback	General recommendations about methodology and other aspects of the course	"I recommend that the class is taught in the computer room, because the use of EXCEL as a tool was useful to understand the topic when using the formulas and table tools, which could not be done in a classroom without computers."
1	Good professor, dedication, thank you, evaluation criteria, listen to students	Projects, evaluations and grading schemes	"I think that the professor should reestablish her evaluation criteria since she establishes them but she does not accept them when evaluating and this is not fair, since the work is done as she demands, but nothing seems enough for her and she does not value the effort."
2	Best professor, virtual, virtual clasroom, support, feedback	Aspects of the class methodology	"Pedagogical strategies are good. The time could be distributed to use all the time of the session since the topics are very extensive. In the virtual sessions, it was necessary to use more resources to help students understand, perhaps the board and drawings."
3	Dynamic classes, virtual class, entertaining, class preparation, slow	Management of time in the projects and class	"The teacher is very well prepared, however, he must control the time available for each activity, since, I give more time to the daily activities but I do not give enough time to the topics and how to develop them in each project."
4	Excellent professor, human being, professional, patience, attention	Professor's attitude and respect towards the class and the students	"The teacher explains the topics of the class clearly, but he lacks courtesy, charisma and decency when addressing his students. From a simple greeting, to respectfully answering a question in the middle of the class."

Figure 4 shows a box plot of the score that students gave to professors, grouped by topic and polarity. We observe that there is a positive correlation between positive/negative polarity (as predicted by the FastText model) and the score given by students. Notice also, that comments with negative polarity have a wider score distribution compared to positive and neutral comments for which the score distributions are narrow and have shorter tails. The mean value in positive and negative comments is almost the same throughout all topics, but for neutral comments, we observed that the mean value is lower in the topic 1. This is because FastText wrongly predicts negative comments as neutral for that topic. This box plot allows us to explore which topics are perceived as better or worst by students when evaluating their professors. In other words, this analysis allows us to know which aspects of professors' teaching generate more discomfort in the students.

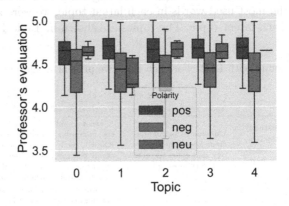

Fig. 4. Box plot of the score given by students to professors, grouped by topic and assigned polarity.

One of the most important aspects of surveys is their response rate (RR). We calculated the RR for each course of the university. The value of RR can expose what topic is more relevant for the students positively or negatively. In general the RR in this data is low, but we can do some analysis. For instance, for the topics in Table 1, the highest RR corresponds to topic 0 and the lowest RR to topic 3. This means that the students give recommendations for the methodology of the class, but are more indifferent to the professors' time management. In general, the RR in positive comments is greater than the RR in negative comments, except for topics 1 and 3, where the students tend to have higher RR when expressing their opinions about professors' time management and the way professors evaluate the subjects. On the other hand, the RR is very low in neutral comments for the topics 0 and 1, but these can be biased because of the low quantity of neutral comments in our data set. The results shown above lead us to think that for low RR, we will have low accuracy in polarity prediction. For this reason, it is necessary to encourage the completion of surveys, which leads to the generation of better models and better analysis of the students' comments.

Finally, we train an XGBoost model to predict the professors' evaluation score intervals (very high, high, and moderate). The confusion matrix for the model is shown in Fig. 6. We observed that our model is efficient to predict scores greater than 4.5 (very high scores), but the model fails in moderate scores (less than 4.0). This happens because the database is imbalanced, as it does not have

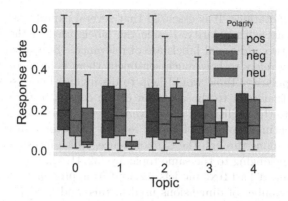

Fig. 5. Box plot of the response rate grouped by topic and polarity.

enough comments with moderate scores. The average accuracies of the model, as defined in Eq. (1), are 0.52 and 0.53 in train and test sets, respectively. Therefore, we conclude that our model does not have a good accuracy to eliminate the closed questions in the professors' evaluation surveys. This is most likely due to the small number of comments in our database. We expect that for a larger comments database, we can build a better model, because it is known that FastText based models (including Word2Vec) have a performance relation with the corpus and vocabulary size [25,29].

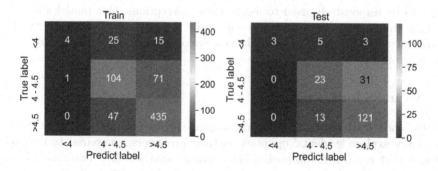

Fig. 6. Confusion matrices in train and test sets for the XGBoost score classifier.

4   Limitations and Perspectives

There is room for improvement in some of our methodological steps. We comment below some of the issues that could be addressed in the future in order to improve the accuracies in polarity prediction, as well as in score prediction:

1. Improve annotations: It is essential that several experts redundantly label the comments with polarity. Beside the labels used in the present work, we believe two additional labels are of relevance: "Subjectivity" and topic. Subjectivity refers to how much sentiment there is on a comment, regardless of its polarity. Topic would help to distinguish between scenarios, e.g. comments that refer to the professor of the course, to the contents of the course, or to the facilities of the university.
2. Find the optimal number of topics for the LDA topic discovering phase. This can be done through the C_V coherence, which measures how coherent comments belonging to the same topic are [32, 41, 42].
3. Use pre-trained FastText models reduced to approximately 20 dimensions (the same number of dimensions used in this study), as this may improve the quality of our predictions.

Furthermore, we shall make explicit some ethical concerns. From an educational perspective, the correct assessment of students' perceptions about their professors and their education is of paramount importance. This assessment allows to take decisions to improve the educational environment, promoting healthier and more productive conditions for students to thrive. However, not only does this assessment affect the lives and projects of the students, but also it affects the professors and universities. Particularly, professors' motivation for delivering high-quality classes can be affected by how their students perceive them. At an institutional level, very important decisions such as removing a professor from a subject, or even firing a professor can be taken using as input the assessment of students' perceptions. Therefore, automated text analysis tools have to be responsively used to assess these perceptions. Our model allows us to take this issue into account, since not only a prediction of the polarity of a comment is given, but also a confidence level over that prediction is also given, as shown in Fig. 3.

5 Conclusions

In this work, we present a new natural language processing methodology to automatically explore students' opinions on their professors, compared to methodologies that use other approaches of sentiment analyses [27]. For this, we use state-of-the-art techniques such as FastText to build classifiers that are able to identify polarity in students' opinions. Furthermore, we discover latent topics in the opinions corpus through Latent Dirichlet Allocation. These two approaches are then combined to predict the score that students give to their professors, so that we can identify professors with non-excellent performance only using the information from students' opinions. We argue that such tools can reduce human burden in this analysis, and can also simultaneously take full advantage of the information found in those text opinions. Nonetheless, the experiments so far exposed in our paper indicate that the amount of information or quality of our annotations hampers the possibility of eliminating closed questions from perception surveys to assess the professors' quality.

We envision students' perception questionnaires based on asking the students' for improvement recommendations, and on opinions about negative and positive aspects of the professor and of the class. This questionnaires will probably be more friendly with students, reaching higher response rates, leaving the tedious part of extracting information to the combined work of humans and NLP algorithms, where the heavy-lifting is done by NLP, and only high-level analysis is left for the human. We hope in the future to use larger opinion databases which allow us to find and train a better model, since a larger database enables us to confidently circumvent the imbalance problem through sampling techniques such as the one presented in Ref. [43].

Acknowledgements. V.V., J.F., L.A. and N.P. would like to thank Carlos Viviescas for his useful insights at the beginning of this study.

References

1. Adams, L.L.M., Gale, D.: Solving the quandary between questionnaire length and response rate in educational research. Res. High. Educ. **17**(3), 231–240 (1982)
2. Ah-Pine, J., Soriano-Morales, E.P.: A study of synthetic oversampling for Twitter imbalanced sentiment analysis. In: Workshop on Interactions between Data Mining and Natural Language Processing (DMNLP 2016). Riva del Garda, Italy, September 2016. https://hal.archives-ouvertes.fr/hal-01504684
3. Anbari, Z., Jamilian, H., Rafiee, M., Qomi, M., Moslemi, Z.A.: The relationship between students' satisfaction with major, mental health and academic achievement in arak university of medical sciences. Iranian J. Med. Educ. **13**(6), 489–497 (2013)
4. Archak, N., Ghose, A., Ipeirotis, P.G.: Show me the money! deriving the pricing power of product features by mining consumer reviews. In: Proceedings of the 13th ACM SIGKDD International Conference on Knowledge Discovery and Data Mining, pp. 56–65 (2007)
5. Baek, S.G., Choi, H.J.: The relationship between students ' perceptions of classroom environment and their academic achievement in Korea. Asia Pacific Educ. Rev. **3**(1), 125–135 (2002)
6. Bergstra, J., Yamins, D., Cox, D.: Making a science of model search: hyperparameter optimization in hundreds of dimensions for vision architectures. In: Dasgupta, S., McAllester, D. (eds.) Proceedings of the 30th International Conference on Machine Learning. Proceedings of Machine Learning Research, vol. 28. PMLR, Atlanta, Georgia, USA, pp. 115–123, June 17–19 2013. http://proceedings.mlr.press/v28/bergstra13.html
7. Blei, D.M., Ng, A.Y., Jordan, M.I.: Latent Dirichlet allocation. J. Mach. Learn. Res. **3**, 993–1022 (2003)
8. Bojanowski, P., Grave, E., Joulin, A., Mikolov, T.: Enriching word vectors with subword information. Trans. Assoc. Comput. Linguist. **5**, 135–146 (2016)
9. Camargo, J.E., Vargas-Calderon, V., Vargas, N., Calderón-Benavides, L.: Sentiment polarity classification of tweets using a extended dictionary. Inteligencia Artificial **21**(62), 1–12 (Sep 2018).https://doi.org/10.4114/intartif.vol21iss62pp1-12, https://journal.iberamia.org/index.php/intartif/article/view/116

10. Chen, T., Guestrin, C.: Xgboost. In: Proceedings of the 22nd ACM SIGKDD International Conference on Knowledge Discovery and Data Mining, August 2016. https://doi.org/10.1145/2939672.2939785, http://dx.doi.org/10.1145/2939672.2939785

11. Chiruzzo, L., Rosá, A.: Retuytinco at TASS 2018: Sentiment analysis in Spanish variants using neural networks and SVM. In: TASS@ SEPLN, pp. 57–63 (2018)

12. Colhon, M., Vlăduţescu, Ş., Negrea, X.: How objective a neutral word is? a neutrosophic approach for the objectivity degrees of neutral words. Symmetry **9**(11), 280 (2017)

13. Correa, J.C., Camargo, J.E.: Ideological consumerism in Colombian elections,2015: links between political ideology, twitter activity, and electoral results. Cyberpsychol. Behav. Soc. Network. **20**(1),37–43 (2017). https://doi.org/10.1089/cyber.2016.0402,https://doi.org/10.1089/cyber.2016.0402, pMID: 28080152

14. Diseth, Ä.: Students' evaluation of teaching, approaches to learning, and academic achievement, Scand. J. Educ. Res. **51**(2), 185–204 (2007)

15. Dobre, I., et al.: Students' satisfaction analysis related to an e-assessment system that uses natural language processing. In: Conference proceedings of eLearning and Software for Education (eLSE), pp. 21–28. No. 03. "Carol I" National Defence University Publishing House (2015)

16. El-Hilali, N., Al-Jaber, S., Hussein, L.: Students' satisfaction and achievement and absorption capacity in higher education. Procedia Soc. Behav. Sci. **177**, 420 – 427 (2015). first Global Conference on Contemporary Issues in Education (GLOBE-EDU 2014) 12-14 July2014, Las Vegas, USA

17. González, J.A., Hurtado, L.F., Pla, F.: Elirf-upv en TASS 2018: Análisis de sentimientos en twitter basado en aprendizaje profundo. In: Proceedings of TASS, vol. 2172, pp. 37–44 (2018)

18. Gottipati, S., Shankararaman, V., Lin, J.R.: Text analytics approach to extract-course improvement suggestions from students' feedback **13**(2), 1793–7078 (2018). https://doi.org/10.1186/s41039-018-0073-0, https://doi.org/10.1186/s41039-018-0073-0

19. Hew, K.F., Hu, X., Qiao, C., Tang, Y.: What predicts student satisfaction with MOOCS: a gradient boosting trees supervised machine learning and sentiment analysis approach. Comput. Educ. **145**, 103724 (2020)

20. Iglesias, C., Torgerson, D.: Does length of questionnaire matter? a randomised trial of response rates to a mailed questionnaire. J. Health Serv. Res. Pol. **5**(4), 219–221 (2000)

21. Jepson, C., Asch, D.A., Hershey, J.C., Ubel, P.A.: In a mailed physician survey, questionnaire length had a threshold effect on response rate. J. Clin. Epidemiol. **58**(1), 103–105 (2005)

22. Joulin, A., Grave, E., Bojanowski, P., Mikolov, T.: Bag of tricks for efficient text classification (2016)

23. Kumar, K.L.S., Desai, J., Majumdar, J.: Opinion mining and sentiment analysis on online customer review. In: 2016 IEEE International Conference on Computational Intelligence and Computing Research (ICCIC), pp. 1–4 (2016)

24. Le, Q., Mikolov, T.: Distributed representations of sentences and documents. In: International Conference on Machine Learning, pp. 1188–1196 (2014)

25. Li, B., Drozd, A., Guo, Y., Liu, T., Matsuoka, S., Du, X.: Scaling word2vec on big corpus. Data Sci. Eng. **4**(2), 157–175 (2019). https://doi.org/10.1007/s41019-019-0096-6,https://doi.org/10.1007/s41019-019-0096-6

26. Liu, Y., Huang, X., An, A., Yu, X.: ARSA: a sentiment-aware model for predicting sales performance using blogs. In: Proceedings of the 30th Annual International ACM SIGIR Conference on Research and Development in Information Retrieval, pp. 607–614 (2007)
27. Nelson, S.C., Baktashmotlagh, M., Boles, W.: Visualising student satisfaction. In: Tse, N., Huda, N., Town, G., Inglis, D. (eds.) Proceedings of the 28th Annual Conference of the Australasian Association for Engineering Education (AAEE 2017), pp. 722–730. School of Engineering, Macquarie University, Australia (2017)
28. Ong, C.S., Day, M.Y., Hsu, W.L.: The measurement of user satisfaction with question answering systems. Inf. Manag. **46**(7), 397–403 (2009)
29. Patel, K., Bhattacharyya, P.: Towards lower bounds on number of dimensions for word embeddings. In: Proceedings of the Eighth International Joint Conference on Natural Language Processing (Volume 2: Short Papers), pp. 31–36. Asian Federation of Natural Language Processing, Taipei, Taiwan, November 2017. https://www.aclweb.org/anthology/I17-2006
30. Permana, F.C., Rosmansyah, Y., Abdullah, A.S.: Naive Bayes as opinion classifier to evaluate students satisfaction based on student sentiment in Twitter social media. J. Phys: Conf. Ser. **893**, 012051 (2017)
31. Řehůřek, R., Sojka, P.: Software framework for topic modelling with large corpora. In: Proceedings of the LREC 2010 Workshop on New Challenges for NLP Frameworks, pp. 45–50. ELRA, Valletta, Malta, May 2010. http://is.muni.cz/publication/884893/en
32. Röder, M., Both, A., Hinneburg, A.: Exploring the space of topic coherence measures. In: Proceedings of the Eighth ACM International Conference on Web Search and Data Mining, pp. 399–408 (2015)
33. Rolstad, S., Adler, J., Rydén, A.: Response burden and questionnaire length: is shorter better? a review and meta-analysis. Value Health **14**(8), 1101–1108 (2011)
34. Sahlqvist, S., et al.: Effect of questionnaire length, personalisation and reminder type on response rate to a complex postal survey: randomised controlled trial. BMC Medical Res. Methodol. **11**(1), 62 (2011)
35. Samdal, O., Wold, B., Bronis, M.: Relationship between students' perceptions of school environment, their satisfaction with school and perceived academic achievement: An international study. Sch. Effect. Sch. Improv. **10**(3), 296–320 (1999)
36. Skrbinjek, V., Dermol, V.: Predicting students' satisfaction using a decision tree. Tert. Educ. Manag. **25**(2), 101–113 (2019)
37. Smith, N.A.: From tweets to polls: linking text sentiment to public opinion time series. In: Proceedings of the International AAAI Conference on Weblogs and Social Media (2010)
38. Smith, R., Olah, D., Hansen, B., Cumbo, D.: The effect of questionnaire length on participant response rate: a case study in the us cabinet industry. Forest Prod. J. **53**(11/12), 33 (2003)
39. Sun, S., Luo, C., Chen, J.: A review of natural language processing techniquesfor opinion mining systems. Inf. Fus. **36**, 10 – 25(2017). https://doi.org/10.1016/j.inffus.2016.10.004, http://www.sciencedirect.com/science/article/pii/S1566253516301117
40. Tumasjan, A., Sprenger, T.O., Sandner, P.G., Welpe, I.M.: Predicting elections with Twitter: what 140 characters reveal about political sentiment. In: Fourth International AAAI Conference on Weblogs and Social Media. Citeseer (2010)

41. Huertas-Herrera, B., Góez Sánchez, D., ReyesVera, E.: Spectral power map generation based on spectrum scanning in the ism band for interference effects. In: Narváez, F.R., Vallejo, D.F., Morillo, P.A., Proaño, J.R. (eds.) SmartTech-IC 2019. CCIS, vol. 1154, pp. 3–15. Springer, Cham (2020). https://doi.org/10.1007/978-3-030-46785-2_1
42. Vargas-Calderón, V., Parra-A., N., Camargo, J.E., Vinck-Posada, H.: Event detection in Colombian security Twitter news using fine-grained latent topic analysis (2019)
43. Wang, S., Li, D., Zhao, L., Zhang, J.: Sample cutting method for imbalanced text sentiment classification based on BRC. Knowl.-Based Syst. **37**, 451–461 (2013).https://doi.org/10.1016/j.knosys.2012.09.003, http://www.sciencedirect.com/science/article/pii/S0950705112002602
44. Wright, K.B.: Researching internet-based populations: advantages and disadvantages of online survey research, online questionnaire authoring software packages, and web survey services. J. Comput.-Mediated Commun. **10**(3) (2017). jCMC1034
45. Zhang, W., Skiena, S., et al.: Trading strategies to exploit blog and news sentiment. In: ICWSM (2010)

Health Care Information Systems

A Framework for BYOD Continuous Authentication: Case Study with Soft-Keyboard Metrics for Healthcare Environment

Luis de-Marcos$^{(\boxtimes)}$ [ID], Carlos Cilleruelo, Javier Junquera-Sánchez, and José-Javier Martínez-Herráiz

Departamento de Ciencias de la Computación, Universidad de Alcalá. Edificio Politécnico.
Campus Universitario, Ctra. Madrid-Barcelona km, 33, 600 Alcalá de Henares. Madrid, Spain
`{luis.demarcos,carlos.cilleruelo,javier.junquera,`
`josej.martinez}@uah.es`

Abstract. Mobile authentication is a hot topic because organizations can adopt BYOD (bring your own device) policies that allow to use personal devices, rather than require the use of officially provided devices. However, this brings additional access control issues like intentional or unintentional unauthorized uses of devices (e.g., stealing a mobile phone) that may eventually result in access to sensitive information. Continuous authentication (CA) aims to mitigate and provide a solution to access control by monitoring user activity. CA can then be particularly useful in mobile BYOD environments. However, each CA solution has to be implemented and integrated ad-hoc and tailored for each particular information system that wants to use it. This paper presents a modular, extensible framework for CA that enables to integrate new agents and models to implement access control with mobile devices. The framework includes three main types of components: Endpoint Detection and Response (EDR) Agents that run on the mobile device to gather user metrics and evaluate user's trust, APIs that collect information and return trustworthiness levels of users, and AI models that predict the trust of users. The framework also integrates authorized third parties that can ask for trust levels of individual users and are responsible for implementing the resulting security measures like raising alerts. The architecture is demonstrated in a healthcare environment which is part of the ProTego project. The proof-of-concept implements a mobile EDR agent and AI model based on the soft-keyboard input data collected on the mobile phone.

Keywords: Continuous authentication · Access control · Bring your own device (BYOD) · Mobile security

1 Introduction

Bring your own device (BYOD) advocates for employees bringing their own devices to work and using them to access corporate information systems, instead of using devices provided by their organization. Although BYOD offers important advantages to both

© Springer Nature Switzerland AG 2020
H. Florez and S. Misra (Eds.): ICAI 2020, CCIS 1277, pp. 347–358, 2020.
https://doi.org/10.1007/978-3-030-61702-8_24

employers and employees, there also significant concerns about security and privacy [1]. Besides careful risk assessment and mitigation, contingency measures include prevention and reaction by employers and security providers [2]. On the side of the employee, it is also important to increase awareness for prevention. Prevention measures consider additional access control and authorization. Since a mobile device is something easy to take and use by unauthorized third parties, continuous authentication (CA) provides a means to monitor user activity and determine whether she is the legitimate user of the device. CA systems are those that do not require an active participation of the user to determine her identity.

CA is particularly relevant in healthcare because health-can providers can deploy BYOD policies for their employees. Also, they can enable patients to access their medical information and records or to provide data to feed these medical records through mobile apps or IoT devices, like fit bands. The ProTego project is an EU funded project that aims to provide a toolkit for health care organizations to assess better and reduce cybersecurity risks related to remote devices access to healthcare data. CA for BYOD is one of these tools.

Current literature on CA provides a variety of methods that can be applied to BYOD mobile healthcare environments. However, currently, there are no architectures or frameworks that assist when CA has to be integrated into a wider context. This is particularly important in healthcare where CA has to be integrated into heterogeneous ecosystems that include a variety of hardware and software by multiple providers, as well as data coming from multiple sources including devices and sensors [3].

This paper contributes to knowledge by providing and showcasing a CA framework for the ProTego healthcare scenario. Further, a flexible framework should also consider multiple CA methods. Since it needs to combine EDR mobile agents, APIs, authorization servers, and third parties, a scalable framework is of interest for researchers and practitioners in a variety of contexts in which they need to design and implement modular architectures that support CA. The rest of the paper is structured as follows. Section 2 summarizes the state of the art of CA. Section 3 presents the modular framework for CA and describes its components and operation. Section 4 describes a CA architecture for the ProTego project that showcases the framework in a specific healthcare BYOD setting. Finally, Sect. 5 summarizes conclusions and future work.

2 State of the Art

Continuous authentication is a procedure of access control that ensures that the identity of the user does not change during her operation of the system. The accuracy of the CA system is usually the indicator of its capabilities. There several approaches that can be based on biometrics or behavioral patterns of the user (e.g., typing). For biometric CA systems, data used ranges from the face, to finger or even electrocardiogram data [4]. For behavioral patterns, CA systems usually define metrics based on the interaction of the user with the system. Data can then be processed using different methods and algorithms that build a prediction function that can be used to determine the probability of the user being legitimate based on future interaction. Approaches can usually be adapted between different systems even if the interaction method varies substantially. For instance, mouse pointer dynamics are similar to touchpad interaction in a mobile phone even though each of them has its particularities [5].

Keystroke and typing patterns was one of the first methods studied [6] given the ubiquity of keyboards or soft-keyboard on each interaction method that requires text input. The different metrics and mechanics of typing sessions studied include typing speed, time between keystrokes or time pressing each key [7]. For mobile devices, touchscreen dynamics drive the most significant amount of research on behavioral biometrics for CA [8] since a touchscreen is also present on most mobile devices including all mobile phones. Interactions with touchscreens also offer a lot of possibilities for exploration since users tend to interact more naturally than with a keyboard in which interaction is limited to press keys. For instance, how the user scrolls through the text provides a significant amount of data [9] that can be used to compute behavioral biometrics. Also, existing knowledge about keystroke dynamics can be combined and adapted to the touchscreen to determine how the user types in a soft-keyboard [10]. Finally, mobile devices also include a variety of sensors (e.g. accelerometer, gyroscope) that provide additional input about the user interaction. Hand Movement, Orientation, and Grasp (HMOG) [11] define a set of behavioral metrics for CA that combines traditional keystroke mechanics with sensor input. HMOG metrics can even provide additional information about the situation in which the user is interacting with a smartphone, e.g., walking or moving, sitting, or lying down. Data to feed these CA systems may come from a variety of sensors like light [12] or position sensors [13], other input and interaction methods with the smartphone like the microphone [14], or other information that can be gathered from the smartphone, like applications or processes running or geolocation.

3   Modular Framework for Continuous Authentication

The framework (Fig. 1) includes three types of components: Clients (AI Clients & Trust Clients), Authorization Server (OAuth), and an API (ProTego JBCA). The framework can also integrate third-party systems getting trust levels, and third party systems with CA capabilities feeding the API. AI Clients have CA capabilities to get user metrics and evaluate the trustworthiness of users. User metrics are specific information or input from the user in the device that can be used to create AI models that predict the trustworthiness of a user. The authorization server secures access to the API. We suggest using OAuth2 standard with PKCE.

To create an AI model, it is necessary to provide the training data and evaluation data. Additionally, it is necessary to define the expiration time of the model. The quality of each model will be based on the values of machine learning metrics. Precision should be larger than 0.5 and recall should be close to 1. To produce AI models, it is necessary to collect and train machine learning algorithms for each particular input metric (e.g., soft keyboard). Trained models can then be incorporated into the framework to provide trust levels through the evaluation of users continuously. Trust values contain a timestamp, a time of validity, the trust value (a number between 0 and 1) and an ID of the AI model. Several AI models can be used to calculate the final trust value of a user using different methods like majority voting or a weighted sum. AI clients continuously retrieve data that send to the API to produce the AI models. When models are produced and

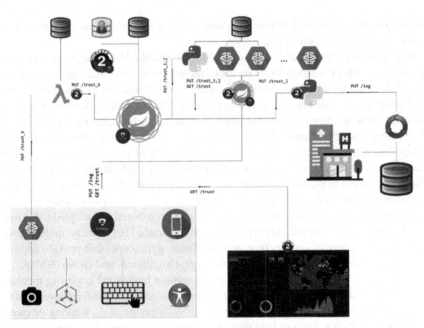

Fig. 1. ProTego continuous authentication framework (Source: created by the authors)

running, AI clients also retrieve new data and periodically evaluate them using the AI model. AI clients may have the capability to generate their own AI models if they have the computational capacity. However, in the first stage of the implementation of the framework, AI models are trained externally in specific servers with data gathered from EDR clients. Clients must be registered and authorized.

The API (ProTego JBCA) can be created in two different ways. In the first stage, the API and the authorization server share a common database of users and clients. When users are created, the relationship between their identity and their data is stored in the same database. The second approach is ad-hoc user creation so that each time that a token correctly generated (i.e., made by a trust authorization server) is received, it is considered to be valid. If the user does not exist, we create it on-the-fly, associating its ID with the client (to avoid collisions). The roles considered in the API are Admin, User and Client. Admins have full access and can create clients and roles. Users can log in and manage the permissions of their clients over their information. Clients can register new AI models and manage their identities.

Figures 2 and 3 show interaction diagrams of two use cases: Authentication with the API (Fig. 2), and Adding Trust Values (Fig. 3). An example of global operation in which trustworthiness is decided based on multiple metrics will be as follows: (1) the AI client can access the API with an OAuth token, (2) AI clients get logs of metrics, generate AI models, and evaluate the trustworthiness of users, (3) AI clients send trust values back to the API, (4) the API combines the results from multiple sources (AI clients, third parties, …), (5) Trust clients ask the API the trust level of the user.

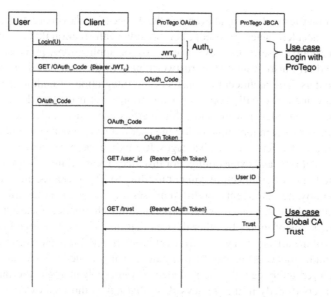

Fig. 2. Use case: authentication with the API (ProTego JBCA) (Source: created by the authors)

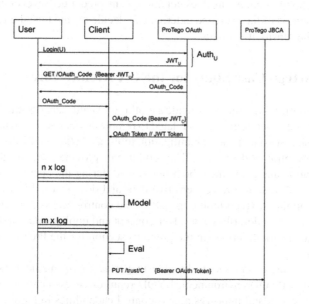

Fig. 3. Use case: AI client produces and sends trust values to the API (Source: created by the authors)

This framework is scalable, enabling flexible integration of new components. Specific architectural models that implement it could be designed and implemented. For instance, each mobile device could run an agent (IA agent) which reports collected metrics to the API. The API would be responsible for storing the metrics collected to be used for CA.

Examples of metrics include input events in the device (e.g., keyboard, touchscreen), its sensors (e.g., accelerometer, gyroscope) or any other information that can be extracted about the individual use of the device (e.g., use of applications, processes run). The AI agents and API also evaluate the trustworthiness of the user based on AI (machine learning) models. The architecture considers the integration of authorized third party systems that can ask the API about the trustworthiness of users and decide how to act based on their own rules. For instance, third parties can send an alert when the user's trust drops below a given threshold or log the user out requiring a new authentication.

This framework offers several advantages. Its modular plugin model facilitates maintainability, scalability, and extensibility. For instance, a new AI model can be developed and integrated into the architecture without needing to add or change any existing component. Similarly, new AI agents for different user metrics or any other information that can be monitored, implemented and incorporated into the model. Please note that this includes new kinds of inputs by other devices that may be used or found useful in the future. State of the art shows a wide variety of biometric and soft-biometric methods for continuous authentication that can be integrated, or novel methods that are not known or fully explored today can also be included. Another advantage is the integration of third-party users directly in the framework so that any authorized external source can ask about the trustworthiness of users and decide how to act, for instance, raising to alert (e.g., SIEM). So the architecture does not impose any predefined level or threshold about the trustworthiness of the user, and external can decide or fine tune the level based, for instance, in the sensitivity of data.

4   The ProTego Case Study for the CA Architecture

The ProTego project [15] aims to provide a toolkit for health care organizations to assess better and reduce cybersecurity risks related to remote devices access to healthcare data. It includes risk assessment and risk mitigation tools, as well as methodologies and protocols for prevention and reaction. The toolkit will provide, among others, tools for risk identification and assessment both before and during the operation of health care applications, and tools to protect sensitive data and devices used to handle it. CA is implemented in the ProTego toolkit as part of the control access tools in BYOD environment. This section describes a proof-of-concept and implementation of the elements of the CA framework described in the previous section for the ProTego mobile access control scenario.

Authorized care-takers should be able to get access to medical data using their own device in a BYOD environment. BYOD requires access control, and continuous authentication offers and improves access control capabilities in mobile scenarios, for instance, in the case of stealing a device or similar unauthorized accesses. This case study (Fig. 4) focuses on providing a proof-of-concept of the framework by showing an implementation of an agent that stores information about the keyboard, accelerometer, and the processes running on the mobile phone. The EDR responses include blocking the mobile device or logging-out the user in case of unauthorized access from the mobile device using an AI model that predicts the probability of being a legitimate user based on previous interaction and use of the mobile device.

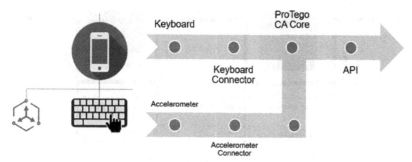

Fig. 4. Proof-of-concept of the CA framework for the ProTego case study. (Source: created by the authors)

4.1 Soft-Keyboard Biometrics

So, for this particular implementation of the framework, the AI client is an EDR mobile agent with CA capabilities to generate the trust level of a user. In this case, the agent does not need AI capabilities since AI models are trained in a backend. The EDR mobile agent component retrieves behavioral metrics and sends them to the API. Some of these metrics could be the keystroke dynamics, sensors data or gestures in the screen. When sensors generate a new log, it is sent through an internal bus to the core component (ProTego CA Core). Then, the core component processes its content to determine whether it is a continuous authentication log, and uploads to the backend. The application has been designed as a plugin model. An interface is provided that facilitates that each new feature can connect for sending logs. With this architecture, to get a new metric, it is not necessary to modify all the app, but just get the new metric and send it to the core using the interface provided. Logs are transferred as a Data Transfer Object (DTO) (Fig. 5).

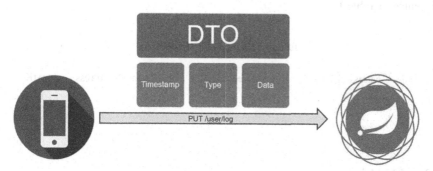

Fig. 5. Data Transfer Object (DTO) of an event log. (Source: created by the authors)

Mobile phone soft-keyboard events include the pressing and release of keys. These events can be used to generate a variety of metrics that identify individual users, which are used to train AI models that predict the trust level of a user. Literature of keyboard-based CA for desktop applications usually focus on the following metrics (Fig. 6):

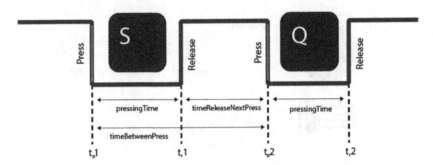

Fig. 6. Soft-keyboard events (Source: created by the authors)

- Pressing time of each key (pressingTime)
- Time between a key release and the following key pressed (timeReleaseNextPress)
- Time between a keypress and the next keypress (timeBetweenPress)

Additionally, the codes of the key pressed can also be captured. Machine learning models eventually decide about the importance that each metric has in defining a typing pattern of the user that can be used to determine her trust level. Although the keys pressed may not seem determinant to determine identity, existing research suggests that individuals express differently and this is reflected in their wording, punctuation, etc. Since the text is composed of characters, these may be significant to determine identity. Further, although characters pressed may not be representative of a typing pattern by themselves, the combination with other metrics can provide more accurate predictive models (for instance pressing time of different characters can be different for each user). All these metrics that result from soft-keyboard interaction are gathered by the EDR mobile agent and send to the API. An example of a key event stored in the log is presented in Table 1.

Table 1. Example of key event log

keyCode	pressingTime	timeBetweenPress	timeReleaseNextPress	nextKey
107	53.2	143.2	90.0	101

4.2 AI Models

Data of several users was collected by EDR mobile agents and used to train the AI models. Different supervised and unsupervised machine learning algorithms were selected and test for this scenario. Unsupervised algorithms included EllipticEnvelope, Isolation-Forest, and OneClassSVM. Supervised algorithms included RFC, SGD, and SVC. The datasets to train, test, and validate models tried to recreate real-world scenarios (Fig. 7). Particularly, the test dataset included 30% of new non-authorized user data different from the data included in the train and validation datasets. The 70:30 is a common ratio of separation used by many researchers. Implementation used a k-fold cross-validation. Initially k was established to 10.

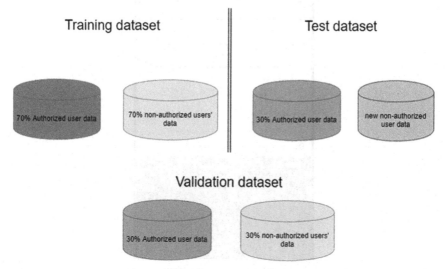

Fig. 7. Datasets for the AI model (training, test & validation) (Source: created by the authors)

It is an unbalanced problem since positive cases (authorized use) significantly outweigh negative cases. A negative occurs when there is an unauthorized use of a device. In most of the cases, the user is who she says she is. Because of this, we focused on unsupervised algorithms intended for use in outlier or anomaly detection and change detection (One-Class SVM, Isolation Forest, Elliptic Envelope), and on supervised algorithms that can deal with unbalanced data. The inclusion of a different test dataset with new unused data was also intended to test the accuracy of the machine learning algorithms and its capacity to deal with the unbalance data of this particular classification problem. As future work we plan to generate and use synthetic data to further mitigate this issue.

The AI models trained can then be used by the API to answer requests of trust levels of users. In the initial prototype, the trust level is shown in a progress bar on the mobile phone (Fig. 8).

The backend of this architecture centralizes the logs and associates them with the users' identity. All the system's information is stored in a relational database, and the logs are saved in a NoSQL database. Periodically, the backend generates the AI models using the logs stored to feed the machine learning process. The backend also evaluates new logs retrieved against these models. When an EDR agent asks for the trust of a user, the backend checks all the logs stored since the model's creation and returns a value between 0 and 1.

Fig. 8. Example of the trust level of the user of the CA EDR agent running in the mobile phone (Source: created by the authors)

4.3 Next Steps to Complete the Architecture

The components will be rearranged to improve and complete the architecture. The API will be divided in three different parts: an authorization server to manage the users, a central backend to manage the trust generated by the different AI models, and an EDR backend that would implement the AI models. It would illustrate how a third party should create his own backend acting as an AI client.

The Android mobile agent will also undertake several changes and improvements. Only the central part will be part of the integration. The EDR agent will be divided in two components: the EDR client itself and a library for third party integration which will provide an interface that facilitates integrating new apps into the CA archirecture.

We also plan to add OpenID capabilities to the OAuth2 implementation upgrading either through the use of MitreID or through the integration in the ProTego authorization system. Another significant point is the enhancement of privacy. We are working on detecting the most appropriate data protection techniques for each scenario, as we could store a large amount of behavioral metrics. Even though in the new model the most critical data could be stored in the users' device, it can be used to generate a fingerprint of the user. We are going to study which security measures could protect the users' privacy allowing to compute with the data. These security measures over the data go from the use of secure multi-party computation to homomorphic encryption, and the evaluation of AI models under different perspectives (like differential privacy).

5   Conclusions and Future Work

BYOD policies require additional access control to guarantee the identity of the users of mobile devices. CA offers this additional access control, but CA functionalities have to be included in existing information systems. This paper presented a modular framework that integrates clients, an API, authorization servers and third parties to provide a scalable model for BYOD CA. The framework was showcased in a healthcare scenario of the ProTego project which implements CA based on soft-keyboard metrics of the mobile phone. The main components of the architecture are the EDR agents and the AI model.

As future research, the ProTego project aims to complete the architecture and toolkit to provide state-of-the-art high security in healthcare environments. Future research lines include network slicing [16] for securing wifi access inside the facilities of health care providers for users (patients and healthcare staff). Future work also includes modular encryption systems that enable transmitting and computing securely with data which can be also complemented with full memory encryption systems that enable computation with encrypted data, like homomorphic encryption [17]. Future research that is specific for continuous authentication and the framework proposed in this paper include using ensemble learning based on multiple AI models and using machine learning models based on image classification. Key events as well as touchscreen events (gestures) can be used to create heatmaps that can feed new AI models. EDR capabilities could also be augmented through malware software detection in mobile devices. Finally, the architecture will consider the presence of a local model on the user side. For instance, a model can locally generate trust levels based on a picture taken o some other local events or information. The architecture will include a local model agent to check the integration with this kind of systems.

Acknowledgments. This project has received funding from the European Union's Horizon 2020 Research and innovation programme under grant agreement No. 826284.

References

1. Miller, K.W., Voas, J., Hurlburt, G.F.: BYOD: security and privacy considerations. IT Prof. **14**(5), 53–55 (2012)
2. Sequeiros, J.B.F., Chimuco, F.T., Samaila, M.G., Freire, M.M., Inácio, P.R.M.: Attack and system modeling applied to IoT, cloud, and mobile ecosystems. ACM Comput. Surv. **53**(2), 1–32 (2020)
3. Shuwandy, Moceheb Lazam., Zaidan, B.B., Zaidan, A.A., Albahri, A.S.: Sensor-based mhealth authentication for real-time remote healthcare monitoring system: a multilayer systematic review. J. Med. Syst. **43**(2), 1–30 (2019). https://doi.org/10.1007/s10916-018-1149-5
4. Zhang, Y., Gravina, R., Lu, H., Villari, M., Fortino, G.: PEA: parallel electrocardiogram-based authentication for smart healthcare systems. J. Netw. Comput. Appl. **117**, 10–16 (2018)
5. Mondal, S., Bours, P.: Continuous authentication using mouse dynamics. In: 2013 International Conference of the BIOSIG Special Interest Group (BIOSIG) (2013)
6. Shepherd, S.J.: Continuous authentication by analysis of keyboard typing characteristics. In: European Convention on Security and Detection (1995)

7. Pisani, Paulo Henrique, Lorena, Ana Carolina: A systematic review on keystroke dynamics. J. Braz. Comput. Soc. **19**(4), 573–587 (2013). https://doi.org/10.1007/s13173-013-0117-7

8. Frank, M., Biedert, R., Ma, E., Martinovic, I., Song, D.: Touchalytics: on the applicability of touchscreen input as a behavioral biometric for continuous authentication. IEEE Trans. Inf. Forensics Secur. **8**(1), 136–148 (2013)

9. Siirtola, P., Komulainen, J., Kellokumpu, V.: Effect of context in swipe gesture-based continuous authentication on smartphones. In: European Symposium on Artificial Neural Networks, Computational Intelligence and Machine Learning, Bruges (Belgium). pp. 639–644 (2018)

10. Gascon, H., Uellenbeck, S., Wolf, C., Rieck, K.: Continuous authentication on mobile devices by analysis of typing motion behavior. In: Proceedings of GI Conference "Sicherheit" (Sicherheit, Schutz und Verlässlichkeit), Vienna (2014)

11. Sitová, Z., Šeděnka, J., Yang, Q., Peng, G., Zhou, G., Gasti, P., Balagani, K.S.: HMOG: new behavioral biometric features for continuous authentication of smartphone users. IEEE Trans. Inf. Forensics Secur. **11**(5), 877–892 (2016)

12. Basar, O.E., Alptekin, G., Volaka, H.C., Isbilen, M., Incel, O.D.: Resource usage analysis of a mobile banking application using sensor-and-touchscreen-based continuous authentication. Procedia Comput. Sci. **155**, 185–192 (2019)

13. Katevas, K., Haddadi, H., Tokarchuk, L.: SensingKit: a multi-platform mobile sensing framework for large-scale experiments. In: Proceedings of the 20th Annual International Conference on Mobile Computing and Networking, MobiCom 2014. Association for Computing Machinery, Maui Hawaii, pp. 375–378 (2014)

14. Bonastre, J.-F., Bimbot, F., Boe, L.-J., Magrin-Chagnolleau, I.: Person authentication by voice: a need for caution. In: 8th European Conference on Speech Communication and Technology, EUROSPEECH 2003 - INTERSPEECH 2003, Geneva, Switzerland (2003)

15. ProTego: Data-protection toolkit reducing risks in hospitals and care centers. ProTego project. https://protego-project.eu/. Accessed 10th June 2020

16. Isolani, P.H., et al.: Airtime-based resource allocation modeling for network slicing in IEEE 802.11 RANs. IEEE Commun. Lett. **24**(5), 1077–1080 (2020)

17. Naehrig, M., Lauter, K., Vaikuntanathan, V.: Can homomorphic encryption be practical? In: Proceedings of the 3rd ACM Workshop on Cloud Computing Security Workshop. Association for Computing Machinery: Chicago, Illinois, USA, pp. 113–124 (2011)

Diabetes Link: Platform for Self-control and Monitoring People with Diabetes

Enzo Rucci[1,3]($\boxtimes$) (ORCID), Lisandro Delía[1] (ORCID), Joaquín Pujol[2], Paula Erbino[2],
Armando De Giusti[1] (ORCID), and Juan José Gagliardino[3]

[1] III-LIDI, Facultad de Informática, UNLP – CeAs CICPBA, 1900 La Plata,
Bs As, Argentina
`erucci@lidi.info.unlp.edu.ar`
[2] Facultad de Informática, UNLP,1900 La Plata, Bs As, Argentina
[3] CENEXA,UNLP – CONICET – CeAs CICPBA,1900 La Plata, Bs As, Argentina

Abstract. Diabetes Mellitus (DM) is a chronic disease characterized by an increase in blood glucose (sugar) above normal levels and it appears when human body is not able to produce enough insulin to cover the peripheral tissue demand. Nowadays, DM affects the 8.5% of the world's population and, even though no cure for it has been found, an adequate monitoring and treatment allow patients to have an almost normal life. This paper introduces Diabetes Link, a comprehensive platform for control and monitoring people with DM. Diabetes Link allows recording various parameters relevant for the treatment and calculating different statistical charts using them. In addition, it allows connecting with other users (supervisors) so they can monitor the controls. Even more, the extensive comparative study carried out reflects that Diabetes Link presents distinctive and superior features against other proposals. We conclude that Diabetes Link represents a broad and accessible tool that can help make day-to-day control easier and optimize the efficacy in DM control and treatment.

Keywords: Diabetes · Diabetes control · Blood sugar monitoring · Health informatics · Mobile application · eHealth · mHealth

1   Introduction

According to the American Institute of Medical Sciences & Education, the term mobile health (*mHealth*) is used to refer to mobile technology focused on health care and medical information. There are currently more than 100,000 mobile applications associated with the health field. In the United States, 80% of medical professionals use mobile phones and medical applications, 25% of which are used for patient care [2].

Diabetes Mellitus (DM) is a chronic disease characterized by an increase in blood glucose (sugar) above normal levels [7]. Affected people need ongoing and long-term treatment, as well as periodic self-monitoring of blood glucose

© Springer Nature Switzerland AG 2020
H. Florez and S. Misra (Eds.): ICAI 2020, CCIS 1277, pp. 359–373, 2020.
https://doi.org/10.1007/978-3-030-61702-8_25

(SMBG) mainly, but also of other clinical and metabolic parameters, such as body weight, food intake (measured mainly in carbohydrates), blood pressure, medications used, insulin dose and physical activity performed. Failure to adequately control the disease or comply with the prescribed treatments can not only have irreparable consequences on overall health, but it can also affect the quality of life of people with diabetes (namely, chronic complications affecting the eyes, kidneys and heart, among other organs; as well as psychological and mental damage). At the same time, it also affects patients from and economic and social perspective, due to the high costs of treatment and the impact on work discrimination [6].

Globally, according to the latest figures presented by the World Health Organization (WHO) in October 2018, the number of people with diabetes has increased significantly [9]. In 1980, it affected 4.7% of the world's population, and this increased to 8.5% by 2014, with a total of 422 million people affected. Among people with diabetes, those with type 1 diabetes (T1D) and some with type 2 diabetes (T2D) receive daily insulin injections and perform SMBG to define the insulin dose they need to inject and optimize blood sugar control. This process is required to reduce the development and progression of the chronic complications of the disease and its negative impact in quality of life.

In this paper, we present *Diabetes Link*, a comprehensive platform to simplify the control and monitoring of people with DM. Diabetes Link combines a mobile application and a web portal, making the best of each platform. It allows recording various parameters relevant for the appropiate treatment and calculating different statistical charts using them. Also, it allows connecting with other users (supervisors) so they can monitor the controls. In addition, Diabetes Link offers all its functionality for free, and it is available on multiple platforms. Through an extensive comparative analysis, we show the distinctive and superior features of Diabetes Link against other available tools.

The remaining sections of this article are organized as follows: Sect. 2 describes the recommended treatment for people with DM. Section 3 introduces Diabetes Link, and Sect. 4 presents a comparative analysis with other available options. Finally, Sect. 5 summarizes the conclusions and and possible future lines of work.

2   Treatment for Diabetes Mellitus

So far, no cure for DM has been found, but sustained control and adequate treatment allow patients to lead an almost normal life. In addition, an active participation of the patients in the control and treatment of their disease is required to achieve this goal.

Treatment is based on four pillars — education, healthy meal plan, regular practice of physical activity, and various medications (oral antidiabetic drugs and insulin if required). It is very important that people with diabetes keep their condition under continuous and tight control and adhere to their prescribed treatment throughout their lives. In addition, depending on patient and disease severity, different clinical and metabolic parameters should be monitored, such as body weight, blood glucose, blood pressure, the amount of ingested carbohydrates, and physical activity performed. All these parameters have an impact on the long-term level of control and the simultaneous monitoring prevents the development/progression of the chronic complications that deteriorate quality of life and increase their costs of care [6–8].

Recording the various parameters associated with the treatment allows physicians to monitor patient evolution over time and to adjust the treatment accordingly in order to optimize results. In that sense, the ultimate goal is that the patient can maintain certain degree of stability.

The lack of an adequate control of the disease, together with non-adherence to prescribed treatments, leads to the development and progression of the chronic complications of the disease. They affect various organs such as the retina, kidneys, and cardiovascular system, decreasing their quality of life and their psychophysical ability as well as increasing their costs of care. Equally important, the decrease in psychophysical capacity also affects the ability to work, with the consequent socio-economic impact.

3   Diabetes Link

3.1   Work Methodology

To analyze the potential of the proposal and subsequently define its scope, clinical researchers from the CENEXA (UNLP-CONICET-CeAs CICPBA)[1] were contacted, due to their long career devoted to diabetes epidemiology, care programmes and derived costs. Their advice allowed us to learn about basic concepts of the disease and multiple aspects of its treatment. In addition, they emphasized the importance of keeping an adequate record of relevant data to achieve a good metabolic control.

Two physicians specialized in DM (with experience in therapeutic education of people with diabetes and co-authors of a manual oriented to the complementation of this activity [7]) were also interviewed. They provided useful information related to the statistical indicators that specialists frequently analyze when assessing the status of a patient and adjusting their treatment.

Finally, this development phase was complemented with a state-of-the-art study of mobile applications oriented to diabetes, which allowed us to discover possible uncovered needs in the area. It is important to remark that this study was repeated once again after the platform was released to carry out the comparative analysis of Sect. 4.

3.2   Requirements Analysis and Design

For the first release of Diabetes Link, a set of functional and non-functional requirements of the platform was agreed among all the participants. Require-

---

[1] www.cenexa.org.

ments analysis and design modelling were required phases in the plataform development to guarantee the quality of the final product.

Functional Requirements. Table 1 shows the functional requirements of Diabetes Link in a simplified manner.

Use Cases Model. Figure 1 shows the use cases model of Diabetes Link. It is important to note that as these functional requirements are fine-grained, it was possible to translate each one into a particular use case.

Non-Functional Requirements. Table 2 shows the non-functional requirements of Diabetes Link.

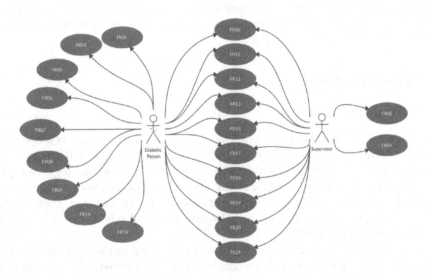

Fig. 1. Use cases

Architecture. The platform can be accessed through a mobile application (available now for Android[2] and soon for iOS), and/or a web application[3]. Figure 2 shows a general model of service-oriented architecture.

The mobile application is used for both supervised and supervisor users. It was developed using web technologies (HTML5, CSS3 and Javascript) and the frameworks Angular 6[4] and Ionic v3[5]. The latter, on its behalf, uses Apache

---

[2] https://play.google.com/store/apps/details?id=lidi.diabetes.link.
[3] http://diabeteslink.info.unlp.edu.ar.
[4] https://angularjs.org/.
[5] https://ionicframework.com/docs/v3/.

Table 1. Functional requirements of Diabetes Link

ID	Functional Requirement *The systems must allow the*	Web app	Mobile app
FR01	Login/Logout of patient/supervised user		✓
FR02	Login/Logout of physician/supervisor user	✓	✓
FR03	Creation of supervised user		✓
FR04	Creation of supervisor user		✓
FR05	Record of relevant information for metabolic control: blood glucose measurements, carbohydrates intake and injected insulin. For each variable, the time of day (before/after breakfast/lunch/snack/dinner) must be included, and additional comments can be added to help understand the information entered		✓
FR06	Record of medications		✓
FR07	Record of physical activity (detailing intensity and duration)		✓
FR08	Record of body weight		✓
FR09	Record of blood pressure		✓
FR10	Analysis of the evolution of blood glucose	✓	✓
FR11	Analysis of the evolution of body weight and BMI	✓	✓
FR12	Analysis of the evolution of blood pressure	✓	✓
FR13	Weekly summary of daily records detailing, for each day and meal, physical activity, carbohydrates intake, and blood glucose and injected insulin measurements before and after each intake	✓	✓
FR14	Supervisor search		✓
FR15	Association/Dissociation of supervisors		✓
FR16	List of supervisor users	✓	✓
FR17	Access to supervised user profile	✓	✓
FR18	Access to the FAQs section about DM. There, patients can read about the disease, including its causes, consequences, and specifications about treatment goals.		✓
FR19	Setting target values for blood glucose and blood pressure to customize the statistical analysis	✓	✓
FR20	Support for different units of measurement: User can choose their preferred units of measure for blood glucose (mg/dL or mmol/L) and weight (kg or lbs)		✓
FR21	Support for different languages	✓	✓

Cordova[6] for packaging web solutions in modules that can be later installed in mobile devices. It is for that reason that the mobile application of Diabetes Link can be categorized as a multi-platform, hybrid one [4].

---

[6] https://cordova.apache.org/docs/en/latest/guide/overview/index.html.

Table 2. Non-functional requirements of Diabetes Link

ID	Non-functional requirement
NFR01	Security. The system must ensure all information of the registered end users are secured and not accessible by other party
NFR02	Security. The system should back up its data every 12 hours and the copies must be stored in a secure off-site location
NFR03	Usability. The system should provide a systematic, simple and user-friendly interfaces
NFR04	Usability. The system should provide internationalization support (at least, English and Spanish)
NFR05	Platforms Constraint. The mobile application should work under Android and iOS platforms. Also, a web application is needed for supervisors access
NFR06	The system must have a "Terms & conditions" section

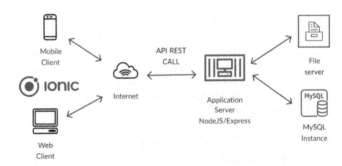

Fig. 2. General model of service-oriented architecture

Nowadays, Android and iOS are the main mobile operating systems. The mobile application of Diabetes Link is ready to work on both of them due to its multi-platform, hybrid feature. In that sense, the Android version was released first allowing Diabetes Link to cover more than 70% of the market share [10]. On its behalf, the iOS version will be released next.

Most of the mobile application code could be reused for the development of a web application, which is now only available for supervisor users. However, supervised users will be able to access to it in the near future.

Both mobile and web applications communicate through the HTTP protocol using an API developed with Node.js[7] and the framework Express[8]. Finally, the data is managed using a MySQL database[9].

---

[7] https://nodejs.org/es/.

[8] https://expressjs.com/es/.

[9] https://www.mysql.com/.

User Interface. Figures. 3, 4, 5 and 6 show the implementation of several functional requirements, that were described in Table 1.

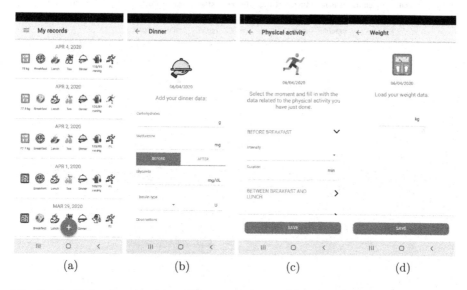

Fig. 3. (a–b) Implementation of FR05 and FR06. (c) Implementation of FR07. (d) Implementation of FR08.

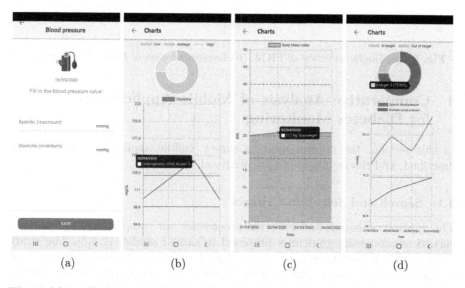

Fig. 4. (a) Implementation of FR09. (b) Implementation of FR10. (c) Implementation of FR11. (d) Implementation of FR12.

← **Weekly summary**

April	Physical activity	Breakfast Before	Breakfast After	Physical activity	Lunch Before	Lunch After	Physical activity	Tea Before	Tea After	Physica activity
Friday 3	-	100 mg/dL	200 mg/dL	-	100 mg/dL	230 mg/dL	High(30 min)	100 mg/dL	-	-
		·	·		·	5 U		5 U	·	
		1000 g			·			1000 g		
Saturday 4	-	90 mg/dL	-	-	100 mg/dL	-	High (30 min)	-	180 mg/dL	-
		3 U	-		·	·		·	5 U	
		·			1500 g			500 g		

(a)

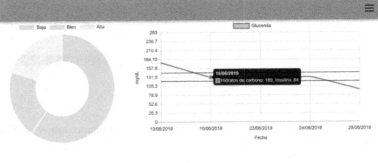

(b)

Fig. 5. (a) Implementation of FR13. (b) Implementation of FR10 (Web access).

4 Comparative Analysis of Mobile Applications for Diabetes Monitoring

In this section, the criteria used to survey mobile applications for DM are described, and the results found are analyzed.

4.1 Search and Selection Criteria

The application search and selection process for our comparative analysis was carried out following guidelines proposed in similar studies [1,3,5]. The study focused just on the Android operating system due to two reasons: first, Android is currently the most popular option, having more than 70% of the market share [10]; second, even though the mobile application of Diabetes Link will be soon available in iOS, now it is just present in Android.

Today, Google Play does not offer filters to apply to search results. In addition, search terms are matched against app title and/or description, which usually leads to false hits, sometimes caused by spam techniques. To ensure that our

Fig. 6. (a) Implementation of FR15. (b) Implementation of FR19. (c) Implementation of FR20. (d) Implementation of FR21.

analysis is representative, the search on Google Play was carried out on a specific date (Feb. 18, 2020), and all apps found were recorded. The phrase "diabetes control" was used since it is sufficiently general to ensure that every relevant app is detected. As a result, 246 applications were listed (incognito mode on). To be included in the analysis, an application must meet the following characteristics:

– It must offer functionality that facilitates self-monitoring and control by people with diabetes;
– It must allow blood glucose registration as a minimum requirement;
– It must offer Spanish or English language interfaces.

After filtering out those apps that did not meet these requirements, 75 applications remained[10]. In order to evaluate these applications, the first 10 were selected according to three criteria: (1) greater popularity (order of appearance on results list); (2) higher score; and (3) greater number of downloads. The 3 partial listings were combined to obtain a single final one. In total, 22 applications were reviewed (30% of the total).

4.2 Comparative Analysis

After selecting the applications for the comparative analysis, their primary features were surveyed and analyzed. We have considered previous similar stud-

---

[10] Considering the applications that were not used, 2% offer functionality for control, but do not support Spanish or English; 67% are about DM, but only for educational purposes; and 31% are not relevant to this study (poorly classified).

ies [1,3,5] to determine the feature selection criteria. This comparison allows to quickly and easily see their strengths and weaknesses.

Table 3 presents the main features of each app regarding Google Play information (order of appearence (#), number of downloads, score and version), web access support, its adquisition cost, its communication features, and if it offers diabetes information. First of all, it can be noted that just 32% of the apps offers web access. As described in Sect. 3, Diabetes Link is cross-platform and both mobile and web accesses are supported. The former becomes more significant at the time of analizying the information and statistical graphics, since its more user-friendly view.

In relation to adquisition costs, 78% of the applications studied require paying a monthly or annual fee to access advanced features (for instance, calculating statistics based on the information entered, adjusting target values, exporting reports or sending them by e-mail, supporting connectivity, among others). As regards connectivity, just four applications (18%) offer this star feature but only one does it for free. Other four applications do not offer any feature for communication support while the rest (14 apps) rely on generating PDF/XLS reports or sending them by e-mail. Diabetes Link, on its behalf, supports connectivity and offers all features for free.

Table 4 summarizes the funcionality features of each application regarding data register and statistical analysis. Each app was surveyed to determine if it supports recording blood glucose, insulin, carbo-hydrates, body weight, blood pressure, medication, and physical activity. Additionally, wether the application analyzes blood glucose, body weight, and blood pressure data or not. Last, if it offers a tabular summary of registered data or not.

Between 59% and 82% of the selected applications allow recording measurements for blood glucose, insulin, carbohydrate intake, physical activity, food and medications intake. In addition, 77% allow recording body weight, and less than 73% allow recording blood pressure. As for the ability of adding labels or notes to the records, all applications offer this feature. Diabetes Link, on the other hand, allows recording of all of these measurements.

All of the applications that were reviewed offer statistical charts/tables for blood glucose measurements. As regards the other parameters, the percentages of applications that analyze them are 59% and 41%, they correspond to body weight and blood pressure, respectively. Furthermore, only 27% are capable of generating summary tables to report all recorded values. In contrast, Diabetes Link generates statistics for all these parameters, as well as a weekly summary tables for blood glucose, insulin and carbohydrate intake measurements, as well as physical activity done. It should be noted that the idea of adding these weekly summaries was suggested by the physicians during their interviews. They stated that they usually ask their patients to provide written records (diary) with this information to analyze patient status and adjust treatment accordingly.

From Tables 3 and 4, it can be observed that none of the applications provides information about diabetes, statistics and connection with monitors simultane-

Table 3. Google Play information and features of selected diabetes applications.

Application	Google Play #	Downloads	Score	Version	Web Access	Cost	Communication Connectivity	E-mail / External report	Diabetes Info
mySugr	5	100K	4.6	3.66.1		PVIP[a]		✓	
OneTouch Reveal	63	100K	4.1	4.5		Free			✓
Alarma de Medicina	118	1M	4.7	3.61.1	✓ (Beta)	Free	✓ (Beta)	✓	
Diabetes - Diario de glucosa	4	500K	4.7	4.1.5		PVIP		✓	
Diabetes:M	8	500K	4.4	8.0	✓	PVIP	✓	✓	✓
One Drop	23	500K	4	2.0.0		Free		✓	
Índice y Carga Glucémicos	115	500K	4.3	3.3.1		PVIP		✓	
OnTrack Diabetes	125	500K	3.6	3.2.7	✓	Free		✓	
BloodPressureDB	207	500K	4.4	6.2.7		PVIP		✓	
SocialDiabetes	1	100K	4.7	4.15	✓	PVIP	✓	✓	
Açúcar no sangue	30	100K	4.9	3.2.5		PVIP		✓	
Blood Glucose Tracker	21	100K	4.7	1.8.12		PVIP		✓	
BG Monitor Diabetes	73	50K	4.6	8.0.17		PVIP		✓	
RT Diabetes	171	500	4.7	2.03		PVIP[b]		✓	✓
Diario de diabetes	33	50K	4.6	1.2		PVIP		✓	✓
SugarFree	34	100	4.6	1.2.22		Free			
Control de la Glucosa	2	50K	4.5	1.81	✓	PVIP		✓	✓
forDiabetes	7	10K	4.3	1.15.0		PVIP		✓	
Diabetes Tracker	9	100K	3.6	1.11	✓	PVIP			✓
SiDiary Diabetes Management	10	50K	4.4	1.45		PVIP			
gluQUO	12	100K	4.3	2.8.0		PVIP		✓	
Diabetes Connect	16	100K	4.4	2.5.0	✓	PVIP	✓	✓	

[a] Premium version is paid
[b] Trial version is free

Table 4. Features for data register and analysis of selected diabetes applications.

Application	Data register							Data analysis			
	Blood glucose	Insulin	Carbo-hydrates	Body weight	Blood pres-sure	Medi-cations	Physical activity	Blood glucose	Body weight	Blood pres-sure	Tabular sum-mary
mySugr	✓	✓	✓	✓	✓	✓	✓	✓			✓
OneTouch Reveal	✓	✓	✓			✓	✓	✓			✓
Alarma de Medicina	✓	✓		✓	✓	✓	✓	✓	✓	✓	
Diabetes - Diario de glucosa	✓			✓				✓	✓		✓
Diabetes:M	✓	✓	✓	✓	✓	✓	✓	✓	✓		
One Drop	✓	✓	✓	✓	✓	✓	✓	✓			✓
Índice y Carga Glucémicos	✓		✓	✓		✓		✓	✓		
OnTrack Diabetes	✓	✓	✓	✓	✓	✓	✓	✓	✓	✓	
BloodPressureDB	✓			✓	✓	✓		✓	✓	✓	
SocialDiabetes	✓	✓	✓	✓	✓	✓	✓	✓	✓	✓	
Açúcar no sangue	✓	✓		✓	✓	✓		✓	✓	✓	
Blood Glucose Tracker	✓	✓	✓	✓	✓	✓		✓			
BG Monitor Diabetes	✓	✓	✓			✓	✓	✓			
RT Diabetes	✓	✓		✓	✓	✓		✓	✓		
Diario de diabetes	✓	✓		✓	✓	✓	✓	✓	✓		✓
SugarFree	✓	✓	✓			✓		✓			
Control de la Glucosa	✓	✓	✓	✓	✓	✓	✓	✓	✓	✓	
forDiabetes	✓	✓		✓	✓	✓	✓	✓		✓	
Diabetes Tracker	✓				✓	✓		✓		✓	
SiDiary Diabetes Management	✓	✓	✓	✓			✓	✓	✓		
gluQUO	✓	✓	✓	✓				✓			
Diabetes Connect	✓	✓	✓	✓	✓	✓	✓	✓	✓	✓	✓

ously for free. In that context, Diabetes Link sets itself apart by providing all these features at no charge.

Table 5. Features for customization of selected diabetes applications.

Application	Customization		
	Language	Target valures	Units of measurement
mySugr	✓	✓	✓
OneTouch Reveal	✓	✓	
Alarma de Medicina	✓	✓	✓
Diabetes - Diario de glucosa	✓	✓	✓
Diabetes:M	✓	✓	✓
One Drop	✓	✓	✓
Índice y Carga Glucémicos	✓	✓	✓
OnTrack Diabetes		✓	✓
BloodPressureDB	✓		✓
SocialDiabetes	✓	✓	✓
Açúcar no sangue	✓	✓	✓
Blood Glucose Tracker		✓	✓
BG Monitor Diabetes	✓	✓	✓
RT Diabetes	✓		
Diario de diabetes		✓	✓
SugarFree	✓	✓	✓
Control de la Glucosa			
forDiabetes	✓	✓	✓
Diabetes Tracker		✓	✓
SiDiary Diabetes Management	✓	✓	✓
gluQUO	✓	✓	✓
Diabetes Connect	✓	✓	✓

Finally, Table 5 shows the customization features of each application considering user language, target values and units of measurement. First, 22% of the applications does not include multi-language support. Having this feature allows Diabetes Link to offer an expanded reach, which means more people can use it. Both target values and units of measurement can be configured in most applications; in particular, 86% for the former and 82% for the latter. Diabetes Link support these two configuration options allowing users to customize their level of control and preferred units of measurement.

4.3 Limitations

Due to the great number of existing diabetes apps and the large amount of work required to revise them, some limitation of the comparative analysis were imposed. First, the review study just considered the Android OS. Although Android has more than 70% of the market share [10], currently available mobile applications for other OS's (especially iOS) were not considered.

In addition, the comparative analysis carried out only gathered the presence or absence of a given feature, as a way of simplifying the large collection task. In that sense, neither the quality of functions nor their effectiveness were evaluated. However, useful information could still be extracted.

5 Conclusions

Adequate diabetes control is fundamental to improve the quality of life of people who suffer from this disease. This paper presented Diabetes Link, a comprehensive platform to simplify the control and monitoring of people with DM. The exhaustive comparative analysis carried out shows that Diabetes Link presents distinctive and superior features against other current proposals. In particular, we can highlight it is cross-platform, it supports connectivity, and it allows users to record/analyze various parameters relevant for the appropiate treatment (all for free). It is for that reason that Diabetes Link is expected to help make day-to-day control easier and optimize the efficacy in DM control and treatment.

Future work focuses on the extension of the comparative analysis to include two aspects: first, considering advanced features like IoT integration; second, considering mobile applications from iOS, especially when the iOS version of Diabetes Link is available.

References

1. Arnhold, M., Quade, M., Kirch, W.: Mobile applications for diabetics: a systematic review and expert-based usability evaluation considering the special requirements of diabetes patients age 50 years or older. J. Med. Internet Res. 16(4), e104 (2014). https://doi.org/10.2196/jmir.2968
2. Banova, B.: Global illumination for point modelsthe impact of technology in healthcare. Am. Inst. Med. Sci. Educ. (2019). https://www.aimseducation.edu/blog/the-impact-of-technology-on-healthcare/
3. Chomutare, T., Fernandez-Luque, L., Årsand, E., Hartvigsen, G.: Features of mobile diabetes applications: review of the literature and analysis of current applications compared against evidence-based guidelines. J. Med. Internet Res. 13(3), e65 (2011). https://doi.org/10.2196/jmir.1874
4. Delia, L., Galdamez, N., Thomas, P., Corbalan, L., Pesado, P.: Multi-platform mobile application development analysis. In: 2015 IEEE 9th International Conference on Research Challenges in Information Science (RCIS), pp. 181–186 (2015)
5. El-Gayar, O., Timsina, P., Nawar, N., Eid, W.: Mobile applications for diabetes self-management: status and potential. J. Diabetes Sci. Technol. 7(1), 247–262 (2013). https://doi.org/10.1177/193229681300700130

6. Elgart, J.F., Asteazarán, S., De La Fuente, J.L., Camillucci, C., Brown, J.B., Gagliardino, J.J.: Direct and indirect costs associated to type 2 diabetes and its complications measured in a social security institution of Argentina. Int. J. Pub. Health **59**(5), 851–857 (2014). https://doi.org/10.1007/s00038-014-0604-4
7. Gagliardino, J.J., et al.: Cómo Tratar Mi Diabetes. CENEXA, 3 edn. (2016)
8. Gæde, P., Vedel, P., Larsen, N., Jensen, G.V., Parving, H.H., Pedersen, O.: Multifactorial intervention and cardiovascular disease in patients with type 2 diabetes. N. Engl. J. Med. **348**(5), 383–393 (2003). https://doi.org/10.1056/NEJMoa021778. pMID: 12556541
9. Organización Mundial de la Salud: Informe mundial sobre la diabetes (2018). https://www.who.int/es/news-room/fact-sheets/detail/diabetes
10. Stat Counter: Mobile operating system market share worldwide, May 2020. https://gs.statcounter.com/os-market-share/mobile/worldwide/

Human-Computer Interaction

Design and Prototyping of a Wearable Kinesthetic Haptic Feedback System to Support Mid-Air Interactions in Virtual Environments

Ekati Ekaterini Maria Sagia and Modestos Stavrakis(✉) ⓘ

University of the Aegean, Hermoupolis TK84100, Syros, Greece
sagiaekati@gmail.com, modestos@aegean.gr

Abstract. This paper focuses on the study of mid-air gestural interaction and haptic means of immersion in virtual environments to design a wearable kinesthetic feedback system based on vibro-tactile feedback mechanisms. The paper gives special attention to the design and prototyping of the wearable system and the use of low-cost optical hand tracking devices. The complete implementation of the system is comprised of a motion tracking sensor, used to identify and monitor the user's hand position and gestures, and a wearable device based on low-cost micro-controller technologies and vibration motors for producing the haptic rendering. The wearable device is mounted on the user's hand (fingers, palm and wrist), with the aim of producing feedback in real time when interacting with virtual objects in virtual environments. In this paper we present the design of the wearable kinesthetic feedback system, the implementation of the haptic rendering mechanisms and a preliminary evaluation of its usability from a user experience perspective.

Keywords: Mid-air interaction · Wearables · Vibro-tactile feedback · Haptics

1 Introduction

Gestural interactions and more specifically mid-air interactions present a number of benefits and problems [1, 2]. One of the most mentioned difficulties users experience when interacting with natural interfaces that involve touchless manipulations is related to the absence of tactile feedback. This results in a number of consequent issues such as the inability to differentiate between intended and unintended interactions referred to as the Midas Problem [3], the continuous-active nature of the gestural interaction [4], and among others the lack of haptic feedback that assists in fine tuning and refining manipulations [5] by combining multiple senses, perceptions and actions such as visual, haptic, sense of depth, spatial proximity, grasping etc [6–9]. While the cutaneous system employs receptors embedded in the skin, and the kinesthetic system those receptors that are located in muscles, tendons, and joints, the haptic sensory system acts on the basis of combinatory mechanism which employs both cutaneous and kinesthetic receptors [10]. The haptic system is characterized in terms of a bidirectional communication channel that living organisms incorporate to sense and interact with their environment. The haptic

© Springer Nature Switzerland AG 2020
H. Florez and S. Misra (Eds.): ICAI 2020, CCIS 1277, pp. 377–391, 2020.
https://doi.org/10.1007/978-3-030-61702-8_26

system is coupled by an active procedure controlled by both movement and touch and therefore combine both mid-air and touch interactions.

Thus, as a key point in the mitigation of the weaknesses of mid-air interaction, the aim of this paper is to study the use of vibro-tactile feedback in mid-air interactions by implementing a wearable device that will provide haptic feedback based on the creation of haptic rendering patterns. Towards this goal, the paper discusses a number of research and design challenges. First, it outlines related concepts, mid-air interaction, vibro-tactile and cutaneous haptic feedback, and haptic rendering. Next, it reviews a number of related projects and research works that employ tactile and mid-air interaction technologies. It provides a detailed description of the design decisions and prototyping steps towards the implementation of a vibro-tactile wearable device for supporting tactile feedback in mid-air interactions. Finally, we include a short report on a pilot study and outline current research activities of the design team of an ongoing research experiment that utilizes the device in use cases that involve interactions in virtual environments.

2   Mid-Air Interaction and Haptic Feedback

In recent years the combination of haptic, wearable technologies uncovered new ways in providing tactile feedback while gesturing in mid-air [11]. These interfaces are very useful in situations where the actual device or interface poses limitations and thus restrict user performance. These limitations arise for a number of reasons and are related to a) the physical characteristics of the interface or the device, b) the users' concurrent activities, c) the context of use including the cultural or physical environment. For example, small device interfaces such as touchscreens on smart-watches often hinder users from interacting with them. Concurrent activities that the users perform might prohibit them to interact by using interaction styles such as touch, tangible or voice. Context is also playing an important role, for example in environmental conditions where the users are unable to employ other interaction styles such as underwater, or in severe weather conditions, or even in contexts where cultural rules, rituals and behavior regulations direct users to use only gestural interactions.

2.1   Mid-Air Interaction

Mid-Air Interaction is defined as a form of human computer interaction in which an action is carried out without the mechanical contact between the user and any part of a device or system. It is considered a particular form of a natural user interaction, more specifically a kinesthetic and gestural interaction, that employs touchless or contact-free manipulations of digital content and is based on the identification of bodily movements, usually of the hands [12]. It imparts greater naturalness from what we are used to in our everyday lives when we interact with traditional human-computer interfaces, and thus provides new ways of interacting through simple and intuitive body movements [13, 14].

The most notable mid-air interaction systems, at the time of writing this paper, are the Nintendo Wii platform which incorporates the Wiimote remote controller and has motion sensing capabilities that allow the user to interact with and manipulate items on screen via gesture recognition and pointing, the Microsoft Kinect which is based on the

MS Kinect sensor and implements two cameras (color and depth camera) and an array of microphones. Kinect is accompanied by an SDK that provides tracking of human movements by the use of two skeletons of 25 points in total [15] and the Leap Motion Controller (Ultraleap), an optical hand tracking module that specifically captures the movements of hands.

2.2 Vibro-Tactile Haptic Feedback

Tactile interaction is related to all aspects of touch and body movements and the application of these senses to the field of human-computer interaction [16]. Tactile interaction is a field that refers to the ways in which people communicate and interact through the sensation of touch. This kind of interaction offers an extra dimension in virtual environments, adds a sense of immersion in them and are usually encountered in the use of vibrations in contact with the skin. When referring to tactile feedback, we usually mean vibrations while the vibrotactile feedback is the feedback offered by the vibrations of a device in the hand of the user.

Dynamic feedback also works through haptic vibrations, but particularly in conjunction with an on-screen action. Dynamic feedback is typically found on controllers in computer games, for example, the pursuit of naturalness and resistances. These are, therefore, essential forces that stop the user's movement providing an additional sense of immersion. These two feedback mechanisms are often combined. In most tactile feedback systems, vibrotactile feedback is used either by vibration sensors or by other feedback techniques and mechanisms such as ultrasound or air pressure. These vibrational stimuli when they come into direct contact with the skin cause different sensations in proportion to the frequency and intensity used.

2.3 Haptic Rendering and Haptic Patterns

Haptic rendering is the process by which the user can touch, feel, and manipulate virtual objects [10, 17]. It aims to improve the user's experience in a virtual environment and provide a natural and intuitive interface. A case of tactile performance is the transmission of information about the physical properties of the object such as shape, elasticity, texture, mass, etc. The tactile performance, based on the method used, can provide many different feedback senses. According to Salisbury et al. [18], the tactile performance algorithms calculate the correct interaction forces between the visual representation of the interface within the virtual environment and the virtual objects that constitute it. A typical tactile feedback algorithm is synthesized by many factors to be effective. In this paper, we study a simple collision-detection algorithm that identifies collisions between objects in the virtual environment and provides information on where, when, and ideally, to what extent collisions have occurred. This is represented as a haptic feedback pattern that is rendered according to specific interaction scenario needs and aims to produce the appropriate feedback to the users. Haptic patterns are leveraged to enhance perceptual and sensory feedback and response, convey useful information, and enhance usability instead of 'beautifying' interactions unnecessary to the user experience.

2.4 Related Projects

There is a growing number of research projects that explore the potentials of using a combination of haptic feedback and mid-air interactions. In this section we present an overview of the research works that are related to our project. These can be grouped in two major categories, mid-air interactions that make use of electromechanical means to produce haptic feedback, and experimental methods that investigate alternative methods to produce haptic feedback. We also present research works related to mid-air interaction that combine depth camera motion tracking and haptics. According to Freeman et al. [19], there are four types of tactile feedback that can be used in mid-air interactions, tactile ultrasonic measurements, remote feedback from a ring worn on the pointer, remote feedback from a clock set worn on the wrist, and feedback directly from the phone (when held). In their experiment they focused on two different tactile responses: continuous and discrete. The results of this study identified that the discrete feedback did not give a great sense of feeling compared to the continuous, but many users preferred it as it was less disturbing compared to the continuous vibration. In their study Mazzoni et al. [20] presented the development of a wearable device that aims to enhance musical mood in cinematic entertainment through tactile sensations (vibration feedback). This research showed that vibrational stimuli at low intensity and frequency, causes tranquility to users, while vibrational stimuli with low intensity, but in higher frequencies, increase their motivation to interact. Vibrations of high intensity and high frequency had a major impact on the user's experience. A method that combines mid-air interactions and haptic feedback was developed by Feng et al. [21] who presented a waterproof, lightweight and small tactile device, worn on the finger, which consists of 4 3D printed microscopic airbags. The implementation is based on air pressure by a high-frequency speaker to provide tactile feedback to the user. Vivoxie introduced a pair of gloves (PowerClaw) that can produce temperature senses to its users (cold and heat). This device stimulates the skin and allows the senses of heat, cold, vibration and roughness of objects to simulate virtual reality. The device has limited power management and the actuators consume a big amount of electricity when switching between hot and cold, so it is not yet possible to wirelessly use the gloves [22].

The Leap Motion sensor is well known in this research field for mid-air interactions but still there are a few consumer products developed to provide vibrotactile feedback while using this sensor. Thought there are some good research examples around this field, as presented by Nguyen et al. [4], who developed a tactile feedback glove, with vibration sensors and an Arduino Mini Pro microcontroller, in mid-air interaction with the Leap Motion sensor. The conclusions of the evaluation showed that generally with the use of the glove the work was better compared to that without it [4]. A wearable device presented by Kim et al. [23], is based on vibration and heat feedback. They present a similar comparative evaluation to Nguyen et al. study, and identify that tactile support provide greater immersion to users.

In the following, some of the consumer products mentioned before, which provide vibrotactile feedback in addition to Leap Motion sensors interactions, are presented.

A well-known product is UltraHaptics, a multipoint, tactile, ultrasonic airborne system that uses ultrasound to deliver tactile feedback to specific parts of the user's hands.

For the evaluation of this system some experiments were performed to highlight feedback points with different touch properties and their recognition in smaller divisions. The results of this evaluation showed that it can create individual feedback points with high precision and that users have the ability to distinguish between different frequencies and vibrations [24]. Another example in tactile interaction with the Leap Motion sensor is Gloveone, which is a wearable device that provides users with tactile feedback by allowing them to interact with virtual objects on the computer screen or in virtual reality headsets. Users can feel the shape, weight, textures of the objects displayed on the screen, and can interact with them. In addition, they are able to feel sound waves, raindrops even the intensity of a virtual fire. It uses ten vibration sensors, which, depending on the object or the desired sensation, adjusts the provided vibration intensity. Finally, for better motion detection it uses independent finger tracking with 6 IMU (3 axes), manual orientation with 1 IMU (9 axes) and contact areas for digital and reliable gesture recognition. The VRtouch is also a wearable tactile feedback device, except that this technology is worn on each finger individually. It has a magnetic fastening system that makes it easier to place on each finger, it is light-weighted and has well-designed ergonomics, helping to exploit the natural and enjoyable user experience. It also supports the Leap Motion sensor and other similar positioning and movement systems.

3 Research and Design Considerations

The design phase of the wearable system followed an iterative process and initially involved research and data gathering, the modeling of collected data, and finally the formation of the design framework and the definition of design requirements and design specifications [25]. The research and framework definition phase were followed by a design phase which mainly involved the production of prototypes of the wearable system and a formative evaluation.

3.1 Design Requirements and Specifications

Based on desktop research, user research and contextual inquiry we collected requirements for the design of the wearable device [26]. By using recent research work on guidelines for designing wearable devices [27, 28], we have identified a need for a wearable device that can deliver tactile feedback to the user, be portable and have good ergonomics. It should provide a sense of safety and security and support users to wear it even in scenarios that require long term usage. It should be capable of adapting to the different needs of each user (anthropometric/physiology factors, hygiene, aesthetics, comfort, wearability, physical activity interference, supporting mid-air movement). Requirements for the wearable should be related to its ergonomics and ease of use, while tactile feedback should focus on providing immersion. The following table represents some design requirements and specifications that guided our design (Table 1).

Table 1. Design requirements and specifications for the wearable system.

Design requirements	Design specifications
Product aesthetics: Be aesthetically simple, not to attract the attention of the user	Simple aesthetic, use of black fabric. Small number of additional components on the device
Wearability: Size	Thin fabric and components (board and sensors) of small size
Wearability: Be light-weighted	Lightweight fabric, components, board and sensors
Comfort: Do not warm up the user's hand when wearing it	Thin fabric and no use of fabric in the inside part of the device
Comfort: Be easy to wear and remove, non-slippery	Use Velcro in two places for easy placement and removal from the hand
Anthropometry/Physiology: Respond to many users with different hand sizes	Elastic fabric and Velcro to change its size depending on the size of the user's hand
Appropriate Body Placement: The fabric shouldn't be tight on the user's hand	Do not consist of tight fabrics
Learnability: The user should understand how the device is worn	Have external and internal indications in order to be easier for the user to place it on his/her hand
Physical Activity Interference: Do not hinder the user's movements when wearing it	Place the objects on the device in appropriate points to facilitate movements of the hand
Wearability: portable	Portable device operation using battery
Safety: The user shouldn't perceive sensors and cables, so that they feel safe when wearing it	Sensors and cables covered with fabric in such a way not to be perceived by the user
Interaction and Ease of use: The vibrotactile feedback shouldn't be too intense, so that it doesn't cause annoyance to the user	Low intensity and short duration of vibrotactile feedback
Interaction and Ease of use: Vibrotactile feedback should have a good match to real time actions and be realistic	Match vibrotactile feedback with the depiction of the application, for example, when the tool comes into contact with the figurine to trigger feedback
Operational Lifetime: Long battery life	Use of a long-life lithium battery (750 mAh)
Connectivity: Easy connection of the device with the application	Connect the device to the computer via Bluetooth
Compatibility: The technology used should be compatible with Unity engine	Using the ESP32 DevKit, compatible with the Unity engine
Reliability and Fault Tolerance: Make the system efficient and effective	Fast and accurate system response without interference due to the use of the wearable device

3.2 Prototyping

The prototyping phase focused on enhancing an existing application [29] on the basis of the wearable device prototype that included the haptic feedback mechanisms. In this context the research team designed and developed a wearable prototype system, to enhance mid-air interaction and usability in the Cycladic sculpture application through vibrotactile feedback.

The focus was to enrich the interactions of the existing application using the wearable device prototype developed in this work. In this application the user constructs a Cycladic sculpture with mid-air hand movements using the Leap Motion controller. The interaction scenario involved three sub-scenarios or stages where the user is using three different sculpting tools to perform a number of tasks.

To amplify usability and user experience, we incorporated vibro-tactile haptic feedback in mid-air interactions. The first vibro-tactile feedback (user's palm) is activated upon tool selection while a wrong tool selection is expressed by a vibration with different intensity and sharpness. The vibration responses vary at each stage in terms of their intensity, duration, and the actual location on the hand in which they are activated. The focus of the designed haptic patterns was to provide a realistic feedback to the user depending on the interaction scenario at hand. For these reasons we carefully identified the points where the user would feel pressure and vibration if he performed the task in real life and based on these, we designed the haptic patterns for each feedback mechanism on every scenario.

Physical Prototype of the Wearable Device
The prototyping of the wearable device took place in two different phases (low-fidelity and medium-fidelity prototypes). The first focused in designing iteratively the early model of the actual wearable glove and initiate the technological tests of the actual hardware while the second mainly focused in understanding and designing the actual interactions and combine hardware, software and the physical wearable product.

The hardware that was used for the prototyping of the wearable device included, a desktop computer for running the actual application that the users interacted with, a Leap Motion controller for the capturing the position and the movements of the users' hand, a microcontroller devkit based on Espresif ESP32 board for doing the calculations related to the haptic feedback mechanisms and providing the means of wireless communication (Wi-Fi and Bluetooth) with the desktop computer, six coin vibration motors for the vibrotactile feedback placed on the edges of each finger and the center of the palm (Fig. 1), a rechargeable lithium battery (750 mAh). The physical product was designed by the use of elastic fabric for the main body of the wearable device glove, black Velcro stripes for controlling and providing variable size fit for the wearable device and flexible ribbon cables for connecting the vibration motors to the microcontroller.

The software used in this project was based on Arduino IDE for compiling the code of the microcontroller and Unity and the Unity Scripting API for the developing the desktop application and calculating the interactions. The schematic presented on the figure below provides an overview of the final wearable device configuration at a prototyping level (Fig. 1).

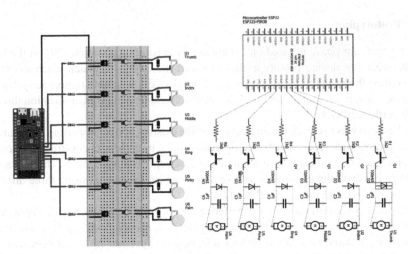

Fig. 1. Circuit Layout and Schematic of the vibration sensor circuit, ESP32 Devkit microcontroller, vibration motors, 1 KΩ resistors, 2N2222 NPN transistors, 1N4001 diode rectifiers, 1 μF ceramic capacitors and a breadboard.

Table 2. Pins to which the motors are associated, their designation in the code, the position on the board and the position on the wearable device.

MotorPin (code)	Pin (on board)	Correspondence with location to the wearable device
MotorPin1	22	Thumb
MotorPin2	28	Index
MotorPin3	27	Middle
MotorPin4	26	Ring
MotorPin5	25	Pinky
MotorPin6	24	Centre of the palm

Vibrotactile Feedback

As mentioned earlier, the vibro-tactile feedback was designed on the basis of a haptic mechanism that provided variable intensity, customizable duration, and location on the hand depending on the desirable interaction (Fig. 2).

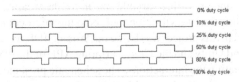

Fig. 2. Circuit diagram generated by the frequency of the PWM signal.

Intensity

The vibration intensity in each case on the sensor is defined by the frequency of the PWM signal, which in most pins is about 490 Hz. At Arduino Uno and similar boards, pin 5 and 6 have a frequency of about 980 Hz. Pulse Width Modulation (PWM) is a technique for achieving analogue results with digital media. The digital control is used to create a square wave, a signal that is on and off. The PWM signal is a digital square wave, frequency being constant, but this fraction of the time at which the signal is activated (the duty cycle) can be between 0% and 100%. This on-off pattern can simulate the voltages between on (5 V) and off (0 V) by changing the amount of time the signal passes over the time the signal erases. The variable value is the operating cycle: between 0 (always closed) and 255 (always open) and only integer numbers (int) are allowed. In this case, the variable value was set to 255 and in each case divided by a number. That is, the operating cycle is always 100% until it changes. The larger the number by which this variable is divided, the lower the vibration sensor intensity.

Duration

The duration of a vibratory feedback is defined by the Delay command. This command determines how long the sensor is running and any other command. The syntax of the command is: delay (ms) and the number entered in brackets is measured in milliseconds.

Location on the Wearable Device

In each interaction of the user with the system, the vibrational responses differ with respect to the palm points of the user on which they are activated each time.

Prototyping the Physical Wearable Device

In the first stage of fabrication of the wearable device we used leather that was cut and punched with special tools. Velcro was placed in two points so that it can be easily worn and adjust in size and four black elastic fabrics were sewn, for placement at the fingertips. This construction did not go further due to difficulties encountered with the material. Leather, although was a durable material, it finally appeared heavy and rigid and the addition of extra parts to it was difficult. It did not meet the design specifications of the wearable device in terms of weight and aesthetics as well as the proper operation of the leap motion sensor. Hand detection was tested with the Leap Motion sensor while the wearable device was placed in the user's hand and there were significant errors in the detection of hand and finger movements due to reflections developed from the material's surface.

In the second stage, the ends of the positive and negative cable of the vibration sensors were attached with wires so that they have longer length when placed on the device.

Materials that have been considered most suitable for the construction of the wearable device were then selected based on the criteria and specifications set above. The basic material for the "body" of the device is a black elastic fabric. At this stage, the central vibration motor was placed and sewed at the center of the palm on a 16 × 17 cm cut fabric. Velcro was also glued (as shown in Fig. 3) across the main area of the palm closed at the point between the thumb and the index. Further on, the fabric was sewed around the rest of the actuator motors and their cables and across the body of the wearable glove above the finger areas. An additional key part of the device is the elastic ribbons

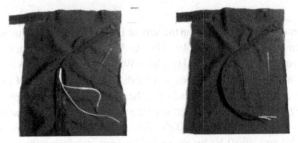

Fig. 3. Vibration motor sewed on elastic fabric.

(1.5 * 3.5 cm), which act as rings/fasteners and make it easy to place the sensors on the user's fingers. These parts were placed and then glued around the fingertips so that when the glove is worn the motors lie at the inner part of the fingertips and the cables goes around and over the fingers. At this stage, the different pieces of the device were placed on the hand in order to proceed with its construction. The purpose of this was to make some tests before sewing these parts to the rest of the device, to be as customizable as possible and applied to different hand sizes (Fig. 4).

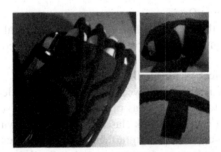

Fig. 4. Elastic "runner" joint stitched around a sensor cable

At this point, the first motor, which is placed on the user's thumb, was stitched at a distance of 10.5 cm from the fabric located at the middle left, at the distance between the two Velcros. This distance corresponds to the measurements of the average distance of the thumb from the rest of the palm. When a user bends his thumb, there must be the appropriate margin to make this move. The same applies for the rest of the motors. Still to achieve a greater fluctuation in the size of the parts ending at the fingertips, in addition to the elastic fabric surrounding the wires, the wires were positioned in such a way so that this flexible behavior to exist. More specifically, the two wires on the inside of the fabric form small folds, resulting in the fabric being elongated, the wires being unaffected but helping to form this movement. Hereupon, the five actuator motors where attached to the area close to the fingertips and were sewed on the main body of the wearable device. For the flexible wires not to be exposed at the top of the device they were boxed/ woven together with the actual fabric.

During the final design iteration few changes were made regarding the form of the device. These changes were made on the inside of the device, as some tests showed

Fig. 5. Medium fidelity prototype

that the fabric inside the palm made it difficult to accurately detect the hand by the leap motion sensor. A part of the fabric was removed from the inside of the device as shown above on Fig. 5.

4 Early Evaluation of Usability

During the iterative design processes, analyzed in the previous sections, we completed a number of formative evaluations with regards to the use of the wearable device in terms of the application scenarios. The purpose of the experimental evaluation of the wearable device was to determine its usability, the expediency of using haptic feedback in the specific application and whether it improves the users experience. On this basis, we also performed a comparative study regarding the use of the application in two distinct situations, one where interactions took place with mid-air interactions only and a second where the application was enhanced by the haptic wearable device. The evaluations criteria are divided in four categories, based on their characteristics. These are portability, usability, tactile feedback and user experience.

4.1 Evaluation Objectives and Criteria

Evaluation Protocol. First, we briefly described the system to the participants, then they were given a questionnaire, which included demographic characteristics, so that we could separate them into categories. After that, they used the system with and without the wearable device. Each time they used the system the participants completed a NASA TLX questionnaire, in order to compare the factors between the two. Finally, they completed a questionnaire based on their overall experience and the SUS usability questionnaire (Brooke, 1996), for the wearable device.

User Participants and Tasks. We interviewed 32 users (16 women, 16 men), most of whom where students (ages 18–30) and academics (ages 30 and above) who completed the sculpting scenarios in two situations (with and without haptic feedback).

The participants were separated at random in two groups:

- Group 1: Participants who used the application first using the wearable device and then without the wearable device.
- Group 2: Participants who used the application first without the wearable device and then with the wearable device.

These groups were also divided into two sub-groups based on their age:

- Sub-group A: Participants under the age of 30, mainly students participated in this group.
- Sub-group B: Participants over the age of 30, mainly academics and staff of the university community participated in this group.

4.2 Early Observations and Evaluation Results

The majority of users 75% indicated that the haptic feedback session was more immersive. Some male users 12.5%, experienced problems in wearing the device because their actual physiological characteristics (larger hands) where beyond the upper limits of the devices size. These users indicated problems in performing the tasks primarily because they were not able to fully or easily close their hands when grasping the virtual tools. The majority of users (more than 90%) stated that they better understood the sculpting operations they performed, they felt more confident in grasping, manipulating and using the virtual tools as well as touching and exploring solid geometric objects in the 3D environment. We identified that users tented to explore by touching objects in the 3D scenes when wearing the haptic device something that was not performed without it. Six users 19% experienced problems when the motion sensor stopped tracking their hands and had to re-initialize the scenarios. This happened in both sessions, 4 times with the wearable device and 2 times without it. One of these users found a workaround to initialize the identification of the hands in runtime by inserting and removing spontaneously both hands in the detection area. Three users stated that they preferred the vibration feedback generated from the motor located in their palm while others showed no preference. Most users 65.6% preferred transient vibration events (short-lived vibrations) compared to continuous events while most users 84.5% proposed to implement a calibration mechanism for the vibration intensity, something we implemented in later versions (Fig. 6).

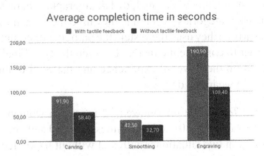

Fig. 6. Results of the comparative study of the average time taken to complete tasks, with and without haptic feedback, in seconds.

Design Considerations After the Evaluation
The results of the experiment were positive in terms of adding the wearable device to this system. Things to improve include, the improvement of the haptic textures related to

the scenarios, the introduction of a better calibration mechanism of the haptic feedback intensity depending on user preference and finally the actual re-design of the physical wearable device to afford a better leap sensor detection, left handed users and the possibility for multiple gloves for both hand support.

5 Conclusion and Future Work

This paper presented the research, design and prototyping of a vibro-tactile wearable device that adds haptic feedback when performing mid-air interactions. The role of vibro-tactile feedback has been extensively analyzed and similar commercial interaction systems and applications have been reviewed and presented. The wearable device was designed for complementing a VR sculpting application that incorporates mid-air interactions. The haptic feedback provided by the device, aims to simulate specific tasks related to the sculpting scenarios at hand.

The comparative study performed during the formative evaluation sessions, revealed the differences in the interaction between the original mid-air only application and the one enhanced with haptic feedback. We identified that the difficulty of understanding depth in the virtual environment in the first case was heavily improved when the haptic feedback was introduced with the wearable. User's perception of depth and the identification of the exact location of her/his hand in space was improved both in terms of actual performance based on metrics (time and accuracy) but also based on evidence acquired from interviews that captured usability and user experience (ease of use, cognitive overload in performing the tasks).

Moreover, an interesting finding indicated that the overall user's immersion was also enhanced because of the haptic feedback mechanisms. The majority of users stated that they better understood the sculpting operations they performed, they felt more confident in grasping, manipulating, and using the virtual tools as well as touching and exploring solid geometric objects in the 3D environment.

This work provided an initial starting point for further research in this area and set the basis for further investigation of other aspects related to the use of vibro-tactile feedback mechanisms in mid-air interaction. We currently perform a second comparative study related to the evaluation of workload when using or not mid-air haptic feedback mechanisms in tasks performed in virtual environments.

References

1. Attwenger, A.: Advantages and Drawbacks of Gesture-Based Interaction. Grin Verlag (2017)
2. Bruder, G., Steinicke, F., Sturzlinger, W.: To touch or not to touch? Comparing 2D touch and 3D mid-air interaction on stereoscopic tabletop surfaces. In: Proceedings of the 1st Symposium on Spatial User Interaction. pp. 9–16. ACM, New York (2013). https://doi.org/10.1145/2491367.2491369
3. Spano, L.D.: Developing touchless interfaces with GestIT. In: Paternò, F., de Ruyter, B., Markopoulos, P., Santoro, C., van Loenen, E., Luyten, K. (eds.) AmI 2012. LNCS, vol. 7683, pp. 433–438. Springer, Heidelberg (2012). https://doi.org/10.1007/978-3-642-34898-3_39
4. Nguyen, V.T.: Enhancing touchless interaction with the leap motion using a haptic glove. Comput. Sci. (2014)

5. O'hara, K., Harper, R., Mentis, H., Sellen, A., Taylor, A.: On the naturalness of touchless: putting the "interaction" back into NUI. ACM Trans. Comput. Hum. Interact. (TOCHI) **20**, 25 (2013)
6. Ernst, M.O., Banks, M.S.: Humans integrate visual and haptic information in a statistically optimal fashion. Nature **415**, 429 (2002)
7. Ernst, M.O., Banks, M.S., Bülthoff, H.H.: Touch can change visual slant perception. Nat. Neurosci. **3**, 69 (2000)
8. Ernst, M.O., Bülthoff, H.H.: Merging the senses into a robust percept. Trends Cogn. Sci. **8**, 162–169 (2004)
9. Gepshtein, S., Burge, J., Ernst, M.O., Banks, M.S.: The combination of vision and touch depends on spatial proximity. J. Vis. **5**, 7 (2005)
10. Lin, M.C., Otaduy, M.: Haptic Rendering: Foundations, Algorithms, and Applications. CRC Press, Boca Raton (2008)
11. Maereg, A.T., Nagar, A., Reid, D., Secco, E.L.: Wearable vibrotactile haptic device for stiffness discrimination during virtual interactions. Front. Robot. AI **4**, 42 (2017). https://doi.org/10.3389/frobt.2017.00042
12. Fogtmann, M.H., Fritsch, J., Kortbek, K.J.: Kinesthetic interaction: revealing the bodily potential in interaction design. In: Proceedings of the 20th Australasian Conference on Computer-Human Interaction: Designing for Habitus and Habitat, pp. 89–96. ACM, New York (2008). https://doi.org/10.1145/1517744.1517770
13. de la Barré, R., Chojecki, P., Leiner, U., Mühlbach, L., Ruschin, D.: Touchless interaction-novel chances and challenges. In: Jacko, J.A. (ed.) HCI 2009. LNCS, vol. 5611, pp. 161–169. Springer, Heidelberg (2009). https://doi.org/10.1007/978-3-642-02577-8_18
14. Vogiatzidakis, P., Koutsabasis, P.: Gesture elicitation studies for mid-air interaction: a review. MTI **2**, 65 (2018). https://doi.org/10.3390/mti2040065
15. Zhang, Z.: Microsoft kinect sensor and its effect. IEEE Multimed. **19**, 4–10 (2012). https://doi.org/10.1109/MMUL.2012.24
16. Carter, J., Fourney, D.: Research based tactile and haptic interaction guidelines. In: GOTHI 2005, p. 9 (2005)
17. Bicchi, A., Buss, M., Ernst, M.O., Peer, A. (eds.): The Sense of Touch and Its Rendering: Progress in Haptics Research. Springer Tracts in Advanced Robotics, vol. 45. Springer, Heidelberg (2008). https://doi.org/10.1007/978-3-540-79035-8
18. Salisbury, K., Conti, F., Barbagli, F.: Haptic rendering: introductory concepts. IEEE Comput. Graph. Appl. **24**, 24–32 (2004). https://doi.org/10.1109/MCG.2004.1274058
19. Freeman, E., Brewster, S., Lantz, V.: Tactile feedback for above-device gesture interfaces: adding touch to touchless interactions. In: Proceedings of the 16th International Conference on Multimodal Interaction, pp. 419–426. ACM, New York (2014). https://doi.org/10.1145/2663204.2663280
20. Mazzoni, A., Bryan-Kinns, N.: Mood Glove: a haptic wearable prototype system to enhance mood music in film. Entertain. Comput. **17**, 9–17 (2016). https://doi.org/10.1016/j.entcom.2016.06.002
21. Feng, Y.-L., Fernando, C.L., Rod, J., Minamizawa, K.: Submerged haptics: a 3-DOF fingertip haptic display using miniature 3D printed airbags. In: ACM SIGGRAPH 2017 Emerging Technologies. pp. 22:1–22:2. ACM, New York (2017). https://doi.org/10.1145/3084822.3084835
22. PowerClaw. https://vivoxie.com/en/powerclaw/index. Accessed 4 May 2020
23. Kim, M., Jeon, C., Kim, J.: A study on immersion and presence of a portable hand haptic system for immersive virtual reality. Sensors **17**, 1141 (2017). https://doi.org/10.3390/s17051141

24. Carter, T., Seah, S.A., Long, B., Drinkwater, B., Subramanian, S.: UltraHaptics: multi-point mid-air haptic feedback for touch surfaces. In: Proceedings of the 26th Annual ACM Symposium on User Interface Software and Technology, pp. 505–514. ACM, New York (2013). https://doi.org/10.1145/2501988.2502018
25. Goodwin, K.: Designing for the Digital Age: How to Create Human-Centered Products and Services. Wiley, Hoboken (2009)
26. Benyon, D.: Designing Interactive Systems: A Comprehensive Guide to HCI and Interaction Design. Pearson, Boston (2013)
27. Partheniadis, K., Stavrakis, M.: Design and evaluation of a digital wearable ring and a smartphone application to help monitor and manage the effects of Raynaud's phenomenon. Multimed. Tools Appl. **78**(3), 3365–3394 (2018). https://doi.org/10.1007/s11042-018-6514-3
28. Kordatos, G., Stavrakis, M.: Design and evaluation of a wearable system to increase adherence to rehabilitation programmes in acute cruciate ligament (CL) rupture. Multimed. Tools Appl. (2019). https://doi.org/10.1007/s11042-019-08502-3
29. Vosinakis, S., Koutsabasis, P., Makris, D., Sagia, E.: A kinesthetic approach to digital heritage using leap motion: the cycladic sculpture application. In: 2016 8th International Conference on Games and Virtual Worlds for Serious Applications (VS-GAMES), pp. 1–8. IEEE (2016). https://doi.org/10.1109/VS-GAMES.2016.7590334

Image Processing

Comparison of Gabor Filters and LBP Descriptors Applied to Spoofing Attack Detection in Facial Images

Wendy Valderrama$^{(\boxtimes)}$, Andrea Magadán$^{(\boxtimes)}$, Raúl Pinto, and José Ruiz

TecNM/Centro Nacional de Investigación y Desarrollo Tecnológico, Cuernavaca, Mexico
wendy.valderrama17ca@cenidet.edu.mx, andrea.ms@cenidet.tecnm.mx

Abstract. Spoofing attack detection using facial images is a problem that violates the security of systems that use face recognition technologies. The objective of this research is to show a performance comparison between two texture descriptors: Gabor Filters and Local Binary Patterns applied to the spoofing detection by means of images of the face in order to provide information of interest for future research. These algorithms were evaluated under the same conditions. The results of experimentation show that Gabor filters obtain better discriminant descriptors in synthetic images, making them a good option for applying systems that use facial biometrics.

Keywords: Spoofing · LBP · Gabor filters · Texture · Face biometrics

1 Introduction

The face is one of the most utilized biometric features used in detection authentication systems [1]. A person's face can be obtained more easily than other biometric features such as fingerprint or iris, through social networks or other web media and achieve the attack via photography, tablet, cell phone, mask, among others devices. Thus, these facial recognition systems are vulnerable to spoofing attacks at a relatively low cost. To have a good attack detection system, we propose to have texture descriptor techniques available to detect the difference between the image of a real person and the synthetic image of the person. This problem is further aggravated when it comes to images in an uncontrolled environment. A literature review of the area reveals that the traditional techniques used for the extraction of texture characteristics on the face are the local binary patterns (LBP) and Gabor Filters.

LBP is one of the most used texture description techniques of the last decade. In the specific case of spoofing detection, a combination of LBP with images illuminated by a flash is used, because the flash highlights the texture of the objects helping to obtain better descriptors [2]. They mention that the highest performance was with iPad photographs, reaching 0.50% in the Half Total Error Rate (HTER) metric with a normal lighting environment and 0.66% with poor lighting in the same image database. The percentage increase is derived from the use of the flash since this highlights the reflection and lack

© Springer Nature Switzerland AG 2020
H. Florez and S. Misra (Eds.): ICAI 2020, CCIS 1277, pp. 395–408, 2020.
https://doi.org/10.1007/978-3-030-61702-8_27

of depth of a printed image unlike a person, resulting in a discriminating method for spoofing detection in poor lighting. It is possible to use the light reflection that can exist in an image [3], in this case the reflection is natural and not caused by a flash; the results that they reported with the Equal Error Rate (EER) metric in a percentage of 4.89% with the CASIA image dataset [4] and 2.44% in the MSU image database [5].

Villan et al. developed a system that works like a video where the lighting conditions change according to their location and the time of day [6]. They use LBP to extract texture descriptors and focus on the problem of changes in light intensity and how this affects the description of objects. The results obtained are satisfactory, reaching an accuracy between 84% and 90% according to the lighting present in the image; it is important to mention that the results are relevant because they train with one image database and perform the evaluation with another; this is of a particular interest for research that requires a pre-trained system. There are numerous authors using variants of LBP [7–10], such is the case of Angadi and Kagawde [11], in whose approach they propose to use both structural information and magnitude information of the 3×3 neighborhood of each pixel, with a central gray level value to achieve more discriminative descriptors than were applied in the NUAA image database [12], obtaining results of 98.89% accuracy. A variation of LBP is presented by Kartika et al. where they extract the characteristics by means of LBP and the Local Binary Pattern Variance (LBPV), the union of the two results integrate the final vector of characteristics for the photo attack detection [10]. Another difference from the other works lies in the classifier, since most of these systems use the Support Vector Machine classifier (SVM) and this article uses the k-neighbors classifier. It is important to note that being a classifier that does not need training, the feature vector must be discriminant enough to obtain good classification results; even with the aforementioned limitation they report reaching an 87.22% accuracy with the NUAA image database [12].

Another of the classic algorithms used to describe texture of faces is the Gabor filter family; however, few recent investigations focused on facial attack detection use this technique as a descriptor. Tsitiridis and others use characteristics extracted by Gabor filters, proposing a hierarchical structure of progressive layers that process and train from the visual information of the faces using infrared [13], achieving results of 99% precision in an image bank of their own creation.

Another important aspect within spoofing investigations is the classification algorithms; in their choice it should be considered that it is treated as a two-class classification task where the training set differs from the online attack [14]. In this paper the classification methods used are: random forest, support vector machines and multilayer perceptron (MLP) whose different recognition approaches will allow to objectively evaluate the efficiency of the described descriptors.

The contribution of this work is to compare the performance of the two most used texture descriptors in the task of photo attack detection in images that have poor lighting and considering that the training and testing stages are carried out with different image database and different acquisition conditions We tested the system with a public benchmark: NUAA Photograph Imposter Database [12] that consists of 12614 registers of faces of 15 people, divided into 5105 real images and 7509 of attacks by photographs. The second image database is our own and it has 1000 images of 5 people, divided into

500 real images and 500 photo attacks using images taken with a cell phone. Performance was compared using accuracy, error rate, and F-measure metrics.

The paper is organized as follows: in Sect. 2 the processing, texture descriptors and classification techniques are described, in Sect. 3 the experimentation cases are explained and the results obtained are discussed, and finally in Sect. 4 the paper concludes.

2 Attack Detection System

The development of the spoofing detection system presented here is based on the five stages of an artificial vision system, see Fig. 1, which according to [15] are:

1. *Acquisition* which is covered with the two image databases already mentioned.
2. *Preprocessing* that aims to improve the conditions of the original images, in this case three techniques were implemented that reported good results: histogram equalization [16–19], retina model [19, 20] and multi-scale retinex [19, 20].
3. *Segmentation* tries to locate in the image, as precisely as possible, the object or regions of interest; this process was performed using the Dlib library [21].
4. *Description* of the object or region used its attributes of shape, color or texture, mainly. As already mentioned, the LBP and Gabor Filters descriptor techniques were implemented. It is important to mention that five Haralick texture measurements were calculated on the images resulting from both techniques, which are: contrast, homogeneity, Inverse Difference Moment (IDM), entropy and mean.
5. *Object recognition* was carried out using the random forest, support vector machines and Multi-Layer Perceptron (MLP).

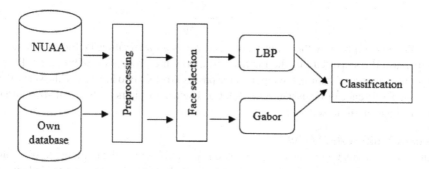

Fig. 1. System stages diagram.

The following subsections follow this stages.

2.1 Preprocessing Techniques

Histogram Equalization [22]
Histogram equalization is a popular and powerful approach to eliminate poor lighting from images. The histogram function distributes the most intensive frequency pixel

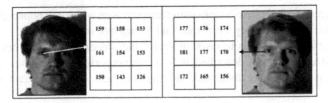

Fig. 2. 3 × 3 pixels values of the left eye portion before and after applying the histogram.

value. As a consequence, the original pixel information that changes the appearance of the face is lost as shown in Fig. 2.

The general histogram formula improves the contrast so that the information that is hidden, due to the lighting factor, becomes visible. G is considered to be the gray level image while i shows the appearance of gray pixels in the image n_t times. Similarly, N is the total number of pixels in the image. Mathematically it can be represented as:

$$F(p_k) = \sum_{i=0}^{k} \frac{n_t}{n} \cdot (G - 1) \tag{1}$$

Retina Model [19, 20]
Retina shaping is used to deal with uneven lighting conditions, mimicking the performance of the human retina. This preprocessing technique is made up of three layers: a) Photo receptor layer, b) External plexiform layer (OPL) and c) Internal plexiform layer.

The photo receiver's layer aims to highlight details at night or under bright signs. To exploit and replace this ability, a nonlinear function based on the Naka-Rushton equation [23] is used, as shown in Eq. 2.

$$Y = \frac{X}{X + X_0} \tag{2}$$

Where X represents the input values and X_0 is an adaptation factor, which varies to increase the sensitivity of the method. To model the processing within the OPL for illumination normalization, the input image passes through two low pass Gaussian filters and one Difference of Gaussian Filter (DoG). The use of filters of different sizes allows the elimination of noise.

Retinex Multi-scale [17–20]
Luminosity model that achieves simultaneous compression of the dynamic range, color consistency and interpretation of luminosity with the aim of improving the fidelity of color images to human observation.

Images with large lighting discontinuities are susceptible to halo effects after being processed by the Single Scale Retinex (SSR) approach. To overcome this problem, an extension of the SSR algorithm called multiscale retinex (MR) was created, it generates a combination of images produced by SSR, but with different Gaussian widths. Reflectante in the MR approach is defined by:

$$R(x, y) = \sum_{n=1}^{N} \omega_n \{ \log[I(x, y)] - \log[F(x, y) * I(x, y)] \} \tag{3}$$

Where $\sum_{n=1}^{N} \omega_n$ represents the weighted sum of the Gaussian filters with different scales N and a weighting factor ω_n

2.2 Texture Descriptor Techniques

LBP

The Local Binary Pattern (LBP) descriptor is a simple and powerful representation of texture characteristics; it is defined as a gray scale invariant measure, derived from a general definition of the texture in a local neighborhood. The original proposal was described by Harwood and Ojala in 1995 [24], later an operator was derived which allows modifying the sizes of the area of interest and the neighborhoods for the pixel of interest described by [25]. The derivation consisting in the establishment of the parameters called R and P, where R corresponds to the distance (radius) taken from the source pixel and P the number of neighbors used to calculate LBP. Mathematically defined for $R > 0$ and $P > 1$ how:

$$LBP_{P,R}(x_C, y_C) = \sum_{P=0}^{P-1} s(g_p - g_c)2^P \tag{4}$$

Where x_C, y_C correspond to the position of the pixel of interest in the image, g_p is the center pixel value, g_c the value the circular neighbors of the central pixel, and 2^P the weight assigned to each operation between the central pixel and the neighbor, finally to $s(g_p - g_c)$ values of 1 and 0 are assigned.

This method and its variants are widely implemented to describe facial information and have achieved good results in detection of photo attack [19]. This work uses the classic form of LBP with default values.

Gabor Filters

Gabor filters are widely used in signal and image processing. It is a linear filter whose impulse response is a sinusoidal function multiplied by a Gaussian function [26]. Each Gabor filter is an oriented, elliptical band pass filter that define a sampling of the frequency space. Gabor filters are characterized by two efficient properties, orientation selectivity and location frequency. These properties resemble those of the human visual system [27].

Gabor filters are functions similar to themselves, if you consider the function $g(x, y)$ like the Gabor Wavelet matrix, where $g(x, y)$ is the center of the Gaussian wave. One can create a bank of filters similar to themselves by scaling and rotating the function $g(x, y)$. For the creation of these filters, a scale and 2 orientations are used ($0°$ and $45°$). The values that were used in the Gabor Filters are, *sigma 4, theta 0, lambda 10* and *gamma 0.5* which were obtained experimentally after a series of tests with the image banks used. The choice of these parameters is a problem in itself and depends a lot on the image to be analyzed, so that some parameters can lead to successful descriptors in one case and not in others. There are works in the literature that evaluate and propose how to determine these parameters [28].

2.3   Texture Measurements of *Haralick*

The measures of contrast, homogeneity, inverse moment of difference (IDM), entropy and mean, are based on the proposal by Haralick [29] and are used in this experiment because they have good texture characteristics used in spoofing detection [16], which are extracted after applying the texture descriptors, where:

- i is the row number and j is the column number
- $C_{i,j}$ It is the probability in the cell i, j
- N is the number of rows or columns

Contrast [30]: It is a measure of the local variation in an image. It reaches a high value when the image has a lot of contrast and has a low value when the high values of the matrix are close to the main diagonal.

$$C_1 = \sum_{i,j} (i-j)^2 . C_{i,j} \tag{5}$$

Homogeneity [30]: It is the opposite of contrast and is calculated using the equation:

$$C_4 = \sum_{i,j} \frac{C_{i,j}}{1 + (i-j)^2} \tag{6}$$

Inverse Difference Moment (IDM) [31]: The IDM increases when the contrast between the pixel pairs decreases.

$$\sum_{i,j=0}^{N-1} \frac{P_{i,j}}{1 + (i-j)^2} \tag{7}$$

Entropy [30]: This descriptor measures the randomness of the image, reaching its maximum when all the elements of the co-occurrence matrix are equal.

$$C_3 = \sum_{i,j} -C_{i,j} . log_2 [C_{i,j}] \tag{8}$$

Mean [30]: The mean is given by the equation.

$$MD_{ni} = 1/N \sum_{j,k} |D_{ni}(b_j, b_k)| \tag{9}$$

2.4 Classification Algorithms

Two classifiers were used to make a comparison with support vector machines, which is the most widely used classifier in the literature, allowing the comparison of performance in spoofing detection under the same conditions.

- Support vector machine (MVS) with polynomial kernel and default parameters in openCV [32].
- Multilayer Perceptron (MLP) [18] with 5 hidden layers.
- Random forest with depth 2000.

2.5 Metrics

Three measures based on the confusion matrix [33] are used to evaluate the classification results, which allows knowing the distribution of the error throughout the classes. The general structure of the confusion matrix is shown in Fig. 3, the values that are along the main diagonal of the matrix, represent the correct classifications and those that are along the secondary diagonal represent mistakes (confusion) between classes. To evaluate the performance of the system, the accuracy metrics (Eq. 10), error rate (Eq. 11) and F-measure (Eq. 12) are calculated; these are briefly described below.

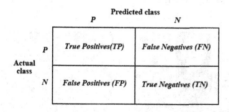

Fig. 3. General structure of the confusion matrix [33].

Accuracy: Overall percentage of correctly classified data. Refers to the dispersion of the set of values, the smaller the dispersion the greater the accuracy. It is represented by the ratio between the number of correct predictions (both positive and negative) and the total of predictions.

$$Accuracy = \frac{TP + TN}{TP + TN + FN + FP} \tag{10}$$

Error Rate: Percentage of incorrectly classified data.

$$Error\ rate = \frac{FP + FN}{TP + TN + FN + FP} \tag{11}$$

F-measure: Provides a way to combine precision and recall in a single measurement that captures both properties.

$$F - Measure = \frac{2 * Precision * Recall}{Precision + Recall} \tag{12}$$

3   Experimentation and Results

For this experimentation, the C++ language was used with the OpenCV library, the NUAA public database and ours own image database.

NUAA Photograph Imposter Database [12]
This image database is made up of 12614 images of which 5105 are real access photographs will refer to images taken of live human subjects and 7509 attack photographs will refer to images of printed photographs or screen-displayed videos. They have an RGB format, the images were taken in three sessions with different lighting, and the participants were in front of the camera and avoided eye and head movements making. The original images have different dimensions, for this project they were normalized to a size of 200 × 200 pixels, see Fig. 4.

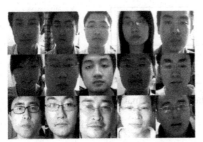 

Real access images   Attack photo images

Fig. 4. Sample of images from NUAA database [12]

Own Batabase
Our own database contains 1000 images of 10 people, acquired in real environments, with different resolution from web cameras, changes in light intensity, scale and background. Of these, 500 are real access data and 500 attack photos replicated by digital means by placing a cell phone in front of a web camera of a TOSHIBA satellite laptop with a resolution of 96 pixels per inch; images were normalized to a size of 640 × 480 pixels, see Fig. 5.

The characteristics vector for the classification was made up of 10 variables: 5 Haralick measurements by description technique (LBP and Gabor Filters). Three experimental cases were carried out.

Real photo images   Attack photo images

Fig. 5. Sample of images from own database.

Case 1: Training and testing with the same image database.
Case 2: Training and testing with a different image database.
Case 3: Preprocessing the images before training, then testing with a different image database.

3.1   Training and Testing with the Same Image Database

The goal of this test is to determine the performance of the system when the database for training and the validation database are the same but the sets are disjoint. Two tests were performed: the first test with the NUAA image database with 5000 images for training and 7814 for testing. The second test was with our own database that included 100 images for training and 900 for testing. Table 1 shows the results obtained with the NUAA image database, while Table 2 shows the results obtained with our own image database.

Table 1. Results of training and testing with the NUAA database.

		Accuracy	Error rate	F-measure
SVM	Gabor	20.44	75.58	20.2
	LBP	30.39	61.35	28.81
MLP	Gabor	92.88	6.33	92.36
	LBP	86.69	13.26	85.68
Random forest	Gabor	**96.3**	**3.79**	**95.94**
	LBP	88.66	12.11	87.58

As can be seen in Table 1 and Table 2, the best results in both datasets are obtained with the Gabor Filters. The random forest algorithm obtained a 95.94% in F-measure of and MLP is in second place with the NUAA database. In our own dataset the MLP neural network in combination with the Gabor Filters reaches 100% with the same metric and a slightly lower value with the LBP descriptor. We expected these results because we use the same database in both stages. Unlike what was reported in the state of the art, the SVM classifier obtained a much lower result with both descriptors in both evaluations. This may indicate that it is necessary to experiment with different kernels and look for the optimal values for their parameters to reach the percentages mentioned in the literature.

Table 2. Results of training and testing with the own dataset.

		Accuracy	Error rate	F-measure
SVM	Gabor	30.67	69.33	30.06
	LBP	46.67	53.33	46.64
MLP	Gabor	**100**	**0**	**100**
	LBP	99.89	0.11	99.89
Random forest	Gabor	99.33	0.67	99.33
	LBP	89.56	10.44	89.54

3.2   Training and Testing with a Different Image Database

This test aims to review the generalization of the model obtained and the ability to describe the techniques used. In this case:

- The training was carried out with the NUAA database: 5000 images were taken for training, of which 2500 are real access images and 2500 photo attack images.
- The testing was carried out with ours own image database: 900 images of which 450 are real images and 450 with cell photo images.

As expected and how we showed in Table 3, the percentage of accuracy decreased considerably, the maximum value reached is 67. 33% with the combination of random forest and LBP algorithms; however, with the F-measure metric, which gives more impartial information, the combination of the LBP descriptor with the MLP classifier reaches a slightly higher value, with the difference between the two being 0.07%. We noted that also in this case, SVM is the worst performing classifier, as already mentioned this could be due to various factors such as the kernel used, the implementation or the classifier configuration.

Table 3. Classification results with different bench for training and testing.

		Accuracy	Error rate	F-measure
SVM	Gabor	44	56	42
	LBP	39.89	60.11	38.98
MLP	Gabor	54.44	45.56	52.13
	LBP	65	35	**64.99**
Random forest	Gabor	60.33	39.67	52.93
	LBP	**67.33**	**32.67**	64.92

3.3 Processing Images and Training and Testing with Different Image Databases

The test goal was to review whether improving the lighting conditions of the images can help to have a better description of the texture and thereby improve the performance of the system in facial spoofing detecting. A problem to consider is that many investigations on facial recognition work uncontrolled environments, therefore, the problem of changes in light intensity present in the images should be analyzed. Three preprocessing algorithms are contemplated for this test: histogram equalization, the retina model and multi-scale retinex, which are the most widely used and best performing techniques for lighting the face. In Fig. 6 you can see a sample of the result of applying the three algorithms to images with poor lighting.

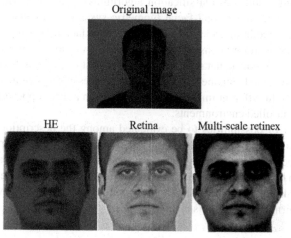

Fig. 6. Results of applying the three preprocessing algorithms to images with poor lighting.

Table 4 shows the results of the accuracy metric of the classification algorithms in combination with the two description techniques used and the applied processing algorithm, where *WP* indicates the results that were obtained Without Preprocessing.

Table 4. Classification results with the accuracy metric.

		WP	HE	RETINEX	RETINA
SVM	Gabor	44	49	45.78	50
	LBP	39.89	50	37.33	57
MLP	Gabor	54.44	69.78	60	31.67
	LBP	65	**79.67**	54.33	**67.33**
Random Forest	Gabor	60.33	32.78	**60**	50
	LBP	**67.33**	37.44	56	66.33

As can be seen, the performance of the system was higher with respect to the values obtained in Table 3. In this case, the best result was achieved with the application of an equalization in combination with LBP and the MLP classifier, reaching 79.67% and in second place, using Gabor filters. Reviewing the results obtained, it is apparent that applying the HE algorithm improves the performance of the descriptors and the performance of the classifiers; however, the random forest classifier has the best results when no processing technique is applied. The application of the RETINA model obtains the second place, with the RETINEX technique contributing least to the improvement of the images. Again, the SVM classifier got the worst results.

Discussion: In many of the investigations on face photo attack detection, training and evaluation are carried out with the same image database [2, 10, 11, 34], reporting high results even with traditional classification algorithms as in test 1. However, we recommend considered that in real facial biometric systems you cannot have the same information for the training and for the testing stage. In fact, in real applications disjoint sets are used and therefore consideration should be given to working with processing and description techniques that support obtaining a best model with high efficiency.

The results obtained with the application of preprocessing algorithms before training and evaluation with different image datasets indicate an area of opportunity to analyze, applied to uncontrolled environments.

The number of possibilities to be evaluated among the description, classifier and preprocessing algorithms are an opportunity area to analyze to find and propose a better solution for spoofing detection systems. An example of this is that, although in the literature it can be found that the most used classifier is SVM, with this experimentation it was observed that it might not be the best option; however, more evidence will be needed to reaffirm or rule out this claim.

4   Conclusions

This article presented the development of an intelligent system for spoofing detection by automatic analysis of real and synthetic facial images. Three preprocessing techniques, two of the best texture descriptors and three classic classification algorithms were evaluated. The results obtained show that the best performance was obtained with the combination of the histogram equalization, the LBP descriptor and the MLP neural network. For future work, variants of the LBP descriptor will be evaluated and will be combined with deep learning techniques.

Acknowledgements. We thanked to TecNM for the financial support provided through the project with the code 9091.20-P.

References

1. Galbally, J., Marcel, S., Fierrez, J.: Biometric antispoofing methods: a survey in face recognition. IEEE Access **2**, 1530–1552 (2014)

2. Chan, P.P.K., et al.: Face liveness detection using a flash against 2D spoofing attack. IEEE Trans. Inf. Forensics Secur. **13**, 521–534 (2018)
3. Kim, I., Ahn, J., Kim, D.: Face spoofing detection with highlight removal effect and distortions. In: IEEE International Conference on Systems, Man, and Cybernetics, pp. 4299–4304 (2016)
4. Zhang, Z., et al.: A face antispoofing database with diverse attacks. In: 2012 5th IAPR International Conference on Biometrics, pp. 26–31 (2012)
5. Patel, K., Han, H., Jain, A.K.: Secure face unlock: spoof detection on smartphones. IEEE Trans. Inf. Forensics Secur. **11**, 2268–2283 (2016)
6. Fernandez Villan, A., Carus Candas, J.L., Usamentiaga Fernandez, R., Casado Tejedor, R.: Face recognition and spoofing detection system adapted to visually-impaired people. IEEE Lat. Am. Trans. **14**, 913–921 (2016)
7. Xiong, F., Abdalmageed, W.: Unknown presentation attack detection with face RGB images. In: 2018 IEEE 9th International Conference on Biometrics Theory, Applications and Systems, pp. 1–9 (2018)
8. Li, L., Feng, X., Jiang, X., Xia, Z., Hadid, A.: Face anti-spoofing via deep local binary patterns. In: IEEE International Conference on Image Processing (ICIP), ICIP 2017, pp. 101–105 (2018)
9. Boulkenafet, Z., Komulainen, J., Hadid, A.: On the generalization of color texture-based face anti-spoofing. Image Vis. Comput. **77**, 1–9 (2018)
10. Kartika, A., Kusuma, I.B., Agung, T., Wirayuda, B., Nur, K.: Image spoofing detection using local binary pattern and local binary pattern variance. Int. J. Inf. Commun. Technol. **4**, 11–18 (2019)
11. Angadi, S.A., Kagawade, V.C.: Detection of face spoofing using multiple texture descriptors. In: 2018 International Conference on Computational Techniques, Electronics and Mechanical Systems (CTEMS), pp. 151–156 (2019). https://doi.org/10.1109/ctems.2018.8769129
12. Tan, X., Li, Y., Liu, J., Jiang, L.: Face liveness detection from a single image with sparse low rank bilinear discriminative model. In: Daniilidis, K., Maragos, P., Paragios, N. (eds.) ECCV 2010. LNCS, vol. 6316, pp. 504–517. Springer, Heidelberg (2010). https://doi.org/10.1007/978-3-642-15567-3_37
13. Tsitiridis, A., Conde, C., Ayllon, B.G., Cabello, E.: Bio-inspired presentation attack detection for face biometrics. Front. Comput. Neurosci. **13**, 1–17 (2019)
14. Li, X., Komulainen, J., Zhao, G., Yuen, P.C., Pietikainen, M.: Generalized face anti-spoofing by detecting pulse from face videos. In: Proceedings of the International Conference on Pattern Recognition (ICPR), pp. 4244–4249 (2017). https://doi.org/10.1109/icpr.2016.7900300
15. Martinsanz, G.P., de la Cruz García, J.M.: Visión por Computador (2002)
16. Wagh, P., Chaudhari, J., Thakare, R., Patil, S.: Attendance system based on face recognition using eigen face and PCA algorithms. In: International Conference on Green Computing and Internet of Things (ICGCIoT), pp. 303–308 (2015)
17. Shah, J.H., Sharif, M., Raza, M., Murtaza, M.: Robust face recognition technique under varying illumination. J. Appl. Res. Technol. **13**, 97–105 (2015)
18. Lumini, A., Nanni, L., Brahnam, S.: Ensemble of texture descriptors and classifiers for face recognition. Appl. Comput. Inform. **13**, 79–91 (2017)
19. Juefei-xu, F., Savvides, M.: Encoding and decoding local binary patterns for harsh face illumination normalization. In: 2015 IEEE International Conference on Image Processing (ICIP), pp. 3220–3224 (2015). https://doi.org/10.1109/icip.2015.7351398
20. Ochoa-villegas, M.A., Nolazco-flores, J.A., Barron-cano, O., Kakadiaris, I.A.: Addressing the illumination challenge in two- dimensional face recognition: a survey. IET Comput. Vis. **9**, 978–992 (2015)
21. King, D.: dlib C++ Library (2015). www.Dlib.Net
22. Pizer, S.M., et al.: Adaptive histogram equalization and its variations. Comput. Vis. Graph. Image Process. **39**, 355–368 (1987)

23. Vu, N.S., Caplier, A.: Illumination-robust face recognition using retina modeling. In: 2009 16th IEEE International Conference on Image Processing (ICIP), pp. 3289–3292 (2009). https://doi.org/10.1109/icip.2009.5413963
24. Harwood, D., Ojala, T., Pietikäinen, M., Kelman, S., Davis, L.: Texture classification by center-symmetric auto-correlation, using Kullback discrimination of distributions. Pattern Recogn. Lett. **16**, 1–10 (1995)
25. Mäenpää, T., Pietikainen, M.: Texture analysis with local binary patterns. In: Handbook of Pattern Recognition and Computer Vision, pp. 197–216 (2005). https://doi.org/10.1142/978 9812775320
26. Gabor, B.D.: Theory of communication. J. Inst. Electr. Eng. III Radio Commun. Eng. **93**, 429–444 (1945)
27. Ameur, B., Belahcene, M., Masmoudi, S., Derbel, A.G. Ben Hamida, A.: A new GLBSIF descriptor for face recognition in the uncontrolled environments. In: Proceedings of the IEEE 3rd International Conference on Advanced Technologies for Signal and Image Processing, ATSIP, pp. 3–8 (2017). https://doi.org/10.1109/atsip.2017.8075591
28. Bovik, A.C., Clark, M., Geisler, W.S.: Multichannel texture analysis using localized spatial filters. IEEE Trans. Pattern Anal. Mach. Intell. **12**, 55–73 (1990)
29. Agarwal, A., Singh, R., Vatsa, M.: Face anti-spoofing using Haralick features. In: 2016 IEEE 8th International Conference on Biometrics Theory, Applications and Systems, BTAS 2016, pp. 1–6 (2016). https://doi.org/10.1109/btas.2016.7791171
30. Jiménez, G.M.: Extracción de características de textura basada en Transformada Wavelet Discreta. Diss. Tesis Grado, Univ. Sevilla, Sevilla, España, pp. 17–29 (2008)
31. Ríos-Díaz, J., Martínez-Payá, J. J., Del Baño Aledo, M.E.: El análisis textural mediante las matrices de co-ocurrencia (GLCM) sobre imagen ecográfica del tendón rotuliano es de utilidad para la detección cambios histológicos tras un entrenamiento con plataforma de vibración. Cult. Cienc. y Deport **4**, 91–102 (2009)
32. Kumar, A., Narain, Y.: Evaluation of face recognition methods in unconstrained environments. Procedia Comput. Sci. **48**, 644–651 (2015)
33. Basso, D.: Propuesta de Métricas para Proyectos de Explotación de Información. Rev. Latinoam. Ing. Softw. **2**, 157 (2015)
34. Song, L., Ma, H.: Face liveliness detection based on texture and color features. In: 2019 IEEE 4th International Conference on Cloud Computing and Big Data Analysis (ICCCBDA), pp. 418–422 (2019)

Deep Transfer Learning Model for Automated Screening of Cervical Cancer Cells Using Multi-cell Images

Vinay Khobragade, Naunika Jain, and Dilip Singh Sisodia[✉]

National Institute of Technology Raipur, Raipur, India
vinay@codevector.in, naunikajain@gmail.com, dssisodia.cs@nitrr.ac.in

Abstract. In the automated screening of cervical cancer using raw micro scoping images, the segmentation of individual cells is time taking and error prone. Therefore, extracting individual cells automatically during inference time is not possible. The automated classification models based on the extraction of hand-crafted features such as texture, morphology, etc. are not very accurate always. In this article, a transfer learning based deep EfficientNet model is used for screening of cervical cancer without any segmentation for reducing manual errors and improving time constraints. Initially, the EfficientNet is trained on the dataset containing original images from the ImageNet dataset and then on the dataset containing the cervical cell microscopic images that consists of different categories of cervix cells. This method has been evaluated on the Herlev Pap smear dataset. Instead of working on individual cells like previous methods, we used to work on images having multiple cells. The number of cells inferred per unit time drastically increases. Results show that EfficientNet model performs well in classification, when applied to the Herlev benchmark Pap smear dataset and evaluated using ten-fold cross-validation. The used model is promising in terms of the time required for the inference as compared to other methods. The performance comparison with other models shows that the accuracy and other scores obtained by EfficientNet is improved with reduction processing time.

Keywords: Cervical cancer · Deep learning · EfficientNet · Transfer learning · Pap smear dataset

1 Introduction

Artificial Intelligence (AI) has helped progress medical sciences. Various AI techniques such as machine learning, deep learning is extensively used for automated screening of various disease using radiology and other images [1]. However, deep learning models requires huge amount of labeled training data from similar domain for proper learning but scarcity of labeled training data in medical field poses challenges in deploying deep learning models [2]. The use of transfer learning supplemented the deep learning algorithms to exceed human abilities and

© Springer Nature Switzerland AG 2020
H. Florez and S. Misra (Eds.): ICAI 2020, CCIS 1277, pp. 409–419, 2020.
https://doi.org/10.1007/978-3-030-61702-8_28

understand the finest details in labeled data scared medical diagnosis. The use of use of transfer learning in training of deep learning models is one of the promising methods of diagnosis of various diseases.

Cervical cancer is very common among women making it the fourth most common cancer in women globally [3]. It is highly treatable if detected at an early stage. There may be few human errors while detecting cancerous blood cells, to improvise this technique and reduce time constraints is the importance of our work. It is highly impossible in real-time to screen the cancerous cell manually with limited certified pathologists in India, so our project aims to reduce the time constraints and human efforts behind the scenes and make the process of screening faster and more accurate by reducing human errors.

Cervical cancer is found in the cells of the Cervix. It is part of the reproductive system in women. Cervix is in the lower part of the uterus that connects to the vagina and is one of the essential parts of a woman's body. Cervical cancer is one of the bog-standard types of cancer that women are suffering. Early-stage cervical cancer generally produces no signs or symptoms, so they are difficult to detect, thus screening regularly is required. Figure 1 shows visual information of normal and cancerous cells from the Herlev Dataset. Figure 1.a, 1.b, and 1.c are normal cells, while the rest are abnormal cells. The healthy cells generally are round. The cytoplasm is not in irregular shape and the nucleus is also present properly inside the cytoplasm. These visual properties of the cells can be exploited to use vision-based algorithms along with machine learning and deep learning to automate the task of screening of cervical cancer.

Cervix are covered by a thin layer of tissue where abnormal growth of cells is seen. The cells tend to grow at a faster rate in comparison to the normal growth, they are seen to develop a tumor. Cervix cancer is caused when the cells growth is very fast and detected in routine checkups through micro scoping images of smear samples. It is important to detect cervical cancer at an early stage before it enters a chronic stage.

The method presented in this paper help in the screening of cervical cancer by detecting cells are cancerous (malignant) or not (normal). The image processing and automated analysis of raw micro scoping images can be done using deep learning. We have used pap smear samples to test for the screening methods and tried to bring results that are both efficient in time and accuracy.

2   Related Work

The research in automated screening of cervical cancer was started back in the year 2000 [4]. The earlier methods used machine learning algorithms such as Support Vector Machine (SVM) for the classification task. The task was broken into steps that required feature engineering. The feature engineering required some help from the experts in the field to understand what is going on in a cervical cancer slide image sample.

Recent advances in the field rely on deep learning based neural networks. Convolution Neural Networks have played a major role in vision-based tasks.

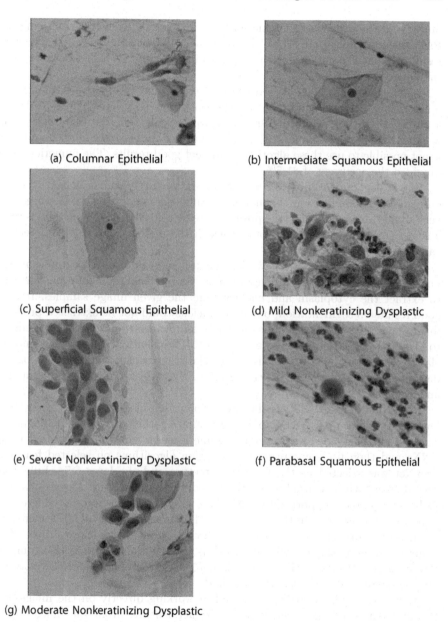

(a) Columnar Epithelial

(b) Intermediate Squamous Epithelial

(c) Superficial Squamous Epithelial

(d) Mild Nonkeratinizing Dysplastic

(e) Severe Nonkeratinizing Dysplastic

(f) Parabasal Squamous Epithelial

(g) Moderate Nonkeratinizing Dysplastic

Fig. 1. Different type of cells in Herlev Dataset (byriel)

The deep learning networks do not require extra feature engineering as was required earlier. Features can be still be extracted as nucleus segmentation of the cells. There is a scarcity of public datasets for cervical cancer screening. The cervical cancer slides can be stained in two different ways. One is called a PAP

Smear and the other is LBC (Liquid-based cytology). Herlev Dataset contains PAP smear samples. HEMLBC Dataset [5] contains LBC samples. The best results obtained to date are from deep learning-based CNN called ConvNet-T in the paper DeepPap.

Mitra P et al. in 2000 [4], worked on Genetic and Interactive Dichotomizer 3 algorithms. It was found out that the work that they had done gives better accuracy than that of multilayer perceptron models. The dataset used in this work was very simple numerical data. When the data becomes more complex, it is not possible to use these algorithms and get good results. The numerical data provided the accuracy of 81.5%.

Zhang J et al. in 2004 [6], used Support Vector Machines which is based on pixel-level classification. Though the results were good, the dataset used was very simple and small. The true positive rate (sensitivity) of this method is 98%. There were 41 cancerous cells out of which the method was able to detect 40 cancerous cells correctly.

Kale A et al. in 2010 [7], worked on the segmentation of cytoplasm and nucleus of cells from a given image sample. Hierarchical segmentation was used to extract the cytoplasm and nucleus from the given image samples. It gave good results on segmentation, but some nucleus could not be extracted properly due to noise. The work was done on Herlev and Haceptte dataset. The accuracy to classify cytoplasm and nucleus was 96%. The mentioned accuracy is not to classify cancerous or normal cells but to classify cytoplasm and nucleus on the dataset generated from Haceptte and Herlev dataset by segmentation for training and evaluation respectively.

Bora K et al. in 2016 [8], used Convolutional Neural Networks to classify Herlev dataset along with 1611 Pap Smear samples gathered from some diagnostic centers. The basic idea was to extract some features from the image first using CNNs and then use some other classification algorithms on selected features. AlexNet was selected as the CNN architecture and the layer fc7 - fully connected layer (7th) was used to use the feature extraction layer. Algorithms such as Least Squared Support Vector Machine (LSSVM) and Softmax Regression were used to classify from the selected set of features. The use of CNN increased the training time as compared to the previous work but is more robust. The accuracy of the method is 90–95% which is good as the dataset is also comparatively larger. However, the dataset is not publicly available and therefore we can't compare it directly to other methods.

Malli PK et al. in 2017 [9], instead of working directly on the images for classification, work has been done to extract features from the images from different computer vision techniques and formulae. This reduced the efficiency of total work. Extracting features itself is a tough task. The cell segmentation work is in fact cannot be relied on all the time. There were some other features such as the nucleus and cytoplasm roundness, perimeter, etc. The extracted features were then trained on KNN and ANN. The results were 88.04% and 54% accuracy, respectively.

Zhang L et al. in 2017 [10], Introduced a novel idea in cervical cancer screening. The previous methods were using feature extraction and then built a classifier on top of it. The problem was the feature extraction methods themselves are not reliable and reduce the accuracy of the whole problem. They introduced 2 networks viz., ConvNet-B and ConvNet-T. ConvNet-B is a simple 5 convolutional, 3 pooling layers and 3 fully connected layers trained on the ImageNet dataset. ConvNet-T has a similar structure to that of ConvNet-B except for some fully connected layers. ConvNet-B is used for transfer learning information and ConvNet-T acts as the final classifier. The transfer learning approach provides good accuracy to the problem statements which do have less amount of data. Zhang L et al. [8] used image augmentation and transfer learning approaches to improvise the accuracy and other metrics such as sensitivity to reduce the problems caused by fewer data. The accuracy increased to $98.3\% \pm 0.7\%$ which is a significant increase in the previous results obtained on Herlev and HEM LBC dataset. This method does not require any external feature extraction mechanism. It works directly on the image samples. It uses a patch augmentation step to improve upon the accuracy. But this causes the network to take around 3.5 s to classify a single patch. This makes it a slow network to be used in real-life cases.

3   Methodology

The used methodology for automated screening of cervical cancer cells using Transfer learning [11] on EfficientNet architecture with ImageNet dataset is shown in Fig. 2. We started with the generation of the new dataset from available Byriel dataset using the methods explained in Sect. 3.1. Moving further, The ImageNet dataset was used to train the EfficientNet model [12]. The images of this dataset were then reshaped and resized and trained on EfficientNet by updating weights. The combination of pretrained EfficientNet model with new densely connected layers gives the final model which is trained further on our generated dataset.

3.1   Dataset and Preprocessing

Herlev dataset [13,14] has been published by Herlev University Hospital, Denmark. It consists of pap smear samples that are clearly understood and well defined. This dataset has been manually classified into seven classes by authorized clinicians and technicians. There are multiple versions of the Herlev dataset. We are using the Byriel version [13] for our work. There is Martin version [14] that has been used for research work in this area. However, the problem with the Martin version is that it contains individual cells from the images that are obtained from the microscope. To get these individual cells in real-world settings is time-consuming and does not guarantee the obtained cells are proper and anything is missed out. The Byriel version contains the images as they are taken from the microscope directly. Table 1 shows distribution of the dataset.

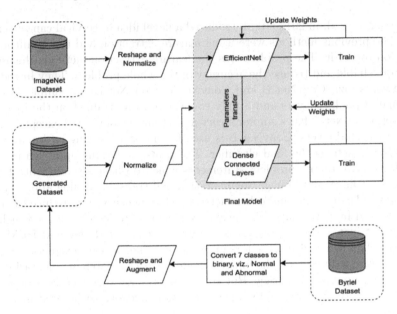

Fig. 2. Visual Illustration of used methodology

Table 1. Herlev Dataset (byriel) distribution

Name	Class	Number of images
Columnar Epithelial	Normal	50
Intermediate Squamous Epithelial	Normal	50
Superficial Squamous Epithelial	Normal	50
Mild Nonkeratinizing Dysplastic	Abnormal	100
Severe Nonkeratinizing Dysplastic	Abnormal	100
Parabasal Squamous Epithelial	Abnormal	50
Moderate Nonkeratinizing Dysplastic	Abnormal	100

3.2   Model Description

We have used different deep learning models based on CNNs [15]. We initially train the models without augmenting the data just to get an idea about what model we should choose from the different models during our exploration. The models selected are used which show good metrics for ImageNet challenge. Transfer learning approaches for Inception v3, MobileNet v2 and EfficientNet. Along with these models, we also worked on a basic CNN model which is trained only on our concerned dataset and not on ImageNet. We further select one of the models which give good results on the normal dataset and then do 10-fold cross-validation on the augmented dataset. Table 2 contains the proposed model layers description. Hyperparameters information of the models are provided in Sect. 4.

Table 2. Model layers description

Layer Name	Details
Input Layer	Shape: (None, 100, 100, 3)
EfficientNet Layers	B3 Architecture, last non convolutional layers removed
Flatten	Output Shape: (None, 24576)
Dropout	Value: 0.5
Dense	Neurons: 64
Activation	ReLU
Dense	Neurons: 2
Activation	Softmax

4 Experimental Results and Discussions

Some work has been done on the Martin version of the Herlev dataset [14]. Table 3 shows the different methods and their accuracy. As mentioned in Sect. 3.1, we have used the Byriel version of the Herlev dataset. The problem with the Martin version is that it contains individual cells from the images that are obtained from the microscope. To get these individual cells in real-world settings is time-consuming and doesn't guarantee the obtained cells are proper and anything is missed out. The Byriel version contains the images as they are taken from the microscope directly.

The limitation of the methods mentioned in Sect. 2 is that they must be dependent on some mechanism to extract individual cells from the images taken from a microscope if they are not readily available. This leads to a drop in the accuracy as well as requires more time to make the inference in real-world settings. Also, in the case of KNN and ANN methods mentioned, there is a need to rely on extracted features that might not be accurate.

Table 3. Comparison table for deep learning methods (Byriel)

SN.	Method name	Accuracy (%)	Sensitivity (%)	Specificity (%)
1	Transfer Learning on Inception V3	76	22.22	95.59
2	Transfer Learning on MobileNetV2	69	54.28	76.92
3	4 CNN + 3 Dense Layers	97.33	100	96
4	Transfer Learning on Efficient Net (B3)	99	100	97.29

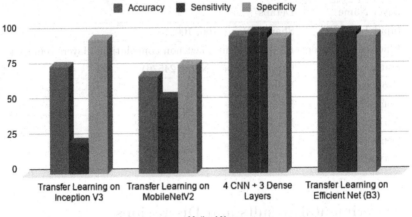

Fig. 3. Comparison of deep learning methods

Table 4. 10 Fold cross validation on transfer learning model (EfficentNet-B3)

TP	TN	FP	FN	FOLD	ACC	SENS	SPEC
67	30	2	1	1	97.00%	97.10%	96.77%
62	35	3	0	2	97.00%	95.38%	100.00%
70	29	0	1	3	99.00%	100.00%	96.67%
71	29	0	0	4	100.00%	100.00%	100.00%
73	24	2	1	5	97.00%	97.33%	96.00%
63	36	1	0	6	99.00%	98.44%	100.00%
74	25	1	0	7	99.00%	98.67%	100.00%
71	27	2	0	8	98.00%	97.26%	100.00%
71	28	0	1	9	99.00%	100.00%	96.55%
68	31	1	0	10	99.00%	98.55%	100.00%
				AVERAGE ->	**98.40%**	**98.27%**	**98.60%**

The dataset (Byriel) consists of 500 images in total. The number of images required for deep learning methods should be large so as the network should learn and generalize the features. Since the dataset contains a smaller number of images, we have used the ImageNet dataset for transfer learning and augmentation methods on the dataset.

To implement binary classification on the dataset, the seven classes were divided into two classes of normal and abnormal (cancerous) cells. The images were reshaped into a 100 × 100 pixel matrix. Further the images were augmented using Augmentor [16], which included 90° and 270° rotations, left-right flips, top-bottom flips, random crops and left-right rotates at the sides by 10° max. For each class, the dataset was augmented to 1000 samples each.

We have worked on 4 different deep learning networks to see how they perform on the generated dataset. All the deep learning models are built using Tensorflow [17]. All experiments are performed on a machine with 4 vCPUs, 15 GB memory along with 1 x Tesla V100 GPU on Google Cloud [18].

The first step we tried was Transfer Learning on Inception V3 [19] which is trained on the ImageNet dataset. Two new layers are added to the bottleneck layer of the Inception model. Both are dense with 1024 and 1 neurons, respectively. The sensitivity is low in this model leads us to think this is because there are a lot of differences in the dataset. Transfer Learning on MobileNetV2 [20] gave better results with the same 1024 and 1 neurons as added layers. We also used Dropout (50%) and ReLU activation.

Both the networks used SGD optimizer with learning rate lr = 0.01, momentum = 0.9, decay = 1e-6 Since, the two transfer learning models we had created did not give good results. We didn't update the weights of the layers till now except for the layers we had created. For new networks, we decided to update the weights of all the layers in the network.

We created a 4 Layer CNN + 3 Layer Dense Layer network. RMSProp [21] is used in this network. This gave us good results. Dropout and MaxPooling are used in this network. EfficientNet [12] was the new state of the art architecture for the ImageNet dataset [22]. It introduced a new concept of compound scaling. Hence B3 architecture of EfficientNet is used to see how well it scales with our dataset. Two new Dense layers are added to the bottleneck features with 64 and 2 neuron units respectively. Dropout [23] (50%) and ReLU activation [24] is used.

Table 3 shows the evaluation of different deep learning methods used. The dataset is bit imbalanced and hence it can be seen that some transfer learning approaches viz., inception v3 [19] and mobile net v2 [20] when used without updating the initial layers give bad results. Transfer Learning on EfficientNet (B3) [12] gave the best results provided that the weight of all layers are updated. Another CNN [15] model works good and is comparable to the best model.

Figure 3 represents the graphical evaluation of different deep learning methods based on accuracy, sensitivity and specificity.

To see if the model is performing well, we performed 10-fold cross-validation. For each fold, the test data and validation data are chosen randomly and trained on the network. After training, each of the individual metrics of accuracy is stored and then the average is calculated of all the metrics.

Table 4 shows the results obtained from the 10-Fold cross-validation of EfficientNet B3 Transfer Learning architecture. Accuracy, Sensitivity and Specificity are derived from the confusion matrix for each fold.

Our method gives just as good accuracy comparable to the methods mentioned in Sect. 2. Here, we solve a couple of problems. The inference time for ConvNet-T [10] is 3.5 s per cell image which is very high. This is because of the augmentation required before the final inference. The proposed method does not require any kind of augmentation during the inference. Moreover, the proposed method works on the images which contain multiple cells instead of just a single cell. This reduces the time required for the inference. Moreover, the backend model that we used i.e. EfficientNet [12] is lighter than most of the previously used models in ImageNet challenge.

5 Conclusion

In this paper a deep transfer learning based automated screening method for cervical cancer cells is discussed. The used cervical cancer method utilizes the features learned from the ImageNet dataset and fine-tuned for cervical cancer cell identifications from generated Byriel dataset. The deep learning models require a huge amount of data, time, and computing power to provide good results. The transfer learning method can be used to reduce the requirement of data, time, and compute power. A model that has its weights trained on a larger dataset can be used and modified for a new case that may have a small amount of data. The other automated screening method for cervical cancer cells are largely relied on different methods of hand-crafted features extraction from the single cell microscopic images such as segmentation. In the proposed deep transfer learning method instead of working on a single cell image we worked on the classification of cells based on the images containing a group of images. This reduces the time required to extract individual cells from the images obtained from the microscope. No feature extraction or augmentation is required at inference time.

References

1. Sisodia, D.S., Verma, S.: Image pixel intensity and artificial neural network based method for pattern recognition. World Acad. Sci. Eng. Technol. **57**, 742–745 (2011)
2. Rai, R., Sisodia, D.S.: Real-time data augmentation based transfer learning model for breast cancer diagnosis using histopathological images. In: Advances in Biomedical Engineering and Technology, pp. 473–488. Springer, Singapore
3. WHO — Cervical cancer.https://www.who.int/cancer/prevention/diagnosis-screening/cervical-cancer/en/
4. Mitra, P., Mitra, S., Pal, S.K.: Staging of cervical cancer with soft computing. IEEE Trans. Biomed. Eng. **47**(7), 934–940 (2000)
5. Zhang, L., et al.: Automation-assisted cervical cancer screening in manual liquid-based cytology with hematoxylin and eosin staining. Cytometry Part A **85**(3), 214–230 (2014)
6. Zhang, J., Liu, Y.: Cervical cancer detection using SVM based feature screening. In: Barillot, C., Haynor, D.R., Hellier, P. (eds.) MICCAI 2004. LNCS, vol. 3217, pp. 873–880. Springer, Heidelberg (2004). https://doi.org/10.1007/978-3-540-30136-3_106
7. Kale, A., Aksoy, S.: Segmentation of cervical cell images. In: Proceedings of the 2010 20th International Conference on Pattern Recognition, IEEE Computer Society, pp. 2399–2402 (2010)

8. Bora, K., Chowdhury, M., Mahanta, L.B., Kundu, M.K., Das, A.K.: Pap smear image classification using convolutional neural network. In: Proceedings of the 10th Indian Conference on Computer Vision, Graphics and Image Processing, p. 55. ACM (2016)
9. Malli, P.K., Nandyal, S.: Machine learning technique for detection of cervical cancer using k-NN and artificial neural network. In: International Journal of Emerging Trends & Technology in Computer Science (IJETTCS) (2017)
10. Zhang, L., Lu, L., Nogues, I., Summers, R.M., Liu, S., Yao, J.: DeepPap: deep convolutional networks for cervical cell classification. IEEE J. Biomed. Health Inf. **21**(6), 1633–1643 (2017)
11. Pan, S.J., Yang, Q.: A survey on transfer learning. IEEE Trans. Knowl. Data Eng. **22**(10), 1345–1359 (2009)
12. Tan, M., Le, Q.V.: EfficientNet: rethinking model scaling for convolutional neural networks. arXiv preprint arXiv:1905.11946 (2019)
13. Byriel, J.: Neuro-fuzzy classification of cells in cervical smears, Master's Thesis, Technical University of Denmark: Oersted-DTU, Automation (1999)
14. Martin, E.: Pap-Smear Classification. Technical University of Denmark DTU. 2003 (2003)
15. LeCun, Y., Bengio, Y., et al.: Convolutional networks for images, speech, and time series. Handb. Brain Theor. Neural Netw. **3361**(10), 1995 (1995)
16. Bloice, M.D., Roth, P.M., Holzinger, A.: Biomedical image augmentation using augmentor. Bioinformatics **35**(21), 4522–4524 (2019)
17. Abadi, M., et al.: Tensorflow: a system for large-scale machine learning. In: 12th USENIX Symposium on Operating Systems Design and Implementation (OSDI 2016), pp. 265–283 (2016)
18. Deep Learning VM — Google Cloud. https://cloud.google.com/deep-learning-vm
19. Szegedy, C., Ioffe, S., Vanhoucke, V., Alemi, A.A.: Inception-v4, inception-resnet and the impact of residual connections on learning. In: 31st AAAI Conference on Artificial Intelligence (2017)
20. Sandler, M., Howard, A., Zhu, M., Zhmoginov, A., Chen, L.-C.: Mobilenetv2: inverted residuals and linear bottlenecks. In: Proceedings of the IEEE Conference on Computer Vision and Pattern Recognition, pp. 4510–4520 (2018)
21. Tieleman, T., Hinton, G.: Lecture 6.5-rmsprop divide the gradient by a running average of its recent magnitude. COURSERA Neural Netw. Mach. Learn. **4**(2), 26–31 (2012)
22. Russakovsky, O., et al.: Imagenet large scale visual recognition challenge. Int. J. Comput. Vision **115**(3), 211–252 (2015)
23. Srivastava, N., Hinton, G., Krizhevsky, A., Sutskever, I., Salakhutdinov, R.: Dropout: a simple way to prevent neural networks from overfitting. J. Mach. Learn. Res. **15**(1), 1929–1958 (2014)
24. Agarap, A.F.: Deep learning using rectified linear units (relu), arXiv preprint arXiv:1803.08375 (2018)

Tissue Differentiation Based on Classification of Morphometric Features of Nuclei

Dominika Dudzińska and Adam Piórkowski[✉][iD]

Department of Biocybernetics and Biomedical Engineering, AGH University of Science and Technology, A. Mickiewicza 30 Av., 30–059 Cracow, Poland
pioro@agh.edu.pl

Abstract. The aim of the article is to analyze the shape of nuclei of various tissues and to assess the tumor differentiation based on morphometric measurements. For this purpose, an experiment was conducted, the results of which determine whether it is possible to determine a tissue's type based on the mentioned features. The measurements were performed on a publicly available data set containing 1,356 hematoxylin- and eosin-stained images with nucleus segmentations for 14 different human tissues. Morphometric analysis of cell nuclei using ImageJ software took 17 parameters into account. Classification of the obtained results was performed in Matlab R2018b software using the SVM and t-SNE algorithms, which showed that some cancers can be distinguished with an accuracy close to 90% (lung squamous cell cancer vs others; breast cancer vs cervical cancer).

Keywords: Nuclei segmentation · Histopathological images · Shape descriptors · Hematoxylin & Eosin staining · Classification

1 Introduction

Pathomorphology is the main procedure used in oncological diagnostics [5]. The key to achieving progress in this field is still the quantitative and qualitative analysis of cancer cells, on the basis of which the presence or progression of the disease can be assessed. This is based on microscopic examination of cell morphology after proper tissue preparation and staining, most often with hematoxylin and eosin. The results of research into the identification of characteristic parameters of cancerous tissues could significantly increase the speed and effectiveness of pathologists' decisions. To this end, various methods developed in the field of digital image processing are used.

Nowadays, many different approaches to determining tissue parameters with the use of microscopic images have been proposed. Huang and Lai [9] tested 14 features of biopsy images, including nuclear morphology and texture. In their work, they focused on local and global parameters, which allowed them to effectively distinguish between cancer malignancy levels. There are many works

© Springer Nature Switzerland AG 2020
H. Florez and S. Misra (Eds.): ICAI 2020, CCIS 1277, pp. 420–432, 2020.
https://doi.org/10.1007/978-3-030-61702-8_29

related to the morphometry of nuclei, especially in the area of nuclear differentiation in terms of disease severity: bladder cancer [23], nodular lesions in HCV cirrhosis [21], gastric adenocarcinoma [13], and nuclear classification based on morphometric context [3, 6].

The use of neural networks [1, 20] which detect and segment nuclei with satisfactory accuracy and, for example, determine the histological grade of a given tissue on the basis of the obtained results, is very popular in the field of tissue microscopic image processing. Many achievements in the field of digital pathology can be found in an article by H. Irshad and others [10] which reviewed the methods used in the comprehensive analysis of cancer cell nuclei.

This article proposes a comparison of the cell nuclei of various neoplasms, analyzing their common and distinguishing features, thanks to which the classification was possible. The document is divided into several sections as follows. Part 1 introduces the topic of scientific achievements in the field of cancer cell analysis. Part 2 provides background information on input data, measuring parameters and selecting the most distinctive features. Part 3 consists of the description of the classification algorithm based on selected features and the reduction of dimensions using t-SNE. In the next stage, the results of the research were presented and a discussion was held which led to the conclusions presented in Part 5 and the proposals for the future direction of research.

2 Materials and Methods

2.1 The Data

The data set used in this experiment was downloaded from The Cancer Imaging Archive (TCIA), which was created for the storage of medical images and their use for scientific purposes [4, 8]. This data contains 1,356 original H&E images with a resolution of 256×256 pixels and nuclei masks obtained from manual segmentation for 14 different types of cancer. There are approximately 100 images for each cancer, therefore a total of 20,592 nuclei were analyzed in order to select the most characteristic features; see Table 1 for details. Figure 1 presents example images with segmentation for different types of cancer.

2.2 Morphometric Analysis

In order to identify the most distinctive morphometric pathological features, nuclear morphometric measurements were performed using the ImageJ software, which was developed by the National Institutes of Health (NIH) [19]. The standard analytical functions of the program were used for the measurements; the MorphoLibJ and BioVoxxel Toolbox libraries, which expand the particle analyzer, were also used [2], Table 2. To avoid taking into account clustered nuclei, and to equalize the number of cell sets for all tissues, the first 840 nuclei were selected for each tissue, ordering by area, ascending.

Table 1. Types of cancer and the number of nuclei in the dataset.

	Type of cancer	# of nuclei
BLCA	Bladder Urothelial Carcinoma	1497
BRCA	Breast Invasive Carcinoma	843
CESC	Cervical Squamous Cell Carc. and Endocervical Adenocarc.	2377
UCEC	Uterine Corpus Endometrial Carcinoma	1945
COAD	Colon Adenocarcinoma	1485
GBM	Glioblastoma Multiforme	1110
LUAD	Lung Adenocarcinoma	1367
LUSC	Lung Squamous Cell Carcinoma	1735
PAAD	Pancreatic Adenocarcinoma	1317
PRAD	Prostate Adenocarcinoma	1246
READ	Rectal Adenocarcinoma	1497
SKCM	Skin Cutaneous Melanoma	1476
STAD	Stomach Adenocarcinoma	1574
UVM	Uveal Melanoma	1123

In the first stage, binary objects were analyzed. When analyzing the particles, overlapping nuclei and those at the edges of the image were rejected (Fig. 2).

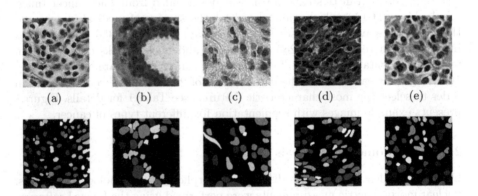

Fig. 1. Examples of dataset images. The first line presents the original images of cancers; the second line shows the generated masks of the nuclei of these images: (a) bladder cancer, (b) breast cancer, (c) lung adenocarcinoma, (d) lung squamous cell cancer, (e) skin melanoma.

Table 2. The list of all morphometric parameters used.

ImageJ	BioVoxxel
Area	**Area**
Perimeter	**Perimeter**
Stnadard deviation	Stnadard deviation
Min & Max gray value	Min & Max gray value
Center of mass	Center of mass
Bounding rectangle (X, Y, Width, Height)	Bounding rectangle (X, Y, Width, Height)
Skewness	Skewness
Area fraction	Area fraction
Mean gray value	Mean gray value
Modal gray value	Modal gray value
Integrated density	Integrated density
Centroid (X, Y)	Centroid (X, Y)
Fit elipse (Major, Minor, Angle)	**Fit elipse (Major, Minor, Angle)**
Feret's diameter	**Feret's diameter**
(XFeret, YFeret, Feret's Diameter, MinFeret, Feret Angle)	**(XFeret, YFeret, Feret's Diameter, MinFeret, Feret Angle)**
Median	Median
Kurtosis	Kurtosis
Stack position (Slice)	Stack position (Slice)
Cricularity	**Cricularity**
AR (Ascpect Ratio)	**AR (Ascpect Ratio)**
Roundness	**Roundness**
Solidity	**Solidity**
	Compactness
	Feret AR
	Coefficient of variation
	Extent

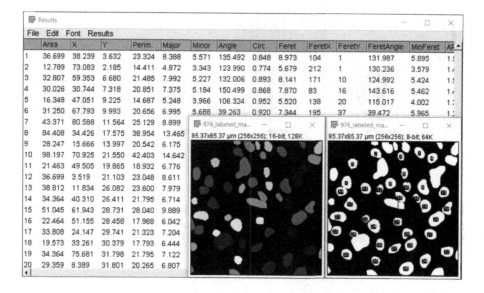

Fig. 2. An example of cell counting in ImageJ

Initial analysis of average parameter values for various tissues, shown in Fig. 3, suggested limiting further analyses to 4 dominant features in the context of tumor tissue differentiation: area, perimeter, roundness and Feret AR. This limitation helped prevent over-matching of classes.

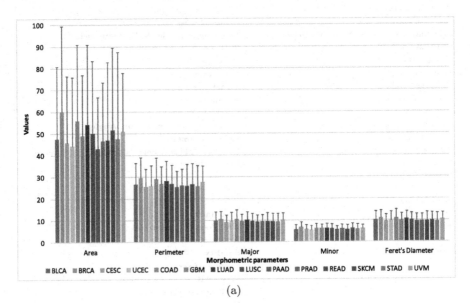

(a)

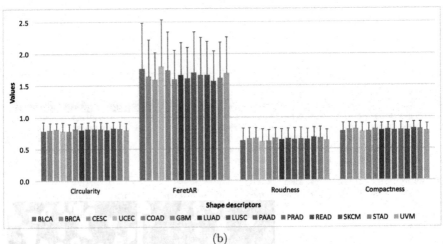

(b)

Fig. 3. Mean morphometric parameters of different types of tumors. (a) Morphometric parameters: from the left, Area - Perimeter - Major - Minor - Feret's Diameter. (b) Shape parameters: from the left, Circularity - Feret AR - Roundness - Compactness

3 Data Analysis

Due to the high efficiency that has been confirmed in other studies [7,11,12,15, 16,23], the study proposed a classification using the Support Vector Machine method (SVM). Then, t-SNE (t-Distributed Stochastic Neighbor Embedding) analysis was performed to obtain visualizations of multidimensional data to assess the effectiveness of the classification [14]. Previous studies have shown that multidimensional visualizations done with t-SNE are superior to those produced by existing dimension-reduction techniques. The main idea of this method is to transform the multidimensional input data set into a matrix of similarities between two points using "t-Student" distribution while maintaining the local data structure [17,18]. The whole grouping analysis was carried out in the MATLAB R2018b environment.

3.1 SVM Classification

Due to the much better distribution of tumors than when using one parameter, it was decided to carry out the classification using two or three characteristic parameters. Additionally, in some cases of analysis, it was noticed that the use of the third parameter increases the accuracy of cancer differentiation, and sometimes this distinction is necessary.

In our study, the SVM classification was carried out with a one-on-one strategy that includes two classes: the first class consists of only one selected cancer images; the second class consists of images of the list of tumors in Table 1. This classification aims to show the best distinction between selected cancer and all other cancers.

It was assumed that the four selected parameters are part of the classifier mechanism. Depending on the parameters indicated, this approach allows tumor classification to be tuned, which in turn makes it possible to determine which parameters are most important in the context of the classification of a particular cancer. In this way, the accuracy of diagnostics is increased.

The following describes the operation of the SVM classifier in several steps:

- Selection of the characteristic parameters of the nuclei, according to which SVM will be carried out.
- Division into training data (80% of input data) and test data (20% of input data).
- Classification using SVM binary classification using the built-in functions in Matlab R2018b (including KernelFunction, rbf kernel function).
- SVM classifies data by finding the best hyperplane that separates all points belonging to one selected class (BLCA, BRCA, LUSC) from the points of the other classes (the next examined tissue).
- The SVM result is a measure of the accuracy of the classification.

3.2 Reduction of Dimension Using T-SNE Method

After classification with the SVM method, in order to confirm the results the data was visualized using the t-SNE technique, which shows the distribution of data in space. The calculations were carried out in MATLAB R2018b environment. In addition, Barness-Hut approximation was used, which enabled analysis with large data sets and accelerated the t-SNE algorithm. This article presents data visualizations on two- and three-dimensional maps.

4   Results and Discussion

4.1   Classic SVM Classification Method in a One-on-One Strategy

In order to assess the effectiveness of the proposed tumor tissue comparison, classification of 14 tumors was performed using SVM, the mechanism of which was to differentiate BRCA, BLCA and LUSC cancers from other tumors. Classification using the SVM mechanism was carried out with the introduction of a cross-validation parameter with a value of 5. Other values of this parameter were also tested, but they produced worse results. From the performed classification, results were obtained in the form of the accuracy of tumor differentiation. The results are shown in Table 3.

The results in Table 3 show the accuracy of distinguishing between two groups of cancers in various combinations. The best distinction (above 90%) is found between LUSC lung cancer and UVM melanoma and PAAD pancreatic cancer. This result is obtained when classification is performed using two or three characteristic parameters, thus indicating a large difference between the nuclei of these cancers when selected parameters are taken into account (Roundness and Feret AR). The next highly differentiated group is BRCA breast cancer and CESC cervical cancer. SVM classification accuracy based on Roundness-Perimeter is as high as 89.41%, and 86.47% accuracy is achieved when Area-Feret AR parameters are considered. In this cancer comparison, it can be seen that the SVM classifier achieves better results when three pairs of parameters are used. There is no a significant increase in the accuracy score after using a third parameter to describe the cancer, as shown in Table 2. This is particularly evident in BLCA bladder carcinoma. In turn, differentiation between LUAD lung cancer and PAAD pancreatic cancer or CESC cervical cancer and UCEC uterine cancer gave poor results. The similarity of the nuclei of these tumors was already visible during the morphometric analysis performed in ImageJ, as shown in Fig. 2.

Table 3. SVM classification accuracy (in %) for two or three parameters.

Cancer	Parameters	BRCA	CESC	UCEC	COAD	GBM	LUAD	LUSC	PAAD	PRAD	READ	SKCM	STAD	UVM
BLCA	Roudness Area	**81.17**	69.70	67.05	65.58	69.41	64.41	54.11	53.82	66.76	57.94	51.76	54.70	70.59
	Roudness Feret AR	56.76	72.05	52.05	53.23	53.35	49.12	**88.23**	51.47	49.70	51.18	55.58	55.58	60.00
	Roudness Perimeter	78.23	66.76	61.20	63.52	68.82	64.11	61.76	54.12	61.76	55.29	58.23	55.29	65.58
	Area Feret AR	**82.94**	70.58	66.18	67.65	67.64	63.82	50.60	55.60	63.52	57.06	55.88	57.94	71.76
BLCA	Roudness Area Feret AR	80.58	70.58	68.82	63.24	73.25	65.58	49.70	52.94	57.35	57.65	51.76	54.11	70.29
	Roudness Area Perimeter	77.65	68.23	67.94	62.94	68.23	67.65	55.00	57.94	68.82	53.23	61.76	56.76	71.50
	Roudness Feret AR Perimeter	79.11	72.35	68.82	65.29	66.76	69.71	81.76	53.53	65.00	56.17	56.76	54.11	65.88

Cancer	Parameters	BLCA	CESC	UCEC	COAD	GBM	LUAD	LUSC	PAAD	PRAD	READ	SKCM	STAD	UVM
BRCA	Roudness Area	81.17	85.00	**85.88**	72.05	70.88	70.29	79.11	77.94	72.05	**82.94**	78.52	81.17	66.47
	Roudness Feret AR	56.76	66.17	54.70	50.58	45.88	47.05	**88.53**	47.94	56.17	50.58	54.41	54.70	56.17
	Roudness Perimeter	78.23	**89.41**	**84.47**	72.35	68.82	68.82	71.47	76.76	70.58	78.82	78.52	81.76	63.53
	Area Feret AR	**82.94**	86.47	**85.88**	73.82	65.88	69.41	**82.35**	78.82	72.35	79.11	79.70	**85.29**	68.24
BRCA	Roudness Area Feret AR	80.58	87.65	87.64	75.29	64.11	71.47	79.70	77.65	72.05	81.47	80.00	81.47	63.82
	Roudness Area Perimeter	77.65	88.24	87.65	74.11	67.94	68.82	82.94	81.47	74.12	80.58	82.94	84.12	65.58
	Roudness Feret AR Perimeter	79.11	85.00	85.88	71.17	65.29	70.58	82.94	77.64	70.58	77.65	77.05	78.53	66.47

Cancer	Parameters	BLCA	BRCA	CESC	UCEC	COAD	GBM	LUAD	PAAD	PRAD	READ	SKCM	STAD	UVM
LUSC	Roudness Area	54.11	79.11	69.70	66.17	61.17	68.82	69.70	59.41	65.29	57.05	53.52	57.05	67.35
	Roudness Feret AR	88.23	88.53	86.47	86.18	88.82	86.18	89.41	**90.29**	88.23	88.83	89.12	85.88	**90.88**
	Roudness Perimeter	61.76	71.47	71.47	68.82	62.05	71.76	63.52	52.64	65.88	57.35	48.23	55.00	67.94
	Area Feret AR	50.60	82.35	72.64	65.00	61.76	72.35	70.29	55.58	62.05	61.76	54.11	53.52	73.23
	Area Perimeter	55.00	81.17	72.64	65.88	68.23	66.17	67.65	60.58	62.05	61.47	52.64	54.70	73.23
	Feret AR Perimeter	59.11	80.29	72.35	69.12	69.41	72.05	64.70	57.05	66.47	62.05	54.11	60.58	72.35

4.2 T-SNE Visualization

Multidimensional visualization of t-SNE was performed to evaluate cancer classification using the SVM algorithm. It allows the successful assessment of which morphometric parameters of tumor tissue are similar and which differ significantly from each other. Deposition of the best differentiating tumor classes in the parameter space using t-SNE is shown in Fig. 4.

The SVM classification results showed that LUSC lung cancer is distinguished with almost 85.88–90.88% accuracy (Roundness-Feret AR), as is further confirmed by the visualization. The distinction between the nuclear morphometry of BRCA breast cancer and CESC cervical cancer (Fig. 4(f)) shows that the use of a three pairs of parameters (Roundness-Perimeter, Area-Feret AR, Roundness-Area) allows high separation of these tumors.

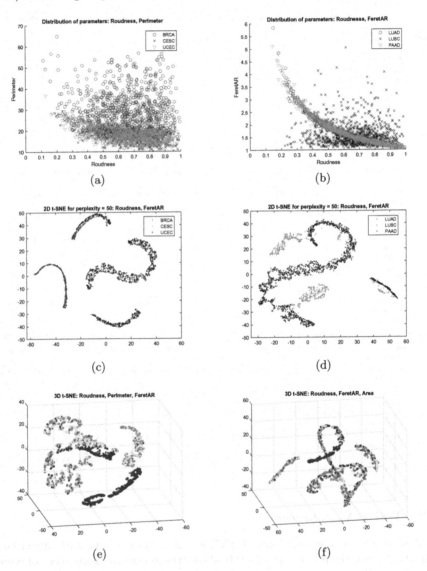

Fig. 4. Multidimensional visualization using the t-SNE method of the two morphometric tumor parameters that are most differentiated in comparison to bladder cancer. The first column shows visualizations for BRCA, CESC, UCEC (a, c, e) and the second column for LUAD, LUSC, PAAD (b, d, f). The first row contains distribution of parameters, the second - 2D t-SNE, and the third - 3D t-SNE visualizations.

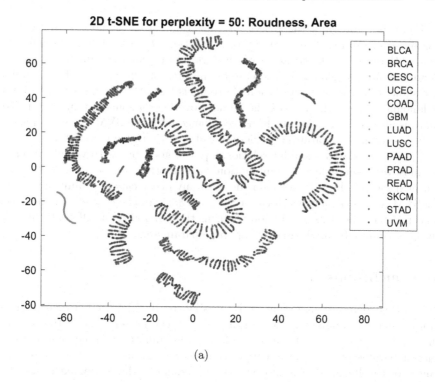

(a)

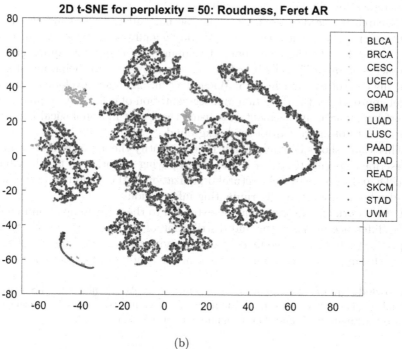

(b)

Fig. 5. Visualization of t-SNE for all tissues using selected parameters.

Figure 5(a) presents the t-SNE visualization for all tumors with the best classification results. The accuracy of separation of some of these tumors was greater than 80%. Visualization of clusters, taking into account all classes of tumors, is not as clear as in the case of the presentation of two classes, but it also shows that the best separation of groups is BRCA breast cancer, and UVM melanoma cancer. The rest of the tumors overlap to some extent, but t-SNE analysis also confirms close to 80% compliance with the SVM accuracy results, and thus the high separation of these morphometric tissue parameters.

Figure 5(b) shows a similar relationship as before, but with visualization for the most different cancer in combination with all other cancers. The LUSC lung cancer most of values do not coincide with any other cancer in any way, hence the SVM results belongs to range of 85.88–90.88%. In the case of squamous cell cancer of the lung, this separation confirms the possibility of differentiating the nuclei of tumors by analyzing two or three parameters.

5   Conclusions

This article demonstrates that it is possible to distinguish between selected tumor tissues by analyzing the morphometry of cell nuclei. This distinction has already been achieved with the use of two and sometimes three characteristic nuclear parameters for selected types of cancers, e.g. breast and squamous cell cancer of the lungs. It was also shown that some of the examined tissues are characterized by similar nuclei morphometry.

Research in the discussed topic may be particularly important in the field of automating the quantitative and qualitative analysis of images of cancer cells and tissues. Due to the continuous development of computer equipment, new approaches to quantify cells based on shape parameters are being investigated, as in the case of the article by S. Wienert et al. [22] who developed a minimal model approach for the detection and segmentation of cells. This approach aims to perform an accurate segmentation using the fewest morphological features to separate cells of interest from the background.

This study shows how important it is to identify the appropriate parameters to describe a specific tissue. It is also worth paying attention to the distribution of nuclei and thus their architectural organization in the examined tissue, which can also be an important discriminating information.

Future work on this issue may be extended to the measurement and analysis of the difference in the shape and distribution of the nuclei of various types of neoplastic tissues in the context of disease advancement and degree of malignancy, this approach has been discussed in the context of breast cancer [24].

Acknowledgement. This publication was funded by AGH University of Science and Technology, Faculty of Electrical Engineering, Automatics, Computer Science and Biomedical Engineering under grant number 16.16.120.773.

References

1. Araújo, T.: Classification of breast cancer histology images using convolutional neural networks. PLoS ONE **12**(6), e0177544 (2017)
2. Arena, E.T., Rueden, C.T., Hiner, M.C., Wang, S., Yuan, M., Eliceiri, K.W.: Quantitating the cell: turning images into numbers with ImageJ. Wiley Interdiscipl. Rev. Dev. Biol. **6**(2), e260 (2017)
3. Chang, H., Borowsky, A., Spellman, P., Parvin, B.: Classification of tumor histology via morphometric context. In: Proceedings of the IEEE Conference on Computer Vision and Pattern Recognition, pp. 2203–2210 (2013)
4. Clark, K., et al.: The cancer imaging archive (TCIA): maintaining and operating a public information repository. J. Digit. Imaging **26**(6), 1045–1057 (2013)
5. Collins, T.J.: ImageJ for microscopy. Biotechniques **43**(S1), S25–S30 (2007)
6. Demir, C., Yener, B.: Automated cancer diagnosis based on histopathological images: a systematic survey. Technical report, Rensselaer Polytechnic Institute (2005)
7. Han, J.W., Breckon, T.P., Randell, D.A., Landini, G.: The application of support vector machine classification to detect cell nuclei for automated microscopy. Mach. Vis. Appl. **23**(1), 15–24 (2012)
8. Hou, L., et al.: Dataset of segmented nuclei in hematoxylin and eosin stained histopathology images of 10 cancer types. Can. Imaging Arch. (2019). https://doi.org/10.7937/tcia.2019.4a4dkp9u
9. Huang, P.W., Lai, Y.H.: Effective segmentation and classification for HCC biopsy images. Pattern Recogn. **43**(4), 1550–1563 (2010)
10. Irshad, H., Veillard, A., Roux, L., Racoceanu, D.: Methods for nuclei detection, segmentation, and classification in digital histopathology: a review-current status and future potential. IEEE Rev. Biomed. Eng. **7**, 97–114 (2013)
11. Jaworek-Korjakowska, J., Kłeczek, P.: Automatic classification of specific melanocytic lesions using artificial intelligence. BioMed Res. Int. (2016). article ID 8934242 https://doi.org/10.1155/2016/8934242
12. Jeleń, Ł., Krzyżak, A., Fevens, T.: Comparison of pleomorphic and structural features used for breast cancer malignancy classification. In: Bergler, S. (ed.) AI 2008. LNCS (LNAI), vol. 5032, pp. 138–149. Springer, Heidelberg (2008). https://doi.org/10.1007/978-3-540-68825-9_14
13. Ji, M.Y., et al.: Nuclear shape, architecture and orientation features from h&e images are able to predict recurrence in node-negative gastric adenocarcinoma. J. Transl. Med. **17**(1), 92 (2019)
14. Kalinin, A.A., et al.: 3D cell nuclear morphology: microscopy imaging dataset and voxel-based morphometry classification results. In: Proceedings of the IEEE Conference on Computer Vision and Pattern Recognition Workshops, pp. 2272–2280 (2018)
15. Kaucha, D.P., Prasad, P., Alsadoon, A., Elchouemi, A., Sreedharan, S.: Early detection of lung cancer using SVM classifier in biomedical image processing. In: 2017 IEEE International Conference on Power, Control, Signals and Instrumentation Engineering (ICPCSI), pp. 3143–3148. IEEE (2017)
16. Kowal, M., Skobel, M., Nowicki, N.: The feature selection problem in computer-assisted cytology. Int. J. Appl. Math. Comput. Sci. **28**(4), 759–770 (2018)
17. Maaten, L.V.D., Hinton, G.: Visualizing data using t-SNE. J. Mach. Learn. Res. **9**, 2579–2605 (2008)

18. Pang, S., Du, A., Orgun, M.A., Yu, Z.: A novel fused convolutional neural network for biomedical image classification. Med. Biol. Eng. Comput. **57**(1), 107–121 (2019)
19. Schneider, C.A., Rasband, W.S., Eliceiri, K.W.: NIH Image to ImageJ: 25 years of image analysis. Nat. Methods **9**(7), 671–675 (2012)
20. Swiderska-Chadaj, Z., et al.: A deep learning approach to assess the predominant tumor growth pattern in whole-slide images of lung adenocarcinoma. In: Medical Imaging 2020: Digital Pathology, vol. 11320, p. 113200D. International Society for Optics and Photonics (2020)
21. Vertemati, M., et al.: Morphometric analysis of hepatocellular nodular lesions in HCV cirrhosis. Pathol. Res. Pract. **208**(4), 240–244 (2012)
22. Wienert, S., et al.: Detection and segmentation of cell nuclei in virtual microscopy images: a minimum-model approach. Sci. Rep. **2**, 503 (2012)
23. Wu, B., Nebylitsa, S.V., Mukherjee, S., Jain, M.: Quantitative diagnosis of bladder cancer by morphometric analysis of HE images. In: Photonic Therapeutics and Diagnostics XI, vol. 9303, p. 930317. International Society for Optics and Photonics (2015)
24. Yamashita, Y., Ichihara, S., Moritani, S., Yoon, H.S., Yamaguchi, M.: Does flat epithelial atypia have rounder nuclei than columnar cell change/hyperplasia? a morphometric approach to columnar cell lesions of the breast. Virchows Arch. **468**(6), 663–673 (2016)

Learning Management Systems

Peer Validation and Generation Tool for Question Banks in Learning Management Systems

Andres Sanchez-Martin[1]([✉]) [iD], Luis Barreto[1] [iD], Johana Martinez[1] [iD],
Nikolay Reyes-Jalizev[1] [iD], Carolina Astudillo[1] [iD], Santiago Escobar[1] [iD],
and Osberth De Castro[2] [iD]

[1] Universidad de San Buenaventura sede Bogotá, Carrera 8H No. 172 -20,
Bogotá, D.C., Colombia
{aasanchez,lbarreto,johmartinez,nreyes}@usbbog.edu.co,
{castudillo,sescobarg}@academia.usbbog.edu.co
[2] Universidad El Bosque, Av. Cra. 9 No. 131A - 02, Bogotá, D.C., Colombia
occastro@unbosque.edu.co

Abstract. One of the biggest challenges in ICT-mediated learning models, such as e-learning and b-learning, is the process of skills assessment. Specifically during the elaboration of random questionnaires based on question banks in Learning Management Systems (LMS), where difficulties such as misspellings or conceptual errors arise. This can make questions difficult for students to understand, and therefore, the possibility of answering wrong by accident. In addition, sometimes questions are not organized by topics or levels of difficulty, which can lead to exams on topics not yet seen in class, or questionnaires with the wrong difficulty level among students in the same course. To reduce this problem, we developed a peer review tool for evaluating and adjusting questions and then exporting them to an LMS as a question bank, organized by topic and difficulty level. This work shows the structure of such a tool, and first validation results for impact and quality using double-blind testing in questionnaire design for a course taught at a higher education institution in Colombia.

Keywords: Learning Management System · e-Learning · Question Banks · Questionnaire · Peer validation

1 Introduction

Learning online is one of the most demanded schemes worldwide. Although higher education was already migrating towards the digital realm, right now, due to the impact of SARS-Coronavirus 2 (SARS - CoV - 2), this process has been accelerated. Proof of this is the statistics presented by UNESCO, showing that by April 20 of 2020, the COVID-19 pandemic related closure of institutes, schools, academies, and universities is estimated to be affecting 91.3% of the

© Springer Nature Switzerland AG 2020
H. Florez and S. Misra (Eds.): ICAI 2020, CCIS 1277, pp. 435–448, 2020.
https://doi.org/10.1007/978-3-030-61702-8_30

student population, or 1,575,270,054 million [28]. Facing this suspension of face-to-face academic activities scenario, the adaptation to new learning models using virtual platforms has become mandatory for institutions.

The incursion of Information and Communication Technologies (ICT) as an educational instrument means a conceptual and methodological turning point in the way universities deal with learning management, especially concerning distance education, which grows rapidly, by adopting the Internet as a medium, which gives rise to the term e-Learning [12]. In this sense, traditional e-Learning platforms, that is, LMS (Learning Management Systems) have a high percentage of penetration. An example of this is the case of Spain, where 100% of universities use at least one LMS and 79.5% of large companies use these platforms for their worker training initiatives [11], leading to the necessity of a serious analysis of the learning assessment component.

The evaluation of learning is a principal component in the development of teaching-learning activities since it provides the elements of feedback to the actors. This feedback process is initially applied on the students learning objectives established in the course syllabus and, therefore, it influences the plan of action in the teaching process and administrative, supervision and control decisions of the educational institution and surveillance and control departments, in curricular management processes, and even in public policy treaties in this regard [8].

In this scenario, the increasing use of ICTs has also begun to permeate traditional evaluation mechanisms. Some virtual education platforms or support to face-to-face education, such as LMS, questionnaire platforms, among others, include extensive modules for the development of evaluation activities. [1]. The pedagogical value of ICT-mediated competency assessment with LMS such as Moodle represents an advantage over traditional assessment systems in terms of student academic performance, [29], feedback times, and support of the learning process [24]. While developing online courses, questionnaires are frequently designed as a mechanism for competency assessment, and making use of technological platforms for creating random questionnaires based on question banks is a widely used mechanism for handling students in large numbers [17].

In this work we show how, in one Colombian higher education institution, 66.6% of the students have problems interpreting questions, 48% identify questionnaires as very difficult or very easy, and 25% say questions were coming up on topics not yet seen in class. On the teachers side, 76% do not organize the questions by topics or levels of difficulty, and 33.3% have doubts about questionnaires. From the information obtained through the survey, the importance of guaranteeing better quality questions organized by topic and difficulty level is evident, and how by missing this as an objective can harm the performance of students. We will also show that both students and teachers have shown difficulties in guaranteeing the right quality of question banks, confirming that the problem exists, so a solution is needed.

Several projects in the field of education, such as the one from Salvin [26], which raises the basis of the impact that students have for the results obtained in the evaluation activities. Similarly, there is the study by Marmolejo et al. [19], which shows the effect it has on academic performance. In the technological aspect, we can see **StudentQuiz** [14], a plugin for the LMS **Moodle** [22] that uses a mechanism for the evaluation of the questions as proposed by students using non double blind peer-review for spelling but not for quality, and the study on **clickers** [27] that showed that the use of ICT for assessment would improve students performance. This work presents some fundamental concepts first, then the case study that motivated the project and the general description of the solution mechanism proposal. The software product that was developed, its functionalities, design, and technologies are described, and finally, the test scenario and validation methods are when applying the tool in a real context, together with analysis of results and conclusions.

2   ICT-Mediated Education

Education mediated by ICT (Information and Communication Technologies) is a concept that defines the use of technologies in the teaching-learning process, whether as support or environment, education can be: face-to-face, blended, remote or virtual [5]. Whatever the modality, ICT-mediated education is charac-terized by the use of technological systems to support activities and processes in the classroom, from content design, topic explanation, learning activities, remote laboratories, and evaluation processes [10]. Higher Education Institutions (HEIs) have seen ICT-mediated education as a tool that enables them to reach large and geographically dispersed populations, with considerable advantages over tradi-tional teaching, but which in turn implies many challenges [23]. At this point, definitions and differences between the different types of ICT-mediated educa-tion begin to impact the design and development of the courses. [21]. Initially, syllabus design or thematic contents of the course should be focused on autonomy in learning [3], and that the acquisition of the skills of the course requires less time of interaction with the teacher [25]. This scenario presents multiple chal-lenges, such as design and implementation of evaluation mechanisms, and how to guarantee an evaluation that allows uniformity, without having as influential factors: the teacher, environment, or modality in which the student is taking the course [6]. For this, platforms such as LMS and questionnaire platforms can be used, which have multiple advantages to be applied in face-to-face or vir-tual modalities [15]. Among the most used technological tools, it is common for Higher Education Institutions to make use of the LMS in both virtual and face-to-face programs, and the LMS becoming information systems with increasingly complex functions, both academic and administrative ([20] and [31]).

2.1   Questions and Questionnaires

The creation of questionnaires, the intention of it is very important, it is not the same to create a questionnaire for a survey, than creating for evaluating the competences of a student [7]. The writing must be in accordance to the type of evaluation. Questions can be open, closed for single answer, or for multiple answers [2]. These questions must evaluate a specific topic, so students at the time of answering the questionnaire has a conceptually correct thematic flow [16]. Questionnaires must also have an adequate number of questions according to the required difficulty, so students don't feel frustrated or pressured time restrictions [4]. Also, for the construction of questionnaires, it is a given that conceptual questions, exercises, case studies, or analysis of results can be used. [9].

All of the above impacts which type of questionnaire or evaluation activity is the most appropriate, taking into account the evaluation scale and the number of topics [30]. Among the types of questionnaires, there are forms specified in question banks, which present students with different questions each, and randomizing answer options. This type of questionnaire makes use of a bank of questions, so students get questions that evaluate the same topics, in the same order and with the same degree of difficulty, but not with the same questions or exercises. For achieving this, the question bank must organize in an specific way [1].

3   Proposal

A tool that aims to support teachers in their face-to-face, remote or virtual courses is proposed, both in the design of thematic content, as in the design of questions and closed exercises with a single answer, classified by level of difficulty in a bank of questions that are exported to LMS. The following stages are taken into account in the software development process of the tool: in the first stage, an analysis of needs was carried out, for which student surveys and interviews with teachers were made to define the validation processes of questions and generation from the bank. In the second stage, the functional and non-functional requirements and use cases were established, as well as the technologies to use. In the third stage, the software architecture, the data model, and the design of the user interface are determined; Lastly, the tool was implemented and tested.

3.1   Processes

For the design of the courses and the validation of the questions, three processes were defined aiming to create a mechanism where a structure of the question bank by topic is produced. Also, the validation of questions by anonymous peer review, and finally the construction and export of the question bank structured by themes and level of difficulty to an LMS.

Our validation model is based on sharing economy by Hamari [13]. In this case, teachers offer their time and effort as reviewers, and can benefit by using the work of other reviewers in the construction of questions and questionnaires. This effort can produce better quality and homogeneity.

Table 1. Software Requirements.

ID	Description	Priority
FR1	The system must allow user management	High
FR2	The system must allow the validation of the user's teaching identity	High
FR3	The system must allow the creation of a course with its thematic content	High
FR4	The system must allow the selection of courses to evaluate	High
FR5	The system must allow the creation of questions	High
FR6	The system must allow anonymous peer review of questions	High
FR7	The system must allow notification of events	High
FR8	The system must allow the export of the questions	High

Course Creation Process. For the creation of courses, the teacher must first register his or her personal data, and the institution to which it belongs, with these data a user profile will be generated, and validated by the administrator, this as a security mechanism. Once the teacher enters, he or she can select from a list of subjects for evaluation, that can be edited later. Also, the teacher can register a new subject where he or she will be the creator of the questions. With this process, the role that the teacher will have is validated, and the subject will be created with its respective topic content (topics and subtopics) organized by weeks.

Question Creation and Validation Process. In our first version, the selected peer review question validation procedure is sequential in nature, following recent results that recommend it instead of the parallel approach usually used in peer review processes [18]. Once a subject is produced with its topic content, teachers can create questions, taking the following steps:

- To create a question, a topic is chosen, and also the type of question, the degree of difficulty, the statement and answer options (correct and incorrect). Once the question has been created, the system sends the question to a first anonymous evaluating teacher (reviewer) who has the subject in his or her profile, to whom an email notification and within the tool arrives, and this first reviewer must approve or reject the question.
- In the case of rejecting the question, the reviewer must attach the reasons, which may be due to: spelling, conceptual errors, writing, error in the correct answer, topic or degree of difficulty. The first reviewer does not know who is the author of the question, this to avoid personal bias. Once the first reviewer finishes making the feedback, the system returns the creator teaching question, where it will make the corrections and re-sends the question to

evaluation, the system will avoid sending the question to the same reviewer. The teacher who created the question (author) also has the option to delete or discard the question.
- If the first reviewer approves the question, the system sends the question to a second reviewer, where the evaluation and feedback process is repeated.
- When the question satisfactorily passes through the two evaluating professors, it is available to be added to the question bank, the questions discarded or that are in the validation process will not be taken into account for the question bank of the subject.

Table 2. List of use cases.

ID	User Case	Description
UC1	Create Account	The teacher can request an account with the institutional card
UC2	Log in	User can login with account created
UC3	Manage courses	The user can create, modify or delete courses. Also, he can follow existing courses to evaluate
UC4	Manage questions	User can create, drop or delete questions
UC5	Validate questions	The system initiates the anonymous peer review process for each question created based on the topic and reviewer load
UC6	Feed back	The system sends feedback, corrections or approval to the creator of the questions
UC7	Notify	The system generates notifications within the platform and via e-mail, for reviews and question corrections
UC8	Export question bank	The user will be able to export the question bank in the selected format and LMS

Question Bank Creation and Export Process. Once the subject has organized and validated the questions according to the thematic content, the teacher can proceed to create the question bank with the outline 1. Once created, the LMS and the bank's export format are selected, the system generates the export file to download.

$$Course : (Topic : (Subtopic(Type : (Difficulty : (Easy, Medium, Hard)))))) \tag{1}$$

This structure, adding the double blind usage for every questionnaire guaranties the difficulty balance for the students.

3.2   Software Requirements Specification

With the definition of the processes for creation of subjects, questions, and bank, together with the peer validation, functional requirements (FR) were established, from these the use cases (UC) of the system that represent the basic functionalities developed the tool.

Software Requirements. In the requirements survey, the previously defined processes are taken into account, indicating inputs, outputs, and priority. These requirements are shown in Table 1. These requirements validated by teachers with experience in ICT-assisted education.

Use Cases. Based on the requirements, a description of the use cases was made. The functions that the user can perform in the system is described, in Table 2, the most relevant are shown.

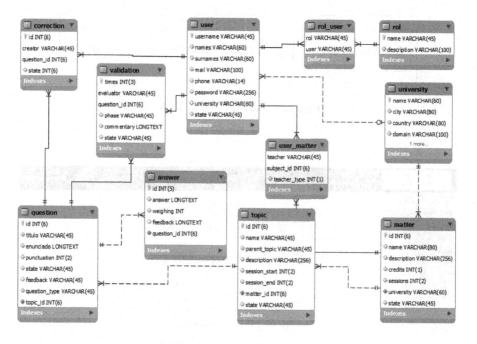

Fig. 1. Relational model

3.3   System Architecture

For the software architecture, the Model-View-Controller (MVC) design pattern was used, divided into three layers: data, logic, and view. MySQL 5.7 connected through the PHP MySQL library used in the data layer. The logic layer, is divided into the CRUDS controller, Business Logic, Model, and Service, the layer developed in PHP 7 on the WEB Apache HTTP 2.4 server. Presentation layer developed with the Bootstrap framework.

Data Model. For the construction of the application, a relational data model was designed, implemented in the MySQL 5.7 relational database management system (RDBMS), which allows data management quickly with SQL commands. This model presents 11 tables that store the data in a structure that allows the implementation of the tool's functions. The model can be seen in Fig. 1.

Deployment. The tool makes use of various technologies, such as PHP, MySQL, and Apache. At this first stage of development, all technologies deploy on the same device (server). This allow queries and requests between the components of the tool to be faster, although the hardware resources are higher to attend to concurrent requests.

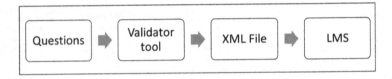

Fig. 2. Export process to LMS

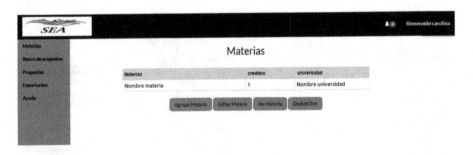

Fig. 3. System MuckUp

LMS Export File. The developed tool implemented the Moodle XML format of the LMS Moodle, however, the system is scalable to other LMS formats (GiFT, WebCT, MS Word, Aikem, Blackboard or Examview). When the user exports the question bank, the tool compiles the XML file and offers it as a direct download. After this, the user can import it from the LMS. The import process is simple since most LMS has a module to perform this task, as shown in Fig. 2.

3.4   User Interface

For the design of the graphical user interface, the strategy of mockup developing was used. Those mockups were evaluated and approved by teachers later on. As a result, a simple web interface was obtained, consisting of a side menu, work area, and notification and administration area. This design allows users to easily manage and remember the functions of the tool. In Fig. 3 you can see the general design of the interface.

4   Validation

Regarding the validation of the tool, a test protocol inspired by the double-blind technique was designed, where two iterations were made in two consecutive semesters (2019-2 and 2020-1). For each iteration, students were divided into groups from the same subject (algorithms and programming). All groups used the LMS Moodle to support the evaluation process, and in both iterations half of the groups used a question bank generated by our tool, being the test groups, and the other half was control groups. Participant peer reviewers are expert teachers from the selected course. An administrative personal validation step was performed for each teacher in order to activate each peer review account in the system. Course groups were difficulty balanced by the teachers from a curricular design perspective, so the questionnaires were fairly generated by the LMS. All course teachers were actively interested in becoming peer reviewers for the project.

Table 3. Data of experiment, semester 2019-2

	With tool	Without tool	Total
Groups	3	2	5
Teachers	3	2	5
Students	45	33	78

Table 4. Data of experiment, semester 2020-1

	With tool	Without tool	Total
Groups	3	3	6
Teachers	3	3	6
Students	47	50	97

4.1   Experiment Data

The **Algorithms and Programming** course was used as a case study during semesters 2019-2 and 2020-1. A total of 11 class groups, 7 teachers and 175 students participated. This is shown in Tables 3 and 4. 5 groups in 2019-2, 6 groups 2020-1, with 5 teachers in 2019-2 and 6 teachers in 2020-1 (4 teachers participated both semesters). 175 students (2019-2 with 78 students participated in 2019-2 and 97 in semester 2020-1. There were no specific student selection based on any performance related bias for participating in the study, and the control and test groups were randomly selected.

In the 2019-2 semester, the students and teachers developed the course in person with the support of the LMS for the evaluation process, facing three joint exam evaluations. By 2020-1, due to the pandemic, students and teachers were in need of developing the course remotely, but as with the 2019-2 groups, the students faced three joint assessments. At the end of each semester, academic performance was measured and a survey was implemented to the students, where they were asked about the quality of the questions, the organization of the questionnaires and the difficulty. As for the teachers, another survey was applied, where they were asked about the academic performance of their students, the organization of the course and the ease and effectiveness of evaluating the students. The surveys used a scale of 1 to 5 satisfaction, where: 0 was very dissatisfied and 5 very satisfied, each survey averaged the results of both the individuals, classifying them in the courses where the tool had been used and where it was not used, It should be noted that the students did not know which group they were in.

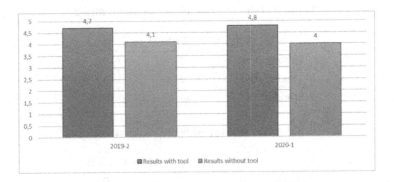

Fig. 4. Teachers Average Survey Results. Scale of 1 to 5 in satisfaction, where: 1 means Very Dissatisfied and 5 means very satisfied.

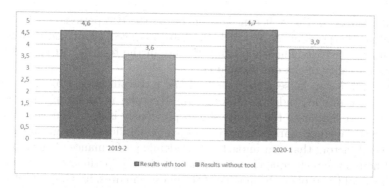

Fig. 5. Student Average Survey Results. Scale of 1 to 5 in satisfaction, where: 1 means Very Dissatisfied and 5 means very satisfied.

4.2   Analysis of Results

The results obtained in the experiments reveal several aspects on the perception of the students, teachers, and academic performance in the course. Starting with the teachers' perception, in Fig. 4, where can be seen that teachers analyzed if evaluation activities were in accordance with the design of the course content, order, and the perception of fraud among the students. The results show that those who used the tool gave a better assessment against those who did not use it, because the teachers who participated with the use of the tool had feedback, and could better control the development of the course in order and time.

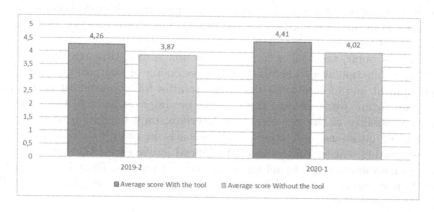

Fig. 6. General average performance Score.

As for the students, a better assessment was also seen by this population, since the groups in which the tool was used, unlike the teachers, did not know which cluster they were in, which makes these results show reliably impact of the tool in the design and implementation of evaluation mechanisms based on question banks. In Fig. 5, it can be seen that in the two periods in which it was evaluated, the population in which the tool was used significantly valued the evaluation activities. This shows that the use of the tool has an impact on the perceived quality of the questionnaires.

In Fig. 6, it can be seen that the tool had a certain impact on the academic performance of the students, although these results must be interpreted with care, a trend similar to the results shown previously is seen; But the difference between the average marks of the courses is not significant, this given that there are several factors that can impact the academic performance of the students.

Although the technique used in the design of the experiment tries to measure the impact of the tool on the quality of the questionnaires, it is important to clarify that it should continue to be applied in more courses from different disciplines to better measure the impact generated and make the necessary adjustments.

5   Conclusions

The question validation tool and the generation of question banks has shown to have a positive impact on the design and implementation of competence assessment activities in learning management systems (LMS) for the particular case study. It also helped teachers to better design the thematic content of the courses, demonstrating that the developed tool has a place on the ICT-mediated education ecosystem.

During development, the pandemic originated by the Covid-19 was faced, forcing the higher education institutions that work in face-to-face mode to migrate their courses to remote or virtual mode. We think that the proposed model and future versions of the tool have a market where it could bring together teachers from multiple universities and generate validated question banks with a variety of teachers.

At this point, the tool is not in production stage. Although the tool has the basic functionalities identified at the beginning of the project, during its development and closure there were opportunities for improvement that could generate future work, among them, could be: improvements in the usability and accessibility of the graphical user interface; implementation of a grading system for questions, corrections, and feedback, in order to give a rating to the evaluating teachers, integration of artificial intelligence (AI) that fueled by teacher interaction learns to automatically assess questions. These improvements could create an ecosystem with more functionalities and more impact on ICT-mediated education.

References

1. Barberà, E.: Aportaciones de la tecnología a la e-Evaluación Technological contributions to e-Assessment Introducción. RED. Revista de Investigación a Distancia, pp. 1–13 (2005)
2. Bécue Bertaut, M.: Análisis estadístico de datos de encuestas. Tratamiento conexo de respuestas a preguntas abiertas y cerradas. Papers. Revista de Sociologia **37**, 113 (1991). https://doi.org/10.5565/rev/papers/v37n0.1599
3. Belloch, C.: Entornos Virtuales de Aprendizaje. Unidad de Tecnología Educativa (UTE). Universidad de Valencia, pp. 1–9 (2009)
4. Blosser, P.E.: How to ... Ask the Right Questions. National Science Teachers Association, Nov ember 2015. https://doi.org/10.2505/9780873551021
5. Rafael, C.J.: Evaluación del aprendizaje en espacios virtuales -TIC. Ediciones Uninorte (2011)
6. Carnoy, M.: Las TIC en la enseñanza: posibilidades y retos. Lección inaugural del curso académico **10**(1), 20 (2004)
7. Cuervo-Arango, M.A.: Metodología de cuestionarios: Principios y aplicaciones. Boletín de la Anabad **43**(3), 263–272 (1993)
8. Fernández, F.: La evaluación y su importancia en la educación. Distancia por tiempos (2018). https://educacion.nexos.com.mx/?p=1016
9. Fernández Núñez, L.: ¿Cómo se elabora un cuestionario? Bulletí LaRecerca **1**(2002), 1–9 (2007). ISSN 1886–1964
10. García-Martínez, R., Lage, F., Pessaq, R., Cataldi, Z.: Metodología extendida para la creación de software educativo desde una visión integradora. RELATEC: Revista Latinoamericana de Tecnología Educativa **2**(1), 1–32 (2003)
11. García-Peñalvo, F.J., García-Holgado, A.: Open source solutions for knowledge management and technological ecosystems. IGI Global, October 2016. https://doi.org/10.4018/978-1-5225-0905-9
12. García-Peñalvo, F.J., Seoane Pardo, A.M.: Una revisión actualizada del concepto de eLearning. Décimo Aniversario. Education in the Knowledge Society (EKS) **16**(1), 119 (2015). https://doi.org/10.14201/eks2015161119144
13. Hamari, J., Sjöklint, M., Ukkonen, A.: The sharing economy: Why people participate in collaborative consumption. J. Assoc. Inf. Sci. Technol. **67**(9), 2047–2059 (2016). https://doi.org/10.1002/asi.23552
14. Informatik, A., Manente, D., Schaefer, S., Koch, P.F.: Moodle Plugin StudentQuiz Bachelorarbeit. HSR Hochschule für Technik Rapperswil, Bachelorarbeit (2017)
15. Jefferson, R., Arnold, L.: Effects of virtual education on academic culture: perceived advantages and disadvantages. Online Submission **6**(3), 61–66 (2009)
16. Koufetta-Menicou, C., Scaife, J.: Teachers' questions - types and significance in science education. Sch. Sci. Rev. **81**(296), 79–84 (2000)
17. Lezcano, L., Vilanova, G.: Instrumentos de evaluación de aprendizaje en entornos virtuales. Perspectiva de estudiantes y aportes de docentes. Informes Científicos Técnicos - UNPA **9**(1), 1–36 (2017). https://doi.org/10.22305/ict-unpa.v9i1.235
18. Luxton-Reilly, A., Lewis, A., Plimmer, B.: Comparing sequential and parallel code review techniques for formative feedback. In: ACM International Conference Proceeding Series, pp. 45–52. Association for Computing Machinery, New York, New York, USA, January 2018. https://doi.org/10.1145/3160489.3160498
19. Marmolejo, E.K., Wilder, D.A., Bradley, L.: A preliminary analysis of the effects of response cards on student performance and participation in an upper division university course. J. Appl. Behav. Anal. **37**(3), 405–410 (2004). https://doi.org/10.1901/jaba.2004.37-405

20. Medved, J.: LMS Industry User Research Report (2017). http://www.capterra. com/learning-management-system-software/user-research
21. Mirzakhani, M., Ashrafzadeh, H., Ashrafzadeh, A.: The virtual university: advantages and disadvantages. In: ICDLE 2010–2010 4th International Conference on Distance Learning and Education, Proceedings, pp. 32–36 (2010). https://doi.org/ 10.1109/ICDLE.2010.5606048
22. Moodle: Moodle - Open-source learning platform | Moodle.org (2018). https:// moodle.org/
23. O'Donoghue, J., Singh, G., Dorward, L.: Virtual education in universities: a technological imperative. Br. J. Educ. Technol. 32(5), 511–523 (2001). https://doi.org/ 10.1111/1467-8535.00221
24. Roldán López, N.: Ambientes virtuales de aprendizaje (AVAS): ¿Cómo quieren aprender los estudiantes? Revista Virtual Universidad Católica del Norte 1(19) (2011)
25. Salinas Quiroz, J.: Diseño y moderación de entornos virtuales de aprendizaje (EVA). Editorial UOC (Universitat Oberta de Catalunya), S.L, Barcelona (2011)
26. Slavin, R.E.: Student teams and comparison among equals: effects on academic performance and student attitudes. J. Educ. Psychol. 70(4), 532–538 (1978). https:// doi.org/10.1037/0022-0663.70.4.532
27. Stowell, J.R., Nelson, J.M.: Benefits of electronic audience response systems on student participation, learning, and emotion. Teach. Psychol. 34(4), 253–258 (2007). https://doi.org/10.1080/00986280701700391
28. UNESCO: El Coronavirus COVID-19 y la educación superior: impacto y recomendaciones - UNESCO-IESALC (2020). https://www.iesalc.unesco.org/2020/04/02/ el-coronavirus-covid-19-y-la-educacion-superior-impacto-y-recomendaciones/
29. Vera, J.: Valor Pedagógico De La Evaluación Mediada Por Las Tic. Technical report, Universidad Nacional de Colombia, Medellín, Colombia (2013)
30. Wilson, G., Randall, M.: The implementation and evaluation of a new learning space: a pilot study. Res. Learn. Technol. 20(2) (2012). https://doi.org/10.3402/ rlt.v20i0/14431
31. Zhang, D., Zhao, J.L., Zhou, L., Nunamaker, J.F.: Can e-learning replace classroom learning? (may 2004). https://doi.org/10.1145/986213.986216

Simulation and Emulation

Early Breast Cancer Detection by Using a Sensor-Antenna

Hector F. Guarnizo-Mendez[1]([⊠]), N. P. Rodríguez Rincón[1], P. P. Plata Rodríguez[1], M. A. Polochè Arango[2], and D. F. Márquez Romero[1]

[1] Universidad El Bosque, Bogotá, Colombia
{hguarnizo,nprodriguezr,pplatar,dmarquezr}@unbosque.edu.co
[2] Universidad de San Buenaventura, Bogotá, Colombia
mpoloche@usbbog.edu.co

Abstract. In the last decades, the early detection of cancer has motivated many researches works because these increases the possibilities of survival of patients and positive responses to different treatments. Particularly, this work concerns the preliminary results obtained in the detection of a cancerous tumor (5 mm cube) at early stage that concerns a breast using a sensor-antenna. The sensor-antenna operates at a frequency of 2.45 GHz. A breast model was implemented in ANSYS® with electrical properties (conductivity and permeability) of the tissues (fat, skin, and tumor). The detection of cancerous tumor (5 mm cube) at early stage was carried out for five different tumor positions (center, west, north, east, and south) inside the breast (XY plane). Furthermore, in each of the five different tumor positions, the tumor was located at 5 different depths (YZ or XZ plane) with the spacing of 10 mm. The simulation results obtained show that the sensor-antenna is fit for detect a 5 mm tumor. The tumor was detected in the 5 different positions (XY plane) and in the 5 different depths (XZ or YZ plane).

Keywords: Sensor-antenna · Possibilities survival · Positive responses · Breast cancer detection

1 Introduction

The spread and uncontrolled growth of abnormal cells are the characteristics of the disease called cancer. Nowadays, the second leading cause of death worldwide is cancer [1]. In the study carried out in 2018 by the Global Cancer Observatory with respect to new cancer cases in the world, it was estimated that 11% correspond to new Brest cancer cases. Moreover, it was estimated that 6.6% of deaths (men and women) in the world will be caused by breast cancer. For both sexes, the incidence of cancer in North America and Europe is 12.6% and 25% respectively. For both sexes, mortality in North America and Europe is 7.5% and 22% respectively [2]. The probability of death by breast cancer can be reduced, detecting the tumor at early stage [3]. Standard methods such as Ultrasound (US) [4], X-ray Mammography [5], Biosensor [6], and Biomarker [7] are implemented in the context of the breast cancer detection.

© Springer Nature Switzerland AG 2020
H. Florez and S. Misra (Eds.): ICAI 2020, CCIS 1277, pp. 451–466, 2020.
https://doi.org/10.1007/978-3-030-61702-8_31

Along with these methods, another method implemented is the detection of the breast cancer by using the microwave. This method is based mainly on the differences between the conductivity and dielectric constant of the tumor and the healthy breast tissues [8]. Microwave cancer detection has taken a great interest in the context of breast cancer because it is cost effective, low health risk, cozy for the patient, non-ionizing and noninvasive procedure and has a potential to detect small tumors [9]. Microwave cancer detection includes techniques such as Radar-Based Microwave Imaging [10] and Microwave Tomography [11]. In the context of breast cancer detection are used antipodal Vivaldi antenna [12], patch antenna [13], dielectric resonator antenna [14], monopole antenna [15], horn antenna [16], printed inverted-F antenna [17], slot antenna [18], bowtie antenna [19], Hilbert fractal antenna [20], dielectric waveguide [21] and inverted cone antenna [22].

In this paper, the detection of a cancerous tumor at early stage is presented. A sensor-antenna (at 2.45 GHz) and an interrogator system were used to carry out the detection of a cancerous tumor at early stage. A 0.5 cm tumor located in 5 different positions (XY plane) inside the breast was detected. Moreover, in each of the 5 different positions, the tumor was detected at 5 different depths (YZ or XZ plane) with the spacing of 10 mm. In the breast model were considered the skin, fat, and tumor. The breast model was implemented in ANSYS® by using electrical properties (conductivity and permittivity) of the breast tissues.

2 Methodology

To model the breast were taken into account the fat, skin, muscle and tumor [23]. The tumor has the shape of a cube. The cube edge length was of 0.5 cm. The electromagnetic model of the breast was implemented with a radius of 6.5 cm. The simulation setup is showed in the Table 1. The simulation process was carried out in the software ANSYS®. The simulation process flow chart is showed in [24].

Table 1. Configuration setup implemented in ANSYS®.

Properties	Values
Maximum number of passes	20
Maximum delta S	0.01
Minimum converged passes	4
Order of basis function	Mixed order

The electrical properties (relative permittivity and conductivity) of the fat, skin, lobes, muscle, and tumor used in the electromagnetic model are presented in the Table 2 [25, 26].

Table 2. Electrical properties of the breast tissues.

Tissue	Relative permittivity	Conductivity (S/m)
Muscle	52.7	1.7
Tumor	60	2.5
Fat	5.3	0.3
Skin	38	1.5

3 Detection Proposed System

The system raised to detect a cancerous tumor at early stage within the breast consists of two parts, 1) a sensor which is comprised by a resonant cavity whose resonance frequency is 2.45 GHz, this frequency is used because it is part of the spectrum reserved for industrial, scientific and medical (ISM) purposes. Planar technology was used to implement the resonant cavity [27]. Furthermore, on the top wall of the cavity a meandered antenna at 2.45 GHz is printed. This meandered antenna is spotted as magnetic dipole [28], it has two functions. First function, it is to capture the electromagnetic energy in the cavity. Second function, it is to provide information about the concentration of energy within the cavity. 2) A system of interrogation, this name is due to the fact that the system has the function of energizing the sensor and pick up information about the concentration of electromagnetic energy within the cavity. System of interrogation consists of two patch antennas at 2.45 GHz. Planar technology was used to implement the patch antennas too [29, 30]. The first antenna (TX) sends the electromagnetic energy to the sensor. The second antenna (RX) pick up the information on the concentration of electromagnetic energy within the cavity, this information is provided by the sensor (see Fig. 1) [30].

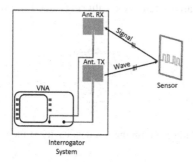

Fig. 1. Interrogator system and proposed sensor-antenna.

3.1 Operation Principle and Detection of a Cancerous Tumor at Early Stage

The sensor is composed of a resonant cavity, a meandered antenna printed on the top wall of the resonant cavity. The two side walls, the front wall and the back wall of resonant cavity were implemented by using through-holes [30, 31], Through-holes are used because the cavity is implemented in Substrate integrated waveguide (SIW) technology, in this technology the two side walls, the front wall and the back wall of the cavity are implemented by means of through-holes.

For the operation of the system, initially the meandered antenna must be irradiated-illuminated by electromagnetic energy (constant power). This electromagnetic energy is generated by the first antenna (TX) of the interrogator system (see Fig. 1 and Fig. 2). From the electromagnetic energy captured by meandered antenna and which is sent inside of the cavity, the sensor is energized [30, 31].

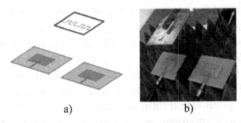

a)   b)

Fig. 2. Interrogator system and sensor-antenna a) system implemented in ANSYS®, b) experimental setup carried out in laboratory.

The captured electromagnetic energy will be reflected on the internal walls of the resonant cavity producing an accumulation of energy within it. This accumulated energy will be radiated outside. The energy radiated outside is read in the form of short-wave pulses by the second antenna (TR) of the interrogator system (see Fig. 4 and Fig. 6). These short-wave pulses are called backscattering. (see Fig. 3) [30, 31].

Fig. 3. Electric field distribution within the resonant cavity of the sensor-antenna at 2.45 GHz.

In Fig. 4, the interrogator system, the sensor, and the vector network analyzer (VNA) are presented. The vector network analyzer is instrument used to carry out the measurement of parameter S21. Parameter S21 is the transmission coefficient, it is a measure of the transmitted energy from the first antenna (TX) to second antenna (TR)

Detection of cancerous tumor at early stage was carried out based on the operation principle described above. First, a circular slot (radius = 6 mm) was printed on the

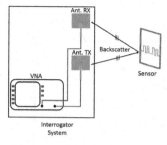

Fig. 4. Sensor-antenna and interrogator system.

bottom wall of the sensor. This circular slot generates a variation in the energy of the resonant cavity; this energy variation produces a shift in the frequency of the sensor. Second, the sensor-antenna with the circular slot in its bottom wall was placed over the breast model (without the tumor) (see Fig. 5), the substrate of the sensor and the breast model are in contact. The sensor-antenna was retuned to 2.45 GHz due to the shift produced by the energy variation.

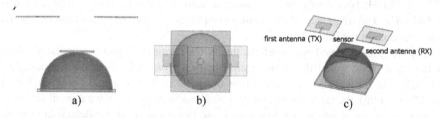

Fig. 5. 3D breast model (without the tumor) and interrogation system

Lung disease is another disease that has a high mortality rate in the world. To detect the disease at an early stage, technologies such as x-ray images are implemented.

Lung diseases at an early stage may not be detected by using X-ray images because they may be camouflaged by adjacent tissues or anatomical structures, or poor image quality, or radiologist's decision criteria. To improve the efficiency of x-ray images and reduce the number of false positives, computer-aided diagnosis (CAD) is being implemented. However, in computer-aided diagnosis (CAD) data processing is complex and difficult.

Based on the above, in the context of early detection of lung diseases, the early detection system for breast cancer presented in this article can be used as a Neoadjuvant system because the operating principle of this system is based on the variation of the permittivity of the breast when a tumor appears in it.

The reading (simulated S_{21} parameter) carried out by the interrogator system from breast model without tumor is presented in the Fig. 6.

The Fig. 6 shows that the short-wave pulses present in simulated S_{21} parameter occurs at 2.45 GHz. The process to obtain the short-wave pulses in parameter S21 is described down below: the first antenna (TX) (see Fig. 5 c) sends electromagnetic energy to the sensor (see Fig. 5 c), this energy is captured inside the cavity. The captured

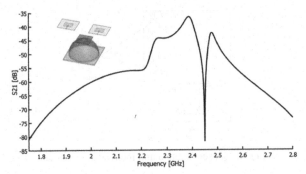

Fig. 6. Simulation of the short-wave pulses reading by the interrogator system from breast model without tumor.

electromagnetic energy will be reflected on the internal walls of the resonant cavity, producing an accumulation of energy inside the cavity. This accumulated energy will radiate outside. The energy radiated to the outside is read in the form of short-wave pulses by the second antenna (TR) (see Fig. 5 c). Short wave pulses appear in parameter S21 at 2.45 GHz because the first antenna, the second antenna and the sensor are tuned to 2.45 GHz. The frequency where short wave-pulses occurs will present a shift when a tumor appears in the breast.

For the case presented in this article, that is, the permittivity and conductivity values of the breast tissues and the tumor were obtained from [25, 26] for a frequency of 2.45 GHz. In the case of early detection of breast cancer in a real breast or breast model (phantom), the values of permittivity and conductivity may have a small variation for different women which would cause a low performance of the detection system. Therefore, it is necessary to perform tests with different real breasts in order to improve and adjust the performance of the early detection system for breast cancer.

4   Results

For the early breast cancer detection, five tumor positions (XY plane) were considered (see Fig. 7).

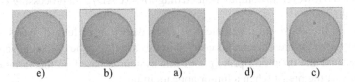

Fig. 7. Tumor positions inside the breast model a) center, b) west, c) north, d) east, e) south.

First, the tumor was located as shown Fig. 7 a. Second, the tumor was located as shown Fig. 7b. Third, the tumor was located as shown Fig. 7c. Fourth the tumor was located as shown Fig. 7 d. Finally, the tumor was located as shown Fig. 7e.

For the 5 tumor positions, the tumor location has a shifting from 3 mm to 55 mm under the skin (XZ and YZ plane). Figure 8 shows the interrogator system, sensor-antenna, and breast model (with tumor) implemented in ANSYS®. The frequency will present a shifting where short wave-pulses occurs because the electrical properties (relative permittivity and conductivity) of the breast have changed. The electrical properties of the breast have changed due to the presence of the electrical properties (relative permittivity and conductivity) of the tumor within the breast. The electrical properties of the tumor have a value greater than the electrical properties of the other breast tissues (see Table 2).

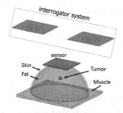

Fig. 8. 3D model of interrogator system, sensor, and breast model (skin, fat, muscle, and tumor).

Figure 9 shows the simulated S_{21} parameter (short-wave pulses) reading by the interrogator system when the tumor is located as shown Fig. 7 a (XY plane). The tumor location was shifting from 4 mm to 44 mm (Table 3, column 1, row 2, 3, 4, 5 and 6) under the skin (YZ plane) with a spacing of 10 mm.

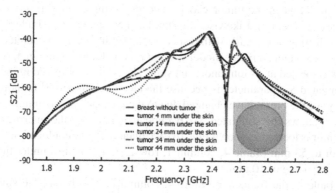

Fig. 9. Simulated S_{21} parameter (short wave pulses) read by the interrogator system when the tumor is located in breast's center (Fig. 7a).

In the Table 3, the frequency (Table 3, column 2, row 1) and the simulated S_{21} parameter (Table 3, column 3, row 1) reading by the interrogator system from the breast model (without tumor) are presented. Next, the frequency (Table 3, column 2, row 2, 3, 4, 5 and 6) and the simulated S_{21} parameter (Table 3, column 3, row 2, 3, 4, 5 and 6) reading by the interrogator system from the breast model when the tumor is presented and its location shifting from 4 mm to 44 mm under the skin (YZ plane) with a spacing of 10 mm are presented.

Table 3. Simulated S_{21} parameter (short wave pulses).

Tumor position under skin (mm)	Frequency (GHz)	Simulated S21 parameter (short wave pulses) (dB)
breast model without tumor	2.4498	−81.91
4	2.4705	−49.99
14	2.4493	−52.36
24	2.4504	−55.91
34	2.4416	−50.51
44	2.4479	−69.35

In the Fig. 9 and Table 3, it is observed that the frequency (Table 3, column 2, row 2 and 3) reading by the interrogator system has a 0.9% shifting (with respect to the frequency reading by the interrogator system on breast model without tumor, Table 3, column 2, row 1) when the tumor was located to 4 mm and 14 mm under the skin. For the other locations (Table 3, column 1, row 4, 5 and 6) of the tumor, the frequency (Table 3, column 2, row 4, 5 and 6) reading by the interrogator system has a 0.2% shifting (with respect to the frequency reading by the interrogator system on breast model without tumor, Table 3, column 2, row 1). With respect to the simulated S_{21} parameter (Table 3, column 3, row 2, 3, and 4), it shows a shifting of −30 dB (with respect to the simulated S_{21} parameter reading by the interrogator system on breast model without tumor, Table 3, column 3, row 1) when the tumor was located in the three initial positions (Table 3, column 1, row 2, 3 and 4). Likewise, the simulated S_{21} parameter (Table 3, column 3, row 6) has a shifting of −10 dB (with respect to the simulated S_{21} parameter reading by the interrogator system on breast model without tumor, Table 3, column 3, row 1) when the tumor was located at 44 mm under the skin. The shifting observed in the frequency and the simulated S_{21} parameter is because the electrical properties (conductivity and permeability) of the breast have changed due to the presence of the tumor.

Figure 10 shows the simulated S_{21} parameter reading by the interrogator system when the tumor is located as shown Fig. 7b (XY plane). The tumor location was shifting from 13 mm to 53 mm (Table 4, column 1, row 2, 3, 4, 5 and 6) under the skin (YZ plane) with a spacing of 10 mm.

In the Table 4, the frequency (Table 4, column 2, row 1) and the simulated S_{21} parameter (Table 4, column 3, row 1) reading by the interrogator system from of the breast model without tumor are presented. Likewise, the frequency (Table 4, column 2, row 2, 3, 4, 5 and 6) and simulated S_{21} parameter (Table 4, column 3, row 2, 3, 4, 5 and 6) reading by the interrogator system from the breast model when the tumor location was shifting from 13 mm to 53 mm under the skin (YZ plane) with a spacing of 10 mm are presented.

In Fig. 10 and Table 4, it can be observed that the frequency (Table 4, column 2, row 2 and 3) reading by the interrogator system has a 0.1% shifting (with respect to the

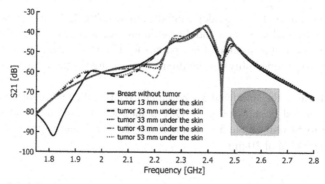

Fig. 10. Simulated S_{21} parameter (short-wave pulses) reading by the interrogator system when the tumor is located as shown Fig. 7b.

Table 4. Simulated S_{21} parameter (short wave pulses).

Tumor position under skin (mm)	Frequency (GHz)	Simulated S21 parameter (short wave pulses) (dB)
breast model without tumor	2.4498	−81.91
13	2.4475	−53.59
23	2.4504	−51.50
33	2.4494	−60.46
43	2.4482	−58.43
53	2.4548	−52.83

frequency reading by the interrogator system on breast model without tumor, Table 4, column 2, row 1) when the tumor was located to 13 mm and 23 mm under the skin. The frequency reading (Table 4, column 2, row 4 and 5) by the interrogator system has a 0.05% shifting (with respect to the frequency reading by the interrogator system on breast model without tumor, Table 4, column 2, row 1) when the tumor was located to 33 mm, and 43 mm under the skin.

Finally, the frequency reading (Table 4, column 2, row 6) by the interrogator system has a 0.3% shifting (with respect to the frequency reading by the interrogator system on breast model without tumor, Table 4, column 2, row 1) when the tumor was located to 53 mm under the skin. With respect to the simulated S_{21} parameter (Table 4, column 3, row 2, 3 and 6), it can be observed a shifting of −30 dB (with respect to the simulated S_{21} parameter reading by the interrogator system on breast model without tumor, Table 4, column 3, row 1) when the tumor was located at 13 mm, 23 mm, and 53 mm under the skin. Moreover, the simulated S_{21} parameter (Table 4, column 3, row 4 and 5) has a shifting of −20 dB (with respect to the simulated S_{21} parameter reading by the interrogator system on breast model without tumor, Table 4, column 3, row 1) when the tumor was located at 33 mm and 43 mm under the skin. The shifting observed in the frequency and in the simulated S_{21} parameter is because the electrical properties (conductivity and permeability) of the breast have changed due to the presence of the tumor.

Figure 11 shows the simulated S_{21} parameter read by the interrogator system when the tumor is located as shown Fig. 7c (XY plane). The tumor's location was shifting from 14 mm to 54 mm (Table 5, column 1, row 2, 3, 4, 5 and 6) under the skin (XZ plane) with a spacing of 10 mm.

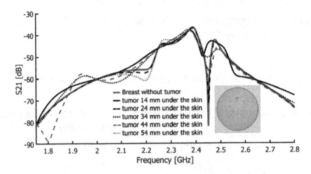

Fig. 11. Simulated S_{21} parameter (short-wave pulses) reading by the interrogator system when the tumor is located as shown Fig. 7 c.

Table 5. Simulated S_{21} parameter (short wave pulses).

Tumor position under skin (mm)	Frequency (GHz)	Simulated S21 parameter (short wave pulses) (dB)
breast model without tumor	2.4498	−81.91
14	2.4287	−49.90
24	2.4519	−71.55
34	2.4482	−50.33
44	2.4550	−56.77
54	2.4501	−61.57

In the Table 5, the frequency (Table 5, column 2, row 1) and the simulated S_{21} parameter (Table 5, column 3, row 1) reading by the interrogator system from the breast model without tumor are presented. Likewise, the frequency (Table 5, column 2, row 2, 3, 4, 5 and 6) and the simulated S_{21} parameter (Table 5, column 3, row 2, 3, 4, 5 and 6) reading by the interrogator system from breast model when the tumor location was shifting from 14 mm to 54 mm under the skin (XZ plane) with a spacing of 10 mm are presented.

In Fig. 11 and Table 5, it can be observed that the frequency reading (Table 5, column 2, row 2 and 3) by the interrogator system has a 0.9% shifting (with respect to the frequency reading by the interrogator system on breast model without tumor, Table 5, column 2, row 1) when the tumor was located to 14 mm and 24 mm under the skin. The frequency reading (Table 5, column 2, row 4 and 6) by the interrogator system has a 0.2% shifting (with respect to the frequency reading by the interrogator system on breast model without tumor, Table 5, column 2, row 1) when the tumor was located to 34 mm and 54 mm under the skin. Finally, the frequency reading (Table 5, column 3, row 5) by the interrogator system has a 0.3% shifting (with respect to the frequency reading by the interrogator system on breast model without tumor, Table 5, column 2, row 1) when the tumor was located to 44 mm under the skin. With respect to the simulated S_{21} parameter (Table 5, column 3, row 2 and 4), it can be observed a shifting of -30 dB (with respect to the simulated S_{21} parameter reading by the interrogator system on breast model without tumor, Table 5, column 3, row 1) when the tumor was located at 14 mm and 34 mm under the skin. The simulated S_{21} parameter (Table 5, column 3, row 5 and 6) has a shifting of -20 dB (with respect to the simulated S_{21} parameter reading by the interrogator system on breast model without tumor, Table 5, column 3, row 1) when the tumor was located at 44 mm and 54 mm under the skin. Finally, the simulated S_{21} parameter (Table 5, column 3, row 3) has a shifting of -10 dB (with respect to the simulated S_{21} parameter reading by the interrogator system on breast model without tumor, Table 5, column 3, row 1) when the tumor was located at 24 mm under the skin. The shifting observed in the frequency and the simulated S_{21} parameter are because the electrical properties (conductivity and permeability) of the breast have changed due to the presence of the tumor.

Figure 12 shows the simulated S_{21} parameter reading by the interrogator system when the tumor is located as shown Fig. 7 d (XY plane). The tumor location was shifting from 13 mm to 53 mm (Table 6, column 1, row 2, 3, 4, 5 and 6) under the skin (YZ plane) with a spacing of 10 mm.

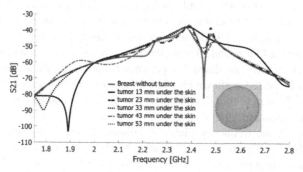

Fig. 12. Simulated S_{21} parameter reading by the interrogator system when the tumor is located as shown Fig. 7 d.

In the Table 6, the frequency (Table 6, column 2, row 1) and the simulated S_{21} parameter (Table 6, column 2, row 1) reading by the interrogator system from the breast model without tumor are presented. Likewise, the frequency (Table 6, column 2, row 2,

Table 6. Simulated S_{21} parameter.

Tumor position under skin (mm)	Frequency (GHz)	Simulated S21 parameter (short wave pulses) (dB)
breast model without tumor	2.4498	−81.91
13	2.3899	−37.58
23	2.4503	−54.36
33	2.4482	−50.49
43	2.4507	−66.16
53	2.4493	−63.87

3, 4, 5 and 6) and the simulated S_{21} parameter (Table 6, column 3, row 2, 3, 4, 5 and 6) reading by the interrogator system from of the breast model when the tumor location was shifting from 13 mm to 53 mm under the skin (YZ plane) with the spacing of 10 mm are presented.

In Fig. 12 and Table 6, it can be observed that the frequency (Table 6, column 2, row 2 and 3) reading by the interrogator system has a 2.4% shifting (with respect to the frequency reading by the interrogator system on breast model without tumor, Table 6, column 2, row 1) when the tumor was located to 13 mm and 23 mm under the skin. For the other locations of the tumor (Table 6, column 1, row 4, 5 and 6), the frequency (Table 6, column 2, row 4, 5 and 6), reading by the interrogator system has a 0.1% shifting (with respect to the frequency reading by the interrogator system on breast model without tumor, Table 6, column 2, row 1). With respect to the simulated S_{21} parameter (Table 6, column 3, row 3 and 4), it can be observed a shifting of −30 dB (with respect to the simulated S_{21} parameter reading by the interrogator system on breast model without tumor, Table 6, column 3, row 1) when the tumor was located at 23 mm and 33 mm under the skin. The simulated S_{21} parameter (Table 6, column 3, row 5 and 6) has a shifting of −20 dB (with respect to the simulated S_{21} parameter reading by the interrogator system on breast model without tumor, Table 6, column 3, row 1) when the tumor was located at 43 mm and 53 mm (Table 6, column 3, row 5 and 6) under the skin.

Figure 13 shows the simulated S_{21} parameter reading by the interrogator system when the tumor is located as shown Fig. 7 e (XY plane). The tumor location was shifting from 12 mm to 52 mm (Table 7, column 1, row 2, 3, 4, 5 and 6) under the skin (XZ plane) with the spacing of 10 mm.

In the Table 7, the frequency (Table 7, column 2, row 1) and the simulated S_{21} parameter (Table 7, column 3, row 1) reading by the interrogator system from of the breast model without tumor are presented. likewise, the frequency (Table 7, column 2, row 2, 3, 4, 5 and 6) and the simulated S_{21} parameter (Table 7, column 3, row 2, 3, 4, 5 and 6) reading by the interrogator system from of the breast model when the tumor location was a shifting from 12 mm to 52 mm under the skin (XZ plane) with a spacing of 10 mm are presented.

In the Fig. 13 and Table 7, it can be observed that the frequency (Table 7, column 2, row 3 and 4) reading by the interrogator system has a 4.5% shifting (with respect

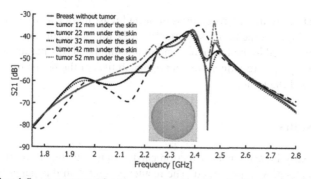

Fig. 13. Simulated S_{21} parameter (short wave pulses) reading by the interrogator system when the tumor is located as shown Fig. 7 e.

Table 7. Simulated parameter S_{21} (short wave pulses).

Tumor position under skin (mm)	Frequency (GHz)	Simulated S21 parameter (short wave pulses) (dB)
breast model without tumor	2.4498	−81.91
12	2.4492	−49.57
22	2.3404	−39.90
32	2.4548	−55.18
42	2.4449	−50.61
52	2.4494	−73.68

to the frequency reading by the interrogator system on breast model without tumor, Table 7, column 2, row 1) when the tumor was located to 22 mm and 32 mm under the skin. The frequency (Table 7, column 2, row 5) reading by the interrogator system has a 0.4% shifting (with respect to the frequency reading by the interrogator system on breast model without tumor, Table 7, column 2, row 1) when the tumor was located to 42 mm under the skin. For the other locations of the tumor (Table 7, column 1, row 1 and 6), the frequency (Table 7, column 2, row 1 and 6) reading by the interrogator system has a shifting of 0.01% (with respect to the frequency reading by the interrogator system on breast model without tumor, Table 7, column 2, row 1). With respect to the simulated S21 parameter (Table 7, column 3, row 2, 4 and 5), it can be observed a shift of − 30 dB (with respect to the simulated S21 parameter reading by the interrogator system on breast model without tumor, Table 7, column 3, row 1) when the tumor was located at 12, 32 and 42 mm under the skin. The simulated S21 parameter (Table 7, column 3, row 6) has a shifting of −10 dB (with respect to the simulated S21 parameter reading by the interrogator system on breast model without tumor, Table 7, column 3, row 1) when the tumor was located at 52 mm under the skin. Finally, the simulated S21 parameter (Table 7, column 3, row 3) has a shift of −40 dB (with respect to the simulated S21 parameter reading by the interrogator system on breast model without tumor, Table 7, column 3, row 1) when the tumor was located at 22 mm under the skin.

The shift observed in the frequency and in the simulated S21 parameter are because the electrical properties (conductivity and permeability) of the breast have changed due to the presence of the tumor.

5 Conclusions

In this work, early breast cancer detection carried out by using an interrogator system and a sensor-antenna was presented. The results presented in this paper were obtained from simulations carried out in the HFSS software, currently a breast model (phantom) is being manufactured. With this breast model (phantom), the measurements will be carried out. From results, it can be asserted that a 5 mm tumor can be detected by using the sensor-antenna. The tumor was detected in 5 different positions (under the skin, XY plane). Moreover, the tumor was detected (under the skin) when its location shifting from 4 mm to 54 mm under the skin (XZ or YZ plane) with a spacing of 10 mm.

Currently, the interrogator system and antenna-sensor to detect a cancerous tumor at early stage are in manufacturing process. Also, an interrogator system and a sensor-antenna at 5 GHz are being developed to detect a cancerous tumor at early stage.

References

1. American Cancer Society, Global cancer facts & figures. 4th edn. (2018)
2. G. The Global Cancer Observatory, "Breast Cancer. Source: Globocan 2018," World Health Organization (2018). http://gco.iarc.fr/today
3. Bassi, M., Caruso, M., Khan, M.S., Bevilacqua, A., Capobianco, A.D., Neviani, A.: An integrated microwave imaging radar with planar antennas for breast cancer detection. IEEE Trans. Microw. Theor. Tech. 61(5), 2108–2118 (2013)
4. Kelly, K.M., Dean, J., Comulada, W.S., Lee, S.J.: Breast cancer detection using automated whole breast ultrasound and mammography in radiographically dense breasts. Eur. Radiol. 20(3), 734–742 (2010)
5. Gur, D., et al.: Changes in breast cancer detection and mammography recall rates after the introduction of a computer-aided detection system. J. Natl Cancer Inst. 96(3), 185–190 (2004)
6. Arif, S., Qudsia, S., Urooj, S., Chaudry, N., Arshad, A., Andleeb, S.: Blueprint of quartz crystal microbalance biosensor for early detection of breast cancer through salivary autoantibodies against ATP6AP1. Biosens. Bioelectron. 65, 62–70 (2015)
7. Loke, S.Y., Lee, A.S.G.: The future of blood-based biomarkers for the early detection of breast cancer. Eur. J. Cancer 92, 54–68 (2018)
8. Mashal, A., et al.: Toward carbon-nanotube-based theranostic agents for microwave detection and treatment of breast cancer: Enhanced dielectric and heating response of tissue-mimicking materials. IEEE Trans. Biomed. Eng. 57(8), 1831–1834 (2010)
9. Fear, E.C., Meaney, P.M., Stuchly, M.A.: Microwaves for breast cancer detection? IEEE Potentials 22(1), 12–18 (2003)
10. Vemulapalli, S., Khan, M., Chatterjee, D.: Analysis of ultrawideband microwave imaging via space time beamforming algorithm in the frequency domain. In: 2007 Canadian Conference on Electrical and Computer Engineering, no. 1 (2016)

11. Kwon, S., Lee, S.: Recent advances in microwave imaging for breast cancer detection. Int. J. Biomed. Imaging **2016** (2016)

12. Tangwachirapan, S., Thaiwirot, W., Akkaraekthalin, P.: Antipodal vivaldi antenna with non-uniform corrugation for breast cancer detection. In: 2019 16th International Conference on Electrical Engineering/Electronics, Computer, Telecommunications and Information Technology (ECTI-CON) (2020)

13. Rahayu, Y., Hilmi, M.F., Masdar, H.: A novel design rectangular UWB antenna array for microwave breast tumor detection. In: 2019 16th International Conference on Quality in Research QIR 2019 - International Symposium on Electrical and Computer Engineering (2019)

14. Fokoa Makiela, G.L., Uyguroğlu, R.: Conical, stair-shapedand cylindrical dielectric resonator antenna for early breast cancer detection application. In: 2019 27th Signal Processing and Communications Applications Conference (SIU) (2019)

15. Brinda, K., Kumar, S.P., Priyadharshini, N.: Design of ultra-wideband planar monopole antenna for breast tumor detection. In: 2019 International Conference on Vision Towards Emerging Trends in Communication and Networking (ViTECoN) (2019)

16. Al-Zuhairi, D.T., Gahl, J.M., Abed, A.M., Islam, N.E.: Characterizing horn antenna signals for breast cancer detection. Can. J. Electr. Comput. Eng. **41**(1), 8–16 (2018)

17. Wada, M., Fujimoto, T., Takenaka, T.: Breast cancer detection system using printed inverted-F antennas. In: 2017 IEEE International Conference on Computational Electromagnetics, ICCEM 2017, pp. 148–149 (2017)

18. Khan, M.A., Aziz Ul Haq, M.: A novel antenna array design for breast cancer detection. In: IEACon 2016 - 2016 IEEE Industrial Electronics and Applications Conference (2017)

19. Song, H., Kubota, S., Xiao, X., Kikkawa, T.: Design of UWB antennas for breast cancer detection. In: 2016 International Conference on Electromagnetics in Advanced Applications (ICEAA) (2016)

20. Katbay, Z., Sadek, S., Le Roy, M., Lababidi, R., Perennec, A., Dupre, P.F.: Microstrip back-cavity Hilbert Fractal Antenna for experimental detection of breast tumors. In: 2016 IEEE Middle East Conference on Antennas and Propagation, MECAP 2016 (2016)

21. Diaz-Bolado, A., Memarzadeh-Tehran, H., Laurin, J.J.: Implementation of a dielectric waveguide configuration for microwave tomography applied to breast cancer detection. In: 2016 10th European Conference on Antennas and Propagation, EuCAP 2016 (2016)

22. Woten, D.A., El-Shenawee, M.: Broadband dual linear polarized antenna for statistical detection of breast cancer. IEEE Trans. Antennas Propag. **56**(11), 3576–3580 (2008)

23. Korkmaz, E., Isık, O., Sagkol, H.: A directive antenna array applicator for focused electromagnetic hyperthermia treatment of breast cancer. In: 2015 9th European Conference on Antennas and Propagation, vol. 1, pp. 1–4 (2015)

24. Guarnizo Mendez, H.F., Polochè Arango, M.A., Coronel Rico, J.F., Rubiano Suazo, T.A.: Hyperthermia study in breast cancer treatment using a new applicator. In: Florez, H., Leon, M., Diaz-Nafria, J.M., Belli, S. (eds.) ICAI 2019. CCIS, vol. 1051, pp. 215–229. Springer, Cham (2019). https://doi.org/10.1007/978-3-030-32475-9_16

25. Lazebnik, M., et al.: A large-scale study of the ultrawideband microwave dielectric properties of normal, benign and malignant breast tissues obtained from cancer surgeries. Phys. Med. Biol. **52**(20), 6093–6115 (2007)

26. Porter, E., Fakhoury, J., Oprisor, R., Coates, M., Popovic, M.: Improved tissue phantoms for experimental validation of microwave breast cancer detection. In: EuCAP 2010 - The 4th European Conference on Antennas and Propagation, pp. 4–8 (2010)

27. Carlos, J., et al.: Reconfigurable planar SIW cavity resonator and filter. In: 2006 IEEE MTT-S International Microwave Symposium Digest, pp. 947–950 (2006)

28. Bohórquez, J.C., Pedraza, H.A.F., Pinzón, I.C.H., Castiblanco, J.A., Peña, N., Guarnizo, H.F.: Planar substrate integrated waveguide cavity-backed antenna. IEEE Antennas Wirel. Propag. Lett. **8**, 1139–1142 (2009)
29. Mohammad, I., Huang, H.: An antenna sensor for crack detection and monitoring. Adv. Struct. Eng. **14**(1), 47–53 (2011)
30. Polochè Arango, M.A., et al.: Implantable intraocular pressure sensor using principles of electromagnetic radiation. In: 2014 IEEE 9th IberoAmerican Congress on Sensors, Bogota, pp. 1–5 (2014). https://doi.org/10.1109/IBERSENSOR.2014.6995543
31. Polochè Arango, M.A., Guarnizo Mendez, H.F., Diaz Pardo, I.E.: Crack detection using an electromagnetic sensor-antenna for structures. In: 2019 Congreso Internacional de Innovación y Tendencias en Ingenieria (CONIITI), BOGOTA, Colombia, pp. 1–6 (2019). https://doi.org/10.1109/CONIITI48476.2019.8960835

Temperature Sensing in Hyperthermia Study in Breast Cancer Treatment Using Optical Fiber Bragg Gratings

Andrés Triana[1]([✉])[ID], C. Camilo Cano[1][ID], Hector F. Guarnizo-Mendez[1][ID], and Mauricio A. Poloche[2][ID]

[1] Universidad El Bosque, Bogota, Colombia
{ctrianai,ccanov,hguarnizo}@unbosque.edu.co
[2] Universidad de San Buenaventura, Bogota, Colombia
mpoloche@usbbog.edu.co

Abstract. This paper presents the simulation results of an optoelectronics temperature monitoring system intended to be used in a hyperthermia breast-cancer treatment. This treatment involves the use of electromagnetic fields in order to generate a concentrated heat pattern around tissues affected by cancer. Therefore, all-optical fiber sensors which are immune to electromagnetic signals should be used to determine the relationship between the applied electromagnetic power density and the actual temperature in the modeled tissue. The proposed optoelectronic system is an electro-optic dual-comb fiber Bragg grating interrogation system, which uses a simple architecture with a continuous wave laser and a Mach-Zehnder modulator at an specific bias voltage to generate additional modes around the central wavelength of the laser. The photo-detected response of the sensor at the modulation frequency makes it possible to read the changes in the sensor's Bragg wavelength. In the simulation study, the modulation frequency of the Mach-Zehnder modulator was swept in order to find the best configuration in terms of amplitude temperature resolution.

Keywords: Fiber Bragg grating · Electro-optic frequency comb · Mach Zehnder modulator · Interrogation system

1 Introduction

It is well known that one of the biggest concerns of humanity nowadays is the cancer disease, cancer is the second leading cause of death to humans worldwide [24,30]. Breast cancer affects both women and men indistinctly and poses at large risk over their health, in Colombia it is estimated that around 24% of women with some sort of cancer are prone to being diagnosed with breast cancer [13]. Several treatments and care techniques are used when any sort of cancer is detected in the human body, the most frequently used between them are surgery,

© Springer Nature Switzerland AG 2020
H. Florez and S. Misra (Eds.): ICAI 2020, CCIS 1277, pp. 467–478, 2020.
https://doi.org/10.1007/978-3-030-61702-8_32

immunotherapy, radiotherapy and chemotherapy [3,11,16,21,31]; another supporting techniques are cell transplantation and hyperthermia. The hyperthermia treatment can be used alone or in conjunction with other treatments or therapies to effectively treat the cancer tissues [7,9,14,19]. The hyperthermia treatment consists on using focused electromagnetic waves in order to heat selectively the cancer cells and consequently to stop the tumoral cells reproduction [22]. To achieve this, the tumoral cells' temperature should reach 39 °C to 45 °C [8], a critical challenge in the hyperthermia process is to guarantee that only the tumor cells are increasing their temperature but not the surrounding healthy tissues around the tumor [10].

Given the nature of the hyperthermia treatment and its potential to enhance the breast cancer treatment, several studies have been proposed to assess the magnitude, spectral density and type of antennas needed to guarantee the thermal therapy is applied consistently over the affected area [17,28,29]. Optical fiber sensors are a convenient way to seize the correct amount of energy applied to a breast model or 'phantom' consisting of layers of materials that emulate the health and tumoral cells. Given its own nature, optical fiber sensors are made of Silica which is transparent to any electromagnetic (microwave) signal.

Between the optical fiber sensors, Fiber Bragg Gratings (FBG) are optical devices built inside the optical fiber that have been proven to be one of the most robust and used optical sensors in the market, FBGs have been widely used in different applications since 1978 when the studied these kind of devices [12]. Some of these applications are in the telecommunications field, acting as wavelength filters. Another important use is in the field of sensing, where the main advantages of FBG technology are exploited, such as the immunity to electromagnetic interference, multiplexation of many sensors on the same fiber and the long distance to the measurement point that could be reached [15].

On sensing applications, measurement schemes that convert optical-domain variations into electrical signals are needed, where many signal processing methods are available. Such schemes are known as optical interrogation systems [2]. On the other hand, the dual-comb spectroscopy concept [6] was applied to these systems using electro-optic generated dual-combs, reaching picometer resolutions sensing variables such as dynamic strain and with fast acquisition speeds [26].

Figure 1 shows the schematic representation of the breast model (phantom) where different kind of tissues are modeled according to Table 1 [23,25]. The antenna applicator is located approximately at a distance of 2 cm from the model to irradiate microwave frequencies with a distinct spectral density intended to heat only the cancer area. The main idea is to embed the optical fiber inside the phantom to take single-point temperature measurements at each point of interest inside the phantom. In this process we take advantage of the fact that optical fiber is transparent to these microwave radiation waves. The sensors are illuminated, and their signals detected, by the interrogation system proposed in this paper, which is based on an electro-optic dual-comb interrogation signal with a few modes that illuminate the sensor, then the reflected modes by the optical FBG sensor are detected at the modulation frequency by means of a standard

PIN photodetector (PD) obtaining, consequently, the temperature change as a change in the detected AC power from the PD.

Table 1. Electrical properties for different breast tissues

Tissue	Relative permittivity $[\varepsilon_r]$	Conductivity $[\sigma]$
Muscle	52.7	1.7
Tumor	56	1.8
Fat	5.3	0.3
Skin	38	1.5
Lobes	35	1

The rest of the paper is organized as follows: first, a general background of FBG sensors, the interrogation systems and the dual comb architecture are presented in Sects. 2 and 3 respectively; then, the simulation setup and equations used to build the model are explained in Sect. 4; and finally the simulation results are presented and analyzed in Sect. 5.

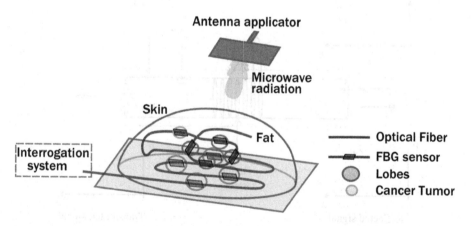

Fig. 1. Schematic representation of the emulated hyperthermia process over a breast phantom, an antenna applicator is located close to the breast phantom in order to irradiate it with electromagnetic waves at 2.45 GHz. Different types of tissues are modeled inside the breast phantom which includes a set of optical FBG sensors distributed at places of interest inside the phantom. The optoelectronics system is completed with an optical interrogator system used to illuminate the sensors in the optical fiber and capture their reflected signals.

2 FBG Sensors

An FBG is a periodic perturbation of the effective refractive index, η_{eff}, in the core of an optical fiber [15]. The spatial period of the grating, Λ, is defined as the distance between a layer with a refractive index value η_c and the next one with $\eta_c + \Delta\eta_c$. When a broadband spectrum illuminates the FBG inside an optical fiber, the device reflects a narrowband set of wavelengths around its resonance wavelength called the Bragg wavelength (λ_B), defined as follows [15]:

$$\lambda_B = 2\Lambda\eta_{eff} \tag{1}$$

Figure 2 shows the FBG principle of operation. As the resonance wavelength defined by Eq. (1) depends on the spatial period of the grating, it would be affected by external variables such as axial tension or temperature. These effects could be quantified as follows [15]:

$$\Delta\lambda_B = \lambda_B(1 - p_e)\Delta\epsilon_x + \lambda_B(\alpha_\Lambda + \alpha_\eta)\Delta T \tag{2}$$

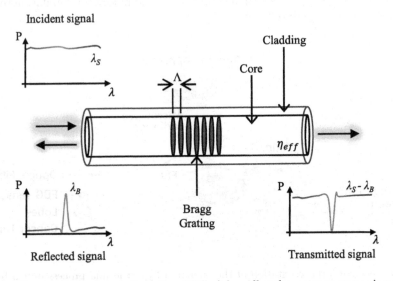

Fig. 2. The principle of operation of an FBG. A broadband spectrum source is applied to the sensor, the reflected signal contains a peak wavelength defined by the Eq. (1), while the transmitted signal is the remaining incident signal

The first term considers the variations in the Bragg wavelength due to the existence of an axial strain in the fiber, and it is related to the effective tenso-optic constant p_e and the corresponding applied strain $\Delta\epsilon_x$. The second term responds to a temperature change ΔT in the sensor and is related with the thermal coefficient, α_n, and the thermo-optic coefficient, α_Λ of the optical fiber.

3   Interrogation System

An optical interrogation system performs the detection of the reflected wave-length of one or a set of FBG sensors. This allows to monitor changes on that wavelength due to external variables. Knowing the information obtained, and with the values of the sensor sensitivity to the specific variable, it is possible to obtain the measured variable value [2].

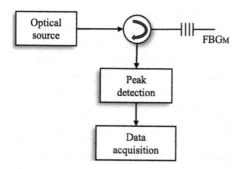

Fig. 3. A general block diagram of an optical interrogation system [2]. A broadband spectrum source covering the Bragg wavelength of the sensor illuminates the optical fiber through an optical circulator. A peak detection system is implemented using different technologies in order to obtain the response of the reflected signal. Finally, the optical to electrical conversion and the calculation of the variable value are implemented on the data acquisition system [2].

A general block diagram of an FBG sensor interrogation system is depicted in Fig. 3. The simplest scheme includes an optical spectrum analyzer (OSA) or a wavelength meter to perform the direct measure of the central wavelength reflected by the grating. The main disadvantages of this scheme are the elevated cost of the used equipment and their manipulation. Some other schemes allow to have robust topologies with reduced costs and for specific purposes, but fulfilling the general requirements for an optical interrogation system [2].

3.1   Dual-Comb Spectroscopy Applied to Fiber Bragg Gratings Interrogation

The dual-comb spectroscopy consist on the superposition of two optical fre-quency combs with slightly different repetition rates, allowing to map each tooth of the comb in the optical domain, into the radio-frequency domain [20]. This technique have been used to interrogate FBG sensors, replacing the broad-band spectrum source in the general interrogation scheme shown on Fig. 3, for a dual-comb generated near the Bragg wavelength of the sensor [18].

If only one pair of teeth of the comb is located on each side of the sensor spectrum, the interrogation scheme is called differential, because when a central wavelength shift occurs, the magnitude of one tooth will increase, while the other decreases. Some studies report measurement resolutions near $1pm$ [5], taking advantage of the properties of any differential scheme, such as common-noise rejection and signal-to-noise ratio augmentation [1,4,26,27].

4   Simulation Setup

The proposed simulation setup to interrogate FBG sensors was implemented in the Optiwave software Optisystem as depicted in Fig. 4, the FBG sensor is characterized with a bandwidth of 100 GHz and reflectivity of 30%. A Mach-Zehnder optical modulator is used to generate the frequency comb interrogating signal, this was achieved by modulating a continuous wave laser centered at a frequency of 193.1030 THz with radio frequency signals in the range of 1 to 20 GHz. When the central wavelength of the interrogating signal falls into the wavelength range of the FBG sensor, it is reflected and photo-detected by a PIN photodetector (PD) with responsivity of 1 A/W. The gathered signal from the PD have frequency components corresponding with the beating between the wavelengths in the frequency comb. Finally, an electrical filter is used to obtain the response of the sensing device at a fixed microwave frequency, namely, the modulation frequency.

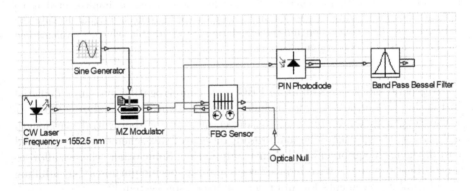

Fig. 4. Interrogation system based on the modulation of a continuous wave laser centered around the Bragg wavelength of the FBG sensor. A frequency comb is obtained through modulating the laser wavelength at a microwave frequency ranging from 1 to 20 GHz. The reflected signal from the FBG sensor is photo-detected and filtered at the modulation frequency, the wavelength change in the sensor due to changes in temperature is then translated to a change in the detected power at this frequency.

Figures 5 and 6 show the frequency comb generated through modulation of a continuous wavelength laser at a radio frequency between 1 and 20 GHz, in Fig. 5 a radio frequency of 5 GHz is used to generate a frequency comb with 5 lines in a 10 dB bandwidth, the same procedure is exemplified in Fig. 6 with a

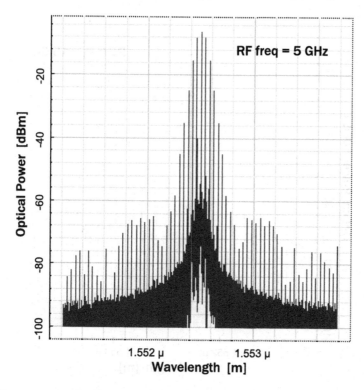

Fig. 5. Frequency comb obtained from the external modulation of a continuous wavelength laser centered at a wavelength of 1552 nm. In the plot, it is exemplified the signal obtained at a radio frequency of 5 GHz.

radio frequency of 15 GHz, again, it is obtained a frequency comb with 5 lines in a 10 dB bandwidth. These are the wavelengths generating the beating terms at which the response of the sensor is retrieved. The lines falling outside the 10 dB bandwidth do not have a considerable contribution to the photo-detected signal.

The simulation setup is intended to retrieve the electrical power corresponding to the Bragg wavelength of the sensor. Therefore, the FBG sensor is simulated for different temperature values consistent with a hyperthermia process, i.e. 10 to 45 °C. The simulation purpose is to validate the detection of the sensor central wavelength and also to find the RF frequency value that produces a better distinguishing slope to the system, therefore the RF frequency is swept from 1 to 20 GHz.

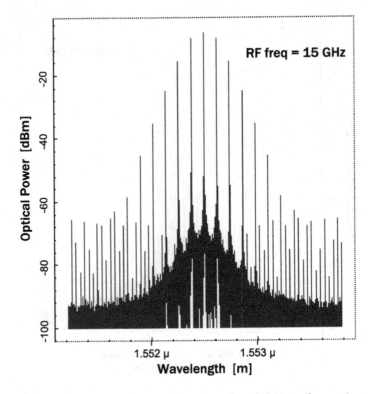

Fig. 6. Frequency comb obtained from the external modulation of a continuous wavelength laser centered at a wavelength of 1552 nm. In the plot, it is exemplified the signal obtained at a radio frequency of 15 GHz.

5   Results

As explained above, the simulation setup is intended to find the variation in the photo-detected electrical current due to the change of temperature experimented by the optical FBG sensor. Figure 7 shows the normalized values for the AC power detected at the photodetector at different values of the modulation frequency. The photo-detected amplitude is obtained as the temperature changes linearly from 15 to 45 °C at each frequency, the slope of these curves determines the temperature resolution of the interrogation system.

From the results presented in Fig. 7, it is possible to conclude that the signal detected at the PD contains more power for small values of the modulation frequency, this is expected given that the additional modes generated after the modulation of the laser are closer to its central wavelength and consequently they have similar amplitude values. On the contrary, for larger values of the modulation frequency, the additional modes are more distanced from the central wavelength and therefore are affected differently for the fiber Bragg grating sensor.

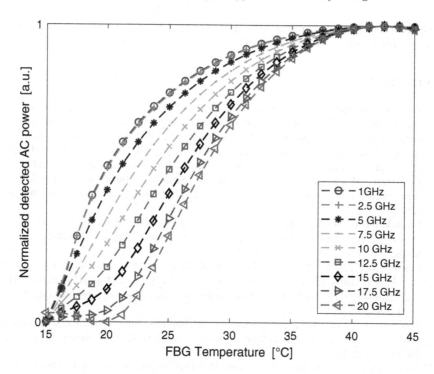

Fig. 7. Normalized photo-detected current obtained for different radio frequency values while sweeping the FBG sensor temperature.

The slope of these curves determines the direct relationship between the optical power collected by the photo-detector and the central wavelength of the FBG sensor. A modulation frequency of 10 GHz offers the best performance given that presents a more linear behavior in the first part of the curve and has an average amplitude amongst all the obtained curves.

6   Conclusion

This paper presented an interrogation technique for optical fiber Bragg grating sensors based on the photo-detection at a single frequency of frequency combs obtained from external modulation of a continuous wave laser around the central wavelength of the sensor. The proposed setup was proven to effectively detect the change in temperature of an FBG sensor in the working range of an hyperthermia treatment (15 to 45 °C).

The simulation of the system permitted to find the adequate modulation frequency to implement the system based on the trade off between detected optical power and slope of the response curve. Therefore, values of modulation frequency of 10 GHz would lead to a better discrimination of the temperature of the sensor embedded in the breast phantom.

Acknowledgment. This research is partly financed by the government of Colombia through Minciencias call No. 844-2019.

References

1. Bonilla-Manrique, O.E., Garcia-Souto, J.A., Martin-Mateos, P., Jerez-Gonzalez, B., Acedo, P.: Fast interrogation of fiber Bragg grating sensors using electro-optic dual optical frequency combs. In: International Conference on Optical Fibre Sensors (OFS24), vol. 9634, 963422 (2015). https://doi.org/10.1117/12.2195288, http://proceedings.spiedigitallibrary.org/proceeding.aspx?articleid=2441947
2. Bosiljevac, M., Komljenovic, T., Babic, D., Sipus, Z.: Interrogating FBG based temperature sensors; Practical issues. In: ELMAR, 2012 Proceedings, pp. 305–308 (2012)
3. Chalakur-Ramireddy, N.K., Pakala, S.B.: Combined drug therapeutic strategies for the effective treatment of triple negative breast cancer. Biosci. Rep. **38**(1) (2018). https://doi.org/10.1042/bsr20171357
4. Cheng, R., Xia, L.: Interrogation of weak Bragg grating sensors based ondual-wavelength differential detection. Opt. Lett. **41**(22), 5254 (2016). https://doi.org/10.1364/OL.41.005254. https://www.osapublishing.org/abstract.cfm?URI=ol-41-22-5254
5. Clement, J., Torregrosa, G., Maestre, H., Fernández-Pousa, C.R.: Remote picometer fiber Bragg grating demodulation using a dual-wavelength source. Appl. Opt. **55**(23), 6523–6529 (2016)
6. Coddington, I., Newbury, N., Swann, W.: Dual-comb spectroscopy. Optica **3**(4), 414 (2016). https://doi.org/10.1364/OPTICA.3.000414. https://www.osapublishing.org/abstract.cfm?URI=optica-3-4-414
7. Crezee, J.: SP-0299: technical aspects of hyperthermia: present and future. Radiother. Oncol. **115**, S151 (2015). https://doi.org/10.1016/s0167-8140(15)40297-x
8. Datta, N., et al.: Local hyperthermia combined with radiotherapy and-/or chemotherapy: recent advances and promises for the future. Cancer Treat. Rev. **41**(9), 742–753 (2015). https://doi.org/10.1016/j.ctrv.2015.05.009
9. Dutta, J., Kundu, B.: Two-dimensional closed-form model for temperature in living tissues for hyperthermia treatments. J. Therm. Biol. **71**, 41–51 (2018). https://doi.org/10.1016/j.jtherbio.2017.10.012
10. Guarnizo Mendez, H.F., Polochè Arango, M.A., Coronel Rico, J.F., Rubiano Suazo, T.A.: Hyperthermia study in breast cancer treatment using a new applicator. In: Florez, H., Leon, M., Diaz-Nafria, J.M., Belli, S. (eds.) ICAI 2019. CCIS, vol. 1051, pp. 215–229. Springer, Cham (2019). https://doi.org/10.1007/978-3-030-32475-9_16
11. Hadi, F., et al.: Combinatorial effects of radiofrequency hyperthermia and radiotherapy in the presence of magneto-plasmonic nanoparticles on MCF-7 breast cancer cells. J. Cell. Physiol. **234**(11), 20028–20035 (2019). https://doi.org/10.1002/jcp.28599
12. Hill, K.O., Fujii, Y., Johnson, D.C., Kawasaki, B.S.: Photosensitivity in optical fiber waveguides: application to reflection filter fabrication. Appl. Phys. Lett. **32**(10), 647–649 (1978). https://doi.org/10.1063/1.89881. http://scitation.aip.org/content/aip/journal/apl/32/10/10.1063/1.89881
13. IARC, G.: Cifras y estimaciones de cáncer en el mundo. Web, September 2018. https://www.cancer.gov.co/sites/default/files/boletin-prensa/archivo/boletin_globocan.pdf

14. Iero, D.A.M., Crocco, L., Isernia, T., Korkmaz, E.: Optimal focused electromagnetic hyperthermia treatment of breast cancer. In: 2016 10th European Conference on Antennas and Propagation (EuCAP). IEEE (2016). https://doi.org/10.1109/eucap.2016.7481515
15. Kersey, A., et al.: Fiber grating sensors. J. Lightwave Technol. **15**(8), 1442–1463 (1997). https://doi.org/10.1109/50.618377
16. Kheirolomoom, A., et al.: Combining activatable nanodelivery with immunotherapy in a murine breast cancer model. J. Controlled Release **303**, 42–54 (2019). https://doi.org/10.1016/j.jconrel.2019.04.008
17. Korkmaz, E., Isık, O., Sagkol, H.: A directive antenna array applicator for focused electromagnetic hyperthermia treatment of breast cancer, pp. 1–4. Lisbon (2015)
18. Kuse, N., Ozawa, A., Kobayashi, Y.: Static FBG strain sensor with high resolution and large dynamic range by dual-comb spectroscopy. Opt. Express **21**(9), 11141–11149 (2013). https://doi.org/10.1364/OE.21.011141. http://www.ncbi.nlm.nih.gov/pubmed/23669971
19. Mallory, M., Gogineni, E., Jones, G.C., Greer, L., Simone, C.B.: Therapeutic hyperthermia: the old, the new, and the upcoming. Crit. Rev. Oncol./Hematol. **97**, 56–64 (2016). https://doi.org/10.1016/j.critrevonc.2015.08.003
20. Martin-Mateos, P., Ruiz-Llata, M., Posada-Roman, J., Acedo, P.: Dual-comb architecture for fast spectroscopic measurements and spectral characterization. IEEE Photonics Technol. Lett. **27**(12), 1309–1312 (2015). https://doi.org/10.1109/LPT.2015.2421276
21. Naz, S., Shahzad, H., Ali, A., Zia, M.: Nanomaterials as nanocarriers: a critical assessment why these are multi-chore vanquisher in breast cancer treatment. Artif. Cells Nanomed. Biotechnol. **46**(5), 899–916 (2017). https://doi.org/10.1080/21691401.2017.1375937
22. Nguyen, P., Abbosh, A.: Focusing techniques in breast cancer treatment using non-invasive microwave hyperthermia, pp. 1–3. Hobart, TAS (2015)
23. Nikita, K.S.: Handbook of Biomedical Telemetry. Wiley, Hoboken (2014). https://doi.org/10.1002/9781118893715
24. Observatory, T.G.C.: Breast Cancer. Globocan 2018 (2018). https://gco.iarc.fr/today/data/factsheets/cancers/20-Breast-fact-sheet.pdf
25. Porter, E., Fakhoury, J., Oprisor, R., Coates, M., Popović, M.: Improved tissue phantoms for experimental validation of microwave breast cancer detection. In: Proceedings of the Fourth European Conference on Antennas and Propagation, pp. 1–5, Barcelona (2010)
26. Posada-Roman, J.E., Garcia-Souto, J.A., Poiana, D.A., Acedo, P.: Fast interrogation of fiber Bragg gratings with electro-optical dual optical frequency combs. Sensors **16**(12) (2016). https://doi.org/10.3390/s16122007
27. Posada-Roman, J.E., Poiana, D.A., Garcia-Souto, J.A., Acedo, P.: Interrogation of FBG sensors based on electro-optic dual optical frequency combs. In: Latin America Optics and Photonics Conference, pp. 2–4 (2016)
28. Singh, S., Sahu, B., Singh, S.P.: Conformal microstrip slot antenna with an AMC reflector for hyperthermia. J. Electromagn. Waves Appl. **30**(12), 1603–1619 (2016). https://doi.org/10.1080/09205071.2016.1207568
29. Singh, S., Singh, S.P.: Water-loaded metal diagonal horn applicator for hyperthermia. IET Microwaves Antennas Propag. **9**, 814–821 (2015). https://doi.org/10.1049/iet-map.2014.0699

30. Society, A.C.: Global Cancer Facts and Figures 4th Edition (2018). https://www.cancer.org/content/dam/cancer-org/research/cancer-facts-and-statistics/global-cancer-facts-and-figures/global-cancer-facts-and-figures-4th-edition.pdf
31. Zhou, J., Wang, G., Chen, Y., Wang, H., Hua, Y., Cai, Z.: Immunogenic cell death in cancer therapy: present and emerging inducers. J. Cell. Mol. Med. **23**(8), 4854–4865 (2019). https://doi.org/10.1111/jcmm.14356

Software Design Engineering

A Computer-Based Approach to Study the Gaussian Moat Problem

Hector Florez[1]($\boxtimes$) and Alejandro Cárdenas-Avendaño[2]

[1] Universidad Distrital Francisco Jose de Caldas, Bogota, Colombia
haflorezf@udistrital.edu.co
[2] Programa de Matemática, Fundación Universitaria Konrad Lorenz,
Bogotá, Colombia
alejandro.cardenasa@konradlorenz.edu.co

Abstract. In the year 1832, the well known German mathematician Carl Friedrich Gauss proposed the set of Gaussian integers, which corresponds to those complex numbers whose real and imaginary parts are integer numbers. A few years later, Gaussian primes were defined as Gaussian integers that are divisible only by its associated Gaussian integers. The Gaussian Moat problem asks if it is possible to walk to infinity using the Gaussian primes separated by a uniformly bounded length. Some approaches have found the farthest Gaussian prime and the amount of Gaussian primes for a Gaussian Moat of a given length. Nevertheless, such approaches do not provide information regarding the minimum amount of Gaussian primes required to find the desired Gaussian Moat and the number and length of shortest paths of a Gaussian Moat, which become important information in the study of this problem. In this work, we present a computer-based approach to find Gaussian Moats as well as their corresponding minimum amount of required Gaussian primes, shortest paths, and lengths. Our approach is based on the creation of a graph where its nodes correspond to the calculated Gaussian primes. In order to include all Gaussian primes involved in the Gaussian Moat, a backtracking algorithm is implemented. This algorithm allows us to make an exhaustive search of the generated Gaussian primes.

Keywords: Gaussian primes · Gaussian Moat · Backtracking

1 Introduction

Finding the distribution of prime numbers in the natural numbers has proven to be a difficult task and a definite pattern has not been found [5,10]. Nevertheless, several simple and quite powerful interesting theoretical properties of prime numbers have been found. In particular, there are arbitrarily large distances between consecutive primes and therefore it has been proved that it is not possible to walk to infinity on the real line using prime numbers of bounded length [9]. In addition, prime numbers can be defined in fields other than the

© Springer Nature Switzerland AG 2020
H. Florez and S. Misra (Eds.): ICAI 2020, CCIS 1277, pp. 481–492, 2020.
https://doi.org/10.1007/978-3-030-61702-8_33

integer field. In the complex number field they are called Gaussian primes and many problems on ordinary primes can be reformulated for Gaussian primes [5].

A Gaussian integer is a complex number $a + ib$, where $a, b \in \mathbb{Z}$ and a Gaussian prime is a Gaussian integer that cannot be decomposed into a product of two Gaussian integers $z_1 = a_1 + ib_1$, $z_2 = a_2 + ib_2$ such that $a_1, b_1, a_2, b_a \neq \pm 1$ and $i = \sqrt{-1}$.

Basil Gordon in 1962 at the International Congress of Mathematicians in Stockholm presented the following question: *Is there an unbounded walk starting from the origin and stepping along Gaussian primes with steps of bounded length?* [9]. This question is often coined as the Gaussian Moat problem. Despite several theoretical [11,14,16] and numerical [2,3,7,13] approaches to solve this problem, it still remains open [3].

Bearing this in mind, the aim of the paper is to present a computer-based approach to calculate the minimum amount of generated Gaussian primes required to find a Gaussian Moat with a desired length as well as the corresponding shortest paths, in order to study a possible connection with the gap size. We believe that this information is very valuable to push forward the current record holder and will allow us to optimize the current approaches, which are at the moment very computational expensive.

The rest of the paper is structured as follows. Section 2 presents a brief historical background. Section 3 describes our approach and presents the algorithms used to solve the problem. Section 4 presents our results that include graphical representations of the Gaussian Moats. Finally, Sect. 5 concludes the work and points to future work.

2   Historical Background

In 2005 Tsuchimura [13] provided computational results for the Gaussian Moats, by computing the maximum reachable distance for all k-connected components surrounded by Moats up to size $\sqrt{32}$ and suggested the existence of Moats up to size $\sqrt{36}$, which is, to the best of our knowledge, the largest Moat ever found. Table 1 summarizes the current reported results for a certain given length, i.e., the farthest Gaussian prime reached, the distance from the origin of the farthest Gaussian prime, and the amount of Gaussian primes included in a Gaussian Moat. The results reported by Tsuchimura have been recently verified by West and Sittinger [16] up to the $\sqrt{20}$-Moat, since there was a discrepancy with the results presented by Gethner et al. [3].

The reported results lack of an important information: the minimum amount of Gaussian primes required to find the Gaussian Moat. For instance, when the length is $\sqrt{2}$ the amount of primes that compose the Gaussian Moat is 14; however, more Gaussian primes are required. Specifically, this Gaussian Moat is made up of the Gaussian primes: $1 + i$, $2 + i$, 3, $4 + i$, $3 + 2i$, $5 + 2i$, $6 + i$, 7, $7 + 2i$, $8 + 3i$, $9 + 4i$, $8 + 5i$, $10 + 3i$, and $11 + 4i$. Nevertheless, it is necessary to generate more primes because their distance from the origin is less than the farthest distance which is 11.7. In this case, those primes are: $5 + 4i$, $6 + 5i$,

Table 1. Reported results in Ref. [13]. The Farthest prime achieved has been $2106442 + 1879505i$.

Length	Farthest prime	Farthest distance	Amount of primes
$\sqrt{1}$	$2 + i$	2,23	2
$\sqrt{2}$	$11 + 4i$	11,7	14
$\sqrt{4}$	$42 + 17i$	45,31	92
$\sqrt{8}$	$84 + 41i$	93,47	380
$\sqrt{10}$	$976 + 311i$	1024,35	31221
$\sqrt{16}$	$3297 + 2780i$	4312,61	347638
$\sqrt{18}$	$8174 + 6981i$	10749,4	2386129
$\sqrt{20}$	$120510 + 57857i$	133679,06	273791623
$\sqrt{26}$	$943460 + 376039i$	1015638,76	14542615005
$\sqrt{32}$	$2106442 + 1879505i$	2823054,54	103711268594

$6 + 7i$, $10 + i$, and 11. Furthermore, the following primes are also necessary because they have to be compared to the farthest prime in order to find that they do not satisfy the length $\sqrt{4}$: $10 + 7i$, $11 + 6i$, and $13 + 2i$. As a result, albeit the amount of primes of the Gaussian Moat with length $\sqrt{4}$ is 14, it is necessary to generate 22 Gaussian primes. In addition, these results do not present the shortest paths from the initial Gaussian prime to the farthest Gaussian prime. For instance, when the length is $\sqrt{2}$ there are two paths in the Gaussian Moat, each with 11 Gaussian primes. They are: a) $1 + i$, $2 + i$, 3, $4 + i$, $5 + 2i$, $6 + i$, $7 + 2i$, $8 + 3i$, $9 + 4i$, $10 + 3i$, $11 + 4i$ and b) $1 + i$, $2 + i$, $3 + 2i$, $4 + i$, $5 + 2i$, $6 + i$, $7 + 2i$, $8 + 3i$, $9 + 4i$, $10 + 3i$, $11 + 4i$.

3 Computer-Based Approach

The approach we follow is composed by three main components, each one defined by its own algorithm. The first one generates the necessary Gaussian primes, the second one calculates the Gaussian Moat, and the third one calculates the shortest paths. The source code of the approach is distributed under git version-control system at: https://gitlab.com/florezfernandez/GaussianMoat.

3.1 Generating Gaussian Primes

The first part of the approach is focused on the mechanism to generate Gaussian primes. It is based on the integer primes; then, we calculate whether $p \in \mathbb{N}$ is prime using the Algorithm 1. Thus, to calculate if p is prime, it is enough to iterate from 2 to $\sqrt{p}$ because if p is not prime it can be factored into two factors a and b such that $p = a * b$. Then, a and b cannot be both greater than $\sqrt{p}$, since the product $a * b$ would be greater than $\sqrt{p} * \sqrt{p} = p$. Thus, for any factorization of p, at least one of the factors must be smaller than $\sqrt{p}$.

Algorithm 1. *Integer primes*

---

function IsPrime(p)
   for $i \leftarrow 2$ **to** $\sqrt{p}$ **do**
      if p **mod** $i == 0$ **then**
         return *false*
      end if
   end for
   return *true*
end function

Then, for each integer prime p, a Gaussian prime is calculated based on the following criteria:

- $p \equiv 1 (mod\ 4)$. In this case, the Gaussian prime $z = a + ib$ is obtained based on the integer prime p, where $a^2 + b^2 = p$.
- $p \equiv 2 (mod\ 4)$. This case occurs just in one case that is when $p = 2$; then, the Gaussian prime is $z = 1 + i$
- $p \equiv 3 (mod\ 4)$. In this case, the imaginary part of the Gaussian prime is 0, Thus, the Gaussian prime is $z = a + ib$, where $a = p$ and $b = 0$.

Based on the previous criteria, Algorithm 2 generates and collects the corresponding Gaussian prime of an integer prime p.

Thus, when a integer prime p is calculated, it is possible to calculate and collect the corresponding Gaussian prime. Nevertheless, once collecting all Gaussian primes, there are several Gaussian primes that are not able to be reached. Such

---

Algorithm 2. *Gaussian primes*

---

function GenerateGaussianPrimes(p)
   if p **mod** $4 == 1$ **then**
      $a \leftarrow 2$
      $b \leftarrow 1$
      while $pow(a, 2) + pow(b, 2) \neq p$ **do**
         $b \leftarrow b + 1$
         if $b == a$ **then**
            $a \leftarrow a + 1$
            $b \leftarrow 1$
         end if
      end while
      collect(Gaussianprime(a, b))
   else if p **mod** $4 == 2$ **then**
      collect(Gaussianprime(1, 1))
   else if p **mod** $4 == 3$ **then**
      collect(Gaussianprime(p, 0))
   end if
end function

Algorithm 3. *Remove unnecessary Gaussian primes*

---

function REMOVEUNNECESSARYGAUSSIANPRIMES(*gaussianPrimes*)
   done ← *false*
   i ← *size(gaussianPrimes)* − 2
   while not *done* **do**
      if *imaginaryPart(gaussianPrimes[i])* == 0 **then**
         remove(gaussianPrimes[i])
         i ← *i* − 1
      else
         done ← *true*
      end if
   end while
end function

Gaussian primes are some of those p that satisfy $p \equiv 3(mod\ 4)$. Then, it is necessary to remove them. However, before removing it is necessary to ensure that the collected Gaussian primes are sorted based on the distance of the Gaussian prime with the origin. Then Algorithm 3 proceeds to remove all the unnecessary Gaussian primes.

3.2 Creating a Gaussian Moat

To build the Gaussian Moat, we create a graph with one node which is the first Gaussian prime (i.e., $z = 1 + i$), and then we verify every Gaussian prime p_j to know if it must be included in the Gaussian Moat. In this way a Gaussian prime, p_j, is verified by calculating its distance to the last Gaussian primes already included in the Gaussian Moat p_i, as follows:

$$d = \sqrt{(a_j - a_i)^2 + (b_j - b_i)^2}. \tag{1}$$

Algorithm 4. *Gaussian Moat*

---

function NEXTGAUSSIANPRIME(p_i, *gaussianPrimes*, *k*)
   i ← 0
   while *i* < *size(gaussianprimes)* **do**
      p_j ← *gaussianprimes[i]*
      if not *isIncluded(p_j)* **then**
         if *distance(p_i, p_j)* < *k* **then**
            $p_i \rightarrow p_j$
         end if
         remove(gaussianPrimes, p_j)
         NextGaussianPrime(p_j, gaussianprimes, k)
      end if
      i ← *i* + 1
   end while
end function

When the distance is less or equal than the square root of the given length, $\sqrt{k}$, the Gaussian prime p_j is added as a connected Gaussian prime to p_i and it is removed from the collected Gaussian primes. The algorithm is applied recursively. Algorithm 4 creates recursively the Gaussian Moat, where the function *distance* returns the result of Eq. 1, and k is the given length. This algorithm corresponds to a *Backtracking* algorithm, which is successfully used for exhaustive search in graphs and decision trees [4,6].

The *Backtracking* algorithm searches recursively for all possible options to build the solution and ignore the options that do not satisfies the search requirements [4,8,12]. Backtracking is a proper algorithm to solve problems that depend on given constraints. Thus, since the Gaussian Moat problem includes the distance between Gaussian primes constraint, backtracking fits perfectly to this problem. In addition, using backtracking, we can not only find the desired results (i.e., farthest prime, farthest distance, amount of primes, required primes), but also we can find the actual path, which we represent graphically.

3.3   Calculating Shortest Path

Once the points of the Gaussian Moat are found, it is possible to calculate their shortest paths. To achieve this, the Dijkstra algorithm [1] is used. Based on this algorithm, the points of the Gaussian Moat are validated just once in order to determine whether or not certain point belongs to the shortest path. The Dijkstra algorithm finds a shortest path from a single source node, which in this case corresponds to the Gaussian prime $1 + i$ and explores the adjacent nodes i.e., Gaussian primes whose the distance to the origin are close to the evaluated Gaussian prime. This process is repeated recursively until the farthest Gaussian prime is found.

4   Results

In our approach, we developed a software, which is able to calculate and deploy desired Gaussian Moats and trace the corresponding Gaussian Primes [15]. The approach provides the results presented in Table 2, where we have included for the lengths from $\sqrt{1}$ to $\sqrt{18}$, the farthest Gaussian prime for each length, the

Table 2. Results

Length	Farthest prime	Farthest distance	Amount of primes	Amount of required primes	Size of primes files	Time
$\sqrt{1}$	$2 + i$	2,236	2	5	25 B	0 ms
$\sqrt{2}$	$11 + 4i$	11,705	14	22	182 B	1 ms
$\sqrt{4}$	$42 + 17i$	45,310	92	160	1.7 kB	2 ms
$\sqrt{8}$	$84 + 41i$	93,472	380	558	6.1 kB	4 ms
$\sqrt{10}$	$976 + 311i$	1.024,352	31.221	41.078	604.7 kB	7,884 s
$\sqrt{16}$	$3297 + 2780i$	4.312,610	347.638	596.647	10.5 MB	24,735 s
$\sqrt{18}$	$8174 + 6981i$	70.749,355	2.386.129	3.309.126	62.1 MB	5,11 m

farthest distance that correspond to the distance from the origin to the farthest
Gaussian prime, the amount of primes that belong to the Gaussian Moat, the
amount of required Gaussian primes to be evaluated, the size of files that store
the generated Gaussian primes, and the execution time of the algorithms.

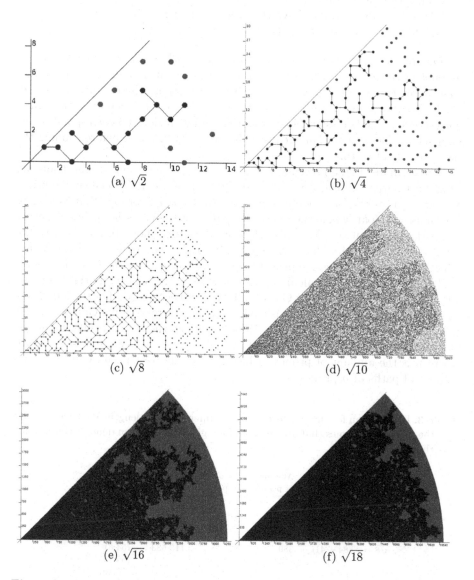

Fig. 1. Gaussian Moat of different sizes. The blue points represent the Gaussian primes
that belong to the Gaussian Moat, while the red points represent the Gaussian primes
that are nor part of the Gaussian Moat.(Color figure online)

We tested our approach with lengths from $\sqrt{1}$ to $\sqrt{19}$. We found that there are length (e.g., $\sqrt{3}$) that have exactly the same previous results. Consequently, those lengths are not included in the report results. For example:

- $\sqrt{3}$ has the same results that $\sqrt{2}$
- $\sqrt{11}, \sqrt{12}, \sqrt{13}, \sqrt{14}, \sqrt{15}$ have the same results that $\sqrt{10}$
- $\sqrt{19}$ has the same results that $\sqrt{18}$

Our results agree with previous works, and include more information: the amount of required primes to find the Gaussian Moat and the size of the files that stores the required primes. In addition, we report the execution times of the backtracking algorithm. It is important to clarify that such execution times correspond to the Gaussian Moat construction i.e., it does no correspond to the Gaussian primes calculation because this process is executed before running the backtracking algorithm.

Furthermore, Fig. 1 presents the graphical representations of the Gaussian Moat for lengths $\sqrt{2}, \sqrt{4}, \sqrt{8}, \sqrt{10}, \sqrt{16}$, and $\sqrt{18}$ as an additional contribution. In these figures the blue points represent the Gaussian primes that belong to the Gaussian Moat, whole the red points represent the Gaussian primes that are nor part of the Gaussian Moat. In addition, the figure allows to observe also the farthest Gaussian prime for each representation in the boundary of the figure. Thus, no additional Gaussian primes where used to calculate the Gaussian Moat.

In this work, we also calculated the shortest path from the initial Gaussian Prime i.e., $1+i$ to the furthest Gaussian Prime for each length. For the length $\sqrt{1}$ there is one shortest path, which is trivial since the corresponding Gaussian Moat just includes two Gaussian Primes. Table 3 presents the actual results found for various lengths. In the last column of the table, there are two values n and m, where n is the amount of primes included in the shortest path, while m is the amount of paths of n primes.

Table 3. Information for the shortest paths for different Moat length. We have denoted by n the amount of primes that are included for a given path and m denotes the amount of path with n primes.

Length	Farthest prime	Amount of primes	Amount of paths	Path length	n:m
$\sqrt{1}$	$2+i$	2	1	1.0	(2:1)
$\sqrt{2}$	$11+4i$	14	2	13.728	(11:2)
$\sqrt{4}$	$42+17i$	92	6	56.799	(34:6)
$\sqrt{8}$	$84+41i$	380	32	113.533	(54:6)
					(55:14)
					(56:10)
					(57:2)

Interestingly, we found that the shortest path length is not unique. Figure 2 presents the Gaussian Moat with the corresponding shortest paths for length

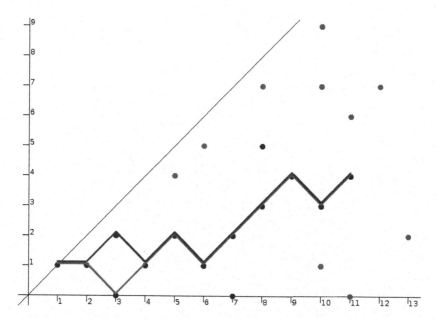

Fig. 2. The two shortest paths for $\sqrt{2}$. These paths only differ only by one prime, located in the third node.

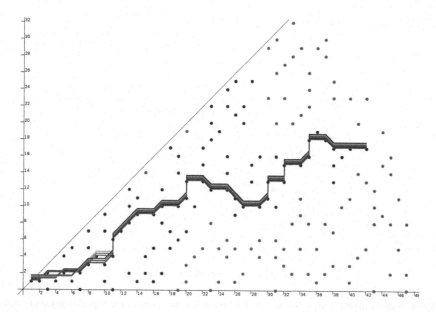

Fig. 3. The shortest paths for $\sqrt{4}$. In this case there are 6 different paths with the same minimum length.

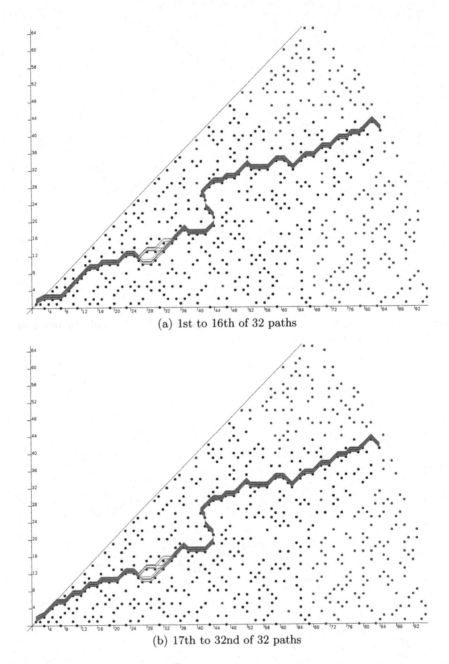

(a) 1st to 16th of 32 paths

(b) 17th to 32nd of 32 paths

Fig. 4. The shortest paths for $\sqrt{8}$. For illustration porpoises, each panel presents only 16 paths.

$\sqrt{2}$, which are just different by the last Gaussian prime i.e., the third prime of the first path shown is $3 + 0i$, while the third prime of the other path is $3 + 2i$. Similarly, Fig. 3 presents the Gaussian Moat with the corresponding shortest path for length $\sqrt{4}$, where there are six paths with the same minimum length. From the eighth prime to the last prime, all six paths are the same. The first eight primes for the six paths are:

- Path 1: $1 + i \to 2 + i \to 3 + 2i \to 5 + 2i \to 7 + 2i \to 8 + 3i \to 9 + 4i \to 11 + 4i$
- Path 2: $1 + i \to 2 + i \to 3 + 2i \to 5 + 2i \to 7 + 2i \to 8 + 3i \to 10 + 3i \to 11 + 4i$
- Path 3: $1 + i \to 2 + i \to 4 + i \to 5 + 2i \to 7 + 2i \to 8 + 3i \to 9 + 4i \to 11 + 4i$
- Path 4: $1 + i \to 2 + i \to 4 + i \to 5 + 2i \to 7 + 2i \to 8 + 3i \to 10 + 3i \to 11 + 4i$
- Path 5: $1 + i \to 2 + i \to 4 + i \to 6 + i \to 7 + 2i \to 8 + 3i \to 9 + 4i \to 11 + 4i$
- Path 6: $1 + i \to 2 + i \to 4 + i \to 6 + i \to 7 + 2i \to 8 + 3i \to 10 + 3i \to 11 + 4i$

In this particular case, when running the backtracking algorithm over the third prime, note that it can continue either through $3 + 2i$ or $4 + i$; in the fourth prime, it can continue either through $5 + 2i$ or $6 + i$; and in the seventh prime, continue either through $9 + 4i$ or $10 + 3i$, which accounts for the six different shortest paths.

In a similar fashion, Fig. 4 presents the 32 paths for $\sqrt{8}$, where for illustration porpoises, each panel presents only 16 paths. Note that from the prime $12 + 7i$ to the prime $26 + 11i$, and from the prime $34 + 15i$ to the prime $84 + 41i$, all paths are equal. However, there are different possible primes from $3 + 2i$ to $12 + 7i$ and from $26 + 11i$ to $34 + 15i$, which account for the 32 different paths. As it can be seen, the multiplicity of primer for each path increases significantly. For example, 10 paths have 56 primes.

5   Concluding Remarks

Despite several theoretical and numerical attempts to know if it is possible to walk to infinity using the Gaussian primes separated by a uniformly bounded length, this problem is still open. In this work we presented computer-based algorithms capable to produce useful information that may provide insight into further theoretical studies of this problem. In particular, our approach is able to compute correctly the Gaussian Moat, the required amount of Gaussian primes for a given length, and produces visualizations that can also help to understand how the Gaussian Moats are formed.

This is still work in progress and we have only shown explicitly examples for lengths less than $\sqrt{18}$. Improvements of the algorithm must be devoted to reduce the execution time, which necessary when studying larger Moats, as the amount of Gaussian primes increase considerably. For instance, albeit we required a little less than 600.000 Gaussian primes to reach $\sqrt{16}$, we need to calculate over a 3.000.000 to reach $\sqrt{18}$. Current work is under way to modify the algorithms presented here to allow for parallel processing, which can in principle greatly speed up the calculations.

Acknowledgments. A.C.-A. acknowledges funding from Fundación Universitaria Konrad Lorenz (Project 5INV1). Computational efforts were performed on the High Performance Computing System, operated and supported by Fundación Universitaria Konrad Lorenz.

References

1. Dreyfus, S.E.: An appraisal of some shortest-path algorithms. Oper. Res. **17**(3), 395–412 (1969)
2. Gethner, E., Stark, H.M.: Periodic Gaussian moats. Exp. Math. **6**(4), 289–292 (1997)
3. Gethner, E., Wagon, S., Wick, B.: A stroll through the Gaussian primes. Am. Math. Mon. **105**(4), 327–337 (1998)
4. Ginsberg, M.L.: Dynamic backtracking. J. Artif. Intell. Res. **1**, 25–46 (1993)
5. Guy, R.: Unsolved Problems in Number Theory. Springer, Heidelberg (2004). https://doi.org/10.1007/978-0-387-26677-0
6. Hernandez, J., Daza, K., Florez, H.: Alpha-beta vs scout algorithms for the Othello game. In: CEUR Workshops Proceedings, vol. 2846 (2019)
7. Jordan, J., Rabung, J.: A conjecture of Paul Erdo's concerning Gaussian primes. Math. Comput. **24**(109), 221–223 (1970)
8. Knuth, D.: The Art of Computer Programming 1: Fundamental Algorithms 2: Seminumerical Algorithms 3: Sorting and Searching. Addison-Wesley, Boston (1968)
9. Loh, P.R.: Stepping to infinity along Gaussian primes. Am. Math. Mon. **114**(2), 142–151 (2007)
10. Oliver, R.J.L., Soundararajan, K.: Unexpected biases in the distribution of consecutive primes. Proc. Nat. Acad. Sci. **113**(31), E4446–E4454 (2016)
11. Prasad, S.: Walks on primes in imaginary quadratic fields. arXiv preprint arXiv:1412.2310 (2014)
12. Sanchez, D., Florez, H.: Improving game modeling for the quoridor game state using graph databases. In: Rocha, Á., Guarda, T. (eds.) ICITS 2018. AISC, vol. 721, pp. 333–342. Springer, Cham (2018). https://doi.org/10.1007/978-3-319-73450-7_32
13. Tsuchimura, N.: Computational results for Gaussian moat problem. IEICE Trans. Fundam. Electron. Commun. Comput. Sci. **88**(5), 1267–1273 (2005)
14. Vardi, I.: Prime percolation. Exp. Math. **7**(3), 275–289 (1998)
15. Velasco, A., Aponte, J.: Automated fine grained traceability links recovery between high level requirements and source code implementations. ParadigmPlus **1**(2), 18–41 (2020)
16. West, P.P., Sittinger, B.D.: A further stroll into the Eisenstein primes. Am. Math. Mon. **124**(7), 609–620 (2017)

Numerical Model-Software for Predicting Rock Formation Failure-Time Using Fracture Mechanics

Emmanuel E. Okoro[1]([✉]) [ID], Samuel E. Sanni[2] [ID], Amarachukwu A. Ibe[3] [ID],
Paul Igbinedion[1], and Babalola Oni[2]

[1] Department of Petroleum Engineering, Covenant University, Ota, Nigeria
emeka.okoro@covenantuniversity.edu.ng
[2] Department of Chemical Engineering, Covenant University, Ota, Nigeria
[3] Department of Physics, Nigeria Maritime University, Okerenkoko, Nigeria

Abstract. Real-time integrated drilling is an important practice for the upstream petroleum industry. Traditional pre-drill models, tend to offset the data gathered from the field since information obtained prior to spudding and drilling of new wells often become obsolete due to the changes in geology and geo-mechanics of reservoir-rocks or formations. Estimating the complicated non-linear failure-time of a rock formation is a difficult but important task that helps to mitigate the effects of rock failure when drilling and producing wells from the subsurface. In this study, parameters that have the strongest impact on rock failure were used to develop a numerical and computational model for evaluating wellbore instability in terms of collapse, fracture, rock strength and failure-time. This approach presents drilling and well engineers with a better understanding of the fracture mechanics and rock strength failure-prediction procedure required to reduce stability problems by forecasting the rock/formation failure-time. The computational technique built into the software, uses the stress distribution around a rock formation as well as the rock's responses to induced stress as a means of analyzing the failure time of the rock. The results from simulation show that the applied stress has the most significant influence on the failure-time of the rock. The software also shows that the failure-time varied over several orders of magnitude for varying stress-loads. Thus, this will help drilling engineers avoid wellbore failure by adjusting the stress concentration properly through altering the mud pressure and well orientation with respect to in-situ stresses. As observed from the simulation results for the failure time analysis, the trend shows that the time dependent strength failure is not just a function of the applied stress. Because, at applied stress of 6000–6050 psi there was time dependent failure whereas, at higher applied stress of 6350–6400 psi there was no time dependent strength failure.

Keywords: Time-to-failure · Numerical model · Software development · Rock strength · Stress distribution · Fracture mechanic · Oil and gas operation

© Springer Nature Switzerland AG 2020
H. Florez and S. Misra (Eds.): ICAI 2020, CCIS 1277, pp. 493–504, 2020.
https://doi.org/10.1007/978-3-030-61702-8_34

1   Introduction

Well instability is a major factor that affects well failure, and it can contribute to several problems during drilling and well completion. Wellbore instability often increases the cost and time of drilling, and sometimes causes the well to be abandoned without reaching the target depth. The cost of these challenges is approximately 10% of the total drilling time (Aslannezhad et al. 2020). In recent years, great efforts have been made to improve wellbore stability, and various numerical models and analytical methods have been used to analyze wellbore stability. However, drilling and wellbore instabilities remains a serious problem because, about a third of the non-productive time during drilling is due to borehole problems that occur in most shale formations (Li et al. 2019). Most of the processes in rock deformation are multi-scale evolutionary processes, presented in the form of accumulation of many micro-damages, growth of clusters and the final large-scale catastrophe (Edalat-Behbahani et al. 2016).

During the process of evolution, some minor scale, irregular structural influences may increase and become significant on a large scale, which ultimately lead to rock failure (Huang et al. 2020). Studying the basic rule of the failure-process is helpful in predicting the occurrence of instabilities (Potirakis et al. 2017; Rahimi and Nygaard 2015). The mechanical properties of the inherent discontinuities also contribute to the decrease in the overall strength of the rock. The effects of tensile properties are mostly focused directly on shear strength during shear tests, and these have shown that shear strength and other tensile properties further complicate the problem (Mokhtarian et al. 2020). More attention has also been paid to the effect of discontinuity in orientation of the unfilled jointed rock strength under tri-axial stresses and the parameters of rock failure criteria (Wu et al. 2018; Igwilo et al. 2020). A number of researchers have investigated the applicability of various model materials to simulate rock properties. Also, materials of several combinations have been used for various types of modeling works (Thirukumaran and Indraratn 2016).

This study presents a numerical model that investigates the Time Dependent Strength Failure of rock using fracture mechanics principle. The numerical model was used to develop software, based on the deformation characteristics of the rock mass around the wellbore. The developed software was used for validation of the proposed numerical model via simulation using field data. The aim of this study is to develop a numerical model to determine the failure function and the rock time dependent strength-failure of a rock.

Time dependent deformation and failure mechanisms have been considered by other authors (Lajtai 1991; Liu et al. 2020), but most of these studies did not integrate time dependent factor in the failure function. Other approaches in studying time dependent behaviour of rock formation, requires some form of laboratory data and these results in some form of complex models that cannot be easily resolved via numerical computation. This study integrates the failure function and time dependent behaviour of rock formation. Based on the characteristics of rock strength and damage mechanics, it has been proven that there is a close relationship between macroscopic deformation and the mesoscopic damage of a drilled rock. This was done in order to predict the deformation time-dependent strength of the rock mass around the borehole with the help of a well-defined easy to use model whose solution was determined via numerical simulation.

2 Methodology

2.1 Numerical Model – Fracture Mechanics Principle-Based Model

This section shows the mathematical presentation of stress orientation and magnitude around the borehole and their application in forecasting the time-to-failure of the rock when stress-load is applied. To achieve this purpose, it is important to establish the shear and tensile strength of the rock formation. Underground formations are subject to vertical and horizontal stresses due to the weight of the rock's upper layers and lateral restrictions, respectively. Usually, the rock mass is assumed to be in a state of equilibrium prior distortion by drilling. Equation (1) shows that the magnitude of stress (σ) around a uniformly loaded formation is the force (F) divided by the area (A) of application.

$$\sigma = \frac{F}{A} \tag{1}$$

When a well is drilled, the load carried by the rock formation cuttings is absorbed by the adjacent rock, thereby re-establishing the stress equilibrium. To assess the potential mechanical instability of a wellbore, a constitutive model is desired in order to estimate the magnitude of the stresses around the wellbore. To effectively analyze the wellbore stability, it was assumed that the rock formation exhibits isotropic elastic properties and that the wellbore stresses are in the cylindrical co-ordinate system.

The vertical principal stress can be estimated numerically as the weight of the overburden stress.

$$\sigma_v = \rho g h \tag{2}$$

where ρ = average mass density of the overlying rock, g = acceleration due to gravity, and h = the depth.

According to Al Ajmi (2006), the maximum stress for a vertical well is always at $\theta = \pm 90°$; and according to Fjaer et al. (2008), the stress equations at the wall of a vertical wellbore is as follow:

$$\left.\begin{array}{c} \sigma_r = P_w, \\ \sigma_\theta = \sigma_H + \sigma_h - 2(\sigma_H - \sigma_h)cos2\theta - P_w + 2\eta(P_f - P_{fo}), \\ \sigma_z = \sigma_v - 2v(\sigma_H - \sigma_h)\cos 2\theta + 2\eta(P_f - P_{fo}), \\ \tau_{\theta z} = 0, \\ \tau_{r\theta} = 0, \\ \tau_{rz} = 0. \end{array}\right\} \tag{3}$$

$$\tau_{r\theta} = 0,$$

$$\tau_{rz} = 0.$$

Al Ajmi and Zimmerman (2005, 2006) developed a linearized form of Mogi's criterion and established that the failure criterion is a linear envelope in the $\tau_{oct} - \sigma_{m,2}$ space.

$$\sigma_{m,2} = \frac{\tau_{max}}{\sin \varnothing} - Ccot\varnothing \tag{4}$$

And

$$\tau_{oct} = \frac{1}{3}\sqrt{(\sigma_1 - \sigma_2)^2 + (\sigma_2 - \sigma_3)^2 + (\sigma_3 - \sigma_1)^2} \tag{5}$$

The failure surface of a rock can be expressed using an appropriate function F of the major, intermediate and minor principal stresses as given in (6).

$$F(\sigma_1, \sigma_2, \sigma_3) = 0 \tag{6}$$

Thus, the failure function can be expressed mathematically as:

$$F = a + b\left[\frac{\sigma_1 + \sigma_3}{2}\right] - \frac{1}{3}\sqrt{(\sigma_1 - \sigma_2)^2 + (\sigma_2 - \sigma_3)^2 + (\sigma_3 - \sigma_1)^2} \tag{7}$$

The parameters (a, b) in the Mogi-Coulomb expression are related to the (c, Ø) parameters for Coulomb failure as given in (8) and (9):

$$a = \frac{2\sqrt{2}}{3} cCos\emptyset \tag{8}$$

$$b = \frac{2\sqrt{2}}{3} Sin\emptyset \tag{9}$$

Failure occurs when $F \leq 0$. $\emptyset$ = friction angle of the shear plane, c = shear strength or cohesion of the material, $\emptyset$ = internal friction angle, a = intersection of the line with the τ_{oct} axis, b = the slope, and σ_1, σ_2, σ_3 = vertical principal stress, intermediate stress and minimum stress respectively.

Intrieri et al. (2019) classified time-of-failure prediction methods that are based on kinematic parameters, as empirical and semi-empirical methods. Amitrano and Helmstetter (2006) proposed time-to-failure models with the assumption that failure occurs when the crack velocity diverges or when it reaches a given threshold. The threshold in this study is taken as the maximum rock strength. The evolution of microstructure is a time-dependent progressive damage process, and the rock degradation with time is due to the degradation of its internal material properties (Davarpanah et al. 2020). Equation (10) shows the failure of each element when subjected to a constant stress and σ_i (maximum stress) which is smaller than its short-term strength, $\sigma_{0,i}$. Thus, the time-dependent strength, σ_{t_i} at time, t_i can be expressed as:

$$\sigma_{t_i} = \sigma_\infty + (\sigma_{0_i} - \sigma_\infty)e^{-a_1 t_i} \tag{10}$$

Where σ_∞ = long-term failure strength at time, t when t approaches infinity, σ_{0_i} = initial short-term failure strength of each element, and a_1 = coefficient of strength degradation of the element. According to Xu et al. (2012), an element fails either when the time, t is equal to its failure time (t_i) or when the stress σ_i on this element reaches its rupture criterion, σ_{0_i}. The ratio of long and short term failure strengths can be expressed as:

$$\frac{\sigma_\infty}{\sigma_0} = k \tag{11}$$

Thus, considering Eqs. 10 and 11, Eq. (10) can then be rewritten as:

$$\sigma_{t_i} = \sigma_0\left[k + (1 - k)e^{-a_1 t_i}\right] \tag{12}$$

One way to interpret the long-term strength of a rock is to consider the mobilized strength when the rock fails at an extremely slow strain rate. But there is need to consider the field conditions and the stain rates induced by drilling. According to Damjanac and Fairhurst (2010), "the effect of time on rock deformability and strength is a topic of considerable interest in rock mechanics". Lajtai (1991) asserted that the slope of the failure rate curve of a stressed rock can be expressed mathematically as;

$$b = \ln\left(\frac{\sigma - \sigma_\infty}{\sigma_0 - \sigma_\infty}\right) \tag{13}$$

When the three stress parameters are known, the long-term strength can be expressed as:

$$\sigma_\infty = \frac{\sigma_0 e^b - \sigma}{e^b - 1} \tag{14}$$

Substituting Eq. (14) into (11);

$$k = \frac{\sigma_0 e^b - \sigma}{e^b - 1} \cdot \sigma_0 \tag{15}$$

The long term strength of the rock mass depends on the time-dependent response of the intact rock and the friction components of the rock-mass' strength. On a large scale, rocks are mostly continuous and homogeneous, but quite often, faults, bedding planes, or different formations appear (Okoro et al. 2020). Thus, rocks often do not behave homogeneously as metals. Under specific scenarios, the resulting micro/macrostructures result in a rather complicated mechanical behaviour.

2.2 Software Development

Without proper planning, drilling operations cannot be done successfully. Well planning depends on the information available and this information is usually provided from already drilled fields around the current location (also known as offset well/field data). After designing and planning a well with these offset data, the exploratory well or real-time data from the actual drilling process is used for validation of the existing parameters. However, real-time data are crucial for predicting potential problems in a well because they help drillers make quick and timely decisions during drilling. But, it should be noted that the acquisition of these real-time well data during drilling can also be expensive. The question then is, how much planning needs be carried out without providing preliminary information on the relevant processes. In lieu of the fact that real-time data acquisition is key to the success of drilling operations, but pre-drilling or offset data is also very important at the planning phase. These well data can be used to predict, analyze and forecast the possible scenarios that may occur during drilling. Therefore, a reliable and efficient software that integrates these real-time pre-drilling models for optimal drilling

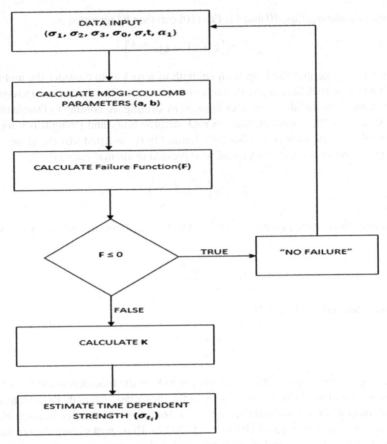

Fig. 1. Software development flow chart

is the optimum choice for stress analysis of different physical parameters around the wellbore. Figure 1 shows the flowchart for the developed model using the modified numerical model proposed in this study.

The software was developed with the Visual Basic (VB) Programming Language by using the platform of Microsoft Visual Basic.Net. Visual Basic is a third-generation object-oriented programming language which is known for its ability to generate Component Object Models (COMs). The software contains a public class with private subs which aid the deployment of mathematical functions that make up the analysis. The software contains two sections which allow for the analysis of both single and multiple datasets (Fig. 2(a) and (b) respectively). The section for single dataset analysis contains panes for both data input and result output. The section for multiple dataset analysis allows for the importation of data from Microsoft excel sheets; the analysis is then done with the results plotted for clarity. The plot is separated by a dark blue horizontal line which identifies the failure status. The data points are further distinguished by their shapes and colors.

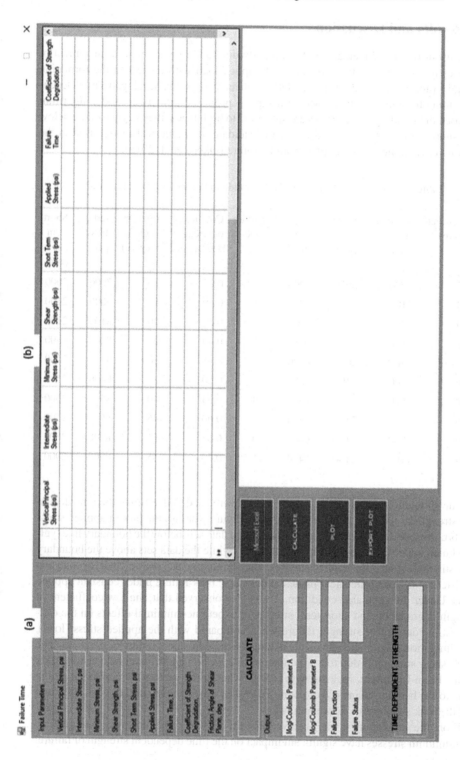

Fig. 2. The time dependent strength failure software user-interphase (Color figure online)

3   Results and Discussion

The anisotropy of sedimentary rocks is mainly due to the geometrical arrangement of particles that depend on the orientation of applied load with respect to the formation strength. Table 1 was used for the validation and analysis of the developed Time Dependent Strength Failure Software Model using the proposed numerical model algorithm proposed in this study. When rocks are subjected to high loads, they begin to sidle below their short-term strengths. The data used to validate the numerical model used in the software development was adopted from literature (Okoro et al. 2019).

Table 1. Range of field data used for the validation of the model and software.

Intermediate stress (psi)	Minimum stress (psi)	Shear strength (psi)	Applied stress (psi)	Failure time	Coefficient of strength degradation	Friction angle (degree)	Vertical stress (psi)	Short term stress (psi)
7000	7000	2050	6000	2	0.25	10	7900	2000
7100	7100	2060	6050	3	0.30	15	8000	2100
7200	7200	2070	6100	4	0.35	20	8100	2200
7300	7300	2080	6150	5	0.40	25	8200	2300
7400	7400	2090	6200	6	0.45	30	8300	2400
7500	7500	2100	6250	7	0.50	35	8400	2500
7600	7600	2110	6300	8	0.55	40	8500	2600
7700	7700	2120	6350	9	0.60	45	8600	2700
7800	7800	2130	6400	10	0.65	50	8700	2800
7900	7900	2140	6450	11	0.70	55	8800	2900

The simulation runs and calculated outputs were used to determine the time dependent strength of the rock under consideration. Figure 3 shows the plot of applied stress and its corresponding failure function. The plotted data sets below the boundary line (yellow) failed under the individual applied stresses; while the data sets above the boundary were still intact under the applied stresses. The simulation also showed that the high and low friction angles of the shear plane cannot cause rock failure under constant applied stress. Under the stipulated condition, it was also observed that, the low coefficient of strength degradation and short term stress will experience minimal effects on the estimated time dependent strength failure when compared with the applied stress (load). The simulation gives an insight on the nature of time-dependent failure of the rocks. The rock's shear strength is due to a combination of cohesion and friction between the rock grains. From Literature, rock strength is high when force vectors are applied at a high angle to the bedding-plane (Okoro et al. 2019). At lower angles, in the order of 15 and 30°, the rock's compressive strength is low.

From the simulation, it was observed that the vertical principle stress, intermediate and minimum stresses have significant impact on the time dependent strength of failure.

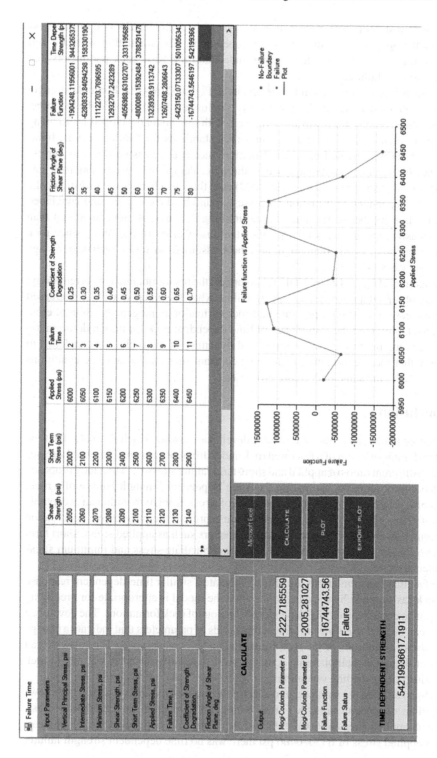

Fig. 3. Simulation runs and results from the developed time dependent strength failure software (Color figure online)

The borehole instability over time will in most cases be a direct reflection of the stress states and the applied stress during drilling operations. The simulation software will help the drilling engineers to identify and understand the basic rock parameters that contribute to rock failure.

The trends observed from simulation results in Fig. 3, shows that borehole strength failure starts gradually and builds up with time, t before the failure around the wellbore. These simulated results are in strong agreement with the model developed by Kemeny et al. (2016); their study assessed long term rock stabilities for dam and bridge foundations, and the first method considered fracture mechanics as is seen in this current study. They highlighted that damage occurs through calculation of decreasing rock size from subcritical crack growth. Drescher (2002) used three mechanisms to investigate the various time-dependent deformation processes around hard rock types, and concluded that the relationship between grain size and infilling thickness is more important than was previously assumed. This then justifies the observations in this study since rock materials react more slowly than might have been assumed during the well design stage of an oil and gas well.

The findings of Xu and Zhou (2017) also support the results obtained in current study; their study observed an increase in time to failure when the creep strain rate decreased with an increase in confining pressure and rock formation homogeneity. Brantut et al. (2013) also highlighted the importance of time dependent rock formation deformation in understanding the long-term evolution and dynamics of the rock, and concluded in their study that rock deformation under both constant stress and strain rate conditions are controlled by the same underlying processes.

4   Conclusion

The proposed numerical model was used to develop a software which simulates the time dependent failure situation of a fractured rock under different applied differential stresses (i.e. within different ratios of applied and short-term failure stresses). This study proposed a simulation procedure for estimating the Time Dependent Strength Failure of a rock, which is also referred to as the time of collapse of a rock formation within an acceptable margin of error. The stages that precede failure represent the progressive degradation of the formation and, during these stages, parameters such as applied stress, short term stress, shear strength, vertical principal stress, intermediate stress and minimum stress were calculated.

The fact that the simulations are able to simulate a similar time-dependent response of the rocks as supplied by the data implies that the model is appropriate for predicting the non-linear complicated time-dependent behaviour of rock formations. The developed software can be used to define the critical thresholds of parameters that indicate a change in the stability conditions of the rock formation under consideration. The software can also be considered in well planning activities so as to identify the early warning of rock deformation during drilling operations.

As observed from the simulation results for the failure time analysis, the trend shows that the time dependent strength failure is not just a function of the applied stress. Because, at applied stress of 6000–6050 psi there was time dependent failure whereas, at higher applied stress of 6350–6400 psi there was no time dependent strength failure.

Limitations and Recommendation

The model proposed in this study was not applied to simulate the time dependent failure of weak bedding planes and jointed rock slopes. Hence, there is need to investigate the ability of the proposed model and simulation technique adopted in this study, in predicting the time dependent failure of weak bedding planes, which are influenced by the nature and variation in the geometry of micro-cracks that exist in these rock-formations. Furthermore, the data used for validation was obtained from published literature, hence, it is limited to some specified field conditions within which it was generated.

Acknowledgments. The authors appreciate the management of Covenant University for providing the enabling environment to carry out this research, as well as her timely financial assistance as regards the publication of this manuscript.

References

Al-Ajmi, A.M., Zimmerman, R.W.: Stability analysis of vertical boreholes using the Mogi Coulomb failure criterion. Int. J. Rock Mech. Min. Sci. **43**(8), 1200–1211 (2006)

Al-Ajmi, A.M.: Wellbore stability analysis based on a new true-triaxial failure criterion. Ph.D. thesis. Royal Institute of Technology, Stockholm (2006)

Al-Ajmi, A.M., Zimmerman, R.W.: Relationship between the parameters of the Mogi and Coulomb failure criterion. Int. J. Rock Mech. Min. Sci. **42**(3), 431–439 (2005)

Amitrano, D., Helmstetter, A.: Brittle creep, damage, and time to failure in rocks. J. Geophys. Res. **111**, B11201 (2006). https://doi.org/10.1029/2005JB004252

Aslannezhad, M., Keshavarz, A., Kalantariasl, A.: Evaluation of mechanical, chemical, and thermal effects on wellbore stability using different rock failure criteria. J. Nat. Gas Sci. Eng. **78**, 103276 (2020). https://doi.org/10.1016/j.jngse.2020.103276

Brantut, N., Baud, P., Heap, M., Meredith, P.G.: Mechanics of time-dependent deformation in crustal rocks. In: Poromechanics V: Proceedings of the Fifth Biot Conference on Poromechanics (2013)

Damjanac, B., Fairhurst, C.: Evidence for a long-term strength threshold in crystalline rock. Rock Mech. Rock Eng. **43**(5), 513–531 (2010)

Davarpanah, M., Somodi, G., Kovács, L., Vásárhelyi, B.: Experimental determination of the mechanical properties and deformation constants of Mórágy granitic rock formation (Hungary). Geotech. Geol. Eng. **38**, 3215–3229 (2020)

Drescher, K.: Investigation into the mechanisms of time dependent deformation of hard rocks. Safety in Mines Research Advisory Committee, GAP 601, February, pp. 1–88 (2002)

Edalat-Behbahani, A.E., Barros, J.A.O., Ventura-Gouveia, A.: Application of plastic-damage multidirectional fixed smeared crack model in analysis of RC structures. Eng. Struct. **125**, 374–391 (2016)

Fjaer, E., Holt, R.M., Horsrud, P., Raane, A.M., Risnes, R.: Petroleum Related Rock Mechanics, 2nd Ed., vol. 53, pp. 102–265. Elsevier Science (2008)

Okoro, E.E., Alaba, A.O., Sanni, S.E., Ekeinde, E.B., Dosunmu, A.: Development of an automated drilling fluid selection tool using integral geometric parameters for effective drilling operations. Heliyon **5**, e01713 (2019)

Huang, F., Zhang, M., Wang, F., Ling, T., Yang, X.: The failure mechanism of surrounding rock around an existing shield tunnel induced by an adjacent excavation. Comput. Geotech. **117**, 103236 (2020)

Igwilo, K.C., Okoro, E.E., Ohia, P.N., Nwanro, P., Izuwa, N.C.: A new approach to wellbore stability models using diagnostic iteractive design: case study-Niger Delta. Pet. Coal **6**(2), 429–441 (2020)

Intrieri, E., Carlà, T., Gigli, G.: Forecasting the time of failure of landslides at slope-scale: a literature review. Earth Sci. Rev. **193**, 333–349 (2019)

Kemeny, J.M., Roth, K., Wu, H.: Modeling of time-dependent rock failure in abaqus and PFC3D. In: 50th US Rock Mechanics/Geomechanics Symposium, Houston, United States, 26–29 June (2016)

Lajtai, E.Z.: Time-dependent behaviour of the rock mass. Geotech. Geol. Eng. **9**, 109–124 (1991). https://doi.org/10.1007/BF00881253

Li, G., Cheng, X.F., Pu, H., Tang, C.A.: Damage smear method for rock failure process analysis. J. Rock Mech. Geotech. Eng. **11**, 1151–1165 (2019). https://doi.org/10.1016/j.jrmge.2019.06.007

Liu, H., Li, L., Li, S., Yang, W.: The time-dependent failure mechanism of rocks and associated application in slope engineering: an explanation based on numerical investigation. Math. Probl. Eng. **2020**, 1–19 (2020). https://doi.org/10.1155/2020/1680265. Article ID 1680265

Mokhtarian, H., Moomivand, H., Moomivand, H.: Effect of infill material of discontinuities on the failure criterion of rock under triaxial compressive stresses. Theoret. Appl. Fract. Mech. **108**, 102652 (2020). https://doi.org/10.1016/j.tafmec.2020.102652

Okoro, E.E., Okolie, A.G., Sanni, S.E., Joel, E.S., Agboola, O., Omeje, M.: Assessment of naturally occurring radiation in lithofacies of oil field in Niger Delta region and its possible health implications. J. Environ. Manag. **264**, 110498 (2020)

Potirakis, S.M., Hayakawa, M., Schekotov, A.: Fractal analysis of the ground-recorded ULF magnetic fields prior to the 11 March 2011 Tohoku earthquake (Mw-9): discriminating possible earthquake precursors from space-sourced disturbances. Nat. Hazards **85**(1), 59–86 (2017)

Rahimi, R., Nygaard, R.: Comparison of rock failure criteria in predicting borehole shear failure. Int. J. Rock Mech. Min. Sci. **41**(8), 1251–1275 (2015)

Thirukumaran, S., Indraratn, B.: A review of shear strength models for rock joints subjected to constant normal stiffness. J. Rock Mech. Geotech. Eng. **8**, 405–414 (2016)

Wu, Q., et al.: Investigation on the shear properties of discontinuities at the interface between different rock types in the Badong formation, China. Eng. Geol. **245**, 280–291 (2018)

Xu, T., Tang, C.-A., Zhao, J., Li, L., Heap, M.J.: Modelling the time-dependent rheological behaviour of heterogeneous brittle rocks. Geophys. J. Int. **189**, 1781–1796 (2012). https://doi.org/10.1111/j.1365-246X.2012.05460.x

Xu, T., Zhou, G.-L.: Thermomechanical time-dependent deformation and fracturing of brittle rocks. In: Tanski, T., Sroka, M., Zielinski, A. (eds.) Creep. IntechOpen (2017). https://doi.org/10.5772/Intechopen.72326

Validation of Software Requirements Specifications by Students

Alberto Sampaio$^{(\boxtimes)}$ and Isabel Braga Sampaio

Interdisciplinary Studies Research Center (ISRC),
Institute of Engineering of Porto – Polytechnic of Porto (ISEP/IPP), Porto, Portugal
{acs,ais}@isep.ipp.pt

Abstract. Context: Requirements validation is an important activity in software development, but frequently neglected in computing courses. This paper describes a study where requirements specifications produced by students are validated by their peers.

Objective: To evaluate how well students perform the validation of requirements specifications.

Methods: A correlational study.

Results: Group' grades correlate with teachers' marks for a level of significance of 5%.

Conclusion: Students reviews can be used for peer assessment, but with some care.

Keywords: Requirements · Requirements specification · Validation · Peer review · Inspection

1 Introduction

Software requirements engineering is a basilar activity for software development [1] and its quality considered important [2]. Boehm [3] showed that the cost of defect repairing increases significantly along the software product life cycle, which implies that errors in requirements should be detected as early as possible. Concomitantly, cost factors require the implementation of the just needed requirements demanded by the client [4]. In an iterative development model, the software engineer is concerned with smaller sets of requirements, usually a subset by iteration. Smaller sets makes requirements validation lighter for each iteration, although a validation for a larger initial set (e.g. backlog) can be needed. Even if agile methods use distinct ways to validate requirements (e.g. acceptance criteria) validation is still performed and needed as shown in a meta study [2].

In a more traditional development model the engineer must do an initial validation of all elicited requirements. Traditional models like waterfall have not being abandoned. Recently there was an increase in the use of hybrid methodologies [5]. The emphasis on requirements elicitation at upfront is also a characteristic of model based development. To sum up, independently of the development

© Springer Nature Switzerland AG 2020
H. Florez and S. Misra (Eds.): ICAI 2020, CCIS 1277, pp. 505–518, 2020.
https://doi.org/10.1007/978-3-030-61702-8_35

model, requirements validation needs to be performed reinforced by the recent increase use of hybrid methodologies.

Following the importance of requirements validation and its possible benefit for the classroom (see e.g. [6]) it was decided to introduce requirements validation in a course. It was also decided to introduce it through a practical exercise of requirements review. The review has been considered an adequate method for requirements validation (e.g. [7]). Reviews can be more or less formal, being the inspection the more formal. There are several kinds of inspections and in this initiative it was decided to opt for one based on a checklist, but without all the formalism of a common inspection. Furthermore, the checklist is one of the methods also used in agile projects [2]. Another important motivation for this research is that even if students can badly design, they are considered able to evaluate others designs [8]. Being able to evaluate other designs, we extrapolate that students should also be able to evaluate others specifications. All this is reinforced by the fact that peer assessment is considered an effective way of assessment [9]. The main goal of this research is to know how well students perform requirements validation. To that, it was performed an empirical study where students validate requirements specified by their peers. The study is the main subject of this paper.

The paper is organized as follows. After this introduction, background and related work are reviewed in Sect. 2. Section 3 presents the empirical study. The paper finishes with the main conclusions in Sect. 4.

2   Background and Related Work

Review is a general term referring to defect detection by the examination of software work products (artefacts), including requirements. The term defect is used in a broad sense that includes quality criteria the requirements specification should satisfy. The most common types of reviews are inspections, walkthroughs and actual reviews [10] by descent order of formalism. An inspection is a kind of review but with a well defined process where participants follow specific roles. Inspections can be ad-hoc, checklist based reading or scenario based reading [11] according the technique employed.

In the case of ad-hoc inspections there is not a systematic way of inspecting the artefacts. In the case of a checklist based technique the inspectors follow a list of certain characteristics or classes of defects to search for. For a requirements specification a checklist would a list of items about the document specification the reviewer should focus, like correctness, priorities or others. Scenario based means that participants follow specific scenarios of possible defects according their expertise. Each scenario provides more detailed guidance to the inspectors than a checklist. A common scenario based technique is perspective based reading (PBR) [12] where the artefacts are read from the perspectives of the roles of the software stakeholders, like user and tester.

The use of reviews to teach requirements validation is not original. For example, in [6] the authors used a N-fold inspection with that aim. In a N-fold inspection the requirements document is reviewed by several groups and their results compared in a meeting. In [6] each group of students could choose between two techniques: checklist and PBR. After the exercise the students answered a survey and, from the survey results, the authors considered that the exercise goals were achieved and that the exercise did contribute to students have a better understanding of the engineering requirements process.

It is also common to use students as experimental subjects in requirements validation studies. An example is [10] where the authors performed 2 experiments with students to determine if checklist based inspections would improve defect detection of use case models. In the first study the use of a checklist was considered beneficial. In the second, their authors concluded that a checklist (p. 133) "may not be particularly useful when inspectors already have good knowledge of the defects they are expected to find as had the inspectors in this case". Also in the second experiment, the students with the checklist found more defects than the students that did not use it. The used checklist was based on a taxonomy of defects developed by the authors and is specific for use case models.

There are several tools available for requirements engineering (e.g. DOORS) but these tools, although providing help, do not allow the full automation of the process. This is also true for requirements reviews. In the case of agile approaches, there are tools (e.g. Cucumber) that can be useful to express requirements and to validate their implementation but not very helpful to evaluate the quality of the specifications. Recent research intend to develop new tools as discussed in [13] that can evaluate some requirements characteristics. Automation is essential in modern code reviews (e.g. [14] and so more automation is needed to achieve what could be called "modern requirements reviews". Anyway, requirements validation still remains a process requiring significant human intervention.

In the present paper, besides the use of a review to teach requirements validation, the review is performed by students' peers.

3   The Study

3.1   Background and Methodology

The main goal of this study is to find how well students perform requirements validation, more specifically, of software requirements specifications (SRS) documents.

The study was performed in a course from the third semester of an informatics program. This is a special course because it is implemented as a project with a duration of approximately 4 weeks including the final evaluation. Each week is an iteration. Before the project start, the students are grouped in teams. During the project one of the team members speaks directly with the teacher responsible for the course who acts as the client. The meetings with the client are face-to-face and occur at least once by week. The meetings involve all the groups in simultaneous, so all have to solve the same problem.

In the project, most of the requirements have been elicited at the first week, but new requirements have been added weekly. During the course, students produce several artefacts, in particular use cases to model software requirements.

The result of their work during the first week (iteration) is a document with the software requirements specification (SRS). The study focus is on the SRS document and not on the use case descriptions alone. After the students submit the SRS, the SRS was marked by the teachers and supplied a draw of the expected solution.

The initiative of introducing requirements validation in the course was implemented via inspections performed by students using a checklist. In the exercise the students only review the specification, that is, they not perform any other inspection role. Because students are organized in teams, the teams (or groups) are the experimental units.

This study was elaborated as a case study [15] in a learning context. As such, the study followed several steps, namely, preparation, data collection, analysis of the data and reporting. This research has an exploratory intent and, as such, the study can be considered as exploratory.

3.2   Research Questions

To validate the success of the initiative, it is necessary to evaluate the quality of the reviews performed by the students. If reliable, these reviews can be used as a form of peer assessment.

RQ1 - Do students perform well requirements reviews?

The answer to that question can also give some light to the viability to classify students works with the help of the classifications produced by their own peers.

Besides knowing if the reviews performed by the students can be considered of quality, it was decided to have a deeper understanding of the phenomenon. That is, to know if students "quality" affects the quality of their validation work. This second goal was considered relevant in order to find some indicator of trust that can be assigned to the results of students validations, so these results can be used for peer assessment. The goal was translated into a second research question.

RQ2 - There is a relation between the quality of the group and the quality of its validation?

Because there was no access to the marks of the students in other courses of the program, the quality of the groups is restricted to the course so far and specifically to their SRS documents.

3.3   Environment and Participants

The participants are all the groups formed at the beginning of the course. Context factors should be considered as they can play an important role [16]. At the time of the study, the knowledge area of requirements engineering was part of the program syllabus and taught in the previous semester, the second one. At the beginning of the study, students had no experience with requirements validation. Because all students took the same previous course, the experience of the students in the use of UML, particularly for requirements analysis, and their academic experience using the methods should be similar. However, it was known that a small number of participants had industrial experience in software development, but this was not taken into consideration for the study.

For the course, it was a defined a template for the SRS document to be produced by the teams. Not all teams completely followed the template.

Briefly, the main topics of the template are:

- System objective;
- Glossary;
- Use case diagram;
- Table with requirements and their priorities and possible dates;
- Actors/use cases;
- Constraints;
- Conceptual diagram (domain model).

Students could develop their specifications using any tool they know. For the study we were not concerned with tools usage and no tool was used to accomplish the reviews. The study was conducted during the normal classes schedule, so for teachers it was a regular class. The course involves fifteen teachers.

3.4 The Instrument

Students are from the 3rd semester and being in the first half of the course, they are expected to have a limited experience about software development and, as pointed before, they had no experience in requirements validation. A checklist seemed to be adequate because it provides concrete guidance [6]. Furthermore, the use of well designed check-lists in learning is a recommended approach to support students learning and performance [17] as intended with this exercise.

The quality of a requirements specification possess several dimensions and so it was necessary for the developed checklist to covers such dimensions. According the IEEE 830 standard [18] the characteristics of a good SRS are:

- Correct;
- Unambiguous;
- Complete;
- Consistent;
- Ranked for importance and/or stability;
- Verifiable;
- Modifiable;
- Traceable.

Those characteristics plus some guidance about quality issues with requirements that could be found in the literature (e.g. [10,19]) were used to develop a first version of the checklist with 22 items.

Before the study, it was performed a small pilot study with students from another course in order to evaluate the checklist and, possibly, to improve it. The most important issue pointed out by the students was some lack of clarity about what was intended with each question. To improve clarity it was added some guidance to each question of the checklist and its organization changes.

The 22 items are the following:

1. Are references to other requirements correct? Guidance: In case in a use case there is any reference to another use case this should be correct.
2. Has a priority been set for each requirement? Guidance: Whether the priority of each requirement has been defined and whether both the requirements table and the requirements descriptions are sorted by priority.
3. Is the definition of priority judicious? Guidance: If the priority is based on importance and difficulty.
4. Is the requirements detail adequate and consistent? Guidance: Whether the requirements are suitable to be used later in the next phase of design.
5. Specification is complete? Guidance: All known customer needs are included.
6. Are the anomalous (error) conditions that can be predicted documented? Guidance: These situations will be described in the alternative scenarios contained in the descriptions of the use cases.
7. Are there requirements that conflict with other requirements (how many)? Guidance: For example, contradictory requirements.
8. Is the language used in the requirements clear, concise and unambiguous? Guidance: Do you understand, refer only to what matters and do not raise doubts about what is intended?
9. Is the terminology consistent with that of the problem? Guidance: The terminology must be identical to that of the problem.
10. Do the requirements not present Portuguese errors ? Guidance: For example: spelling and grammatical errors.
11. Are the requirements within the scope of the project problem? Guidance: Requirements must not exceed the limits of the desired system.
12. Are the scenarios described correctly? Guidance: The order of the event stream is correct, and you can see who starts the events, what the inputs, outputs, and the processing are.
13. Are requirements testable? Guidance: If there are objective tests for each requirement.
14. Are there redundant requirements? Guidance: If a requirement is duplicated, or can be obtained from another part of the requirements.
15. Is each requirement uniquely identified? Guidance: The identification of each must be unique.
16. Is each requirement really a requirement? Guidance: A requirement should not concern design or implementation, i.e. other phases.
17. Is the documentation compliant? Guidance: If you agree with the standards of the documents defined for the project and the disciplines involved.
18. Do the requirements seem to be achievable in the time stipulated? Guidance: If the time set for the implementation of each requirement is realistic.
19. Conceptual diagram is complete? Guidance: For example, if there are actors that did not match classes and should, or if there are names in use cases that do not appear as classes and that should also.
20. Conceptual Diagram does not present unjustified classes? Guidance: You should not have classes outside the scope of the problem domain.

21. Are class relations correct? Guidance: To evaluate the type of association and its multiplicity.
22. Are the classes clear? Guidance: Is it understood the role of the class and its name (and attributes) is suggestive?

For each item in the checklist it was necessary to add 3 columns. One column to allow the participants to classify the SRS quality for each item. The classification scale defined was from 1 to 5. A second column for annotation of the number of defects (violations) for each item and a third to specify those defects were also added in order to gather more complete data. The instrument can be seen as a questionnaire.

3.5 Variables and Measures

The research questions involve two main concepts: quality of the reviews performed by the groups; and the quality of the groups. We start by analyzing the latter. Before the exercise each group received a mark for its SRS document (TM - teacher mark) given by the teachers. This is a numeric value between 0 and 20. The TM, besides being used to classify each SRS document, it is also a measure of the quality of each group (GQ - group quality).

During the exercise, each group should produce a grade for the SRS document they review (GG - group grade). For the exercise it was decided to not overload teachers with additional work, which implied that the validations made by the groups were not marked by the teachers. Without such information, there was no direct measure of the quality of each group review (RQ - review quality).

However, it is reasonable to expect that for a good review, the grade attributed by a group to a SRS would not be very distinct from the mark produced by the teachers to the same SRS. This can be seen as an indicator of the quality of the review. Assuming this, RQ was evaluated in the study through the proximity between the mark given by the teachers to the SRS (TM) and the grade attributed by the group to the same SRS (GG). More specifically, the proximity is computed as the absolute difference between the two measures.

3.6 Hypothesis

The original research questions were divided into statistical hypotheses as follows.

$RQ1$. To answer this question it was decided to see if there was a correlation between the grades attributed by the groups (GG) and the marks attributed by the teachers (TM) to the same SRS document.

$H1_0$ The grades attributed by the groups and the marks attributed by the teachers are independent. That is, TM and GG are mutually independent, $\rho = 0$.
$H1_a$ There is a correlation between the grades attributed by the groups are independent of the marks attributed by the teachers. That is, $\rho <> 0$.

RQ2. To answer this question it was determined to use the correlation between the mark received by the validation group for its SRS document (GQ) and the quality of the review $(RQ = abs(TM - GG))$.

$H2_0$ The quality of the reviews are independent of the quality of the groups. That is, RQ and GQ are mutually independent, $\rho = 0$.

$H2_a$ There is a correlation between the quality of the reviews and the quality of the groups. That is, $\rho <> 0$.

The group classifies the SRS document according the items of the checklist using a scale 1 to 5. To obtain a unique value for the GG it will be used the median of the classification given to each item. TM is a continuous variable in the range 1 to 20, so GG was first normalized to that range.

For both research questions, the main interest is to see if relationships are monotonic. To that, it was decided to use the Spearman coefficient, with an alpha of 5% for two-tails.

3.7   Process

The process for this study involving participants inspect SRS documents possess the following steps:

1. Selection of participants.
2. Explanation of the exercise to the teachers.
3. Explanation of the exercise to the team leaders.
4. Conduct the exercise in the class with teacher supervision.
5. Gathering and analysis of the results.

3.8   Preparation and Execution

Before the exercise, there was a meeting with all teachers about the exercise. Later, but before the exercise start, the team leaders met with the course responsible. At this meeting, the course responsible presented the exercise, its goal and the procedure to be followed during the exercise. The students became aware that they need to review a SRS from another group.

In order to guarantee the anonymity of the authors, the validation groups must be not aware of the identification of the SRS authors, their colleagues. To achieve this, previously to the study, each group was told to submit two versions of their reports: one report with identification and another without groups's identification. To each of latter documents, it was given a random number, so they could be identified later. All SRS documents were verified about their anonymity. After that they were uploaded to a server from where they could be read but not downloaded.

At the beginning of the exercise the teachers explained briefly to the students what should be done by the teams. After that teachers supplied the teams with the questionnaire (checklist) and the URL of the SRS document the team should review. The questionnaire was supplied in paper and no tool was used to help in the validation task. Because it was not possible to download the document, then each group read it online.

Each group inspected the respective SRS document and classified it according the checklist points giving a classification between 1 and 5 to each point. The team leader was responsible for filling the checklist with the group classifications and return it to the teacher. Group classifications to each checklist item where given by consensus. After the exercise the teacher delivered the filled checklists to the course responsible.

The exercise had an indicative time for completion of one hour but it was not rigid. Soon it was verified that one hour was not enough and some groups extend it to nearly two hours, but the time required by each group was not registered by the teachers.

As a quality measure, teachers were instructed to classify the group commitment to the exercise. After the exercise, several teachers showed many doubts about their classification.

3.9 Results

Forty five (groups) filled the questionnaire. Two questionnaires were removed because the respective team leaders did miss the kick-off meeting. The result was forty three (43) answers to be analysed. Also the third and forth columns of the checklist could provide relevant information, some were incomplete and many present several discrepancies in the way they were filled. Although more correlations and information would be interesting to obtain using those columns, they have to be ignored.

For each group it was determined the median and mean of their answers to each item of the questionnaire. The median and mean of those medians and means is showed in Table 1. All computations were done using the R package. For both statistical tests was used the *cor.test* function.

Table 1. Overall median and mean.

Groups	Median	Mean
43	4	3.7482

Regarding **RQ1**, Spearman's rank correlation was $\rho = 0.3844098$ and *p-value* $= 0.01092$. So, since *p-value* is less than the defined significance of 0.05, the null hypothesis for *RQ1* was rejected.

About **RQ2**, to obtain the value for the review quality (RQ), firstly was computed the mean of the classifications (1–5) that each group attributed to each questionnaire item ($GGmean$). The computation of the mean was done despite the problem with scales because this is an exploratory study. Next, the value was normalized to the range 0–20, *GGmean*20. Finally, it was computed the absolute value of the difference between TM and *GGmean*20.

Spearman's rank correlation was $\rho = -0.04078396$ and *p-value* $= 0.7951$. According the obtained *p-value* for a the significance level of 5%, the null hypothesis for $RQ2$ could not be rejected.

3.10   Analysis and Discussion of Results

Regarding the first research question, the observed correlation between the teachers' marks and the groups' marks is statistically significant, but not high. However the criteria used by the groups and the teachers were not the same. The teachers didn't follow the students' checklist, but all follow the same set of criteria. So, the question was to know if the correlation would be higher if criteria were the same. If higher, it would give more confidence on peer reviews and on their use for peer assessment.

The result of the second research question was negative, that is, the correlation between the quality of the groups and their reviews as was measured was not statistically significant. Possibly, if instead it was used the mean of the marks of the students during the program and not simply of their SRS, the result would be different. Furthermore, the quality of the reviews was measured as the distance between the groups' grades and the teachers marks. This is not a direct measure and could have had some effect on the results.

As seen, the checklist covers quality criteria for traditional requirements specifications. It is relevant to know its adequacy to agile development. A recent study [2] about agile requirements specifications investigated 16 papers and found 28 different quality criteria used on those papers. The authors grouped the criteria, if cited by 3 or more papers, in three global criteria: completeness, uniformity and, consistency and correctness. Uniformity is about the adherence to some specific agile format for the specification. Completeness, should be interpreted in an agile context, that is, as just-enough and just-in-time requirements, where requirements are incomplete. The three global criteria are more detailed in [20]. Looking to our checklist, can be seen that in general it covers those quality criteria, except for uniformity, which is specific to agile. This means that the checklist can be easily adapted to agile development with smaller sets of requirements.

Anyway, it is necessary a more in-depth analysis to align the checklist with the quality criteria used in agile projects. Currently, and contrary to the time of the study, the project is supported by a project tracking tool that allows the course responsible to keep track of the work performed by the groups.

For the study it was used a large set of requirements. The difficulty to validate a large set of requirements would be higher than for a small set, but, at the same time, it is expected to better prepare the students to validate requirements specifications of any size and, in this way, using any development methodology. As stated, most of the requirements have been elicited at an early stage of the project, but new requirements have been added at each new iteration. However, the study refers only to specification documents submitted with the initial requirements. Anyway, this means that the methodology used can be considered hybrid.

3.11   Threats to Validity

The validity of measures used can not be regarded as guaranteed, in particular, the review quality (RQ) and group quality (GQ) measures. It is not obvious the possible negative impact on validity of RQ because it was observed some correlation between groups' grades and teachers' marks, the two measures RQ depends. The GQ is equal to the teachers' marks to the same SRS the group reviewed. The use of columns 3 and 4 of the checklist would help to improve the validity of the results, but, as explained, their use was not possible.

The criteria used in the teachers' assessment of the SRS documents were distinct from the criteria used by the groups. Teachers' assessments also incorporate pedagogical dimensions (as the report presentation, or the formalism of the UML diagrams) and did not use the checklist. There is some percentage of common criteria but we were not able to achieve a value for that. We speculate that the different criteria could have been a main bias factor for the unobservable correlation between RQ and GQ. So, in future research we intend to assure common criteria. The large number of teachers involved could also affect the correlations between their marks and the students grades.

Another threat has to do with the use of the supplied SRS template because not all groups respected completely this template, which should have affected the SRS document presentation and the corresponding reading by the validation groups. Also, it should had some impact on the examination by teachers. Because each group possess their own view of the problem, it is possible some bias when evaluating others SRS.

The time indicated initially for the exercise was not enough for all groups. Although this could apparently had some impact on the quality of the answers, it was overcome by the fact that teachers gave additional time to the groups.

We are aware that students commitment to the exercise could have an important impact on the results. However, we have no reliable measure about students commitment to the exercise and, consequently, the possible impact on the performance of the several groups. Possibly the teachers that supervise the exercise could also have an effect on the groups' performance but all validations were done in identical circumstances, with the presence of a teacher.

In [21] were found some differences between students (freshman and graduates) due to their experience. As stated in Sect. 3.3 a small number of students possess industrial experience in software development. However, we did not identify such situations.

Also, the grouping and ordering of the questions in the checklist may not be the most correct. Possibly, it should start from the more general and substantive to the detailed an less substantive questions. For example, questions like the 5th and the 11th could be placed in the first positions. This needs to be further investigated.

4   Conclusions

This paper presented a study of an exercise performed during regular classes where groups of students reviewed requirements specifications developed by their peers. In the study it was observed a correlation with statistical significance between the grades attributed by students and the marks given by the teachers to the same requirements specifications. That correlation was not high. So, peer reviews can be considered reliable to some extent. This means that teachers can use those reviews as a form of peer assessment to aid them in marking students work, but carefully. This was the main contribution of this paper.

At the same time, the study found no correlation between the quality of students' groups and the quality of the requirements reviews they do. However, indirect measures to classify the quality of the groups and of their reviews were used. Researchers that intend to develop similar studies should pay attention to guarantee that criteria used by teachers and students to evaluate their requirements specifications, or other relevant artefacts, are as identical as possible.

The software development model used on the exercise can be classified as hybrid, that is, using weekly iterations, but with a strong emphasis on requirements engineering up front. With such approach, students are faced with a large amount of requirements to validate. This should have increased the difficulty of the exercise, turning it more challenging to the students, which was considered positive for training purposes. The current increase in the use of hybrid models by the industry, as stated before, makes this kind of studies more relevant.

The effectiveness of reviews in software development is well documented [22] and the use of checklists in inspections is considered as having a positive effect in requirements engineering in agile projects (e.g. [23]). As shown, the checklist used by the groups requires some changes to be suitable for use in pure agile projects, including the use of tools, as done in modern code reviews. But using tools should not avoid having the knowledge underlying performing validations. From the limitations presented, this research should continue by improving the checklist, the measures and, if possible, its integration with tools to be in complete line with a modern requirements review perspective.

Acknowledgment. The authors would like to thank their colleagues and students.

References

1. Ambreen, T., Ikram, N., Usman, M., Niazi, M.: Empirical research in requirements engineering: trends and opportunities. Requirements Eng. **23**(1), 63–95 (2016). https://doi.org/10.1007/s00766-016-0258-2
2. Heck, P., Zaidman, A.: A systematic literature review on quality criteria for agile requirements specifications. Software Qual. J. **26**(1), 127–160 (2016). https://doi.org/10.1007/s11219-016-9336-4

3. Boehm, B.W.: Software Engineering Economics, 1st edn. Prentice Hall PTR, Upper Saddle River (1981)
4. De Lucia, A., Qusef, A.: Requirements engineering in agile software development. J. Emerg. Technol. Web Intell. **2**(3), 212–220 (2010)
5. Kuhrmann, M., et al.: Hybrid software development approaches in practice: a European perspective. IEEE Softw. **36**(4), 20–31 (2019). https://doi.org/10.1109/MS. 2018.110161245
6. He, L., Carver, J.C., Vaughn, R.: Using inspections to teach requirements validation. CrossTalk: J. Defense Softw. Eng. **21**(1) (2008)
7. Gigante, G., Gargiulo, F., Ficco, M.: A semantic driven approach for requirements verification. In: Camacho, D., Braubach, L., Venticinque, S., Badica, C. (eds.) Intelligent Distributed Computing VIII. SCI, vol. 570, pp. 427–436. Springer, Cham (2015). https://doi.org/10.1007/978-3-319-10422-5_44
8. Loftus, C., Thomas, L., Zander, C.: Can graduating students design: revisited. In: Proceedings of the 42nd ACM Technical Symposium on Computer Science Education, SIGCSE 2011, pp. 105–110. ACM, New York (2011). https://doi.org/ 10.1145/1953163.1953199
9. Topping, K.: Peer assessment between students in colleges and universities. Rev. Educ. Res. **68**(3), 249–276 (1998). https://doi.org/10.3102/00346543068003249
10. Anda, B., Sjøberg, D.I.: Towards an inspection technique for use case models. In: Proceedings of the 14th International Conference on Software Engineering and Knowledge Engineering, pp. 127–134. ACM (2002)
11. Lahtinen, J.: Application of the perspective-based reading technique in the nuclear I&C context: CORSICA work report 2011. VTT Technical Research Centre of Finland, No. 9. VTT Technology (2012). http://www.vtt.fi/inf/pdf/technology/ 2012/T9.pdf
12. Basili, V.R., et al.: The empirical investigation of perspective-based reading. Empirical Softw. Eng. **1**(2), 133–164 (1996). https://doi.org/10.1007/BF00368702
13. Atoum, I.: A scalable operational framework for requirements validation using semantic and functional models. In: Proceedings of the 2nd International Conference on Software Engineering and Information Management, ICSIM 2019, pp. 1–6. ACM, NY (2019). https://doi.org/10.1145/3305160.3305166
14. Nazir, S., Fatima, N., Chuprat, S.: Modern code review benefits-primary findings of a systematic literature review. In: Proceedings of the 3rd International Conference on Software Engineering and Information Management, ICSIM 2020, pp. 210–215. ACM, NY (2020). https://doi.org/10.1145/3378936.3378954
15. Runeson, P., Host, M., Rainer, A., Regnell, B.: Case Study Research in Software Engineering: Guidelines and Examples. Wiley, Hoboken (2012)
16. Laitenberger, O., Atkinson, C., Schlich, M., Emam, K.E.: An experimental comparison of reading techniques for defect detection in UML design documents. J. Syst. Softw. **53**(2), 183–204 (2000). https://doi.org/10.1016/S0164-1212(00)00052-2
17. Rowlands, K.D.: Check it out! Using checklists to support student learning. Engl. J. **96**(6), 61–66 (2007)
18. IEEE-SA: IEEE Std 830-1998 - Recommended Practice for Software Requirements Specifications, IEEE-SA (1998). https://doi.org/10.1109/IEEESTD.1998.88286
19. van Lamsweerde, A.: Requirements Engineering: From System Goals to UML Models to Software Specifications. Wiley Publishing, Hoboken (2009)
20. Heck, P., Zaidman, A.: Quality criteria for just-in-time requirements: just enough, just-in-time?. In: 2015 IEEE Workshop on Just-In-Time Requirements Engineering (JITRE), pp. 1–4 (2015). https://doi.org/10.1109/JITRE.2015.7330170

21. Runeson, P.: Experiences from teaching PSP for freshmen. In: Proceedings of the 14th Conference on Software Engineering Education and Training, CSEET 2001, pp. 98–107. IEEE Computer Society, Washington, DC (2001)
22. Jones, C.: A Guide to Selecting Software Measures and Metrics. CRC Press, Boca Raton (2017)
23. Kalinowski, M., et al.: Supporting defect causal analysis in practice with cross-company data on causes of requirements engineering problems. In: Proceedings of the 39th International Conference on Software Engineering: Software Engineering in Practice Track, pp. 223–232. IEEE Press (2017)

Author Index

Printed in the United States
By Bookmasters